Die Design Fundamentals

A step-by-step introduction to the design of stamping dies including material, punches, die sets, stops, strippers, gages, pilots and presses

Second Edition

Die Design Fundamentals

J. R. Paquin

Registered Professional Engineer
Supervisor, Tool Engineering Department
Cleveland Engineering Institute
Senior Member, ASTME

and

R. E. Crowley, CMfgE, PE

Regional Manager
Engineering Systems
Electronic Data Systems
Indianapolis, Indiana

Industrial Press Inc.

Library of Congress Cataloging-in-Publication Data
Paquin, J. R.
Die design fundamentals.

Includes index.
1. Dies (Metal-working) 2. Punching machinery.
I. Crowley, R. E. II. Title.
TS253.P3 1986 671.3'3 86-19132
ISBN 0-8311-1172-0

Industrial Press Inc.
200 Madison Avenue
New York, New York 10016

Second Edition

DIE DESIGN FUNDAMENTALS

12 13 14 15 16

Preface to Second Edition

This second edition of *Die Design Fundamentals* has not changed the fourteen basic steps in designing stamping dies. As in most areas of tool design, the fundamentals are still the same, and these fundamentals should be learned by any student who is serious about his field. Once these basics have become a part of the designer's natural thought processes, shortcuts and more exotic techniques may be utilized.

While the fundamentals may not have changed, the equipment, such as machine tools and die cushions, has. These changes have been reflected in the pictures and illustrations that have replaced those of 20 or more years ago. An example will be the added emphasis that has been placed on hydraulic presses in the 1980s. These changes will be noted primarily in Section 2 of the second edition.

The plan of the book remains unique. After the introductory material, the design of a representative die is separated into fourteen distinct steps. Each division or step is illustrated in two ways; first, as a portion of an engineering drawing, that is, as the component is actually drawn on the design. Second, it is shown pictorially, to improve the student's visualization. In succeeding sections of the book each step is expanded and explained in detail as it is applied in the design of various types of dies. The final section shows 20 of those dies.

Line drawings are given both a pictorial view and a conventional two-view or three-view illustration. Thus, the student sees, in three dimensions, just how the component appears and how it must be visualized in the design process. At the same time he learns exactly how it should be shown in a tool design. The student is therefore exposed to accurate and proportioned data, which becomes his learning mode.

Special thanks must be given to those who were so helpful in contributing not only pictures, but also considerable time and effort. While it is impossile to name them all, Dave Gruelich, and Reuben Nystrom, of Cincinnati, Inc., and Bill Ardis, of The Minster Machine Company, should be singled out for these efforts.

Preface to First Edition

This book is a more comprehensive compilation of the information contained in a series of articles that appeared in American Machinist/Metalworking Manufacturing under the title, *Fourteen Steps to Design a Die*. The number of illustrations and the length of the text have been almost doubled.

The series was well-received. A large number of requests for additional copies of the magazine installments showed that a definite need exists for a book of this type. Inquiries came from students; from draftsmen, tool designers, die designers, toolmakers and diemakers. They came from virtually every state and from a number of European countries. Some arrived from India and Japan. Many requests for additional copies came from instructors in technical schools who found the material helpful in their classes.

This book was written by a member of the tool engineering profession whose practical experience has spanned more than twenty years. He was formerly Tool and Die Designer for such companies as Republic Aircraft Corp., Frigidaire Division of General Motors Corp., Underwood Corp., Torrington Manufacturing Co., and Associated Engineers. He was formerly Chief Engineer of Worcester Automatic Machine Company. The terms of the book are those that die men are familiar with and understand. In addition, over eight years of teaching prospective tool and die designers have provided insights into the special requirements of students.

The plan of the book is unique. After the introductory material, the design of a representative die is separated into fourteen distinct steps. Each division or step is illustrated in two ways; 1. As a portion of an engineering drawing, 2. Pictorially, to improve the student's visualization. In succeeding sections of the book, each step is expanded and explained in detail as it is applied in the design of various types of dies. The final section shows the twenty types of dies in use in industry.

Line drawings are given both a pictorial view and a conventional two-view or three-view engineering drawing. Thus, the student sees, three dimensionally, just how the component appears and how it must be visualized in designing. At the same time he learns exactly how it should be drawn on a die drawing. Thus students are exposed to accurate and proportioned data and this becomes their experience.

It has been the author's intention to present the information about fundamentals of die design in the form of underlying principles. After an analysis has been conducted to identify the principles involved, each is clearly explained with appropriate illustrations and text as a complete unit of information presented in the modern picture-story form. The engineering principles then stand out clearly for adaptation to an unlimited variety of die designs. Numbered side headings are used to provide a quick and easy reference from text to illustration and vice versa.

Mathematics is an indispensable ally of any type of mechanical design. It is the cement that fixes the relationship between all the parts of any mechanical assembly and it determines the shape, size, and strength of each of the components, as well as the clearances between them. The elements of mathematics required for the design of die components have been introduced throughout the book where required for solution of specific problems instead of being grouped together in a final section that would be too often overlooked or neglected.

The author is pleased to acknowledge the valuable contributions made by many friends and associates in the preparation of this book. First among them is Rupert Le Grand, Senior Associate Editor of American Machinist/Metalworking Manufacturing, who provided encouragement in developing the articles in the series. Mr. Le Grand's perceptive suggestions and able editing of serial installments helped materially to establish direction.

Special credit is due to Isaac Hart and Charles Zelenko, Directors of Cleveland Engineering Institute for their encouragement. Robert Leuthner, Registrar, and V. J. Costanzo, Instructor extended many courtesies.

E. E. Kalman made finished drawings for a number of the illustrations and for the problem book. Messrs. Robert Moyer, Charles Einsiedler, and Lester Horne of Standard Die Set Co., Providence, R.I. provided assistance in development of Sections 13 and 14.

Considerable material was originated as a result of questions posed by the author's former students in the tool and die design classes of Porter School of Tool Design, Hartford, Conn., Worcester Junior College, Worcester, Mass., and Cleveland Engineering Institute, Cleveland, Ohio.

Credit is also due to Professor Casimir Rakowski, Department of Mechanical Technology, State University Agricultural and Technical Institute, Farmingdale, N.Y., who conducted a penetrating review of the book in manuscript form.

Many press and equipment manufacturers contributed photographic illustrations. Each is acknowledged where the illustration appears in the book. Special credit is due to Robert Rhodes of Federal Press Co., Elkhart, Ind., and to E. C. Monell of F. J. Littell Machine Co., Chicago, Ill., who contributed outstanding line drawings of press and equipment constuction for Section 2.

J. R. Paquin

Cleveland, Ohio
July, 1962

Contents

Section 1

INTRODUCTION TO DIE DESIGN

Die design, a large division of tool engineering, is a complex, fascinating subject. It is one of the most exacting of all the areas of the general field of tool designing.

The die designer originates designs of dies employed to stamp and form parts from sheet metal, assemble parts together, and perform a variety of other operations.

1-1. BLUEPRINTS

After a die has been designed on tracing paper, blueprints or ozalid prints are produced for use in the die shop where the dies are actually built by die makers. This is how a blueprint of a die drawing appears. From such prints die makers build the die exactly as the designer has designed it. The drawing must be complete with all required views, dimensions, notes, and specifications. If the die maker is obliged to ask numerous questions, a poor job of drawing was done.

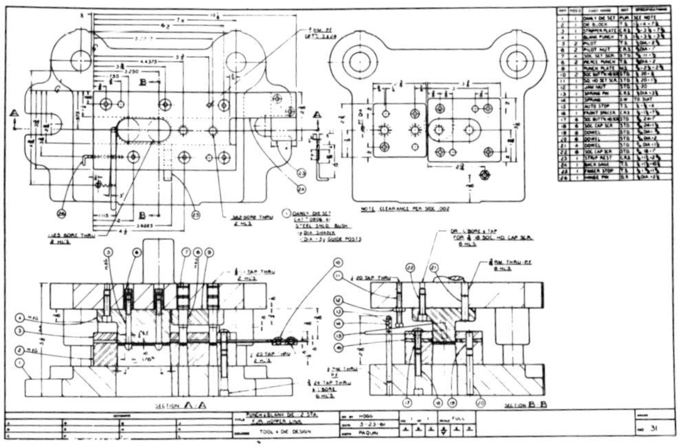

Fig. 1-1. A typical blue print.

Good die designers have no trouble in finding employment for their talents. They are always in short supply because the pressed metal industry with which they are associated is a dynamic, highly exciting field.

STAMPINGS

Stampings are parts cut and formed from sheet material. Look around you! Wherever you may be, there you will find stampings. Many are worn on your own person; the ring on your finger is probably a stamping. Most of the parts in your wrist watch are stampings, including the case. Your belt buckle, the metal grommets through which your shoe laces pass, eyeglass frame, the clip on your ball point pen, and zipper; all these are stampings. There are small stamped washers in your shoe heels against which the heel nails bear.

Look around the room, any room, and you will find products of the pressed metal industry. Most of the parts in the lighting fixture are stampings; so are threaded portions of light bulbs, door knobs, radiator covers, ash trays; the list is a long one indeed! In the home we find stampings by the score: Pots and pans, knives, forks, and spoons, coffee pot, canister set, pie plates and muffin pans, cabinet handles, kettle, can opener, etc.

The refrigerator is almost entirely made of stampings. So are the stove, toaster, and other appliances. And each single part in all these requires an average of from three to six dies to produce it.

Every automobile contains hundreds of stampings. The largest are the tops, quarter-panels, doors, etc. Even the wheels are stampings. There are hundreds of smaller parts, many of which are covered and seldom seen. For example, even the points require very complex dies with multiple stations each, costing thousands of dollars to build, in addition to assembly dies for joining the components.

Office machines provide another big stamping field. Typewriters contain hundreds of stampings. So do adding machines, calculators, and dictating machines. I could go on and on because the list is almost endless. Radio and television components require thousands of dies. So do streamlined trains, aircraft, and missiles. All of these are improved from year to year, so an enormous number of new dies are constantly required.

The foregoing should give you some idea of the great size and importance of the pressed metal industry. Stampings engineering has grown in the last fifty years into a vast field, one filled with opportunity for the alert.

1-2. SCRAP STRIP

Shown here is the scrap strip and finished injectors for Schick razors. These parts are cut and formed in a nine station progressive die. Once the strip has been started through the die, a complete injector is produced with each stroke of the press. This layout illustrates perfectly how complex, accurate stampings can be produced in large quantities when operations are carefully planned and dies are properly designed.

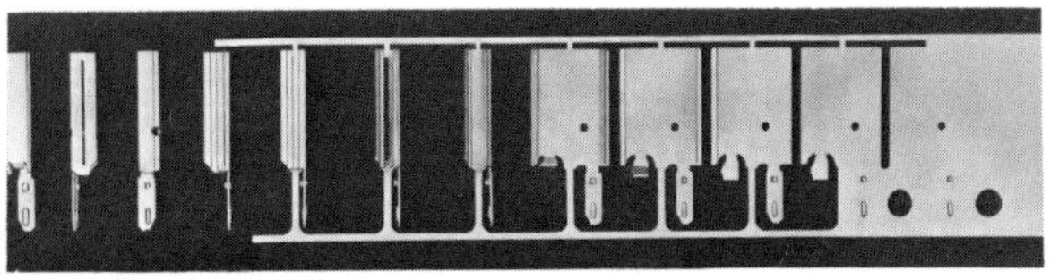

Jahn Mfg. Co.

Fig. 1-2. An injector for a razor (at left) and scrap strip from which it was cut.

DIE DESIGN

How then shall we enter into the study of die design? Obviously, we shall have to begin cautiously, learning each principle thoroughly before proceeding to the next one. Otherwise it is quite likely that we should soon become hopelessly involved in the complexities of the subject and in the bewildering number and variety of principles which must be understood. What, then, is a die?

The word "die" is a very general one and it may be well to define its meaning as it will be employed in our work. It is used in two distinct ways. When employed in a general sense, it means an entire press tool with all components taken together. When used in a more limited manner, it refers to that component which is machined to receive the blank, as differentiated from the component called the punch which is its opposite member. The distinction will become clear as you proceed with the studies.

In this introduction you are to learn the names of various die components and to get some idea of how they go together and are operated. In addition, we will consider the steps taken in designing, building, and inspecting a die in a representative press shop. Finally, operations which are performed in dies will be listed and illustrated. In other sections of the book, the design of dies and die components will be explained in a far more thorough manner so that your understanding will be complete in every respect.

1-3. PUNCH PRESS

Figure 1-3 is a photograph of a typical punch press in which dies are operated to produce stampings. The bolster plate **A** is a thick steel plate fastened to the press frame. The complete die is clamped securely on this bolster plate. The upper portion of the die is clamped in ram **B** which is reciprocated up and down by a crank. As the material strip is run through the die, the upper punches, fastened to the moving ram of the press, remove blanks from it. The subject of punch presses will be covered in detail in Section 2, "Presses and Press Accessories."

Minster Machine Co.

Fig. 1-3. A typical punch press.

1-4. DIE SET

Figure 1-4 shows a die set, and all parts comprising the die assembly are built within it. Die sets are made by several manufacturers and they may be purchased in a great variety of shapes and sizes. Punch shank **A** is clamped in the ram of the press. In operation, the upper part of the die set **B**, called the punch holder, moves up and down with the ram. Bushings **C**, pressed into the punch holder, slide on guide posts **D** to maintain precise alignment of cutting members of the die. The die holder **E** is clamped to the bolster plate of the press by bolts passing through slots **F**. In Section 17, "How to Select a Die Set," all types of die sets will be described and illustrated, and rules will be given to help you determine the correct type to employ under specific conditions.

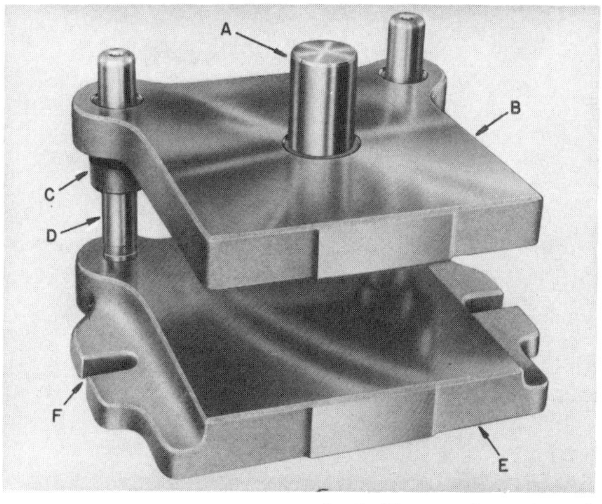

Danly Machine Specialties, Inc.

Fig. 1-4. A typical die set.

1-5. PART DRAWING

To begin our study of the various components which make up a complete die, let us consider the drawing of the link illustrated here. This part is to be blanked from steel strip and a die is to be designed for producing it in quantity. The first step in designing any die is to make a careful study of the part print because the information given on it provides many clues for solving the design problem.

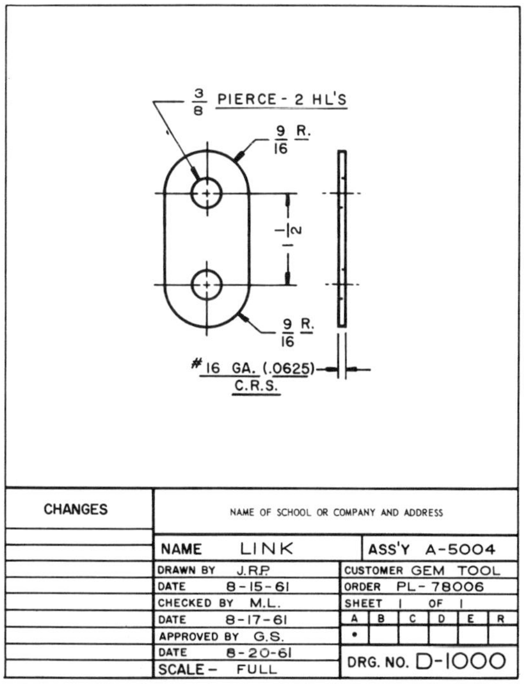

Fig. 1-5. A typical part drawing.

1-6. SCRAP STRIP

Next, a scrap strip would be designed as a guide for laying out the views of the actual die. This illustration shows the material strip as it will appear after holes have been pierced and the blank has been removed from it. We would first consider running the blank the wide way as shown at **A**. When blanks are positioned in this manner, the widest possible strip is employed and more blanks can be removed from each length of strip. In addition, the distance between blanks is short and little time is consumed in moving the strip from station to station. However, for this particular blank there occurs a serious disadvantage in this method of positioning. Since the grain in a metal strip runs along its length, the grain in each blank would run across the short width and the blanks would be weak and lacking in rigidity. This defect is important enough for the method to be discarded and, instead, the blanks will be positioned the long way in the strip as shown at **B**. The grain will then occur along the length of each blank for maximum stiffness and strength.

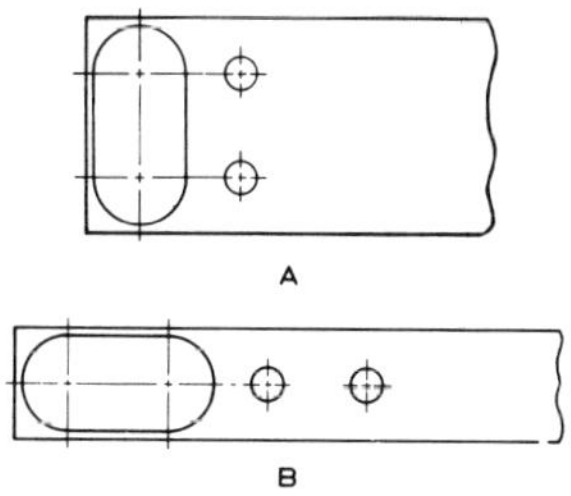

Fig. 1-6. Typical scrap strip layouts.

1-7. DIE DRAWING (See page 4)

Figure 1-7 is a complete die drawing ready to be printed in blueprint form. To the uninitiated, it might appear to be just a confusing maze of lines. Actually, however, each line represents some important information which the die makers must have to build the die successfully. In illustrations to follow, we will remove the individual parts from this assembly and see how they appear both as three or two view drawings and as pictorial views to help you to visualize their shapes. As you study further, keep coming back to this illustration to see how each component fits in. When you get through, you should have a good idea of how the various parts go together to make up a complete die.

1-8. DIE ASSEMBLY

Figure 1-8 is a pictorial view of the entire die shown in Fig. 1-7. The die pierces two holes at the first station, and then the part is blanked out at the second station. The material from which the blanks are removed is a cold-rolled steel strip. Cold-rolled steel is a smooth, medium-hard steel, and its gets its name from the process by which it is produced. It is rolled, cold, between rollers under high pressure to provide a smooth surface. The strip **A** is shown entering the die at the right.

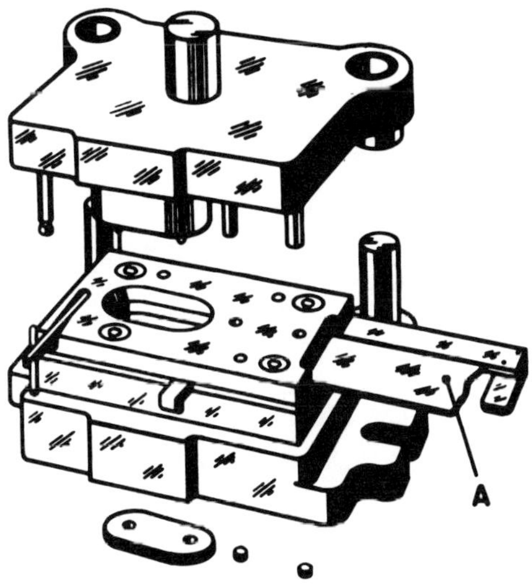

Fig. 1-8. A pictorial view of an entire die.

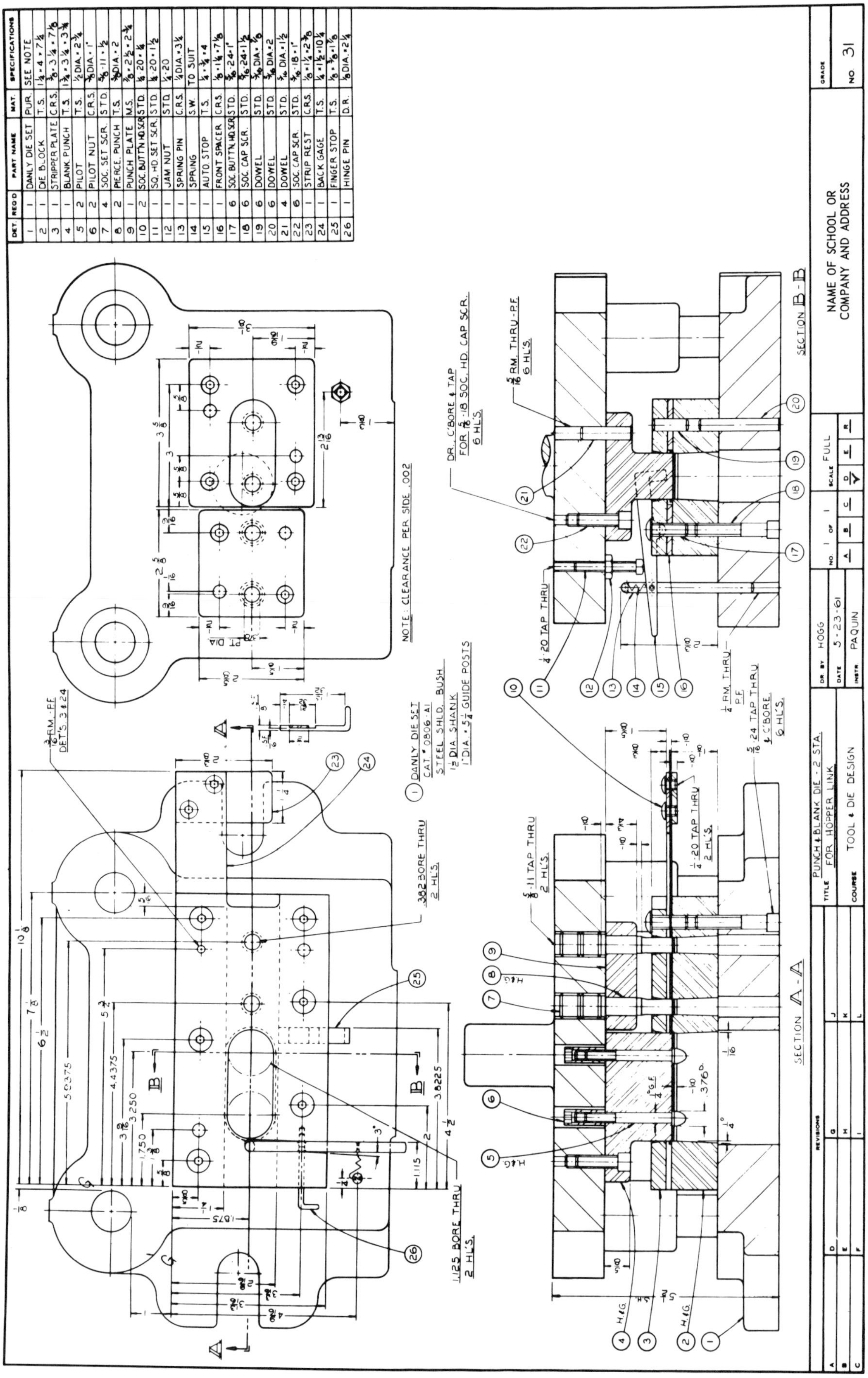

Fig. 1-7. A complete die drawing.

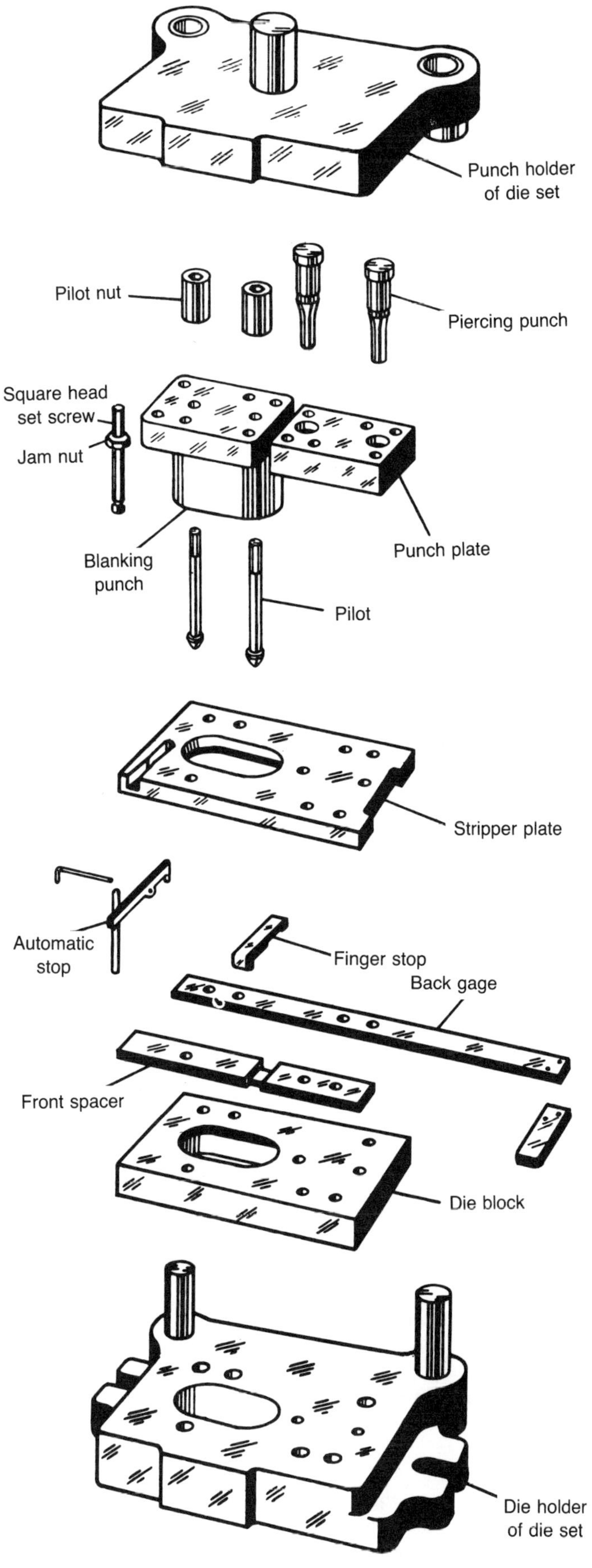

Fig. 1-9. An exploded view of the die shown in Fig. 1-8.

1-9. DIE PARTS

Figure 1-9 is an exploded drawing of the die shown in Fig. 1-8. Listed are names of various die components. These names should be memorized because we will refer to them many times in future work.

Figures 1-8 and 1-9 show the operation of a typical "pierce and blank" die. The strip is advanced until it contacts the finger stop which has been pushed forward by the operator. The press is tripped and the piercing punches pierce two holes in the strip end. The finger stop is then retracted and the strip is advanced until it contacts the automatic stop. Tripping the press again causes two holes to be pierced in the strip at the first station, while, at the second station, the blanking punch removes a blank from the strip and pushes it into the die block. The acorn shaped pilots then engage the previously pierced holes to register the strip correctly before recycling.

1-10. THE SCRAP STRIP

Three views of the material strip are shown here exactly as they appear in the die drawing in Fig. 1-7. In addition, a pictorial view is applied at the upper right corner to help in visualizing the strip in your mind. In other words, this is the way you would imagine the strip in order to draw it in three views. The top or plan view shows the strip outline as well as all openings. This would be made actual size on the drawing. The holes are represented by circles at the first station, and the blanked opening is shown at the second station. At the lower left, a side view of the strip is

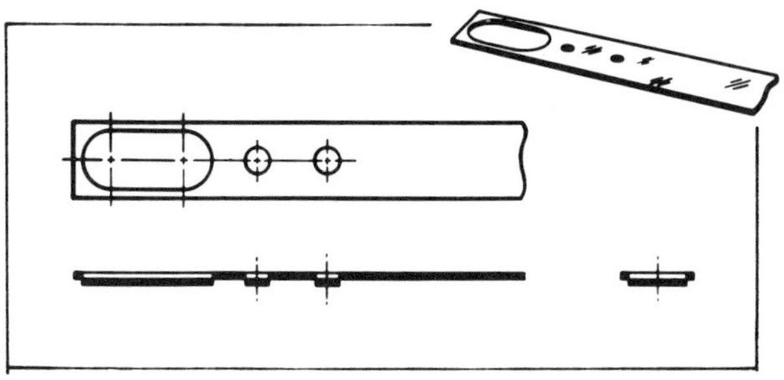

Fig. 1-10. Three views of the scrap strip.

drawn. It is shown exactly as it would appear at the bottom of the press stroke, with the pierced slugs pushed out of the strip at the first station and the blank pushed out of the strip at the second station. The narrow end-view at the lower right corner is shown as a section through the blanking station, and the blank is shown pushed out of the strip. The strip in many instances is drawn shaded to differentiate it from the numerous lines which will represent die members. In the upper plan view, shading lines would appear on the surface of the metal. In the two lower views, the lines are shown in solid black to further differentiate the strip from the die members.

1-11. THE DIE BLOCK

The die block is made of hardened tool steel into which holes have been machined, before hardening, at the piercing station and also at the blanking station. These are the same size and shape as the blank holes

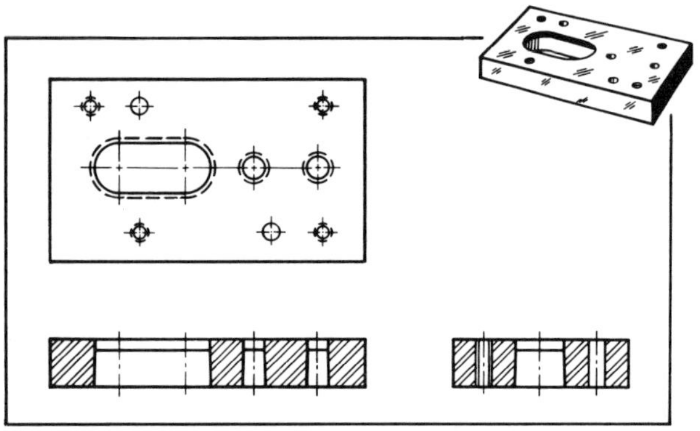

Fig. 1-11. The die block.

and contour. Other holes are tapped holes used to fasten the die block to the die holder, and reamed holes into which dowels are pressed to fix its location relative to other die parts. The top view is a plan view of the die block. The lower left view is a section through the holes machined for piercing and blanking. Lines drawn at a 45 degree angle, called section lines, indicate that the die block has been cut through the center, the lines representing the cut portion. Similarly, the end view is a section cut through the die block at the blanking station. A tapped hole is shown at the left and a reamed hole at the right side. These are for the screws and dowels which hold the die block to other die components. Sectioning a die, that is, showing the die as if portions were cut away to reveal the inside contours of die openings is a very common practice. In fact, practically all dies are sectioned in this manner. The die maker can then "read" the drawing far more easily than if outside views only were shown because they would contain many dotted, or hidden lines. Always remember that all drafting is, in a sense, a language. A die drawing is a sort of shorthand which is used to convey a great deal of information to the die maker. Anything which can be done to make it easier for him to read the drawing will save considerable time in the shop.

Now refer back to Fig. 1-7 and see how easily you can pick out the three views of the die block. That is exactly what the die maker would have to do in order to make the die block.

1-12. THE BLANKING PUNCH

The blanking punch removes the blank from the strip. The bottom, or cutting edge, is the shape and size of the part. A flange at the top provides metal for fastening the blanking punch to the punch holder of the die set with screws and dowels. Two holes are reamed all the way through the blanking punch for retaining the pilots which locate the strip prior to the blanking operation. Locate the views of the blanking punch in the die drawing, Fig. 1-7, to improve your ability to read a die drawing.

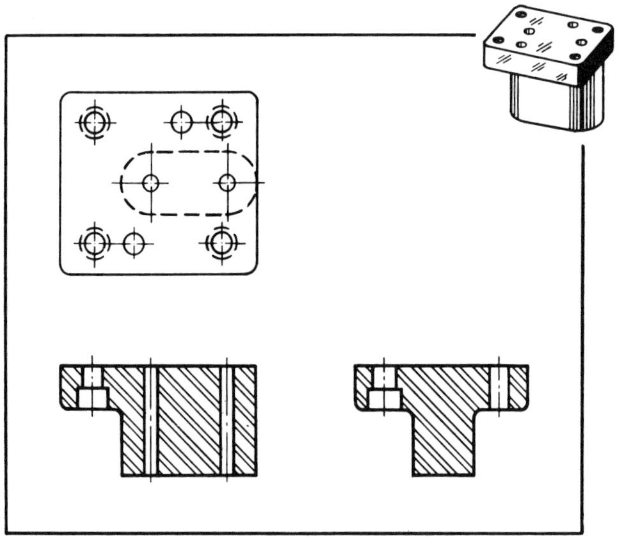

Fig. 1-12. The blanking punch.

1-13. PIERCING PUNCHES

Piercing punches pierce holes through the material strip or blank. They are usually round and are provided with a shoulder to retain them in the punch plate. When a piercing punch penetrates the strip, the material clings very tightly around it and means must be provided to strip, or remove this material from around the punches. Whatever is employed to remove such material is called a stripper.

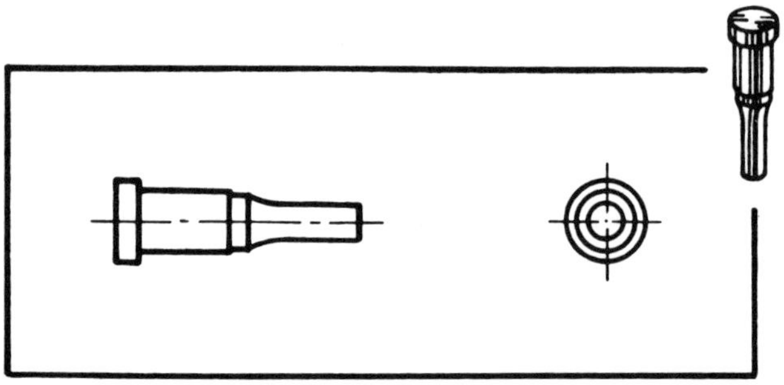

Fig. 1-13. A piercing punch.

1-14. PUNCH PLATES

The punch plate is a block of machine steel which retains punches with their heads against the punch holder of the die set. The punches are held in counterbored holes into which they are pressed. Four screws and two dowels retain the punch plate to the punch holder of the die set. The screws prevent it from being pulled away from the punch holder. Dowels, which are accurately ground round pins, are pressed through both the punch plate and punch holder to prevent shifting. Locate the front view and plan view of the punch plate in the die drawing, Fig. 1-7.

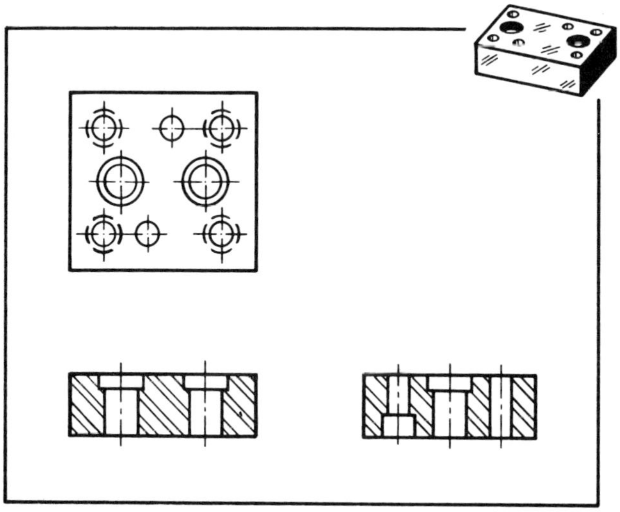

Fig. 1-14. A punch plate.

1-15. PILOTS

Pilots are provided with acorn shaped heads which enter previously pierced holes in the strip. The acorn shape causes the strip to shift to correct register before blanking occurs. Section 11, "How to Design Pilots," will show many different ways of applying these components.

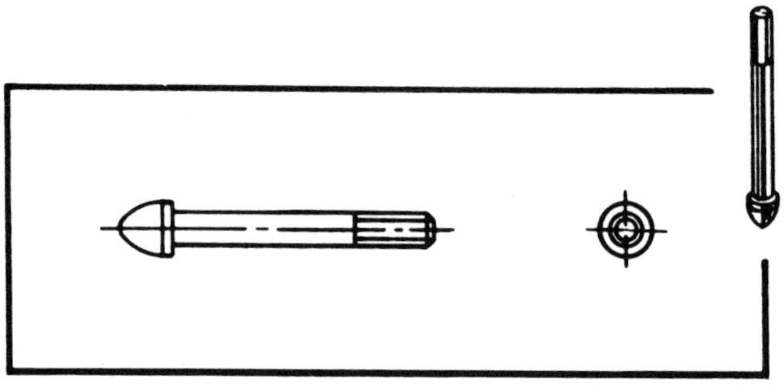

Fig. 1-15. A pilot.

1-16. THE BACK GAGE

The back gage is a relatively thin steel member against which the material strip is held by the operator in its travel through the die. The front spacer is a shorter component of the same thickness. The strip is fed from right to left. It rests on the die block and is guided between the back gage and front spacer. The distance between the back gage and front spacer is greater than strip width to allow for possible slight variations in width.

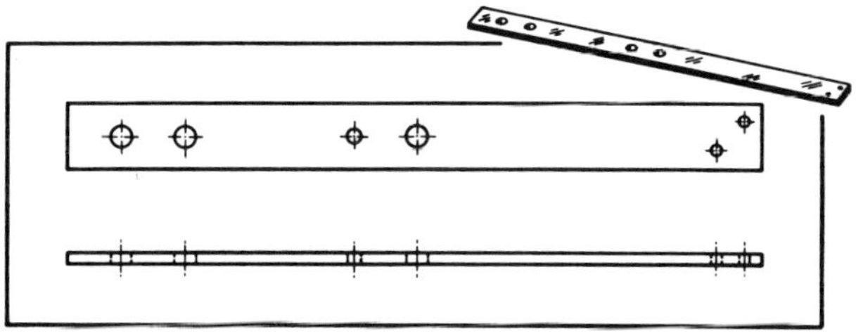

Fig. 1-16. The back gage.

1-17. FINGER STOPS

The finger stop locates the strip at the first station. In progressive dies having a number of stations, a finger stop may be applied at each station to register the strip before its contact with the automatic stop. Finger stops have slots machined in their lower surfaces to limit stop travel. Section 13, "How to Design Finger Stops," will show a number of ways in which these components are applied.

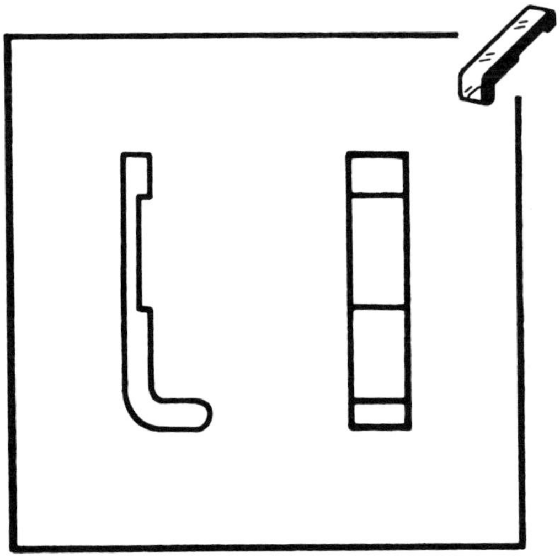

Fig. 1-17. A finger stop.

1-18. AUTOMATIC STOPS

Automatic stops locate the strip automatically while it is fed through the die. The operator simply keeps the strip pushed against the automatic stop toe, and the strip is stopped while the blank and pierced slugs are removed from it, then automatically allowed to move

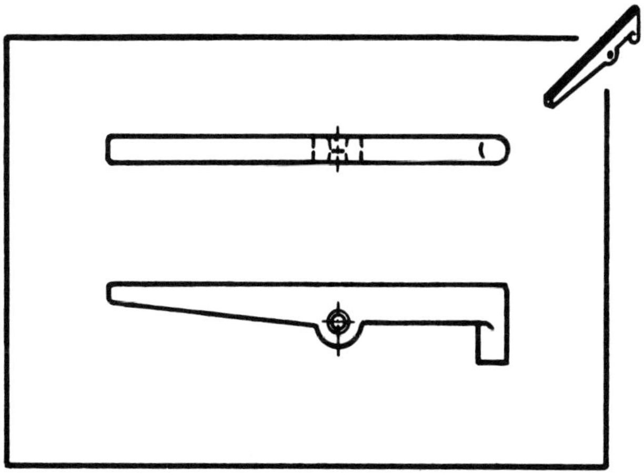

Fig. 1-18. An automatic stop.

one station further and stopped again for the next cutting operation. There are many ways of applying automatic stops, and these will be discussed and illustrated in Section 14, "How to Design Automatic Stops."

1-19. THE STRIPPER PLATE

The stripper plate removes the material strip from around blanking and piercing punches. There are two types: spring-operated stripper plates, and solid stripper plates, like the one illustrated. The stripper plate has a slot **A** machined into it in which the automatic stop operates. Another slot **B** at the right provides a shelf for easy insertion of a new strip when it is started through the die.

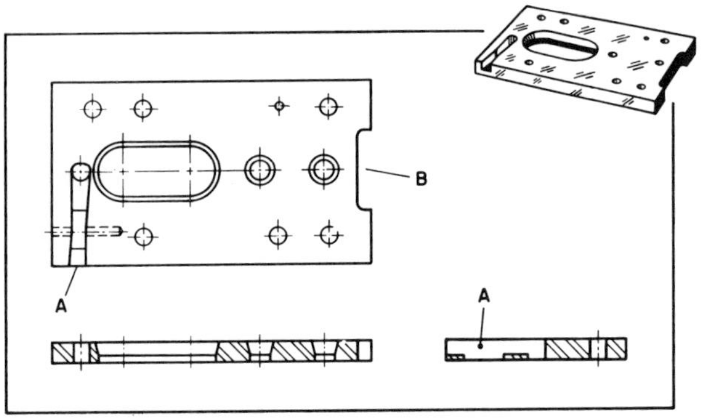

Fig. 1-19. The stripper plate.

1-20. FASTENERS

Fasteners hold the various components of the die together. Figure 1-20 shows the commonly used socket cap screw. These fasteners are available from various suppliers, and all have a threaded portion and a larger round head provided with an internal hexagon for wrenching. All fasteners employed in dies will be discussed in Section 16, "How to Apply Fasteners," and rules will be given for specifying the correct types under given conditions. As you have been doing for previous illustrations, pick out the fasteners shown in the die drawing, Fig. 1-7. Note that in section views, screws are shown on one side and dowels on the other.

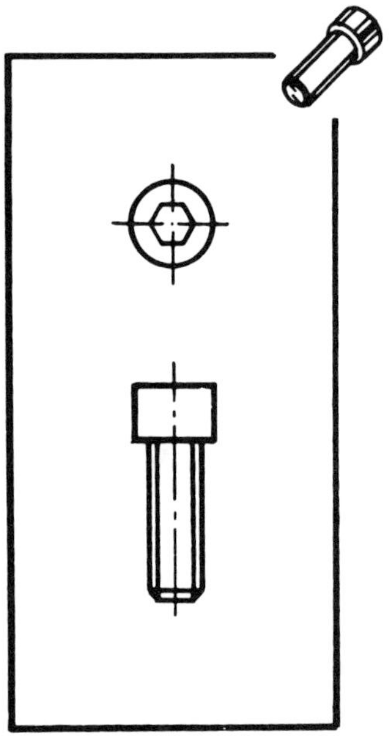

Fig. 1-20. Socket head cap screw for use as a fastener.

1-21. THE DIE SET

The die set is drawn with four views in Fig. 1-21. At the lower left is shown a section through the entire die set. The side view, lower right, is a section view also, with a portion of the die set cut away to show internal holes more clearly. The upper left view is a plan view of the lower die holder with the punch holder removed from it.

The punch holder is shown at the upper right, and it is drawn inverted, or turned over, much like an opened book. In the die drawing, Fig. 1-7 then, all punches are drawn with solid lines. Were the punch holder not inverted, most lines representing punches would be hidden and the drawing would contain a confusing maze of dotted lines.

Another reason for inverting the punch holder is that this is actually the position assumed by the die holder and punch holder on the bench as the die maker assembles the die, and it is easier for him to read the drawing when the views have been drawn in the same position as the die on which he performs assembly motions.

1-22. DIMENSIONS AND NOTES

With the die design completed, all dimensions and notes are applied to the drawing. This is the die set note which tells the die maker exactly what die set to order and which gives required information about punch shank diameter, type of guide bushings, and diameter and length of guide posts.

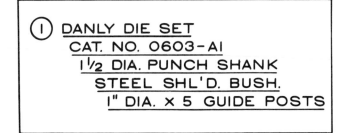

(1) DANLY DIE SET
CAT. NO. 0603-A1
1 1/2 DIA. PUNCH SHANK
STEEL SHL'D. BUSH.
1" DIA. X 5 GUIDE POSTS

Fig. 1-22. A typical die set note.

1-23. BILL OF MATERIAL

The bill of material is filled in last (Fig. 1-23). This gives required information and specifications for ordering standard parts and for cutting steel to correct dimensions. This material is cut and assembled in the stock room and placed in a pan, along with a print of the die drawing. When filled, the pan must contain everything the die maker will require for building the die, including all fasteners and the die set.

PROCESSING A DIE

Let us now consider the steps taken in designing, building, and inspecting a representative die. At the same time, you will gain an insight into the operation of press shops, tool-rooms, and manufacturing plants so your understanding of tooling and manufacturing will be better than average.

The Product

First, we will consider the product to be manufactured. The product engineering department designs the product. In most plants, the work consists in improving the product from year to year to meet changing styles and changing requirements of customers.

After management has decided upon the final form of the new or improved product, a directive is sent to the process planning department to route the various

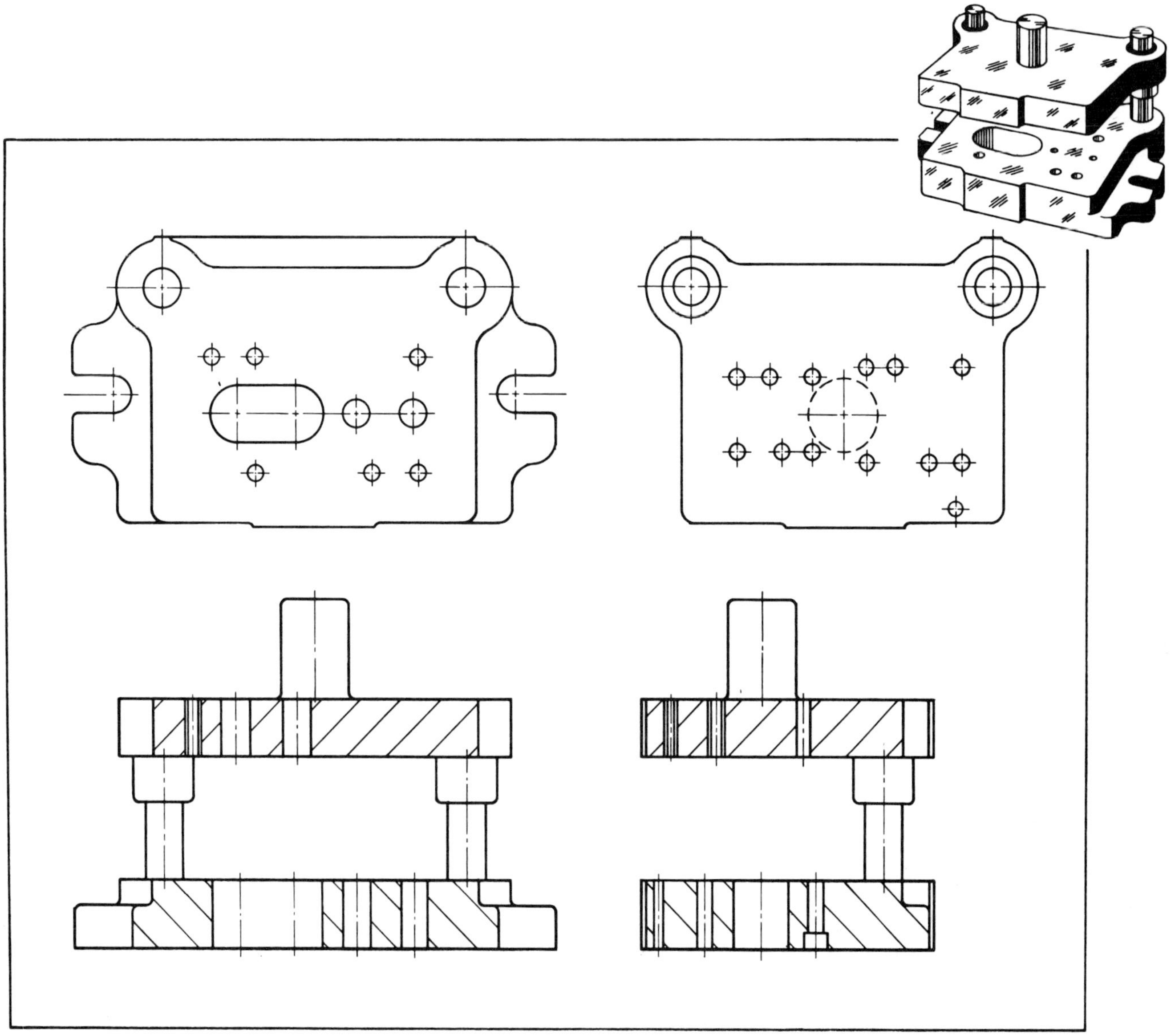

Fig. 1-21. A die set.

parts through the appropriate manufacturing departments. The process or methods engineers then plan the order of manufacturing operations and decide what will be used. They request that the tool design department produce designs of all jigs, fixtures, cutting tools, and dies needed for efficient production of the parts.

The Part

The part which is to be machined, formed, pressed, or inspected is called by one of three names:

1. Part
2. Work
3. Workpiece

Part is the preferred term, but workpiece or simply, work, are often employed as alternate names and all three terms will be used throughout this book.

The print on which this part, work, or workpiece is represented is called a Part Print. It may be a blueprint, or quite often it is a blue and white ozalid print. Therefore, in designing a die for producing a stamping, the die designer works from a part print.

Processing

Following is the sequence of operations or procedure followed in processing a stamping through the planning stages. Substantially the same series of steps would be taken in any large or medium-size manufacturing plant.

After a product designer had prepared layouts and assembly drawings of the product to be manufactured, the engineering department would prepare detail drawings of each individual component which the shop would have to produce. These contain all required views, dimensions, and explanatory notes to represent all detail features of the objects.

Prints of these detail drawings are sent to the process planning or processing department. When stampings are required, it is the function of the men of this department to determine how the stampings are to be made. They decide how many operations will be required and what presses will be employed to make them. This department thus assumes the responsibility of determining the sequence of manufacturing operations. The information is noted on a form called a route sheet.

DET.	REQ'D	PART NAME	MAT.	SPECIFICATIONS
27	4	SOC. CAP SCR.	STD.	3/8 - 16 x 1 1/2
26	1	FRONT SPACER	C.R.S.	1/8 x 3/4 x 4 5/8
25	4	BUTTON HD. SOC. CAP SCR	STD.	3/8 x 16 x 7/8
24	2	DOWEL	STD.	3/8 DIA. x 1 3/4
23	2	DOWEL	STD.	3/8 DIA. x 7/8
22	1	JAM NUT	STD.	1/4 - 20
21	1	SQ. HD. SET SCR.	STD.	1/4 - 20 x 1 3/4
20	2	DOWEL	STD.	3/8 DIA. x 1 1/4
19	4	SOC. CAP SCR.	STD.	3/8 - 16 x 7/8
18	2	DOWEL	STD.	3/8 DIA. x 1 1/2
17	4	SOC. CAP. SCR.	STD.	3/8 - 16 x 1
16	2	RIVET	C.R.S.	1/8 DIA. x 3/8
15	1	STRIP REST	C.R.S.	1/8 x 3/4 x 1 1/2
14	1	BACK GAGE	T.S.	1/8 x 3/4 x 8 1/8
13	2	PIERCE PUNCH	T.S.	3/4 DIA. x 1 7/8
12	1	PUNCH PLATE	M.S.	1 x 2 x 2 1/8
11	1	BLANK-PUNCH	T.S.	1 1/2 x 2 x 2 1/2
10	1	STRIPPER	C.R.S.	3/8 x 2 1/2 x 4 5/8
9	1	DIE BLOCK	T.S.	1 1/4 x 2 3/4 x 4 5/8
8	1	DOWEL	STD.	3/16 x DIA. x 1/2
7	1	FINGER STOP	T.S.	1/8 x 3/8 x 2 1/8
6	1	SOC. CAP SCR.	STD.	#10-24 x 1/4
5	1	SPRING	S.W.	TO SUIT
4	1	SPRING PIN	C.R.S.	1/4 DIA. x 2 5/8
3	1	HINGE PIN	D.R.	1/8 DIA. x 1 7/8
2	1	AUTO STOP	T.S.	1/4 x 1/2 x 2 1/4
1	1	DIE SET	PUR.	SEE NOTE

NAME OF SCHOOL OR COMPANY AND ADDRESS

ASSEMBLY 2 STA. P. & D. FOR – "HOPPER LINK"	TYPE 40-BL
DRAWN BY J. R. P.	CUSTOMER TELECHRON
DATE APR. 25, 1961	ORDER 49268
CHECKED BY C. H. H.	SHEET 1 OF 2
DATE 4-27-61	A B C D E F (● under E)
APPROVED BY R. S.	
DATE 4-28-61	DRG. NO. D-1000
SCALE-FULL	

Fig. 1-23. A typical bill of material.

1-24. ROUTE SHEETS

Route sheets are designed to suit the requirements of the individual plant and therefore the information they contain will vary. However, the following are usually included (Fig. 1-24):

1. The Heading. This is located at the top of the sheet and contains information such as:

Part name
Part number
Drawing number
Number of parts required
Name of product engineer
Date

In addition, the product name and model number may be included.

2. The number of each operation required to make and inspect the part. Numbers are most frequently listed in increments of 5, as 5, 10, 15, 20, etc., to provide numbers in sequence for additional operations which may be found necessary in manufacture or when changes are made in the design of the product.

3. The name of each operation.

4. The name and number of the machine in which the operation is to be performed.

5. Estimates of the number of parts which will be completed per hour for every operation. These estimates are altered after production rates have been measured accurately by the time study department. Route sheets are supplied to the following departments:

Tool design department
Production department
Inspection department

Of course, any machine or product will contain many components which have been standardized and which can be purchased from outside suppliers or vendors. Such items would include screws and dowels, bearings, clutches, motors, and many more. The purchasing department would be supplied with a bill of material, and purchase orders would be issued for all parts to be bought.

1.25. TOOL OPERATION SHEET

The tool operation sheet is prepared from the route sheet and it usually lists the following (Fig. 1-25):

1. Number of each operation.
2. Name of each operation.
3. Machine data.
4. List of all standard and special tools required for the job.
5. Names and numbers of all special tools which are to be designed and built. These numbers are marked on tool drawings and later stamped or marked on the actual tools for identification.

Tool operations sheets are helpful in planning and developing a tooling program. Copies go to the tool designers and to the tool purchasing department. Before proceeding further, study carefully the tool operation sheet illustrated.

1-26. DESIGN ORDER

The design order is a slip of paper authorizing work on an actual design (Fig. 1-26). One is written for each die or special tool required and the information is taken from the route sheet. In addition, it may give instruc-

NAME OF SCHOOL OR COMPANY AND ADDRESS

ROUTE SHEET

PART NAME Housing Cover NO. OF PARTS 800,000 DATE Oct. 19, 1961

PART NO. 10568 DRG. NO. 1225 PROD. ENG. J. Cochran

SHEET NO. 1 OF 1

OPER. NO.	OPERATION	MACHINE	DEPT.	TIME (HOURS)	SET UP (HOURS)
5	Shear Sheet into strips	Bliss Squaring Shears No. 37 (Shop)	30	.0001	---
10	Blank	Federal Press No. 33 No.442 (Shop)	25	.0001	---
15	Form	Federal Press No. 44 No. 337 (Shop)	25	.0002	---
20	Wash and ship to stores	Truck			

Fig. 1-24. A typical route sheet.

tions regarding the type of die preferred. Following is a list of the information usually given on a design order:

1. Department name
2. Tool name
3. Date
4. Tool number
5. Part name
6. Part number
7. Operation
8. Machine in which tool is to be used
9. Department in which machine is located
10. Number of parts to be made

TOOL INSPECTION DEPARTMENT

After a die has been designed, a set of prints is sent to the tool inspection department. After the die has been built they will inspect it to make certain that it was constructed to specifications given in the tool print.

When the die is built by an outside tool shop, it is inspected by the tool inspection department upon delivery and the same inspection procedures are followed to determine if stampings produced by it are held to tolerances specified on the part print.

PRODUCTION

After the tool inspection department has approved its construction and accuracy, the die is delivered to the department where it will be used. The set-up man for that department installs it in the press where it will be operated and he produces a few parts under the same conditions in which the die will run in actual production. These parts are taken to the production inspection department. There, they are inspected to determine whether or not sizes have been held to tolerances specified on the part print.

After the production inspection department has determined that the samples are satisfactory, a form is issued and signed by the chief inspector authorizing production with the die. After the production foreman receives production orders from the production department, he will proceed to go into production of the

NAME OF SCHOOL OR COMPANY AND ADDRESS

PART NAME Housing Cover

PART NO. 10568

TOOL OPERATION SHEET

DATE Oct. 20, 1961

APPROVED BY J. Cochran

Operation Number	OPERATION NAME	TOOL NAME	TOOL NUMBER	Instructions	Dept. No.	EQUIPMENT NAME AND NUMBER
5	Shear Sheet into strips				30	Bliss Squaring
						Shears
						Shop No. 37
10	Blank	Blanking punch and die	T-3073	Des.	25	Federal Press
						No. 33
						Shop No. 442
15	Form	Forming punch and die	T-3074	Des.	25	Federal Press
						No. 44
						Shop No. 337
20	Wash and ship to stores	Truck				

Fig. 1-25. A typical tool operation sheet.

NAME OF SCHOOL OR COMPANY AND ADDRESS

DESIGN ORDER NO.
102

TO Tool Design Department DATE Oct.22, 1961

DESIGN Forming Punch and Die

FOR Forming Lower Flange

PART NAME Housing Cover

PART NO. 10568 TOOL NO. T-3074

USED IN No. 20 Bliss Press SHOP NO. 406

DEPARTMENT Press NO. 22

NUMBER OF PARTS REQUIRED 800,000

COMPLETED CANCELLED

REASON

SIGNED

Fig. 1-26. A typical design order.

stampings. Production orders specify how many parts are to be run, when they will be required, and where they are to be delivered.

After a new die has been in production for a few hours or so and it is found to perform satisfactorily, the order which was issued to the tool-room to build the die is closed and no more time may be charged against it. In this connection it is interesting to note that records are kept of all time devoted to designing, building, inspecting, and trying out the die in order to determine the actual tool cost, illustrating perfectly that "time is money."

DESIGNING THE DIE

Before a designer begins to draw, there are a number of things which he must seriously consider. It is now possible to list all the items which will be required before he can begin designing intelligently. They are:

1. The part print
2. The operation sheet, or route sheet
3. The design order
4. A press data sheet

In addition, he may have a reference drawing of a die similar to the one he is to design or a sketch of a proposed design prepared by the chief tool designer or group leader suggesting a possible approach to solution of the problem. Let us consider further the information required:

Part Print. The part drawing gives all necessary dimensions and notes. Any missing dimension must be obtained from the product design department before work can proceed.

Operation Sheet. The operation sheet or route sheet must be studied to determine exactly what operations were performed upon the workpiece previously. This is very important. When the views of the stamping are laid out, any cuts which were applied in a previous operation must be shown.

The Design Order. This must be studied very carefully because it specifies the type of die to be designed. Consider particularly the operation to be performed, the press in which the die is to be installed, and the number of parts expected to be stamped by the die. The latter will establish the *class* of die to be designed.

The Machine Data Sheet. The die to be designed must fit into a particular press and it is important to know what space is available to receive it and what interferences may be present.

In time you will come to realize the importance of careful and repeated study of the part print, operation sheet, and design order because there can be no deviation from the specifications given.

DRAWING

If the information on a drawing is complete, concise, and presented in the simplest possible manner, the die maker can work to best advantage. The first step in originating plans for a new die is the preparation of a sketch or sketches of significant features of the proposed die. These will become a guide for beginning the actual full-size layout on tracing paper. However, it is a mistake to spend too much time in this phase of the work or to try to develop the entire design in sketch form because then decisions can become too arbitrary and inflexible. Always keep your mind open to possible improvements as you develop the design in layout form. You will find that, often, the first or second idea sketched out can be considerably improved by alteration as work progresses. Often the first idea proves entirely impractical and another method of operation must be substituted.

Before beginning the sketch, place the part print, operation sheet, and design order before you on the drawing table. The three must be studied together so that a complete and exact understanding of the problem will be realized. This study will form the basis for the creation of a mental picture of a tool suitable for performing the operations – one which will meet every requirement. The sketch you make may be a very simple one for simple operations or it may be more elaborate. In fact, a number of sketches may be required for more complex operations and intricate designs. In any event, the sketch will clarify your ideas before a formal layout is attempted. In addition, it will form the basis for a realistic estimate of the size of the finished die so that you may select the proper sheet size for the layout.

LAYOUT

Laying out the die consists of drawing all views necessary for showing every component in its actual position. In the layout stage, no dimensions are applied and neither is the bill of material nor the record strip filled out. After the die has been laid out, the steps necessary for completing the set of working drawings are more or less routine.

A properly prepared assembly drawing contains six general features:

1. All views required for showing the contour of every component including the workpiece.

2. All assembly dimensions. These are dimensions which will be required for assembling the parts and those for machining operations to be performed after assembly.

3. All explanatory notes.

4. Finish marks and grind marks to indicate those surfaces to be machined after assembly.

5. A bill of material listing sizes, purchased components, materials, and number required for all parts.

6. A title block and record strip with identifying information noted properly.

DETAIL DRAWINGS

After the assembly drawing has been completed, detail drawings are prepared unless all dimensions were placed on the assembly, as is done for simple dies. Detail drawings are drawings of individual components and they contain all dimensions, notes, and supplementary information so that each part can be made without reference to the assembly drawing or to other detail drawings. Such information usually includes ten distinct elements:

1. All views required for identifying every detail of the part must be drawn.
2. Every dimension needed for making the part must be given.

3. Suitable notes for furnishing supplementary information which dimensions do not cover must be applied.
4. Finished surfaces must be identified.
5. The name of the part and its number must be given.
6. The material it is to be made from must be specified.
7. The number required per assembly must be stated.
8. The scale to which the drawing has been laid out must be listed.
9. The draftsman's name or initials must be signed.
10. The date must be specified.

CHECKING

After a set of drawings has been completed and the designer has reviewed them for possible omissions or errors, they are turned over to the group leader who will bring them to the checker to be checked. Accompanying them will be the design order, part print, and any notes or sketches which may have accompanied them when the designer received the job. The checker will require all these in order to do his work properly.

The checker will first study the operation of the die to make sure that it will function properly and that its cost will not be excessive for the work it is to perform. After he is satisfied that it has been designed properly, he will check every dimension, note, and specification for accuracy. He usually works from a check print. This is a blue and white print having blue lines and a white background. With a yellow crayon, he will cover with yellow color every dimension he finds to be accurate, and with a red crayon he will cover with red color every dimension he finds to be wrong. Above or to the side he will write the correct dimension in red.

The tracings, along with the check prints, are then returned to the designer for correction. Incorrect dimensions are carefully erased to remove all graphite from the paper. An erasing shield is ordinarily used to prevent smudging of other dimensions or lines. Correct dimensions are then lettered in place.

After the tracings have been corrected, they are returned to the checker and he checks the job again to make sure that no correction was overlooked. He then signs the drawing in the space provided and enters the date the drawing was checked.

After drawings have been completed and checked, they must be approved by the chief designer, chief tool engineer, or possibly the plant superintendent and others who are held responsible by the management for the cost and quality of dies used in the plant. Usually, these approvals are routine after drawings have been approved by the checker. However, it may sometimes happen that someone will refuse to sign because he may feel that the die will not work as well as expected, will not deliver the number of parts required per day, will be too expensive to build, or for some other reason. If he convinces the others that his objections are valid, the drawings will have to be altered or a new design begun, depending upon the extent of the changes to be made.

PRINTS

After approval, blueprints or ozalid prints are made from the tracings, or originals. A small print is taken of the bill of material only. This is sent to the stock cutting department where steel is stored and cut as required. The stock cutter goes over the list, selects bars of proper thickness and width, or diameter, and saws them to the lengths specified for each item listed. These cut blocks and plates are placed in a pan, along with screws, dowels, and other parts which are kept in stock. When purchased components are delivered to the plant, they are also placed in the pan. Finally, the pan contains a set of die prints and a part print and it is delivered to the tool-room where the tool-room foreman turns it over to the die maker who will build the die.

One of the prints is sent to the purchasing department. There, orders are written to authorize purchase of all components which will enter into building the die. If the entire die is to be built by an outside tool shop, a purchase order is sent to them. If it is to be built within the plant, an order authorizing construction is sent to the tool-room. In addition, requisitions are made out for the following:

1. Standard parts or assemblies which are not kept in stock and which must be purchased.

2. Castings, forgings, or weldments required for construction of the die.

3. Steels of special analysis not carried in stock.

4. Special sizes of steels or other materials not stocked.

The purchasing agent must plan for delivery of all these components before the date set for beginning construction of the die.

File cards are then made out for the drawings and they are filed away in drawing files. These are usually kept in the tool and die design department, although some plants keep them in a vault. The file cards list the job by name and number, and they contain the number of the drawing file in which drawings are kept to help in locating them if required again in the future.

1-27. CHECKING A SCRAP STRIP

A die maker examines a scrap strip and finished stamping. This part was produced in a multiple station progressive die in which the operations are done progressively from station to station and a finished part is delivered with every stroke of the press (Fig. 1-27).

1-28. PROGRESSIVE DIE

Figure 1-28 shows photographs of the upper (top) and lower (bottom) sections of the die used to produce the scrap strip and stamping shown in Fig. 1-27. The design of progressive dies requires a thorough knowledge of die principles. A designer capable of designing progressive dies is considered one of the top men in the field.

DIE OPERATIONS

Just exactly what operations are performed in dies? This question is asked often and we have prepared the following illustrated list of the twenty types of operations which are performed in dies.

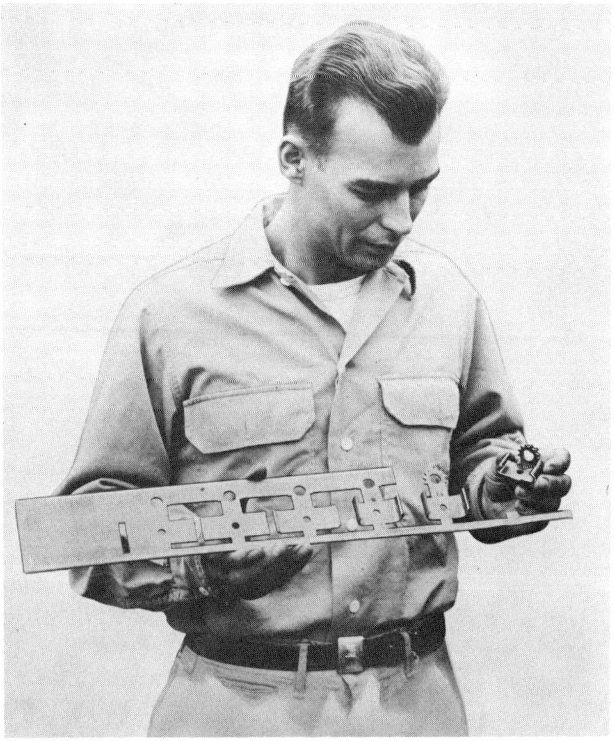

Bethlehem Steel Co.

Fig. 1-27. Examining a scrap strip.

1-29. BLANKING

Stampings having an irregular contour must be blanked from the strip. Piercing, embossing, and various other operations may be performed on the strip prior to the blanking station. (Figure 1-29.)

1-30. CUT OFF

Cut-off operations are those in which strip of suitable width is cut to length. Preliminary operations before cutting off include piercing, notching, and embossing. Although they are relatively simple, many parts can be produced by cut off dies. (Figure 1-30.)

1-31. COMPOUND

Compound dies pierce and blank simultaneously at the same station. They are more expensive to build and they are used where considerable accuracy is required in the part. (Figure 1-31.)

1-32. TRIMMING

When cups and shells are drawn from flat sheet metal the edge is left wavy and irregular, due to uneven flow of metal. This irregular edge is trimmed in a trimming die. Shown is a flanged shell, as well as the trimmed ring removed from around the edge. (Figure 1-32.)

1-33. PIERCING

Piercing dies pierce holes in previously blanked, formed, or drawn parts. It is often impractical to pierce holes while forming or before forming because they would become distorted in the forming operation. In such cases they are pierced in a piercing die after forming. (Figure 1-33.)

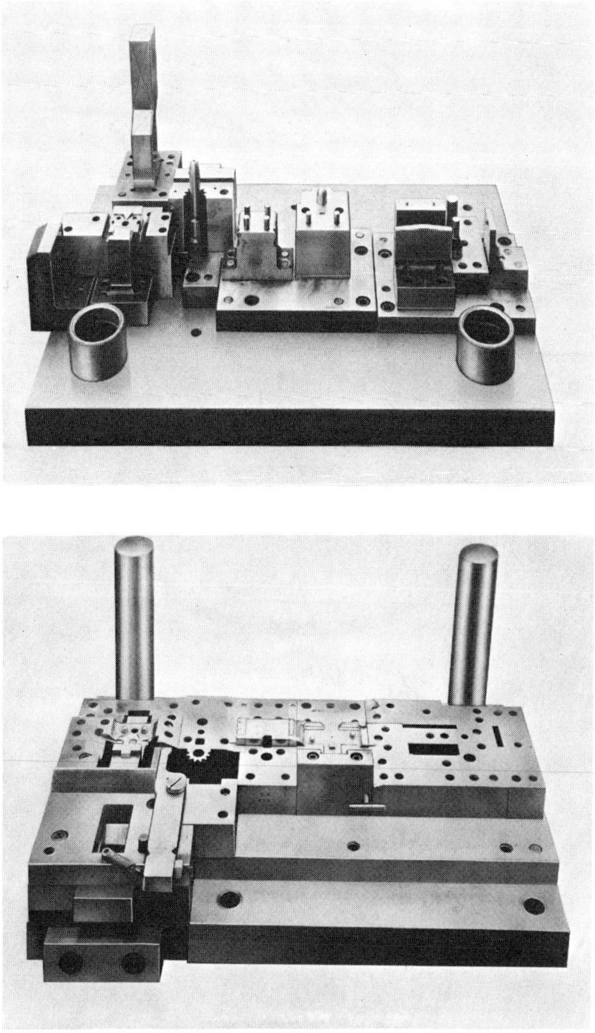

Bethlehem Steel Co.

Fig. 1-28. The upper (top) and the lower (bottom) portions of a typical progressive die.

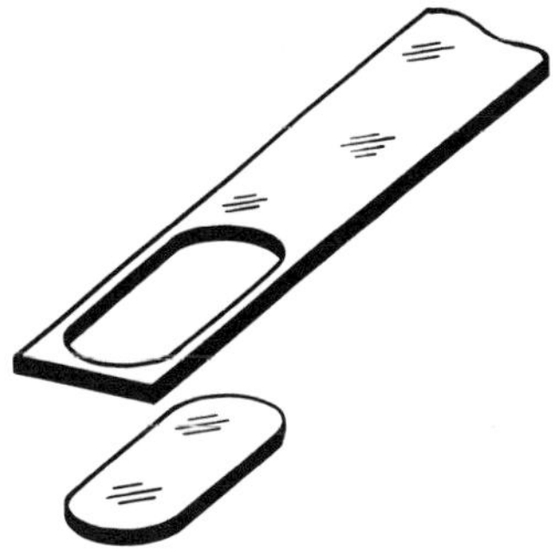

Fig. 1-29. A blank and the strip from which it has been cut.

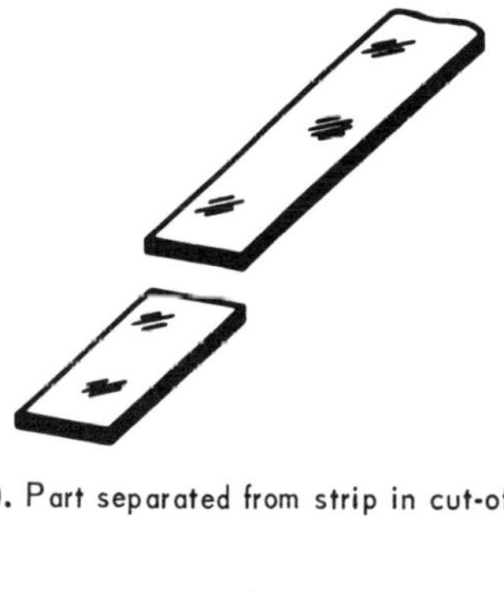

Fig. 1-30. Part separated from strip in cut-off operation.

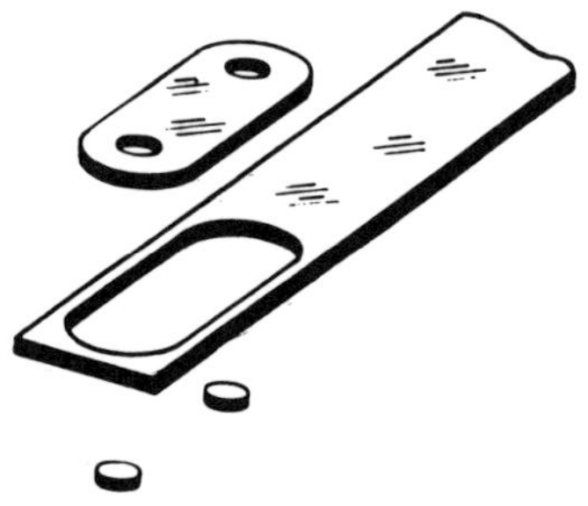

Fig. 1-31. This part is blanked and pierced simultaneously in a compound die.

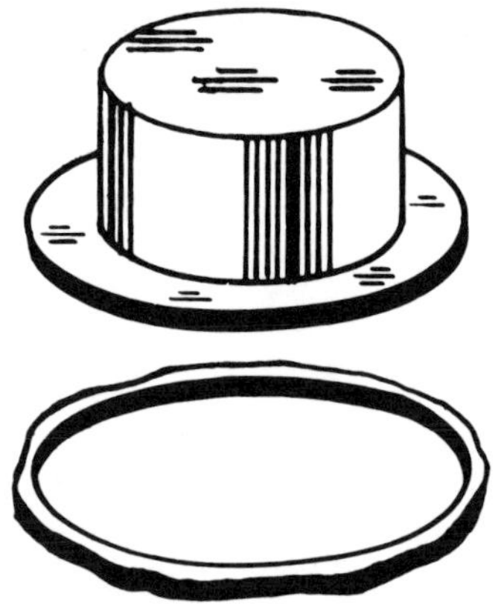

Fig. 1-32. The result of trimming in a trimming die.

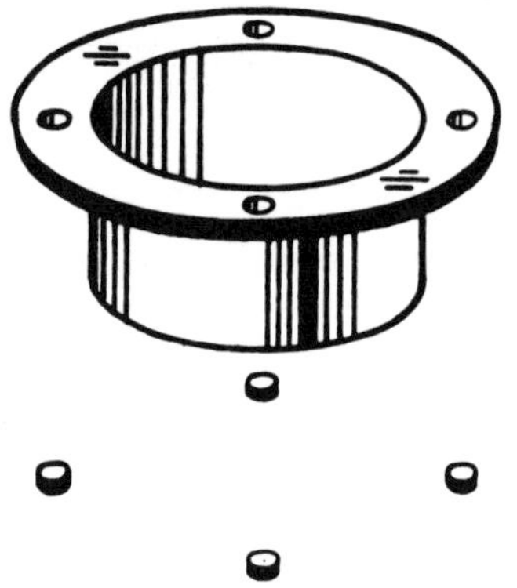

Fig. 1-33. Holes pierced in a previously drawn part.

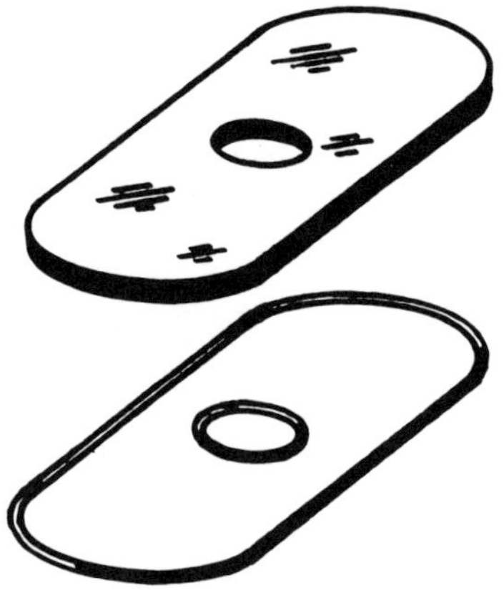

Fig. 1-34. The result of shaving in a shaving die.

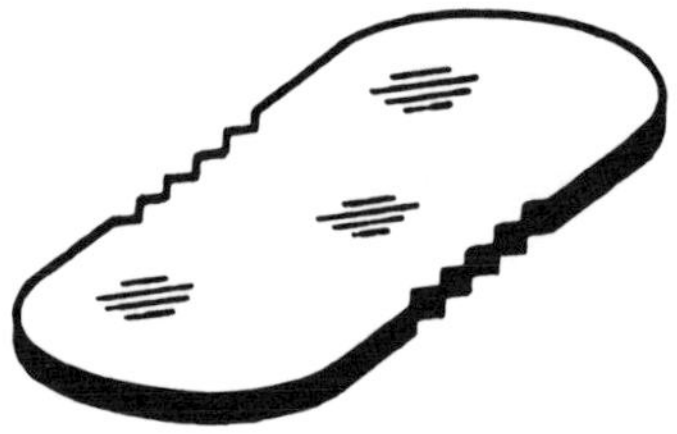

Fig. 1-35. Serrations applied in a broaching die.

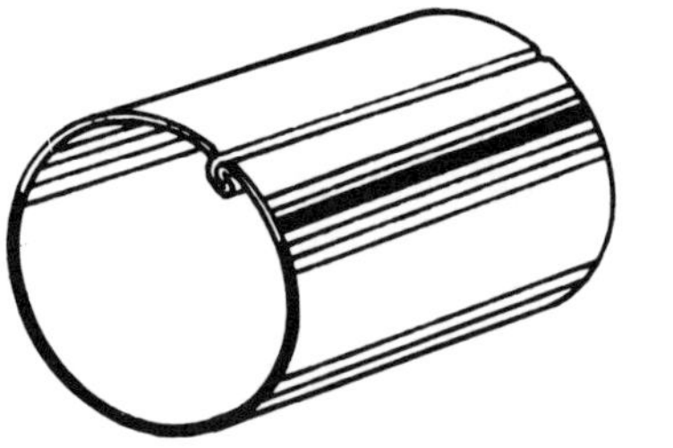

Fig. 1-36. The seam on this part is done as a secondary operation in a horn die.

1-34. SHAVING

Shaving consists in removing a chip from around the edges of a previously blanked stamping. A straight, smooth edge is provided and therefore shaving is frequently performed on instrument parts, watch and clock parts, and the like. Shaving is accomplished in shaving dies especially designed for the purpose. (Figure 1-34.)

1.35. BROACHING

Figure 1-35 shows serrations applied in the edges of a stamping. These would be broached in a broaching die. Broaching operations are similar to shaving operations. A series of teeth removes the metal instead of just one tooth as in shaving. Broaching must be used when more material is to be removed than could effectively be done with one tooth.

1-36. HORNING

Horn dies are provided with an arbor or horn over which the parts are placed for secondary operations such as seaming (Fig. 1-36). Horn dies may also be used for piercing holes in the sides of shells.

1-37. SIDE CAM OPERATIONS

Piercing a number of holes simultaneously around a shell is done in a side cam die. Side cams convert the up-and-down motion of the press ram into horizontal or angular motion when it is required in the nature of the work. (Figure 1-37.)

1-38. BENDING

Bending dies apply simple bends to stampings. A simple bend is one in which the line of bend is straight. One or more bends may be involved, and bending dies are a large and important class of press tool. (Figure 1-38.)

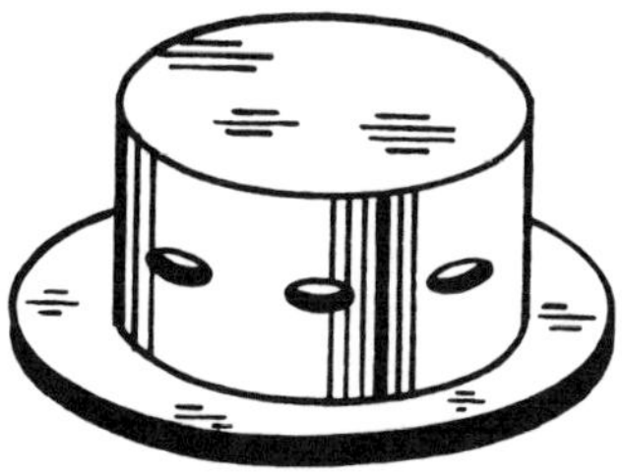

Fig. 1-37. The holes are pierced simultaneously in a side cam die.

Fig. 1-38. Stamping bent in a bending die.

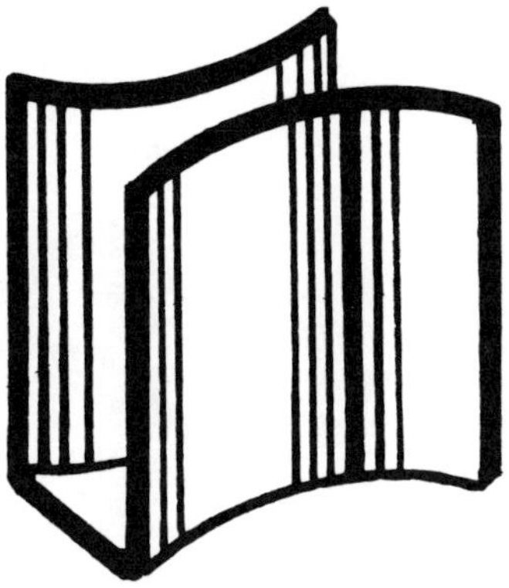

Fig. 1-39. Stamping formed in a forming die.

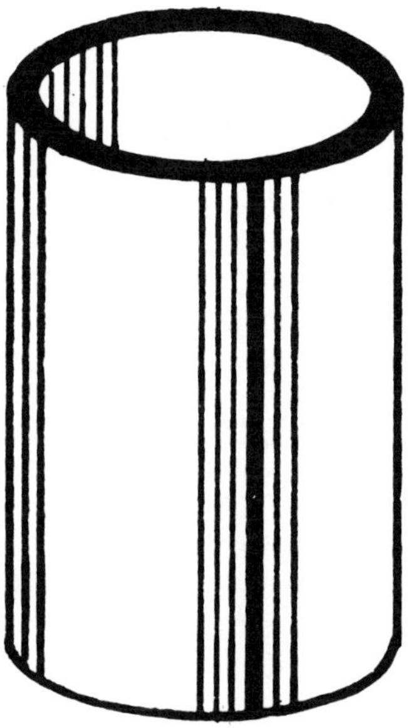

Fig. 1-40. Shell drawn from a flat sheet.

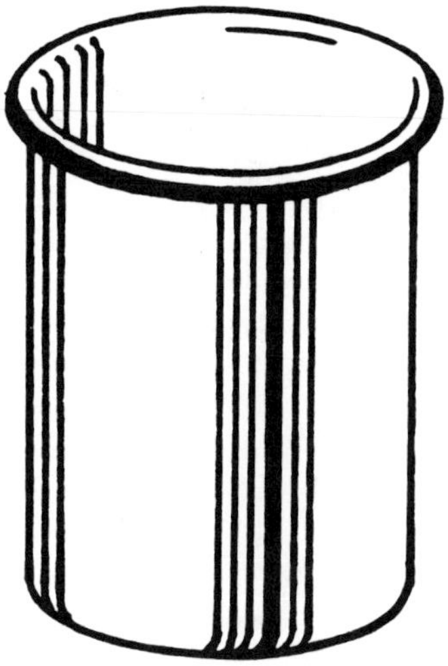

Fig. 1-41. Lip on this drawn shell produced in curling die.

1-39. FORMING

Forming dies apply more complex forms to workpieces. The line of bend is curved instead of straight and the metal is subjected to plastic flow or deformation. (Figure 1-39.)

1-40. DRAWING

Drawing dies transform flat sheets of metal into cups, shells, or other drawn shapes by subjecting the material to severe plastic deformation. Shown in Fig. 1-40 is a rather deep shell that has been drawn from a flat sheet.

1-41. CURLING

Curling dies curl the edges of drawn shells to provide strength and rigidity. The curl may be applied over a wire ring for increased strength. You may have seen the tops of sheet metal pails curled in this manner. Flat parts may be curled also. A good example would be a hinge in which both members are curled to provide a hole for the hinge pin. (Figure 1-41.)

1-42. BULGING

Bulging dies expand the bottom of previously drawn shells. The bulged bottoms of some types of coffee pots are formed in bulging dies. (Figure 1-42.)

1-43. SWAGING

In swaging operations, drawn shells or tubes are reduced in diameter for a portion of their lengths. The operation is also called necking. (Figure 1-43.)

1-44. EXTRUDING

Extruding dies cause metal to be extruded or squeezed out, much as toothpaste is extruded from its tube when pressure is applied. Figure 1-44 shows a collapsible tube formed and extruded from a solid slug of metal.

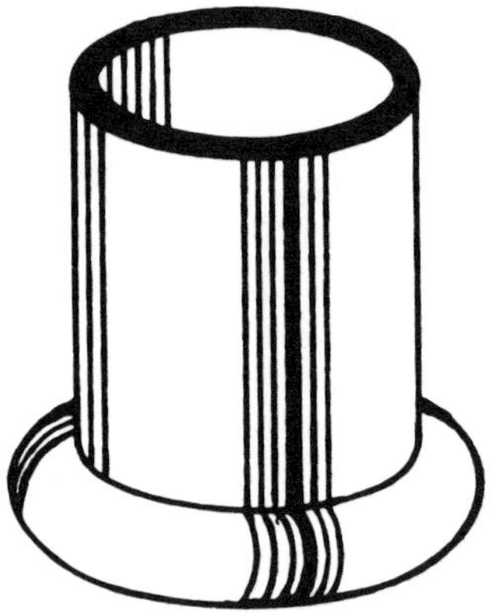

Fig. 1-42. Bulge in this drawn shell produced in bulging die.

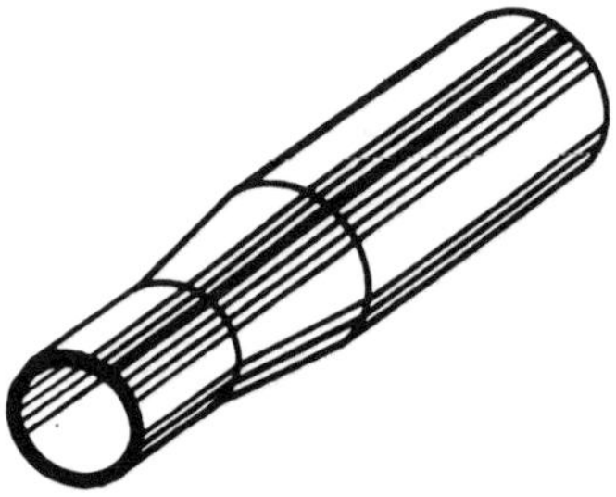

Fig. 1-43. Drawn shell that has been swaged.

Fig. 1-44. Drawn shell that has been extruded.

1-45. COLD FORMING

In cold forming operations, metal is subjected to high pressure and caused to flow into a predetermined form. In coining, the metal is caused to flow into the shape of the die cavity. Coins such as nickels, dimes, and quarters are produced in coining dies.

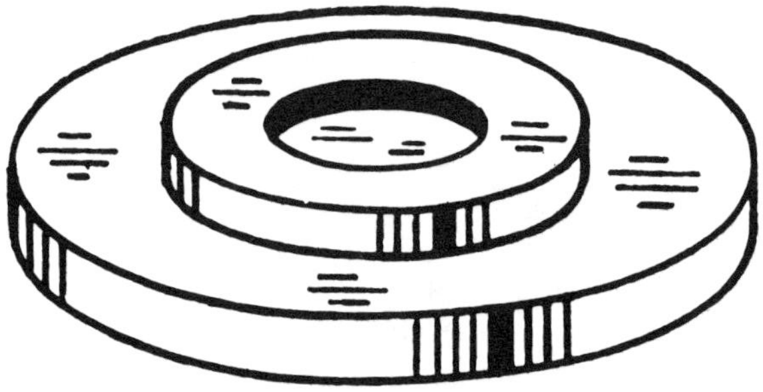

Fig. 1-45. Cold-formed part in which metal flow is caused by high pressure.

1-46. PROGRESSIVE OPERATIONS

Progressive operations are those in which progressive dies perform work at a number of stations simultaneously. A complete part is cut off, at the final station, with each stroke of the press. The die shown in Fig. 1-28 is a progressive die.

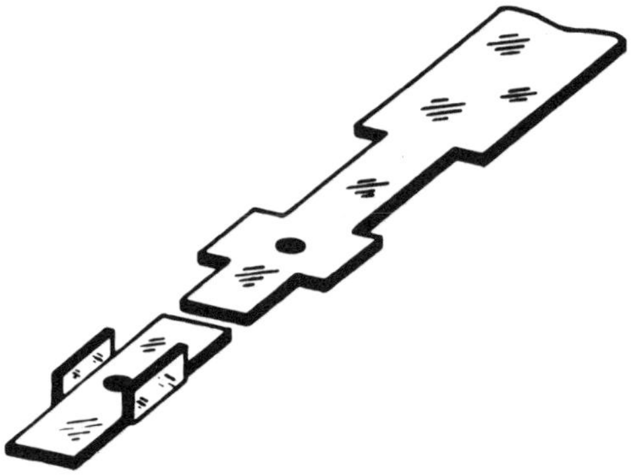

Fig. 1-46. Part and strip produced in a progressive die.

1-47. SUB PRESS OPERATIONS

Sub press dies are used for producing tiny watch, clock, and instrument components, represented by the watch needles shown. Sub presses are special types of die sets used only for such precision work.

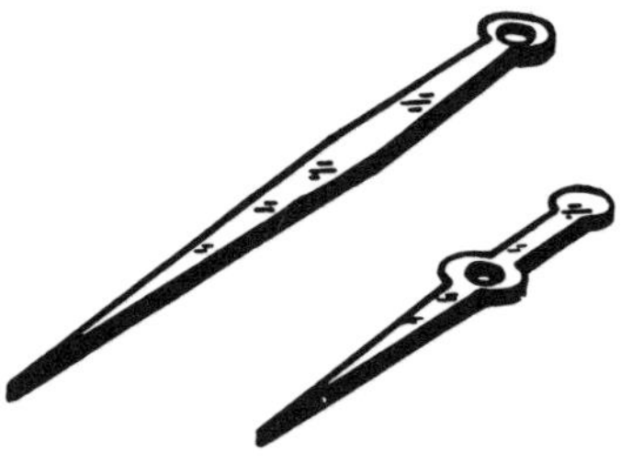

Fig. 1-47. Typical precision parts produced in sub press dies.

1-48. ASSEMBLY DIES

Represented is an assembly operation in which two studs are riveted at the ends of a link. Assembly dies assemble parts with great speed and they are being used more and more.

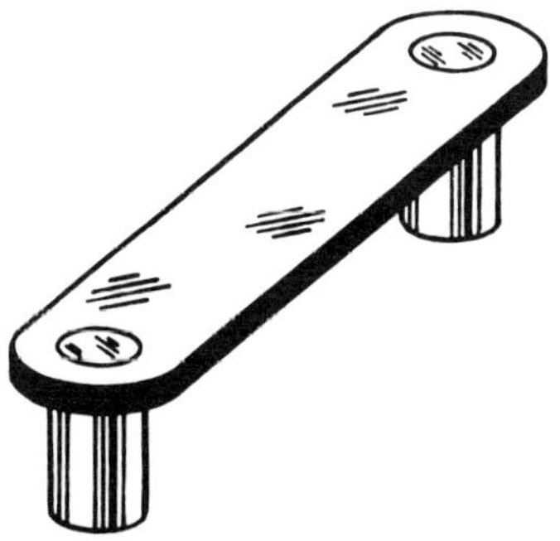

Fig. 1-48. Part produced in an assembly die.

From the foregoing, you can perhaps appreciate what a wide field die design engineering really covers. You must have come to realize that it is indeed a pleasant and interesting occupation, one which will stimulate your mind in much the same manner as working out fascinating puzzles. In addition, you will come to find that is a very profitable one.

As you study the sections to follow, you will be introduced, step by step, to the fundamental die components and you will learn the methods by which die designers assemble these components in designing dies. When you have completed the book you will know the elements of die design quite thoroughly. Knowledge such as this is well paid for by Industry. You will have acquired the foundation of a career that can benefit you for the rest of your life.

Section 2

PRESSES AND PRESS ACCESSORIES

Before studying die design, it will be helpful to have an understanding of the construction and operation of the presses, or machines, in which the dies are operated. In this section you will learn about not only the newer and more modern machines, or presses, but also about some of the older types that are still operating in many of our factories today. Several of these older models have been in use for 30 years or more and are still producing parts.

PRESS TYPES

There are four basic types of presses in which dies are operated. They are:

1. Gap-Frame Presses
2. Straight-Sided, or Four-Post Presses
3. Underdrive Presses
4. Super High Speed Presses

Each type, in turn, contains a number of subtypes in a bewildering variety of sizes and shapes.

PRESS POWER

Today's presses get their power from four basic sources. These sources are:

1. Manual—these presses are hand-operated or foot-operated
2. Mechanical—these presses are motor driven and may have a flywheel, single reduction gear, or multiple reduction gearing
3. Hydraulic—these presses may be oil-operated or water-operated
4. Pneumatic—these presses are operated by compressed air

In this section we will discuss primarily two types of presses—mechanical and hydraulic. While not trying to down play or ignore either manual or pneumatic presses, if you develop an understanding of mechanically and hydraulically driven machines, you will soon discover their similarities and principles can be applied to all four types.

PRESS SPEED

Although some very-high-speed, low-tonnage presses (15–30 tons) run at up to 1800 strokes per minute and typically involve light forming, such as electrical connectors, when cutting dies are operated, the speeds usually range from around 40 to 800 strokes per minute. Because drawing and forming dies must be run more slowly to allow time for the metal to flow, their speeds usually range from around 5 to 100 strokes per minute, depending on part size and severity of the operation being performed.

2-1. GAP-FRAME PRESSES

Gap-frame presses are the most widely used in a large variety of press types. They produce many thousands of different kinds of parts, ranging in size from tiny instrument components to large appliance, automotive, and space vehicle parts. Some operations performed include blanking, trimming, bending, forming, and drawing. The distinguishing characteristic of a gap-frame press is its open throat. Construction of the gap-frame press results in a "C-shape," which provides for easy accessibility in loading and unloading material, parts, and tools. This easy accessibility permits strips or sheets to be fed from right to left or left to right, from front to back or allows individual blanks to be inserted in the dies for either single part production or secondary operations.

Most gap-frame presses are built in capacities ranging from about 100 to 300 tons pressure. These presses can be (1) inclinable, (2) fixed (noninclinable), (3) single-action, (4) double-action, or (5) back-geared.

The frame of an inclinable press can be tilted backward to an angle of around 30° (see Fig. 2-7). This incline permits finished parts, slugs, or both, to slide to the rear of the machine upon completion. As the name implies, a fixed position, or noninclinable machine does not tilt, and parts and/or slugs must either drop vertically or be removed by some other means.

Single-action presses are constructed with a single ram, or slide. These machines are used for blanking, bending, forming, and other operations. They perform a single action with each cycle of the press. A double-action machine is built with dual rams, usually one inner ram sliding within an outer ram. They are used for severe forming and drawing operations. Back-geared presses are provided with gears that mechanically slow the stroke and increase the power of the press.

To enlarge your understanding of the gap-frame press, consider Fig. 2-1-A, which illustrates a typical flywheel-type press. One revolution of the flywheel causes the crankshaft to make one 360° rotation. The rotation of the crankshaft forces the slide to move vertically to the bottom of its stroke distance and return to its original uppermost position, thus completing one cycle of the press. Figure 2-1-B shows the additional components of a back-geared press. As previously mentioned, gearing increases the power capacity of the press.

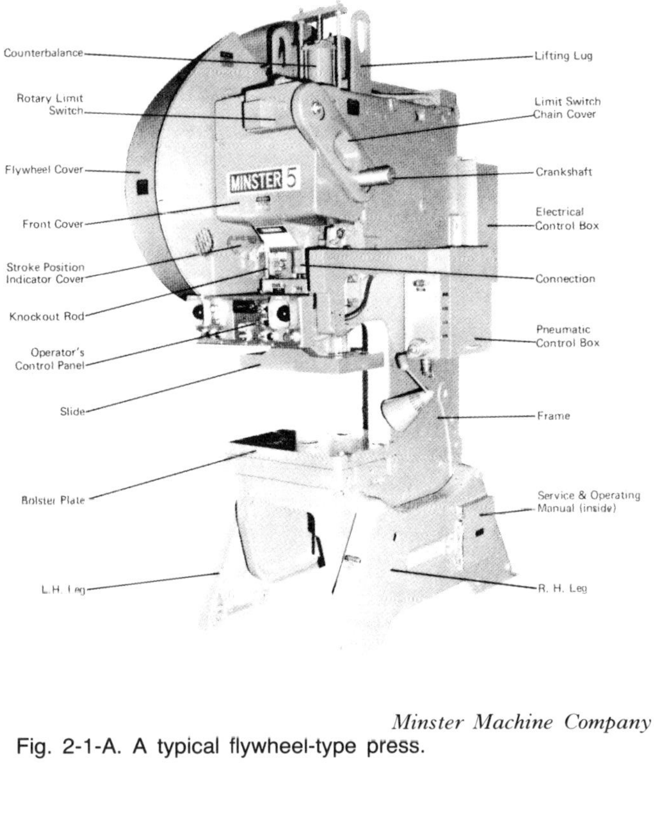

Minster Machine Company

Fig. 2-1-A. A typical flywheel-type press.

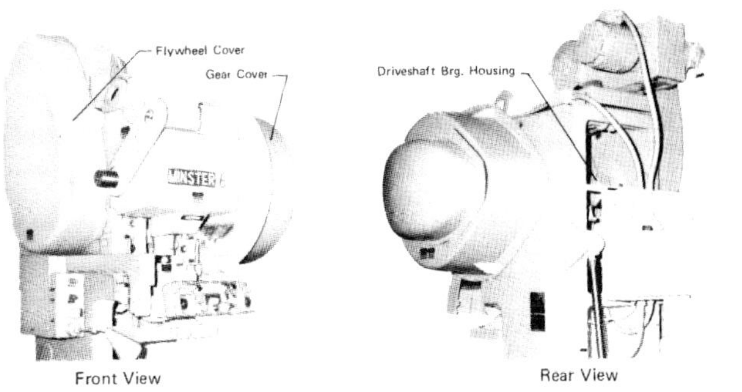

Minster Machine Company

Fig. 2-1-B. The additional components of a back-geared press.

2-2. FRAME ASSEMBLY

The exploded view at Fig. 2-2-A shows the frame assembly of a representative flywheel press. Although some parts have not been identified, for the sake of simplicity, the major components are easily located. Locate each detail in the illustration and become familiar with both the name and function of each.

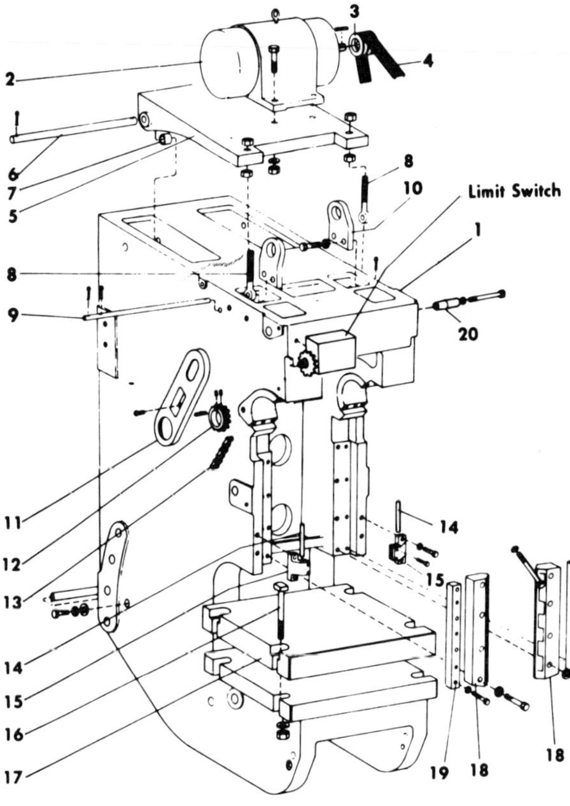

Minster Machine Company

Fig. 2-2-A. Exploded view of the frame assembly of a flywheel-type press.

The exploded view at Fig. 2-2-B is the same as at Fig. 2-2-A, except it illustrates a geared-type press. Again, although some components are not specifically identified, the major ones are. The more familiar you become with the component and its purpose, the faster you will grasp the logic behind both the machine and the tool, as well as the function and purpose of each.

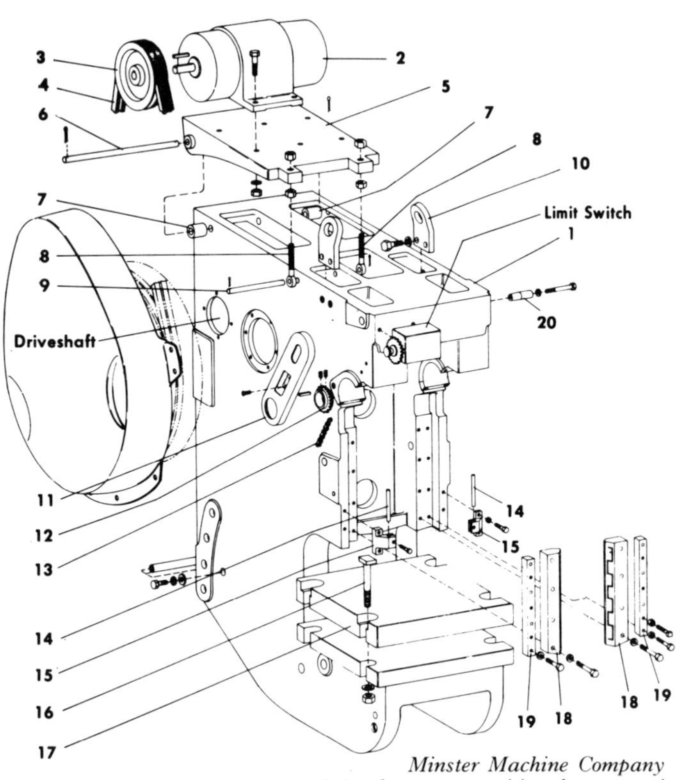

Minster Machine Company

Fig. 2-2-B. Exploded view of the frame assembly of a geared press.

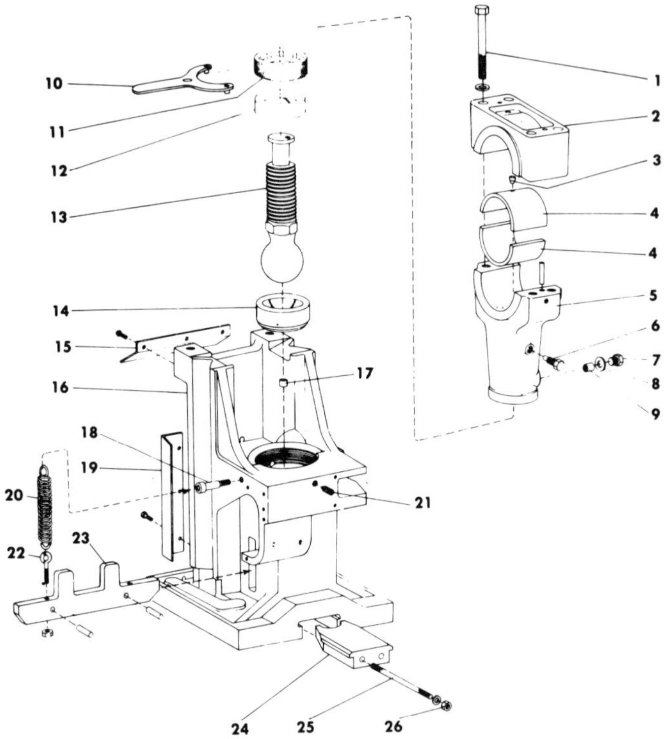

Minster Machine Company

Fig. 2-3. Exploded view of the slide assembly.

Study the following list of names of parts and locate each one in the drawing. You need to familiarize yourself with each component and fully understand its function in the press working process.

1. Frame
2. Drive Motor
3. Motor Sheave
4. Vee Belts
5. Motor Bracket
6. Motor Plate Pin
7. Pivot Shaft Collar
8. Motor Adjusting Screw
9. Motor Adjusting Pin
10. Lifting Lug
11. Limit Switch Cover
12. Limit Switch Sprocket
13. Limit Switch Chain
14. Knockout Rod
15. Knockout Bracket
16. Bolster Bolt
17. Bolster Plate
18. Gib
19. Gib Adjusting Wedge
20. Brake Anchor Pin

2-3. SLIDE ASSEMBLY

The exploded view, Fig. 2-3, illustrates the components that are included in the slide assembly, often referred to as the ram. The slide assembly is the working member of the press and it is important that you understand its construction and purpose thoroughly. The operation of the slide can affect the design of many parts of the die. As mentioned in Section 2-1, the slide is reciprocated up and down by a crank through connection 5 while confined and guided by gibs (Fig. 2-2) attached to the frame. The connection screw 13 is constructed with a hardened ball end, which engages the slide bushing 14. Both the connection screw and slide bushing are confined in the slide by the adjusting nut 11, which is tightened by the spanner wrench 10.

The threads of the connection screw engage a hole tapped in the bottom of connection 5. The position of the connection screw is then fixed by the connection screw stop 6. Position of the slide is therefore adjusted by raising or lowering the connection screw to its proper height. Adjustments are made by loosening the connection screw stop 6, turning the connection screw with spanner wrench 10, either up or down, depending on the direction in which the screw is turned, and finally retightening the connection screw stop 6.

Slide cap 24 grips the shank of the die set for reciprocating the punch half of the die set up and down with each cycle of the machine. Two slide cap studs 25 are threaded into holes in the slide assembly thereby tightening the slide cap against the die shank when the slide cap nuts 26 are tightened. It should be noted, however, that for safety reasons, when large forces are involved, merely gripping the shank of the die set may not be sufficient. It is often necessary to attach the punch half of the die set to the slide assembly with clamps, T-bolts, or other devices.

Study the following list of names of parts and actually locate each one in the illustration to familiarize yourself with the construction of the slide assembly:

1. Cap Screw
2. Connection Cap
3. Bushing Pin
4. Connection Bushing
5. Connection
6. Connection Screw Stop
7. Clamp Plug Screw
8. Laminated Washer
9. Connection Clamp Plug
10. Spanner Wrench
11. Adjusting Nut
12. Ball Bushing
13. Connection Screw
14. Slide Bushing
15. Splash Guard
16. Slide
17. Slide Plug
18. Shoulder Screw
19. Oil Trough
20. Knockout Spring
21. Socket Set Screw
22. Knockout Eye Bolt
23. Knockout Bar
24. Slide Cap
25. Slide Cap Stud
26. Slide Cap Nut

2-4. CRANKSHAFT ASSEMBLY

The crankshaft assembly (Fig. 2-4) drives the slide assembly (Fig. 2-3) in an up and down motion. This up and down action is accomplished by attaching the connection (5 in Fig. 2-3) to the eccentric diameter of the crankshaft 1. The slide assembly is held in place vertically by the gibs (18 in Fig. 2-2) attached to the frame. In a press each revolution of crankshaft 1 drives the slide assembly through one complete up and down cycle of the machine. In a flywheel press, the flywheel is connected directly to the crankshaft and each revolution of the flywheel completes one machine cycle. In a geared-type press, however, it takes several revolutions of a driveshaft to complete one machine cycle. This is explained in more detail in Section 2-5.

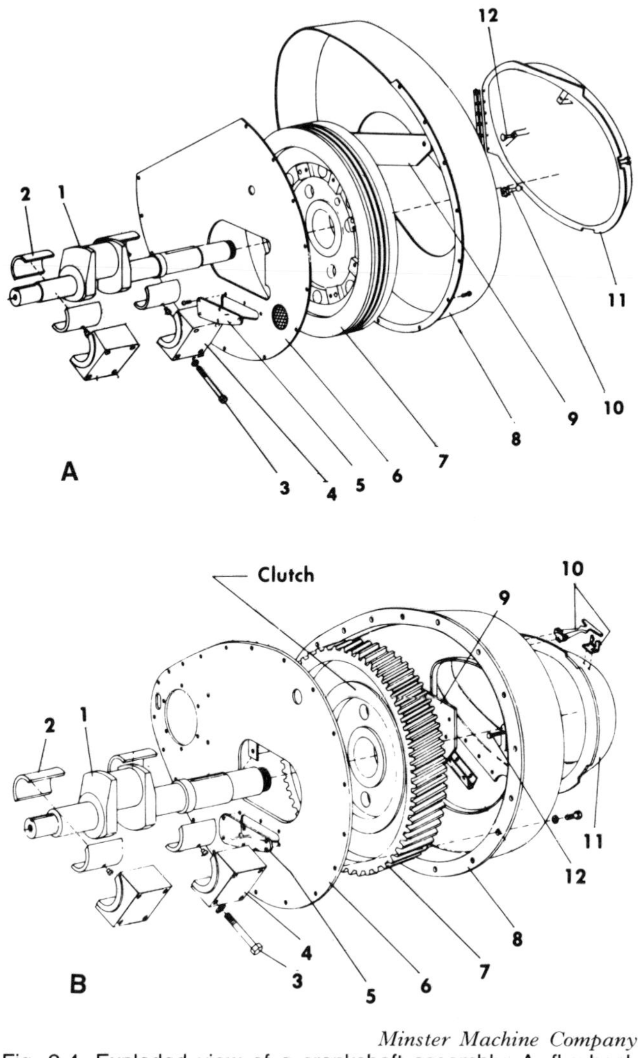

Minster Machine Company
Fig. 2-4. Exploded view of a crankshaft assembly: A, flywheel-type press; B, gear-type press.

Study the following parts lists to determine each component's function in the operation of the machine:

Flywheel-type (Fig. 2-4-A):

1. Crankshaft
2. Main Bearing Bushing
3. Main Bearing Cap Screw
4. Main Bearing Cap
5. Indicator Window
6. Support Plate
7. Flywheel
8. Flywheel Cover
9. Mounting Plate
10. Cover Latch
11. Clutch Valve Cover
12. Elevator Bolt

Geared-type (Fig. 2-4-B):

1. Crankshaft
2. Main Bearing Bushing
3. Main Bearing Cap Screw
4. Main Bearing Cap
5. Indicator Window
6. Support Plate
7. Gear
8. Gear Cover
9. Mounting Plate
10. Cover Latch
11. Clutch Valve Cover
12. Elevator Bolt

2-5. BACKGEAR ASSEMBLY

In a backgeared press, considerable mechanical advantage is realized, thereby generating more force in the slide assembly than obtainable in a flywheel press. This happens because the flywheel 3 (Fig. 2-5) is not mounted directly on the crankshaft for driving the slide assembly, but is connected to the driveshaft 12. Driveshaft 12 turns the drive pinion 11, which, in turn, drives the gear (7 in Fig. 2-4-B). Several revolutions of the pinion gear are required to complete one revolution of the gear. Therefore, several revolutions of the driveshaft are required to complete one revolution of the crankshaft, thus completing one machine cycle and gaining the mechanical advantage previously mentioned.

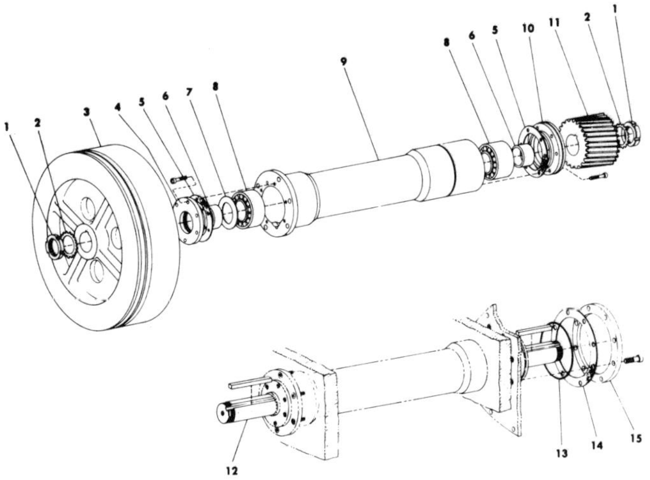

Minster Machine Company
Fig. 2-5. Exploded view of a driveshaft.

A driveshaft parts list is shown in Fig. 2-5. As with the previous parts lists, you should become familiar with these components and their functions:

1. Locknut
2. Lockwasher
3. Flywheel
4. Bearing Cup Clamp
5. Gasket
6. Bearing Spacer
7. Retainer
8. Roller Bearing
9. Bearing Housing Quill
10. Bearing Retainer Clamp
11. Drive Pinion
12. Driveshaft
13. "O" Ring
14. Quill Seal Gasket
15. Quill Seal Plate

2-6. CLUTCH/BRAKE ASSEMBLY

There are several different and varied types of clutch/brake mechanisms for the operation of presses. Federal regulations, such as the Occupational Safety and Health Act (OSHA), are concerned with these mechanisms and require certain rules to be observed. It is not the intent of this text to spell out or interpret these rules; however, one of those regulations requires the automatic deactivation of the press clutch/brake unit in the event of an air supply failure. Furthermore, the clutch must not be able to be reactivated until normal air pressure is restored. We will examine a clutch/brake assembly that meets these requirements.

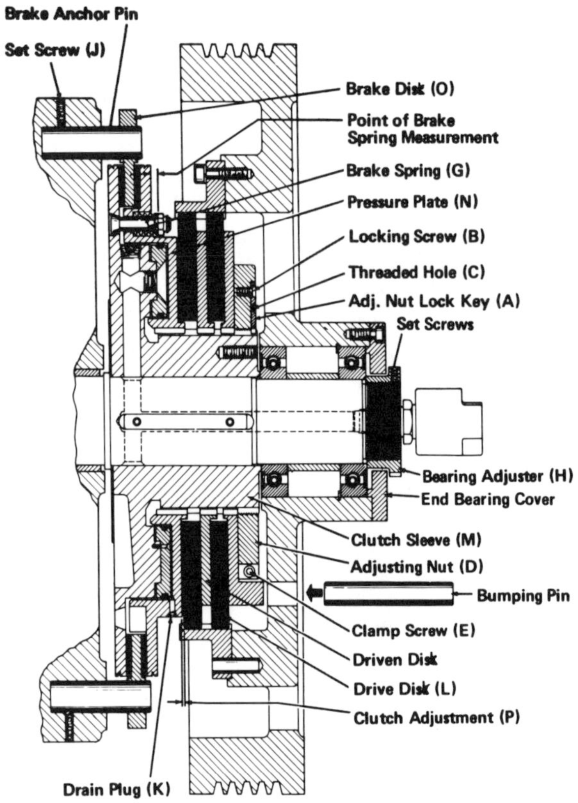

Minster Machine Company
Fig. 2-6-A. Cross-section view of Minster Machine Company's patented combination friction clutch and brake.

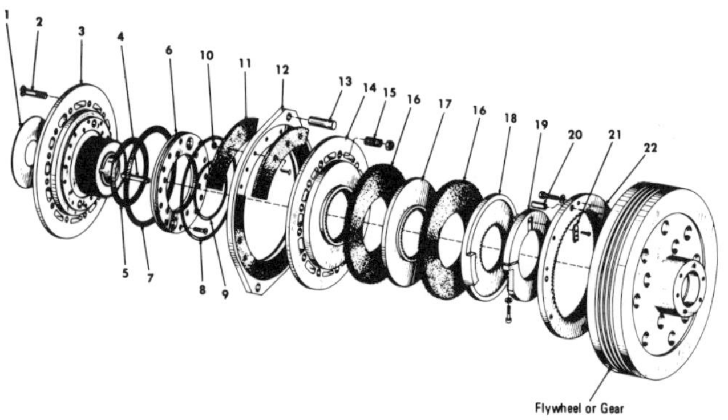

Minster Machine Company
Fig. 2-6-B. Exploded view of the CFC clutch.

Figure 2-6-A is a cross-sectional view of Minster Machine Company's patented Combination Friction Clutch and Brake, referred to as their CFC type. In this mechanism, compressed air is supplied through the end of the shaft. The air flows from the shaft end through air passages in the clutch sleeve, and into the pressure chamber formed by the pressure plate. As air pressure builds up behind the pressure plate, overcoming the brake spring pressure, the pressure plate presses against the moving molded drive disks, forcing them in contact with the motionless cast driven disks. This action transmits drive motion from either the flywheel or gear to the clutch shaft.

Conversely, when the air is exhausted from the pressure plate chamber, brake springs automatically clamp the anchored stationary brake disk between the pressure plate and clutch sleeve, thus stopping rotation of the shaft.

Study both Figs. 2-6-A and 2-6-B to determine the parts and their functions within the clutch/brake assembly:

1. Oil Slinger
2. Brake Spring Bolt
3. Clutch Sleeve
4. Clutch Sleeve Key
5. Inside Gasket
6. Packing Retainer
7. Outside Gasket
8. Outside "O" Ring
9. Inside "O" Ring
10. Rivets and Burrs
11. Brake Disk Facing
12. Brake Disk
13. Brake Anchor Pin
14. Pressure Plate
15. Brake Spring
16. Drive Disk
17. Driven Disk
18. End Driven Disk
19. Adjusting Nut
20. Dowel Pin
21. Adjusting Nut Lock
22. Drive Ring

2-7. INCLINING MECHANISM

The inclining mechanism (Fig. 2-7) is used for tilting the frame to an angular position. This is necessary for some operations when an upper knockout is incorporated in the die. The ejected part then slides to the rear of the press by gravity. One type of inclining mechanism consists of turning the crank handle 3, which is attached to the frame by inclining bracket 9 through the inclining

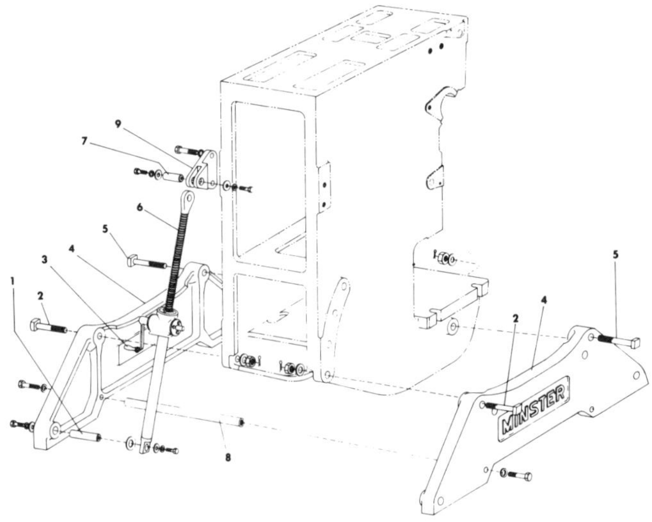

Minster Machine Company
Fig. 2-7. Exploded view of an inclining mechanism.

jack 6. The rear frame bolts 2 are repositioned in the appropriate hole to stabilize the angle of incline when necessary. The parts of the inclining mechanism are:

1. Leg Inclining Pin
2. Rear Frame Bolt
3. Crank Handle
4. Leg
5. Front Frame Bolt
6. Inclining Jack
7. Bracket Pivot Pin
8. Leg Spacer
9. Inclining Frame Bracket

2-8. LARGE GAP FRAME PRESSES

Gap frame presses are manufactured by several different builders and the outer appearances of each make varies considerably from that of other makers. Figure 2-8 is a 250 ton, two-point, meaning it has two connections, photo press. It has a pressurized, recirculating lubrication system and two pneumatic die cushions in the bed. It should also be noted that this particular machine is a twin-drive machine, which means it is driven by gears on both ends of the crankshaft.

Minster Machine Company

Fig. 2-8. Large gap frame press.

2-9. OPERATING A GAP FRAME PRESS

Figure 2-9 shows parts being made in a typical geared-type gap frame press at Quality Tool and Stamping in Muskegon, Michigan. Observe how the operators must use both hands to activate the machine. This is an OSHA regulation and is intended to prevent the operator from accidentally cycling the machine while one of his hands is in the working area. Many fingers and hands were lost before this rule was enforced.

Note also the compressed air-inlet at the end of the shaft in the upper left-hand corner. This is the compressed air used in actuating the clutch/brake assembly discussed in Section 2-6.

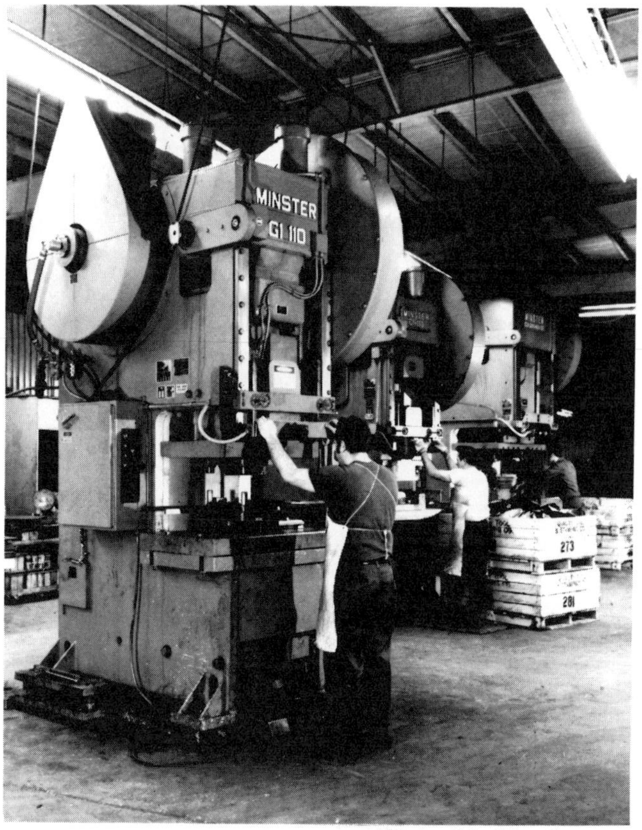

Minster Machine Company

Fig. 2-9. Making parts in a large gap frame press.

2-10. HYDRAULIC PRESSES

As you would imagine, hydraulic presses differ from mechanical ones in several aspects. A hydraulic press (Fig. 2-10) operates from the motion achieved when a piston is guided in a cylinder. This motion is realized when a fluid, usually oil or a mixture of two or more liquids and/or gases, is controlled by pressure. The pressure is regulated by pumps and valves that increase, maintain, or decrease the forces on the fluid, thereby generating the motion required to move the piston. The tonnage available in a hydraulic press, therefore, is determined by the maximum load available on a particular machine.

Characteristics of the hydraulic press make it particularly suitable for certain types of work. For example:

1. The ability to vary the speed of the stroke while maintaining constant force makes them useful when the workpiece thicknesses vary.
2. The force exerted during the working portion of the stroke can be accurately predetermined and regulated, especially with electronic controls.
3. The rate of travel can be adjusted to suit the requirements of particular workpieces.
4. As previously discussed, the stroke can adjust to predetermined forces, depending on the work requirement.

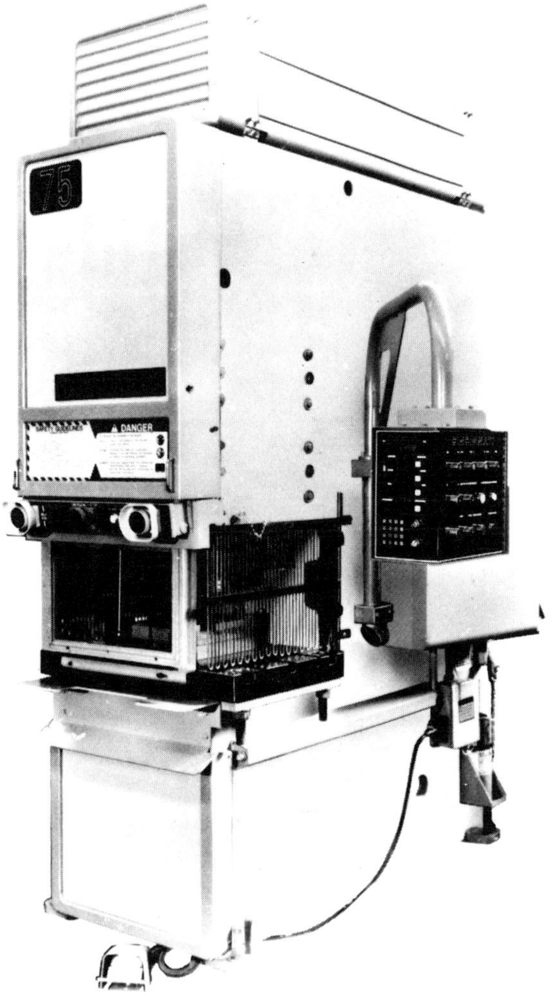

Cincinnati Incorporated
Fig. 2-10. A 75-ton Cincinnati open-back stationary hydraulic press.

Hydraulic presses are particularly adapted to such operations as assembling, stamping, marking, cold forming, broaching, straightening, wax injection, and die casting. Larger hydraulic presses are used for forming and drawing operations, as well as powder metallurgy and forging applications.

2-11. CONSTRUCTION

Figure 2-11-A schematically illustrates the various components that comprise a typical hydraulic press. Fig. 2-11-B shows the front of a hydraulic press, while Fig. 2-11-C is a view of the same machine from the rear. The better die designers will know and understand each of these components. In order to assist in that learning process, we will investigate some of those components in a little more detail.

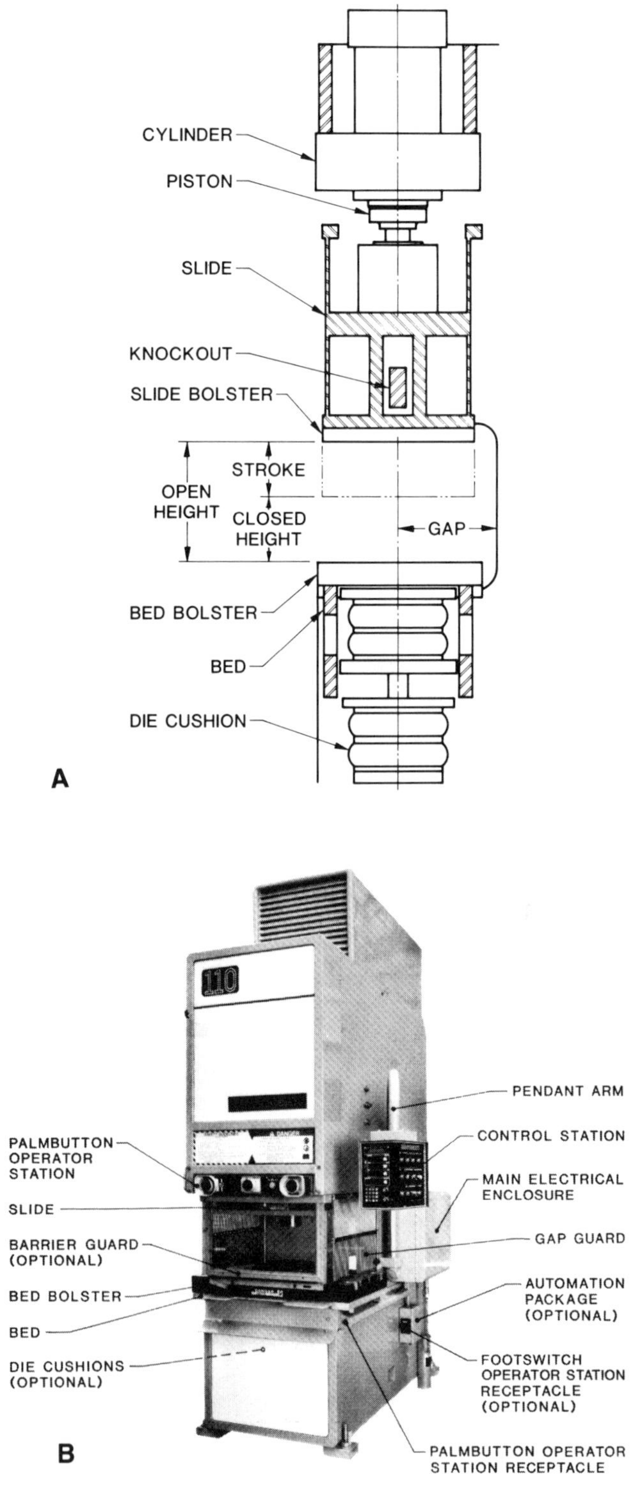

Fig. 2-11.

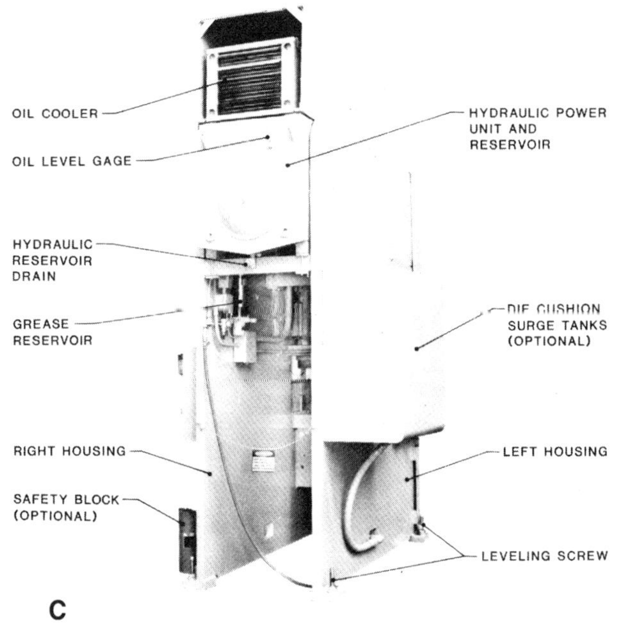

Cincinnati Incorporated

Fig. 2-11. A hydraulic press: A, schematic; B, front of a hydraulic press; C, back of the press shown in B.

2-12. HYDRAULIC CYLINDER

The hydraulic cylinder and piston are shown prior to assembly in the machine (Fig. 2-12). Note the size of the studs and nuts required to connect this assembly, as well as the massiveness of the assembly itself. Extremely large forces can be produced with hydraulic pressures.

2-13. SLIDE ASSEMBLY

The slide assembly is attached to the piston (Fig. 2-13-A) by connecting the holes in the top of the slide assembly to the protruding studs at the bottom of the piston. Then, as pressure is applied to the cylinder, it moves the piston downward, forcing the slide assembly to move in the same direction. Likewise, as the pressure is reversed, the entire assembly moves up, completing one cycle of the machine.

Figure 2-13-B is the front of the press with the front cover open. It shows the arrangement of the hydraulic cylinder and slide assemblies.

Cincinnati Incorporated

Fig. 2-12. Close up view of hydraulic cylinder prior to assembly on the press.

Cincinnati Incorporated

Fig. 2-13-A. Close up view of slide assembly showing eight-point guiding.

Cincinnati Incorporated

Fig. 2-13-B. Close up view of press with front cover open to show arrangement of hydraulic cylinder that operates slide.

2-14. DIE CUSHION

Die cushions consist of two pneumatic actuators connected in series (Fig. 2-14-A). These actuators are single-acting and exert only an upward force. As the cushions are caused to move downward by the tooling pressure pins, the actuators slightly increase in diameter and the air pressure within the system is increased due to compression of the air within the actuators and surge tanks.

Die cushions are sometimes referred to as a pressure pad. They are usually used for blank-holding purposes during a draw operation, but are also used as a lower knockout mechanism. When the die closes, pins push the actuators down against the air pressure by the amount of knockout travel. When the ram goes up, the actuators push the pins upward to operate the knockout.

Figure 2-14-B is a close-up view of the die cushion pressure gage and selector switch. The selector switch gives the operator the choice to either use the die cushion or not, as he sees fit.

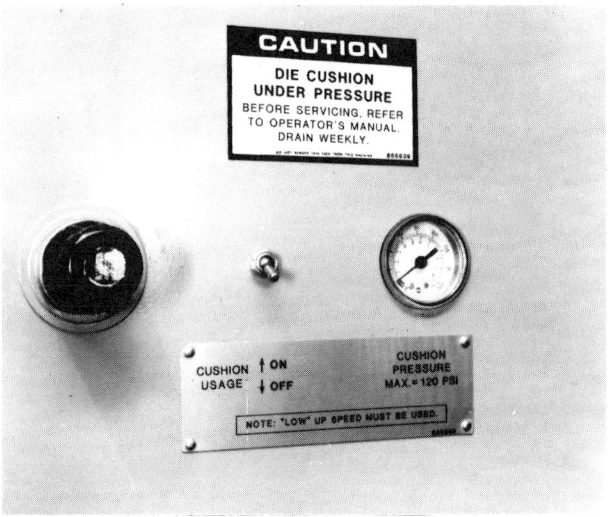

Cincinnati Incorporated

Fig. 2-14-B. Close up view of die cushion pressure gage and selector switch on Cincinnati CNC Press Center.

Cincinnati Incorporated

Fig. 2-14-A. Close up view of die cushion prior to installation into press. Note the positive block.

2-15. CONTROL STATION

A major area of improvement in today's presses is in the area of controls. Figure 2-11-B shows a control station at the end of the pendant arm. The control station, as shown in Figs. 2-15-A and 2-15-B, allows the operator to set up his machine via inputs through the keypad rather than by setting a series of dials inside the cabinet. The set up becomes not only easier, but considerably faster and much more accurate.

The increased use of electronics in this area is also eliminating the need to set up the machine on the shop floor. Microprocessors built into the controls allow the presses to be programmed offline, then the preprogrammed information is sent to the machine controller electronically. This same theory will allow the programming of robots to load and unload the presses, thereby reducing the risk of injury to operators on the shop floor.

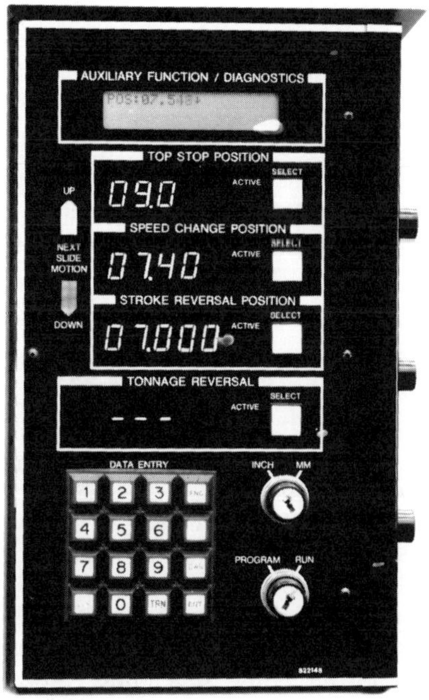

Cincinnati Incorporated

Fig. 2-15-A. Pendant-mounted main control station on Cincinnati CNC Press Center showing LCD (liquid crystal display) of operating information and data entry keypad for press setup instructions.

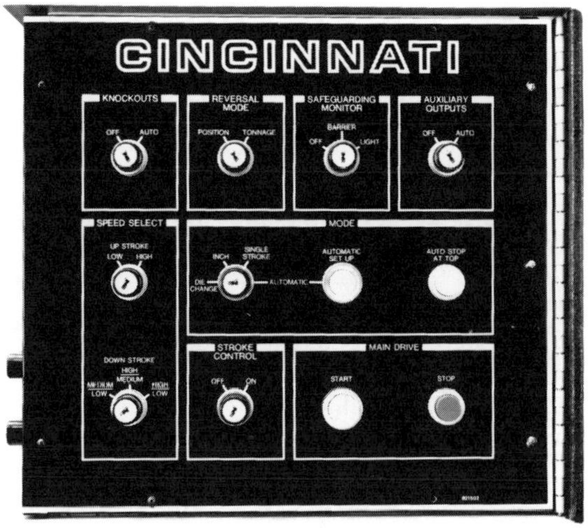

Cincinnati Incorporated

Fig. 2-15-B. Pendant-mounted main control station on Cincinnati CNC Press Center.

ADVANTAGES AND DISADVANTAGES

As in nearly all things, both mechanical and hydraulic presses have advantages and disadvantages. Advantages of the hydraulic press are:

Full power during the stroke—maximum power is maintained during the entire stroke of a hydraulic press. This allows for rapid movement to a position just above the part, then the stroke is slowed for the working stroke. The result is more strokes per minute.

Overload protection—because the pressure is preadjusted, if the pressure exceeds a limit, such as might occur when a part is not properly ejected, the machine shuts down, eliminating catastrophic results to tooling or the machine.

Lower operating costs—hydraulic presses have fewer operating parts, therefore, there are fewer things to break. Automatic lubrication of moving parts helps eliminate maintenance problems.

Flexibility—owing primarily to electronic controls and robotics, hydraulic presses fit well into such areas as flexible manufacturing systems (FMS) and factory automation.

Although hydraulic presses have many advantages, they also suffer from some disadvantages when compared to mechanical presses. Some of the disadvantages are:

Tolerances—While some hydraulic presses do maintain high tolerances, most of them are limited to approximately 0.020 in. When closer tolerances are required on these machines, it usually is held in the tooling, which increases the cost of the die or other tooling.

Speed—Although high speed is attainable in hydraulic presses, for the most part, the mechanical press will produce parts faster. This is especially true when short strokes are used.

Automatic feeding—Because of fewer moving parts, there is less equipment on which to attach automatic feed mechanisms. Therefore, most automatic feed equipment must be integrated into the process via electronics, which increases cost.

Section 3

THE MATERIAL STRIP

Now that you have acquired an understanding of the press and of its accessories, you will have to learn about the material strip – about the ribbon of metal or other material that is run through the press in order to produce stampings. Six elements of information will be included:

1. How strips are produced
2. How strips are planned
3. Materials from which strips are made
4. Deformation of sheet materials
5. Theory of cutting sheet materials
6. Types of strip edges.

3-1. SHEARING

The oldest and simplest method of producing metal strips is by shearing. In the steel mill, metal is formed into large sheets by rolling and trimming. To cut a sheet into strips, it is introduced under the blade of a shear. Gages register the edges of the sheet for cutting correct widths of strips. Descent of the shear blade causes each strip to be parted from the sheet. Advancing the sheet against the gages brings it into position for cutting the next strip and this process is repeated until the sheet has been cut entirely into strips. The illustration at **A** shows a sheet in position under the shear blade **C** ready to be cut. At **B**, the blade has descended and the strip has been cut from the sheet.

The power shear can cut material in any direction – lengthwise of the sheet, across the sheet, or at any angle.

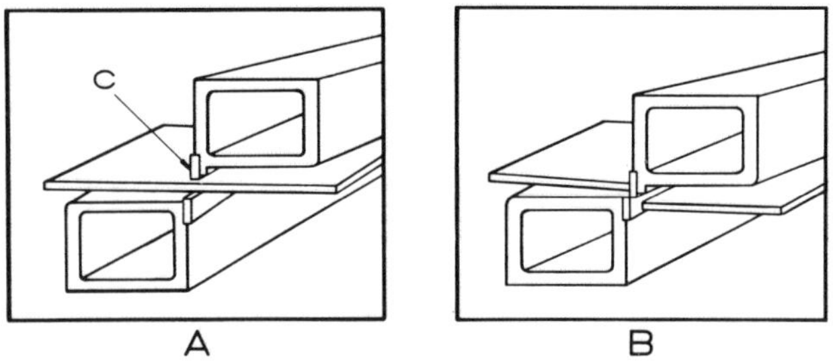

Fig. 3-1. Producing metal strips from sheet by shearing.

3-2. SLITTING

Slitting machines are also used for producing material strips. In slitting operations, the sheet is fed through rotating cutting rolls and all strips are cut simultaneously. In the illustration, cutting rolls **A** are mounted the proper distances apart on arbors **B**. The cutting edges of the rolls are separated by the required amount of clearance to effect cutting of the material as shown in inset **C**. Turning the rolls under power causes the sheet to advance and it is cut into strips. As many as twenty or more strands can be cut at one time. In other types of slitters, the sheets are pulled through the rolls instead, and the rolls are free to turn.

Slit strips are very accurate both in width, flatness, and parallelism of sides because accuracy is built into the machine instead of depending upon the operator. Unlike the shear which can cut strips only as long as the blade, the slitter will cut continuously to any length, without limit.

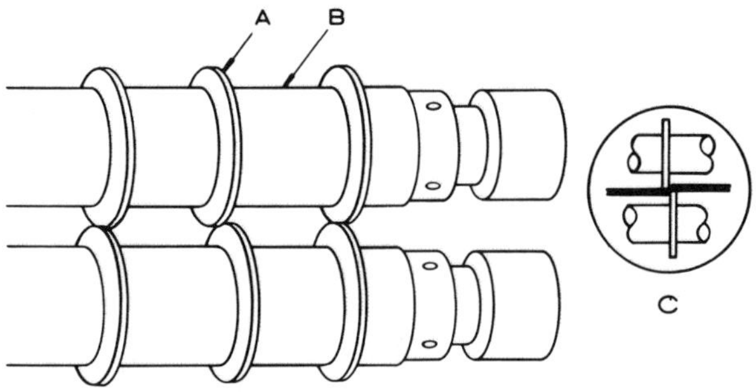

Fig. 3-2. Cutting rolls for slitting strips from sheet.

3-3. PART DRAWING

The first step in the actual production of stampings is to order standard-size sheets of the proper size and thickness from the mill. These are then sheared into strips as described above. The widths of the strips into which the sheets are to be cut is specified by the die design department. Therefore, let us go over the steps taken in determining strip width so your understanding will be complete.

The illustration shows a part drawing of a representative stamping to be produced in a pierce-and-blank die.

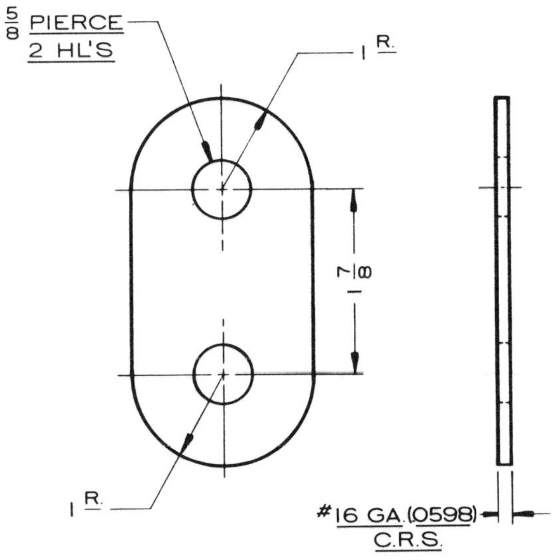

Fig. 3-3. Typical part drawing.

3-4. BLANK LAYOUTS

This shows the two possible ways of running the strip through the die. The blanks may be positioned the wide way necessitating a wide strip, or they may be run the narrow way permitting the use of a narrower strip. These are called blank layouts and it is important that you understand exactly what is meant by the term. A blank layout shows the way in which it is *proposed to produce the blank*. For both the wide-run and narrow-run layouts, two holes are to be pierced at the first station and the part is to be blanked out at the second station. It is customary to show small piercing punches solid black. Section lines are applied through larger piercing punches and through blanking punches, as shown. The strip width and the feed are given directly on the blank layout.

3-5. SIZES OF SHEETS

Sizes of sheets as they are manufactured by the mill are given in steel catalogs. Here is a representative list for #18 Gage (0.0478) cold rolled steel:

30″ × 96″
30″ × 120″
36″ × 96″
36″ × 120″
48″ × 96″
48″ × 120″

3-6. STRIPS PER SHEET – WIDE RUN

The next step is to select the sheet which will be most economical, that is, the sheet from which a maximum number of strips can be cut, leaving a minimum amount of waste. Strip width is taken from the blank layout. Divide the value given into the values for "width of sheet" in the steel catalog, and compare to determine which sheet leaves the smallest remainder. The illustration shows the sheet divided into strips when the representative blank is run the wide way.

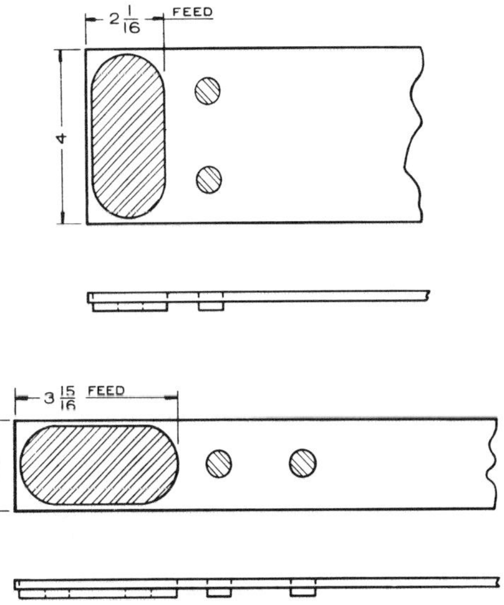

Fig. 3-4. Blank layouts necessitating either wide or narrow strips.

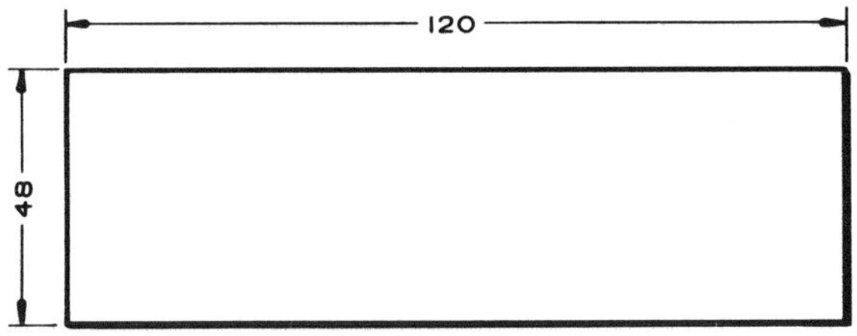

Fig. 3-5. One of the mill sizes available for cold rolled sheet steel.

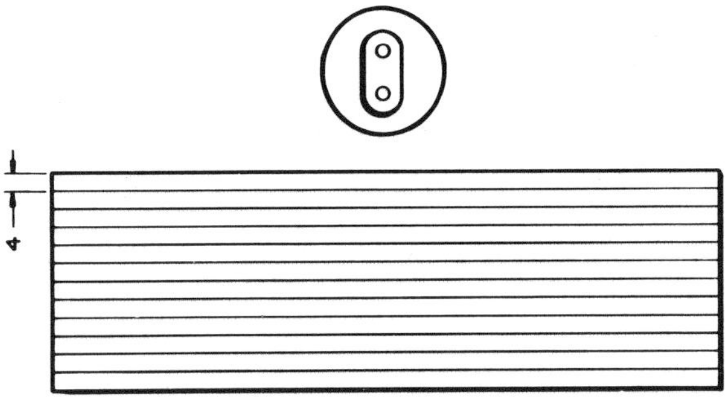

Fig. 3-6. Number of strips obtainable with wide strip blank layout.

3-7. STRIPS PER SHEET – NARROW RUN

This layout shows the same sheet divided into strips when the blanks are to be run the narrow way. More strips are produced from the same size of sheet.

3-8. STRIP LAYOUTS

After it has been decided how the blanks are to be run (wide or narrow way), a stock layout is prepared complete with the following dimensions:

1. Strip width. This dimension is used in selecting the proper width of sheet from which strips are to be cut.

2. Feed. This is the amount of travel of the strip between stations. This dimension is used in selecting the proper length of sheet.

Two views are applied, ordinarily, and these are exactly the views of the strip that will be drawn on the die drawing except that an end view of the strip is added to the die drawing. The die is then actually designed around these views.

Illustrated at **A** is a strip layout for a blanking die in which the blank is run the wide way, and at **B** is shown a layout in which the blank is run the narrow way. For this particular job, more blanks per sheet are produced when the blanks are positioned the wide way and there is less waste; so all else being equal, this method of positioning the blanks would be selected.

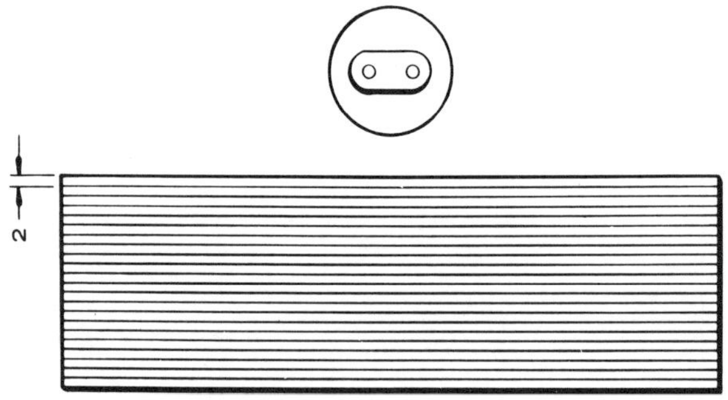

Fig. 3-7. Number of strips obtainable with narrow strip blank layout.

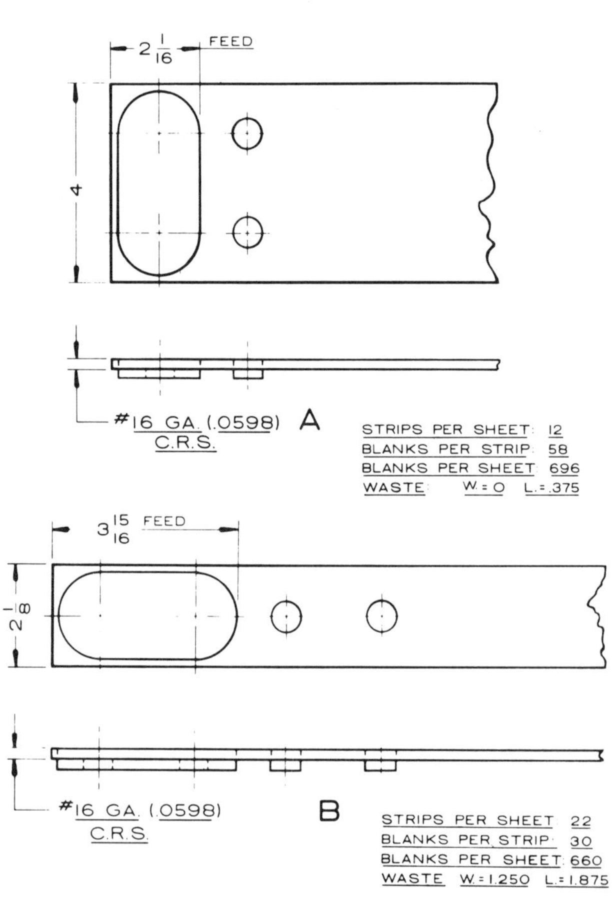

Fig. 3-8. Complete strip layouts for blanks run either the wide (**A**) or narrow (**B**) way.

3-9. STRIPS

At **A** is shown one of the strips ready to be fed through the die with blanks to be removed from it positioned the wide way. At **B**, the blanks are positioned the narrow way in the strip. Five of the parts have been blanked out of each strip. After the strip is run completely through the die, only a narrow scrap bridge is left.

3-10. BLANKS FOR CUT-OFF DIES

Now let us go through the first steps taken in the production of blanks in cut-off dies. Two of the sides of such blanks are originally sides of the material strip and no scrap bridge is produced as in blanking dies. The illustration shows a representative stamping having the parallel sides typical of blanks suitable for production in cut-off dies.

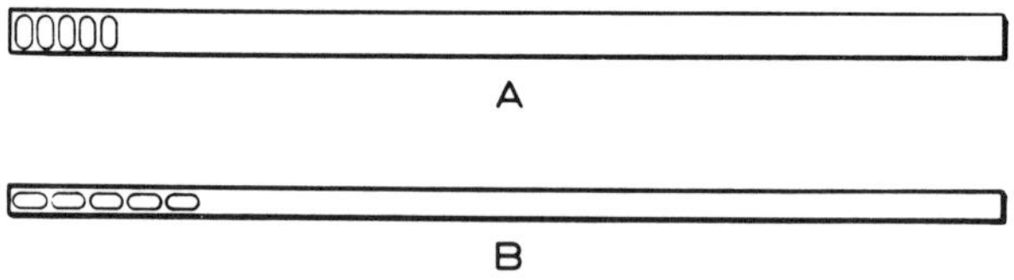

Fig. 3-9. Strips ready for feeding either the wide (**A**) or narrow (**B**) way.

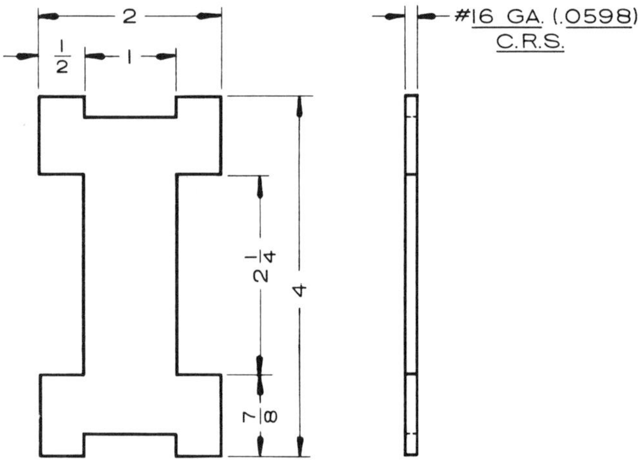

Fig. 3-10. Typical part for production in cut-off die.

3-11. BLANK LAYOUTS

This shows two blank layouts for producing the stamping in the previous illustration. At **A**, the part is positioned the wide way in the strip. The edges of the strip are notched at the first station and a rectangular hole is punched. The blank is cut off from the strip at the second station. At **B**, the part is positioned the narrow way in the strip. Observe how notching punches are sectioned. The heels **C** which prevent deflection of the punches are shown but not sectioned. At **D**, short 45 degree lines and a long vertical line represent the "cut off" line.

Blank layouts are drawn to explain the proposed operation of a die to others. When a die designer is given a part print of a stamping for which a die is to be designed, he proceeds to lay out a suitable scrap strip. Then he sections significant punches and adds cut-off lines to make the proposal layout clearer. This is the blank layout and it must be approved by the group leader or chief engineer before design of the die is begun. When an outside engineering office is doing the work for a manufacturing company, the blank layout is submitted to the customer for approval.

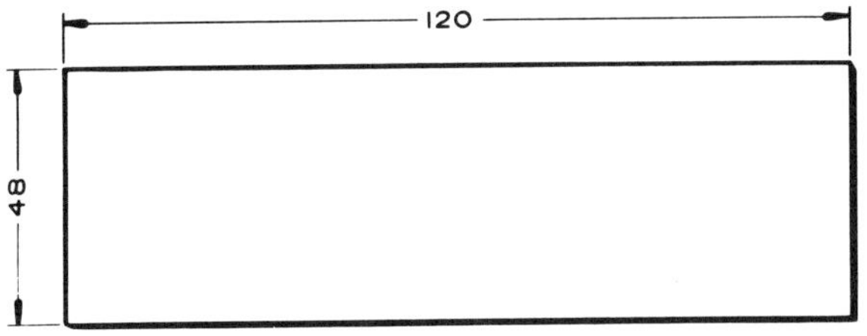

Fig. 3-12. Frequently used size of sheet steel.

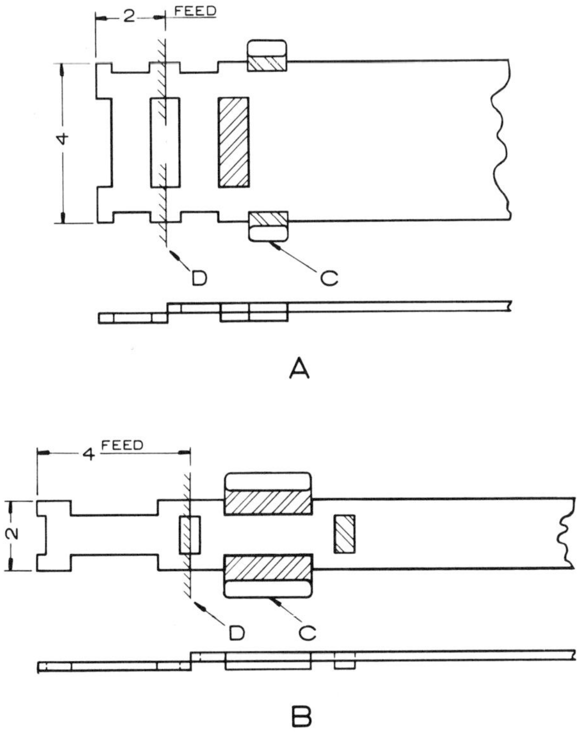

Fig. 3-11. Blank layout for part shown in Fig. 3-10 run, either the wide (A) or narrow (B) way.

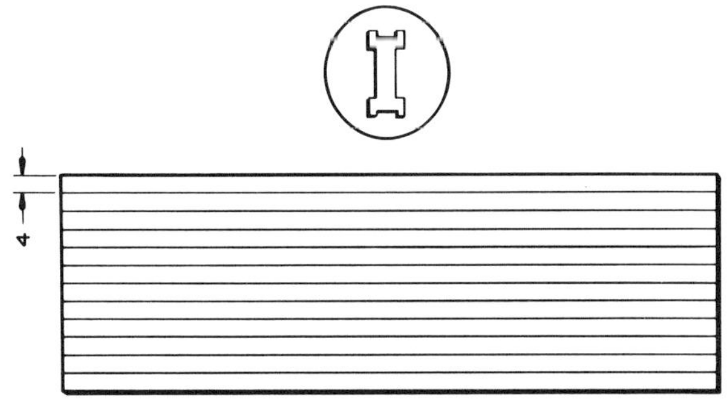

Fig. 3-13. Strips per sheet with wide strip blank layout.

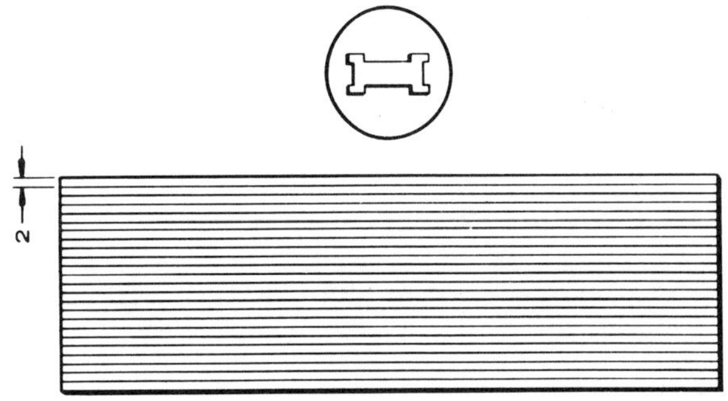

Fig. 3-14. Strips per sheet with narrow strip blank layout.

3-12. SHEET SIZES

Next, a steel catalog is consulted to determine what sizes of sheets are available in the required gage and material. The illustrated sheet, 48 by 120 inches, is a frequently used size.

3-13. STRIPS PER SHEET – WIDE RUN

Now calculations are made to determine how many blanks are produced per sheet with the blanks positioned the wide way in the strip, and also how much waste is left.

3-14. STRIPS PER SHEET – NARROW RUN

Next, we must know how many blanks are produced per sheet with the blanks positioned the narrow way in the strip. With blanks arranged the narrow way, more strips are cut from the sheet, but fewer blanks are contained in each strip.

3-15. STRIP LAYOUTS

Next a strip layout is prepared and copies are sent to the purchasing department and to the shear department. From the layout, sheets are ordered and, upon delivery, they are sheared to the strip width given on the layout. At **A** is shown a representative strip layout for a blank for a cut off die positioned the wide way, and at **B** is shown a layout for a blank positioned the narrow way.

For this job we find that exactly the same number of blanks are produced with blanks positioned the narrow way as for "wide-run positioning" and there is no waste in either method. When blanks can be run either way, select the "wide run" method for three reasons:

1. Fewer cuts will be necessary for producing the strips
2. The feed is shorter when running strips through the die, thus reducing the time required
3. More blanks are produced per strip and fewer strips have to be handled.

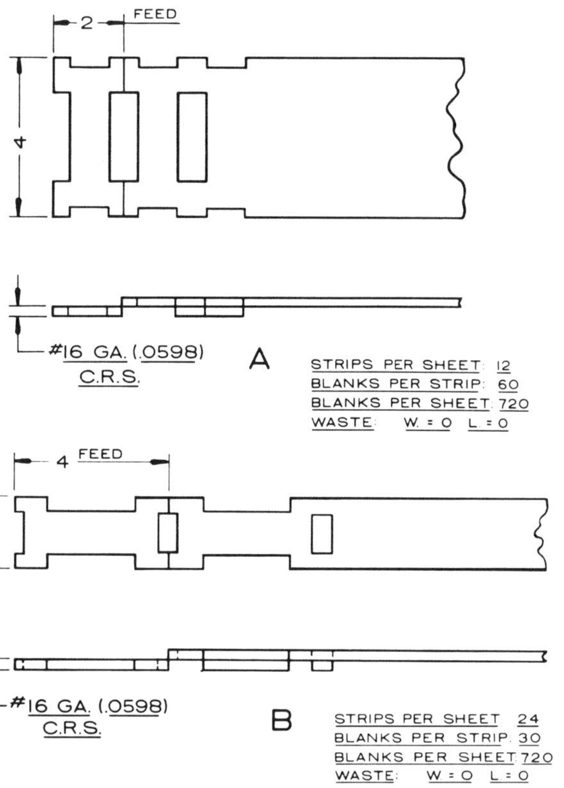

Fig. 3-15. Strip layouts for blanks run either the wide (A) or narrow (B) way.

3-16. STRIPS

At **A** is shown one of the strips ready to be fed through a die with blanks to be removed from it positioned the wide way. At **B** the blanks are positioned the narrow way. Five blanks are shown in each strip. Since they are run in cut off dies, no scrap bridge is produced.

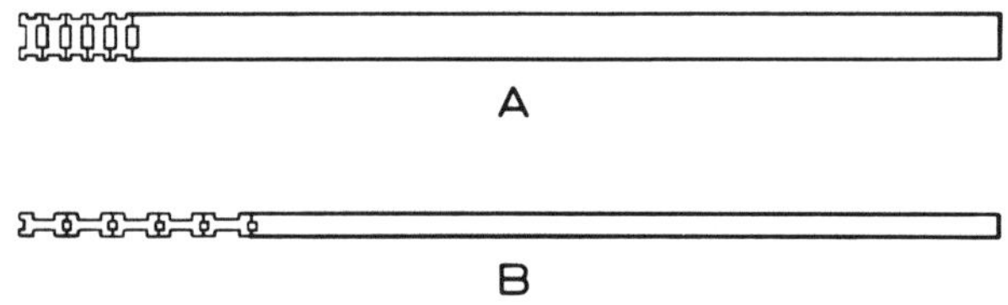

Fig. 3-16. Strips ready for feeding either the wide (A) or narrow (B) way.

MATERIALS

Most stampings are made of steel. Carbon content varies from S.A.E. 1010 to S.A.E. 1030 and therefore most blanks are in the machine or cold rolled steel range. Stampings are also made from the following other materials:

Aluminum
Brass
Bronze
Copper
Stainless steel
Silicon steel
Fiber
Plastic sheet, etc.

HOT ROLLED SHEETS

Hot rolled sheets are formed easily. Low carbon sheets are used for tanks, barrels, pails, farm implements, lockers, cabinets, truck bodies, and other applications where scale and discoloration are not objectionable because surfaces are painted after forming. Hot rolled sheets are readily available in thicknesses ranging from #30 gage (0.012) to #7 gage (0.1875).

Pickled and Oiled Sheets

Pickling, or the immersing of hot rolled sheets in acid solution, results in smooth, clean, scale-free surfaces having a uniform gray color. Oiling protects the surfaces against rust.

These sheets are readily stamped or welded. Long-lasting painting or enameling is possible because of the absence of scale. Pickled and oiled sheets are used for household appliances, automotive parts, toys, and the like.

Copper Bearing Sheets

Copper bearing sheets are hot rolled sheets having a 0.20 per cent minimum copper content. They are used for parts designed for outdoor exposure, or for indoor use under corrosive atmospheres. These sheets have a service life from 2 to 3 times longer than can be expected from non-copper bearing steels. They are used for roofing and siding, farm and industrial buildings, truck bodies, railroad cars, farm implements, signs, tanks, driers, ventilators, washing machines, and other similar applications.

Medium-Carbon Sheets

Hot rolled sheets having a 0.40 to 0.50 per cent carbon content provide hardness, strength, and resistance to abrasion. They can be heat-treated to make the material even harder and stronger and are primarily used for scrapers, blades, hand tools, and the like.

COLD ROLLED SHEETS

Cold rolled sheets have a smooth, de-oxidized satin finish which provides an excellent base for paint, lacquer, and enamel coating. Thicknesses are held to a high degree of accuracy. Cold rolled steel is produced by cold rolling hot rolled sheets to improve size and finish. Among many uses are included refrigerators, ranges, panels, lockers, and electrical fixtures.

3-17. DEFORMATION

Six tempers of cold rolled steel sheets and strips are available and it is important to know exactly what operations can be performed on each. In the illustration:

1. Hard

   Hard sheets and strips will not bend in either direction of the grain without cracks or fracture. These tempers of steel are employed for flat blanks that require resistance to bending and wear. Direction of grain is shown along lines **A** in the illustration. Rockwell hardness is B 90 to 100

2. Three-Quarter Hard

   This temper of steel will bend a total of 60 degrees from flat across the grain. This is shown as dimension **B** in the illustration. Hardness is Rockwell B 85 to 90

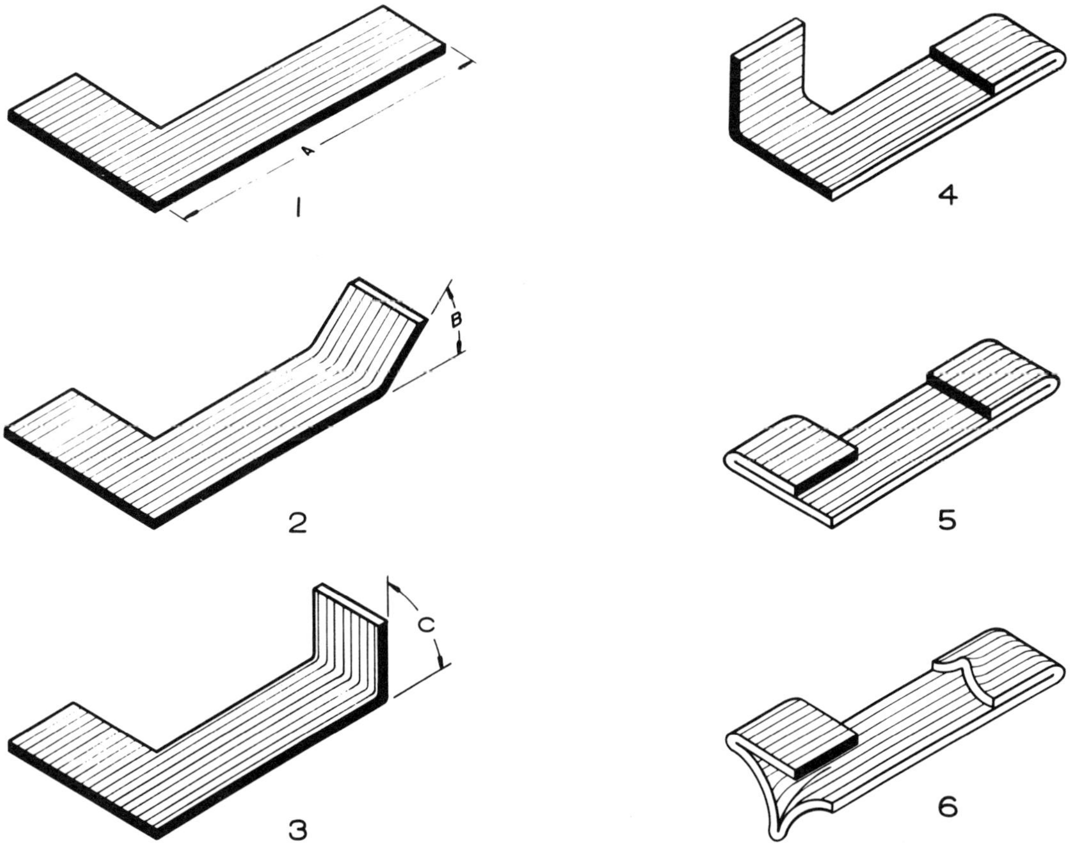

Fig. 3-17. Various tempers of cold rolled steel from hard (1) to dead soft (6) and kinds of deformation possible with each.

3. One-Half Hard

This temper will bend to a sharp 90 degree angle across the grain, shown as dimension **C**. Rockwell hardness is between B 70 and 85

4. One-Quarter Hard

This commonly used temper of steel will bend over flat on itself across the grain and to a sharp right-angle along the grain. Hardness is Rockwell B60 to 70

5. Soft

This temper will bend over flat upon itself both across the grain and along the grain. It is also used for moderate forming and drawing. Hardness is Rockwell B 50 to 60

6. Dead Soft

This temper of steel is used for deep drawing and for severe bending and forming operations. Hardness is Rockwell B 40 to 50.

Finish

Cold rolled steel is furnished in three grades of finish:

1. Dull Finish. This is a gray lustreless finish to which lacquer and paint bond well
2. Regular Bright Finish. This is a moderately bright finish suitable for most work. It is not recommended for plating unless buffed first
3. Best Bright Finish. This finish has a high lustre well suited for electroplating. It is the brightest finish obtainable.

Stretcher-Leveled Sheets

These are cold rolled steel sheets that have been further processed by stretcher leveling and resquaring. They are used in the manufacture of metal furniture, table tops, truck body panels, partitions, and other equipment requiring perfectly flat material.

Deep Drawing Sheets

Deep drawing steel is prime quality cold rolled steel having a low carbon content. Sheets are thoroughly annealed, highly finished to a de-oxidized silver finish, and oiled. Deep drawing sheets are used for difficult drawing, spinning, and stamping operations such as automobile bodies, fenders, electrical fixtures, and laboratory equipment.

SILICON STEEL

Also called electrical steel, silicon steel is extensively used for motors and generators. Lighter gages are suitable for transformers, reactors, relays, and other magnetic circuits.

3-18. SHEARED EDGES

It now becomes necessary that you understand exactly what occurs when sheet material is cut between the cutting edges of a punch and die. This illustration shows the cut edge of a blank enlarged many times to reveal its contour. Observe the following:

The top corner is defined by a small radius **R**. The size of this radius depends upon the thickness and hardness of the strip and on the sharpness of the punch and die members.

A smooth, straight, burnished band goes around the periphery of the blank. The extent of this band, distance **D**, is approximately 1/3 the thickness **T** of the blank when the die is properly sharpened and when the correct clearance has been applied.

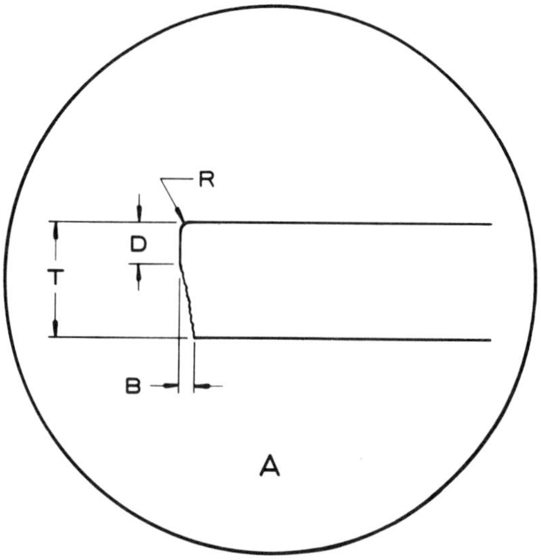

Fig. 3-18. Enlarged view of sheared blank edge.

The remaining 2/3 of the edge is called the breakoff. The surface is somewhat rough and it tapers back slightly. Extent of the taper, distance **B**, is the amount of clearance between cutting edges. If burrs are produced in cutting the blanks, they occur on this breakoff side of the blank. Burrs are produced when improper clearance has been applied and also when cutting edges become dull. The other side of the blank which has the radius and smooth, shiny band is called the burnished side of the blank.

The location of the burnished side and of the burr side of the blank is very important for performing secondary operations such as shaving, burnishing, and the like. In addition, burr side position can influence the functioning or the appearance of the finished stamping.

In blanking, the burnished band goes completely around the blank and the breakoff taper extends completely around the blank on the opposite side. This is not the case for blanks produced in cut off or progressive dies. In such dies, the burnished side may alternate from side to side in a number of positions and careful study is required to determine that any possible burr will not interfere with the function or appearance of the stamping.

Shearing of material occurs in a continuous action. However, to understand the process it will be necessary to "stop" the action in its various stages and to examine what occurs.

3-19. THEORY OF SHEAR

1. This illustration shows the cutting edges of a die with clearance **C** applied. The amount of this clearance is important as will be shown.

2. A material strip is introduced between the cutting edges and it is represented by phantom lines. Cutting a material strip occurs when it is sheared between cutting edges until the material between the edges has been compressed beyond its ultimate strength and fracture takes place.

3. The upper die begins its downward travel and the cutting edge of the punch penetrates the material by the amount **A**. The following stresses occur: The material in the radii at **B** is in tension, that is, it is *stretched*. The material between cutting edges, **C**, is *compressed*, or squeezed together. Stretching continues beyond the elastic limit of the material, then plastic deformation occurs. Observe that the same penetration and stretching is applied to both sides of the strip.

4. Continued descent of the upper cutting edge causes cracks to form in the material. These cleavage planes occur adjacent to the corner of each cutting edge.

5. Continued descent of the upper die causes the cracks to elongate until they meet. Here then is the reason for the importance of correct clearance. If the cracks fail to meet, a bad edge will be produced in the blank.

6. Further descent of the upper die causes the blank to separate from the strip. Separation occurs when the punch has penetrated approximately 1/3 of the strip.

7. Continued descent of the upper die causes the blank to be pushed into the die hole where it clings tightly because of the compressive stresses introduced prior to separation of the blank from the strip. In other words, the material at **C** in Step 3 was compressed and it acts like a compressed spring. The blank, confined in the die hole, tends to swell, but it is prevented from doing so by the confining walls of the die block. Conversely, the material around the punch tends to close in and therefore the strip clings tightly around the punch.

8. The punch has now penetrated entirely through the strip and the blank has been pushed entirely within the die hole. Observe that the edge of the blank and the edge of the strip have identical contours except that they are reversed. The strip will cling around the upper punch with approximately the same pressure as the blank clings within the die hole and a stripper will be required to remove it.

3-20. INSUFFICIENT CLEARANCE

The inset at **A** shows the effects of insufficient clearance. There are four:

a. Radius **R** is smaller than when correct clearance is applied

b. A double burnished band **D** is formed on the blank edge

c. The breakoff angle **B** is smaller than when correct clearance is applied

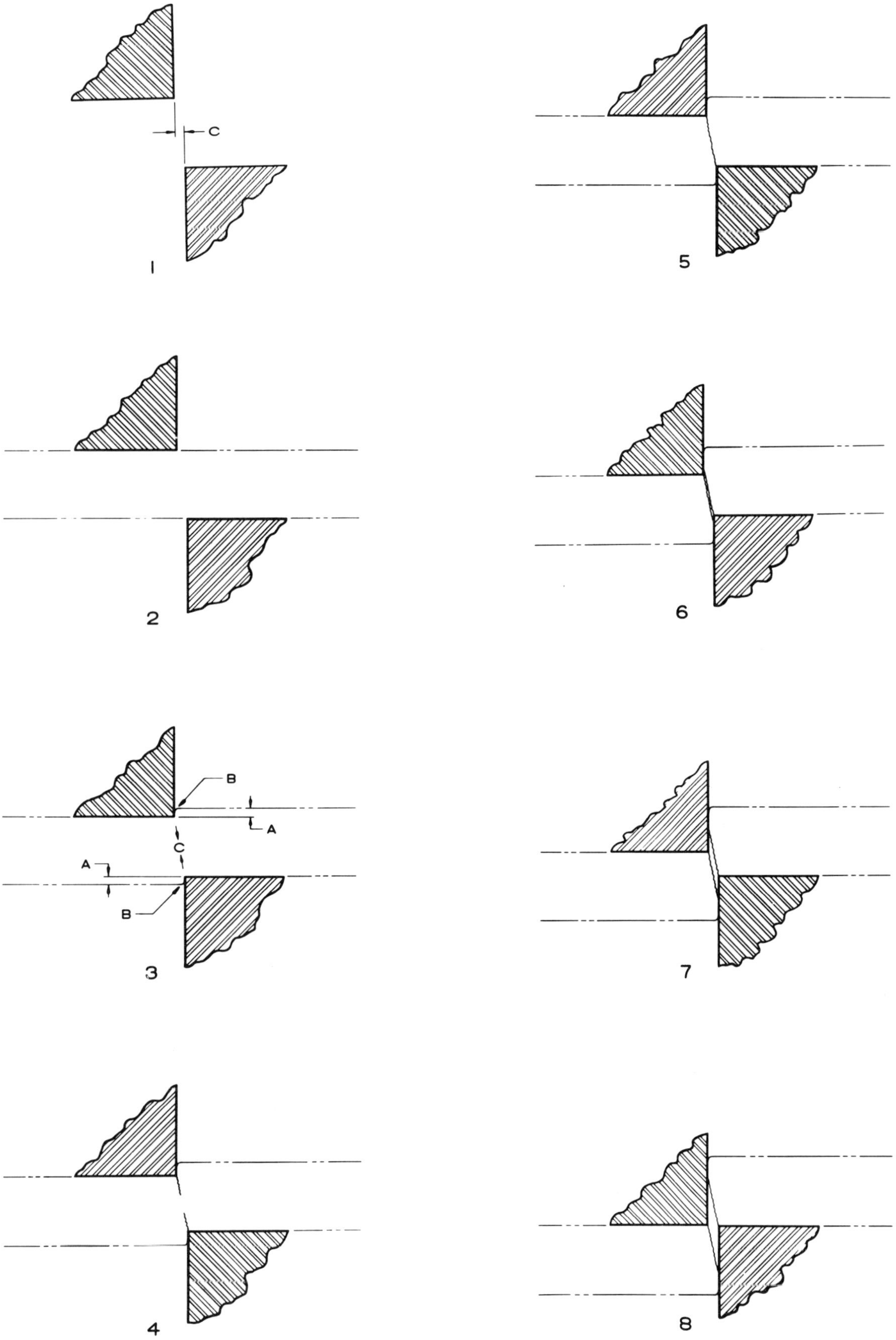

Fig. 3-19. Enlarged views of clearance between cutting edges of a shearing die (1) and material undergoing shear (2 to 8).

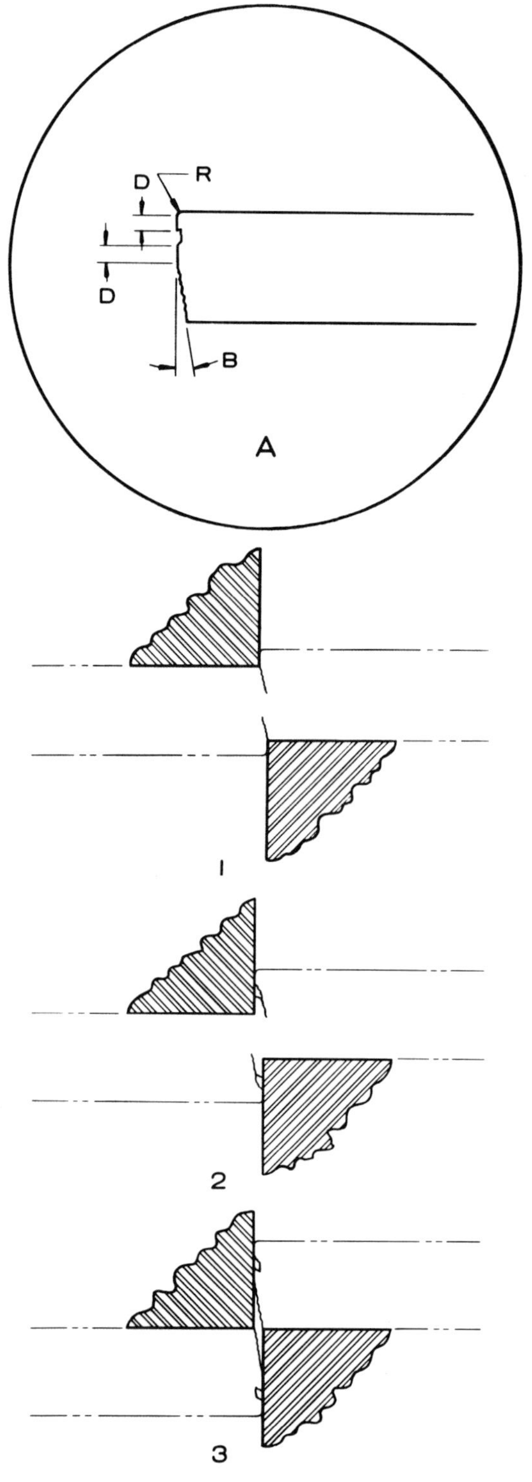

Fig. 3-20. Enlarged views of blank edge sheared with insufficient clearance (**A**) and material undergoing shear with insufficient clearance (**1** to **3**).

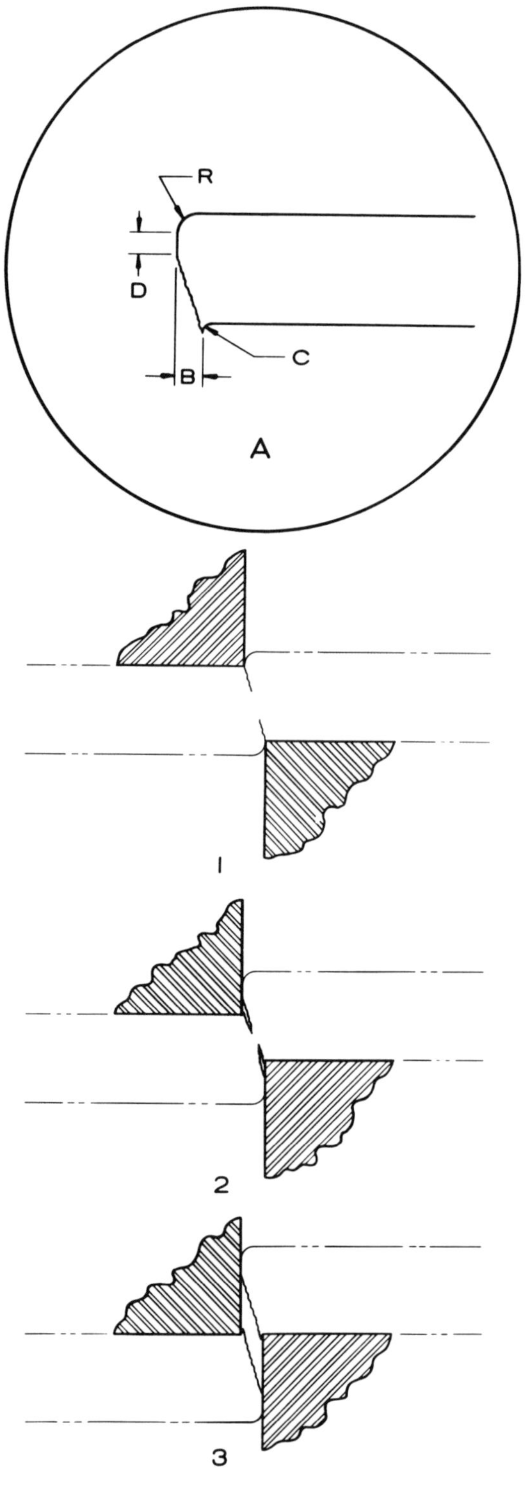

Fig. 3-21. Enlarged views of blank edge sheared with excessive clearance (**A**) and material undergoing shear with excessive clearance (**1** to **3**).

d. Greater pressure is required for producing the blank.

Referring to the illustration:

1. This shows cutting edges of a punch and die in partial penetration. It is obvious that the cracks that have appeared at the punch and die sides will not meet when extended because the clearance is insufficient

2. Continued downward descent of the punch causes elongation of the cracks. The uncut area between them will be broken in a secondary fracture

3. At the bottom of the stroke the secondary fracture has occurred and a second burnished band has been produced on the blank edge and on the strip edge. The characteristic contour shown in the inset at **A** has been formed.

3-21. EXCESSIVE CLEARANCE

The inset at **A** shows the effects of excessive clearance. There are four:

a. Radius **R** is considerably larger than when correct clearance has been applied

b. Burnished band **D** is narrower

c. The breakoff angle **B** is excessive

d. A burr **C** is left on the blank.

Referring to the illustration:

1. This shows cutting edges of a punch and die in partial penetration. Cracks have begun to form at opposite sides

2. Continued downward descent of the punch causes elongation and widening of the cracks. Their alignment is fairly good

3. At the bottom of the stroke, separation has occurred leaving the characteristic blank edges shown in the inset at **A**.

When a die is provided with excessive clearance, less pressure is required to effect cutting of the material. For this reason, more clearance is often specified for blanking the heavy gages of stock to reduce pressure on the press.

3-22. EDGE CONTOUR

The contour of the edge of a strip depends upon the process by which the strip is produced. Five contours may be recognized:

1. Strips produced in a shear have the burnished bands along the edges on *opposite* sides of the strip. If burrs are produced because of dull cutting edges, they will also occur on opposite sides of the strip. In addition, sheared strips often become spiraled or curved because the upper blade of the shear is at an angle to the lower blade. This makes the strips difficult to feed through the die unless they are first straightened

2. Strips produced in the slitter have the burnished bands on the same side of the strip. Blanks produced from these strips in cut off dies have a better appearance and they are fed more easily because they are straighter. Sheared strips or slit strips may be produced in the shear department of the plant, or they may be ordered directly from the mill.

3. Mill edge strips have a radius at each corner. They are produced by rolling sheared or slit strips at the mill. Mill edge strips are used for long stampings such as handles, shelf brackets, and other parts where sharp edges would be objectionable.

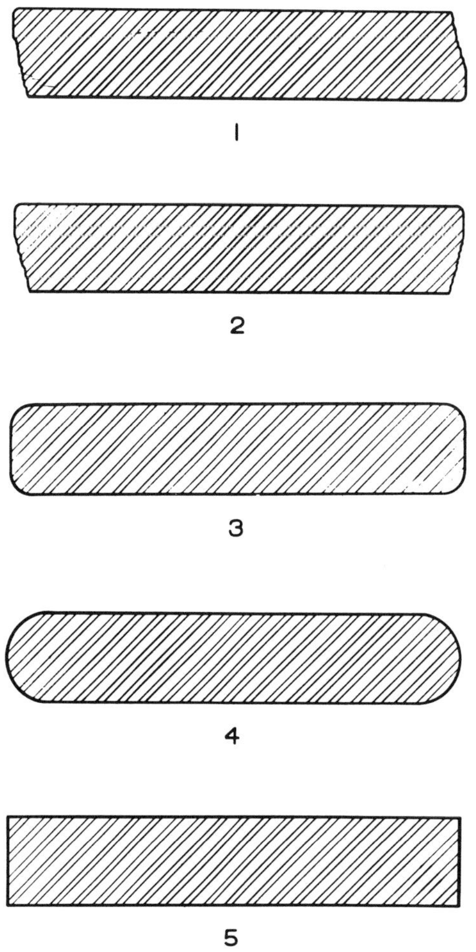

Fig. 3-22. The various edge contours shown are the result of different production processes.

4. Rolled edge strips have a full radius at each side, rolled at the mill. They are used for parts where appearance is a decided factor such as ornamental grills, gratings, and the like.

5. Square edge strips are ordered from the mill when the sides of the strips must be square and smooth. The widths of these strips are held very accurately. Square edge strips are also specified when blanks are to be bent or formed edgewise. The square edges prevent cracking or splitting in the bending or forming operation.

Section 4

THE BLANK

A blank is a piece of flat steel or other material cut to any outside contour. The thickness of a blank may range between 0.001 to 0.500 inch or more depending on its function. However, most stampings are between 0.025 to 0.125 inch in thickness.

Some blanks have simple round, square, or rectangular contours. Others may be very irregular in shape. Many blanks are subsequently bent, formed, or drawn. It is important to realize, however, that when we refer to a blank, what is meant is the flat part before any deformation has been applied.

4-1. TYPES OF BLANKS

There are only two basic types of blanks:

1. Blanks having straight, parallel sides, two of which are originally sides of the material strip. Small blanks of this type are produced in cut off dies. Large blanks are produced by square-shearing and trimming

2. Blanks having irregular contours cut entirely out of the material strip. When they are required in quantity, such blanks are produced in blanking dies. When only a few blanks are required, they may be shaped by contour sawing, nibbling, routing, or other machining operations.

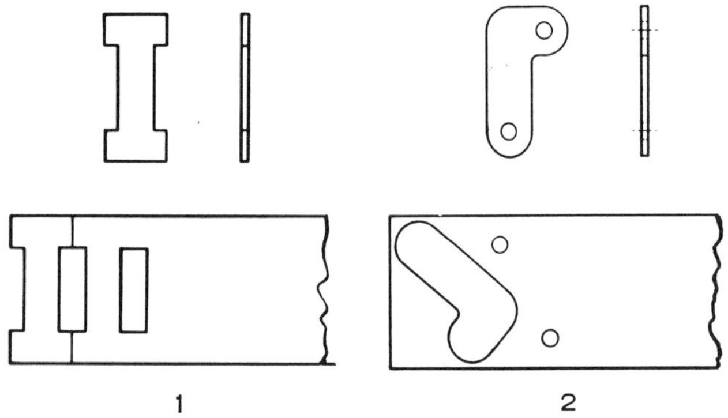

1 2

Fig. 4-1. Two basic types of blanks.

To select the best method of producing a particular blank, consider five factors:

1. *Contour.* If the blank has two parallel sides, determine if it can be produced in a cut off operation. The width between the parallel sides would then become the width of the strip.

Four advantages are realized when cut off dies are used:

a. There is a minimum waste of material

b. Cut off dies cost less to build

c. Faster press speeds are possible

d. There is no scrap strip to handle.

After you have determined that a blank can be produced in a cut off operation, consider three additional factors before making a final decision:

e. Accuracy in strip width. Sheared strips cannot be held to closer accuracy than ±0.010. If the width dimension between parallel sides of the blank must be held to closer limits, discard the idea of using a cut off die.

f. Accuracy of the blank. If the blank must be held to close limits, it should be produced in a blanking die regardless of the number of straight sides that it may have.

g. Flatness. If the part print contains the note, MUST BE FLAT, plan to design a blanking die because it will produce considerably flatter parts. Cut off dies produce blanks by a series of piercing, trimming, and cut off operations and uncut portions can become distorted, especially for heavier gages of strip. In blanking dies the entire periphery is cut in one operation and distortion cannot occur.

Blanking dies produce flat, accurate parts. Whatever accuracy has been "built in" the die is duplicated in the blanks and each is identical to every other blank that the die produces. This is true because the entire blank contour is cut and none of the edges of the strip form any edge of the blank. Blanking is the most widely used method of producing blanks from sheet materials.

If the stamping is intricate and it is to be produced complete in a progessive die, the contour of the blank may be formed by trimming away portions of the strip at one or more of the stations.

2. *Size.* Consider the size of the blank in relation to the number of parts required. This is especially important for large blanks because large dies are very costly to build. Determine if shearing and trimming would do the job, especially if production requirements are low.

3. *Accuracy.* Study the part print carefully to determine the degree of accuracy required in the blank. Very accurate blanks have to be produced in compound

dies in which all operations are performed simultaneously at one station. Blanks requiring a lesser degree of accuracy may be produced in more economical two-station dies.

4. *Number required.* This information is taken from the design order and it often determines the type of die to be designed as well as the class of die.

5. *Burr side.* The burr side must be known when blanks are to be shaved or burnished in a subsequent operation. The same applies for blanks that are to be assembled into other components and those that are to have components assembled into them. The presence of burrs at engaging edges can slow down assembly operations considerably.

PRODUCING BLANKS

Let us now gain an understanding of the various methods of producing blanks. We will begin by considering ways in which blanks may be shaped without the use of dies. These low-cost, but relatively slow methods are employed when only a few blanks are required and it would be uneconomical to design and build special dies for producing them.

Circle Shearing

Large, round blanks may be circle-sheared when quantities required are moderate. Square blanks are clamped in the center of a circle shearing machine. Two disk-shaped cutters are adjusted to the required radius and they apply rotation to the blank and at the same time cut it to circular shape.

For larger quantities it is less expensive to order round blanks precut to the required diameter. Steel companies stock various sizes of round blanks, or they can supply them cut to special sizes.

Contour Sawing

When only a few blanks are required, their contours may be laid out directly on sheet material. After lines have been scribed, the blanks are sawed out in a metal-cutting bandsaw. For contour sawing a number of blanks requiring greater accuracy, a short stack of square or rectangular blanks are clamped in a vise and tack welded together at several places around the edges. The outline of the blank is laid out on the upper sheet and the blanks are sawed directly to this outline. Thus, all the blanks are identical in contour.

Nibbling

The nibbling machine operates by reciprocating a punch up and down at about five strokes per second. The punch is provided with a pilot long enough so it is not raised above the material being cut. As the sheet is moved, the punch cuts a series of partial holes that overlap each other. A jagged edge is left around the edges of the blank and the sharp corners left by the punch must be die-filed after the nibbling operation. Of course, the nibbling process is used to produce blanks when only one, two, or a few are required.

Routing

A routing machine is provided with a long radial arm which can travel over a large area. Mounted at the outer end of the arm is a rapidly revolving cutting tool similar to an end-mill cutter which can cut its way through a stack of blanks. The router bit, as the cutting tool is called, rotates at about 15,000 revolutions per minute and it is guided by a template to produce blanks identical to the template. Routing large aluminum blanks is common practice in the aircraft and missile industries.

Flame Cutting

Flame cutting or torch cutting means the cutting of thick blanks by the use of an acetylene torch. In operation, the torch heats the metal under its flame tip until it melts. Compressed air then blows the molten metal out, forming a narrow channel called the kerf. The width of the kerf ranges from 5/64 inch to 1/8 inch depending upon stock thickness and the speed of the torch. For producing thick blanks in quantity, a template guides the torch by means of a pantograph. Flame cutting is employed for cutting blanks ranging from ¼ to 1 inch or more in thickness.

Holes in blanks can also be torch cut by the same method. Flame cutting leaves the edges somewhat rough and ridged. However, such edges are satisfactory for some parts for trucks, tanks, ships, and other similar applications.

4-2. SQUARE SHEARING

Large, straight-sided blanks are produced in the shear by cutting sheets into strips, then cutting the strips to required lengths or widths. Blanks larger than 8 by 10 inches and composed primarily of straight sides are ordinarily produced by shearing because of the high cost of large dies.

Blanks cut in a modern shear can be held to an accuracy of 0.005. Four factors govern shearing accuracy:

1. The shear must have sufficient rigidity to withstand the cutting load without deflection or spring.
2. Knife clearance must be set correctly and proper rake selected to reduce twist, camber, or bow. Rake is the angle of the upper knife in relation to the horizontal lower knife of the shear. Twist is spiraling of the strip and it is more severe in soft, narrow, or thick strips than it is in hard, wide, or thin strips. Camber is curvature along the edge in the plane of the strip. Bow is curvature perpendicular to the surface of the strip.
3. Good gaging practice must be followed.
4. The sheet must be held down securely while shearing occurs.

In the upper illustration:

For producing square and rectangular blanks shown in the upper inset, the sheet is first cut into strips to length **A** of the blanks. The strips are then run through the shear again and cut into blanks having width **B.** Here is the method of listing operations on the route sheet:

Operation No. 1. Shear to length. (**A**)
Operation No. 2. Shear to width. (**B**)

In the lower illustration:

When the grain of the material must run lengthwise of the blank for extra stiffness, the sheet is cut into strips to width **B** of the blanks. The strips are then run through the shear again and cut into blanks having length **A.** On the route sheet, operations are listed as follows:

Operation No. 1. Shear to width. (**B**)
Operation No. 2. Shear to length. (**A**)

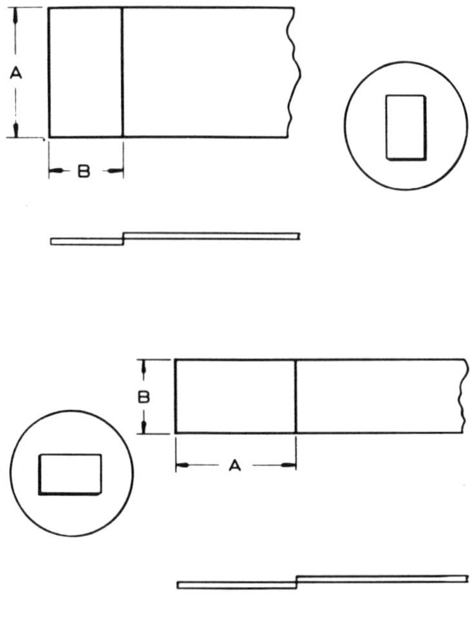

Fig. 4-2. Rectangular blanks sheared from wide and narrow strips.

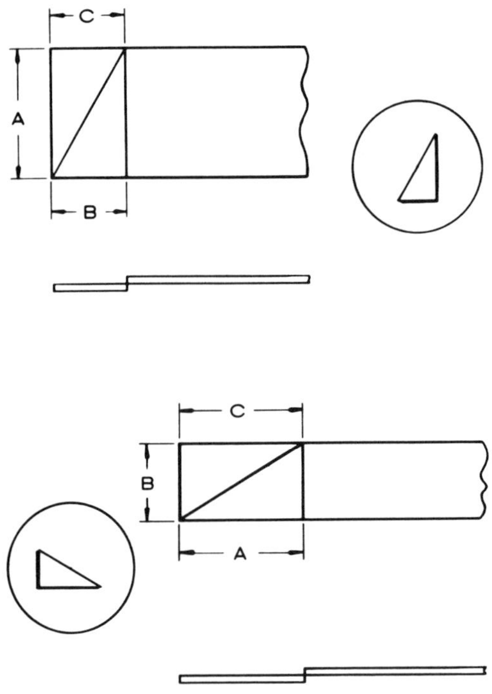

Fig. 4-3. Triangular blanks made by shearing rectangular blanks sheared from wide and narrow strips.

4-3. TRIANGULAR BLANKS

Triangular blanks are produced by shearing square or rectangular blanks, then splitting them to produce two blanks. In the upper illustration:

Operation No. 1. Shear to length. (**A**)
Operation No. 2. Shear to double width. (**B**)
Operation No. 3. Split. (**C**)

Note that although operation No. 2 states "Shear to double width", this does not mean that the strip is to be cut twice the width of a single blank. It simply means that the square or rectangular blanks are to be made wide enough so splitting will produce two full blanks.

In the lower illustration:

For running strips the narrow way, operations are listed as follows:

Operation No. 1. Shear to width. (**B**)
Operation No. 2. Shear to double length. (**A**)
Operation No. 3. Split. (**C**)

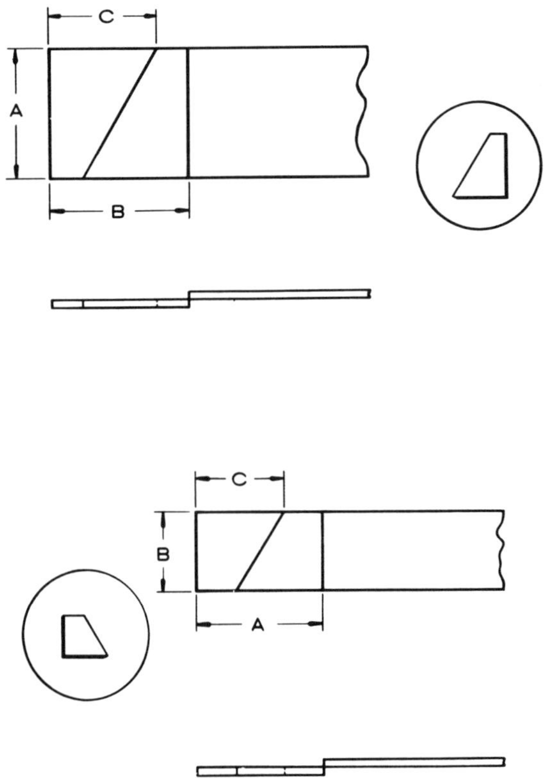

Fig. 4-4. Angular edge blanks made by shearing rectangular blanks sheared from wide and narrow strips.

4-4. ANGULAR EDGE BLANKS

Wider blanks having one angular edge can be produced by the same method employed for triangular blanks. For the upper illustration:

Operation No. 1. Shear to length. (**A**)
Operation No. 2. Shear to double width. (**B**)
Operation No. 3. Split. (**C**)

In the lower illustration:

The function of some blanks renders it necessary to run them the narrow way. Operations are then as follows:

Operation No. 1. Shear to width. (**B**)
Operation No. 2. Shear to double length. (**A**)
Operation No. 3. Split. (**C**)

4-5. ADDED CUTS

One or more extra cuts may be required to complete the blanks. Here is the order of operations for the blank in the upper inset:

Operation No. 1. Shear to length. **(A)**
Operation No. 2. Shear to double width. **(B)**
Operation No. 3. Split. **(C)**
Operation No. 4. Trim. **(D)**

In the lower illustration:

Operation No. 1. Shear to width. (**B**)
Operation No. 2. Shear to double length. (**A**)
Operation No. 3. Split. (**C**)
Operation No. 4. Trim. (**D**)

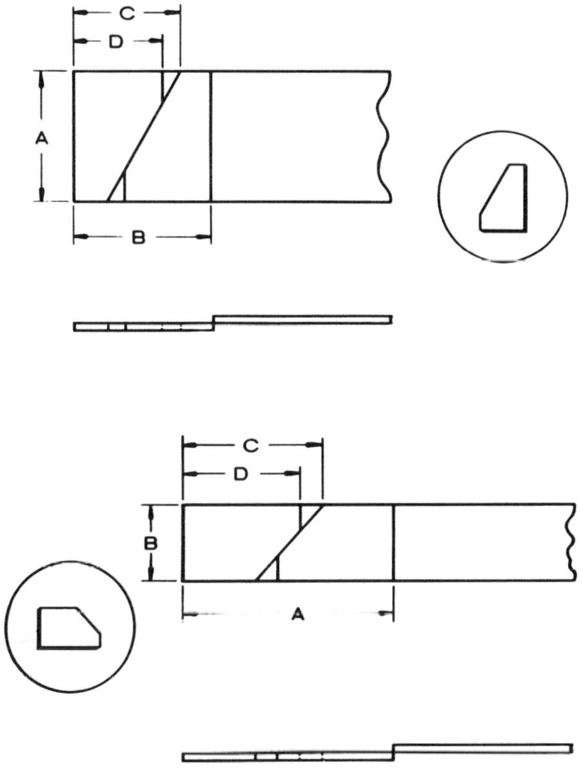

Fig. 4-5. Blanks produced by added cutting of angular edge pieces.

4-6. PARALLELOGRAMS

Blanks in the shape of an angular parallelogram are produced by shearing with the strip positioned at an angle to the shear blade. For the wide strips, upper illustration:

Operation No. 1. Shear to length. (**A**)
Operation No. 2. Shear to width. (**B**)

For narrow strips, lower illustration:

Operation No. 1. Shear to width. (**B**)
Operation No. 2. Shear to length. (**A**)

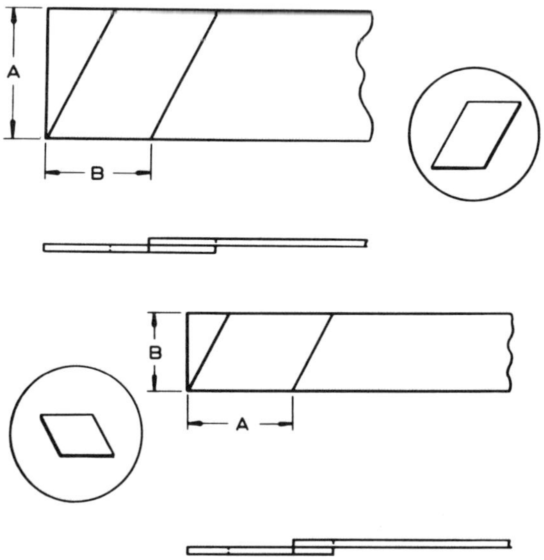

Fig. 4-6. Parallelogram shaped blanks sheared from wide and narrow strips.

4-7. TRIANGULAR BLANKS

Triangular blanks with an acute angle at each of the three apexes are produced by splitting a parallelogram.

For wide strips:

Operation No. 1. Shear to length. (**A**)
Operation No. 2. Shear to double width. (**B**)
Operation No. 3. Split. (**C**)

For narrow strips:

Operation No. 1. Shear to width. (**B**)
Operation No. 2. Shear to double length (**A**)
Operation No. 3. Split. (**C**)

4-8. TRAPEZOIDAL BLANKS

Large trapezoidal blanks are produced by employing the same method.

For wide strips:

Operation No. 1. Shear to length. (**A**)
Operation No. 2. Shear to double width. (**B**)
Operation No. 3. Split. (**C**)

For narrow strips:

Operation No. 1. Shear to width. (**B**)
Operation No. 2. Shear to double length. (**A**)
Operation No. 3. Split. (**C**)

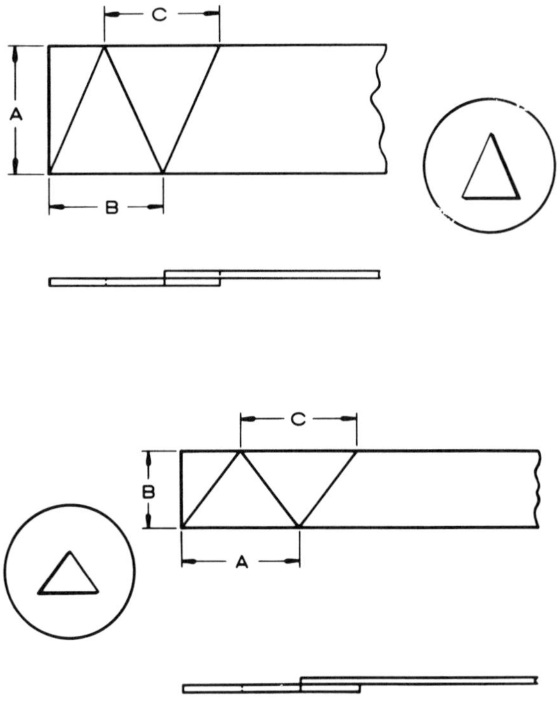

Fig. 4-7. Acute-angle triangular blanks made by shearing parallelogram shaped blanks sheared from wide and narrow strips.

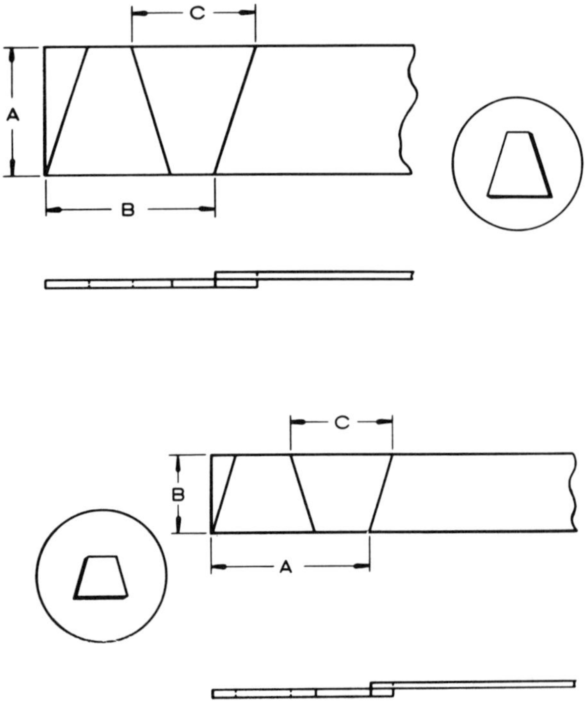

Fig. 4-8. Trapezoidal blanks are sheared in a manner similar to acute-angle triangular blanks.

4-9. ADDED CUTS

One or more extra cuts may be required to complete the blanks.

For wide strips:

Operation No. 1. Shear to length. (**A**)
Operation No. 2. Shear to double width. (**B**)
Operation No. 3. Split. (**C**)
Operation No. 4. Trim. (**D**)

For narrow strips:

Operation No. 1. Shear to width. (**B**)
Operation No. 2. Shear to double length. (**A**)
Operation No. 3. Split. (**C**)
Operation No. 4. Trim. (**D**)

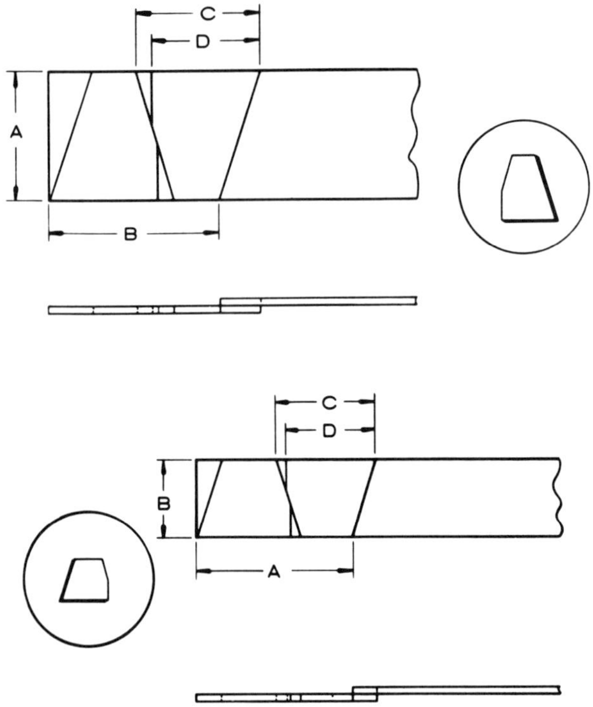

Fig. 4-9. Blanks produced by added cutting of trapezoidal blanks.

4-10. NOTCHING

Irregular notches or cuts are applied in trimming dies after the straight sides of the blanks have been sheared. It is less expensive to design and build a die for trimming small portions of a blank than it would be to design and build a die for producing the entire blank. This is because the length of cutting edges is shorter for trimming than for blanking and less fitting is required. Also, less material is required in the strip when blanks are sheared because there is no scrap bridge.

In this connection, you should know exactly what is meant by the words "notching" and "trimming". Notching is the operation of cutting small portions from the edges of a strip or blank. The area of such portions is no greater than that of average pierced holes. Trimming means the removal of larger portions of metal to alter the form in the area of the trimmed

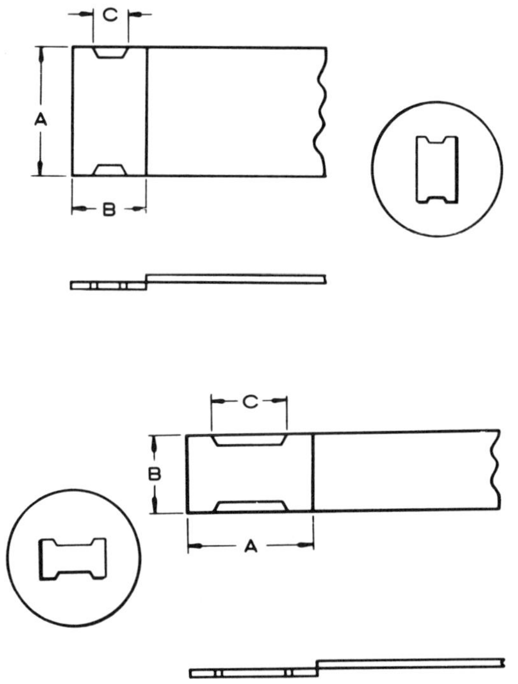

Fig. 4-10. Blanks sheared and trimmed from wide and narrow strips.

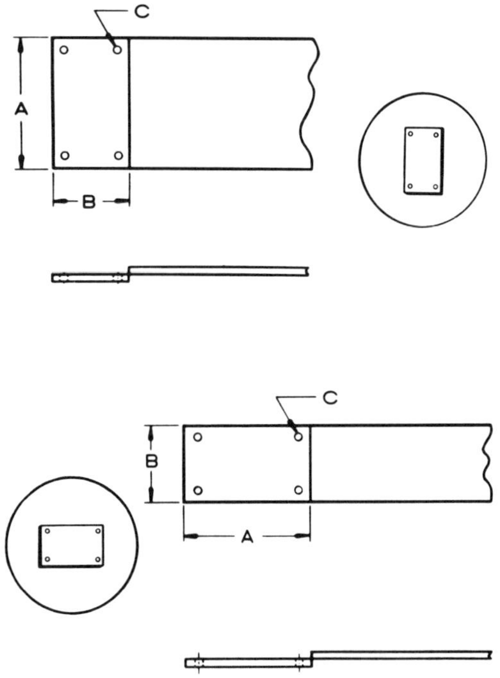

Fig. 4-11. Blanks sheared and pierced from wide and narrow strips.

contour. The difference is one of degree. Trimming thus means the reshaping of blanks on a larger scale than is accomplished by simple notching.

In the illustration, operations for wide strips are:

Operation No. 1. Shear to length. (**A**)
Operation No. 2. Shear to width. (**B**)
Operation No. 3. Trim. (**C**)

For narrow strips:

Operation No. 1. Shear to width. (**B**)
Operation No. 2. Shear to length. (**A**)
Operation No. 3. Trim. (**C**)

4-11. PIERCING

Holes may be pierced in the blanks in a turret punch when required quantities are low. For greater production, a special piercing die is designed and built for the job. After they have been sheared, the blanks are hand-fed into the piercing die.

Operations for wide strips are:

Operation No. 1. Shear to length. (**A**)
Operation No. 2. Shear to width. (**B**)
Operation No. 3. Pierce. (**C**)

For narrow strips:

Operation No. 1. Shear to width. (**B**)
Operation No. 2. Shear to length. (**A**)
Operation No. 3. Pierce. (**C**)

4-12. SHEAR STRENGTH

In cutting any material, a force acting on the area to be sheared (called the shear stress) is applied to the material. The material offers resistance to separation. Its molecular structure resists the shear stress applied to it and the amount of resistance is called the shear strength. To effect cutting, the shear stress applied to the material must be greater than the shear strength. The molecular structure will then fail and fracture and separation will occur.

Shear strengths of various materials have been found by experiment and they are listed in the table. The shear strength **A** is equivalent to the force required to cut a bar one inch square in two and these are the values given.

Expressed differently, the shear strength values in the table are a measure of the force required to cut an *area* one inch square. Given this information it is a simple matter to determine the shear strength for any area to be cut.

4-13. AREA TO BE CUT

The first step in establishing cutting force or blanking force is to determine the area to be cut. For straight cuts as performed in shearing and in some cut off die operations, the area to be cut is found by multiplying the length by the thickness.

Formula: Area = L × T

4-14. AREA TO BE CUT IN BLANKING

In blanking, an area is removed from within the strip and the cut is therefore around an enclosed contour. The area to be cut is found by multiplying the perimeter of the blank by the thickness.

For round cuts: Area = D × 3.1416 × T

For rectangular cuts: Area = (2L + 2W) × T

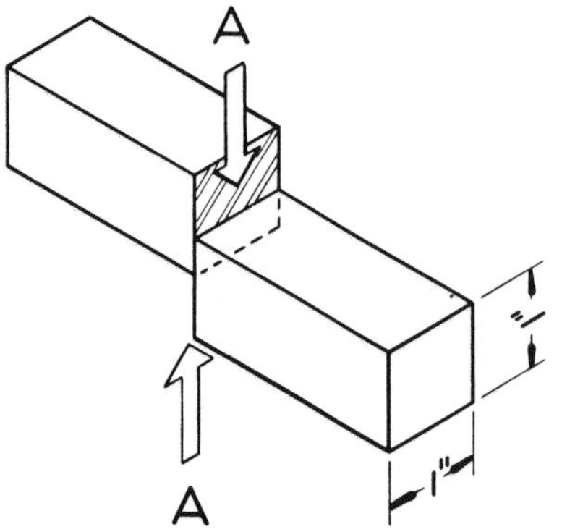

MATERIAL		SHEAR STRENGTH Pounds per square inch
STEEL .10% carbon content	Hot Rolled	35,000
	Cold Rolled	45,000
STEEL .20% carbon content	Hot Rolled	45,000
	Cold Rolled	55,000
STEEL .30% carbon content	Hot Rolled	55,000
	Cold Rolled	65,000
STAINLESS STEEL		60,000
SILICON STEEL		65,000
TIN		5,000
ALUMINUM		10,000
COPPER		25,000
BRASS		30,000
BRONZE		35,000

Fig. 4-12. Drawing which illustrates shear strength and table of shear strengths for various materials.

We are now prepared to use the formula for determining the blanking force.

Blanking force = S × P × T

In which: S = Shear strength as taken from the table in Fig. 4-12.
P = Perimeter. This is the distance around all cut edges.
T = Thickness of material to be cut.

For example, a blank 2 inches by 4 inches is to be cut in a strip of No. 16 gage (0.0598 inch thick), 0.20 per cent carbon, cold rolled steel.

In addition, two ½ inch holes are to be pierced in a previous station, piercing of the holes to occur simultaneously with blanking of the part.

Perimeter of blank (2 + 2 + 4 + 4) =	12	inches
Perimeter of holes (2 × 0.500 × 3.1416) =	3.1416	inches
	15.1416	inches

Formula: 55,000 × 15.1416 × 0.0598 = 49,800.722 lbs.

Since press capacities are rated in tons, this number is divided by 2,000 = 24.9 tons.

A thirty ton press would be selected.

When cutting faces of the punch or die block are ground at an angle so that cutting of the periphery of the blank occurs gradually, the shear strength values given in Fig. 4-12 may be reduced by one-half.

This is called "shearing" the die and the operation will be explained in Section 7, "How to Design Die Blocks," and also in Section 8, "How to Design Blanking Punches."

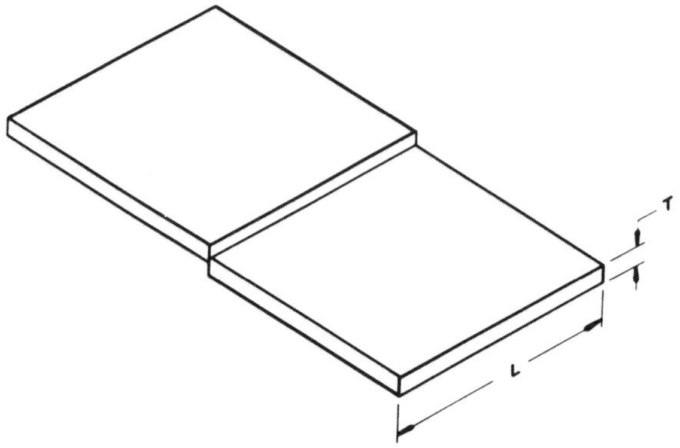

Fig. 4-13. Drawing which illustrates area subjected to shear.

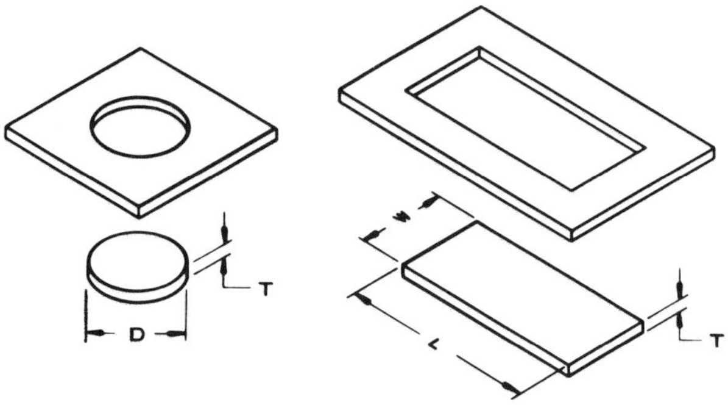

Fig. 4-14. Drawing which illustrates areas subjected to shear in blanking.

Section 5

FOURTEEN STEPS TO DESIGN A DIE

We have completed the introductory portion of our work and we must now come to an understanding of die design itself, of the procedure followed by a die designer in organizing components of different shapes, sizes, and composition into the unified concept called a die. First, it should be understood that a definite order of steps must be taken in originating any die design.

Haphazard design methods waste time and they often result in inefficient press tools, but systematic procedures will provide:

1. Consistently good designs
2. Speedy, effortless work
3. Fewer erasures
4. Improved appearance of drawings
5. Stronger punch and die components.

In this section are illustrated the fourteen steps required for designing a die to produce the sample part shown in Fig. 1-7.

Study this order of steps carefully, because by following it closely, you can begin at once to design a die yourself and when you have completed your design, the results you have achieved will surprise and please you.

By appropriate substitutions the same steps can be taken in the design of any die. For example, in designing a multiple-station progressive die, all die blocks would be laid out at Step 2, The Die Block. If a spring stripper must be employed because of the nature of the operation it simply replaces the solid stripper at Step 10, "The Stripper Plate".

In the top view, outlines of the strip and all holes or openings are drawn with thin, red phantom lines. In the front and side view, the strip thickness is filled in solid red. The blank and slugs are shown pushed out of the strip and they are also drawn solid red. Locate their top surfaces in line, or flush, with the bottom surface of the strip. A pictorial drawing of the strip with the blank and pierced slugs pushed out is shown between views. This is how the strip would be visualized before drawing the actual views. To improve your own faculty of visualization, make a free-hand pictorial sketch of the strip on a separate sheet. In Section 6, rules for properly laying out scrap strips are given, as well as methods for design verification.

In Sections 6 through 19, each step will be explained in far greater detail. As you study each section, keep referring back to the illustrated list in this section to fix the position of each step firmly in your mind.

5-1. THE SCRAP STRIP

The first step in designing any die is to lay out the material strip exactly as it will appear at the bottom of the press stroke. Three views are shown, and the distance between views must be carefully estimated to prevent views from running into each other as the die grows. Always use red lead when drawing the material strip so it will show clearly through the maze of black lines which will represent the punch and die members.

5-2. THE DIE BLOCK

Draw the three views of the die block. In the top view, the die block usually is rectangular in shape. The blank opening and holes for punches are represented by black lines. Simply draw with black lead directly over the red lines. Dotted lines represent edges at the bottoms of blank and slug openings. These are larger because of tapered walls provided for blank and slug relief.

Leave sufficient room for the screws and dowels which will fasten the block to the die set. Because both the front and side views will be section views, the lines representing internal openings are solid lines. The pictorial drawing now shows the die block in position under the strip.

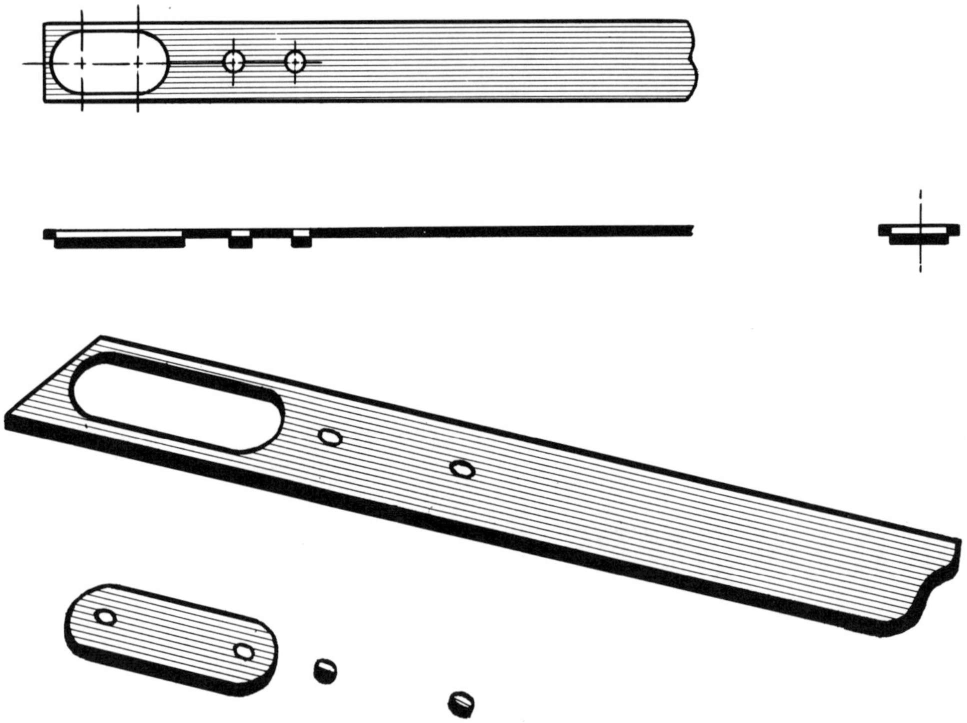

Fig. 5-1. Material strip as it appears at the bottom of the press stroke.

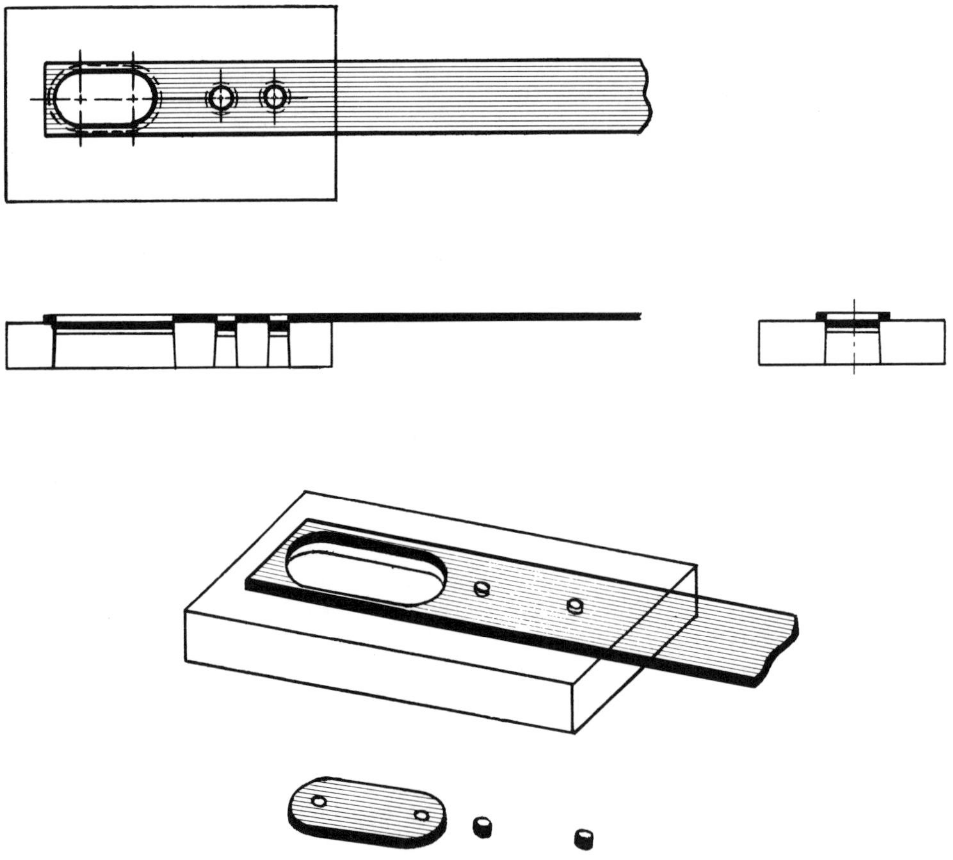

Fig. 5-2. Various views of the die block and material strip.

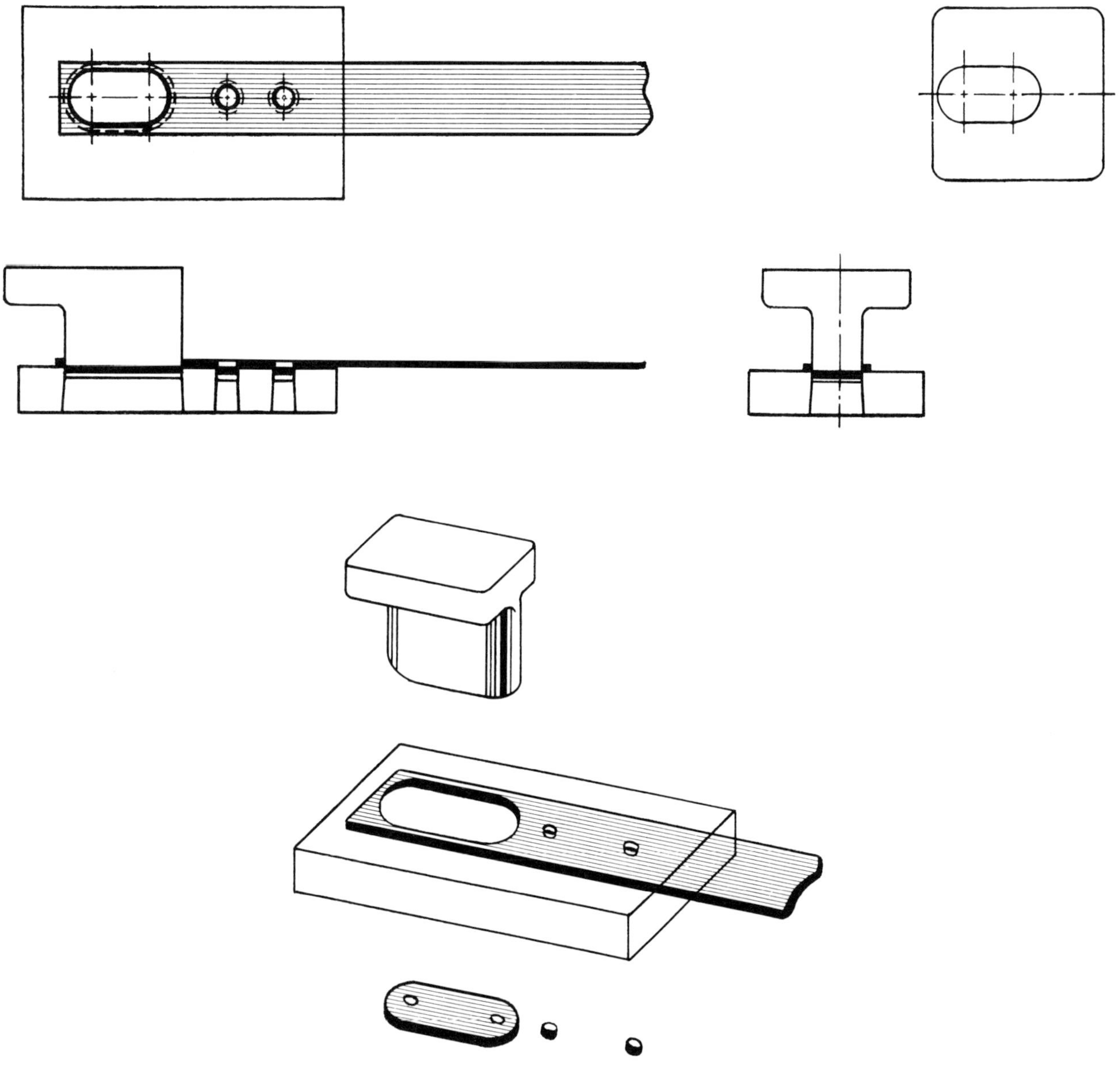

Fig. 5-3. Various views of the die assembly with the blanking punch added.

5-3. THE BLANKING PUNCH

The blanking punch is now drawn in position above the die block. Its plan view is applied in the upper right corner in an inverted position. That is, the punch is drawn as if removed from above the die block and turned over so cutting edges are viewed directly. When outlining the flange width and thickness, take into consideration the screws and dowels which will fasten it to the punch holder of the die set. In the lower section views, the cutting face of the blanking punch is drawn flush with the top of the die block with a single line. To improve your ability to visualize the die in three dimensions, turn to the pictorial drawing and sketch the blanking punch above the blank opening in the die block.

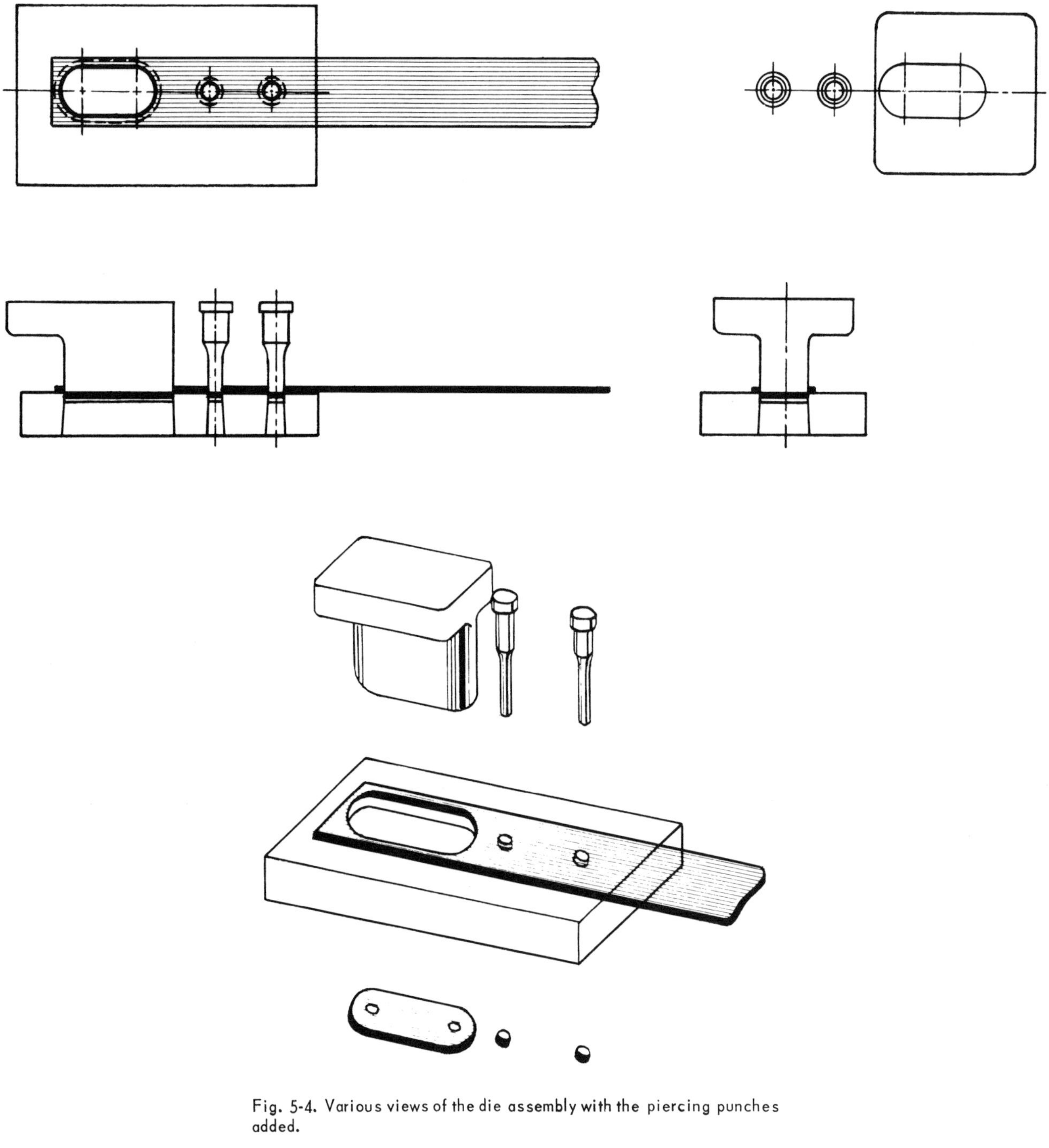

Fig. 5-4. Various views of the die assembly with the piercing punches added.

5-4. PIERCING PUNCHES

Piercing punches are now drawn in their proper positions. Include their plan views, represented by concentric circles, in the upper-right corner, remembering that this view of the piercing punches and blanking punch is opposite from the plan view of the die block. The finished die will appear as if opened, much in the same manner as a book is opened. Sketch piercing punches on the pictorial drawing.

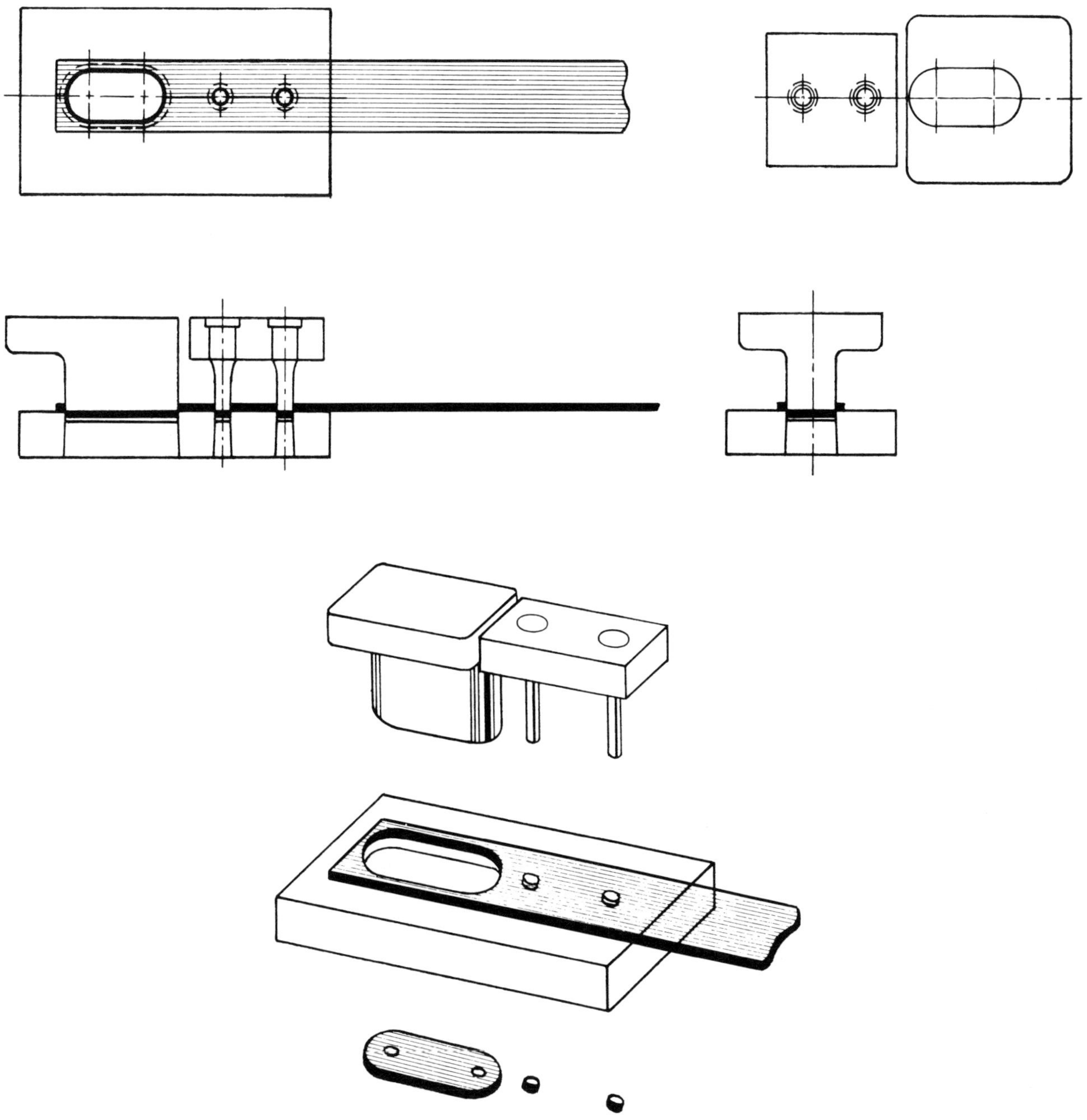

Fig. 5-5. Various views of the die assembly with the punch plate added.

5-5. PUNCH PLATE

In this step, the punch plate, which retains the piercing punches, is drawn in the front and upper-right views. This plate is usually made of a good grade of machine steel. Here again, room must be provided for the screws and dowels which will secure it to the punch holder of the die set.

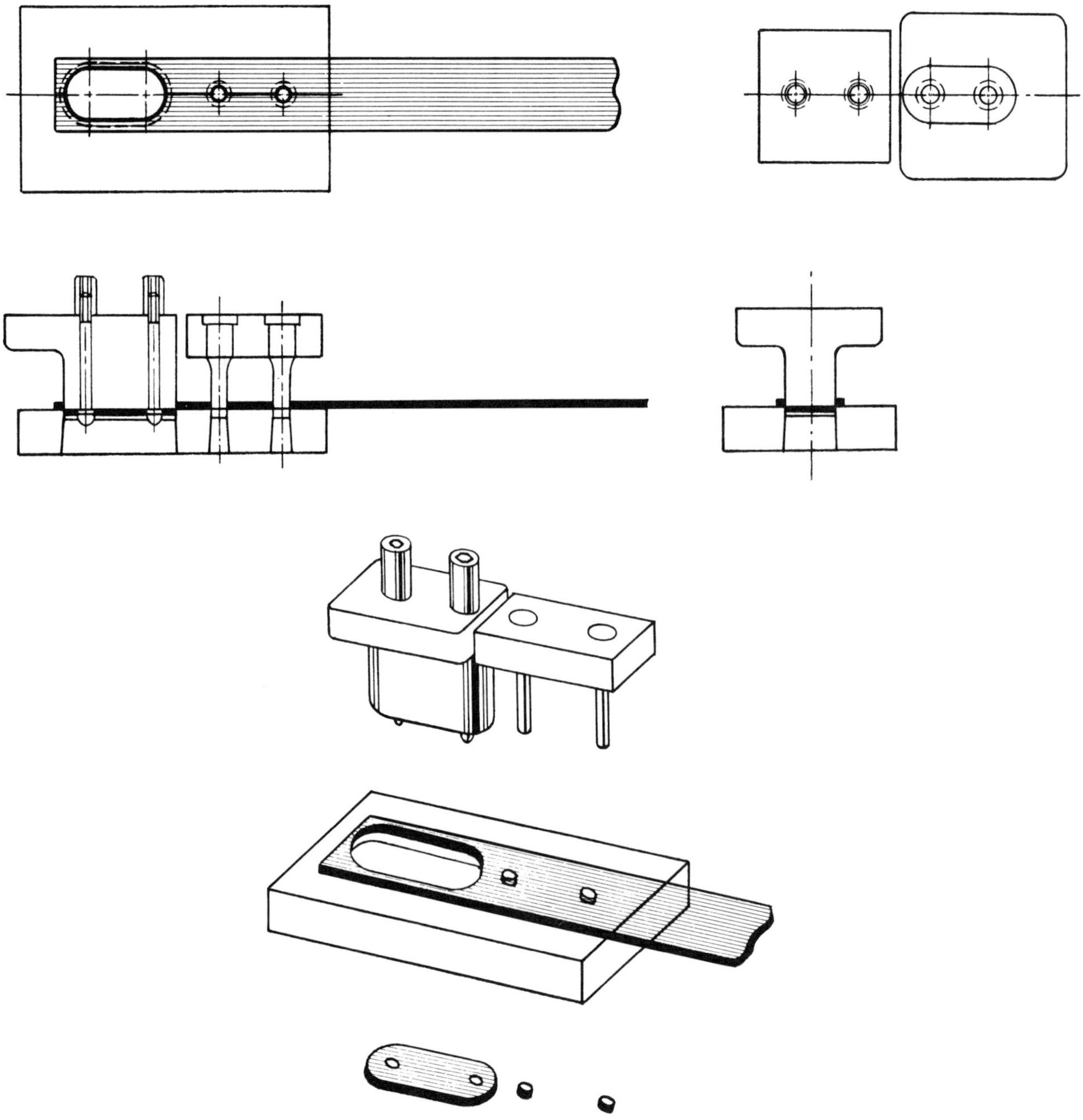

Fig. 5-6. Various views of the die assembly with the pilots added.

5-6. PILOTS

Draw the pilots and the nuts that hold them in the blanking punch. As you know, the pilots accurately locate the strip by engaging the holes pierced in the first station. Only outlines of the parts are drawn, Section lines are not applied until the entire design is completed. Be sure to draw the concentric circles to represent pilots and pilot nuts in the upper-right view in addition to showing them in the front view.

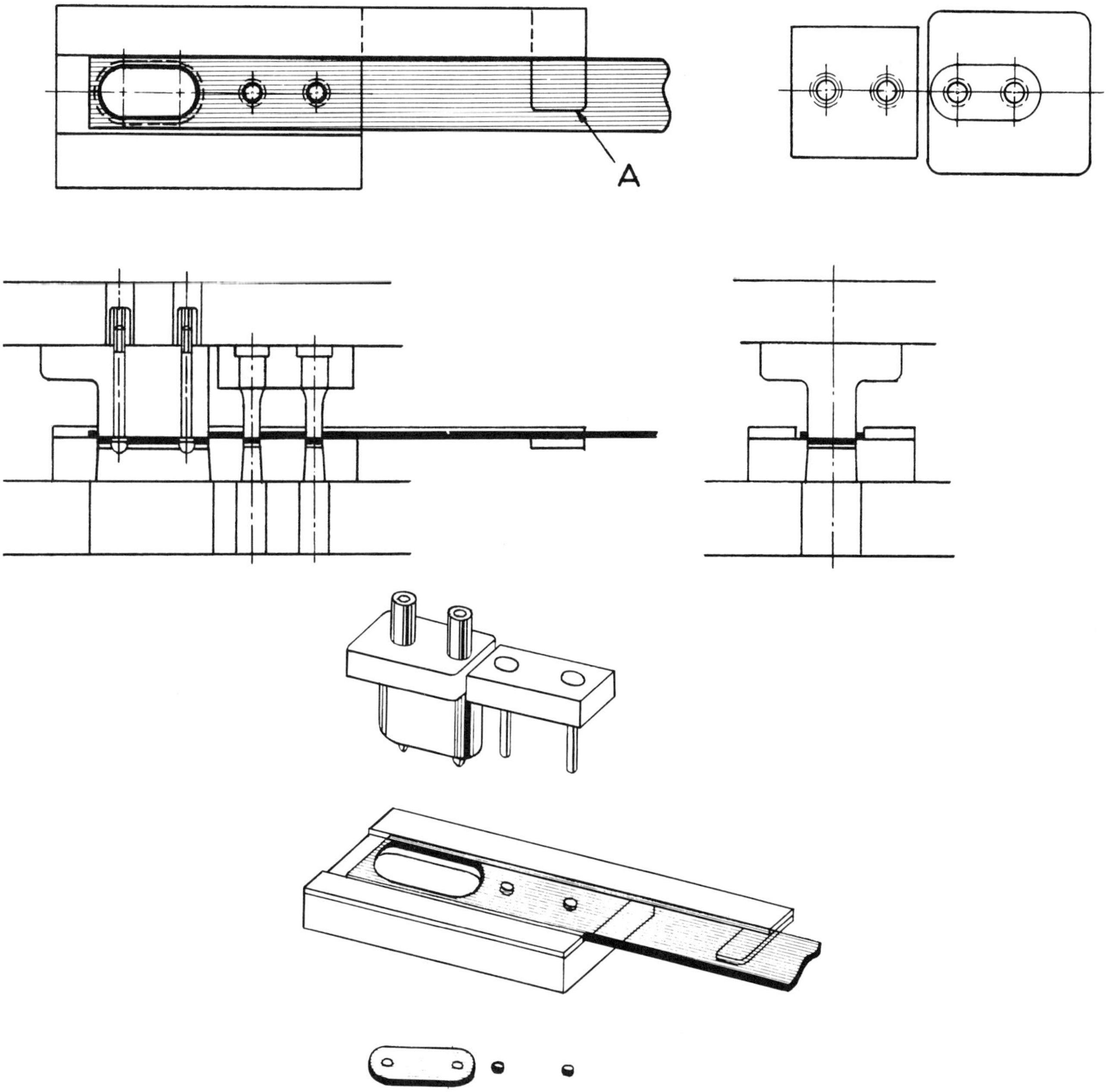

Fig. 5-7. Various views of the die assembly with the back gage and front spacer added.

5-7. GAGES

The strip has not yet been located, it simply lies on top of the die block. We must now draw the back gage and front spacer which guide the strip by its sides. Strip support **A**, if one is used, can be drawn at this time. In the front and side views, draw horizontal lines to represent the top and bottom surfaces of the punch and die holders of the die set. Thicknesses are taken from a die set catalog. For a small die such as this one, a punch holder 1¼″ thick and a die holder 1½″ thick are sufficient.

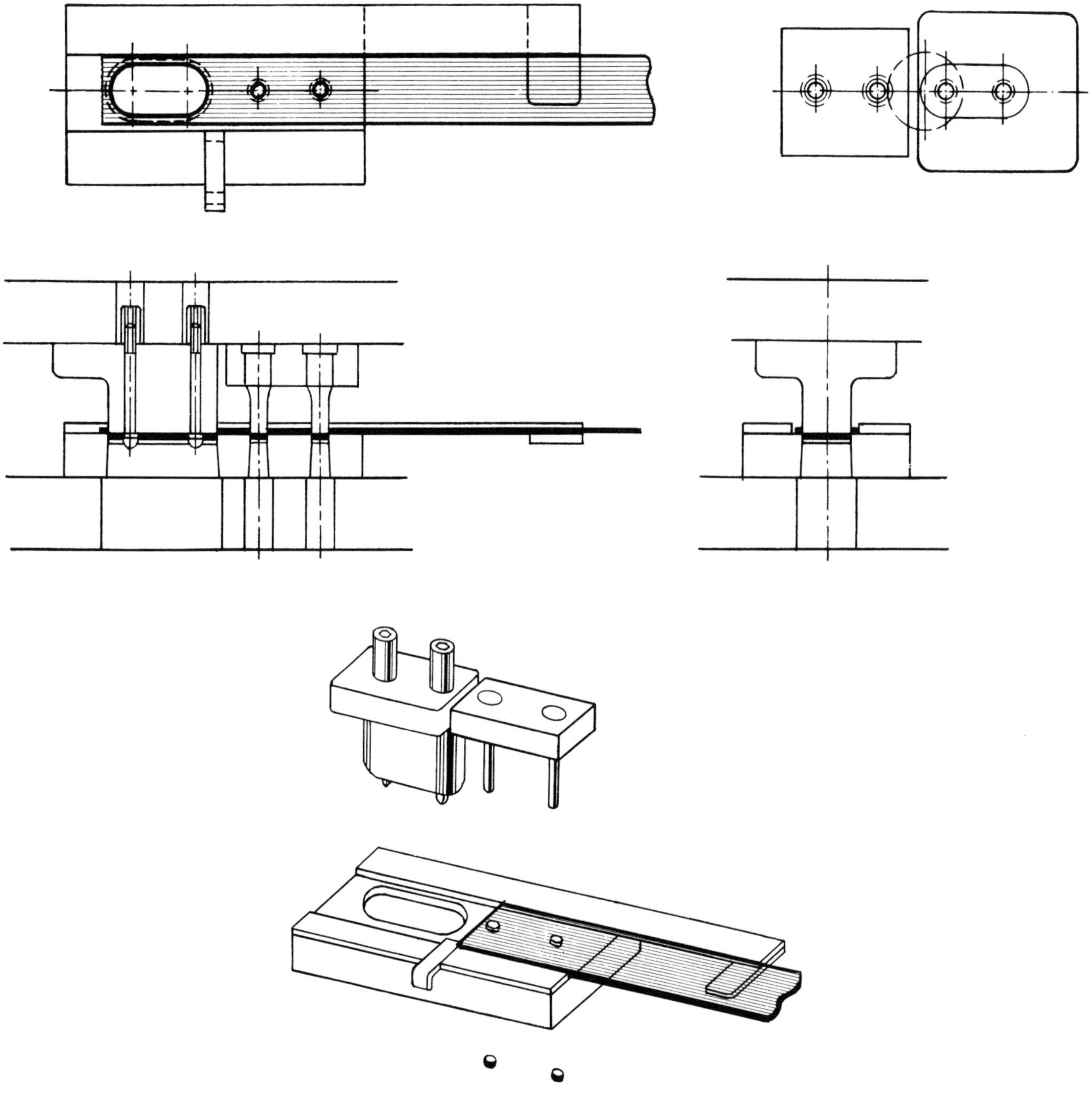

Fig. 5-8. Various views of the die assembly with the finger stop added.

5-8. FINGER STOP

Although the strip is now supported sideways between the back gage and front spacer, no provision has been made for endwise location. Draw a finger stop to position the strip for piercing the two holes in the first blank. In operation, the finger stop is pushed in and the end of the strip engages it. After the press has been tripped to pierce the holes, the strip is then advanced until its end contacts the automatic stop. (See next step.)

Also at this time the punch shank is drawn in the upper right-hand view; being represented by a dotted circle. It should be so placed that any clearance hole will appear entirely within, or completely outside of it.

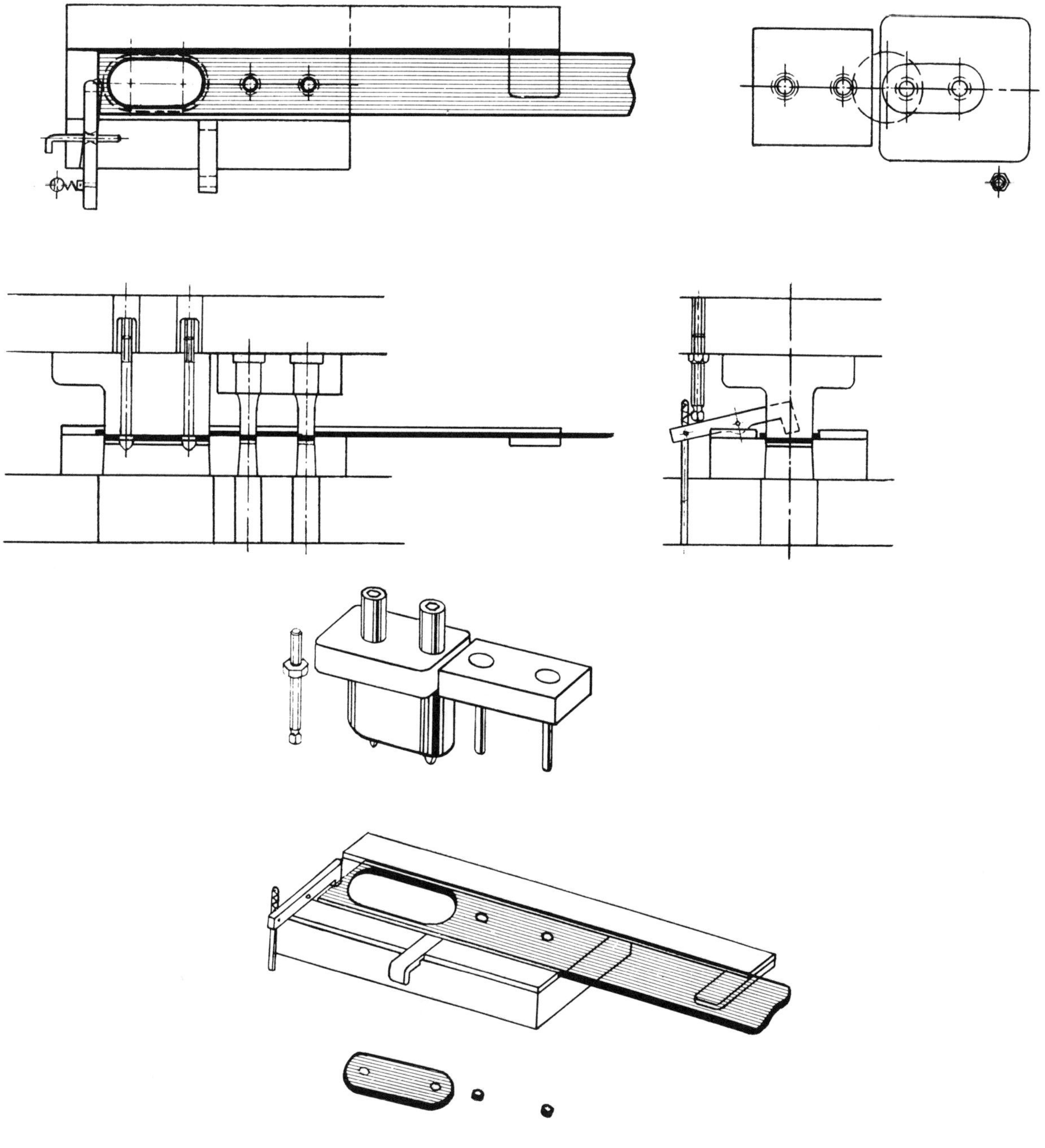

Fig. 5-9. Various views of the die assembly with the automatic stop added.

5-9. AUTOMATIC STOP

An automatic stop, which locates the strip at every punch stroke, is now drawn. There are numerous types of automatic stops, but the one illustrated is perhaps the most widely used. In operation, the end of the strip contacts the toe of the stop locating it in a "set" position. When the press ram descends, a square-head set screw, retained in the punch holder, contacts the opposite end of the stop causing the toe to be raised above the strip. A spring then "triggers" the stop causing it to rotate a few degrees so that the toe of the stop comes to a position above the scrap bridge. When the ram goes up, the stop toe falls on top of the scrap bridge, allowing the strip to slide under it until the toe of the stop falls into the blanked opening. Travel continues until the right edge of the blanked opening contacts the toe, moving it and "resetting" the stop. These motions take place at high speeds, much faster than the time it takes to describe them.

To this point, all lines have been drawn very lightly for easy erasure when sizes of components are altered.

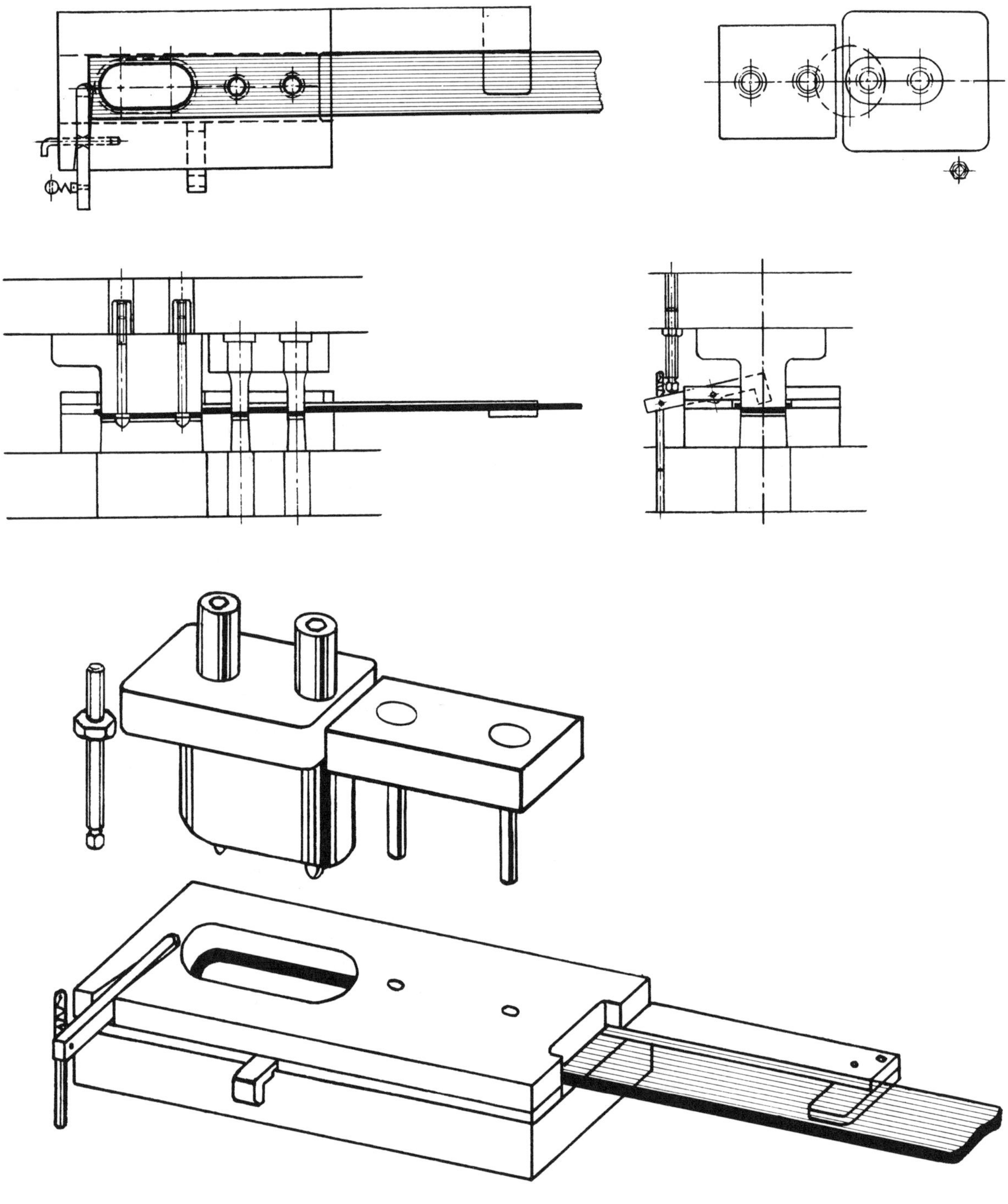

Fig. 5-10. Various views of the die assembly with the stripper added.

5-10. STRIPPER

The stripper is now applied to all three views. Strippers remove the strip from around blanking and piercing punches. For some types of dies, a knockout would be designed at this step. Knockouts are internal strippers and they remove blanks and formed parts from inside cavities of punches and dies. In the upper-left plan view of the die block, all lines under the solid stripper now become dotted lines since they now represent hidden edges of surfaces.

A stripper is required because the material strip always clings tightly around any punch which penetrates it and provision must be made to remove it from the punch.

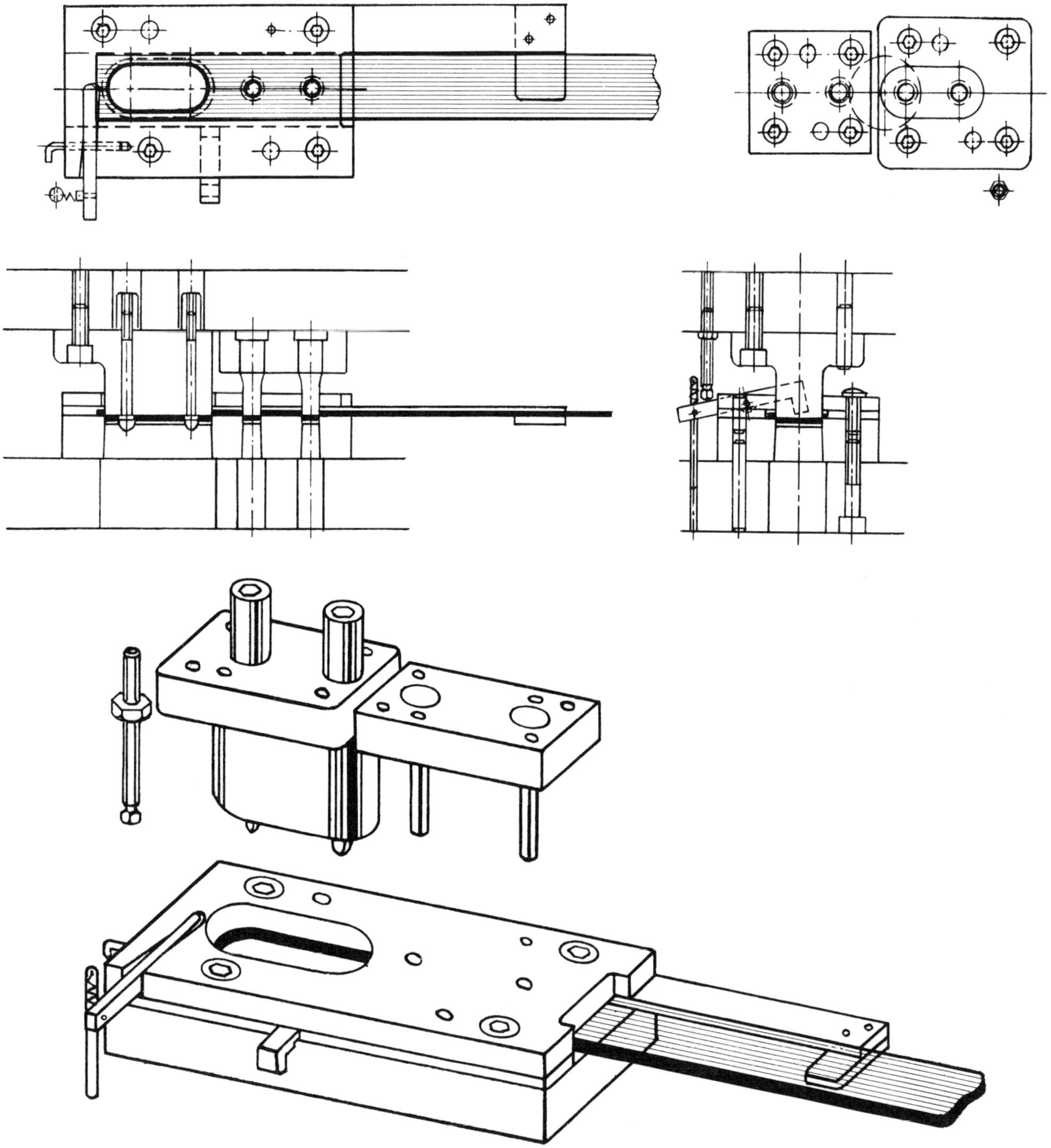

Fig. 5-11. Various views of the die assembly with the fasteners added.

5-11. FASTENERS

In this step, screws, dowels, and other fasteners are drawn. For press tools, all dowels are the same diameter as the screws for any particular member. Note that button-head socket screws are employed to fasten the solid stripper to the die block. Because of their low head height, strength, and clean lines, these are excellent fasteners for this application.

Considerable designing ability is required for applying fasteners properly and there are a number of rules to be learned. This subject will be taken up in detail in Section 16, "How to Apply Fasteners."

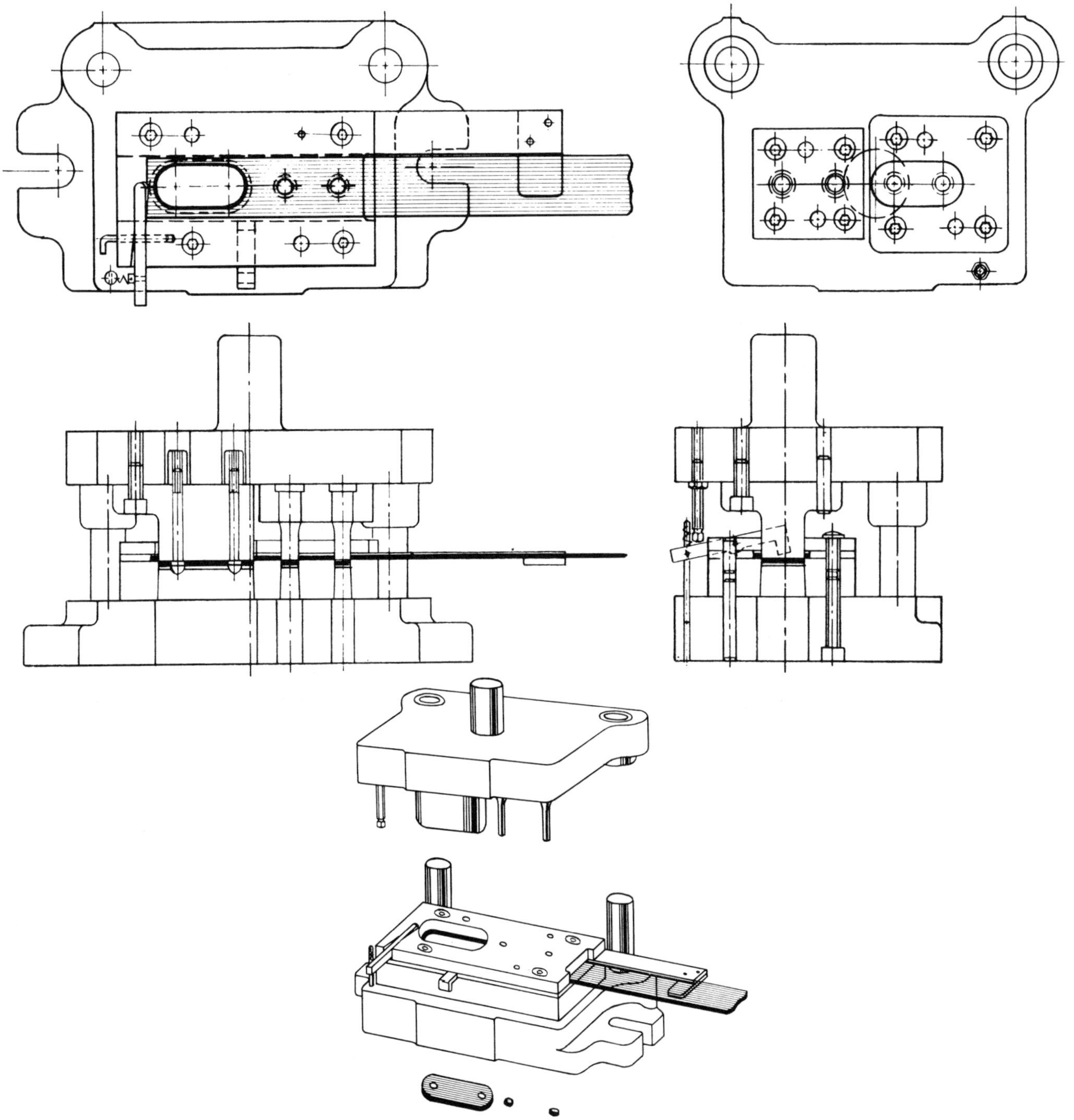

Fig. 5-12. Various views of the die assembly including the die set.

5-12. THE DIE SET

The die set, which was started with horizontal lines in the lower views of Step 7, and with a dotted circle in the upper-right view of Step 8, is now completed. To draw in the die set before this step will very frequently result in considerable erasing when die sections are found to be too small and their sizes are increased.

Die sets are available in a bewildering variety of shapes and sizes, and judgment must be exercised for selecting a suitable one under given conditions. In addition, a definite method of procedure must be followed in applying the views to the drawing. This subject will be explained thoroughly in Section 17, "How to Select a Die Set."

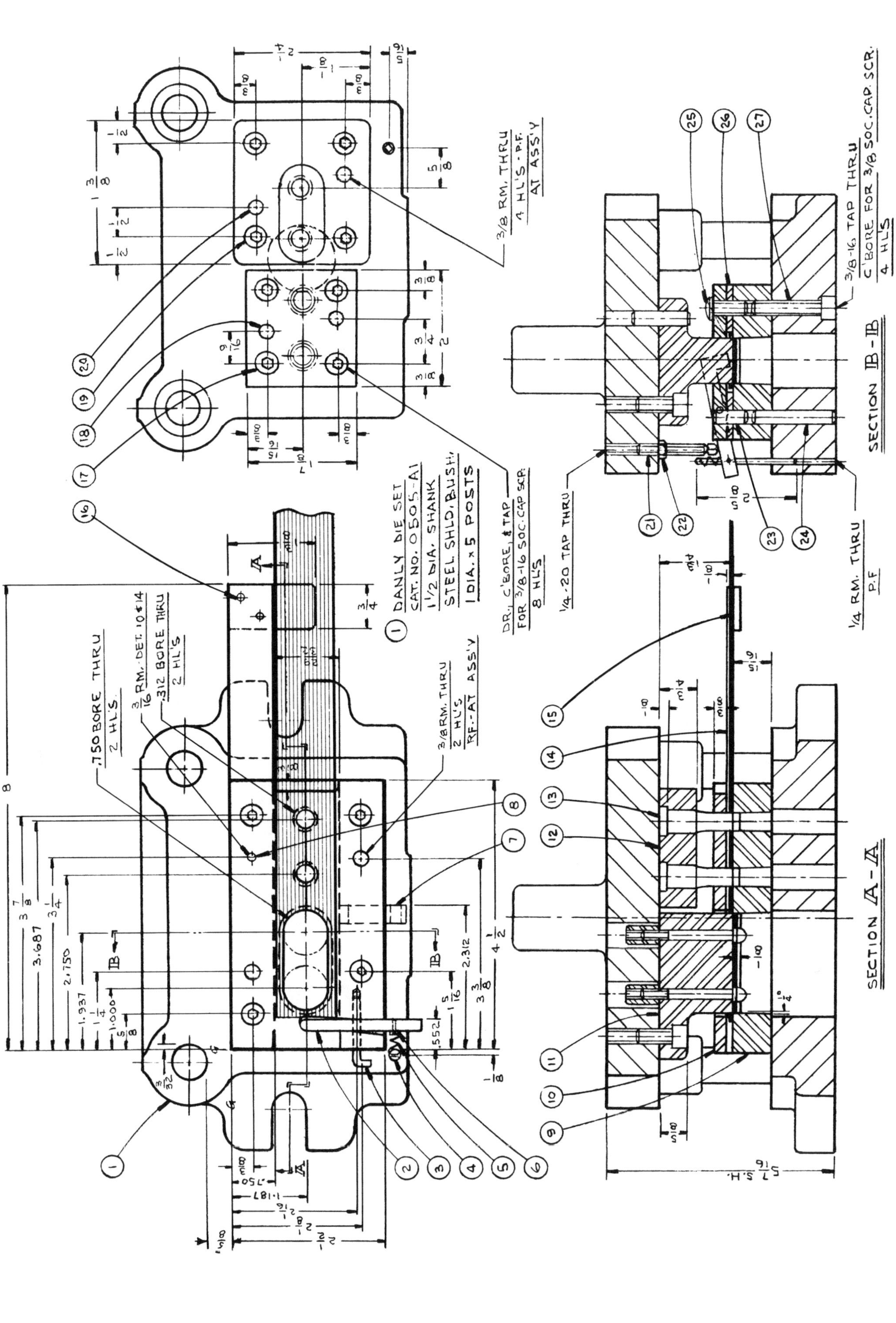

Fig. 5-13. Various views of the complete die with dimensions and notes.

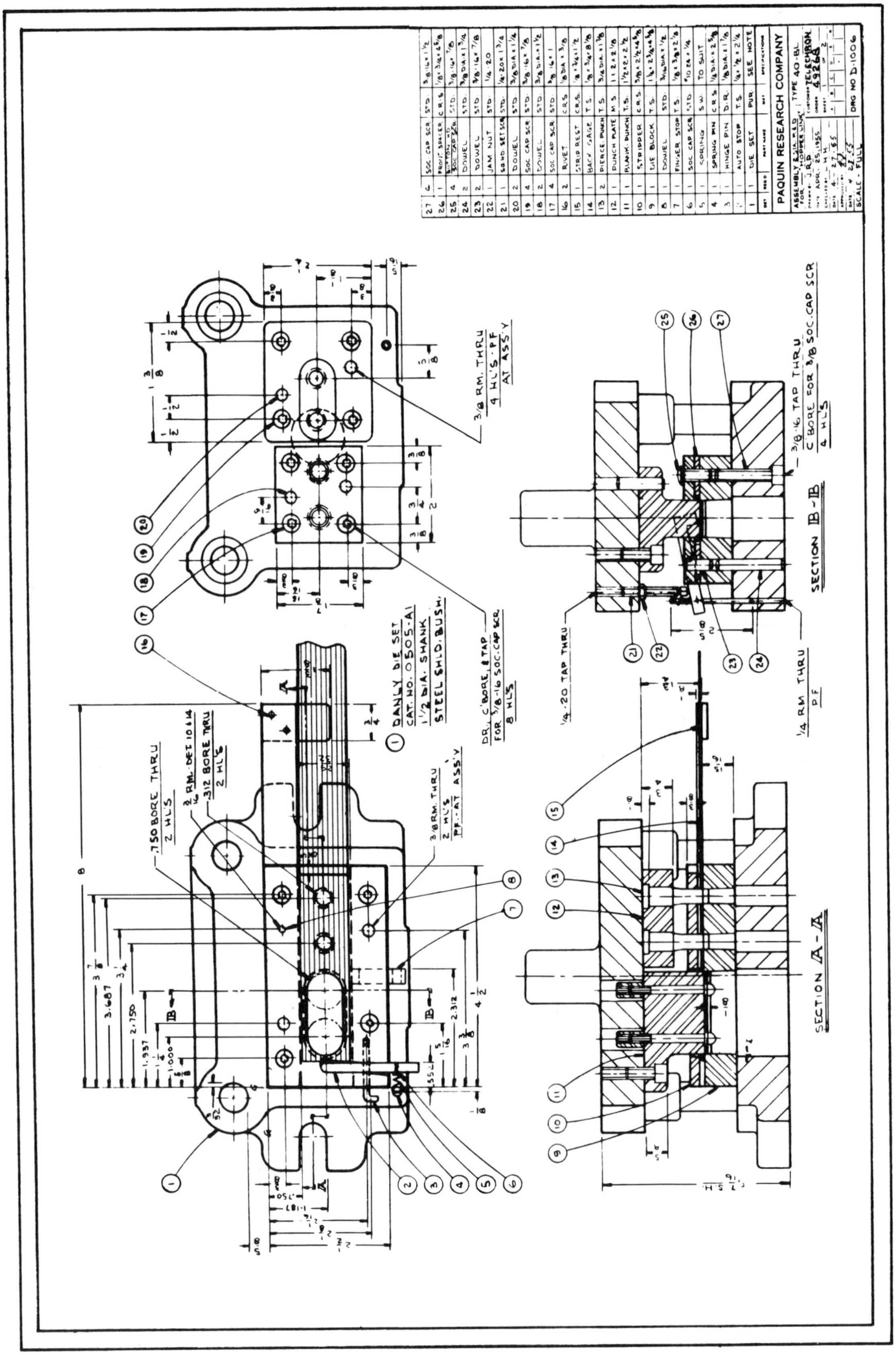

Fig. 5-14. The complete die drawing including the bill of material.

5-13. DIMENSIONS AND NOTES

All dimensions and notes are now lettered in place. Die block dimensions are applied as for a jig borer layout. All information that the die maker might require to complete the die should now be on the drawing, unless components are detailed separately as is done for more complex dies.

5-14. BILL OF MATERIAL

The final step in designing this die is to fill in the bill of material. This lists all components which will enter into building the die. Unless printed sheets are used, the border is applied, the paper is trimmed, and the die design is complete. Each of the fourteen steps will now be taken up in detail.

Section 6

HOW TO LAY OUT A SCRAP STRIP

The first step in designing a die is to lay out the material strip exactly as it will appear after all operations have been performed. It is then called a scrap strip. To be successful, scrap strip designing must follow a definite procedure which will ensure nothing has been omitted or left to chance.

Fifty to seventy per cent of the cost of a stamping is for material. Therefore, the method employed for laying out the scrap strip directly influences the financial success or failure of any press operation. The blank must be positioned so a maximum area of the strip is utilized in production of the stamping. This blank layout is drawn before any work is done on the die design itself. In fact, the scrap strip layout will govern the shapes and sizes of many of the die members.

6-1. SCRAP STRIPS

Illustrated are nine representative scrap strips for different stampings. These are photographs of actual strips of metal as removed from dies and they reveal the progression of steps taken in producing the finished parts. In designing a scrap strip on paper, it is necessary to lay out the contours of outside edges and openings exactly as they will appear in the finished metal strips. Following are the names of the various parts shown:

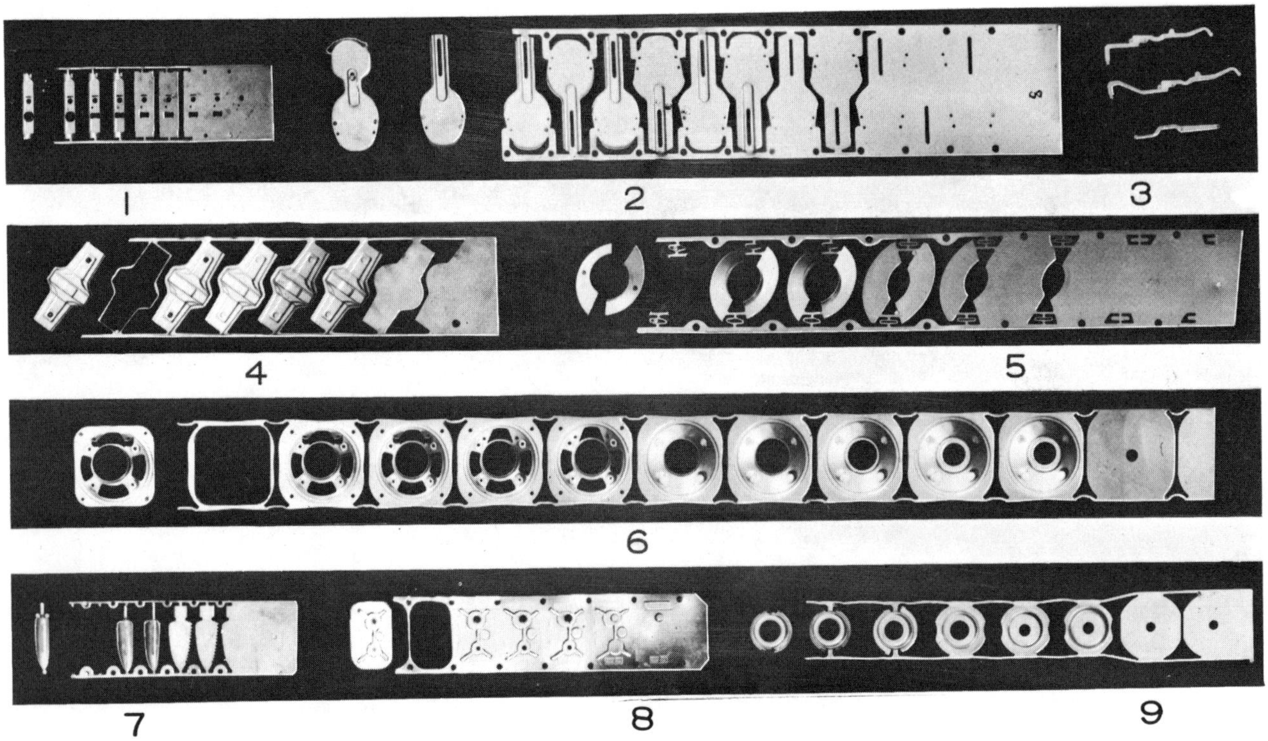

Fig. 6-1. Representative scrap strips. *B. Jahn Mfg. Co.*

1. Part for lock
2. Toe plate for roller skates
3. Key levers
4. Wall bracket
5. Fluid drive coupler
6. Shell for radio loud speaker
7. Fruit parer
8. Camera side plate
9. Automobile radiator cap.

In illustrations to follow, we will consider the steps taken in designing a scrap strip for a pierced link – from the first tentative tries to the finished layout. The same steps applied to the design of a scrap strip for any similar part should assure successful results.

This section of the book further explains Step 1 in Section 5, "Fourteen Steps to Design a Die".

6-2. BASIC BLANK SHAPES

The shape of most blanks will fall into one of the classifications shown here. Accompanying scrap strip designs for these representative part outlines provide a basis for establishing the correct material layout for any similar part to be blanked. As shown, the scrap strip for a circular blank is laid out for a double row. This is more economical than a single-row layout and it is usually specified for such dies except those for large blanks and for low production.

Many blanks have elaborate contours that cannot be readily classified. Upon study, these will be found to be made up of two or more of the basic forms illustrated, and scrap strips for these must take into consideration the particular shape combination.

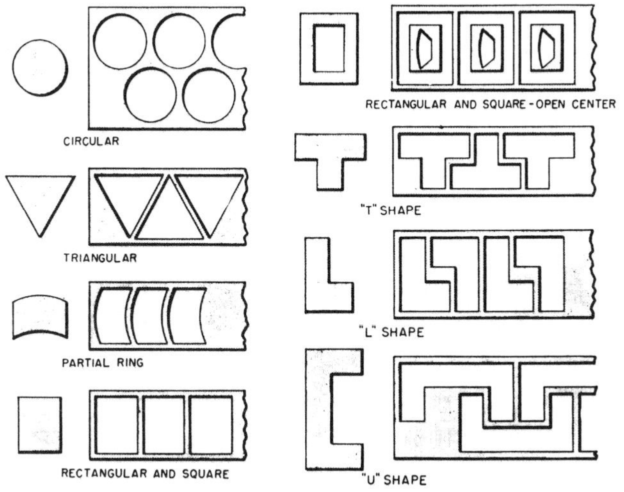

Fig. 6-2. Basic blank shapes.

methods. In the first case the blanks are arranged in a single row and the strip is passed through the die once to cut all blanks from it. At **A**, the parts are located in a vertical position in the strip. This is the preferred method because the maximum number of blanks can be cut from one strip and fewer strips must be handled.

When severe bends are required in subsequent operations, as in flat springs made from strip, method **B** must be used. This procedure involves handling more strips to produce the same number of blanks.

The shape of the part will often lend itself to angular positioning, as at **C**. For some contours, this method is economical of material. Also, it has the further advantage of allowing bends to be made without possible fracture.

Material can be saved by the "single-run, two pass" method (**D**, **E**, and **F**) when employed for certain part shapes. In this case, the blanks are positioned in the strip in a single row. Alternate blanks are turned upside down as shown, and the strip must be passed through the die twice to remove all blanks from it. As the strip goes through the first time, the blanks in the upper row are cut. The strip is then turned over and run through the die again, removing the rest of the blanks.

A ten to fifteen per cent higher labor cost will occur in double-run layouts. The operator must pass the strip through the die twice and employ greater care in gaging it. Extra labor cost is offset by the saving in material when blanks are large and waste is considerable.

Vertical positioning is shown at **D**, horizontal positioning at **E**, and angular positioning at **F**. The contour and bends found in many parts will dictate use of angular positioning.

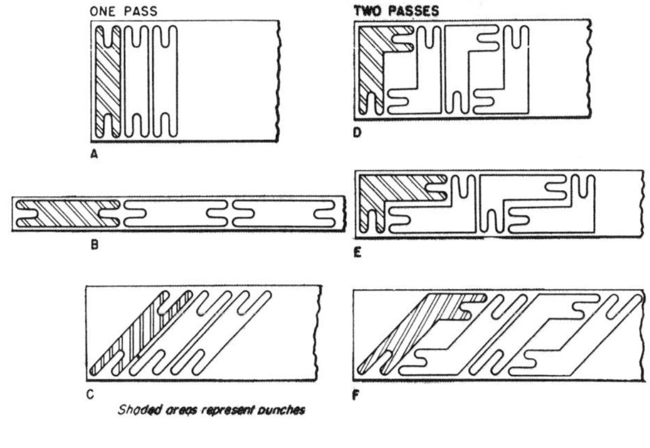

Fig. 6-3. Various ways in which blanks can be positioned.

6-3. BLANK POSITIONING

Blanks can be positioned eleven different ways in the strip. Choice of the correct method depends upon part shape, production requirements, and any bends that must be applied. The illustration shows the "single-row, one pass," and "single-row, two pass" methods.

6-4. DOUBLE-ROW LAYOUTS

Further economy in material can be achieved by use of "double-row, two pass" layouts shown at **A** and **B**. The strip is run through the die twice as in previous examples, but blanking centers are closer together, giving greater operating speed.

The same positioning method may be used for double row gang dies **C** and **D**. An extra punch and die opening is applied to the die, cutting two blanks with each stroke, and the strip is run through only once. Gang dies are high-speed tools and the method should be selected only when the added expense of the extra punch and die hole is warranted.

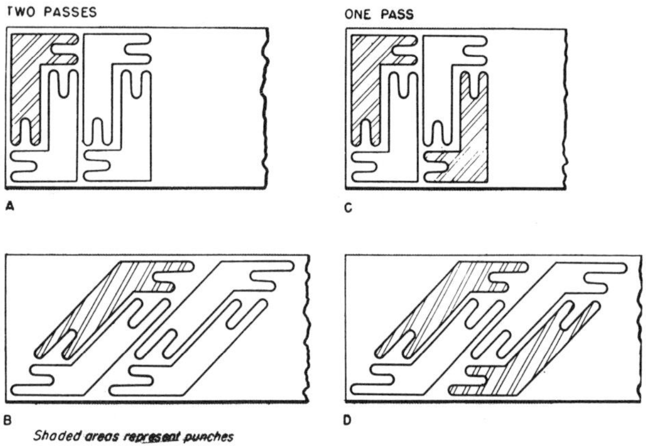

Fig. 6-4. Double-row blank layouts.

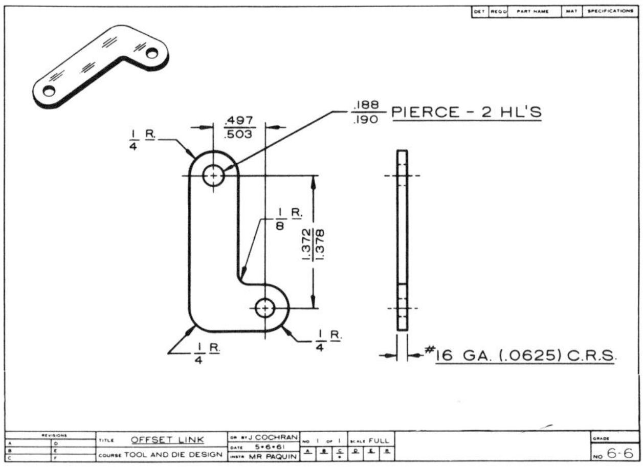

Fig. 6-6. Typical part print.

6-7. PART LAYOUT

The first step is to lay out the part accurately on paper. Check dimensions carefully at this time, as any mistake will result in considerable useless work.

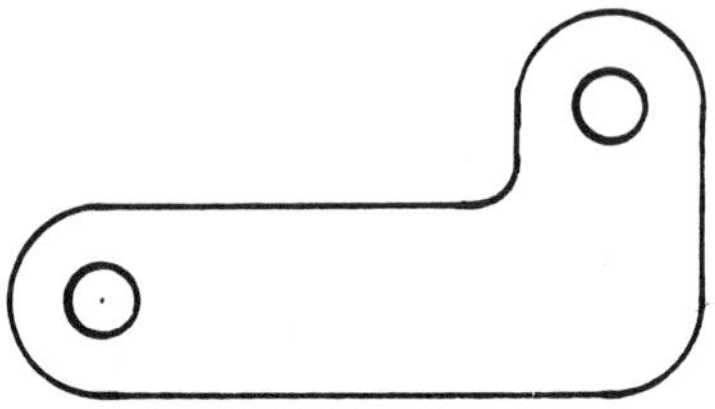

Fig. 6-7. Part layout on paper.

6-5. TRIPLE-ROW LAYOUTS

Illustrated here are two triple-row gang dies of the progressive type. At **A** is the layout for a die used to produce washers at high speed, while at **B** is shown a die to produce elliptical blanks. Such dies may have more than three rows; the number is limited only by press size and production requirements.

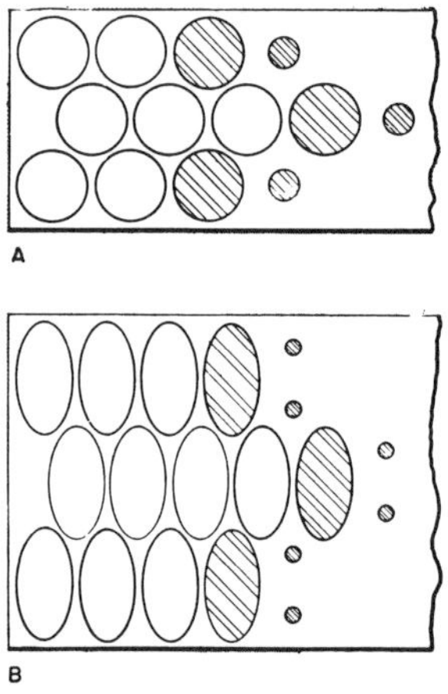

Fig. 6-5. Triple row blank layouts.

6-8. WIDE RUN POSITIONING

Usually, the first thought that comes to mind is to lay out the blanks, side by side, as shown at **A**. Blanks arranged in this manner can be run through the die in any of four different ways, shown further at **B**, **C**, and **D**. It is obvious that this layout is wasteful of material.

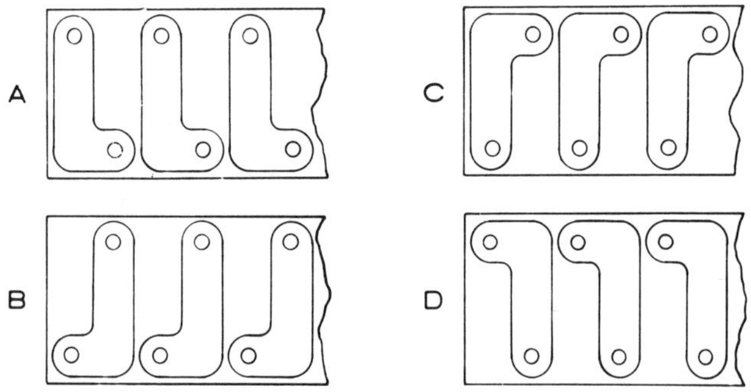

Fig. 6-8. Part positioned for wide run.

6-6. PART PRINT

A scrap strip is to be designed for producing small, elbow-shaped parts called Offset Links. Study of the part print shows that dimensional allowances are liberal enough so a two-station progressive die can be used, instead of a compound die. In such dies the holes are pierced at one station and the part is blanked out at the succeeding station.

6-9. NARROW RUN POSITIONING

If a bend were to be applied to the long arm of this part, the first thought would be to lay it out the narrow way, as shown, because bends should be made across the grain, preferably. However, this layout is also wasteful of material. Again, it is possible to run the strip in four ways.

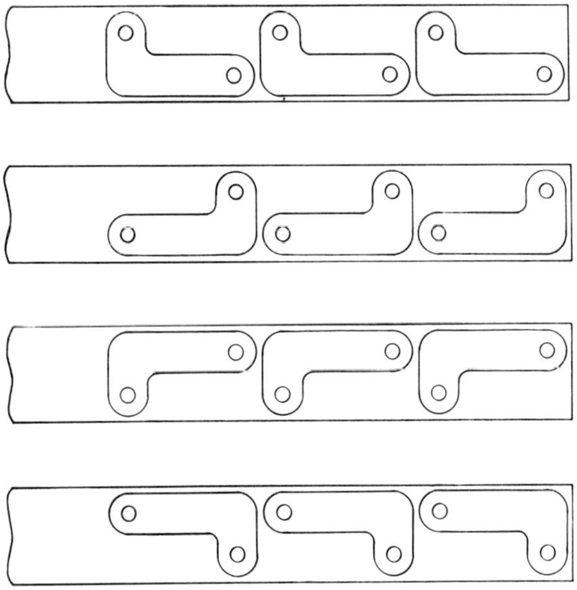

Fig. 6-9. Part positioned for narrow run.

6-10. DOUBLE ROW LAYOUTS

Double-row layouts are economical of material, but they may lure the designer into trouble. At **A**, this part is shown in a wide-run, double-row layout. With No. 1 the blanking station, the strip would be run through, blanking all holes in the upper portion of the strip. It would then be reversed and run through the die a second time. Actually, in running the strip for the first row, it becomes curved and distorted, and this can cause it to stick and bind when running the second time. In fact, there is a ten to fifteen per cent increase in labor cost for double-row dies. Double die layouts, in which both No's 1 and 2 would be blanking stations, present fewer difficulties. But few parts have the high-production requirements which would justify the expense of providing two blanking punches and die openings, and an extra set of piercing punches. A double-row, narrow-run layout is shown at **B**. This can be either a two-pass layout, in which the strip is run through the die twice to extract all blanks, or it can be a double die layout, with both No's 1 and 2 the blanking stations.

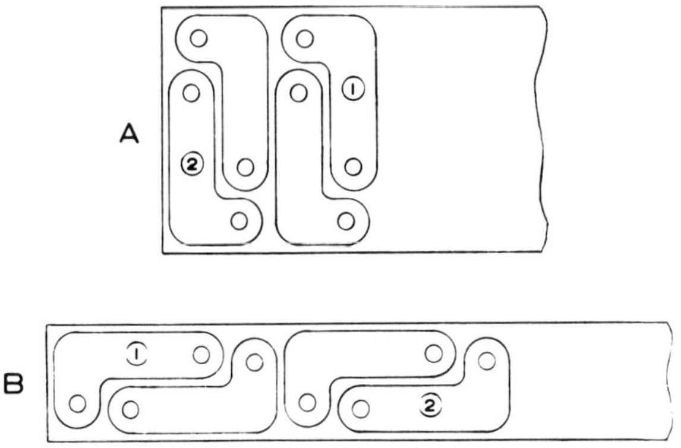

Fig. 6-10. Double-row layouts.

6-11. NESTING

To summarize:

a. The side-by-side layouts, except for some rectangular or round parts, are wasteful of material.

b. Double-run layouts can be a source of trouble and they are seldom used for small parts. Only for very large blanks are the savings in material great enough to justify their use.

c. Double-die layouts are quite expensive except for extremely large quantities.

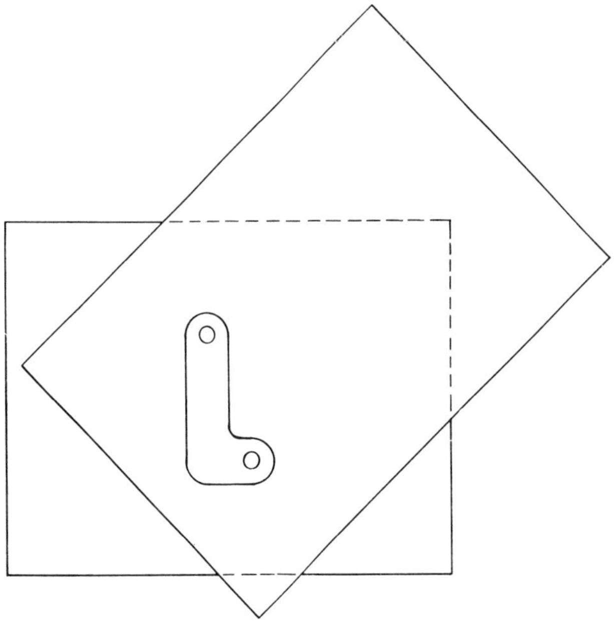

Fig. 6-11. Tracing another part layout from Fig. 6-7.

Most blanks with irregular contours will nest (fit snugly one against another) when placed side by side in the correct position. The best nesting position for the particular part must be found before proceeding with the strip layout. Here is the method to follow: Over the part layout shown in Fig. 6-7, place a sheet of thin, translucent paper and trace the part outline.

6-12. NESTING POSITION

Move the paper over the blank layout until the best nesting position is found. Shown here is the best nesting position for this part. Correct scrap bridge allowances must be allowed between blanks as will be explained later.

6-13. CORRECTING THE LAYOUT

Fasten this layout to the drafting table, straighten inaccurate lines, and check dimensions. Draw guide lines **A** and, leaving the correct scrap bridge allowance, part line **B** of the next blank to help in positioning the paper for tracing it.

6-14. DRAWING THE THIRD BLANK

Place the sheet back over the part layout shown in Fig. 6-7, and draw the third blank as accurately as possible.

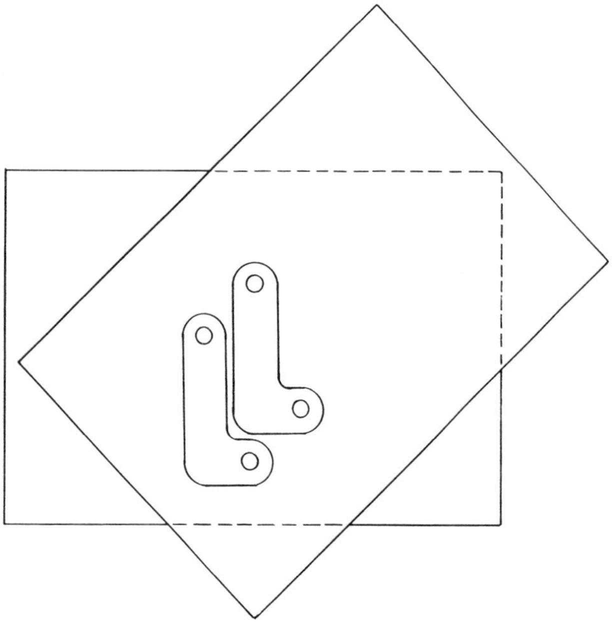

Fig. 6-12. Moving the tracing to the best nesting position.

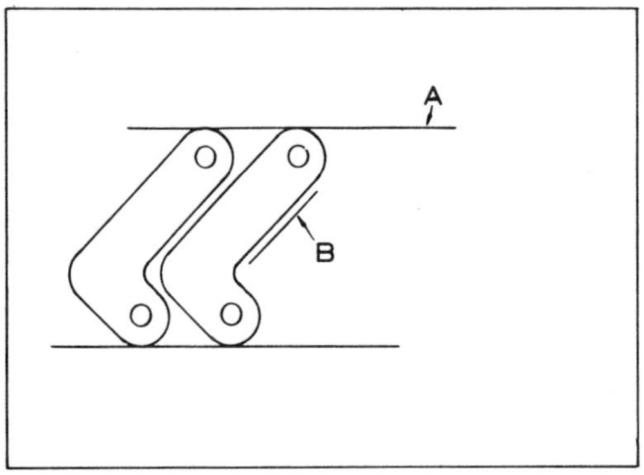

Fig. 6-13. Corrected layout.

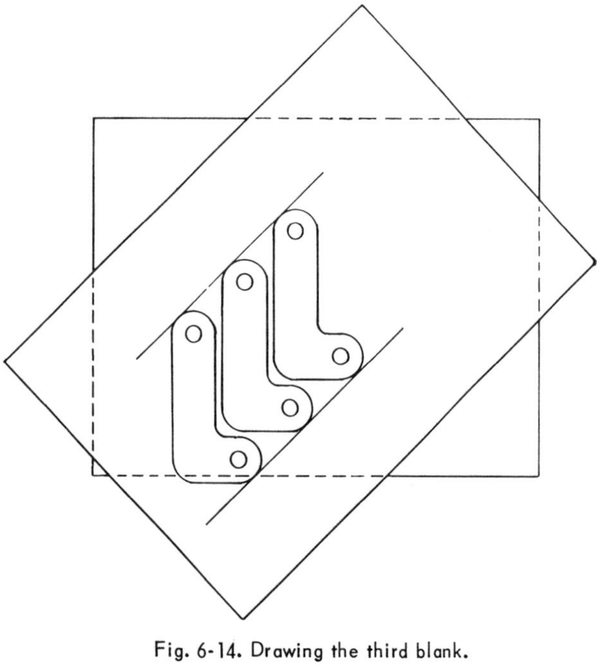

Fig. 6-14. Drawing the third blank.

6-15. COMPLETED LAYOUT

The blank layout is now complete and accurate. It might appear that our task is finished, but much work remains to be done before we can be sure that we have the best possible layout. We must know that it will perform satisfactorily.

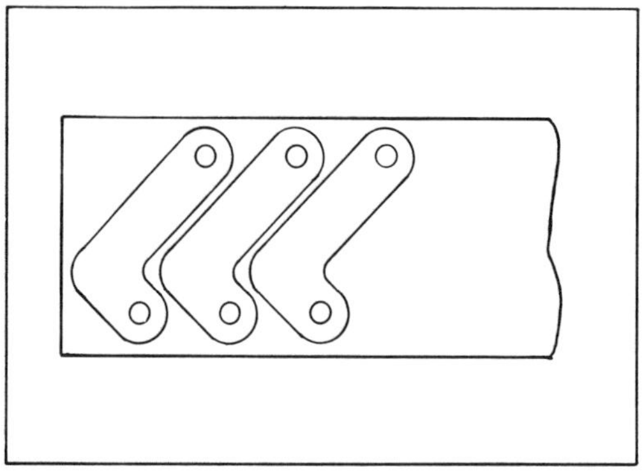

Fig. 6-15. Completed layout.

6-16. RUNNING THE STRIP

There are four ways of running the strip through the die, using the layout just completed. Numbered 1, 2, 3, and 4, one of these will be the best method for a given part, depending on its contour. From the layout in Fig. 6-15, it is possible to trace directly for all four methods of running the strip.

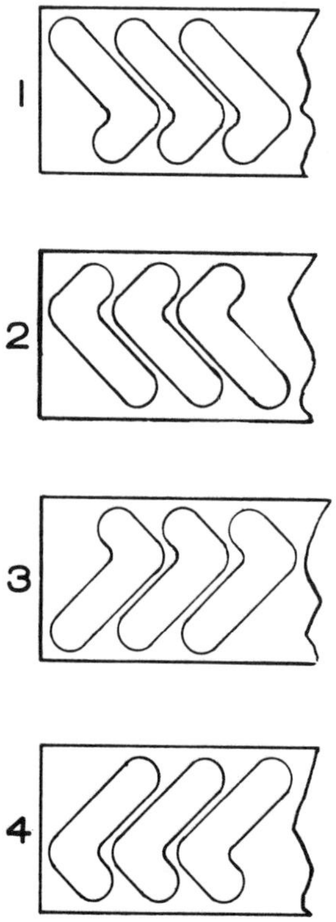

Fig. 6-16. Four ways in which the strip may be run through the die.

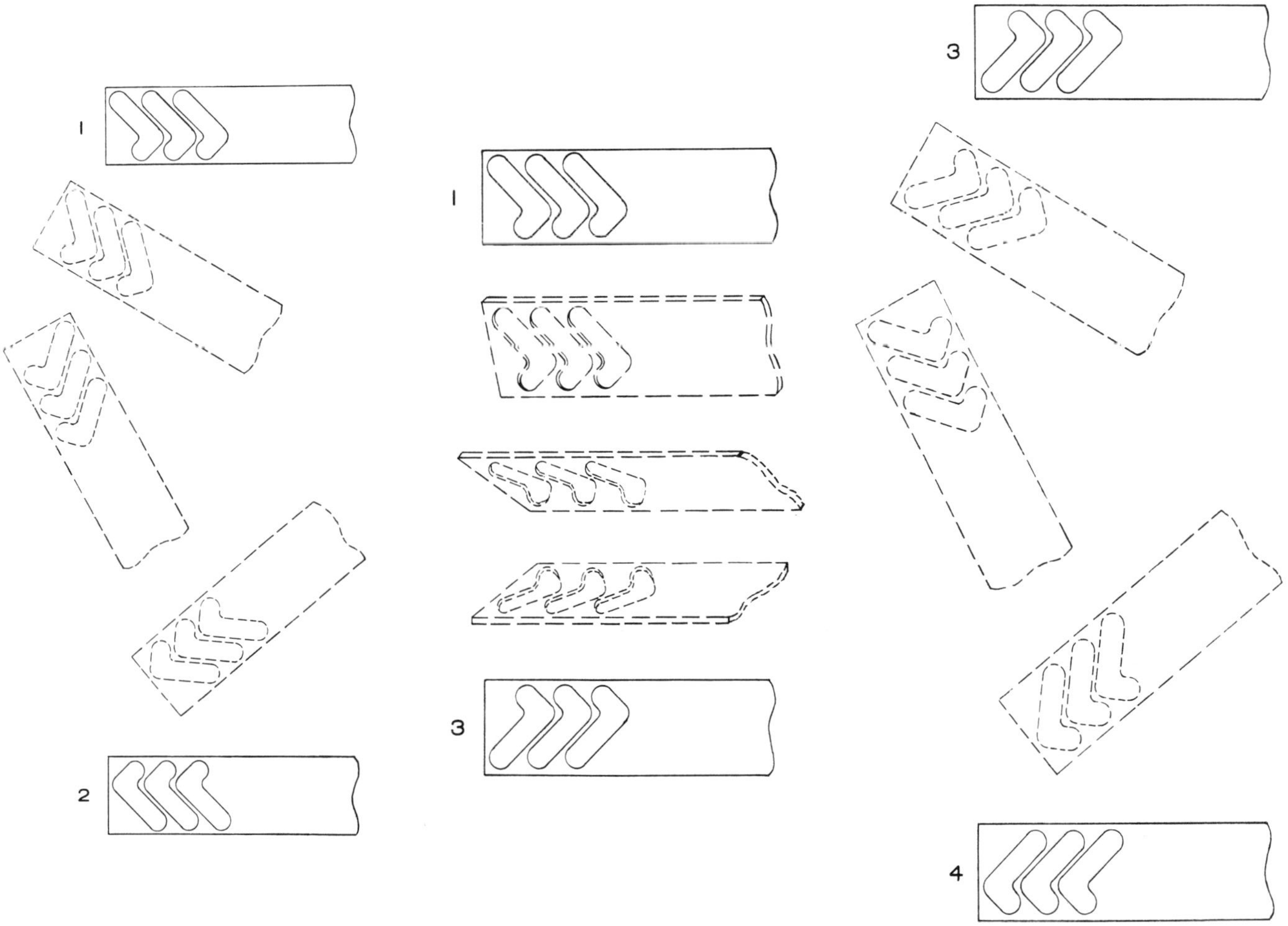

Fig. 6-17. Ways of rotating the strip to obtain the various running methods.

6-17. ROTATING THE STRIP

Method number 2 of running the strip is arrived at by turning around strip number 1 as shown, and tracing it in position. Method number 3 is arrived at by turning strip number 1 upside down as shown, and tracing it in this position. Method number 4 of running the strip is arrived at by turning strip number 3 around as shown, and tracing it in this position. From it, it is possible to trace directly for all four methods of running the strip, shown in Fig. 6-16.

6-18. PIERCE AND BLANK LAYOUTS

The strip laid out in Fig. 6-15 is used in making piercing punch and blanking punch layouts. At **A** is a layout which corresponds to method number 4, Fig. 6-16. At **B** the layout corresponds to method number 3. Piercing punches are usually drawn solid black. (White here for convenience.) Circles **C** are pilots in the blanking punch, used to locate the strip prior to blanking. These are drawn solid red. This shows the importance of drawing three blanks in the layout in Fig. 6-15.

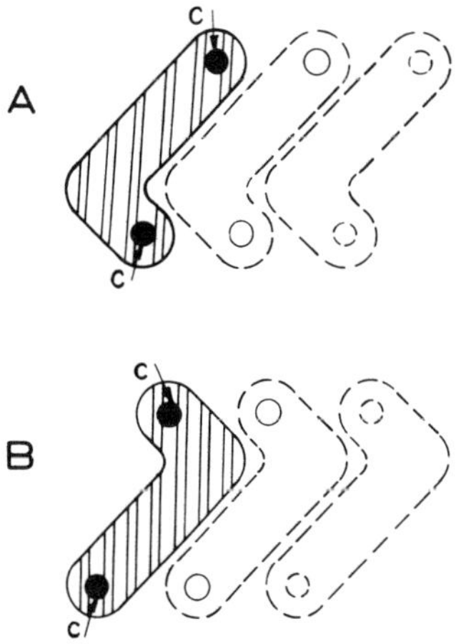

Fig. 6-18. Use of the layout for making the piercing and blanking punch layout.

6-19. TRACING PIERCE AND BLANK LAYOUTS

Four piercing punch and blanking punch layouts are traced from the layout in Fig. 6-15 to correspond to the four methods of running the strip. The line above each of these represents the front edge of the back gage against which the strip is positioned in its travel through the die.

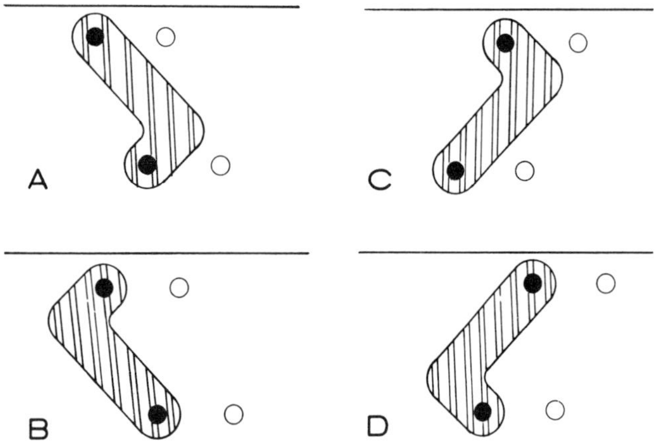

Fig. 6-19. Four piercing and blanking punch layouts traced from Fig. 6-15.

6-20. TRIAL SCRAP STRIP

On another sheet of thin paper, draw the scrap strip as shown at **A**. For experienced men the two lines shown at **B** are sufficient for this tryout work.

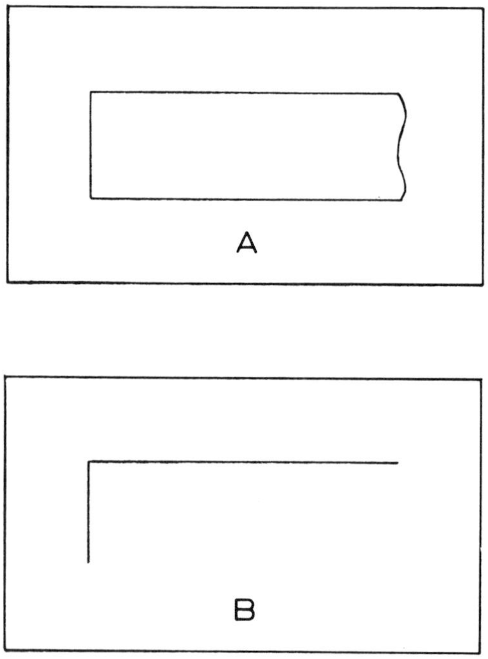

Fig. 6-20. Drawing the trial scrap strip.

6-21. TESTING THE SCRAP STRIP

Run the strip through the piercing and blanking punch layout **A**, Fig. 6-19. At station 1 the strip is advanced as close to the blanking punch as possible. In dimensioning the die, the finger stop should locate the strip 0.010 inch away from the edge of the blanking punch. If the press were tripped, piercing punch **A**

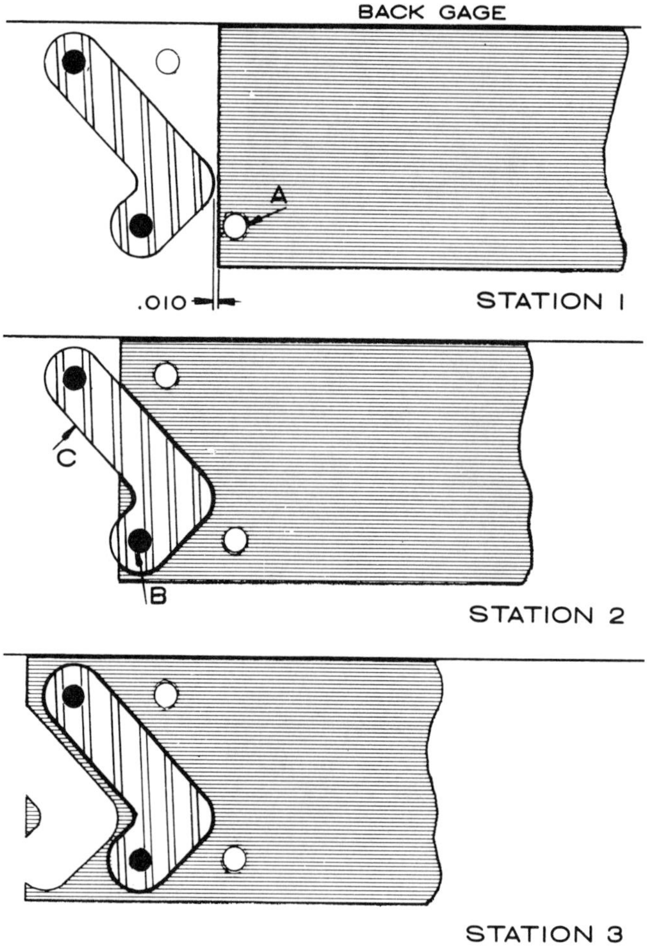

Fig. 6-21. Testing the scrap strip for the first layout.

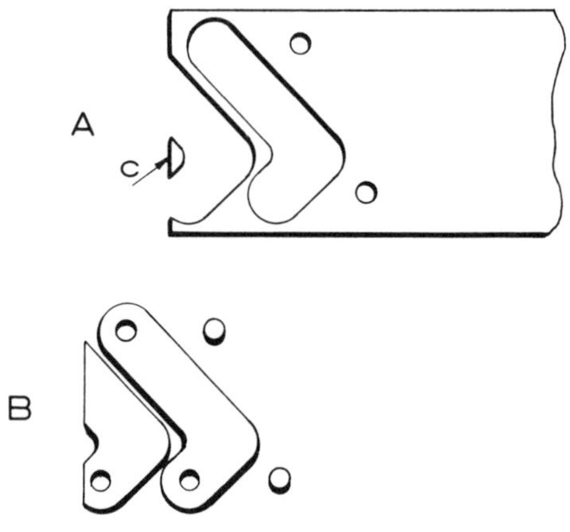

Fig. 6-22. The resulting scrap strip (**A**) and parts removed (**B**) in testing the first layout.

would pierce the first hole. In this paper layout this hole is drawn on the strip as a circle. At station 2 the strip is advanced until the pierced hole is in line with pilot **B** of the blanking punch. If the press were now tripped, blanking punch **C** would produce a partial bank, while the two piercing punches would pierce holes in the strip. In our paper strip we duplicate these operations by tracing around the blanking punch to show this partial removal of a blank, and around the piercing punches, just as the press would do it on an actual strip. This can be done free-hand for the time being.

At station 3, the strip is advanced again until the holes are in line with the pilots. Tripping the press would produce a complete blank, and two more pierced holes at station 1. Draw the outline of the blanking punch and the two holes on the paper strip. With practice these operations can be performed very quickly.

6-22. EVALUATING RESULTS

Our scrap strip layout now looks like the one at **A**, while the parts removed are shown at **B**. By analyzing this scrap strip, we see a serious fault. Tab **C**, cut at station 2, has remained on top of the die block where it can get under the cutting edge of the blanking punch to chip it, or under the piercing punches to break them. The tab would be produced only at the beginning, and possibly at the end of each strip, but many hundreds of strips will be run during the life of the die. Rule Number 1: *Arrange the first partial blank so an unattached piece of metal never remains on top of the die block.*

6-23. TESTING THE SECOND LAYOUT

Run a strip through view **B** of Fig. 6-19. At station 1, we are unable to bring the strip very close to the blanking punch, for to do so would mean a partial cut by piercing punch **A**, which would break it. Use a finger stop to locate the strip close to the piercing punch. Draw the punch **B** in position. At station 2, pilot **C** locates the strip, and blanking punch **D** makes a partial cut. Draw the blanking punch outline and the two piercing punch circles. At station 3 the blanking punch produces a full blank. Draw the blanking punch and the two piercing punch circles.

6-24. EVALUATING THE STRIP

At **A** is shown the scrap strip produced by the die in Fig. 6-23, while at **B** is illustrated the partial blank, full blank, and pierced slugs removed from it. No slug is left on top of the die block as in the previous example. However, it is not good practice to leave a partial slug as at **C**. Because the slug is not gripped securely in the die opening, it can cling to the face of the blanking punch when the press ram goes up and then drop on top of the die block. Another bad feature of this layout is that the blanking punch makes a long, unsupported cut on one side. An unsupported cut, or unbalanced cut, is one in which cutting occurs along one edge only. The cut is not balanced or supported by a cut at the opposite side. As the punch penetrates the material, side thrust is developed tending to cause the punch to back away with consequent wear of the guide posts and bushings of the die set caused by the increased side pressure. In time, as wear of posts and bushings increased, the blanking punch would be deflected sufficiently to strike the

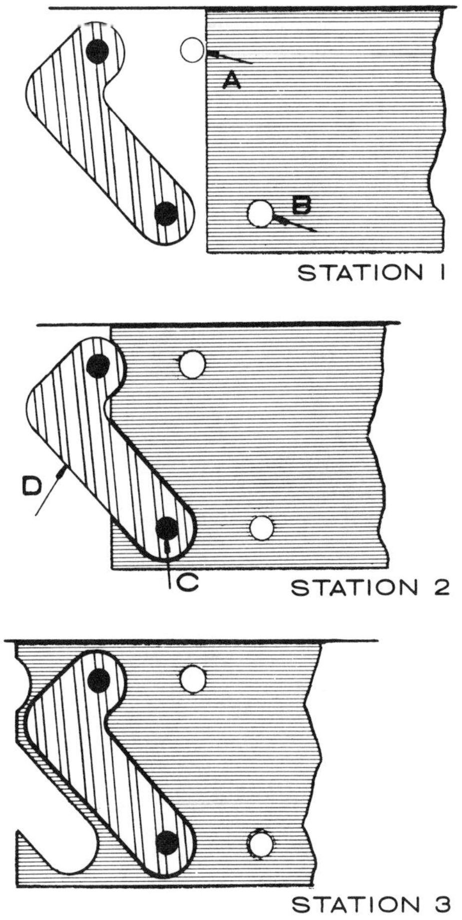

Fig. 6-23. Testing the scrap strip for the second layout.

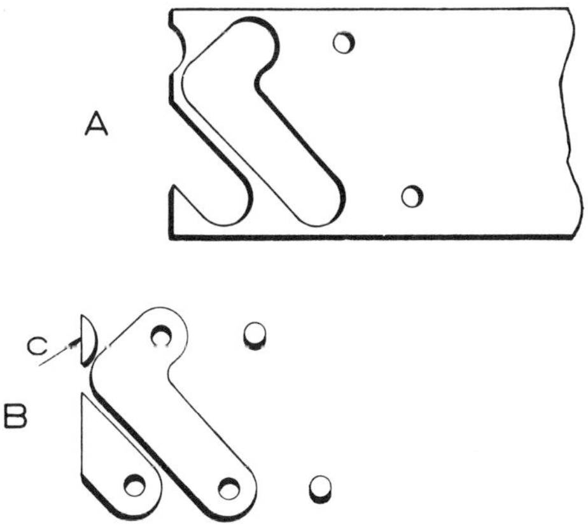

Fig. 6-24. The resulting scrap strip (**A**) and parts removed (**B**) in testing the second layout.

opposite edge of the die block, resulting in nicked cutting edges and shortened die life.

The effect of side deflection may be observed when we try to cut material with scissors that have become somewhat dull. As pressure is applied to cut the material, the blades have a tendency to spread apart or deflect.

Rule Number 2 is: *Avoid cutting long, one-sided portions of a blank unsupported by a balancing cut at the other side.* Rule 3 is: *Avoid cutting small portions of the strip not confined in the die block.*

6-25. TESTING THE THIRD LAYOUT

This layout is opposite to the layout for Fig. 6-21, and the same rules and recommendations apply.

6-26. EVALUATING THE THIRD LAYOUT

This scrap strip is produced by the die in Fig. 6-25. While it does not seem to apply for this particular part, it would be the one to use for some parts with a different contour.

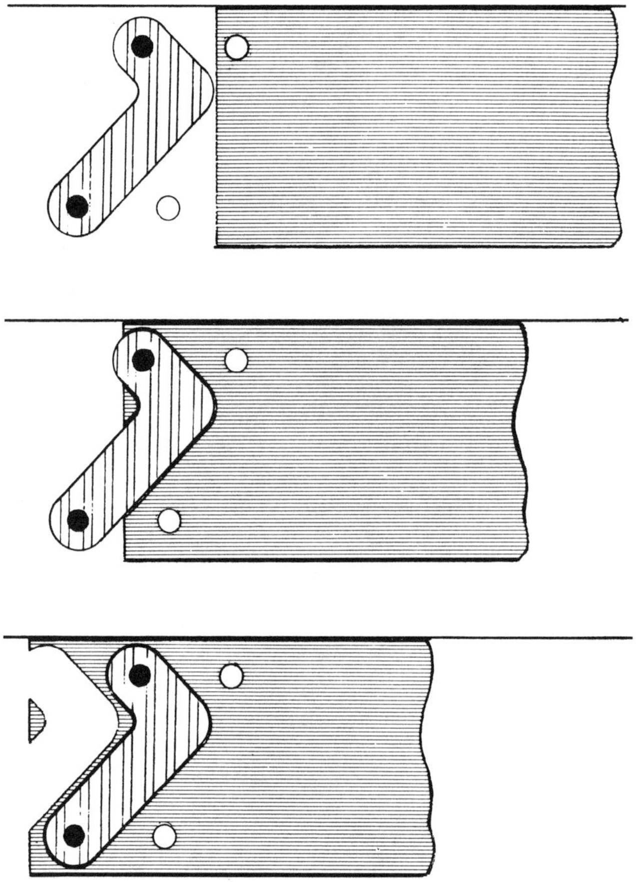

Fig. 6-25. Testing the scrap strip for the third layout.

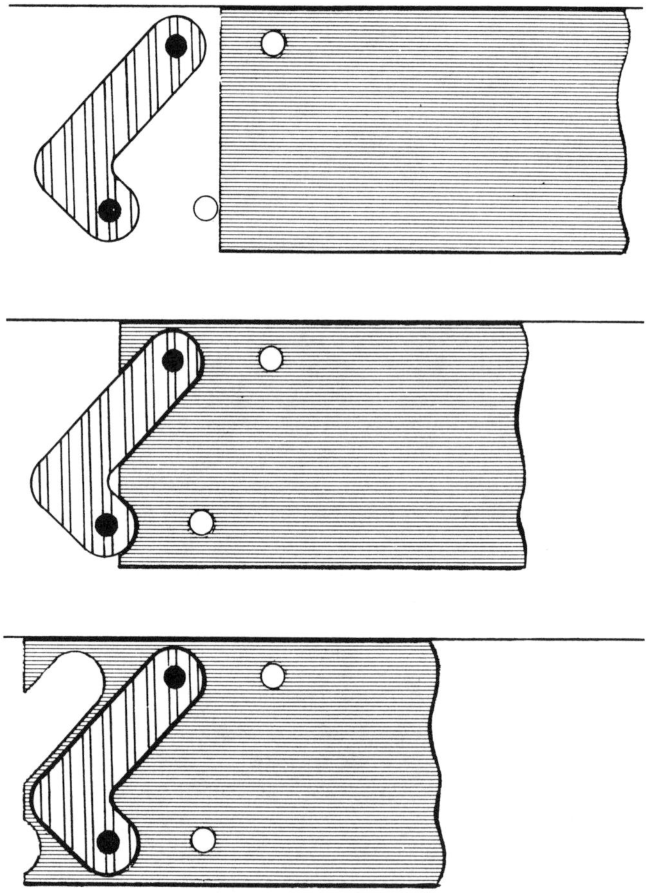

Fig. 6-27. Testing the scrap strip for the fourth layout.

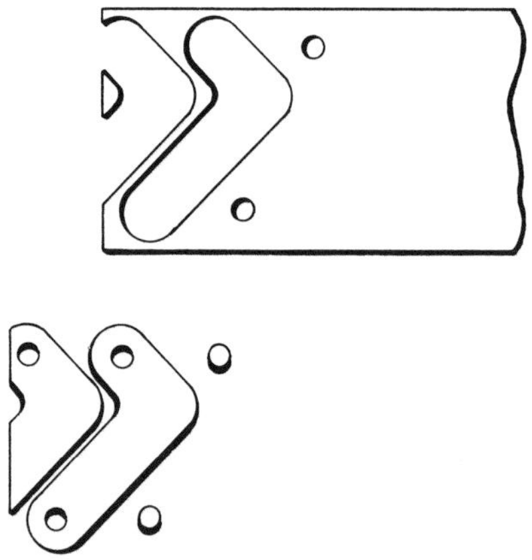

Fig. 6-26. The resulting scrap strip and parts removed in testing the third layout.

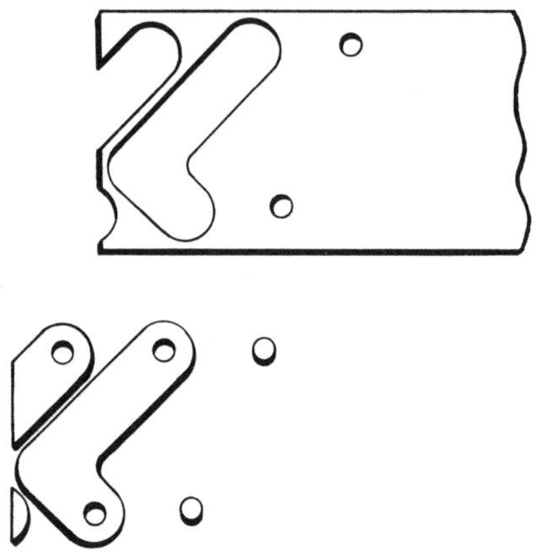

Fig. 6-28. The resulting scrap strip and parts removed in testing the fourth layout.

6-27. TESTING THE FOURTH LAYOUT

This layout is opposite to the layout for Fig. 6-23, and the same rules and recommendations apply.

6-28. EVALUATING THE FOURTH LAYOUT

This scrap strip is produced by the die in Fig. 6-27. It is obvious that none of the four methods produces a trouble free die. These layouts, however, do provide a clue to development of an excellent scrap strip. The layout in Fig. 6-21 appears promising. Inclination of the part is good for gaging purposes. The automatic stop should push the strip against the back gage, rather than pull it forward. But we must find a way to keep tab **C** attached to the strip, possibly by changing the angle of the blank.

6-29. ALTERING THE LAYOUT

Place another sheet of translucent paper over the layout in Fig. 6-7, turned over, and draw two blanks, leaving a greater distance **A** between them.

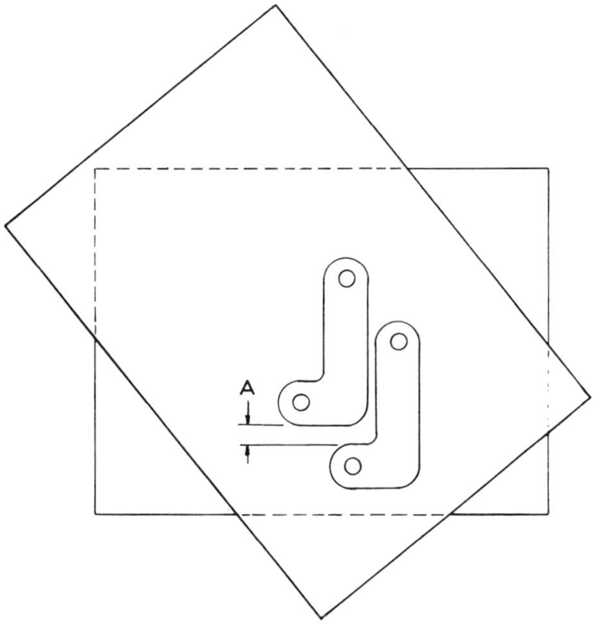

Fig. 6-29. Tracing a new layout allowing for a greater space at **A**.

6-30. CORRECTING OUTLINES

Once again, this layout is fastened to the drafting table and, using the protractor, we go over the outlines, straightening them accurately.

6-31. NEW LAYOUT

After tracing the third blank we have a new layout with the part shown with a smaller angle to the horizontal than we had in Fig. 6-15. From this we make another piercing and blanking punch layout and run the strip through it.

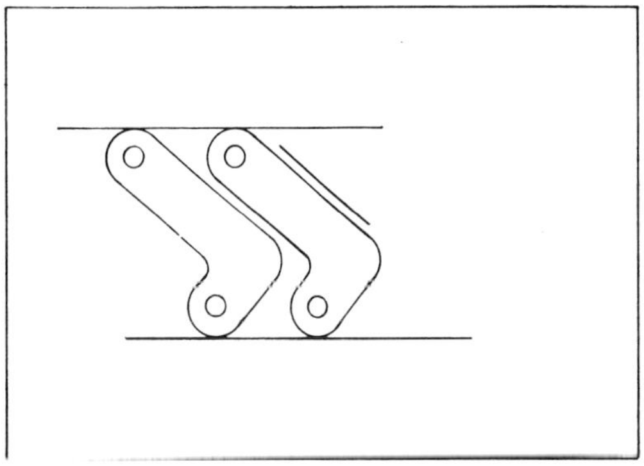

Fig. 6-30. Corrected outlines.

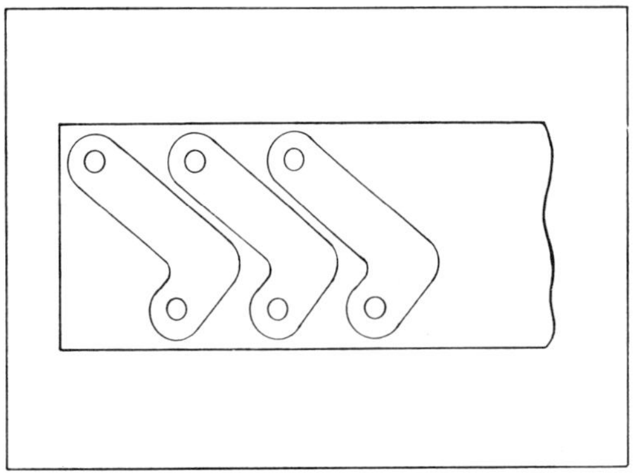

Fig. 6-31. Completed new layout.

6-32. TESTING THE NEW LAYOUT

At station 1, the strip is brought close to the blanking punch to get the maximum "bite," and the first circle is drawn for piercing punch **A**. The altered angle creates a scrap bridge to hold the previously loose tab to the strip. Vary this angle until scrap bridge **B** is same as the scrap bridge between blanks **C**. Cutting forces are fairly well-balanced. There is little tendency for the blanking punch to deflect with this arrangement. At station 3 a full blank is cut from the strip. Note that the toe of the automatic stop **D** is placed to stop the strip for the first blanking cut at station 2, and it also stops the strip for all succeeding cuts.

6-33. COMPLETED SCRAP STRIP LAYOUT

This is how our completed scrap strip appears, along with the partial blank, full blank, and pierced slugs which were removed from it. Die design for this part can now be safely started with full knowledge that a good tool will result.

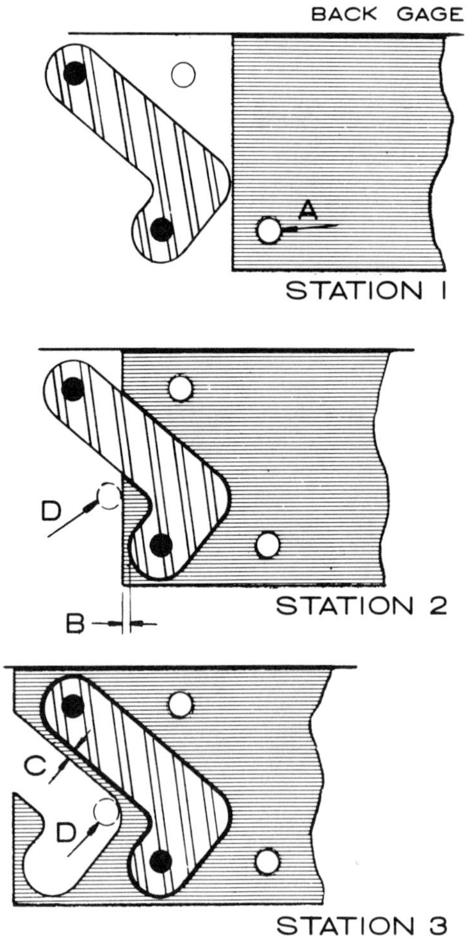

Fig. 6-32. Testing the new scrap strip layout

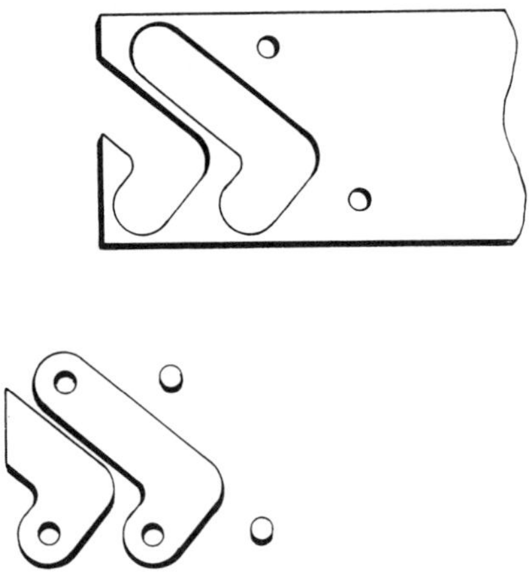

Fig. 6-33. The resulting scrap strip and parts removed in testing the new layout.

6-34. THREE-STATION LAYOUTS

Introduction of another station between the first piercing station and the blanking station does not alter any of the rules, Here is a 3-station die layout for a typical business-machine part. There is one difference. For dies having three or more stations, it is wise to show the outline of the part at every station in either phantom or dotted lines. At station 1 the strip is advanced close to the edge of the center part, and a circle is drawn representing the piercing punch **A**. At station 2 the strip is advanced until the pilot **B** locates in the previously pierced hole. This should bring the end of the strip 0.010 inch away from blanking punch **C**. Round-nosed punches **D** indent three welding projections in the strip. At station 3 the first partial blank is removed from the strip. Note automatic stop toe **E** which stops the end of the strip. At station 4, automatic stop toe **E** stops the strip in the hole of the first partial blank and at the same time the first full blank is produced at station 3, welding projections are applied at station 2, and a hole is pierced at station 1.

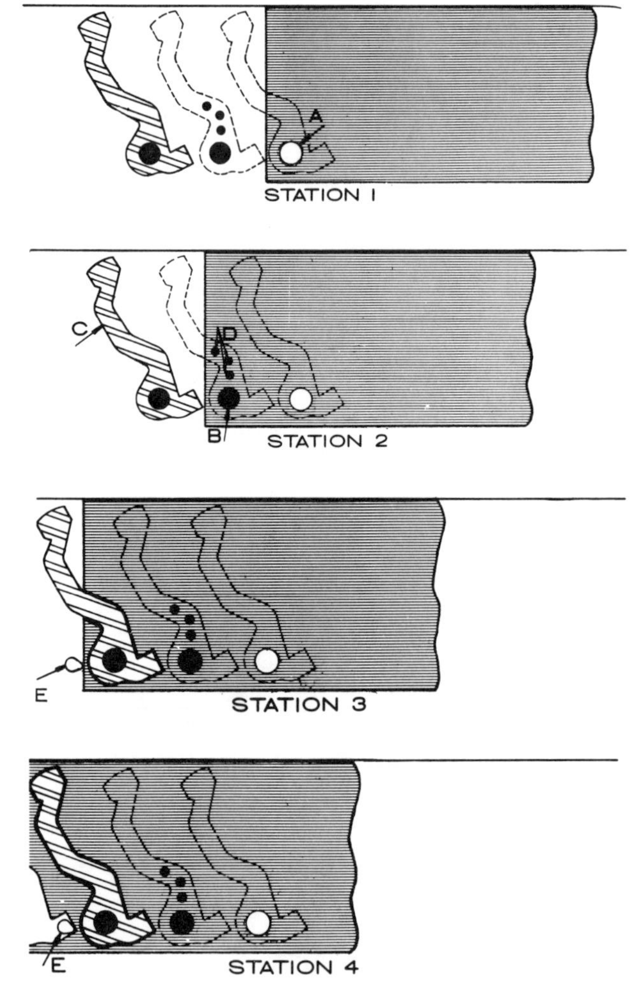

Fig. 6-34. Typical three station layout for a business machine part.

6-35. SCRAP STRIP FOR THREE-STATION DIE

Here is the scrap strip for the die in Fig. 6-34, as well as the parts removed from it.

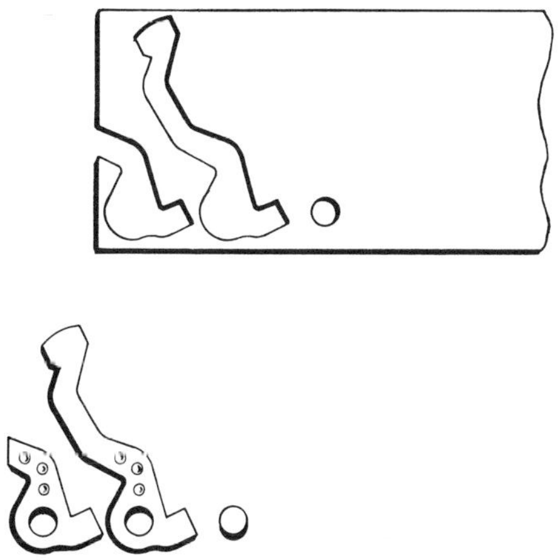

Fig. 6-35. Scrap strip and removed parts for layout in Fig. 6-34.

6-36. FIVE-STATION LAYOUT (See Fig. 6-36)

This shows the scrap strip for a 5 station die. At station 1, the strip is advanced close to the dotted part **A**, and a hole is pierced. At station 2, the strip is located by pilot **B**, hole **C** is pierced, and embossing punch **D** applies a bead to a portion of the strip. At station 3, a marking punch **E** stamps the strip, embossing punch **D** applies a full bead to the strip at station 2, and at station 1 the strip is pierced. At station 4 the blanking punch cuts a partial blank, while members at the previous stations perform their functions. At 5 the blanking punch cuts a full blank.

6-37. SCRAP STRIP FOR FIVE-STATION DIE

At **A** is shown the complete scrap strip for this die, while at **B** the partial blank, finished blank and pierced slug are shown.

SCRAP STRIP ALLOWANCES

It is important that correct bridge allowances be applied between blanks and between blanks and edges of the strip. Excessive allowance is wasteful of material. Insufficient allowance results in a weak scrap strip subject to possible breakage with consequent slowdowns on the press line. In addition, a weak scrap area around the blank can cause dishing of the part.

6-38. SCRAP STRIP ALLOWANCES – ONE-PASS LAYOUTS

Peripheries of blanks may be classified under four distinct outline shapes. In the illustration:

1. Curved outlines. For these, dimensions **A** are given a minimum allowance of 70 per cent of the strip thickness **T**.

2. Straight edges. Dimensions of **B** and **B'** depend upon the length of the bridge, dimensions **L** and **L'**, respectively.

Where **L** or **L'** is less than 2½ inches, **B** or **B'** = 1 **T**, respectively.

Where **L** or **L'** is 2½ to 8 inches, **B** or **B'** = 1¼ **T**, respectively.

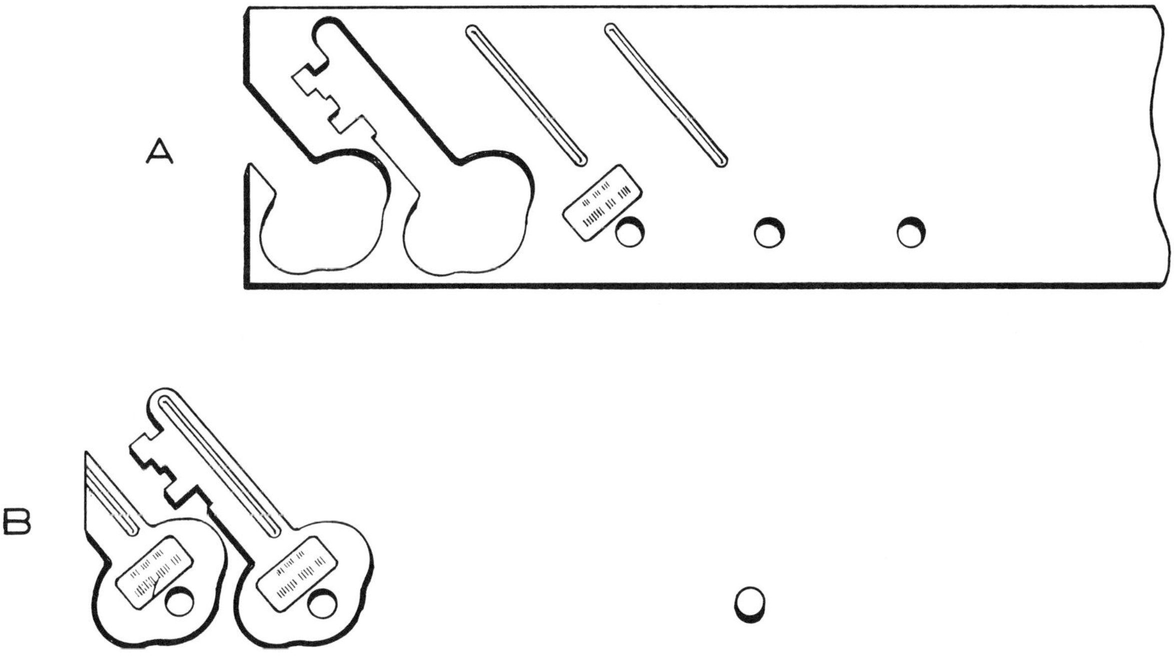

Fig. 6-37. Scrap strip and removed parts for layout in Fig. 6-36.

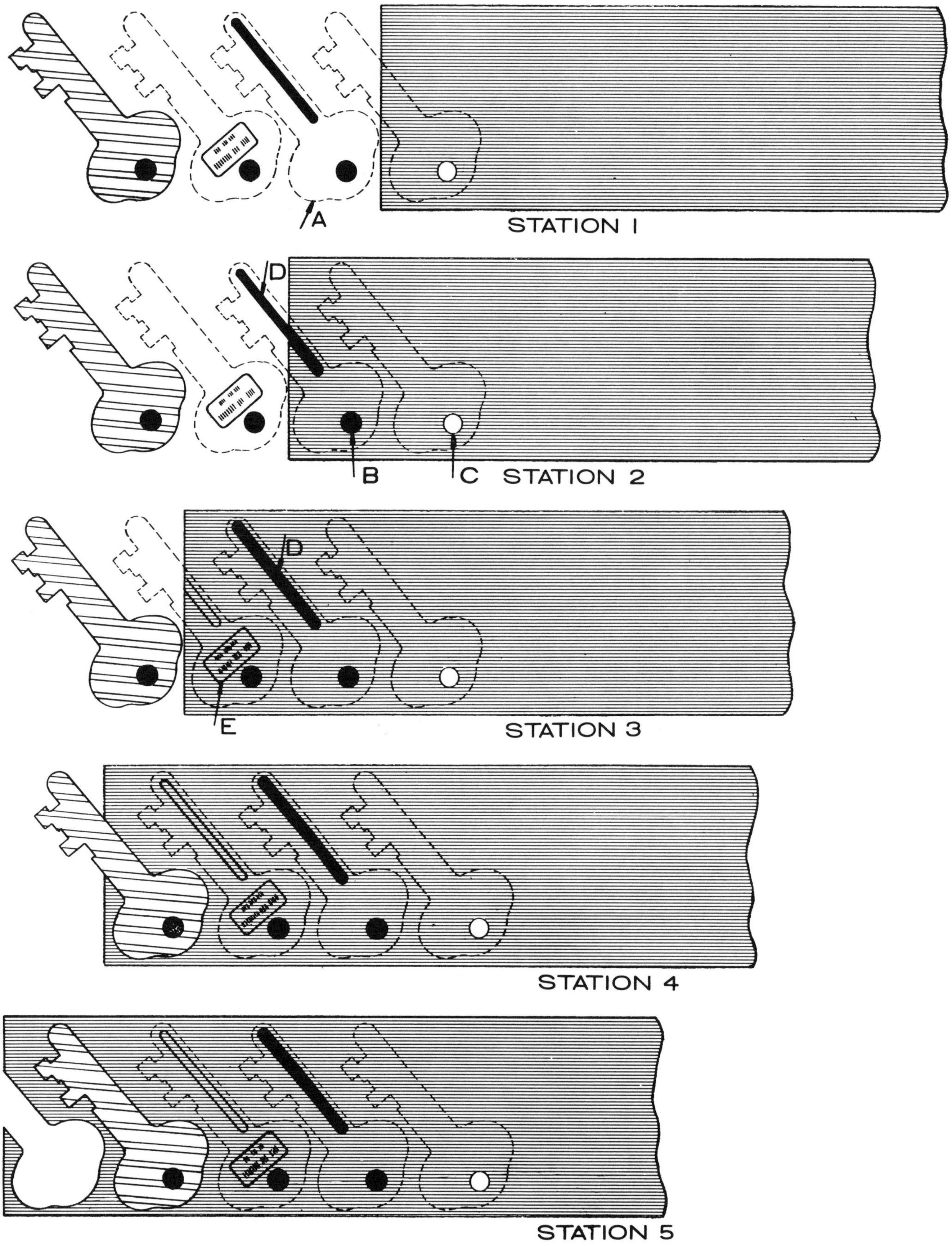

Fig. 6-36. Typical scrap strip for a five-station die.

Where **L** or **L'** is over 8 inches, **B** or **B'** = 1½ **T**, respectively.

3. Parallel curves. For work with parallel curves, the same rules apply as for straight edges and:

Where **L** is less than 2½ inch, **C** = 1 **T**.

Where **L** is 2½ to 8 inches, **C** = 1¼ **T**.

Where **L** is over 8 inches, **C** = 1½ **T**.

4. Adjacent sharp corners. These form a focal point for fractures and minimum allowance is 1¼ **T**, dimension **D** on the drawing.

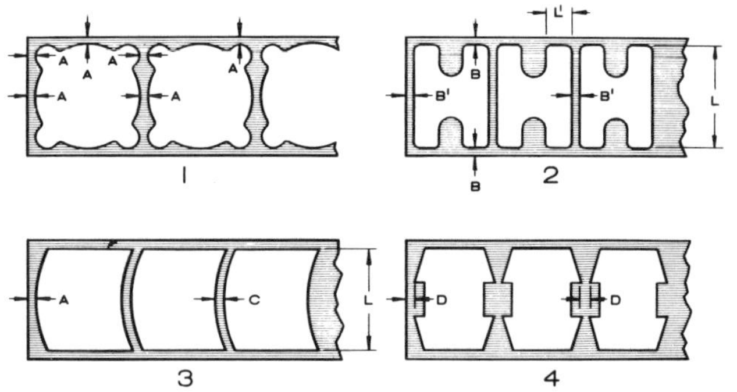

Fig. 6-38. Four classifications of blank peripheries to aid in determining scrap-strip allowances for one-pass layouts.

6-39. SCRAP STRIP ALLOWANCES – TWO-PASS LAYOUTS

When the strip is to be run through the die twice in order to remove all the blanks from it, more allowance must be provided than is required for one-pass layouts. This illustration lists minimum scrap bridge allowances which should be applied under given conditions. Note that single-row layouts **A** are given more allowance than is required for double-row layouts **B** and **C**. This is because the wider double-row strips do not distort as much in cutting the first row and less allowance is required. Because of this minimum strip distortion, double-row layouts are preferred.

6-40. MINIMUM ALLOWANCES

This table lists minimum scrap bridge allowances for both one-pass and two-pass layouts. These values apply for thin gages (less than 3/64 inch) of stock where use of the previous rules would give such small allowances as to be impractical. Select the value for space **A** opposite the appropriate strip width.

6-41. APPLICATION OF ALLOWANCES

This illustration shows how allowances are applied for two representative parts. The upper blank is laid out for single-row, one-pass through the die. The lower blank is laid out for double-row, two-passes through the die. Calculated values are listed under each view. It must be realized that these are minimum allowances and that the next larger fractional dimension would actually be used.

SCRAP-STRIP ALLOWANCES FOR TWO-PASS LAYOUTS

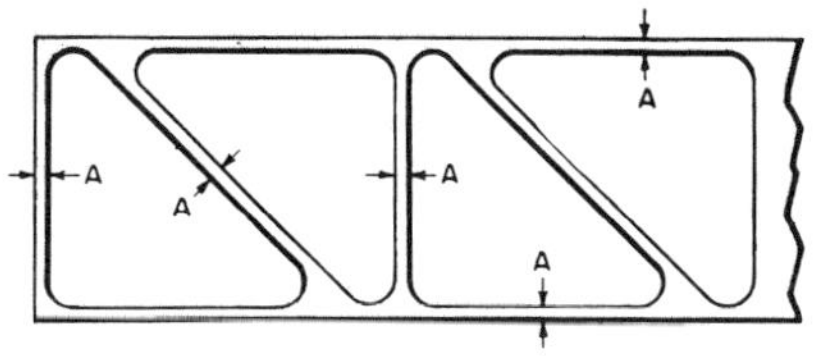

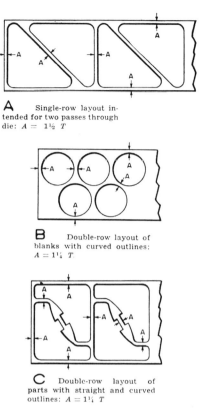

A Single-row layout intended for two passes through die: $A = 1\frac{1}{2}\ T$

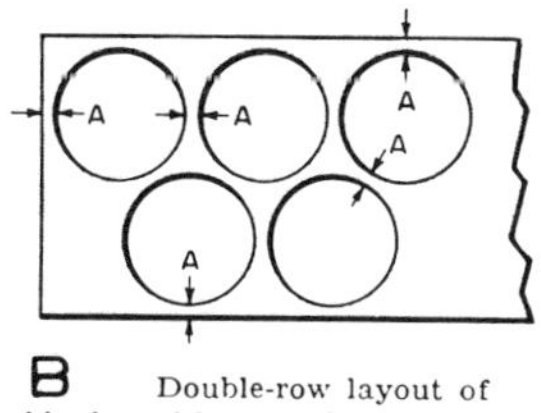

B Double-row layout of blanks with curved outlines: $A = 1\frac{1}{4}\ T$

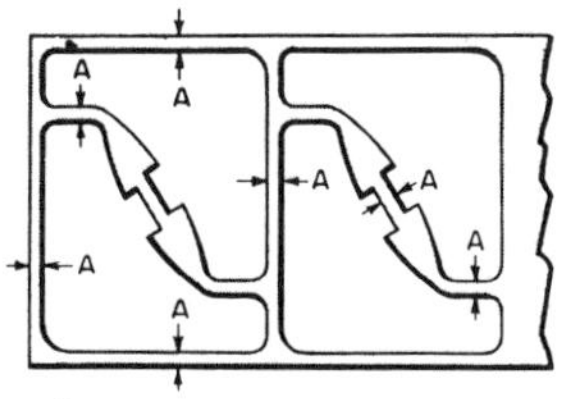

C Double-row layout of parts with straight and curved outlines: $A = 1\frac{1}{4}\ T$

Fig. 6-39. Scrap-strip allowances for two-pass layouts.

MINIMUM SCRAP-STRIP ALLOWANCES

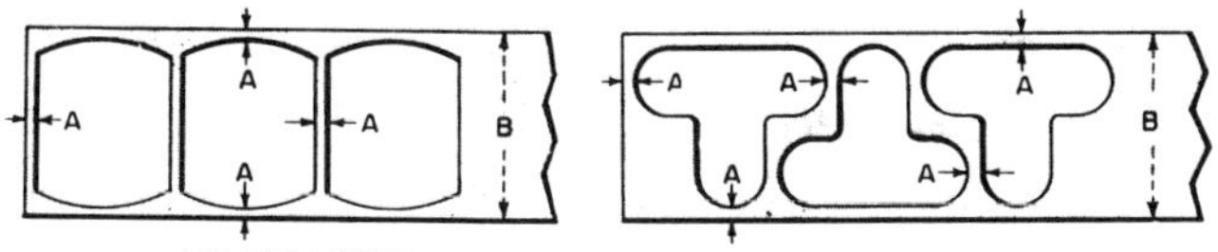

ONE-PASS LAYOUT

Strip Width *B*	Space *A*
0 to 3 in.	1/32 in.
3 to 6 in.	1/16 in.
6 to 12 in.	3/32 in.
Over 12 in.	1/8 in.

DOUBLE-PASS LAYOUT

Strip Width *B*	Space *A*
0 to 3 in.	1/16 in.
3 to 6 in.	3/32 in.
6 to 12 in.	1/8 in.
Over 12 in.	5/32 in.

Fig. 6-40. Minimum scrap-strip allowances.

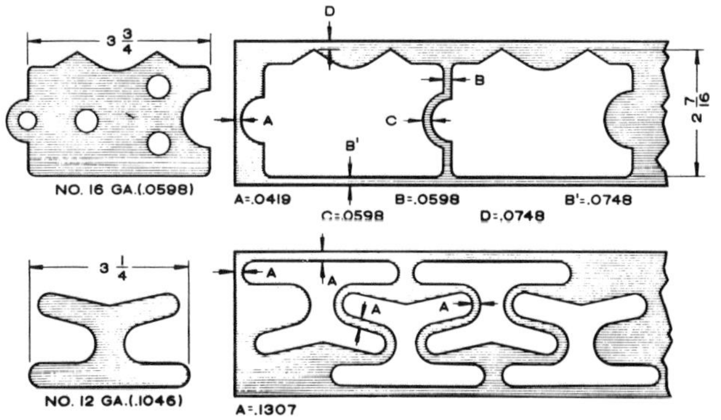

Fig. 6-41. Application of allowances for two representative parts.

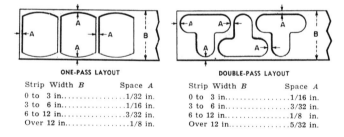

6-42. BLANK AREA CALCULATIONS

When it is possible to position blanks in two or more ways in the strip, the blank area for each method is found and the one most economical of material is selected for the die. At **A** is shown a blank laid out for single-row, one-pass positioning, the most frequently used method. The blank area (the area of the strip which is used for one part) is found by the following formula:

$$\text{Blank area} = A \times B$$

Single-row blanks which must pass through the die twice have their blank area determined by the formula:

$$\text{Blank area} = \frac{A \times B}{2}$$

This formula applies to the blank layout at **B** and also for double-row blanks shown at **C**.

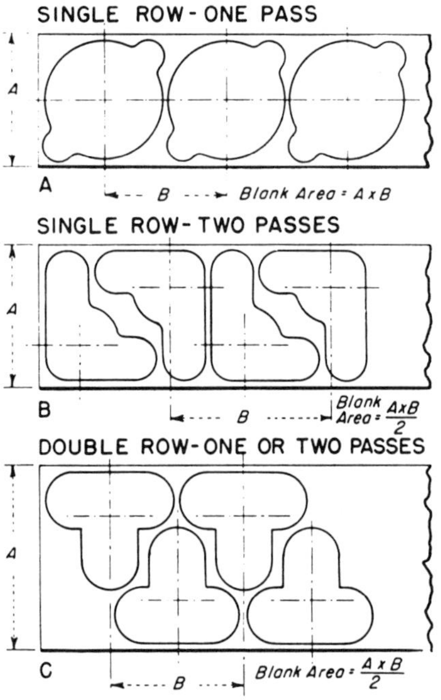

Fig. 6-42. Representative illustrations for calculating blank areas.

6-43. NUMBER OF BLANKS PER STRIP

For large blanks it is often necessary to determine the number of blanks in each strip to establish the extent of the waste end **D**. This has an influence on the blank layout, because too great a waste end is uneconomical. The number of blanks per strip for a single-pass layout is found by the formula:

$$\text{Blanks per strip } A = \frac{S - [X + Y + 2E]}{B} + 1$$

For the waste end:

$$D = S - [B(A - 1) + X + Y + 2E]$$

When strips must make two passes through the die, the following formulas determine the number of blanks per strip and the extent of the waste end:

$$\text{Blanks per strip} = \frac{S - [X + Y + 2E]}{0.5\,B} + 1$$

For the waste end:

$$D = S - [0.5\,B(A - 1) + X + Y + 2E]$$

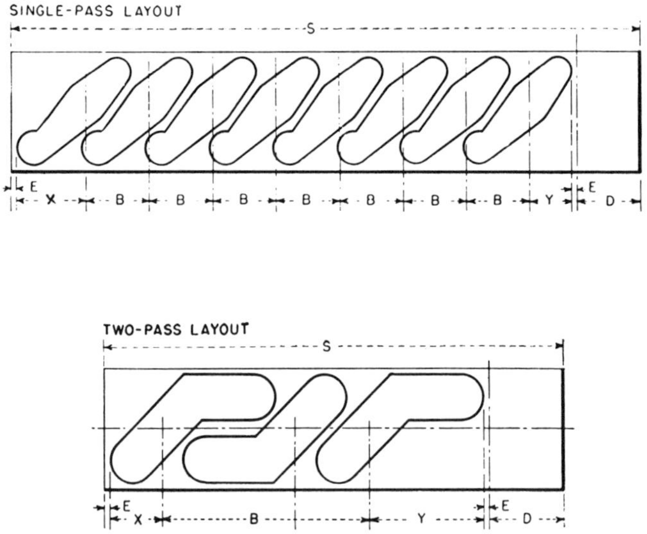

Fig. 6-43. Representative illustrations for determining the number of blanks in a strip.

6-44. BLANKS

Illustrated are a flat blank **A**, and a bent blank **B** for which scrap strips are to be laid out. The flat blank could be positioned vertically, horizontally, or at an angle in the strip. The bent blank should be positioned angularly to prevent possible fracture in the subsequent bending operation.

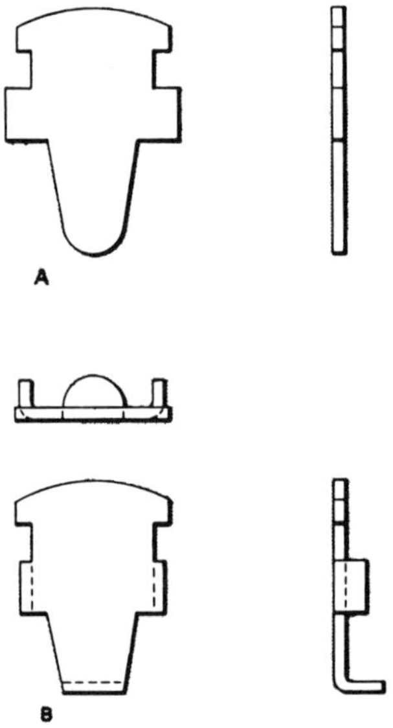

Fig. 6-44. Flat (**A**) and bent (**B**) blanks.

6-45. BLANK POSITIONING

This shows six ways in which the parts illustrated in Fig. 6-44 can be positioned for blanking. The strip width for each position, as well as the feed or distance from station to station, are noted. Observe the considerable difference in strip area per blank for the different methods of positioning.

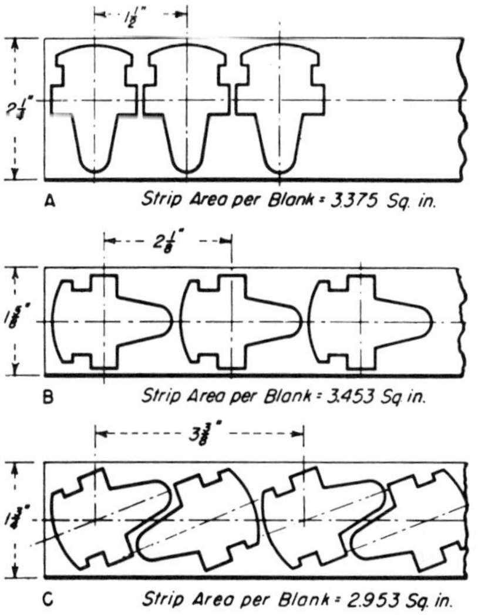

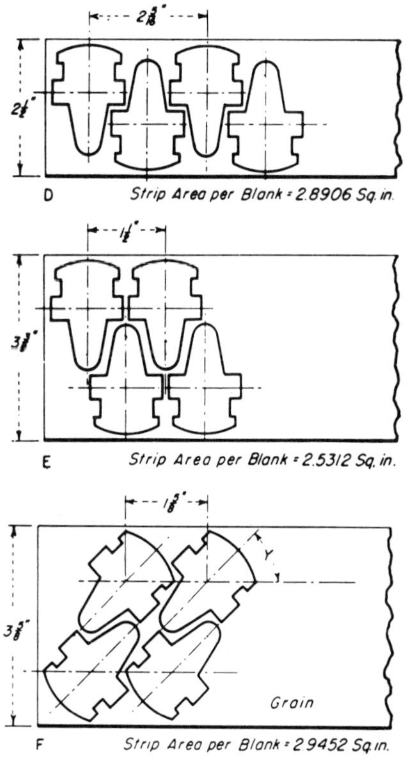

Fig. 6-45. Six ways of positioning blanks.

Section 7

HOW TO DESIGN DIE BLOCKS

Four factors will influence design of the die block for any particular die. They are:

1. Part size
2. Part thickness
3. Intricacy of part contour
4. Type of die.

Small dies, such as those for producing business-machine parts, usually have a solid die block. Only for intricate part contours would the die block be be sectioned to facilitate machining. Large die blocks are made in sections for easy machining, hardening, and grinding. In illustrations to follow are shown twenty-six methods of applying die blocks to small, medium, and large cutting dies. These methods further explain Step 2 in Section 5, "Fourteen Steps to Design a Die."

7-1. DIE BLOCK

This is an actual photograph of a die block for a large piercing die. Large die blocks such as this one are composed of sections for easier machining, hardening, and grinding. Observe that each section is provided with working holes, that is, holes which engage punches to perform cutting operations on the material and with screw and dowel holes which fasten each section to the die set.

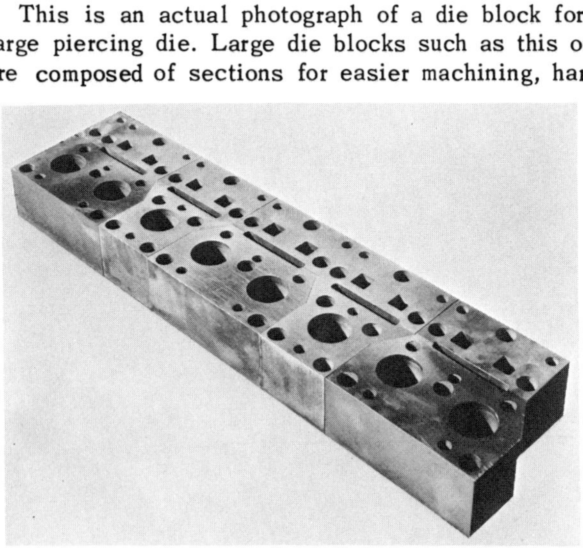

Courtesy of Bethlehem Steel Co.

Fig. 7-1. Die block for a large piercing die.

7-2. APPLYING THE DIE BLOCK

Machined into the die block are blanking opening **C** and piercing holes **D**. Holes **E**, located at each corner, are tapped completely through and two dowel holes **F** are reamed completely through the block.

Section views **A-A** and **B-B** show the fastening method. Four socket capscrews **G** securely hold the die block to the die holder of the die set. Two dowels **H**, pressed into the die set and partly into the die block, prevent any possible shifting in operation. Four button-head socket screws **I** fasten the stripper plate and gages to the die block, while two dowels **J** maintain accurate positioning. Distance **K**, usually ¼ inch, is the grinding allowance, used up when the screws and dowels are lowered in repeated sharpening of the die face.

A small dowel **L** locates the right-hand end of the back gage to the stripper plate. This dowel is made 3/16 inch in diameter. The other screws and dowels are never less than 5/16 inch diameter for any die. Dowels **J** are made a press fit in the stripper and gages, but a sliding fit in the die block. With this construction the stripper, back gage, and front spacer can be removed quickly for sharpening the die face without removing the die block from the die set.

Section **C-C** shows the method of machining the die hole and the piercing punch holes. Straight land **M** is 1/8 inch. Angular relief **N** is made according to values given in the table. Hole **O** in the die set is 1/8 inch larger than opening **P** in the die block to provide 1/16 inch clearance per side.

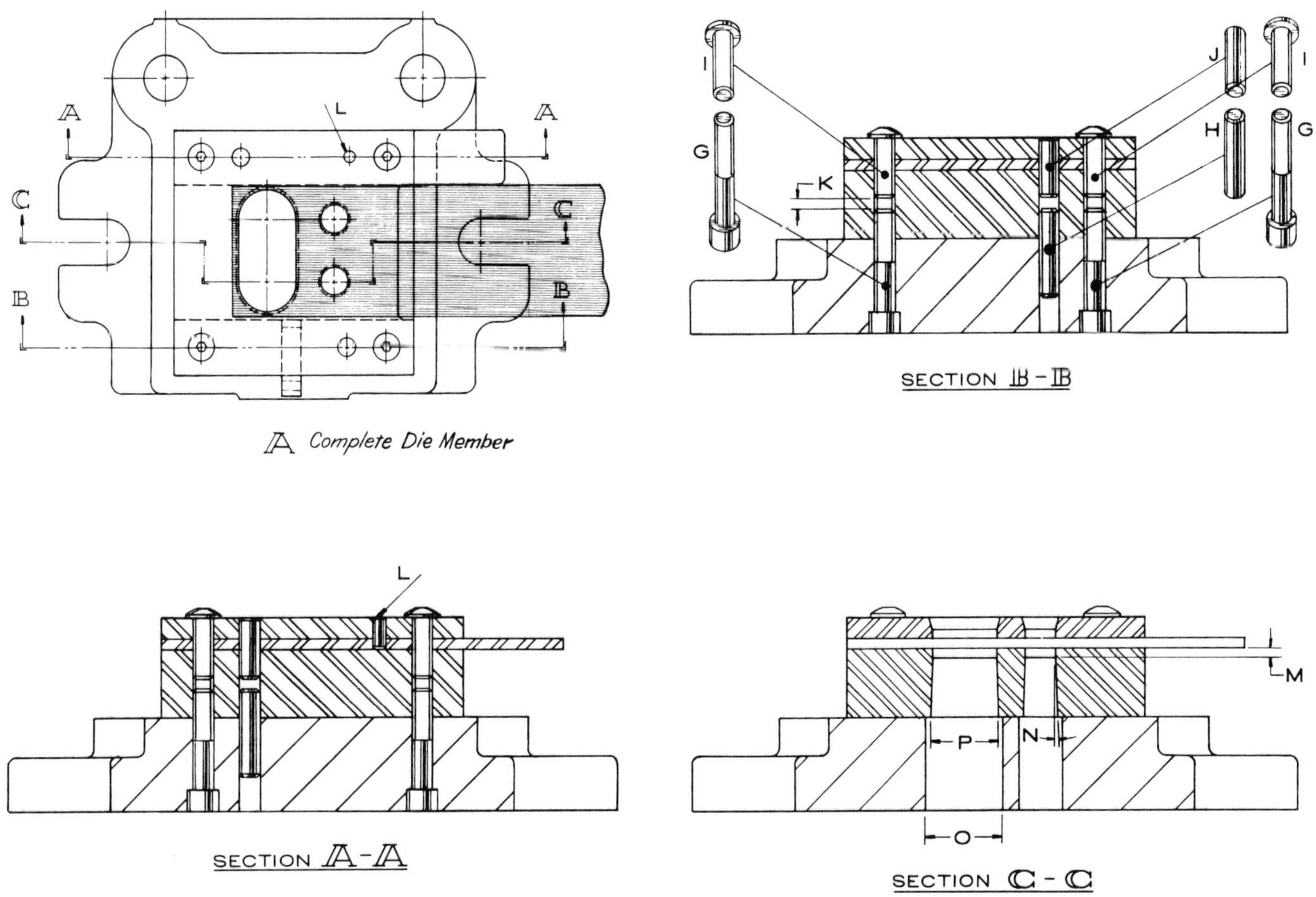

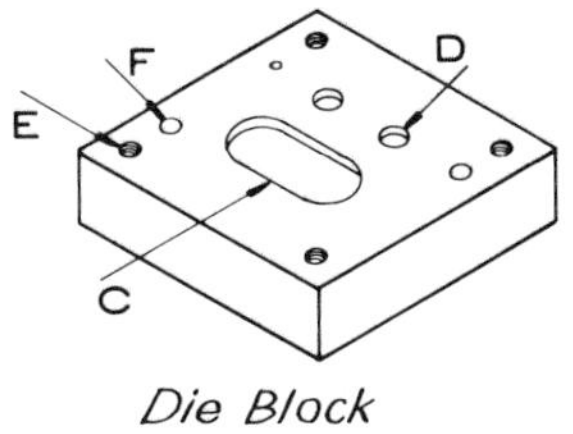

STRIP THICKNESS	ANGULAR RELIEF N
0 to 1/16	1/4°
1/16 to 3/16	1/2°
3/16 to 5/16	3/4°
Over 5/16	1°

Fig. 7-2. Method of applying a die block to a die.

7-3. ALTERNATE METHOD

Because it conserves tool steel, this method of applying a die block is recommended when material shortages exist. Tool steel die block **A**, made one-half the normal thickness, has a machine steel spacer **B** under it. Two long socket capscrews **C** fasten the die block to the die set, while two dowels **D** accurately locate it. Socket button-head screws **E** fasten the stripper plate to the die block, while dowels **F** and **G** are applied as in Fig. 7-2. Section view **C-C** shows the method of machining the die hole and piercing punch hole. Straight land **H** is made 1/8 inch. Angular relief **I** follows the values given in the table in Fig. 7-2. Slug clearance hole **J**, 1/8 inch larger than **K**, is carried through both the die set and spacer **B**.

7-4. PROPORTIONS

The minimum distance **A** from die hole to the outside edge of the die block is normally 1-1/8 the thickness of the die block, **B**, but this would be increased to 1½ times die block thickness for larger dies, or where sharp corners are present in the die hole contour. For very large dies and thick material strip, dimension **A** might well be made twice the thickness of the die block. The table gives recommended die block heights for various strip thicknesses.

7-5. FOOLPROOFING

Dies with symmetrical openings can be assembled incorrectly after repair. This occurrence can result in nicked cutting edges because of slight mismatching of punch and die members. Prevent this by "foolproofing" the die block. In dimensioning, place one of the dowels a different distance from its nearest screw hole than the other.

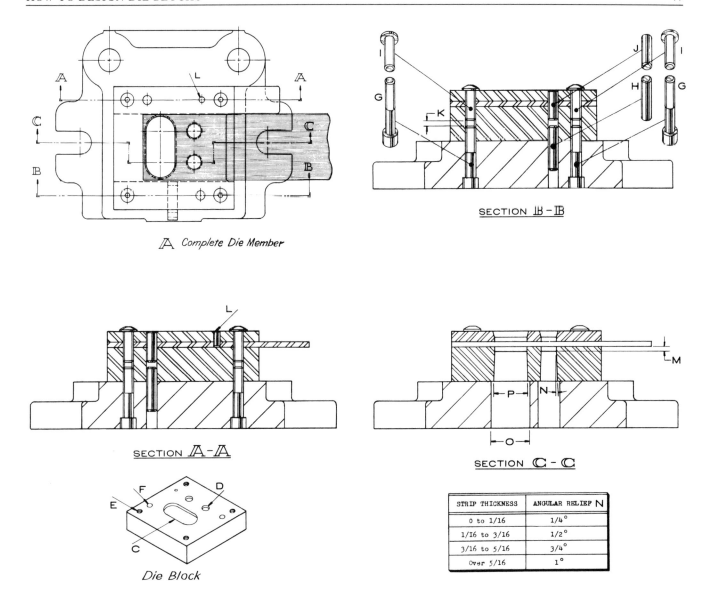

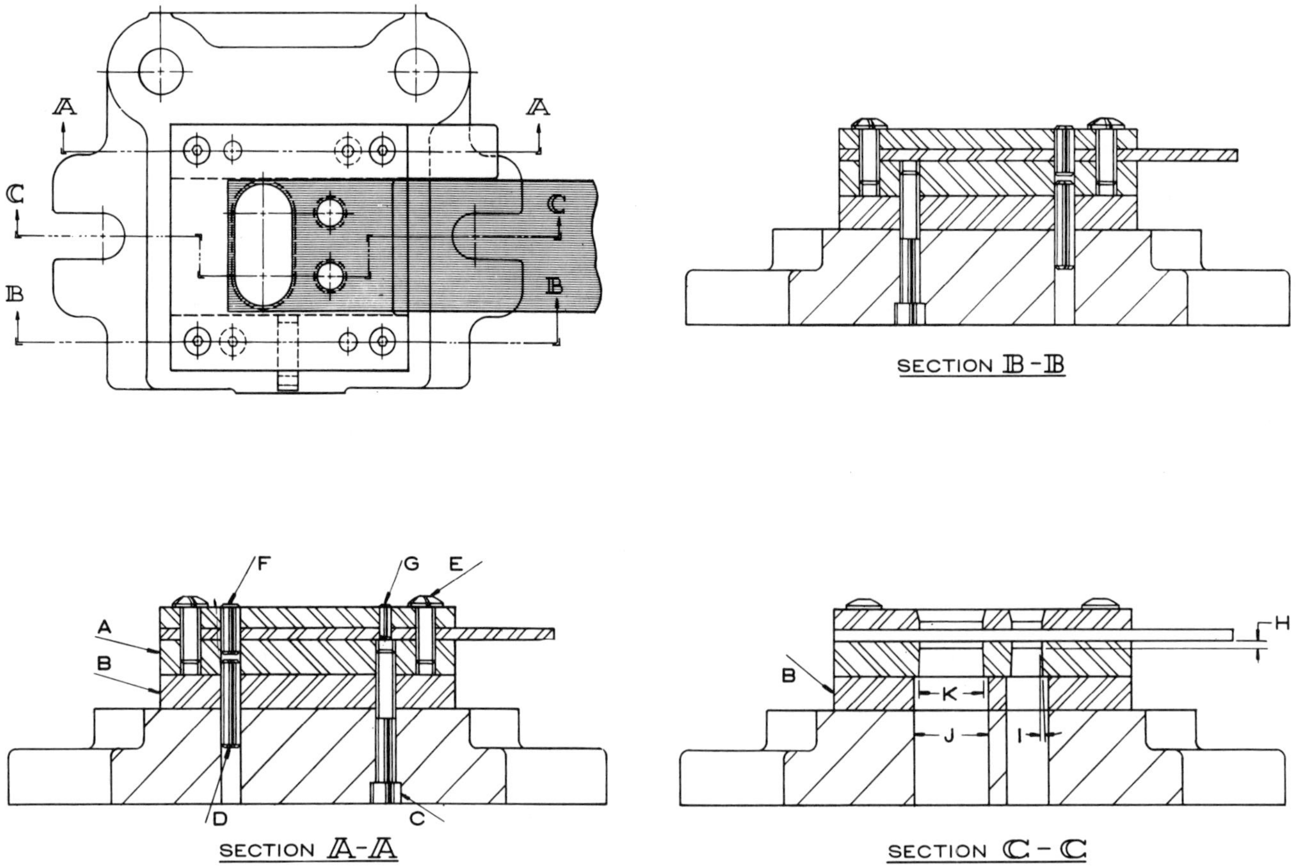

Fig. 7-3. Alternate method of applying a die block to a die.

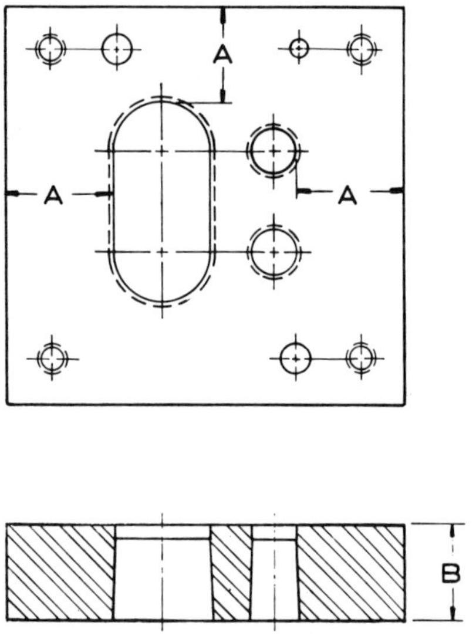

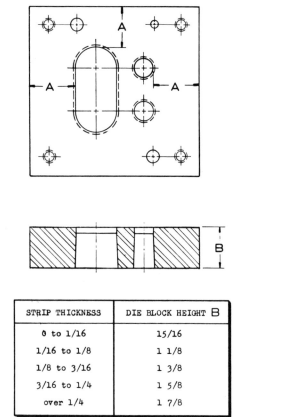

STRIP THICKNESS	DIE BLOCK HEIGHT B
0 to 1/16	15/16
1/16 to 1/8	1 1/8
1/8 to 3/16	1 3/8
3/16 to 1/4	1 5/8
over 1/4	1 7/8

Fig. 7-4. Relationship of die block height to strip thickness.

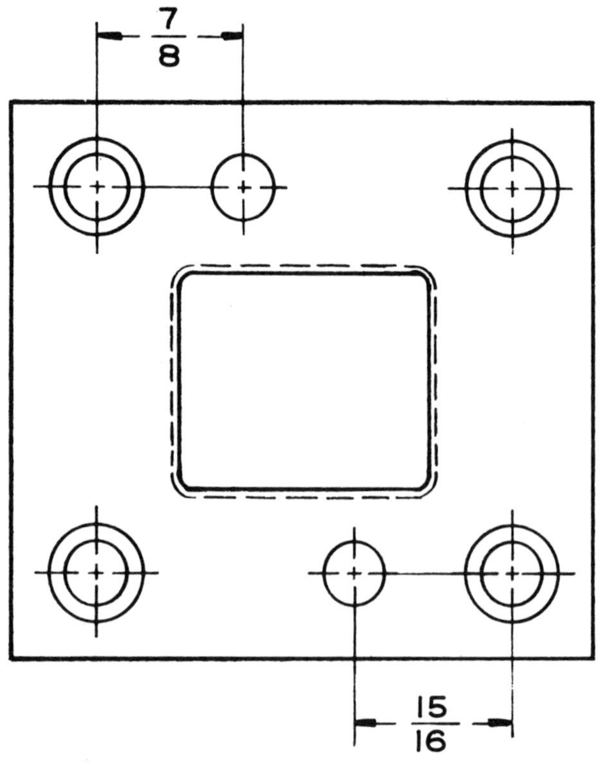

Fig. 7-5. Mismatching of fastener holes called "foolproofing."

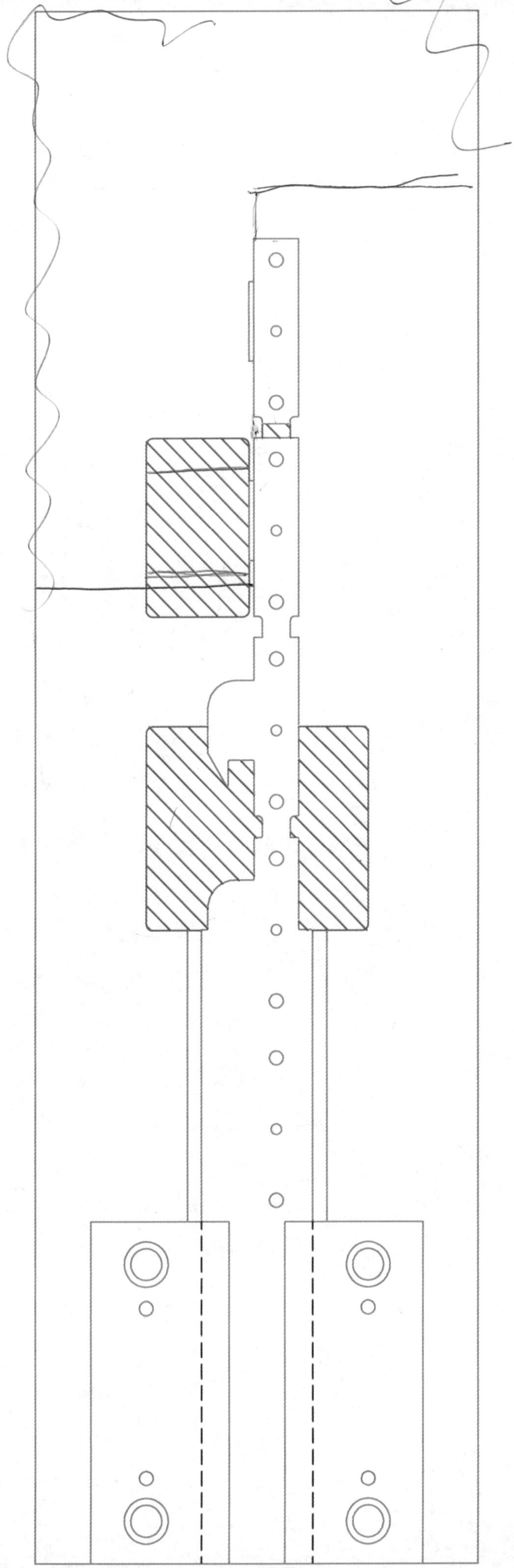

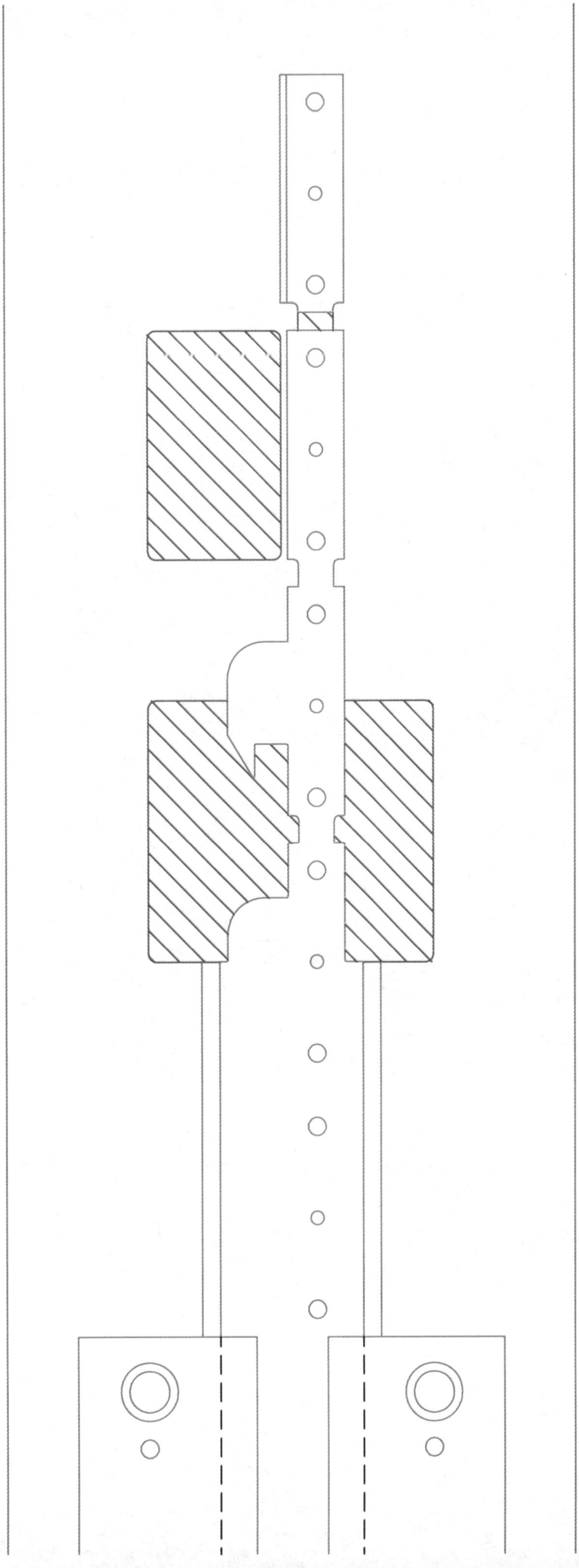

7-6. BLANK ENLARGEMENT

When close part tolerances are present, you should know how much the blank or hole size will increase in die sharpening *past the straight land.* This table lists the amount of growth for each 0.005 inch removed from the face of the die block when ¼ degree angular relief is applied. For ½ degree relief, multiply the values given by 2. For ¾ degree relief, multiply by 3, and for a 1 degree relief, multiply by 4. Of course, there will be no increase in part size for the first 1/8 inch removed from the face of the die block since this is a straight land.

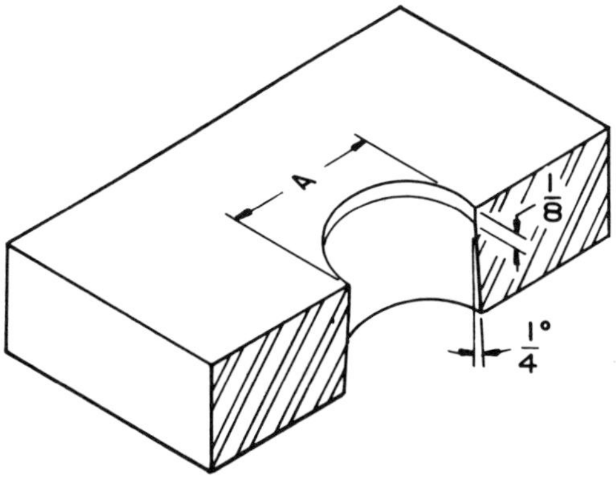

Removed from face of die in sharpening	Blank opening A will increase by this amount
0.005	0.000043
0.010	0.000087
0.015	0.000130
0.020	0.000174
0.025	0.000218
0.030	0.000261
0.035	0.000305
0.040	0.000348
0.045	0.000392
0.050	0.000436
0.055	0.000479
0.060	0.000523
0.065	0.000566
0.070	0.000610
0.075	0.000654
0.080	0.000697
0.085	0.000741
0.090	0.000784
0.095	0.000828
0.100	0.000872
0.105	0.000915
0.110	0.000959
0.115	0.001002
0.120	0.001046
0.125	0.001090

Fig. 7-6. Table for determining hole size when die is sharpened past the straight land.

7-7. STANDARDIZING

Where large quantities of dies are built, time and expense can be saved by standardizing on die block sizes. These standard blocks can be machined during slow periods, or by apprentices, and stocked ready for finish-machining when required. An inexpensive drill jig will assure interchangeability of screw holes. The die block can then be specified on the drawing by part number, reducing time required for dimensioning. This table shows the most comonly used sizes for small dies.

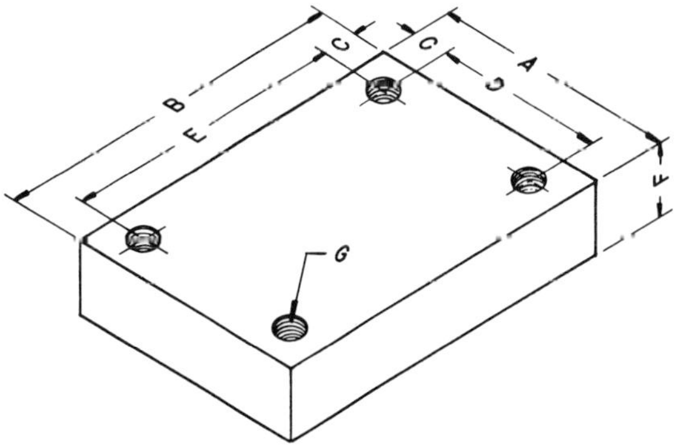

A	B	C	D	E	F	G
3	3 1/2	5/8	1 3/4	2 1/4	15/16	#I (.272) Drill, 5/16-24 Tap Thru
3	5	5/8	1 3/4	3 3/4	15/16	#I (.272) Drill, 5/16-24 Tap Thru
4	4	5/8	2 3/4	2 3/4	15/16	#I (.272) Drill, 5/16-24 Tap Thru
4	5	5/8	2 3/4	3 3/4	15/16	#I (.272) Drill, 5/16-24 Tap Thru
4	6	5/8	2 3/4	4 3/4	15/16	#Q (.332) Drill, 3/8-24 Tap Thru
5	5	3/4	3 1/2	3 1/2	15/16	#Q (.332) Drill, 3/8-24 Tap Thru
5	6	3/4	3 1/2	4 1/2	15/16	#Q (.332) Drill, 3/8-24 Tap Thru

Fig. 7-7. Tabulation of suggested standard die block sizes.

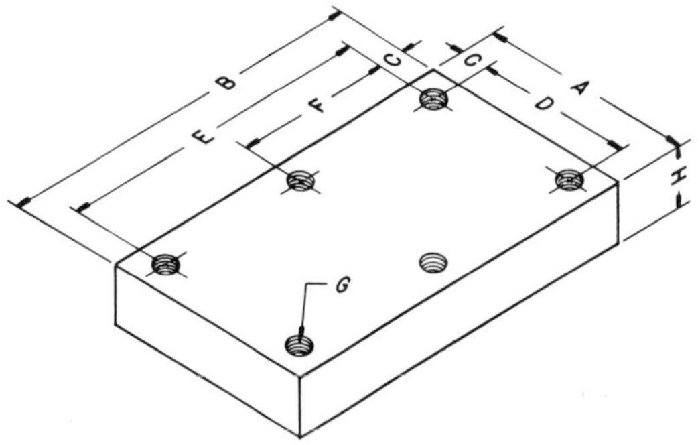

A	B	C	D	E	F	G	H
4	7	3/4	2 1/2	5 1/2	2 3/4	#Q (.332) Drill, 3/8-24 Tap Thru	1 1/8
4	8	3/4	2 1/2	6 1/2	3 1/4	#Q (.332) Drill, 3/8-24 Tap Thru	1 1/8
5	8	3/4	3 1/2	6 1/2	3 1/4	#Q (.332) Drill, 3/8-24 Tap Thru	1 1/8
5	10	3/4	3 1/2	8 1/2	4 1/4	#Q (.332) Drill, 3/8-24 Tap Thru	1 1/8
6	8	3/4	4 1/2	6 1/2	3 1/4	#Q (.332) Drill, 3/8-24 Tap Thru	1 1/8
6	10	3/4	4 1/2	8 1/2	4 1/4	#Q (.332) Drill, 3/8-24 Tap Thru	1 1/8
7	11	3/4	5 1/2	9 1/2	4 3/4	#Q (.332) Drill, 3/8-24 Tap Thru	1 1/8

Fig. 7-8. Tabulation of suggested standard medium-size die block sizes.

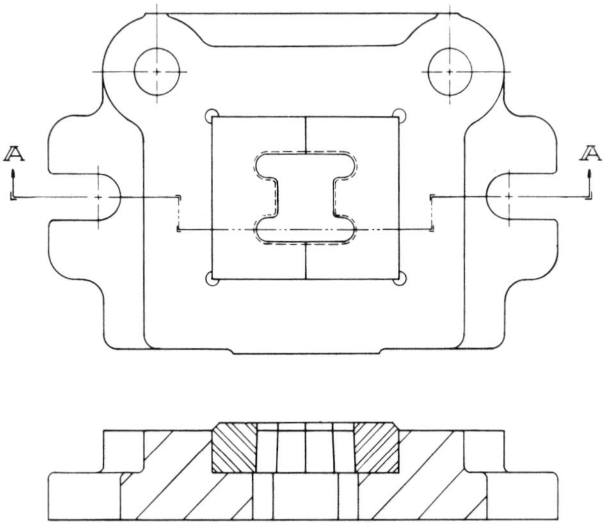

Fig. 7-9. Die block is split for easier machining.

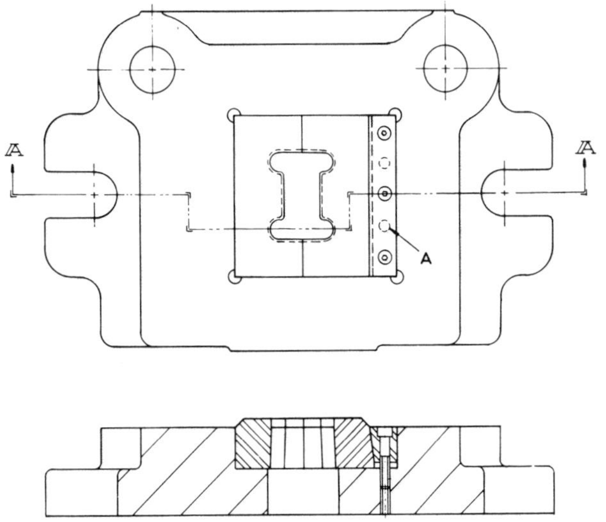

Fig. 7-10. Split die block held in place by a tapered wedge.

7-8. MEDIUM-SIZE DIE BLOCKS

Tabulated are the most comonly used sizes of standard die blocks for medium-size die. Tapped holes are usually National Fine Thread because they resist loosening under vibration better than the Coarse Thread Series.

7-9. SPLIT DIE BLOCKS

When the die block is split for easier machining of the die opening, it is "set into" the die set. This view shows a split block, pressed into a recess machined in the die holder.

7-10. WEDGE LOCK

A tapered wedge, held down by socket capscrews, is often used to clamp split die blocks set into the die set. Knockout pins can be inserted through the holes **A** for pressing out the wedge.

7-11. DIE BUSHINGS

Hardened die bushings, held in machine-steel retainers, are commonly used in large dies where piercing occurs. They conserve tool steel and are easily replaced should edges become chipped or worn. The straight press-fit bushing at **A** is the type most commonly used. The bushing is made a slip fit for approximately 1/8 inch at its lower end. This assures correct alignment while pressing in, an important feature for accurate center-to-center distance between holes. The inside of the bushinghole is ground straight for 1/8 inch. The remainder is given angular relief for proper slug disposal.

With spring strippers, the top of the bushing is made flush with the face of its retainer, as shown at **B**. For heavy material strip, the flanged type **C** is used to provide greater area against the die set. It is also used when upward pressure would tend to work the bushing upward. Shown at **D**, a bushing with an irregular hole is kept from turning by a flat ground in the shoulder. This bears against one edge of a slot machined in the retainer. Where space is limited, die bushings can be kept from turning by a key bearing against a flat ground in the shoulder, as shown at **E**.

7-12. SHEAR

For large blanks, shear is applied to the face of the die to reduce shock on the press, the force required, and blanking noise. Shear, properly applied, reduces the blanking force by 25 per cent for metals thicker than $\frac{1}{4}$ inch. When thinner stock is blanked, the reduction in force is as large as 33 per cent. Shown here is the most common method of providing for shear on the face of a large die block. Shear depth **A** is made 2/3 the thickness of the material strip. Radius **B** removes the sharp edge to avoid a focal point for stock fracture.

7-13. ALTERNATE METHOD

This is a better method of providing angular shear. The material, securely gripped at the corners between the punch and die members, is gradually cut towards the center. Shear is usually applied when blanks are larger than 5 inches by 5 inches, and over 1/16 inch thick.

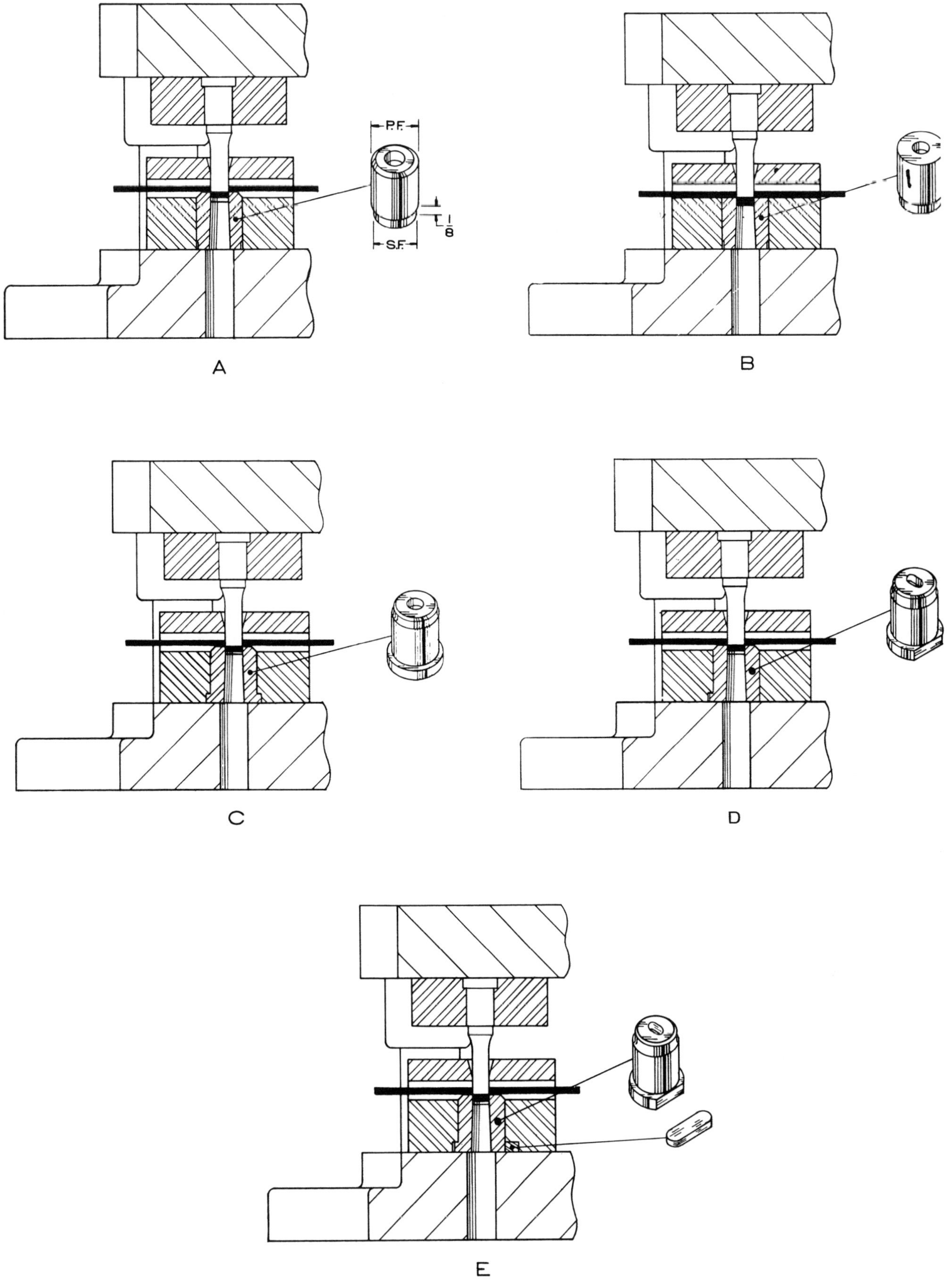

Fig. 7-11. Several versions of hardened die bushings used for piercing.

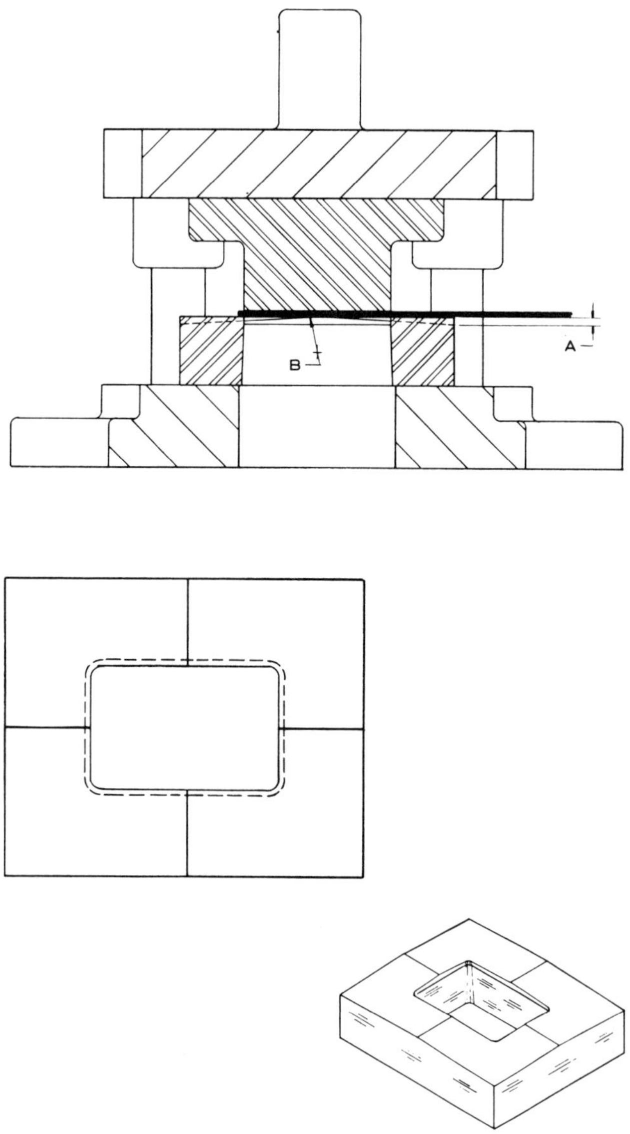

Fig. 7-12. Die block configuration for employing shear in producing large blanks.

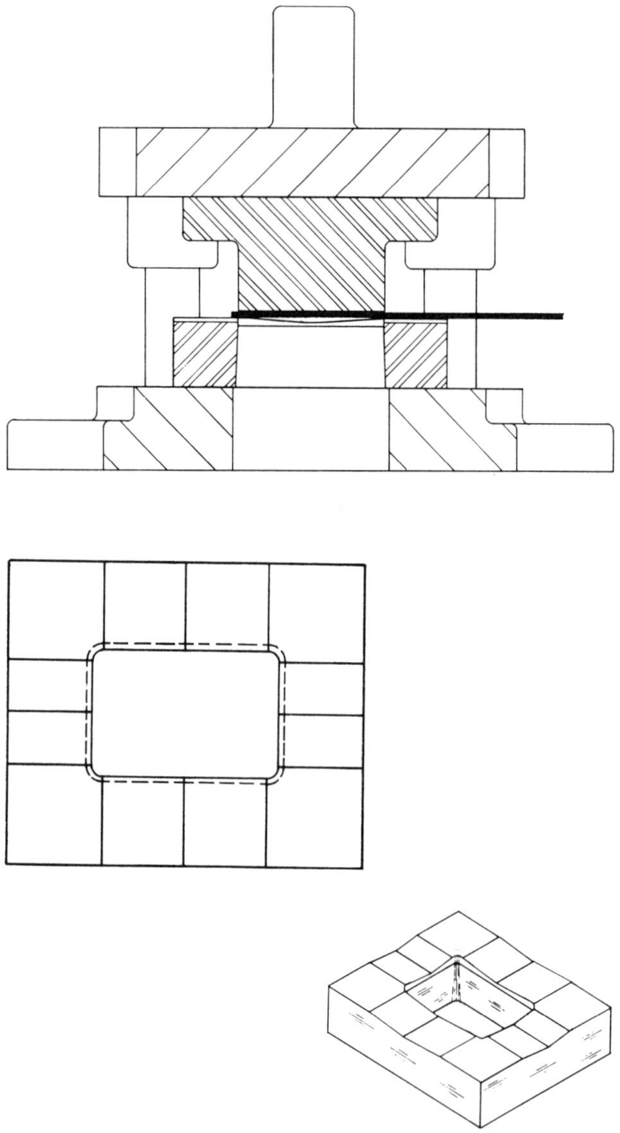

Fig. 7-13. Alternate die block configuration for employing shear in producing large blanks.

7-14. PROVIDING FOR SHEAR IN ROUND DIE BLOCKS

Round die blocks may be given a shearing action by scalloping the face in a series of waves around the periphery. Here again, shear depth should not exceed 2/3 the thickness of the stock.

7-15. DIE SECTIONS

Large die blocks are made of sectional components, screwed and doweled to the die holder of the die set, with the sections butting against each other. A number of types of these composite die sections are available. At **A**, the section is machined from a rectangular bar of tool steel. This method is obviously wasteful of material and labor. At **B** is illustrated a commercially available die section whose original shape is denoted by phantom lines. Far less machining is required to finish this bar than that of the previous example. At **C** is a commercially available composite die section that can be purchased in long bars and cut into required lengths as required by the die design. It can be forged to irregular contours without the tool steel member (**A**) breaking away from the softer machine-steel base (**B**). **D** through **H** are further illustrations of die sections that can be purchased through commercial outlets. Although these are not the only types of die sections available, they do represent a good cross section.

These composites all have a tool steel cutting member electrically welded to a machine steel base which prevents excessive distortion in hardening and provides a soft flange for easy machining for screws and dowels.

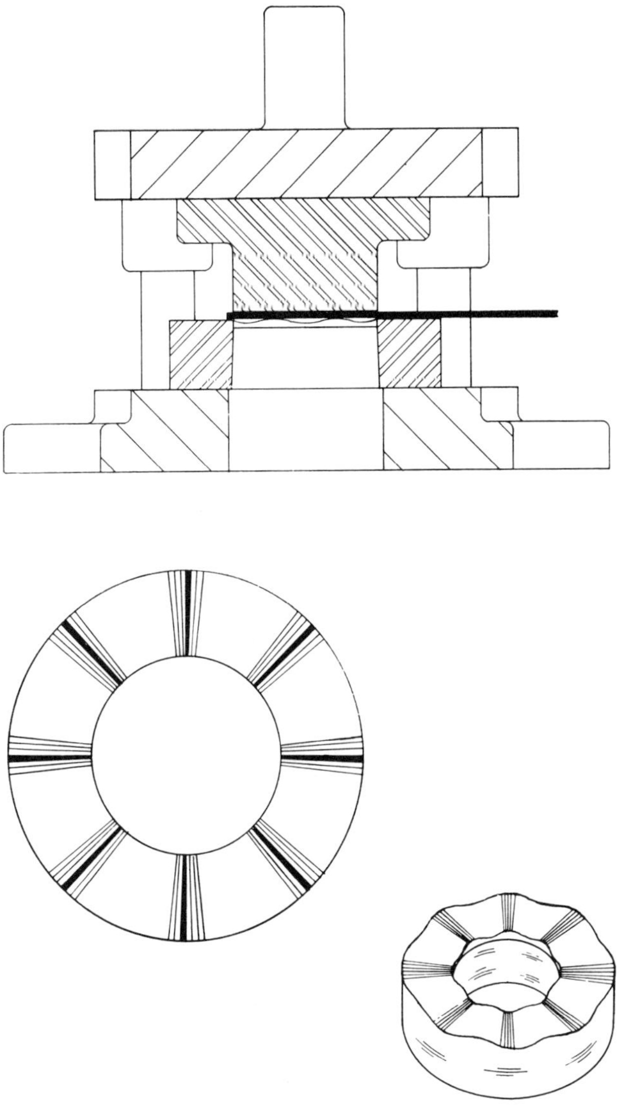

Fig. 7-14. Scalloped round die block for employing shear.

7-16. PROPORTIONS

This table gives recommended proportions of composite die sections. Lengths of straight sections usually do not exceed 12 inches. Curved sections are ordinarily not made longer than 8 inches.

7-17. CONSTRUCTION

Various arrangements of composite sections can be supplied by the manufacturers. It is obvious that almost any large blanking die can be fabricated from composite sections, no matter how intricate the part contour. The following lists the names of the various sections:

A. Straight
B. Ribbed
C. Double
D. Face contoured
E. Contoured and ribbed
F. Forged
G. Forged and ribbed
H. Circular.

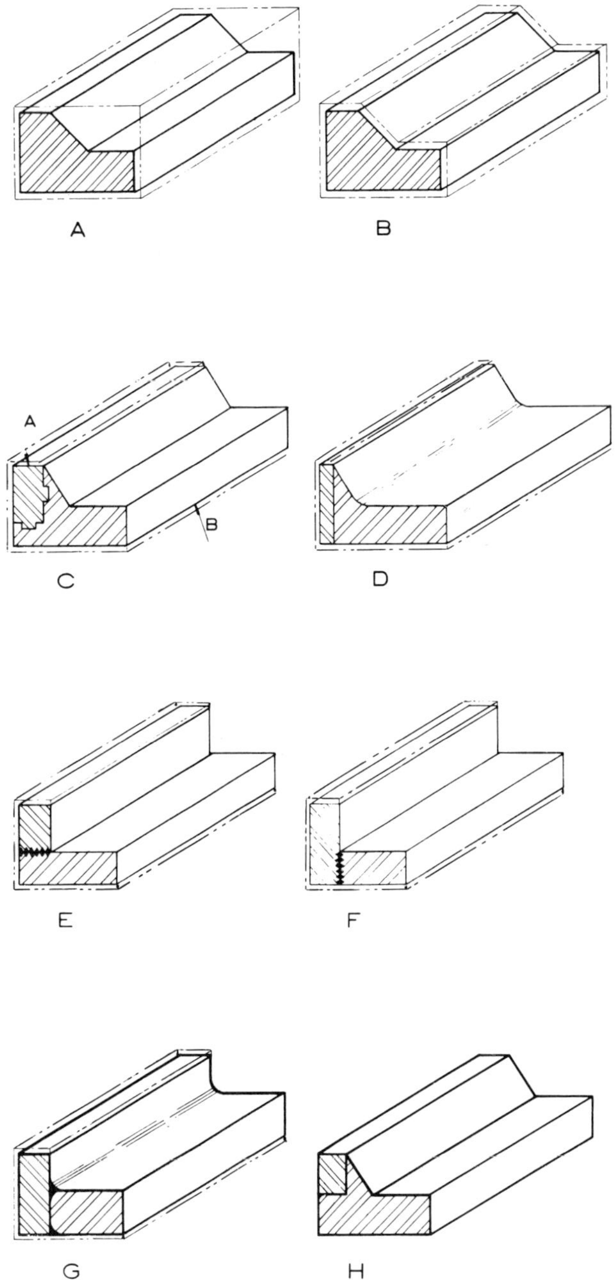

Fig. 7-15. Various types of commercially available plain and composite die sections.

7-18. COMPOSITE LAYOUTS

After a large die has been designed, a composite layout is made on heavy paper or cardboard, exactly to scale. No dimensions are used. However, detail numbers, the type of tool steel, and the number of parts required are specified. Curved members are forged to this layout, with stock allowed for machining. Note that joint lines for the tool steel faces are staggered or offset and that they never should be located opposite each other. Only the tool steel members of the composites bear against each other at the end to reduce fitting time.

PROPORTIONS OF COMPOSITE DIE SECTIONS

STRIP THICKNESS	A	B	C	D	USE RIBS
0 to 3/64	1				
3/64 to 3/32	1 1/4				
3/32 to 9/64	1 1/2				
9/64 to 7/32	1 3/4				
7/32 to 5/16	2				
		2	1	3 min.	
		2 1/2	1	3 min.	
		3	1	3 min.	
		3 1/2	1 1/4	3 1/2 min.	*
		4	1 1/4	4 min.	*
		4 1/2	1 1/4	4 1/2 min.	*
		5	1 1/4	5 min.	*
		5 1/2	1 1/4	5 1/2 min.	*
		6	1 1/4	6 min.	*
		6 1/2	1 1/2	6 1/2 min.	*
		7	1 1/2	7 min.	*
		7 1/2	1 1/2	7 1/2 min.	*
		8	1 1/2	8 min.	*
		8 1/2	1 1/2	8 1/2 min.	*
		9	1 1/2	9 min.	*
		9 1/2	1 1/2	9 1/2 min.	*
		10	1 1/2	10 min.	*

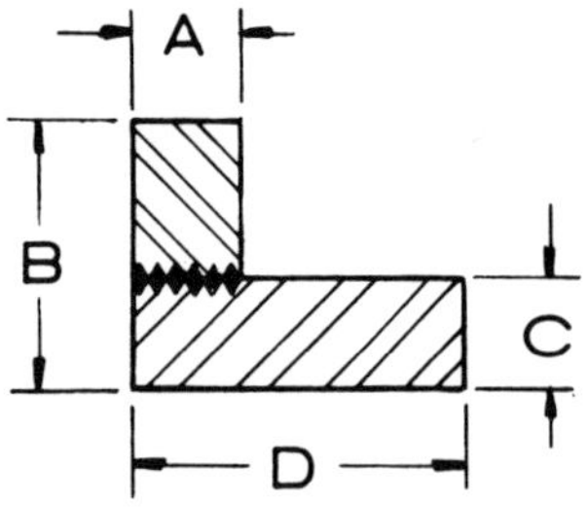

Fig. 7-16. Table of recommended proportions of composite die sections.

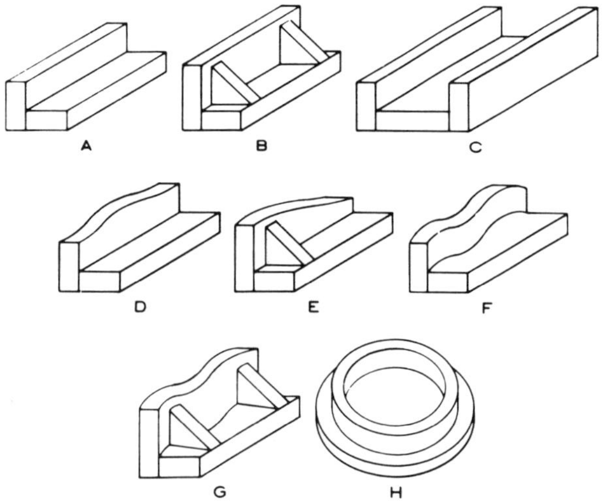

Fig. 7-17. Various configurations of commercially available composite sections.

7-19. COMMERCIAL COMPOSITES

Commercial composites, shown in Fig. 7-15, are also used extensively for large solid die blocks. Here, a solid tool-steel ring **A** is torch cut to the shape shown. A hole of the same outside contour is torch cut in the machine-steel base **B** to receive the tool steel member. The tool steel ring is then welded in position. The machine steel base, which confines the tool steel ring around its periphery, prevents excessive distortion in hardening, and also provides a soft flange for applying screws and dowels which fasten the die block to the die set.

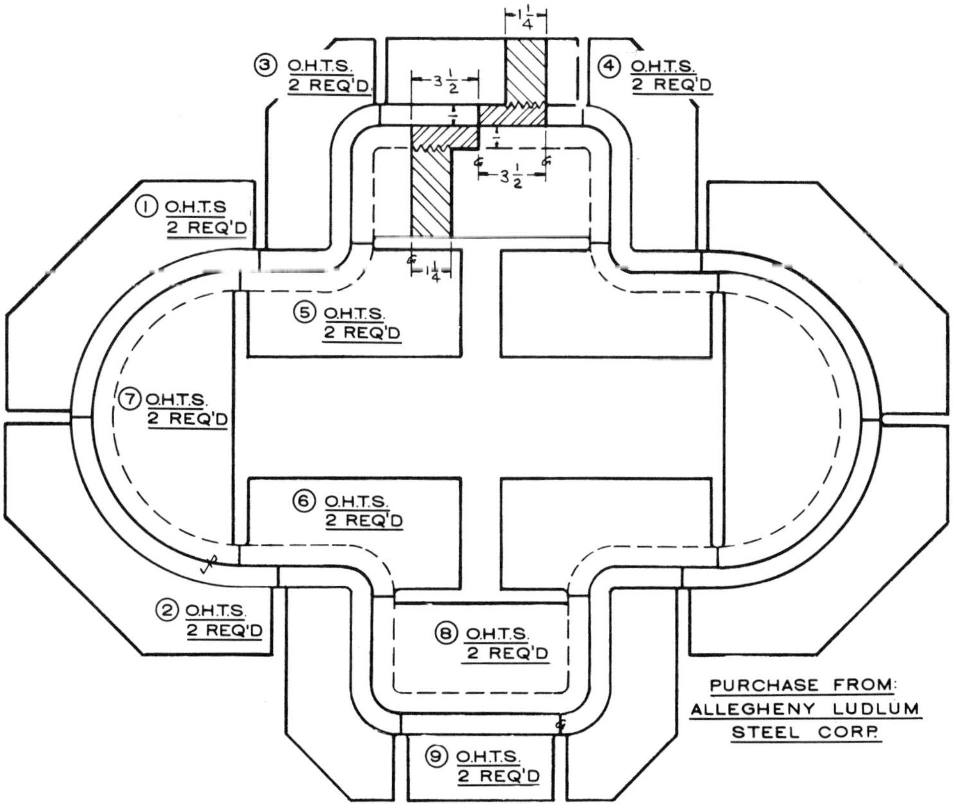

Fig. 7-18. Typical composite layout for a large die.

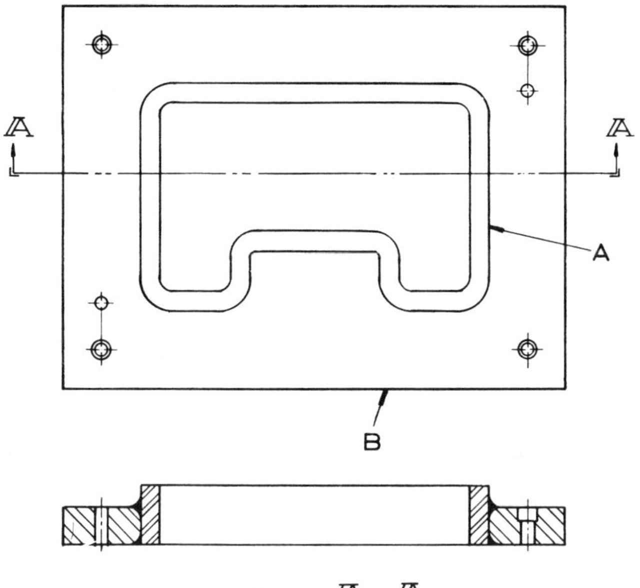

Fig. 7-19. One commercially available composite as used in a large solid die block.

SECTIONING DIE BLOCKS

In Figs. 7-9, 7-10, and 7-15, the subject of sectioning die blocks for ease in hardening and grinding was introduced, and it may be well to enter into a more precise understanding of it at this time. For some die hole shapes, sectioning the die block provides the following distinct advantages:

1. Difficult machining is avoided
2. Less distortion occurs in hardening
3. Any distortion can be corrected by grinding
4. Inserts can be replaced more quickly in case of breakage.

7-20. FASTENING DIE STEELS

Illustrated are two ways of fastening tool steel bars for blanking parts of square or rectangular shape. At **A**, the bars are set on top of the die set and clamping members **C** hold the longer side components **D** from spreading under cutting thrust. The short members are always used as clamps because the greatest amount of side pressure occurs against the longer sides.

At **B** is shown a rectangular sectional die for long runs. It is composed of four bars **E** arranged as shown. This provides for setting the bars to the exact opening required and it obviates the necessity of accurate

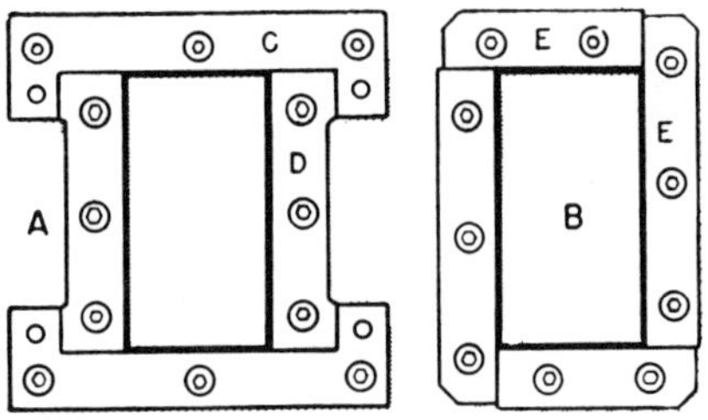

Fig. 7-20. Methods of fastening die steels.

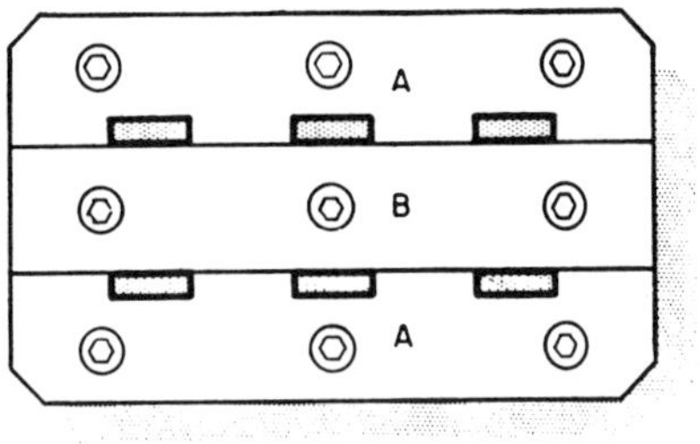

Fig. 7-21. Die block sectioned for piercing two rows of rectangular slots.

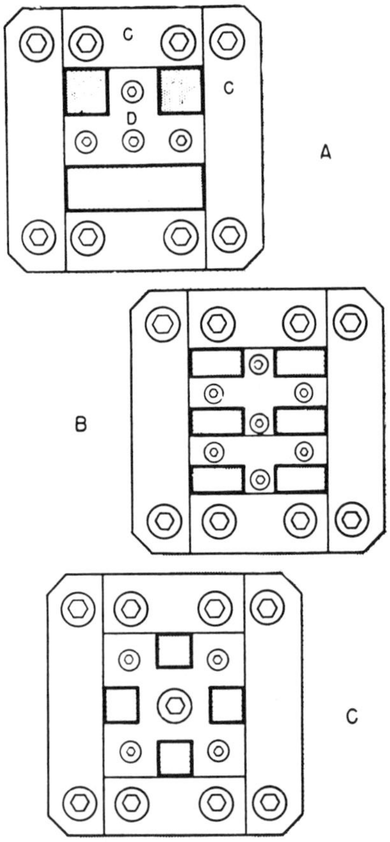

Fig. 7-22. Various sectioned die blocks with center inserts for punching different arrays of square and rectangular holes.

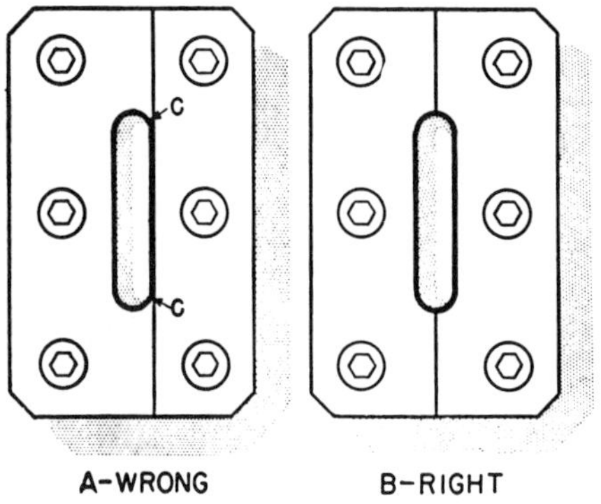

Fig. 7-23. Correct and incorrect ways of applying break lines in sectioned die blocks.

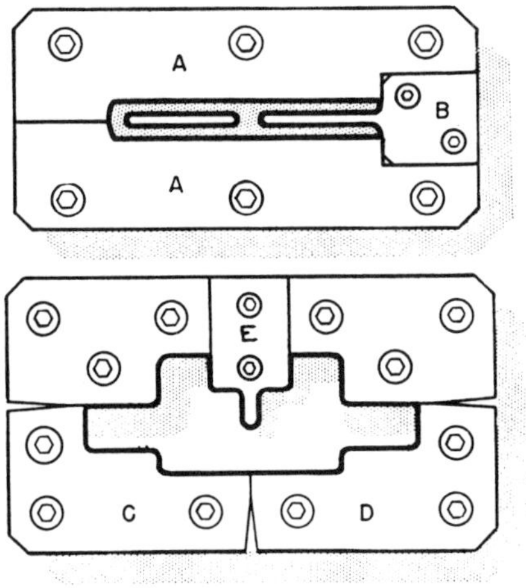

Fig. 7-24. Use of inserts in providing for frail projections.

machining of the members. The assembly is set into the die holder of the die set as in Fig. 7-9.

7-21. SECTIONS FOR SLOTS

Die blocks for piercing rows of square or rectangular slots are often sectioned. In this example, slots are machined in members **A**, and member **B** is a spacer of proper width. The entire assembly is set into a recess in the die set to prevent deflection under cutting pressure.

7-22. CENTER INSERTS

This shows various groupings of square and rectangular holes which can be punched with square sectional dies. The die block shown at **A** consists of four tool steel members **C** and the center insert **D**, both hardened and ground. Construction of die blocks **B** and **C** is similar. Each would be retained in a pocket milled in the die holder of the die set.

7-23. APPLYING BREAK LINES

The first rule in sectioning die blocks having openings with curved outlines is: Never apply the break line tangent to an arc as shown at **A** because sharp projections **C** would be weak and subject to breakage. Break lines should cross the centers of radii as at **B**.

7-24. INSERTS

Frail projections should be designed as inserts for easy machining, heat treating, grinding, and replacement in case of breakage. The upper die block is composed of two side members **A** and insert **B** with a slender, easily broken projection at one end. The lower die block is composed of four corner members **C** and **D** and replaceable insert **E**.

7-25. DIE SEGMENTS

When a portion of the blank outline is circular in shape, the die block may be bored to size and inserts applied to define the remainder of the shape. In the illustration, tool steel block **A** is machined for screws and dowels and the large center hole is bored. The block is then hardened and subsequently ground to size. Segments **B** are machined, hardened, ground, and placed in position. The assembly is then fastened to the die set.

7-26. ROUND SECTIONAL DIE BLOCKS

A round sectional die block consists of a hardened and ground tool steel ring employed to retain inserts or segments and prevent their deflection under cutting pressure. Six representative examples are shown:

1. The insert may consist of a single member. At **A** the center plug **D** of a lamination die is retained in ring **C**. Slot openings and a center hole have been machined in the plug **D** prior to hardening, grinding, and assembly within ring **C**. At **B** is shown a die block for punching two semi-circular openings in a blank. Fitted insert **E** is provided with a shoulder at the bottom to prevent it from pulling out.

2. The insert may consist of two members. At **A** two ground segments are retained in a ring. The die blanks a small ratchet wheel and sectioning simplifies machining of the center opening, At **B**, a die block for electrical contacts is split in two segments for grinding the opposed halves which define the die opening. A ring keeps the segments from deflecting under cutting pressure.

3. The insert may consist of several members because of the shape of the blank opening. At **A**, four identical sections compose the die block. At **B**, the shape of the opening is such that a three-section division is best.

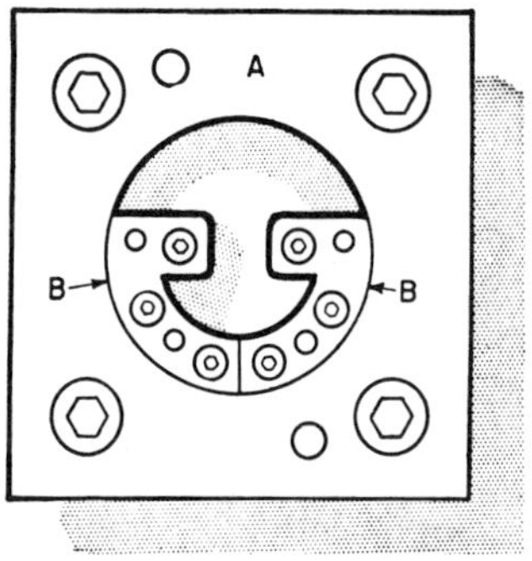

Fig. 7-25. Use of inserts in die block when portion of blank is circular in shape.

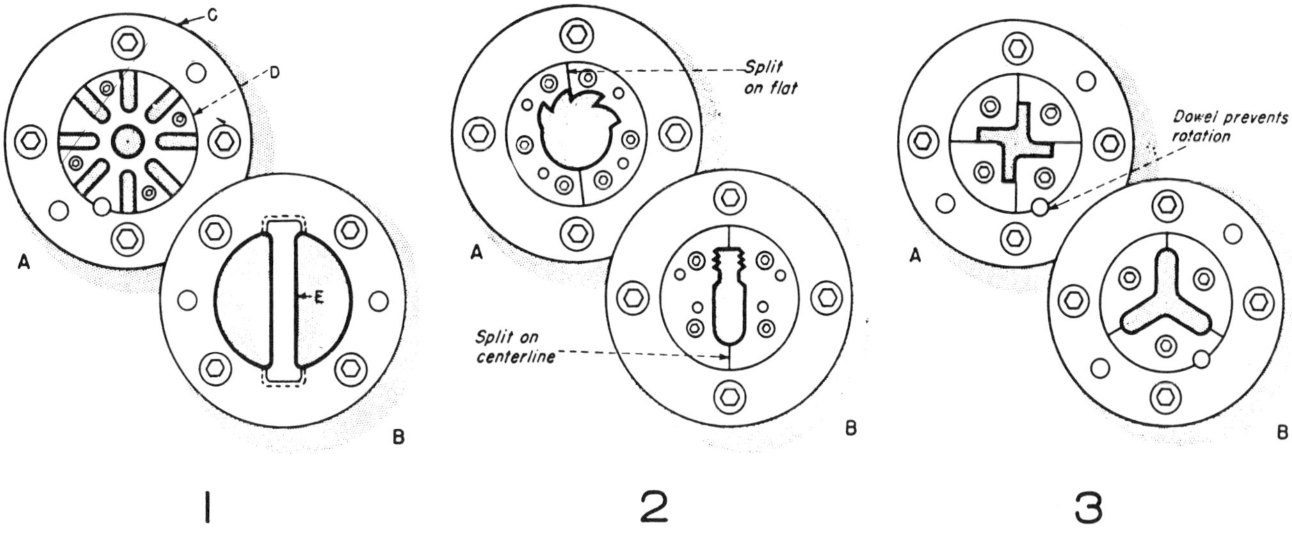

Fig. 7-26. Six representative examples showing use of round sectional die blocks in retaining inserts or segments.

Section 8

HOW TO DESIGN BLANKING PUNCHES

Blanking punches range from tiny components for producing watch and instrument parts to large, multi-unit members for blanking such parts as automobile fenders, doors, and tops. The size of the blank to be produced determines the type of punch to use. Design considerations include:

1. Stability, to prevent deflection
2. Adequate screws to overcome stripping load
3. Good doweling practice for accurate location
4. Sectioning, if required, for proper heat treatment.

In illustrations to follow are shown twenty-two methods of applying blanking punches to small, medium, and large cutting dies. Covered are such considerations as keying the punch in order to keep it from turning, use of inserts for ease and economy of replacement, use of sectioning to facilitate heat-treating and minimize distortion, use of shedders to prevent clinging of blanks to punch faces, and proper proportions of and construction of blanking punches. These methods further explain Step 3 in Section 5, "14 Steps to Design a Die."

8-1. SMALL BLANKING PUNCHES

This shows the method of applying a blanking punch for small instrument washers. Body diameter **A** is made considerably larger than blanking diameter **B**, Radius **C** provides supporting material to give rigidity and prevent deflection of the punch upon contact with the material strip. Section view **A** shows the punch, punch plate, and punch holder as they would appear in the lower left-hand section view of the die drawing. Plan view **B** shows the same components inverted as they would appear in the upper right-hand view of the drawing.

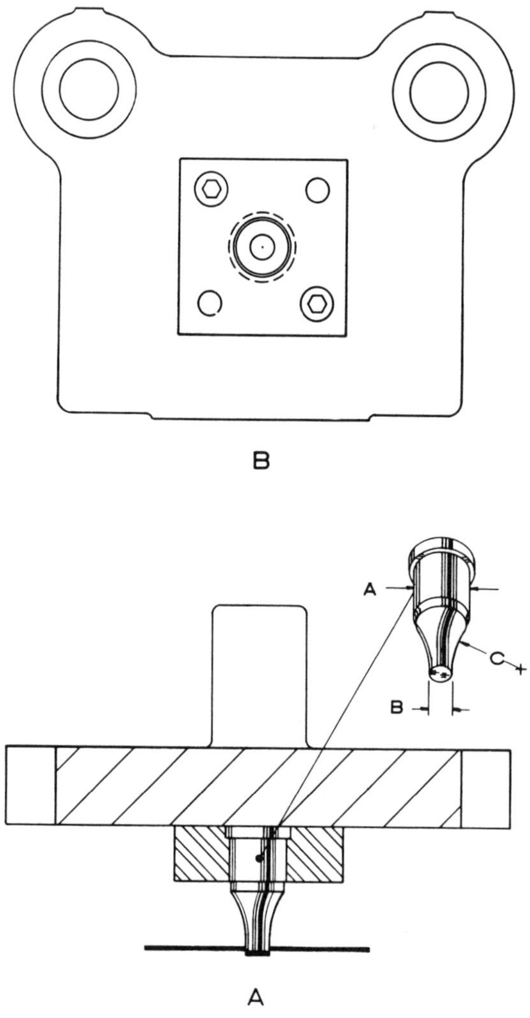

Fig. 8-1. Method of applying a blanking punch for small washers.

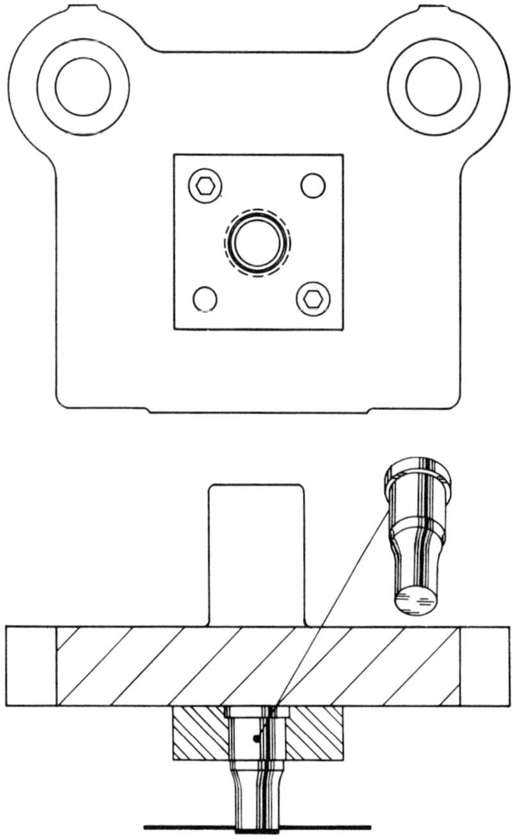

Fig. 8-2. Method of applying a slightly larger blanking punch.

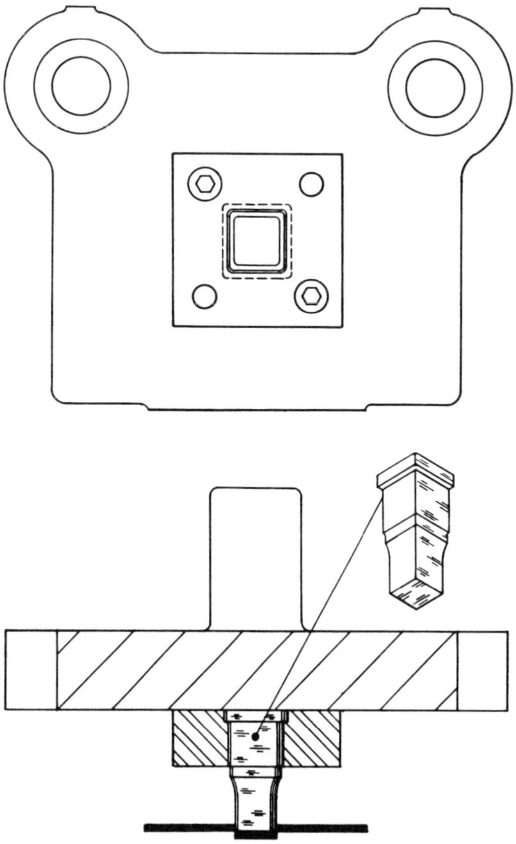

Fig. 8-4. Square-machined punch body for keeping punch from turning.

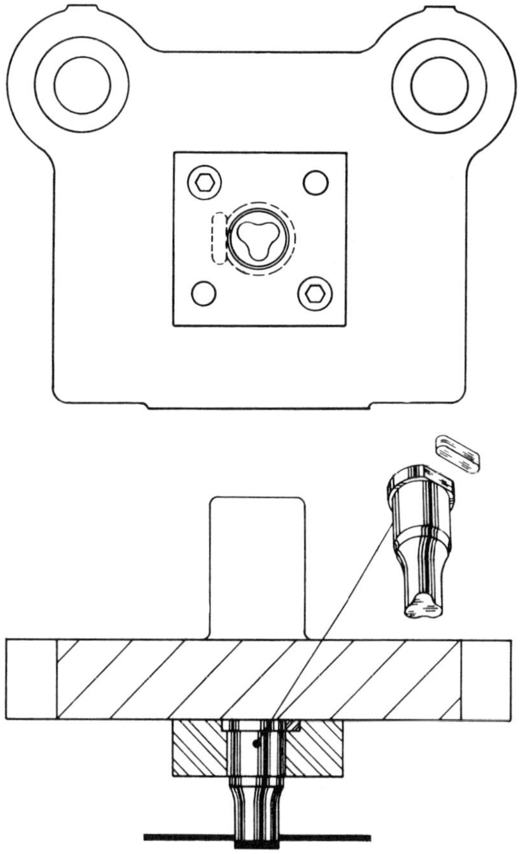

Fig. 8-3. One method of keying a blanking punch.

8-2. PIERCE OR BLANK PUNCHES

Slightly larger blanking punches for producing circular parts are made in much the same manner as piercing punches. Rules for designing piercing punches will be given in the next section of the book.

8-3. KEYING THE PUNCH

Small blanking punches having a cutting end of irregular contour can be kept from turning by a round-end key. This key is retained in an end-milled slot machined in the punch plate and bears against a flat ground in the punch head. Common applications of this construction are small blanking punches for producing clock, watch, and instrument gears.

8-4. ALTERNATE METHOD

Another method of keeping small, irregular blanking punches from turning is to machine the body square or rectangular in shape. The retainer hole is machined to fit the square or rectangular punch body.

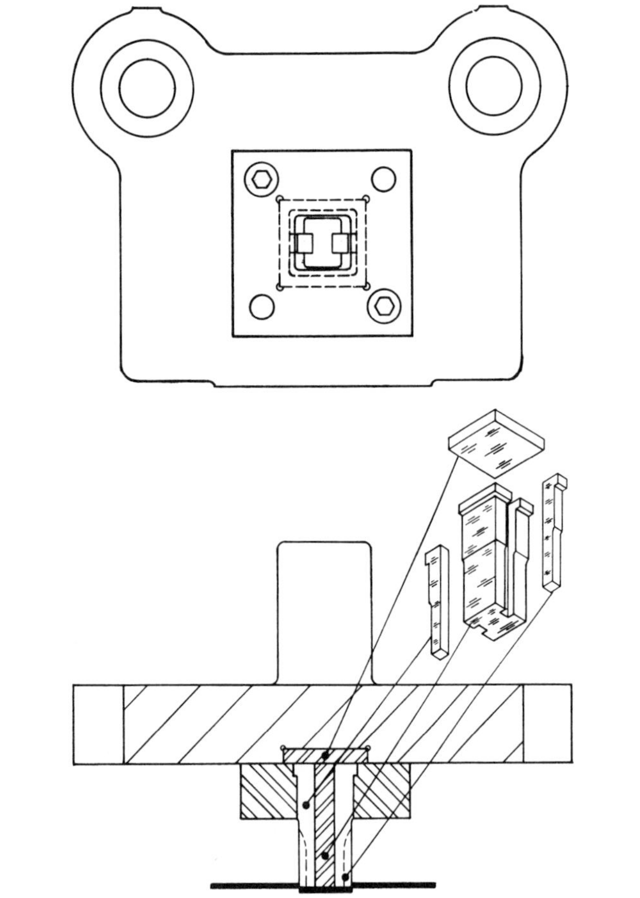

Fig. 8-5. Inserts used in weak areas of small blanking punches.

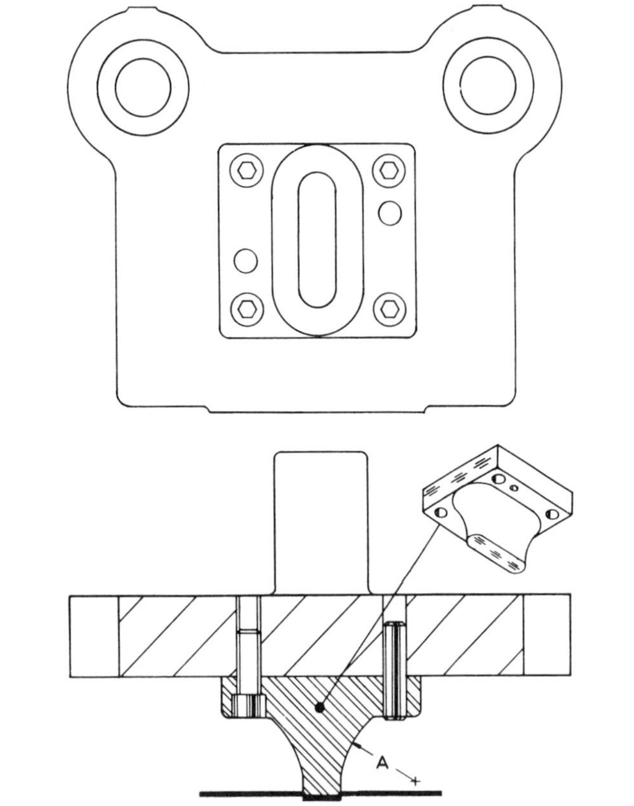

Fig. 8-6. Radius **A** provides extra support in this "narrow-and-long" punch.

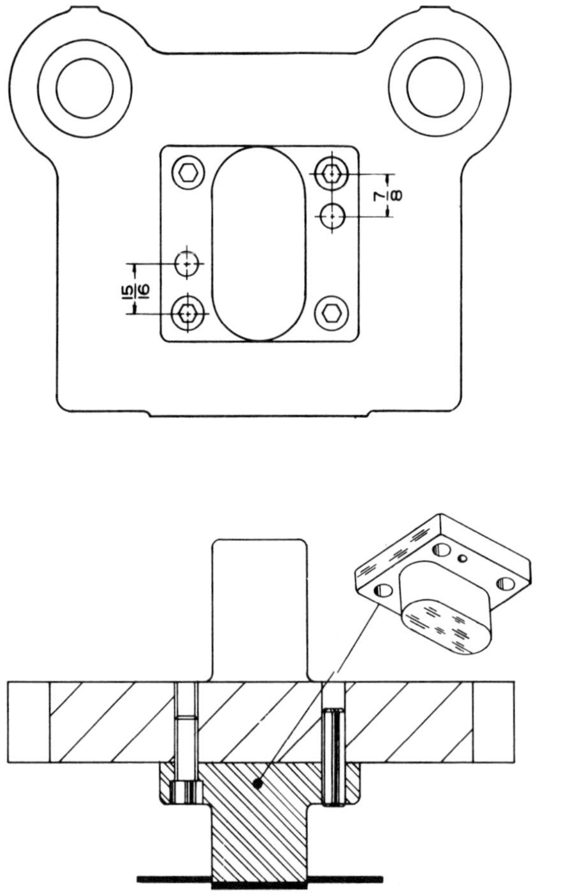

Fig. 8-7. Widely used blanking punch for producing average-size blanks.

8-5. INSERTS

Weak areas of small blanking punches are best applied as inserts for easy and inexpensive replacement of members in case of breakage. When inserts are used, the blanking punch assembly is backed up by a hardened plate.

8-6. PUNCHES FOR LONG BLANKS OR SLOTS

The sides of "narrow-and-long" blanking punches are provided with a radius **A**. This radius provides extra supporting material for stability to prevent deflection of the cutting end upon contact with the material strip.

8-7. FLANGED PUNCHES

This type of blanking punch is the most widely used, because it is employed to produce average-size blanks. As in Fig. 8-6, flanges are provided for fastening the blanking punch to the punch holder with screws and dowels. Only the cutting end of the blanking punch is hardened; the flanges are soft for accurate fitting of dowels at assembly. "Fool-proof" the punch by offsetting one of the dowels to assure correct reassembly in die maintenance.

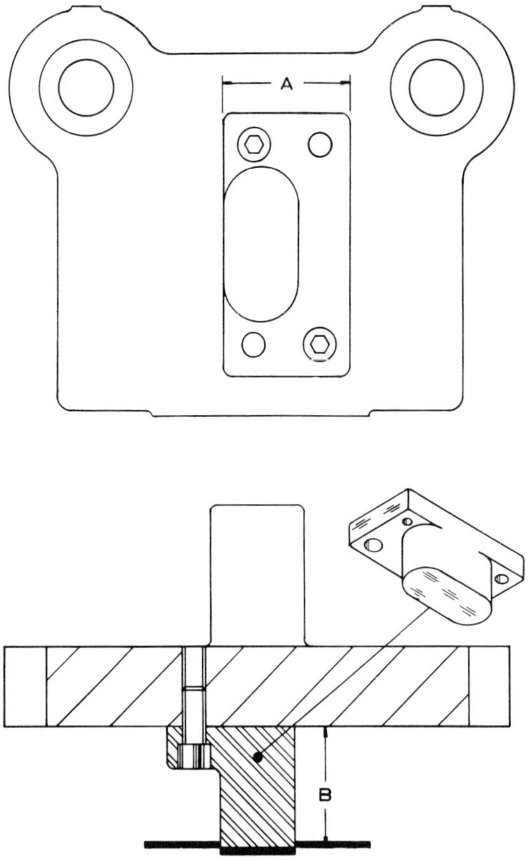

Fig. 8-8. Removing portion of flange to provide clearance for other die components.

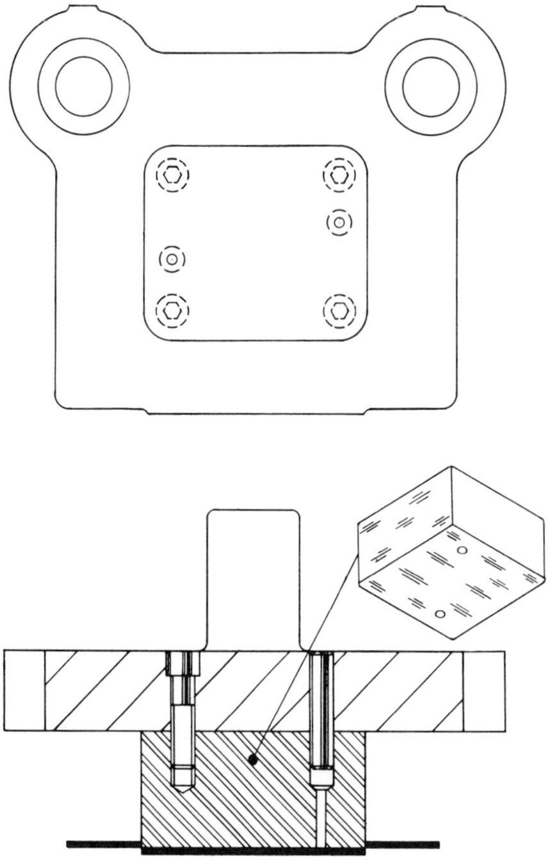

Fig. 8-9. Large blanking punches do not require flanges.

8-8. CLEARING OTHER COMPONENTS

When space is limited, a portion of the flange can be removed to provide room for other die components. For good stability, flange width **A** should not be smaller than punch height **B**.

8-9. LARGE BLANKING PUNCHES

Larger blanking punches do not require flanges. They can be fastened to the punch holder with screws and dowels applied from the back. Dowel holes are shown all the way through the punch, either full size or as a smaller hole to enable pressing out the dowels during die maintenance.

8-10. SECTIONING LARGE PUNCHES

Still larger blanking punches can be made in sections to facilitate heat-treating and minimize distortion. Each section is individually screwed and doweled to the punch holder of the die set.

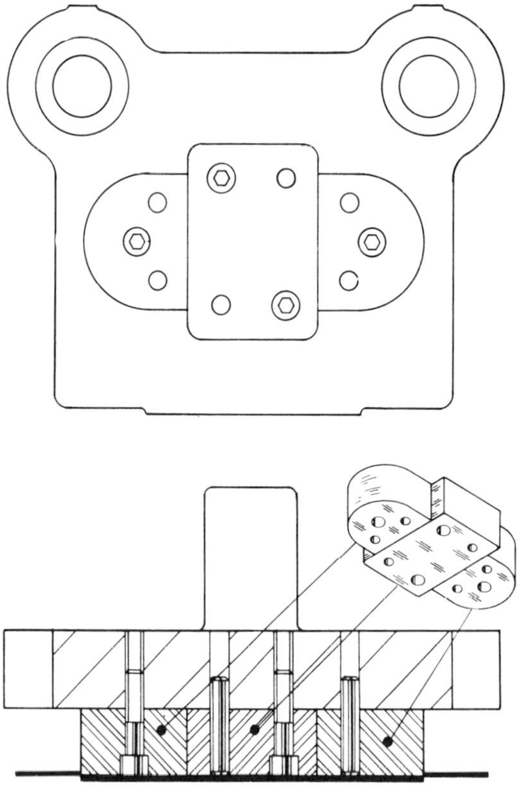

Fig. 8-10. Large blanking punches are sectionalized to facilitate heat-treating and minimize distortion.

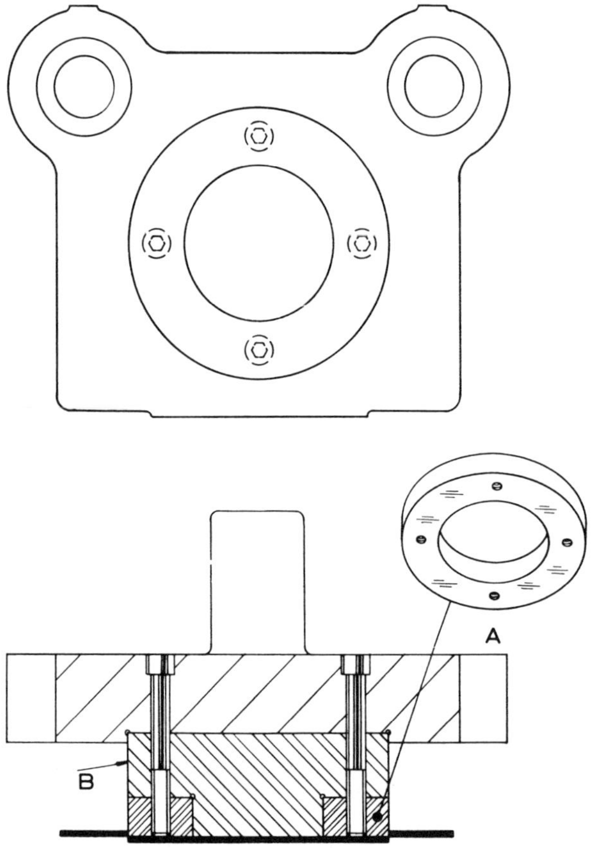

Fig. 8-11. Large circular blanking punch is made in two parts to conserve tool steel.

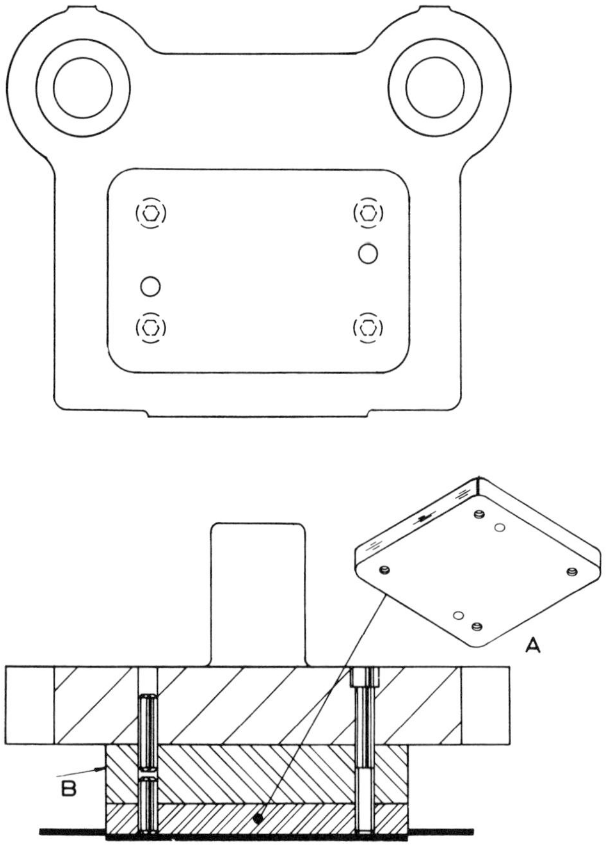

Fig. 8-13. Use of a spacer (**B**) to conserve tool steel.

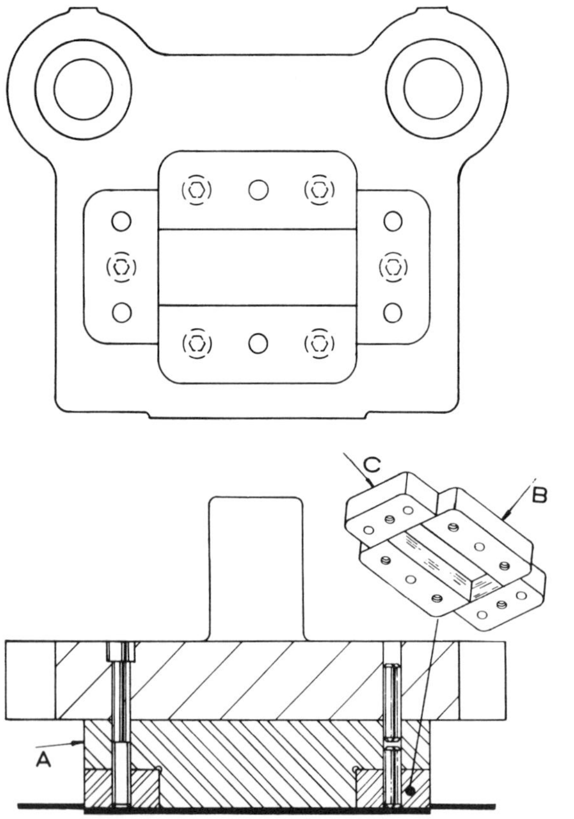

Fig. 8-12. Construction method for large blanking punches with irregular contours.

8-11. CUTTING RINGS

Blanking punches for large circular blanks can be made in two parts to conserve tool steel and simplify heat-treating. Cutting ring **A** is located by a round boss which is part of spacer **B**. This spacer, in turn, is fitted into a recess machined in the punch holder of the die set. With this construction, dowels are not necessary for positioning the punch.

8-12. CUTTING STEELS

The construction method illustrated in Fig. 8-11 can also be used for blanks with irregular contours. Spacer **A** is machined to accommodate hardened tool-steel pads **B** and **C**. Long socket screws, threaded into the tool-steel pads, fasten both the pads and the machine-steel spacer to the punch holder. Dowels accurately locate the entire assembly.

8-13. SPACER

Still another method of conserving tool steel in large dies is to make the cutting member **A** in one piece, but relatively thin, and back it up with a machine steel spacer **B**. The assembly is fastened to the punch holder as in Fig. 8-12, and dowels locate the blanking punch in much the same manner.

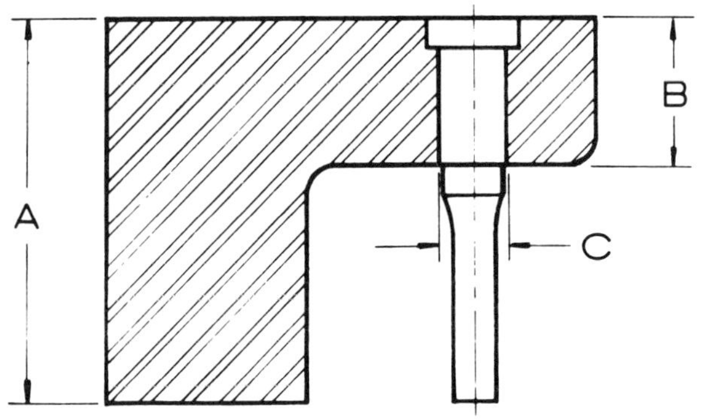

Fig. 8-14. Typical proportions of medium-size blanking punches.

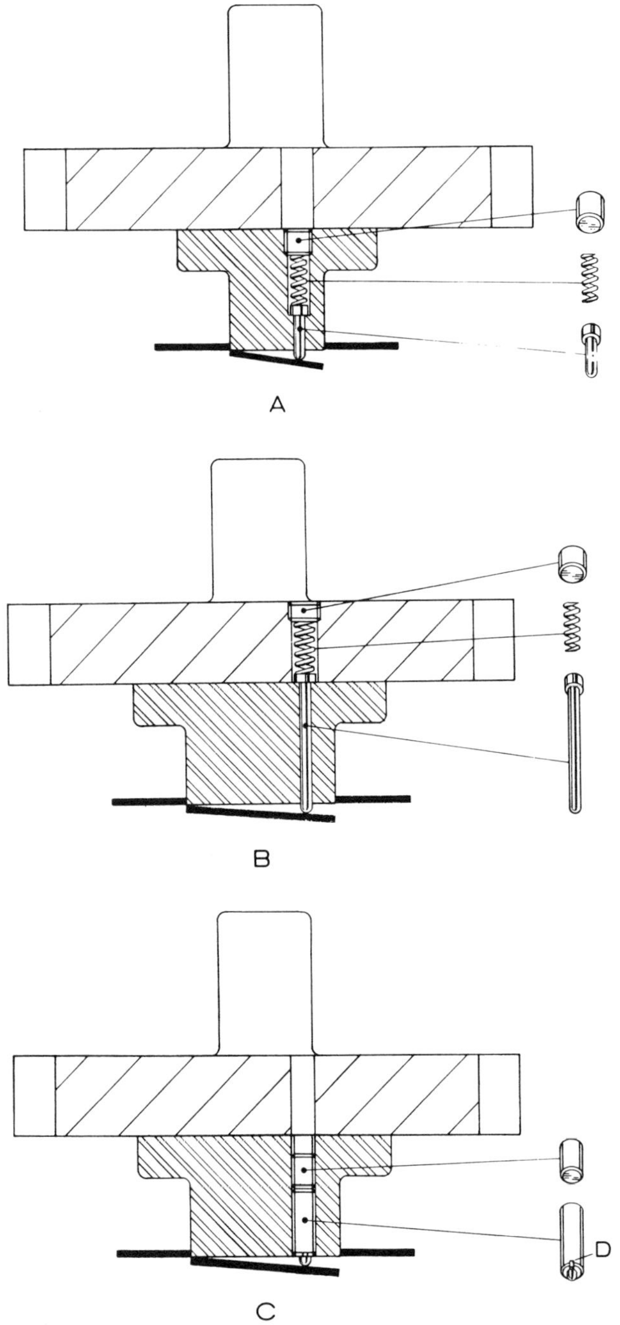

Fig. 8-15. Different versions of a shedder assembly which prevents clinging of blank to punch face.

8-14. PROPORTIONS

Proportions often used for medium-size blanking punches are: Punch length **A** is 1-5/8 inch; flange height **B**, 5/8 inch. However, when the flange in employed to retain a small piercing punch, height **B** should not be less than 1-1/2 times the piercing punch diameter **C** for stability.

8-15. SHEDDERS

Blanks produced from oiled stock tend to cling to the face of the blanking punch. Spring loaded shedder pins, applied to one side of the punch, will break the adhesion and free the blank from the punch face to to prevent "double blanking." Three methods of applying shedder pins are available. At **A,** the shedder pin for a small blanking punch is made short, headed, and backed up by a spring and socket set screw. The pin is made from drill rod, hardened, and polished. A clearance hole is provided in the punch holder for removal of the assembly for punch sharpening.

In another method, the shedder can be made long as at **B.** Its head bears against the top of the blanking punch, and it is similarly backed up by a spring and socket set screw.

At **C,** a Vlier shedder is illustrated. This device is available from the Vlier Engineering Co. A self-contained assembly, the shedder consists of a threaded housing containing a shouldered shedder pin and back-up spring. The assembly is inserted in a hole tapped through the blanking punch, and is backed up by a socket set screw. Screwdriver slot **D** is used to remove it for punch sharpening.

8-16. TO APPLY SHEAR

For cutting large openings in blanks, "shear" (machining punch face so that cutting edge will be presented at an angle to the surface of the material to be cut) is applied to the face of the punch to reduce shock on the press, the force required, and blanking noise. Shear, properly applied, reduces by one quarter the force required to blank metals thicker than ¼ inch. When thinner stock is blanked, the reduction in force is as large as one third. Shown here is the most common method of shearing with the face of a large punch. Shear depth **A** is made two thirds the thickness of the material. Radius **B** removes the sharp corner to avoid a focal point for stock fracture.

8-17. ALTERNATE METHOD

This is a better method of providing angular shear to a punch. The material is securely gripped at the corners between the punch and die members, and is gradually cut toward the center. Shear is usually applied for openings larger than 5 by 5 inches, and over 1/16 inch thick.

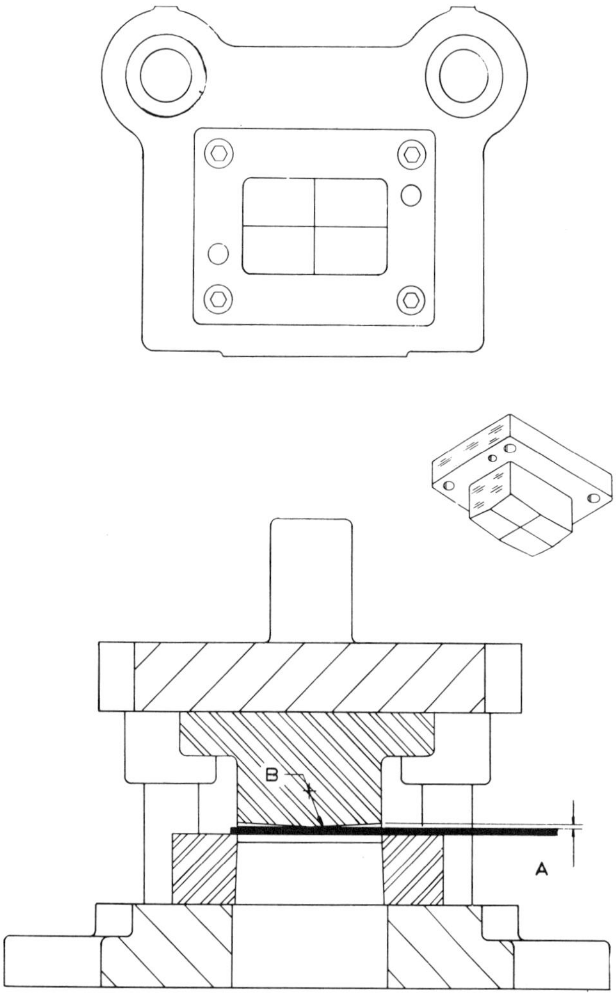

Fig. 8-16. Punch configuration for applying shear in cutting large openings.

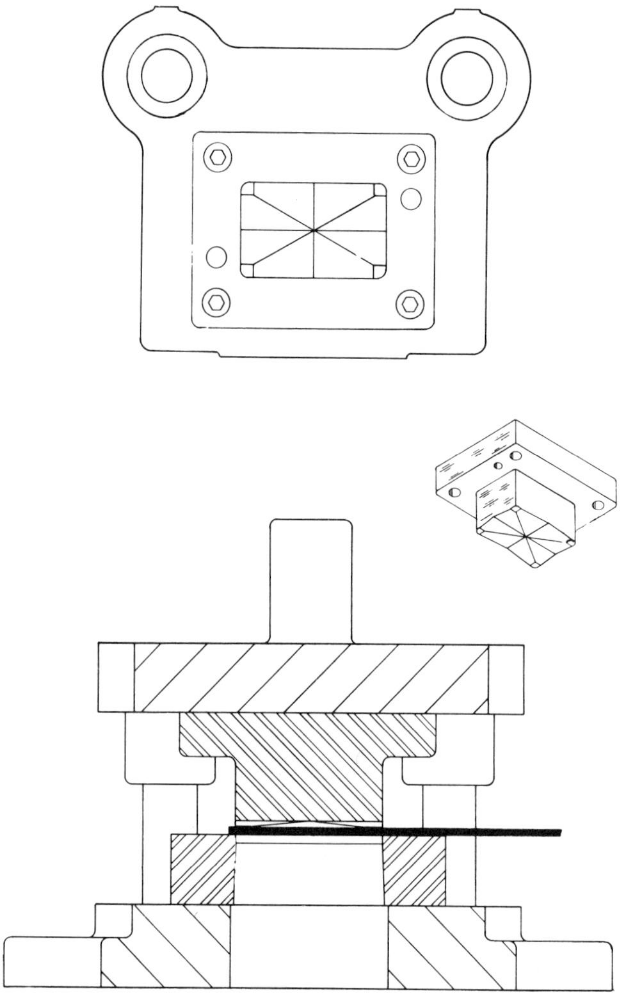

Fig. 8-17. An alternate punch configuration for applying shear.

8-18. PROVIDING FOR SHEAR IN ROUND PUNCHES

Round punches can provide a shearing action by scalloping the face of the punch in a series of waves around the periphery. A hole is first drilled through the center to provide relief for the cutting tool which applies the scalloping. Here again, shear depth should not exceed two-thirds the thickness of the stock.

8-19. COMMERCIAL COMPOSITE PUNCHES

Composite blanking punches can be purchased commercially and are used extensively for large blanks. A tool steel ring **A** is torch-cut to the shape required. Machine steel base **B**, torch-cut to fit within the opening in the tool steel ring, is welded in position. The soft steel base supports the tool steel ring around its inner periphery to prevent excessive distortion in hardening. It also provides a soft inner flange for applying screws and dowels which fasten the blanking punch to the die set.

8-20. PUNCH SECTIONS

Large blanking punches are made of sectional components, screwed and doweled to the punch holder of the die set, with sections butting against each other. A number of types of these composite sections are available to the designer. At **A**, the section is machined from a rectangular bar of tool steel, the original bar being shown in phantom lines. This method is obviously wasteful of material and labor. At **B** is illustrated a commercially available punch section whose original shape is denoted by phantom lines. Far less machining is required to finish this bar than that of the previous example. At **C** is a commercially available punch section that can be purchased in long bars and cut into required lengths as necessitated by the tool design. **D** illustrates another commercial product. It can be forged to irregular contours without the tool steel member (**A**) breaking away from the softer machine-steel base (**B**). **E** through **H** are further examples of punch sections which are available commercially.

These composites all have tool steel cutting members electrically welded to machine steel bases. The soft base prevents excessive distortion in hardening, and it provides a soft flange for easy and accurate machining for screws and dowels.

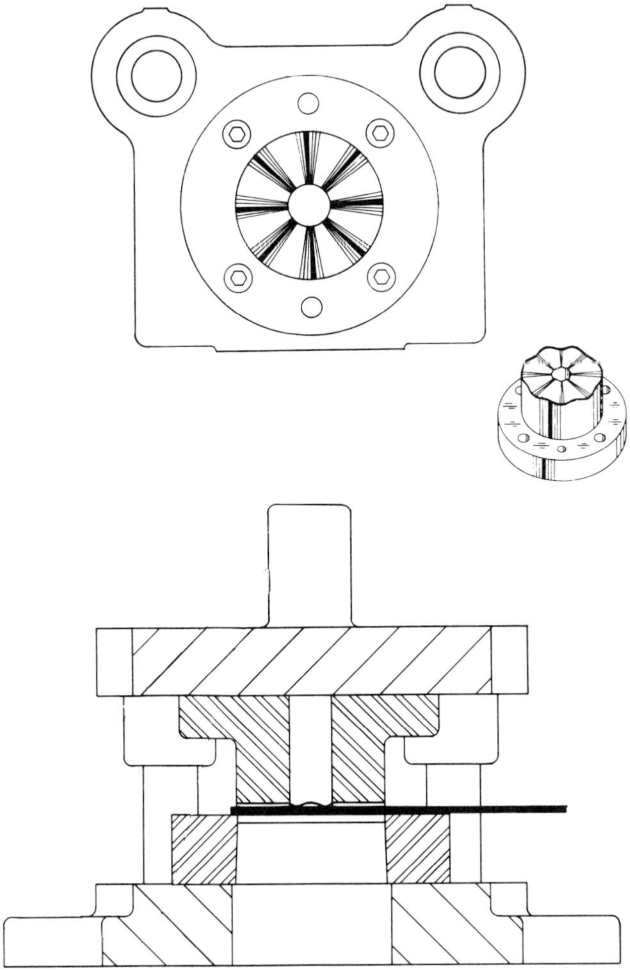

Fig. 8-18. Scalloping provides means of applying shear in cutting round holes.

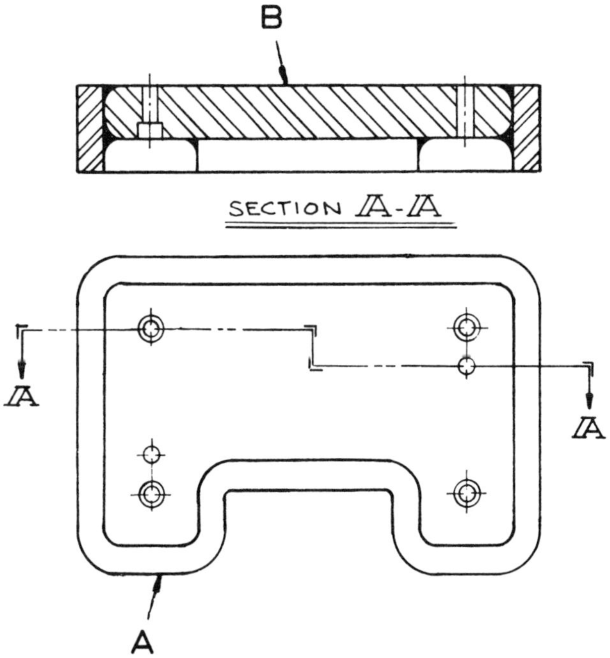

Fig. 8-19. Commercially available composite punch for large blanks.

8-21. CONSTRUCTION

Various arrangements of composite sections are shown. It is obvious from the flexibility with which members can be fabricated that almost any large blanking punch can be built from composite sections no matter how intricate the part contour. Layouts for composite blanking punch sections are drawn at the same time as die sections. This was illustrated in Fig. 7-18 of Section 7, "How to Design Die Blocks." Referring to the illustration, the following list gives the names of the various sections:

A. Straight
B. Ribbed
C. Double
D. Face contoured
E. Contoured and ribbed
F. Forged
G. Forged and ribbed
H. Outside flange
I. Inside flange.

8-22. PROPORTIONS

These are the recommended proportions of composite blanking punch sections. Lengths of straight sections usually do not exceed 12 inches. Curved sections are ordinarily not made longer than 8 inches.

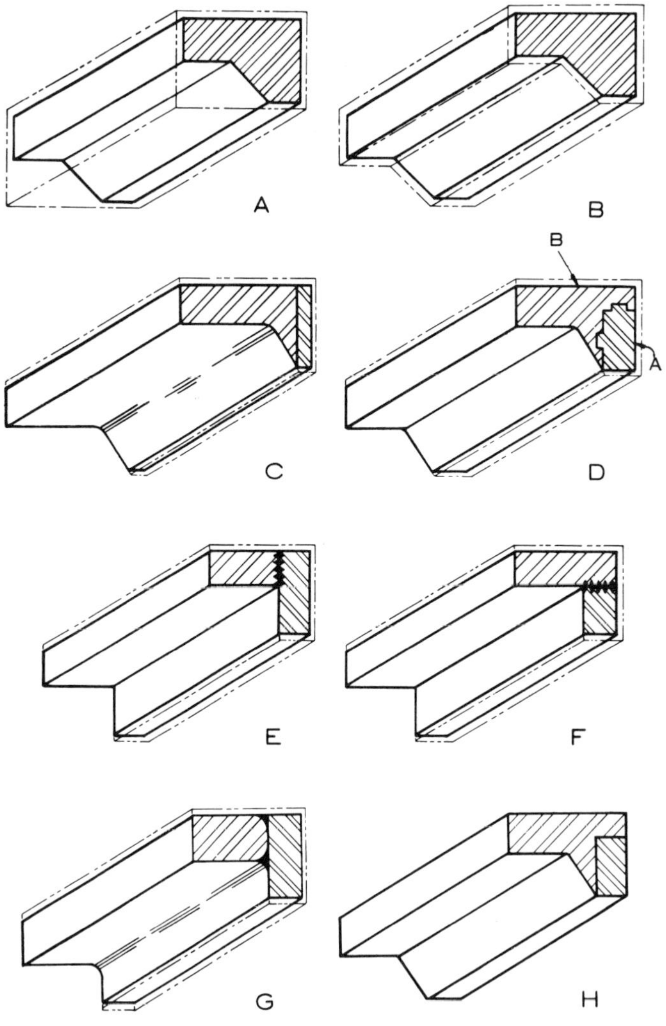

Fig. 8-20. Various commercially available composite sections available to the designer.

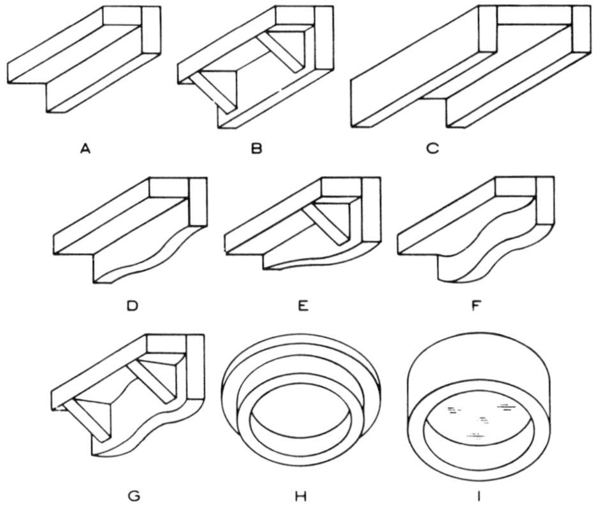

Fig. 8-21. Various arrangements of composite sections.

PROPORTIONS OF COMPOSITE PUNCH SECTIONS

STRIP THICKNESS	A	B	C	D	USE RIBS
0 to 3/64	1				
3/64 to 3/32	1 1/4				
3/32 to 9/64	1 1/2				
9/64 to 7/32	1 3/4				
7/32 to 5/16	2				
		2	1	3 min.	
		2 1/2	1	3 min.	
		3	1	3 min.	
		3 1/2	1 1/4	3 1/2 min.	*
		4	1 1/4	4 min.	*
		4 1/2	1 1/4	4 1/2 min.	*
		5	1 1/4	5 min.	*
		5 1/2	1 1/4	5 1/2 min.	*
		6	1 1/4	6 min.	*
		6 1/2	1 1/2	6 1/2 min.	*
		7	1 1/2	7 min.	*
		7 1/2	1 1/2	7 1/2 min.	*
		8	1 1/2	8 min.	*
		8 1/2	1 1/2	8 1/2 min.	*
		9	1 1/2	9 min.	*
		9 1/2	1 1/2	9 1/2 min.	*
		10	1 1/2	10 min.	*

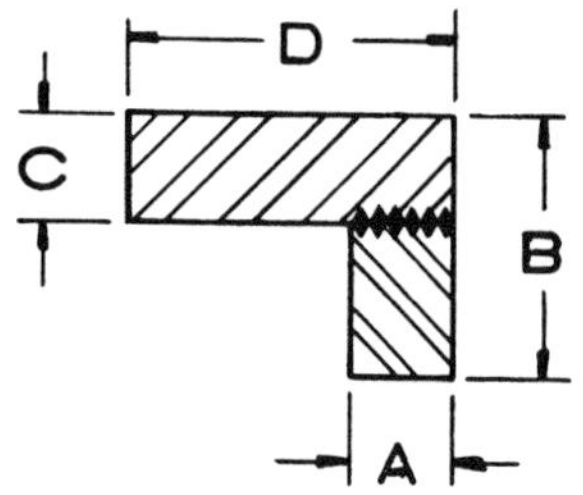

Fig. 8-22. Table of recommended proportions of composite blanking punch sections.

Section 9

HOW TO DESIGN PIERCING PUNCHES

Piercing punches are usually the weakest link in any die design. Therefore, the following factors must always be taken into consideration:

1. Make the punches strong enough so that repeated shock in operation will not cause fracture
2. Slender punches must be sufficiently guided and supported to insure alignment between punch and die members and to prevent buckling
3. Make provision for easy removal and replacement of punches in the event of breakage.

Illustrated are twenty-nine methods of designing and applying piercing punches to aid the designer in selecting the best type for the particular job. This list covers frequently used perforators.

9-1. SHOULDER PUNCHES

Probably the most commonly used type, shoulder punches are made from a good grade of tool steel, hardened, and ground all over. They are readily available from a number of suppliers.

Diameter **A** is a press fit in the punch plate. Diameter **B**, which extends at least 1/8 inch, is a slip fit for good alignment while pressing. Shoulder **C** is usually made 1/8 inch larger in diameter than **A**. Shoulder height **D** is 1/8 to 3/16 inch, depending on size. Piercing diameter **E** is always on the high side of tolerance. For example: If the hole is dimensioned $\frac{0.501}{0.500}$ diameter on the part print, the punch diameter would be made 0.501 inch. The blending radius which connects diameters **B** and **E** should be as large as possible and the surface polished smooth because ridges would present focal points for fracture.

9-2. GUIDING IN THE STRIPPER

In first-class dies, small punches under 3/16 inch in diameter are usually guided in hardened bushings pressed into the stripper. Larger punches are often guided, particularly when cutting heavy stock if there is a possibility of punch deflection upon contact with the strip. These guide bushings are hardened, then ground on both inside and outside surfaces. Headless drill bushings can often be used for the same application.

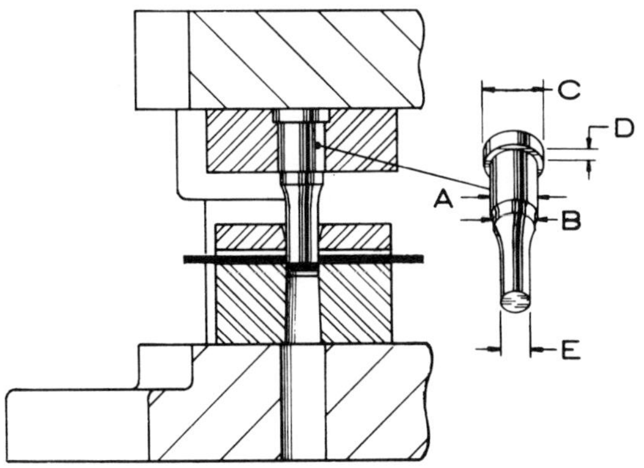

Fig. 9-1. Commonly used shoulder punch.

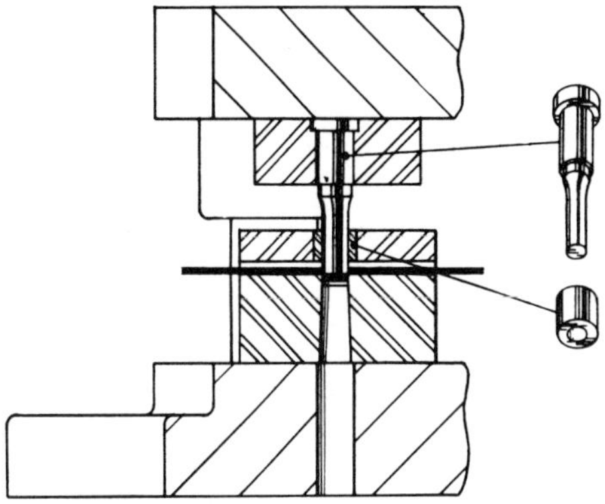

Fig. 9-2. Hardened bushings pressed into the stripper are used for guiding small punches.

9-3. BACKING PLATES

When heavy stock is being pierced, the punch head is backed up by a backing plate, pressed into a counterbored hole in the punch holder. This plate distributes the thrust over a wider area, and it prevents the punch head from sinking into the relatively soft material of the die set. Backing plates are made of tool steel, hardened, and ground. The small hole through the die set serves two purposes: 1. To accomodate the pilot on the counterbore and 2. to allow the backing plate to be pressed out for die repair.

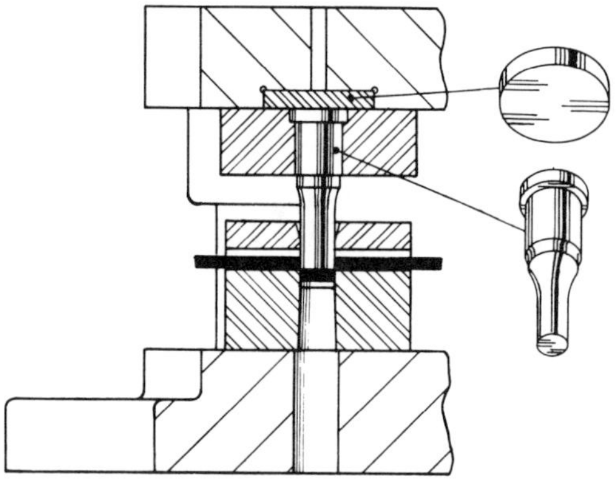

Fig. 9-3. Backing plate distributes thrust over a wide area.

9-4. SET SCREWS BACK UP THE PUNCH

Two socket set screws back up the piercing punch in this application. This method of retaining piercing punches has become widely used in recent years and it should be selected whenever possible. Its main advantage is the ease with which a broken punch can be removed and a new one inserted without the necessity of dismantling any part of the die. When dimensioning, make sure that the tap drill for the threaded hole is larger than the punch head.

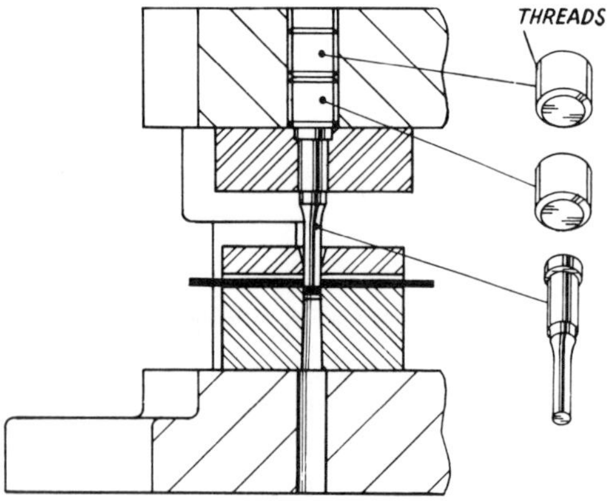

Fig. 9-4. Set screws used for backing up a piercing punch.

9-5. A SET SCREW HOLDS THE PUNCH

For short-run dies, when low accuracy requirements exist, this inexpensive type of punch may be used. It is made of drill rod, machined to size at the cutting end. An angular flat is ground on the punch body for the point of the set screw. However, the set screw has a tendency to "throw over" the punch by the amount of clearance. Therefore, this construction should never be used in first class dies.

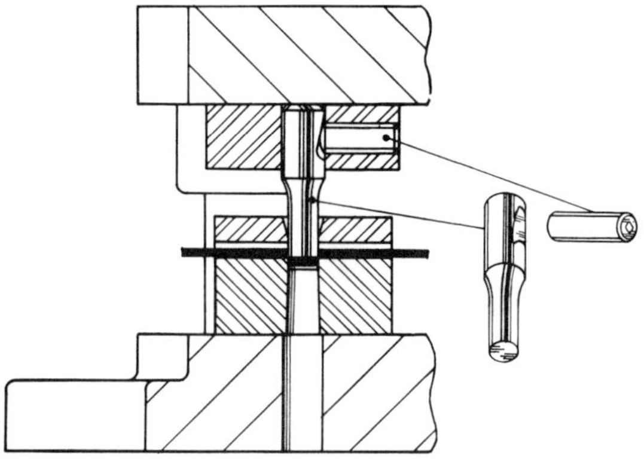

Fig. 9-5. Set screw is used to hold punch in short-run dies.

9-6. BRIDGING THE GAP

When the punch is located a greater distance from the punch plate edge than standard set screw lengths, a drill rod spacer is used between the punch and the set screw.

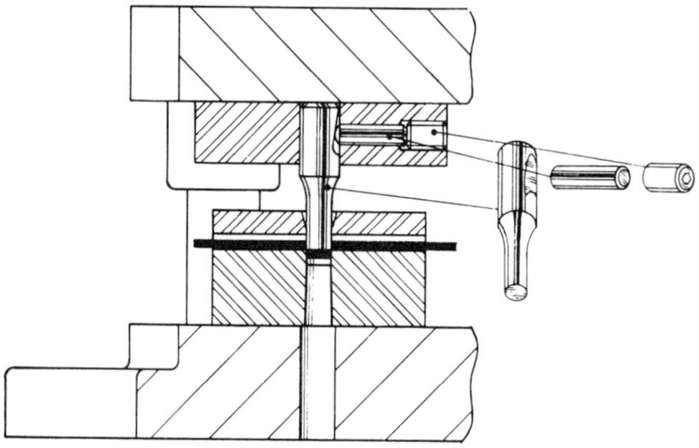

Fig. 9-6. Using a drill rod spacer when punch is a great distance from punch plate edge.

9-7. LARGE PUNCHES

Punches over 1-1/4 inch in diameter are relieved at the center of the cutting face for ease of sharpening. When cutting heavy stock the annular cutting ring **A** is often scalloped to relieve the shock on the press.

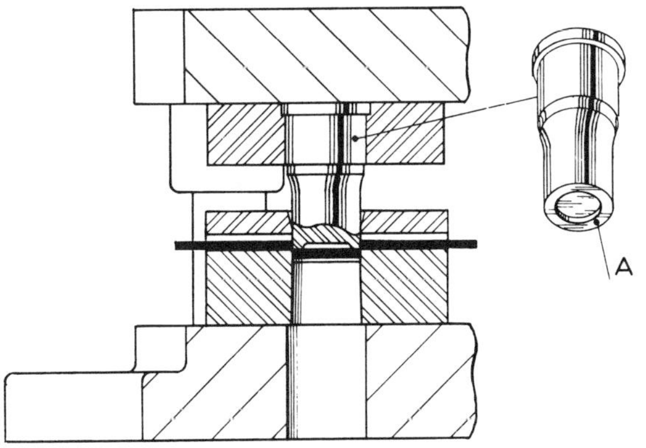

Fig. 9-7. Large punches are relieved at center for ease of sharpening.

9-8. STEPPING SMALL PUNCHES

A small punch adjacent to a large one is made shorter by two-thirds of the stock thickness. Some material flow occurs as the large punch penetrates the strip. With both punches the same length, the small one would deflected slightly, resulting in a nicked cutting edge and eventual breakage.

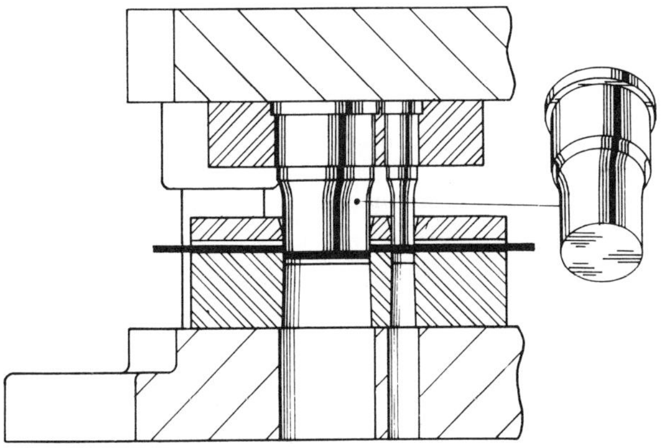

Fig. 9-8. Small punch is made shorter to prevent deflection, nicking and breakage.

9-9. SOFT PLUGS

When a small piercing punch is retained in the flange of a hardened blanking punch, a soft shouldered plug is pressed into the flange, then bored to retain the piercing punch. Modern practice is to harden only the cutting end of the blanking punch leaving the flange soft. No bushing is then required.

9-10. SPLIT-LEVEL PIERCING

To avoid excessively long piercing punches when punching stepped shapes, add an auxilliary die block, as at **A**. In this manner both punches can be made the same length for maximum strength and ease of construction.

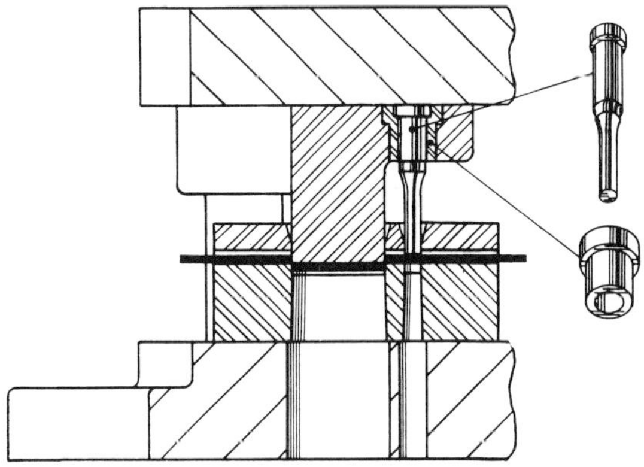

Fig. 9-9. Soft shouldered plug is used to retain small piercing punch in flange of large blanking punch.

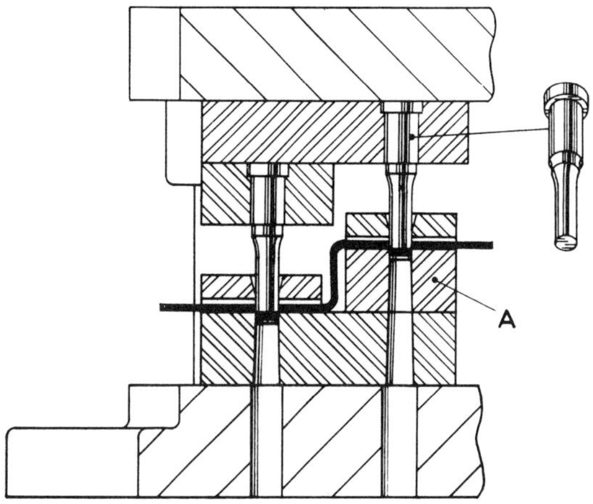

Fig. 9-10. Use of auxiliary die block (A) avoids use of excessively long piercing punches.

9-11. A COMMERCIAL PUNCH

These standardized punches are held in their retainers, and also kept from turning, by spring-backed steel balls. These bear against spherical seats machined in the punches. A simple tool pushes up the ball, depressing the spring, for removal of the punch for sharpening or replacement.

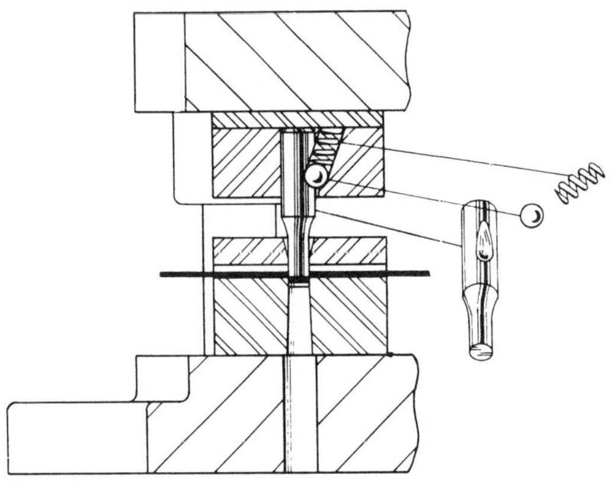

Fig. 9-11. Punch is held in place by spring-backed steel balls.

9-12. ANOTHER COMMERCIAL PUNCH

These standardized punches are held in their retainers, and also kept from turning, by special socket head cap screws, the heads of which bear against grooves machined in the punches. The heads of the retaining screws have milled clearance radii so it is only necessary to give them a quarter turn for removal of the punches.

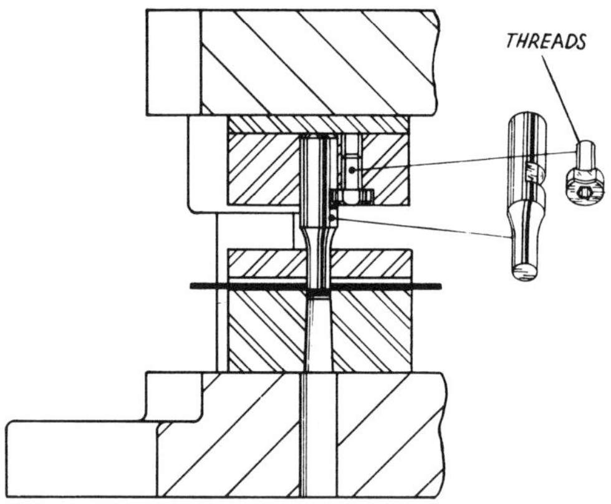

Fig. 9-12. Punch is held in place by a special socket head cap screw.

9-13. PEENING THE HEAD

It is difficult and expensive to machine shoulders on punches of very small diameter. For this reason, they are made of plain drill rod for their entire length. One end is peened to form a head and this is finished to an 82 degree included angle to fit standard countersunk holes. At assembly, the top of the punch plate is ground so the peened heads come flush with its surface. These punches should invariably be backed up by a hardened plate and guided in the stripper. When properly supported in this manner, these punches will pierce holes with diameters as small as twice the thickness of the stock.

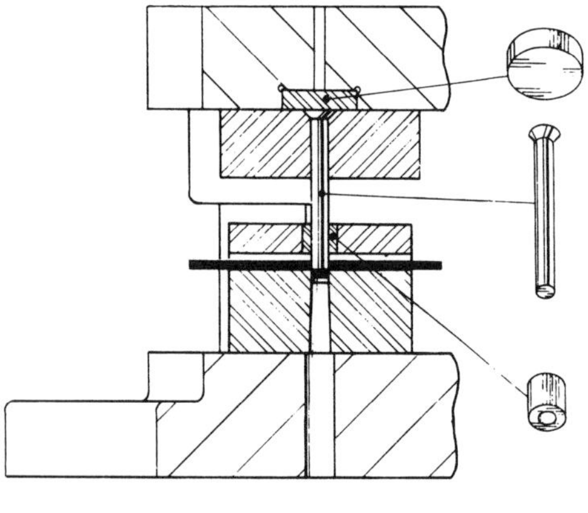

Fig. 9-13. Piercing punch is made by peening head on drill rod and grinding to shape and length.

9-14. CLOSE PERFORATING

Tiny peened-head punches are often arranged in great numbers at very close center distances, as when perforating coffee strainers and similar parts. Such multiple units are backed up by one large hardened plate and the punches are guided in holes in the stripper.

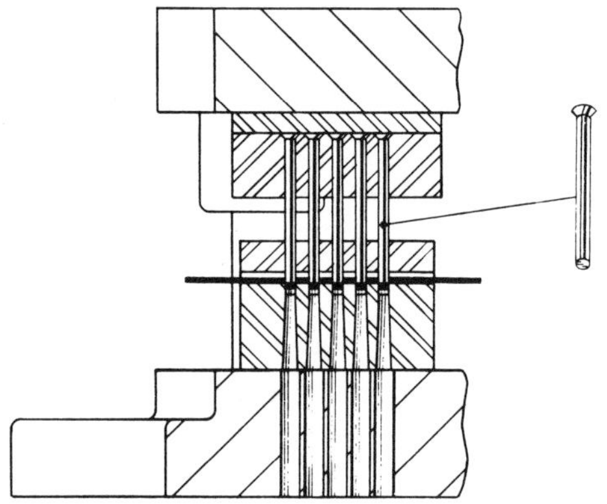

Fig. 9-14. Arrangement of tiny peened-head punches for perforating strainers.

9-15. STEPPED PERFORATORS

Closely spaced peened-head punches, when piercing thicker stock, should be staggered so that not all punches enter the strip at once. This practice prevents excessive punch breakage due to crowding of the metal. Two-thirds of the thickness of the stock is generally allowed as an offset on punch length.

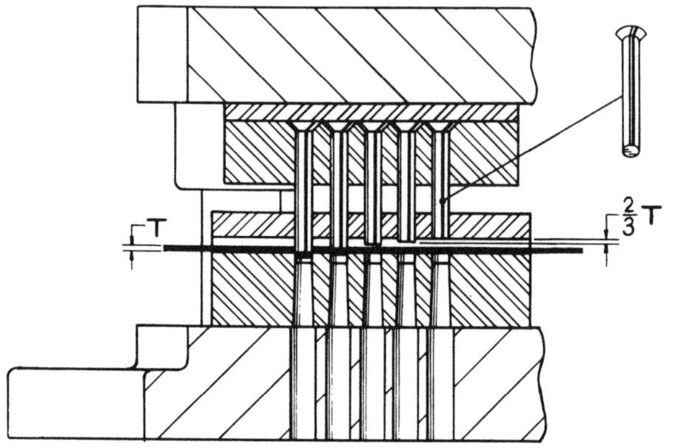

Fig. 9-15. Punches are staggered to prevent breakage and crowding of metal.

9-16. ALTERNATE METHOD

Here is another method of staggering closely spaced punches. The center punch enters the material first. Succeeding punches at either side enter by steps. These, again, are made shorter by two-thirds of the thickness of the stock

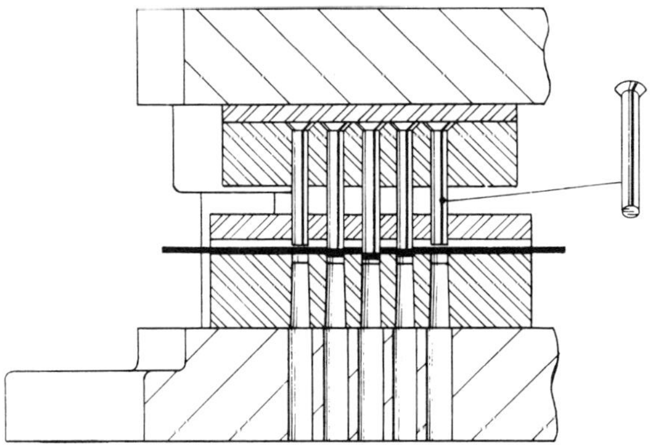

Fig. 9-16. Another method of staggering closely spaced punches.

9-17. QUILL SUPPORT

Very small peened-head punches can be held in quills and guided in hardened bushings pressed into the stripper. When replacing the punches, simply remove them from their quills and insert new ones. They are backed up by either a hardened plate or socket set screws.

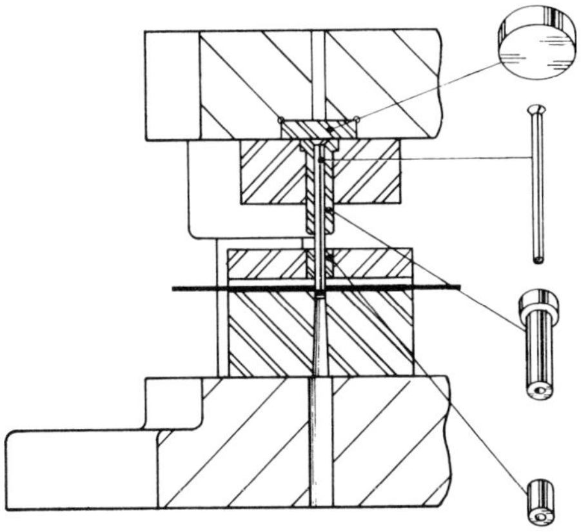

Fig. 9-17. Support for small peened-head punches is provided by a quill in punch plate and hardened bushing in stripper.

9-18. GUIDING THE QUILL

Another method of providing lateral support to a small peened-head punch is to guide the quill itself in a hardened bushing in the stripper plate. In this way the punch extends from the quill only a very short distance for maximum stiffness.

9-19. ONE QUILL – TWO PERFORATORS

Two or more closely spaced peened-head punches can be held in a single quill. The quill is kept from turning by a flat machined on one side of its head. This flat bears against one edge of a slot machined in the punch plate. The quill is guided in a hardened bushing in the stripper and the punches are backed up by a backing plate.

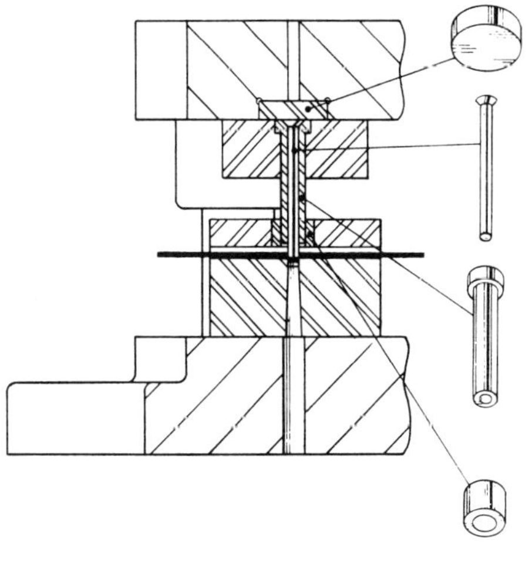

Fig. 9-18. Sometimes the quill itself is guided by a hardened bushing in the stripper.

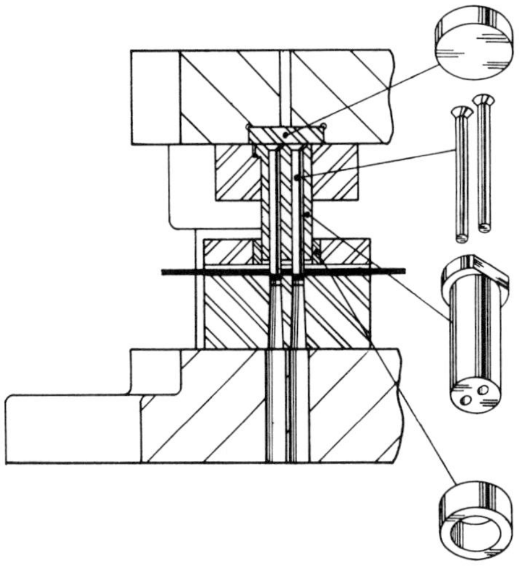

Fig. 9-19. Two very closely spaced peened-head punches held in a single quill.

9-20. BIT PUNCHES

Tiny bit punches, made of top-grade material, are held in a small quill, backed up by a hardened plug. These components are, in turn, held in a larger quill. In this way the punches can be made of expensive material, but the cost compares favorably with larger punches made of lower grade steel.

9-21. DURABLE PUNCHES AND SLEEVES

An ingenious method of supporting and guiding slender punches was patented by the Durable Punch and Die Company. Headed punch **A** is guided and supported for its entire length in two intermeshing sleeves **B** and **C**. The punch extends out of these supporting sleeves only when actually going through the material to be cut. As you may know, a slender needle, passed through a

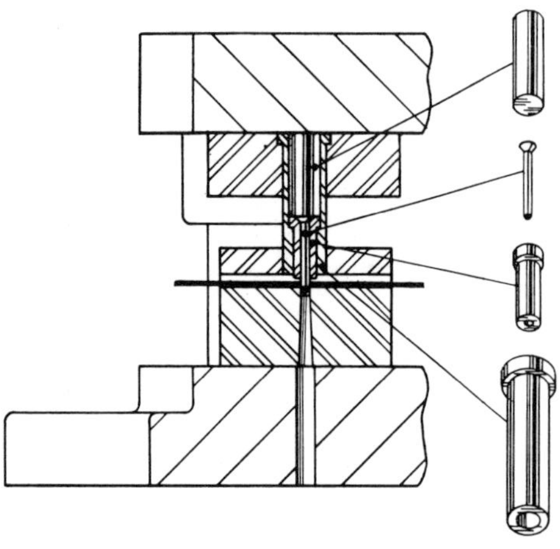

Fig. 9-20. Bit punch enclosed in small quill and in turn enclosed in larger quill and backed up may be made of expensive material.

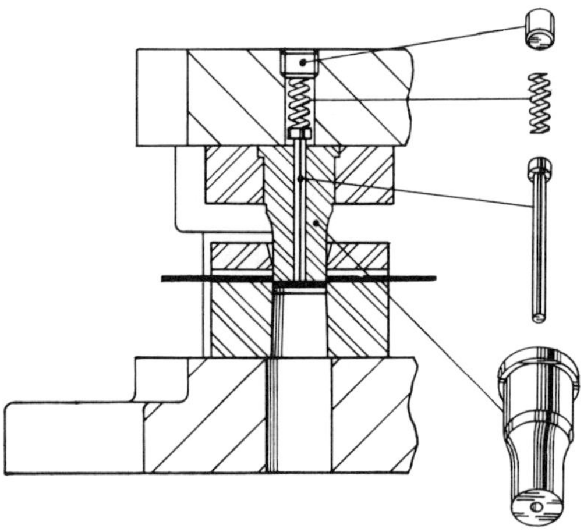

Fig. 9-22. Shedder pin incorporated into piercing punch to overcome tendency of slug to follow piercing punch out of die hole.

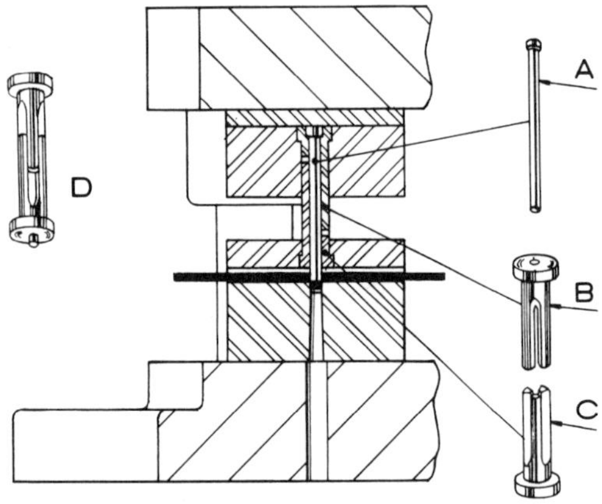

Fig. 9-21. Method of supporting punches with intermeshing sleeves.

cork, can be driven entirely through a coin by a single hammer blow because of the support given by the surrounding cork. The intermeshing action of Durable sleeves supports the punch in much the same manner, allowing the piercing of extremely small holes whose diameters are as little as one-half of the material thickness. A complete Durable assembly is shown at **D**.

9-22. SHEDDER

When piercing some thin materials, the slug tends to follow the piercing punch out of the die hole. This can be a serious problem in progressive dies. To overcome the trouble, incorporate a shedder pin in the punch. This headed pin is backed up by a spring and set screw. Piercing punches provided with shedders are available from a number of suppliers.

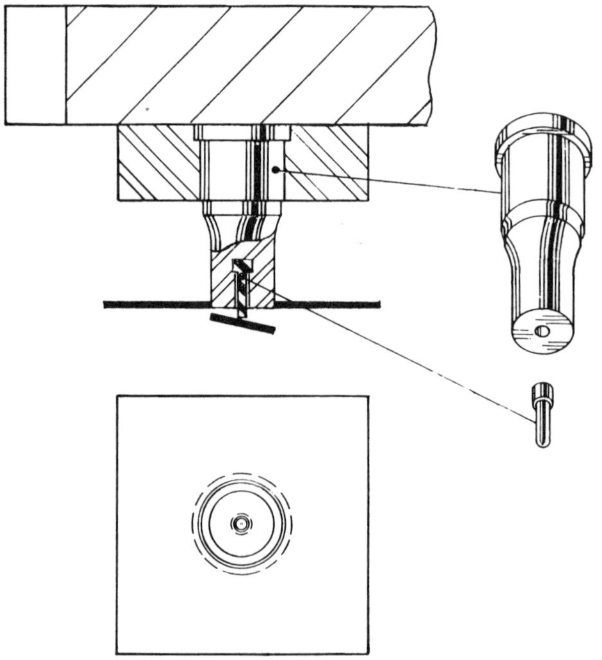

Fig. 9-23. Shedder pin made of rubber.

9-23. RUBBER SHEDDER

Another method of preventing slugs from pulling up out of the die hole is to insert a rubber bumper in a recessed hole in the punch. The rubber shedder is made with a head to keep it from falling out in operation.

9-24. TEMPORARY SOLUTION

If slugs are pulling up in the die tryout stage, grind two slots in the cutting face of the punch as shown. This is a temporary measure and a shedder pin should be applied later.

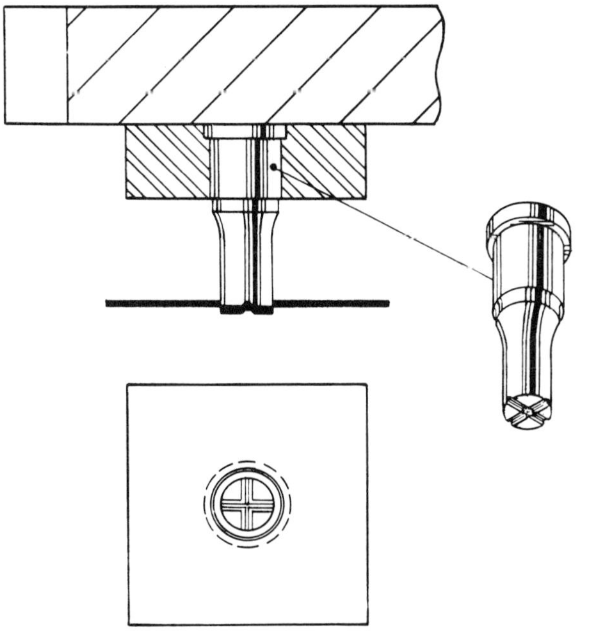

Fig. 9-24. Slots ground on end of punch temporarily serves same purpose as shedder pin.

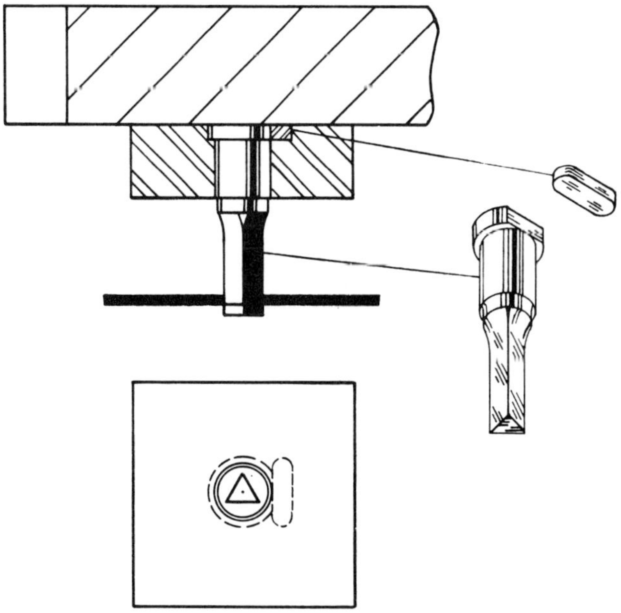

Fig. 9-26. Retaining key keeps punch from turning.

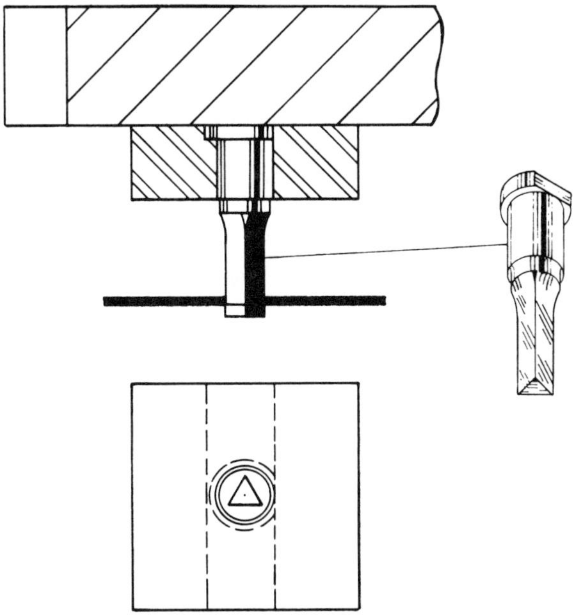

Fig. 9-25. Flat on punch head of irregular punch keeps it from turning.

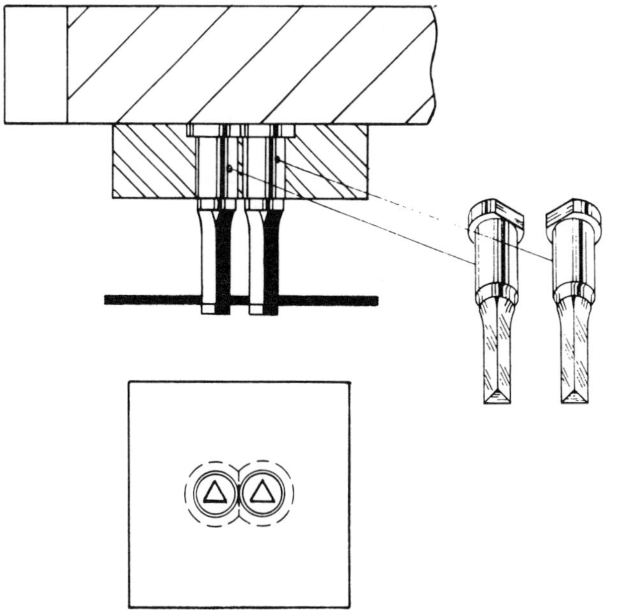

Fig. 9-27. Mating flats of irregular punches keep them from turning.

9-25. IRREGULAR PUNCHES

A good method of keeping an irregular punch from turning is to machine a flat in the punch head. This flat bears against one edge of a slot machined in the punch plate. A snug fit is required.

9-26. RETAINING KEY

Another good method of keeping an irregular punch from turning is to machine a flat in the punch head, as before, and insert a small round-end key in a slot end-milled in the punch plate. This method is particularly useful in multiple station progressive dies where space is limited.

9-27. MATING FLATS

Where irregular punches are close together, an excellent method of keeping them from turning is to machine flats on both punch heads. These flats bear against each other with a good fit, keeping the punches in alignment.

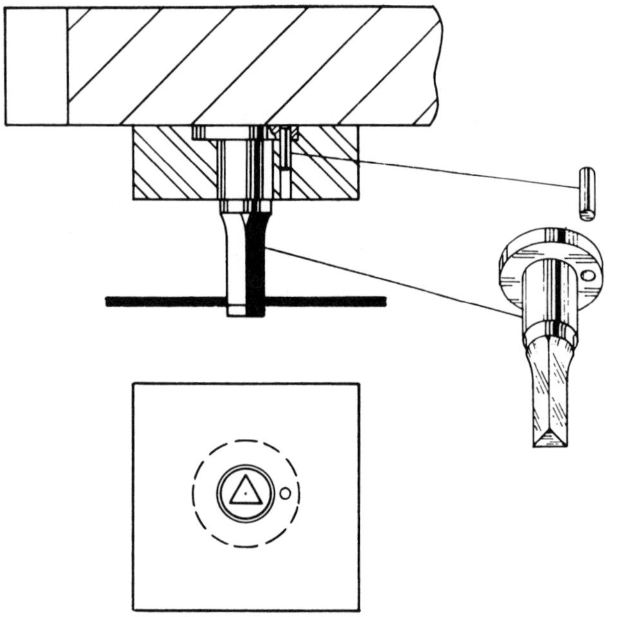

Fig. 9-28. Large punch head may be doweled to keep punch from turning.

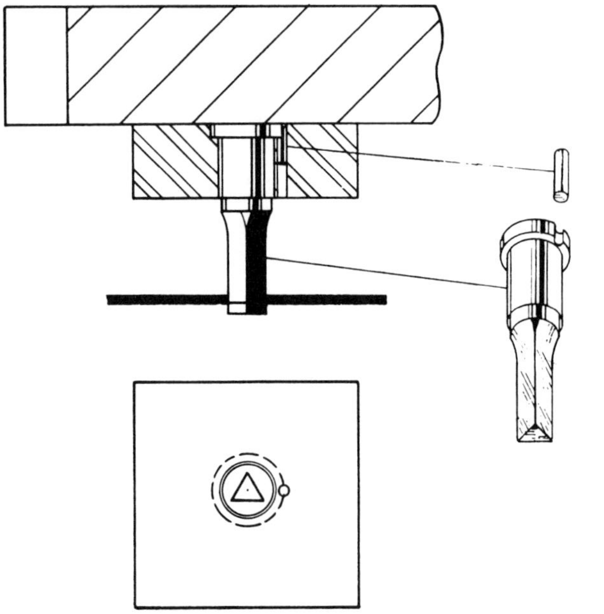

Fig. 9-29. A dutchman (small dowel) may be pressed in place on periphery of punch head to keep punch from turning.

9-28. DOWELED PUNCH HEAD

If an irregular piercing punch is provided with a large head, a small dowel, pressed through both the head and the punch plate will keep the punch in good alignment. This is not considered as good a method as those previously described, but it is used frequently for low and medium production dies.

9-29. DUTCHMAN.

A dutchman, that is, a small dowel pressed half in the punch head and half in the punch plate will keep the punch from turning. As in the previous example, this method should not be used for first-class dies. It is more suitable for temporary dies and dies for low production.

Section 10

HOW TO DESIGN PUNCH PLATES

Punch plates hold and support piercing, notching, and cut off punches. They are usually made of machine steel, but can be made of tool steel, left soft, for high-grade dies. Punch plates range from small simple blocks for holding single piercing punches to large, precision-machined plates for holding hundreds of perforators. Important design considerations include:

1. Adequate thickness for proper punch support
2. Good doweling practice to insure accurate location
3. Sufficient screws to overcome stripping load.

Illustrated are twenty methods of designing punch plates, and applying them to various types of dies. These methods further explain Step 5 in Section 5, "Fourteen Steps to Design a Die".

10-1. PUNCH PLATES FOR SINGLE PUNCHES

A punch plate for holding a single punch is made square, and with sufficient thickness for good punch support. Two socket cap screws, applied at the corners, resist stripping pressure, while dowels at the other two corners provide accurate location. Minimum distance from plate edges to screw centers, **A**, is 1½ times screw diameter **B**.

10-2. PUNCH PLATE BUSHINGS

Slender punches which are subject to breakage and replacement are retained in hardened bushings pressed into the punch plate. The top of the guide bushing is ground flush with the top of the punch plate after pressing in.

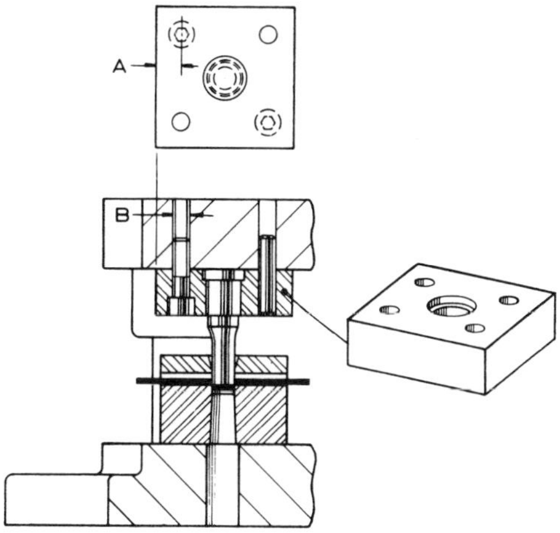

Fig. 10-1. Punch plate for a single punch.

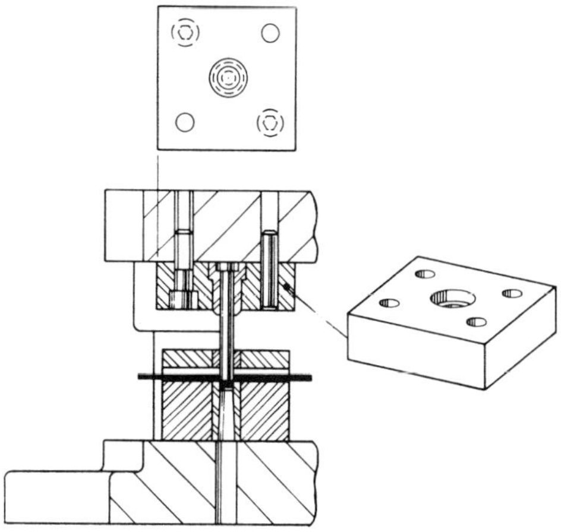

Fig. 10-2. Hardened bushing retains slender punch subject to breakage and replacement.

10-3. IRREGULAR PUNCHES

Punch plates that retain irregular piercing punches should have a slot machined in the top surface to the same depth as the punch head. A flat, ground in the punch head, bears against one edge of this slot to prevent turning.

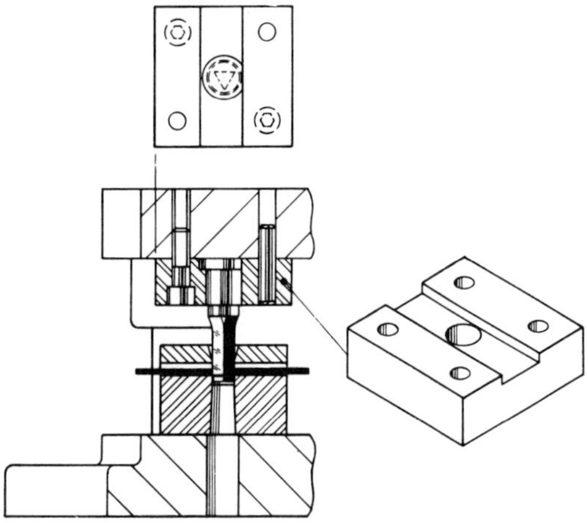

Fig. 10-3. Slot in the top of punch plate provides means of preventing turning of punch.

10-4. MULTIPLE IRREGULAR PUNCHES

Two, or more, irregular punches which are in line can be kept from turning by a single slot machined in the top of the punch plate, against which flats on the punch head bear. This slot should be made large enough to clear the opposite sides of the punch heads.

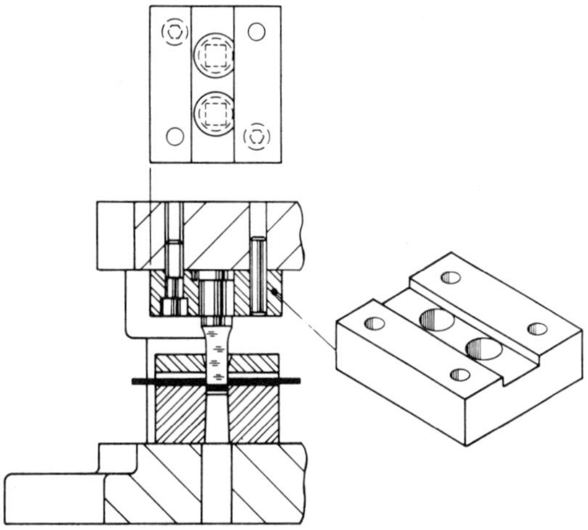

Fig. 10-4. Slot may also be used to keep two or more punches from turning.

10-5. KEYED PUNCHES

Where space is limited a slot is end-milled in the top of the punch plate to the same depth as the counterbored hole for the punch head. A small round-end key is inserted in this slot. The key engages a flat, machined in the punch head, to keep it from turning.

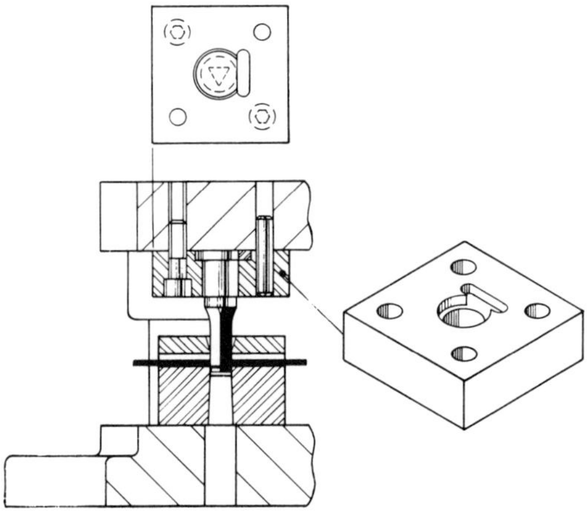

Fig. 10-5. Slot milled in the top of the punch plate retains key for preventing turning.

10-6. STRIPPING FORCE

When center distances are small, a single punch plate can hold a number of piercing punches. When a large number of punches is retained, the stripping force should be calculated to insure that sufficient screws are used to fasten the punch plate to the die set. The formula:

$$P = \frac{L \times T}{0.00117}$$

where: L = Length of cut, in this case the sum of the perimeters of all piercing punch faces.
T = Thickness of stock
P = Force in pounds to effect stripping.

A discussion on the safe strength of screws is given to accompany Fig. 16-30 in the section on fasteners.

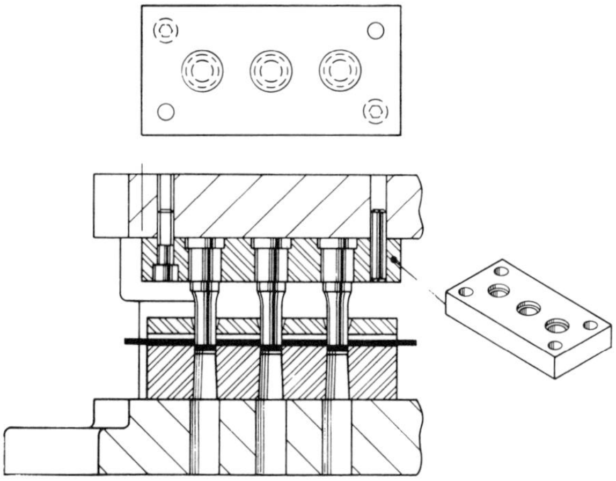

Fig. 10-6. Single punch plate holds three punches as their center distances are small.

10-7. INDIVIDUAL PUNCH PLATES

When piercing punches are some distance from each other, they are preferably held in individual punch plates, as shown. This condition is encountered in large piercing dies.

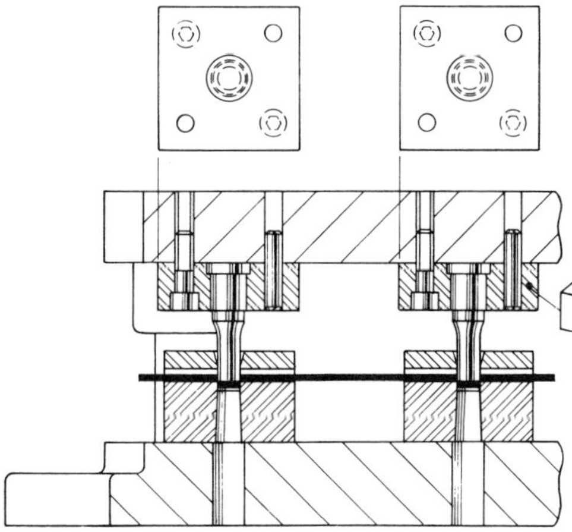

Fig. 10-7. Individual punch plates are used when punches are some distance from each other.

10-8. STEPPED PUNCH PLATES

When the part to be pierced has two levels, double punch plates avoid long piercing punches. Socket cap screws fasten lower to upper plate. The latter is held to the punch holder from the back. Note the double dowels. It is considered poor practice to use extremely long dowels.

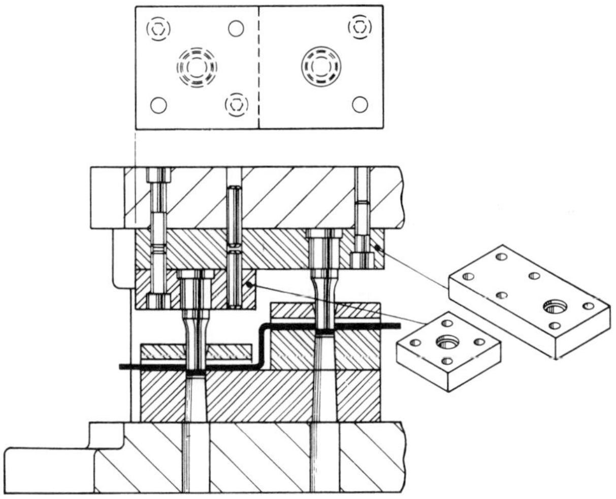

Fig. 10-8. Punch plates are stepped to avoid long piercing punches.

10-9. THICKNESS

Punch plate thickness **B** should be approximately 1½ times diameter **A** of the piercing punch. With the table, the die designer can establish punch plate thickness quickly.

10-10. STANDARDIZED PUNCH PLATES

Where large quantities of dies are produced, time and money can be saved by standardizing punch plate sizes and assigning part numbers to them. The most commonly used sizes are tabulated.

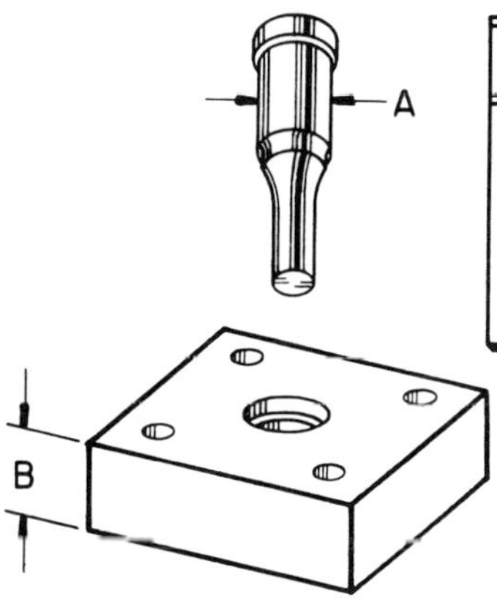

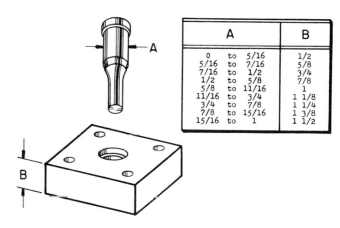

A	B
0 to 5/16	1/2
5/16 to 7/16	5/8
7/16 to 1/2	3/4
1/2 to 5/8	7/8
5/8 to 11/16	1
11/16 to 3/4	1 1/8
3/4 to 7/8	1 1/4
7/8 to 15/16	1 3/8
15/16 to 1	1 1/2

Fig. 10-9. Table for determining punch plate thickness.

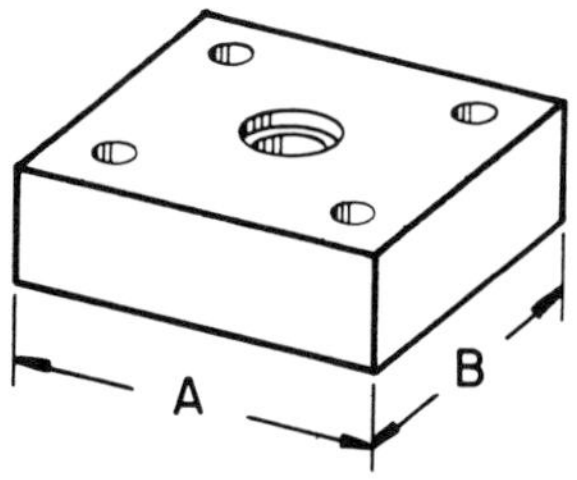

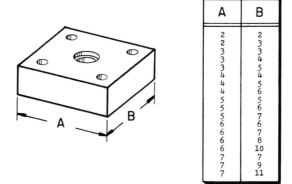

A	B
2	2
2	3
3	3
3	4
3	5
4	4
4	5
4	6
5	5
5	6
5	7
6	6
6	7
6	8
6	10
7	7
7	9
7	11

Fig. 10-10. Commonly used standard punch plate sizes.

10-11. PURCHASED PUNCH PLATES

Available from commercial sources, standard punch plates can be purchased as components to hold the piercing punches. Three styles are illustrated. At **A** is shown a round punch plate. It is machined to accommodate a hardened, spring-backed ball which engages a recess machined in the piercing punch. A hardened backing plate, made the same diameter as the punch plate flange, prevents the punch from sinking into the soft material of the punch holder of the die set. The view at **B** illustrates the more commonly used square punch plate, backed up by a hardened plate of the same size, while at **C** is shown the end-retaining punch plate, used where space is limited.

10-12. ANOTHER PURCHASED PUNCH PLATE

Also available from commercial sources are standard punch plates used to hold a line of piercing punches. They are retained by special quarter-turn screws that provide quick removal of piercing punches for replacement.

10-13. PUNCH PLATES FOR CUT-OFF PUNCHES

There are three commonly used methods of retaining small cut-off punches. At **A** a large slot, machined in the top surface of the punch plate, provides clearance for the punch head. Where space limitations exist, a narrower slot is machined as shown at **B**. End flanges **D** prevent the cut-off punch from pulling out. Where space is still more limited a recess, slightly larger than the punch head, is end-milled in the top of the punch plate, as shown at **C**.

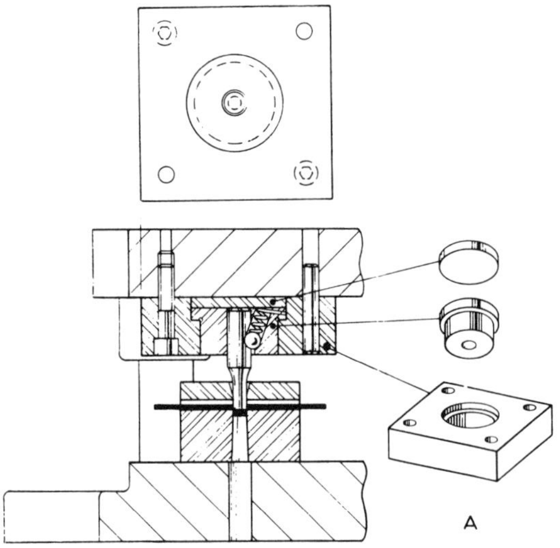

A

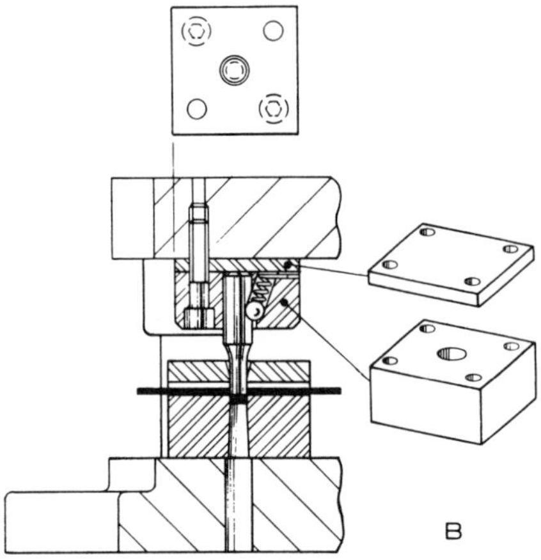

B

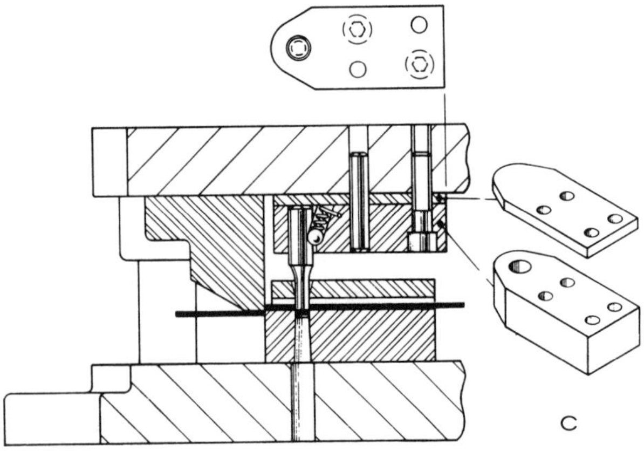

C

Fig. 10-11. Various types of punch plates that are commercially available.

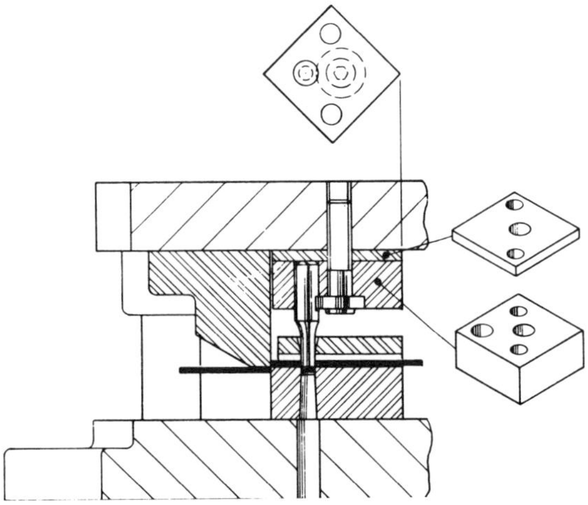

Fig. 10-12. Another type of commercially-available punch plate.

10-14. NOTCHING PUNCHES

Small notching punches are usually held in their punch plate by means of slots machined in the top surface of the plate. Three sides of the punch head bear against the bottom of the machined slot to prevent the punch from pulling out.

10-15. COMPOUND DIES

Punch plates used in compound dies are made large so they can act as a spacer for inverted die block **A**. Long socket cap screws, applied from the top of the die set, pass through clearance holes in the punch plate and are threaded into the die block.

10-16. INDIRECT KNOCKOUTS

When indirect knockouts are used, the punch plate is recessed, as at **A**, to accommodate the knockout plate **B**. In this case, the recess is shaped in the form of the letter X.

10-17. PUNCH PLATES FOR INVERTED DIES

In inverted piercing or shaving dies, the punch plate is fastened to the die holder of the die set instead of being placed in its usual position under the upper punch holder. The illustrated die shaves two holes. The punches have been inverted to make use of the pressure attachment of the press for more effective stripping.

10-18. HORN DIES

Piercing punches used in horn dies are retained in a punch plate fastened to the punch holder of the die set. This die pierces a hole in the side of a drawn cup.

10-19. SIDE-CAM DIES

Punch plates for side cam dies usually have a turned boss that engages a counterbored hole in the slide for accurate punch location. With this construction no dowels are required. The die shown at **A** pierces holes in the sides of shells when the burr is required

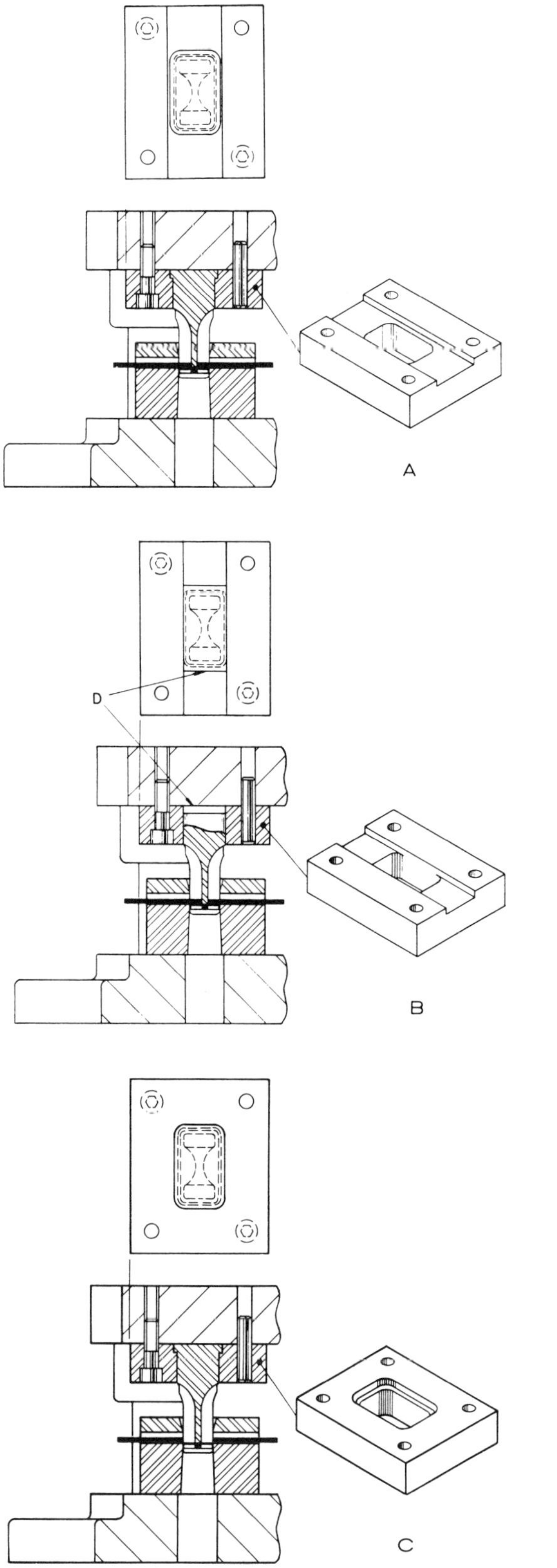

Fig. 10-13. Three commonly used methods of retaining small cut-off punches.

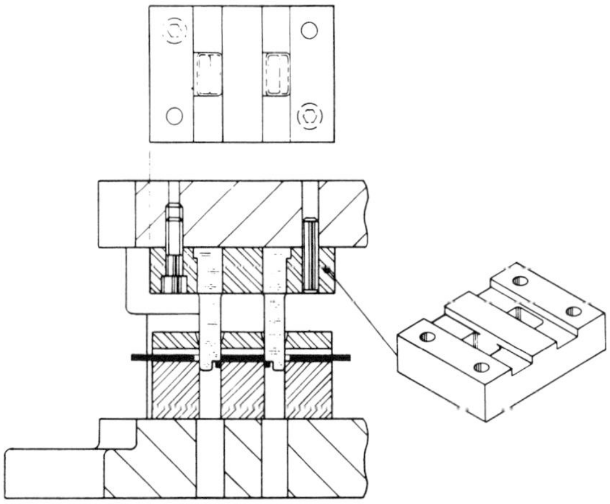

Fig. 10-14. Punch plate for notching punches.

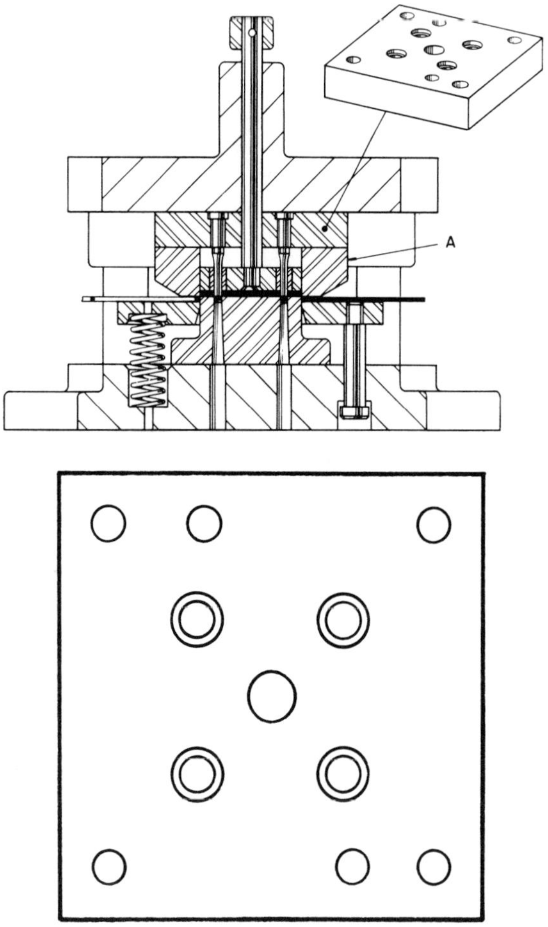

Fig. 10-15. Punch plate for compound die.

to be inside the shell. The die shown at **B** pierces in the sides of shells when the burr is required to come outside the shell. Construction of the punch plate is similar to **A.**

10-20. GUIDED PUNCH PLATES

For piercing angular holes in shells, the punch plate is made large and guided on the die set guide posts. It retains the spring-backed piercing punch **A**, which is guided in a hardened bushing **B** pressed into the punch plate. Hardened buttons limit downward travel of the punch plate.

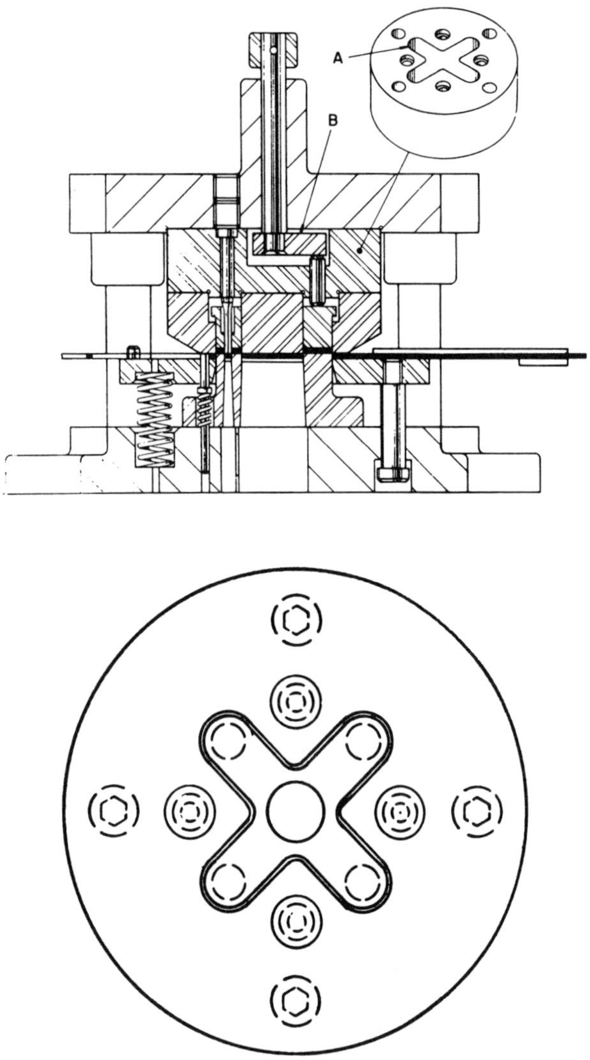

Fig. 10-16. Punch plate for indirect knockouts.

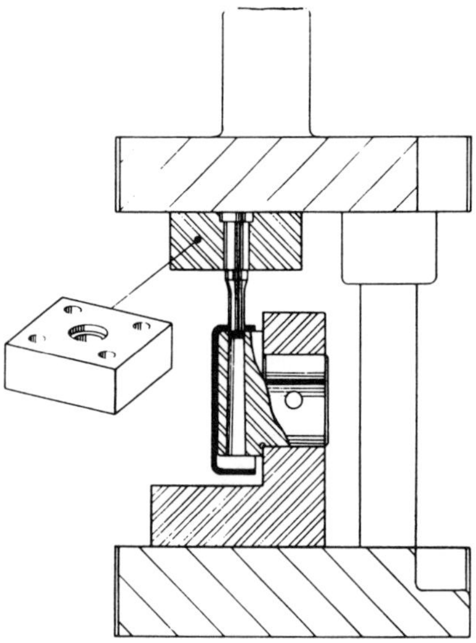

Fig. 10-18. Punch plate for horn die.

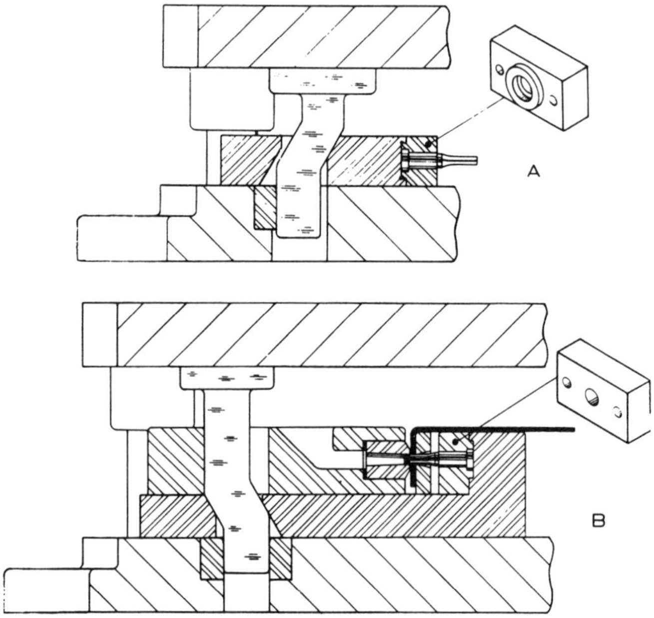

Fig. 10-19. Punch plate for side-cam die.

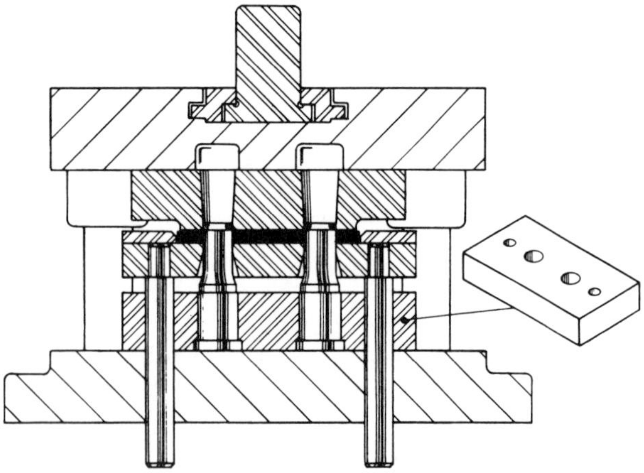

Fig. 10-17. Punch plate for inverted die.

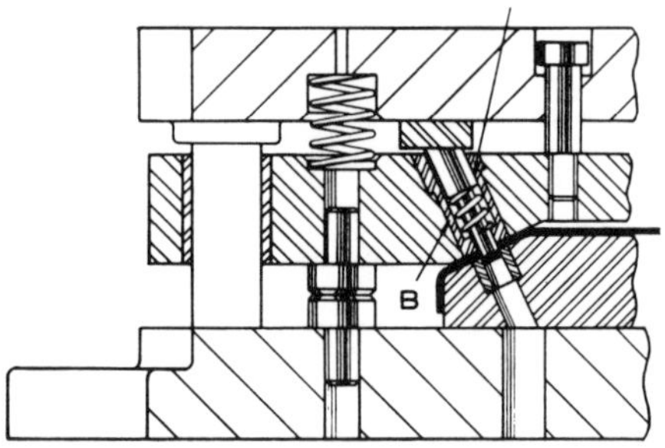

Fig. 10-20. Typical large punch plate that is guided on die set guide posts.

Section 11

HOW TO DESIGN PILOTS

Pilots play a vital role in the operation of multiple-station dies, and many press-line troubles can be traced to their faulty design. In applying pilots the following factors should always be considered:

1. They must be strong enough so repeated shock will not cause fracture. Severe shock is applied to the pilot point more often than is realized. Consider that the pilot moves a heavy material strip, almost instantly, into register. Pilot breakage increases cost of the stamping because hundreds of inaccurate parts may be produced before failures are discovered. Also, there is the danger of costly jams resulting from a broken pilot falling between the cutting edges or forming members of the die.

2. Slender pilots must be sufficiently guided and supported to prevent bending, which can cause faulty strip positioning. They should be made of a good grade of tool steel, heat treated to Rockwell C 57 to 60 for maximum toughness and hardness.

3. Provision should be made for quick and easy removal of the pilots for punch sharpening.

Illustrated in this section are numerous methods of designing and applying pilots to aid the designer in selecting the best type to use for a particular job.

11-1. SHOULDER PILOTS

The frequently used shoulder pilot **A** is retained in blanking punch **B** by a socket pilot nut **C**. Pilot holes are pierced at the first station. The strip is then located by pilots at the second and succeeding stations. The automatic stop is positioned so that the strip is stopped with a previously pierced hole 0.010 inch past its final location. The pilot moves the strip back this amount to bring it into correct register. This overtravel prevents possible cramping of the strip between pilot and automatic stop. As shown, the pilot is just contacting one side of the hole in the strip preparatory to bringing it back to true position.

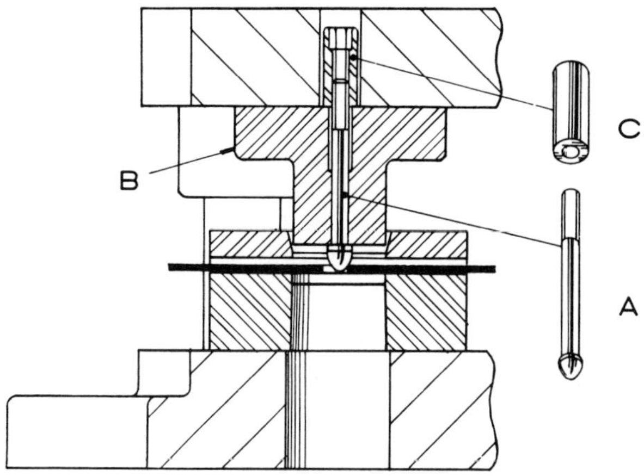

Fig. 11-1. Typical shoulder pilot.

11-2. LOCATING THE STRIP

Descent of the upper die has caused the bullet-shaped nose of the pilot to move the strip back 0.010 inch and the pilot has entered the strip hole, accurately locating it for the blanking operation. The diameter of pilot shoulder **A** is an important dimension. Too small a diameter, in relation to the hole in the strip, will produce inaccurate parts with varying dimensions between hole and part edges. Too large a dimension results in a tight fit in the strip, with a consequent tendency for the blank to be pulled up out of the die hole. This can be a serious problem in progressive dies. A successful formula is: Diameter **A** equals the diameter of the piercing punch, less 3 per cent of the strip thickness. For example: If the piercing punch diameter is 0.500, and the strip thickness is #16 gage (0.0625 inch):

$$\begin{array}{r} 0.0625 \\ \times\ 0.03 \\ \hline 0.001875 \end{array} = \text{Three per cent of strip thickness}$$

Subtracting this from the piercing punch diameter:

$$\begin{array}{r} 0.500 \\ -\ 0.0018 \\ \hline 0.4982 \end{array} = \text{Pilot diameter.}$$

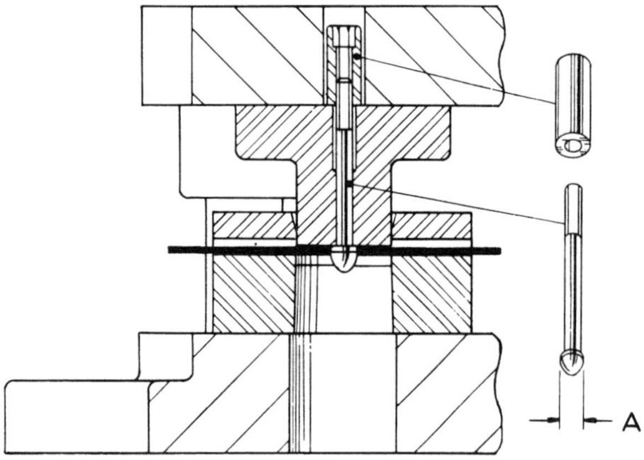

Fig. 11-2. Shoulder pilot in fully descended position accurately locates the strip.

11-3. PILOT PROPORTIONS

Further descent of the upper die has now causec' the blanking punch to penetrate the material strip to produce a blank. The shoulder pilot is used for holes **A** from ¼ to ¾ inch diameter, and it has the following general proportions: Straight engagement length **B** should be from ⅓ to ⅔ of the stock thickness. For example: For #16 gage (0.0625) this length could be made 1/32 inch. Diameter **C** is made an accurate gage fit. The length of this gage fit engagement **D** is made approximately three times pilot diameter **C**. Clearance relief diameter **E** is usually 1/32 inch larger than body diameter **C** of the pilot.

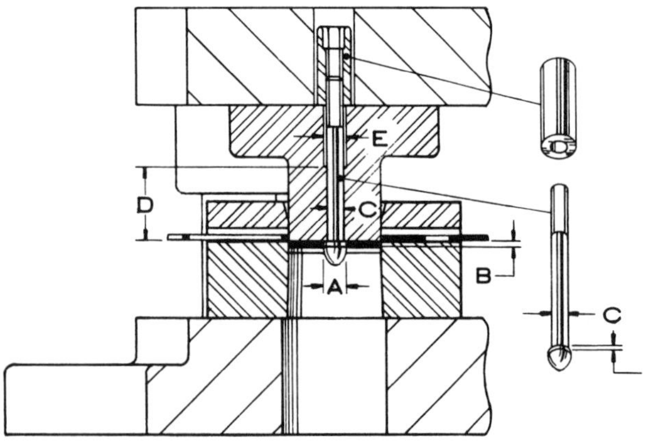

Fig. 11-3. With shoulder pilot accurately locating the strip, punch descends to blank part.

11-4. TO DRAW THE PILOT

Six steps are taken to draw the acorn-shaped head of a pilot:

1. The shank and diameter **A** of the head are drawn with light lines. This is the diameter which actually engages the hole in the strip for register. As previously noted, this diameter is 3 per cent of the stock thickness less than the diameter of the punch that pierces the hole in the strip. Thickness **B** is from ½ to ⅓ of the stock thickness.
2. The point of the compass is applied at the lower right corner and radius **R** is drawn.
3. The point of the compass is applied at the lower left corner and an opposed radius **R** is drawn.
4. A circle template is carefully applied and a smaller blending radius is drawn. This radius should be approximately ¼ of diameter **A**. It should be darkened and the line drawn to finished width at this time.
5. Lines of the two large radii are now blackened and widened to blend with the small radius.
6. The shank is completed and the pilot is now fully drawn.

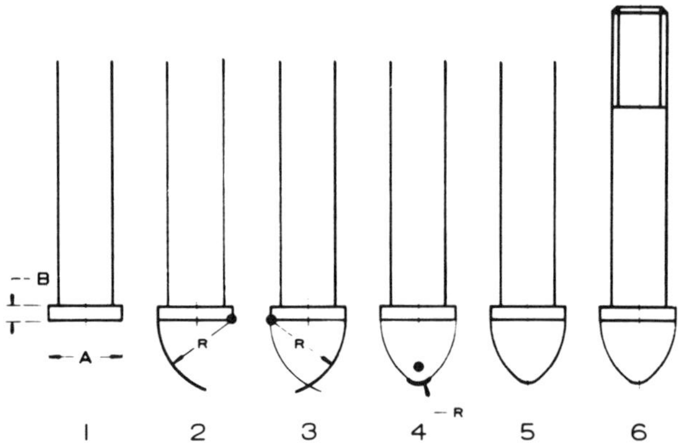

Fig. 11-4. Six steps in drawing the head of a pilot.

11-5. SLOTTED PILOT NUTS

Instead of being driven by internal hexagon wrenches, pilot nuts can be made with a screwdriver slot. While not considered as good as socket nuts, the slotted nuts do provide a quick way of making these components. Dimensions **A** and **B** are grinding allowances, normally ¼ inch, and they are consumed as the blanking punch is sharpened from time to time during the life of the die. Pilots are removed from the punch before sharpening. The gage fit (instead of a press fit) and the pilot nut, allow quick dismantling.

11-6. PILOT NUTS

Pilot nuts represent the fastest and most convenient method of fastening pilots. Their use allows the pilots to be quickly removed for sharpening without the necessity of disassembling other die parts. Standardized, and stocked in the tool crib, the pilot nuts effect substantial savings in both design and manufacture of progressive dies, and further savings on the press line in making possible quick pilot removal and replacement. The most used sizes will vary from shop to shop, depending on the general sizes of stampings to be run. Cold form the double hexagon hole before final turning of the outside diameter. Make the nuts from drill rod, heat treated; or machine steel, cyanide hardened.

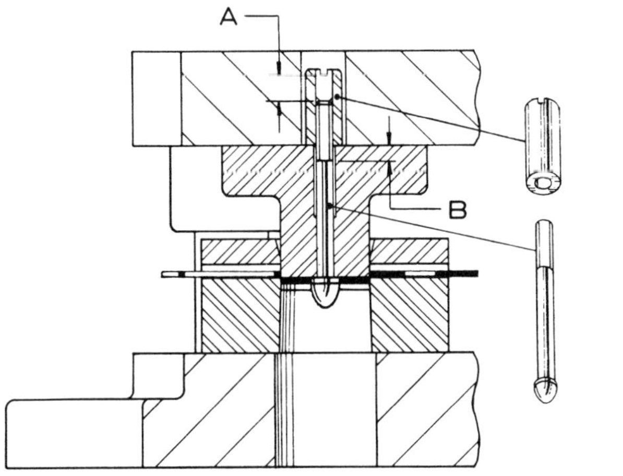

Fig. 11-5. Pilot nut with screwdriver slot may be made quickly.

11-7. SET SCREWS BACK THE PILOT

Straight, headed pilots are used when diameter **A** is from 3/16 to 1/4 inch. The head is backed up by two socket set screws. Grinding allowance **B** is 1/4 inch. Spacer washers are applied under the pilot head each time the blanking punch is sharpened to maintain proper relationship between the end of the pilot and the face of the blanking punch. Gage fit length **C** is again made approximately three times the pilot diameter.

11-8. SMALL PILOTS

For pilots under 1/8 inch in diameter, shank **A** is threaded into pilot nut **B**, and is backed up by a small set screw **C**. The entire assembly is, in turn, backed up by a large set screw **D**, threaded into the punch holder of the die set. The assembly is removed from the punch for sharpening by simply removing set screw **D**. The pilot is moved up to compensate for the amount removed from the punch face in sharpening by loosening the small set screw, raising the pilot slightly, and again locking it in place.

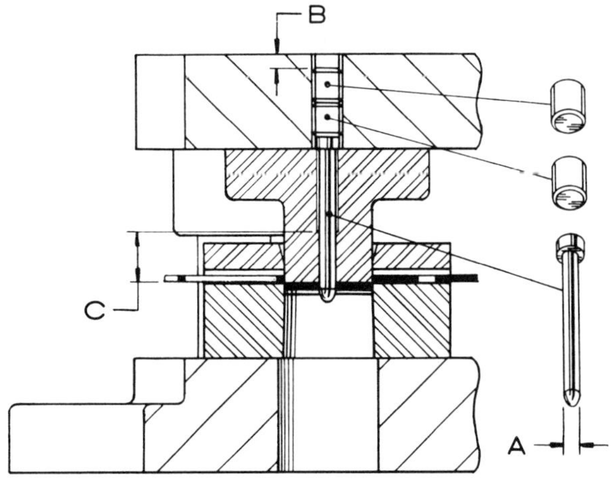

Fig. 11-7. Straight, headed pilot is used when head is backed up by two socket set screws.

11-9. LARGE PILOTS

Pilots over ¾ inch in diameter are held by a long socket cap screw drilled and counterbored into the punch holder of the die set. The pilot is threaded extra distance **A** to provide take-up for punch sharpening.

11-10. PRESS FIT PILOTS

For many years press fitted pilots were almost the only type used in press work, but now they are usually specified only for short run jobs and temporary dies. They can work loose and fall between cutting edges or forming members of the die with disastrous results, or fall through the die allowing perhaps hundreds of parts to be run through the die and spoiled because of faulty location.

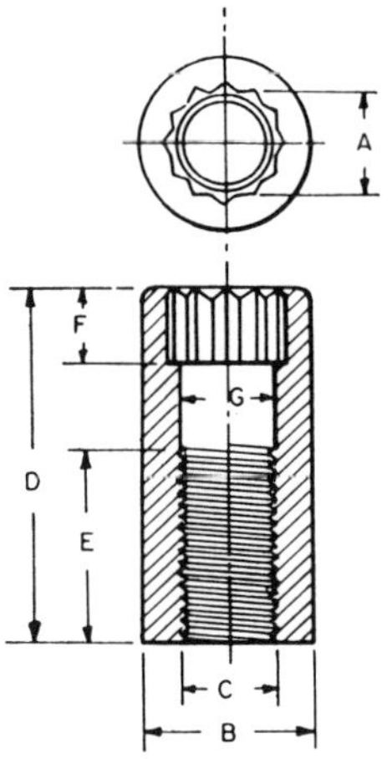

DIMENSIONS OF PILOT NUTS

Nut Size	Socket Width Across Flats	Body Dia	Tap Size NC-3	Body Lgth.	Thd Lgth.	Socket Depth	Clear Hole
	A	**B**	**C**	**D**	**E**	**F**	**G**
No. 4	1/8	0.187	#4-48	1	¼	0.076	#32(0.116)
No. 5	1/8	0.187	#5-44	1	¼	0.082	#30(0.1285)
*No. 6	5/32	0.257	#6-40	1	5/16	0.100	#27(0.144)
*No. 8	3/16	0.280	#8-36	1	3/8	0.112	#18(0.1695)
*No. 10	3/16	0.302	#10-32	1	7/16	0.142	#9 (0.196)
*¼	¼	0.403	¼-28	1	½	0.172	#F(0.257)
5/16	5/16	0.498	5/16-24	1	5/8	0.231	#P(0.323)
3/8	3/8	0.590	3/8-24	1	¾	0.250	#W(0.386)

Note: Hexagon "A" must be double, as shown
*Most frequently used sizes

Fig. 11-6. Suggested dimensions for standardized pilot nuts.

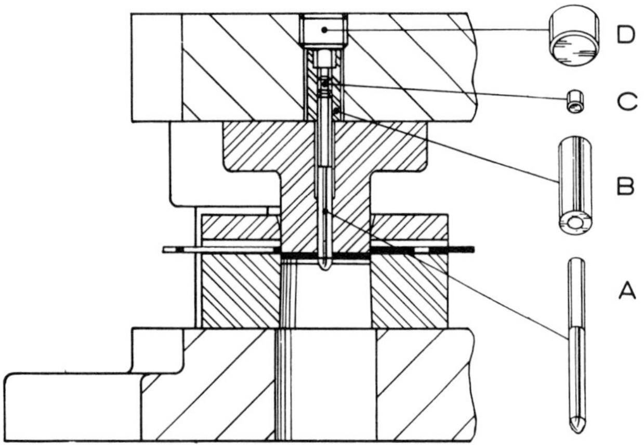

Fig. 11-8. Backing up a small pilot with 2 set screws.

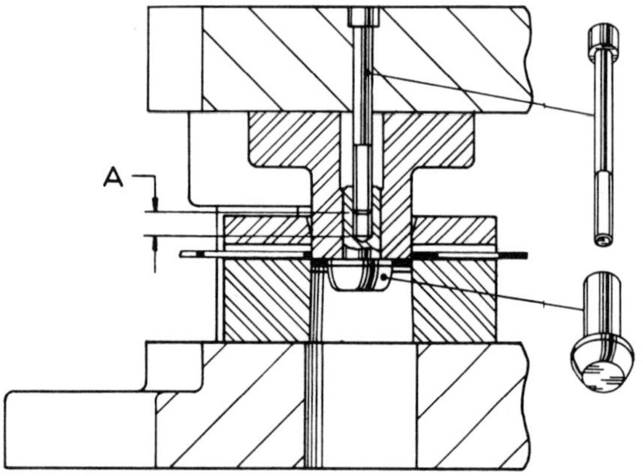

Fig. 11-9. Holding a large pilot in place using a long socket cap screw.

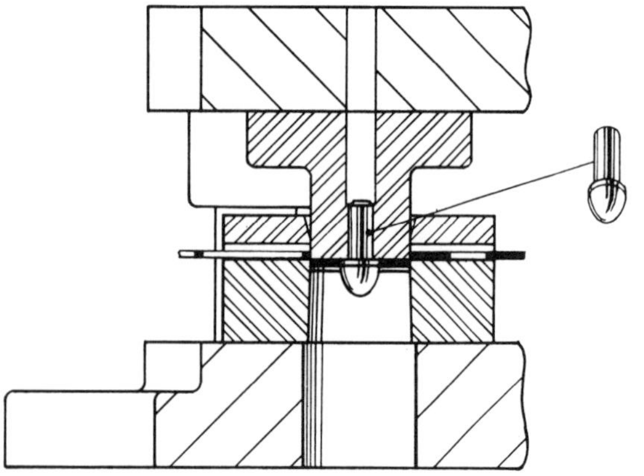

Fig. 11-10. Press fitted pilot for short runs.

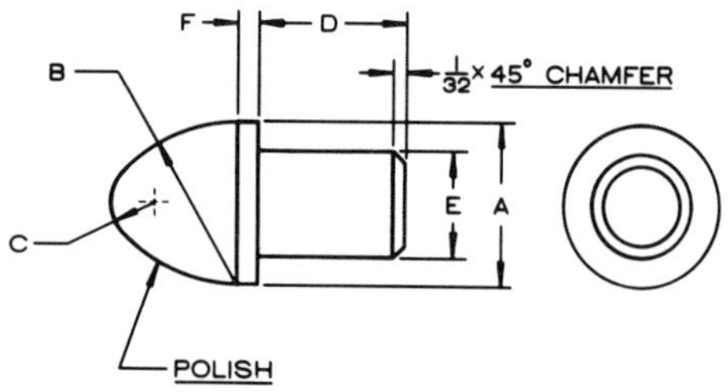

A	B	C	D	E	MAT.
1/8	1/8	1/32	5/32	3/32	D.R.
3/16	3/16	3/64	3/16	1/8	D.R.
1/4	1/4	1/16	9/32	3/16	D.R.
5/16	5/16	5/64	3/8	1/4	D.R.
3/8	3/8	3/32	7/16	9/32	D.R.
7/16	7/16	7/64	1/2	5/16	D.R.
1/2	1/2	1/8	9/16	3/8	D.R.
9/16	9/16	9/64	5/8	7/16	D.R.
5/8	5/8	5/32	11/16	15/32	D.R.
11/16	11/16	11/64	3/4	1/2	D.R.
3/4	3/4	3/16	7/8	9/16	D.R.

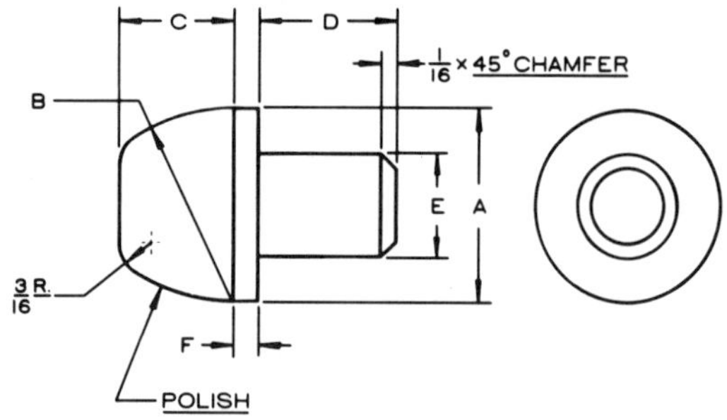

A	B	C	D	E	MAT.
13/16	13/16	1/2	15/16	5/8	T.S.
7/8	7/8	17/32	1	11/16	T.S.
15/16	15/16	9/16	1 1/8	3/4	T.S.
1	1	5/8	1 1/4	13/16	T.S.
1 1/16	1 1/16	21/32	1 5/16	7/8	T.S.
1 1/8	1 1/8	11/16	1 7/16	15/16	T.S.
1 3/16	1 3/16	23/32	1 1/2	1	T.S.
1 1/4	1 1/4	3/4	1 5/8	1 1/16	T.S.
1 5/16	1 5/16	13/16	1 11/16	1 1/8	T.S.
1 3/8	1 3/8	27/32	1 3/4	1 3/16	T.S.
1 1/2	1 1/2	15/16	1 7/8	1 1/4	T.S.

Fig. 11-11. Table of suggested dimensions of press fit pilots.

11-11. PROPORTIONS OF PRESS FIT PILOTS

Although press-fitted pilots are not employed as much as in the past, they do have a place in the design of low-production dies for running strip stock. In addition they are frequently used as locators in secondary operation dies, engaging previously pierced holes for performing other operations. This table gives dimensions of pilots from 1/8 inch to 1-1/2 inches in diameter.

11-12. IRREGULAR PILOTS

Piloting is often done in holes having irregular shape. The pilots must be radially located in a positive manner. In this example, the large, oval-shaped pilot is kept from turning by a dowel inserted half in the pilot body and half in the blanking punch. This dowel is made a press fit in the pilot and a gage fit in the punch to provide for easy removal of the pilot for sharpening the punch face.

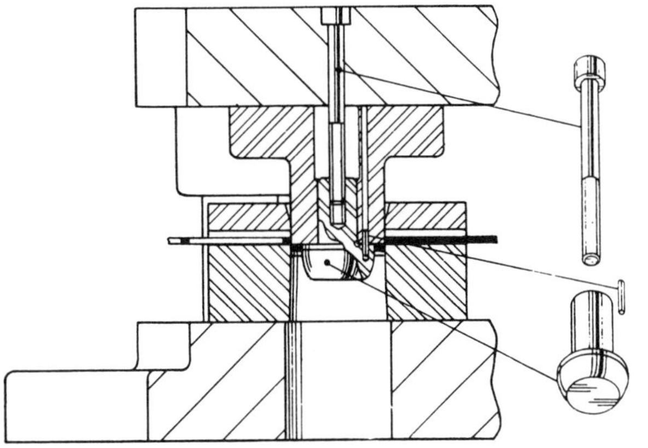

Fig. 11-12. Fixed oval-shaped pilot.

11-13. METHODS OF PILOTING

There are two methods of piloting in progressive dies:

1. Direct piloting consists of piloting in holes pierced in that area of the strip which will become the blank. All pilots described so far have been direct pilots which are retained in the blanking punch. All pilots described hereafter in this section will be indirect pilots.

2. Indirect piloting consists of piercing holes in the scrap area of the strip and locating in these holes at subsequent operations. Direct piloting is the preferred method, but certain blank conditions require indirect piloting, as will be explained.

11-14. PART CONDITIONS

There are seven conditions that require indirect piloting:

1. Close tolerance on holes. Pilots can enlarge holes in pulling a heavy strip to position.

2. Holes too small. Frail pilots can break or deflect in operation.

3. Holes too close to edges of the blank. Distortion can occur in the blank because of enlargement of holes.

4. Holes in weak area. Piloting in projecting tabs is impractical because they may deflect before the strip is pulled to position.

5. Holes spaced too closely. Piloting in closely spaced holes does not provide an accurate relationship between holes and outside edges of the blank.

6. Blanks without holes. Piloting is done in the scrap area whenever the blank does not contain holes.

7. Projections in hole. Whenever the hole in the blank contains weak projections which could be bent down by the pilot, indirect piloting should be selected.

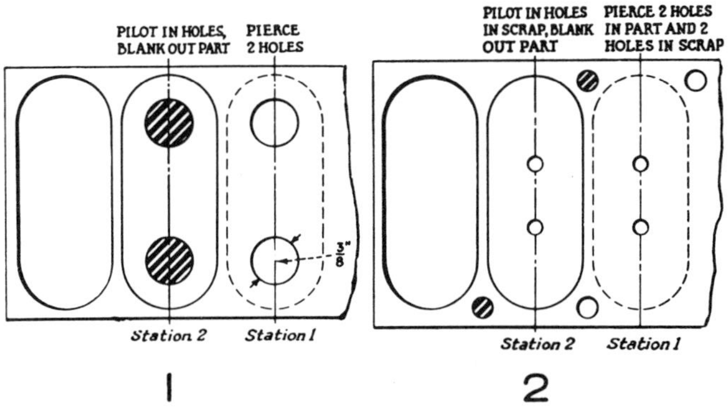

Fig. 11-13. Examples of direct piloting (1) and indirect piloting (2).

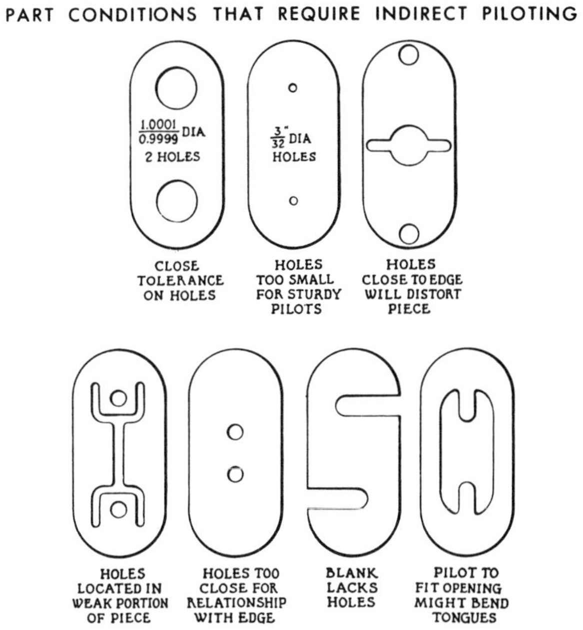

Fig. 11-14. Part conditions that require indirect piloting.

11-15. INDIRECT PILOTS

Indirect pilots are similar in construction to piercing punches. In this view, the pilot is shown contacting the strip prior to moving it back 0.010 inch into correct register. Body diameter **A** is made a light press fit in pilot plate **B**. Diameter **C**, usually 1/8 inch long, is a sliding fit in the pilot plate for accurate alignment while pressing in. Shoulder diameter **D** is generally made 1/8 inch larger than body **A**. Shoulder height **E** is from 1/8 to 3/16 inch, depending on pilot size.

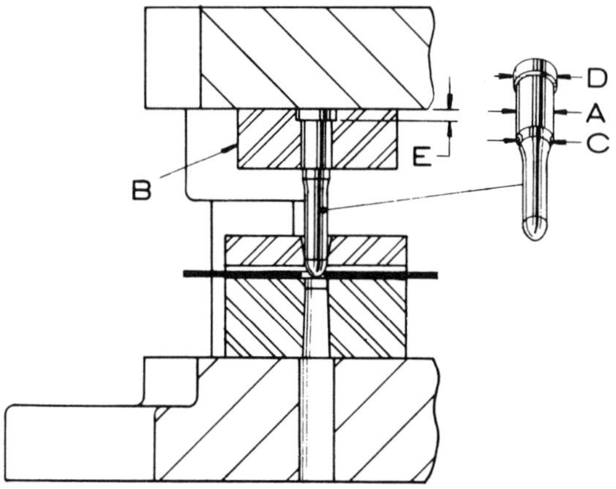

Fig. 11-15. Indirect pilot is similar to piercing punch.

11-16. POSITIONING THE STRIP

Descent of the upper die to the lowest position causes the pilot to move the strip back 0.010 inch to correct position. The pilot then enters the hole in the die block to accurately position the strip. This die block hole is made the same as for piercing punches, with a ¼ degree taper per side. Directly underneath, a clearance hole is applied to the die holder of the die set. In cases of mis-feed, pilots will punch the strip like a piercing punch, and provision must be made for disposal of slugs. Otherwise, they would pile up and in time the pilot would be broken. Pilot diameter **A** should be a good sliding fit in the pilot hole in the die block, with from 0.0002 to 0.0005 inch maximum clearance allowed.

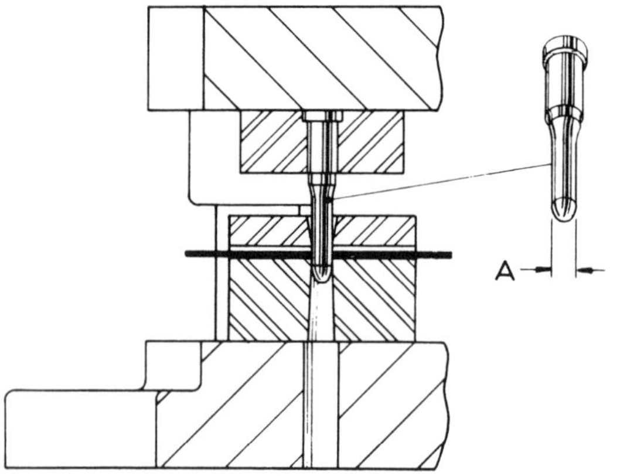

Fig. 11-16. Indirect pilot in full descended position accurately locates the strip.

11-17. GUIDING IN THE STRIPPER

Where considerable accuracy is required, and when moving a large, heavy strip, the pilot is guided and supported in a hardened bushing pressed into the stripper plate. The pilot must be a good sliding fit within this bushing, with from 0.0002 to 0.0005 inch maximum clearance specified.

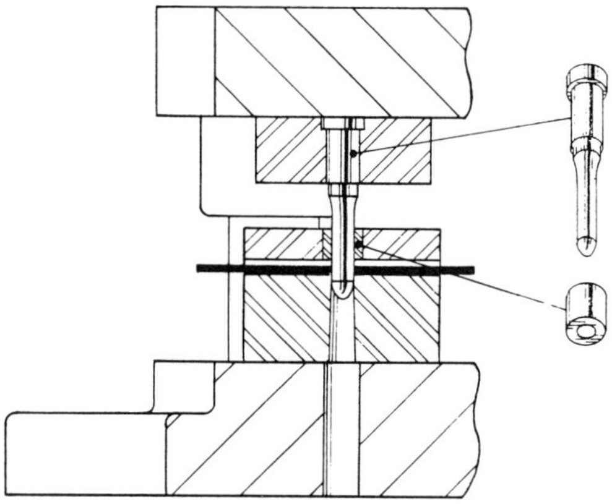

Fig. 11-17. Hardened bushing in stripper provides greater accuracy.

11-18. BACKING PLATES

Considerably more pressure is required for a pilot to pierce a strip than for an equivalent piercing punch. When the possibility is present of repeated mis-feeds, the pilot should be backed up by a hardened plate to prevent its head from sinking into the punch holder.

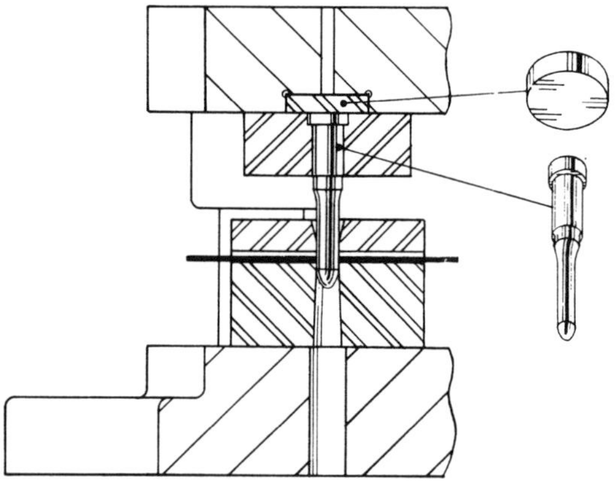

Fig. 11-18. Pilot backed up with hardened plate when chance of repeated mis-feeds is present.

11-19. SMALL INDIRECT PILOTS

Smaller pilots, 3/16 to 1/4 inch in diameter, are made with a turned head, and are guided in a hardened bushing in the stripper plate, and backed up by two socket set screws. In every instance the designer should pay particular attention to grinding allowances, remembering that as punches are sharpened the positions of the pilots will be altered. In this case grinding allowance **A** is applied to assure that, as the pilots are raised with spacer washers when punches are sharpened, the upper socket set screw will not protrude above the punch holder.

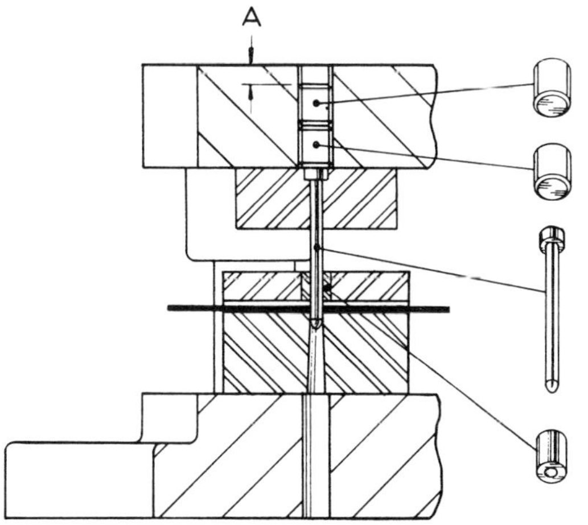

Fig. 11-19. Small indirect pilot is guided through stripper by hardened bushing and is backed up by two set screws.

11-20. PEENING THE HEAD

Smaller pilots, 1/8 to 3/16 inch in diameter can be made of drill rod with a peened head. Such pilots are guided in hardened bushings in the stripper, and are always backed up, either by a hardened plate or with socket set screws. After peening, the head is machined to an 82 degree included angle to fit standard countersunk holes. At assembly the top of the pilot plate is ground so that the peened head is flush with its surface.

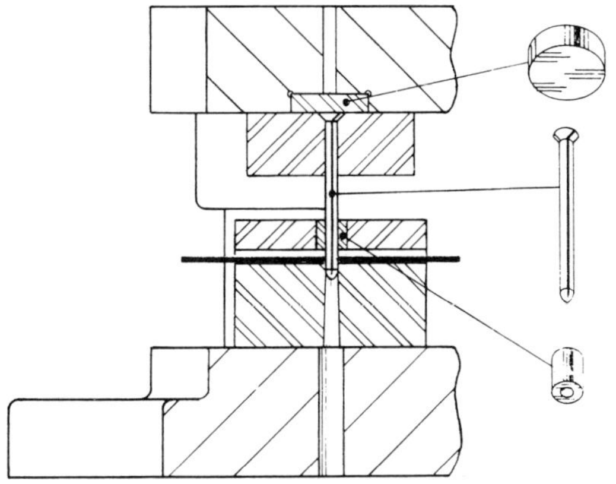

Fig. 11-20. Small indirect pilot made of drill rod has a peened head.

11-21. A SET SCREW HOLDS THE PILOT

For temporary dies, and where low-accuracy and low-production requirements exist, pilots can be held by a socket set screw bearing against a tapered flat machined in the pilot body. These pilots are made of drill rod, and the bullet-shaped end is machined to suit the hole size. Since the set screw has a tendency to "throw over" the pilot by the amount of clearance, this type of pilot should never be used for Class A dies.

11-22. QUILL PILOTS

Small pilots, 1/8 inch diameter and smaller, are of the peened-head type, held in a quill, and backed up by a socket set screw. These quills, made of hardened and ground tool steel, support the pilot close to the piloting end.

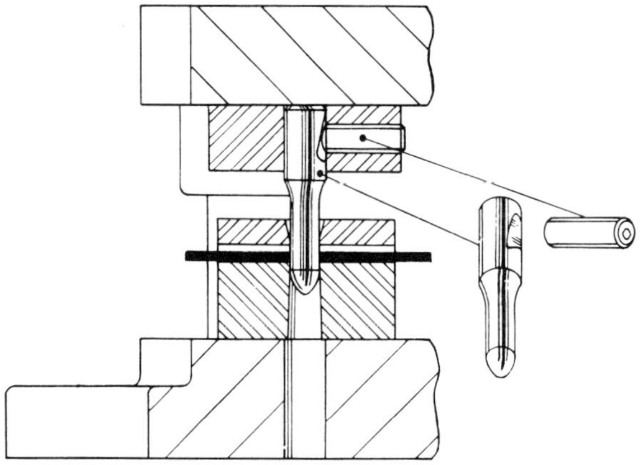

Fig. 11-21. Method of holding pilot with set screw in temporary dies.

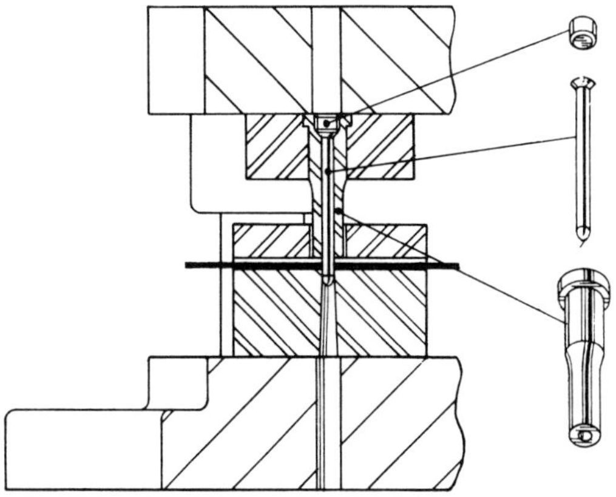

Fig. 11-22. A small peened-head type pilot held in a quill and backed up by a set screw.

11-23. QUILL AND BUSHING

If the quill is made shorter than shown in Fig. 11-22, the pilot is guided and supported in a hardened bushing pressed into the stripper plate. The entire assembly is backed up either by a hardened plate, or by two set screws. Whenever a hardened plate is used to back up a pilot, a through hole should be drilled in the punch holder for pressing the plate out. When the punches are sharpened, an equal amount of stock may be removed from the backing plate to maintain the relationship between the ends of the pilots and the cutting faces of the punches.

11-24. SPRING-BACKED PILOTS

So far, all pilots described have been of the solid variety used for sizes of stock up to and including #16 gage. When piloting in thicker material it is wise to use the spring-backed type of pilot. Pilot **A**, guided in bushings **B** and **C**, is backed up by spring **D** which is, in turn, backed up by set screw **E**. The pilot is made a close sliding fit in bushings **B** and **C**, normally with from 0.0002 to 0.0005 inch clearance.

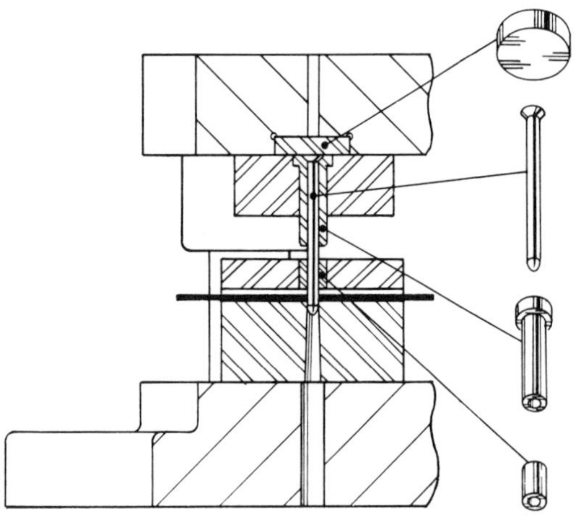

Fig. 11-23. Pilot similar to the one shown in Fig. 11-22 but with hardened bushing in stripper plate and hardened back up plate.

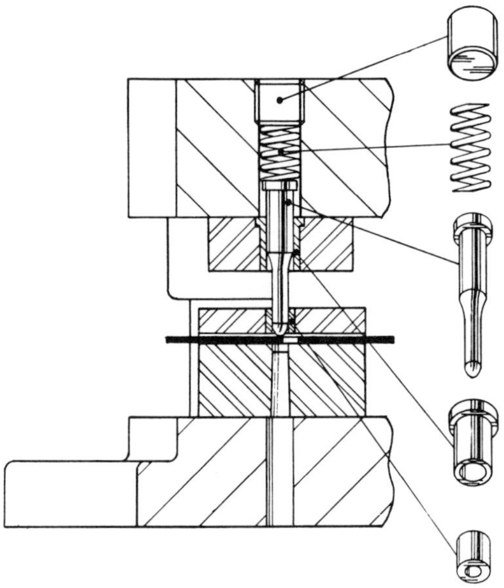

Fig. 11-25. Position of pilot during a mis-feed.

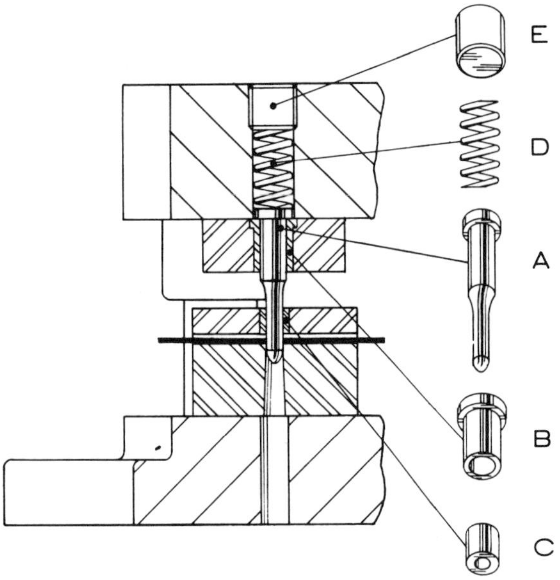

Fig. 11-24. Typical spring-backed pilot.

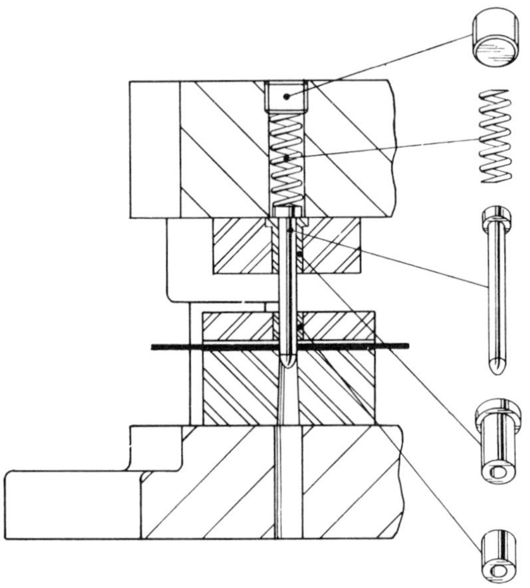

Fig. 11-26. Small spring-backed pilot has shouldered head.

11-25. MIS-FEEDS

In the event of a mis-feed the spring-backed pilot retracts harmlessly, as shown. Spring pressure is determined by trial and error. Sufficient pressure must be applied to move the strip to correct register at every hit. However, the pressure must not be great enough for the pilot to pierce the strip in the event of a mis-feed. Even though a spring-backed pilot is used, the hole in the die block is made as though for a piercing punch. While the pilot is supposed to retract rather than pierce the strip, nevertheless the pilot can become frozen in its bushing and pierce instead of retract. For trouble-free operation, the spring should not be compressed for more than 1/3 of its free length, including the initial compression applied when the set screw is inserted.

11-26. SMALL SPRING-BACKED PILOTS

Pilots from 3/16 to 1/4 inch in diameter are made straight and provided with a shouldered head. These also are guided in hardened bushings pressed into the pilot plate and into the stripper plate. A spring and set screw, inserted in the punch holder, back up the pilot.

11-27. SPRING-BACKED QUILLS

Still smaller pilots can be held in quills and backed up by socket set screws. The quill is then guided in hardened bushings pressed into the pilot plate and into the stripper plate. A spring backs up the quill and it is, in turn, backed up by a large socket set screw. This construction will prevent injury to small pilots and when mis-feeds can occur frequently, this design should be used.

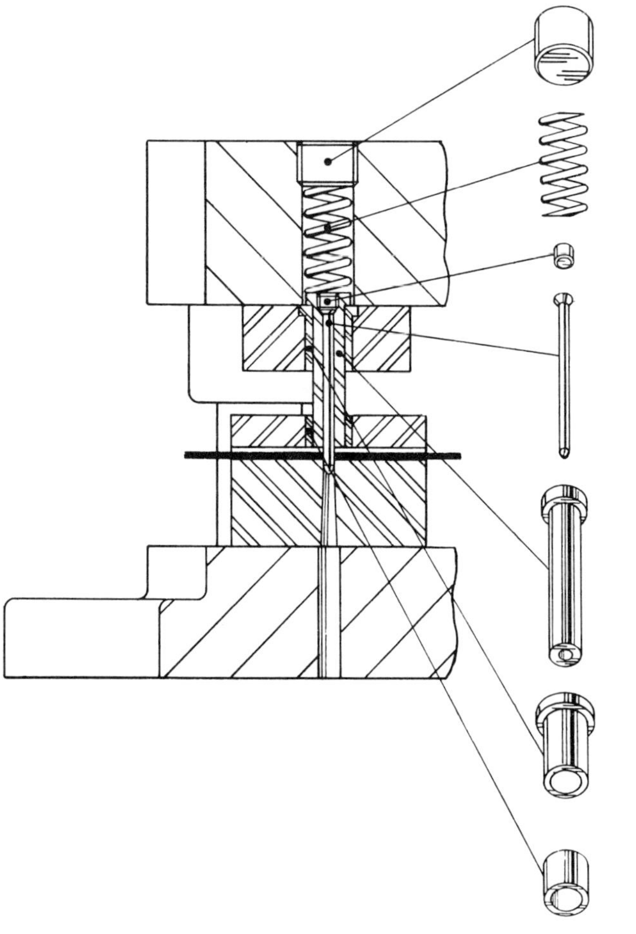

Fig. 11-27. Small spring-backed pilot-bearing quill setup with hardened bushings in pilot and stripper plates.

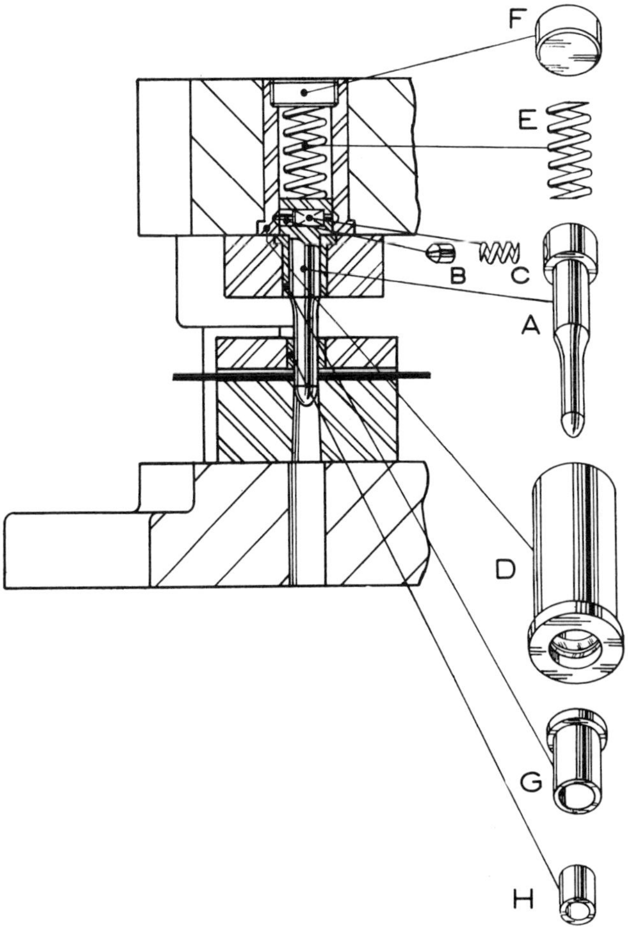

Fig. 11-28. Type of pilot used when stock is thick.

11-28. PILOTING IN HEAVY STRIPS

This type of pilot is provided when the stock is unusually thick, or the strip unusually wide and heavy. Pilot **A** is provided with a thick head into which a hole is drilled and reamed. Detent **B**, backed up by spring **C**, is inserted in this hole, and its angular face fits into a groove machined inside of bushing **D**. Spring **E** and socket set screw **F** back up the assembly. The pilot is guided and supported in bushings **G** and **H**, pressed into the pilot plate and into the stripper plate. The angle on the face of detent **B** is usually made 40 degrees, but it can be varied to release the pilot under any required pressure.

11-29. FLAT ON PILOT HEAD

Some indirect pilots are used at intermediate stations of progressive dies for locating the strip. When these pilots are engaged in holes other than round, they can be kept from turning by grinding a flat on the pilot head. This flat bears against one side of a slot machined in the pilot plate.

11-30. KEYED PILOTS

Where space is limited, the pilot can be kept from turning by grinding a flat in the same way as described for Fig. 11-29, and locating this flat against a key inserted in the pilot plate. Always use the round-end type of key. The fit must be of first-class die quality.

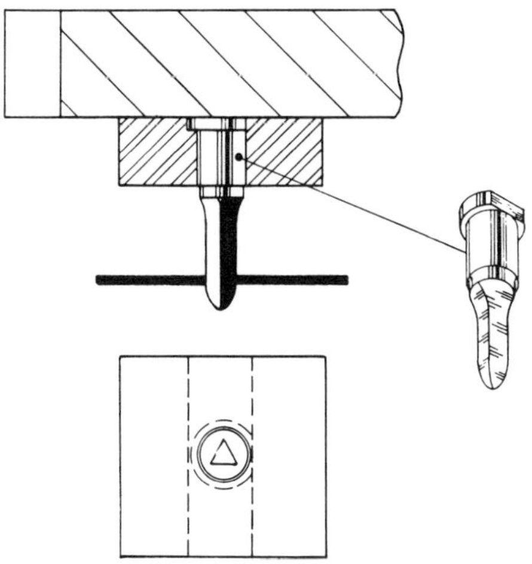

Fig. 11-29. Triangular-shaped indirect pilot that is kept from turning by the flat on the pilot head.

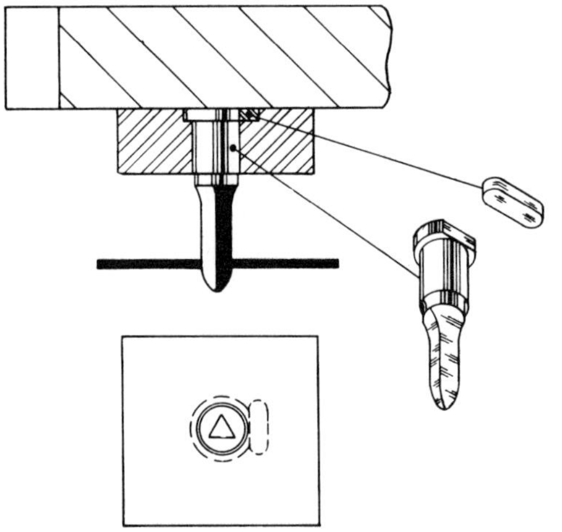

Fig. 11-30. Pilot may be keyed with round-end key where space is limited.

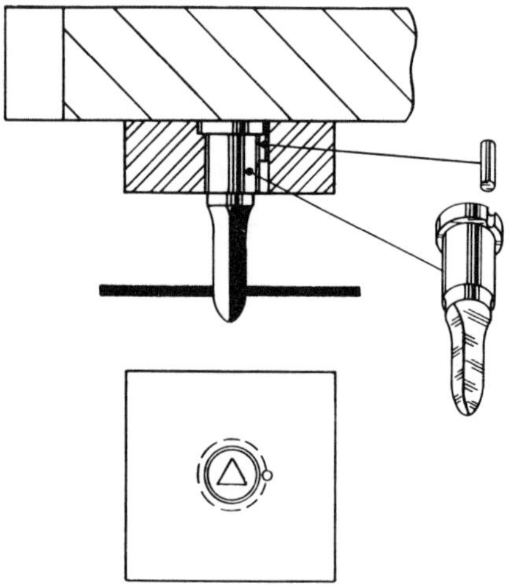

Fig. 11-32. Using a dutchman to keep a pilot from turning in temporary dies.

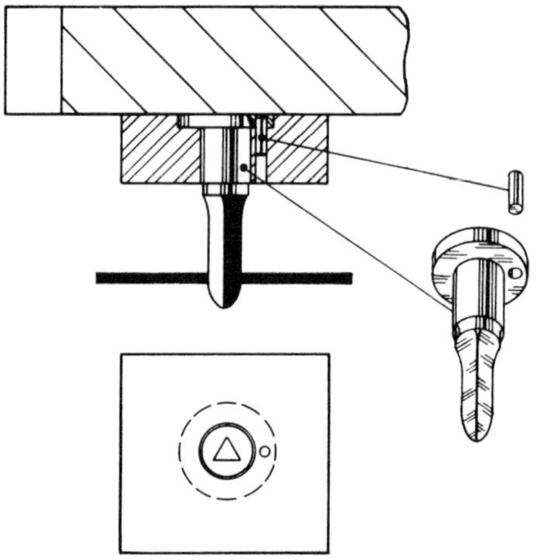

Fig. 11-31. Method of pinning an irregular pilot to keep it from turning.

11-31. PINNED PILOT

Another method of keeping an irregular pilot from turning is to provide a large flanged head on the pilot. Dowel this flange to the pilot plate.

11-32. DUTCHMAN

When space is limited, a dutchman, pressed half in the pilot head and half in the pilot plate, will keep an irregular pilot from turning. This method is not considered as good as those previously described. It should be used only for temporary dies where low-production requirements are present.

Section 12

HOW TO DESIGN GAGES

Gages must be considered in the design of press tools because these components position the strip longitudinally in its travel through the die. In second-operation dies, gages locate the previously blanked or formed part for further processing operations. Design considerations include:

1. Material choice. Commercial gage stock, or an equivalent finished tool steel, is used for gages in first-class dies. Cold-rolled steel should be used only when low-production requirements exist.
2. Adequate thickness. The back gage and front spacer must be thick enough to avoid binding of the strip between stripper plate and die block, because of possible camber in the strip. Camber, or curvature, is more pronounced in coiled stock not passed through a straightener.
3. Good doweling practice. Since gages locate the strip or part, they should always be doweled in position
4. Accuracy of location. Dimensions from die hole to locating surfaces of gages are always given decimally on the drawing.
5. Accuracy of locating surfaces. The gaging surfaces which actually bear against the strip, or part, should be ground, and so marked on the die drawing.

Illustrated in this section are twenty-two methods of applying gages to various types of dies. These methods further explain Step 7 in Section 5, "14 Steps to Design a Die".

12-1. BACK GAGE AND FRONT SPACER

In passing through a two-station pierce and blank die, the strip is positioned against back gage **A** by the operator. Strip support **B** helps to align the bottom of the strip with the top surface of the die block to prevent binding. Dimension **C**, between the back gage and front spacer, is made strip thickness plus 1/32 inch when a roll feed is used; strip thickness plus 1/16 to 3/16 inch for hand feeding. Thickness **D** of both back gage and front spacer is usually made 1/8 inch for strip thicknesses up to #16 gage (0.0625 inch). For heavier strip, dimension **D** is made strip thickness plus 1/16 to 1/8 inch.

Shown at **E**, **F** and **G** are the three methods of fastening the strip support to the back gage. At **E** socket button head screws, passing through the back gage, are threaded into holes tapped in the strip support. At **F** the components are riveted together, while at **G** they are welded together.

The stripper is relieved 3/8 inch, as shown, to help in starting new strips through the die. The relief forms a shelf on which the end of the strip can be dropped, then advanced over the die block surface.

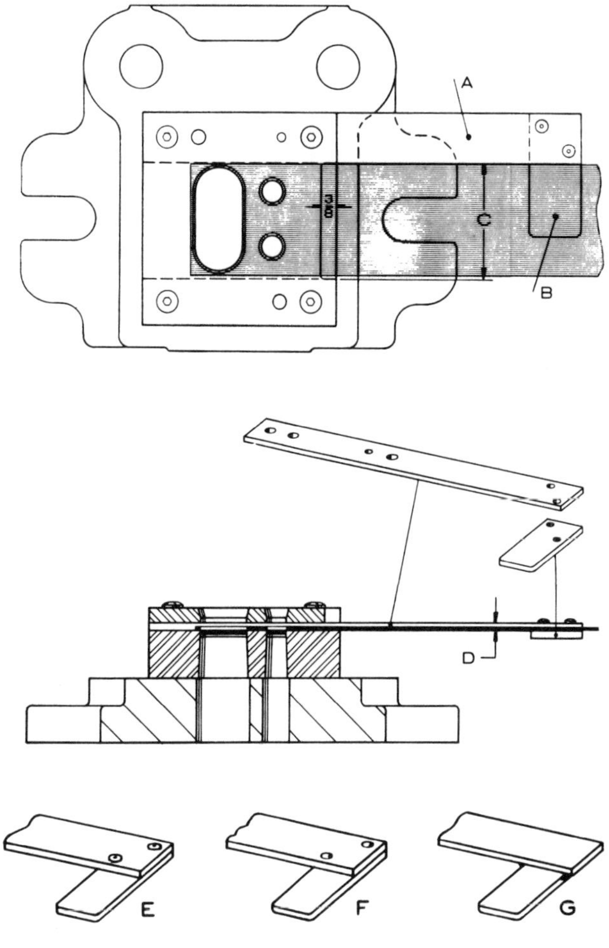

Fig. 12-1. Arrangement of the back gage and front spacer in a two-station pierce and blank die.

12-2. COMPOUND DIES

In compound dies the back end of the spring stripper **A** is extended to provide a pad for fastening back gage **B**. Strip support **C** completes the assembly. A pin **D**, pressed into the spring stripper, helps alignment of the strip.

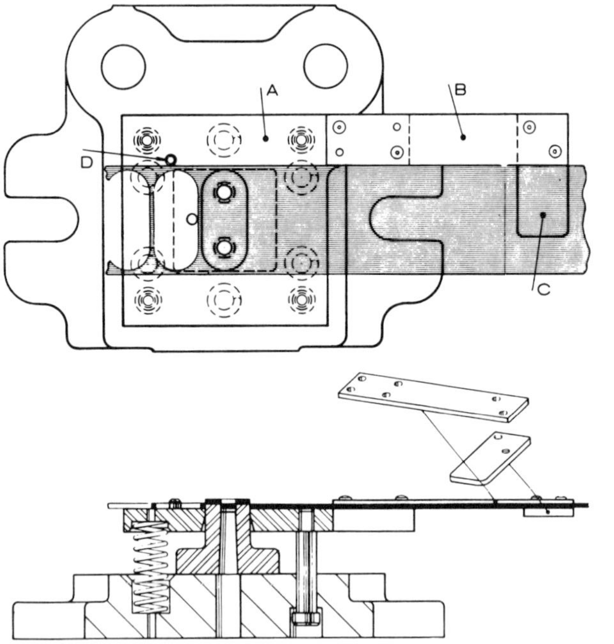

Fig. 12-2. Compound die in which spring stripper (**A**), back gage (**B**) and pin (**D**) help to provide alignment.

12-3. CUT-OFF DIES

A convenient method of providing a stop for cut-off dies for long parts is to extend the back gage to the left and screw and dowel strip stop **A** to it as shown. After they have been cut, the blanks slide to the side of the die by means of the angular relief provided in the die block.

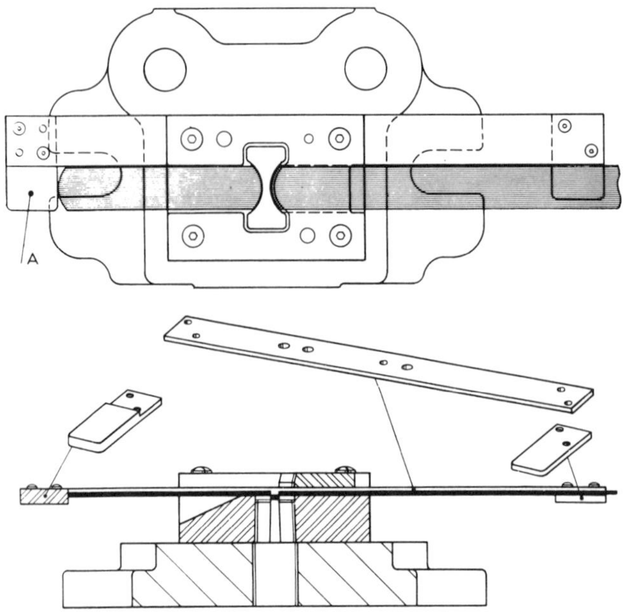

Fig. 12-3. Back gage in this cut-off die has been extended to the left to provide mounting for a stop.

12-4. FEEDING THIN STRIPS

When feeding thin, pliable strips, support **A** is made long and brought up close to the die block to provide better support and guidance. Three socket button-head screws are provided, but no dowels are required.

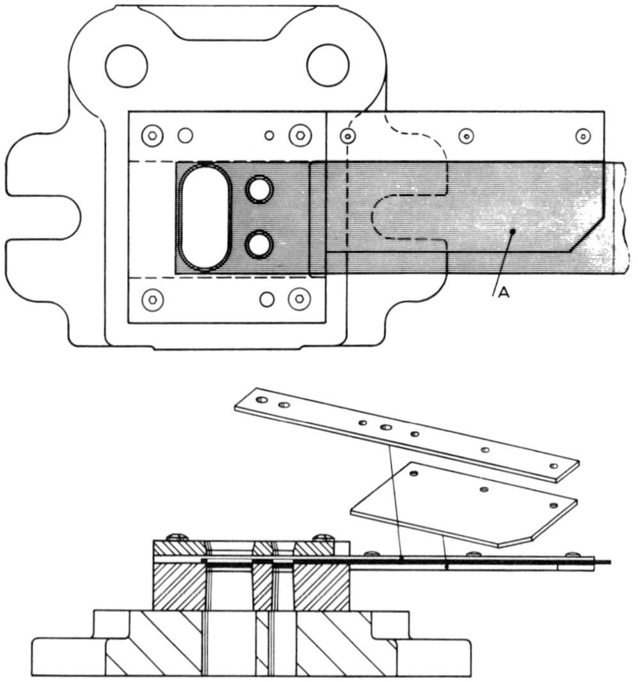

Fig. 12-4. Support (**A**) provides extra support for thin, pliable strips.

12-5. ALTERNATE METHOD

This is a better method of supporting and guiding thin strips and, in fact, may be used for any strip

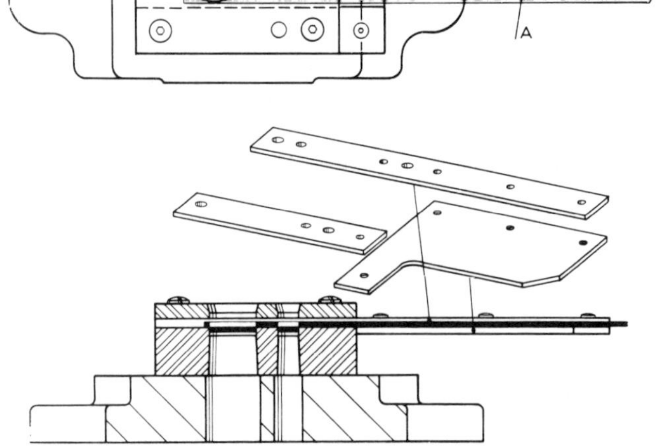

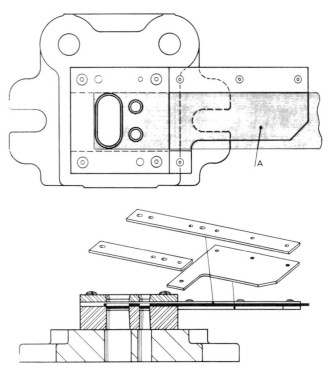

Fig. 12-5. Another method of supporting and guiding thin strips.

thickness. The front spacer is extended to the right and an ear on strip support **A** is fastened under it with a socket button-head screw to provide rigidity. With this method it is not necessary to cut a portion of the stripper for starting the strip.

12-6. ROLL FEEDS

Strip supports are not required when a roll feed is used. The back gage extends to the right a short distance and the stripper plate is relieved to aid in starting a new strip. Guide length **A** is made approximately 1½ times the back gage width **B**.

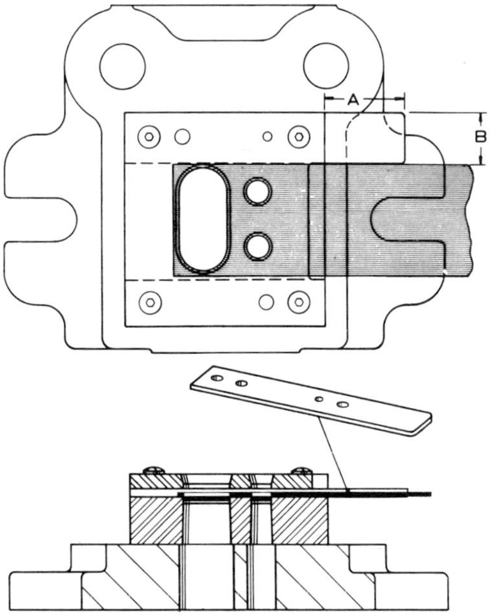

Fig. 12-6. Arrangement of back gage and front spacer when roll feed is used.

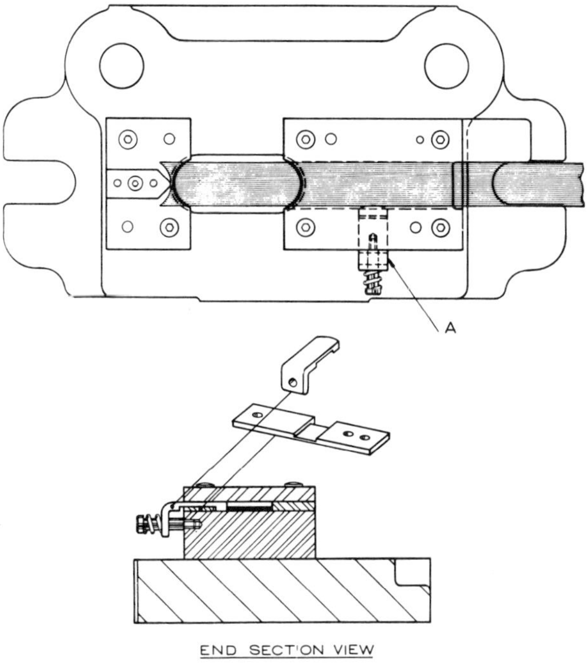

Fig. 12-7. Method of keeping strip firmly against back gage by employing stock pusher (**A**).

12-7. STOCK PUSHERS

Means are often provided to keep the strip firmly against the back gage during its travel through the die, particularly when a roll feed is used. The simplest method is to apply a stock pusher **A**, made much like a finger stop. A spring, held by a shoulder screw, applies pressure to register the strip.

12-8. BAR PUSHER

An alternative method of applying a stock pusher to a die is to use a flat spring **A**. This applies pressure through two pins **B** to pusher bar **C** to locate the strip firmly against the back gage.

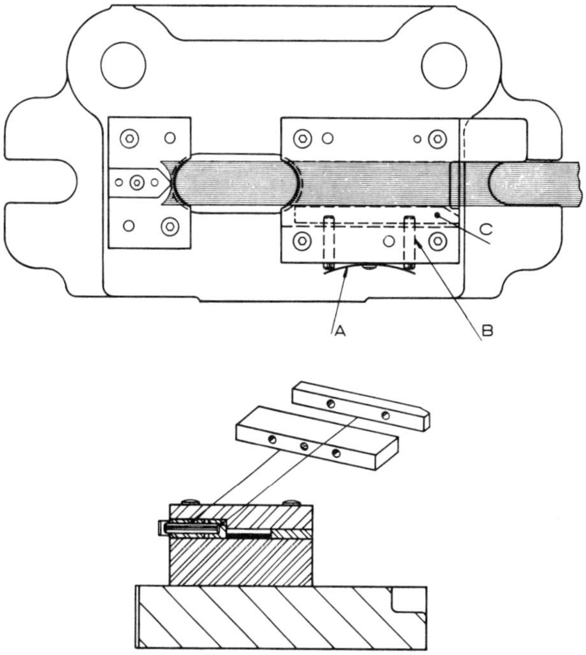

Fig. 12-8. Another method of applying a stock pusher to a die.

12-9. ROLLER PUSHER

This stock pusher incorporates roller **A** which is mounted on pivoting arm **B** by a shoulder screw. Spring **C** pulls the roller toward the back of the die to position the strip.

12-10. STRIP EQUALIZERS

When the strip width tends to vary, a strip equalizer should be used instead of a back gage. This is probably the best type. Arms **A** and **B**, pivoting on shoulder screws **C**, are linked by arm **D**. Four rollers **E** guide the strip, acted upon by spring **F**. Arm **B** is extended to provide a handle for starting the strip through the die.

12-11. PIN GAGING

Gaging methods for secondary-operation dies usually take the form of nests into which the parts are dropped. Shown here is a die for piercing two holes in square-sheared blanks. When low-production requirements are present, the blank is simply located against three pins. Always position the two in-line locating pins against the longer side of the blank and the single pin against the short side.

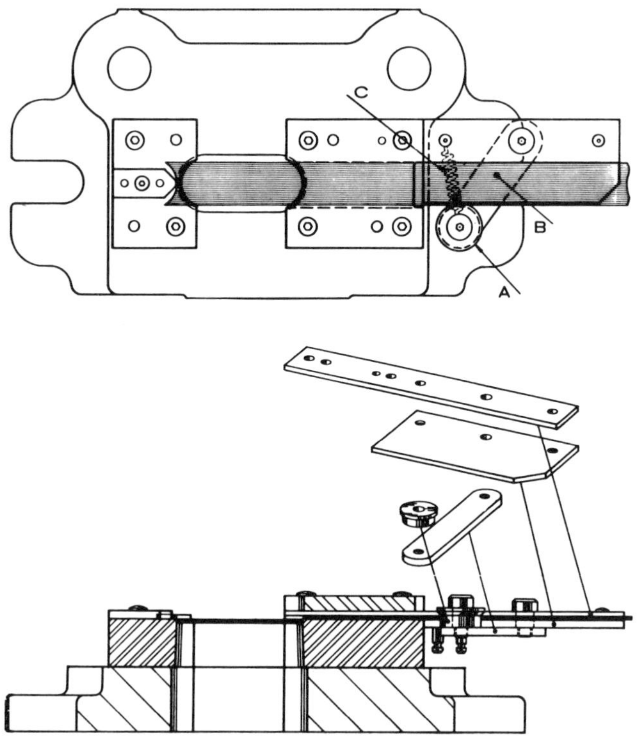

Fig. 12-9. Stock pusher that incorporates a roller.

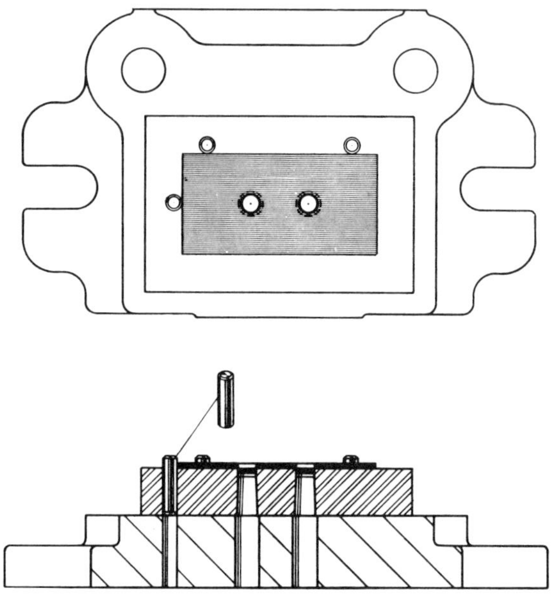

Fig. 12-11. Blank location provided by three dowel pins for low-production secondary requirements.

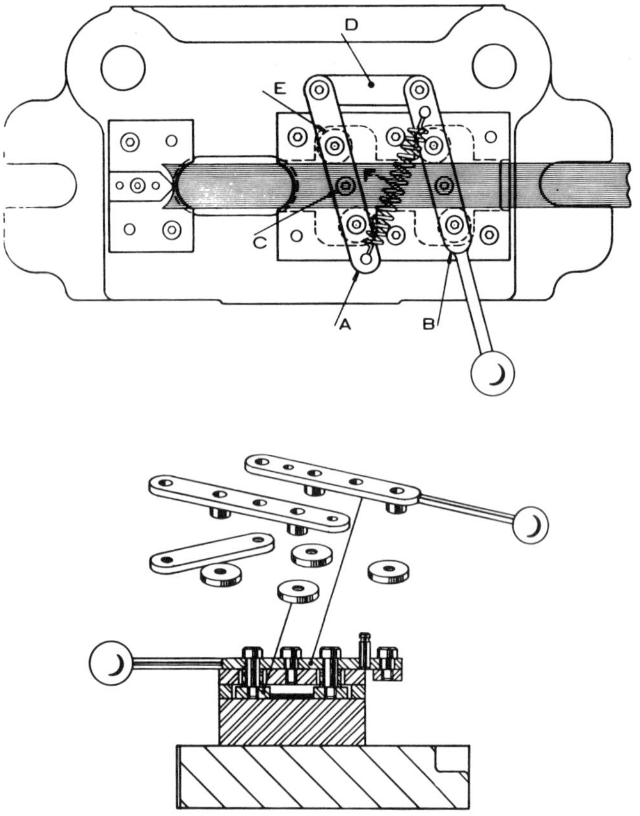

Fig. 12-10. Setup employing a strip equalizer instead of a back gage when the strip width varies.

12-12. BEVELED GAGE PINS

For higher production requirements, the blank is located in a gage composed of six pins. These are beveled leaving a straight land, equal to the stock thickness, for register. The beveled pins help to slide the part to position quickly.

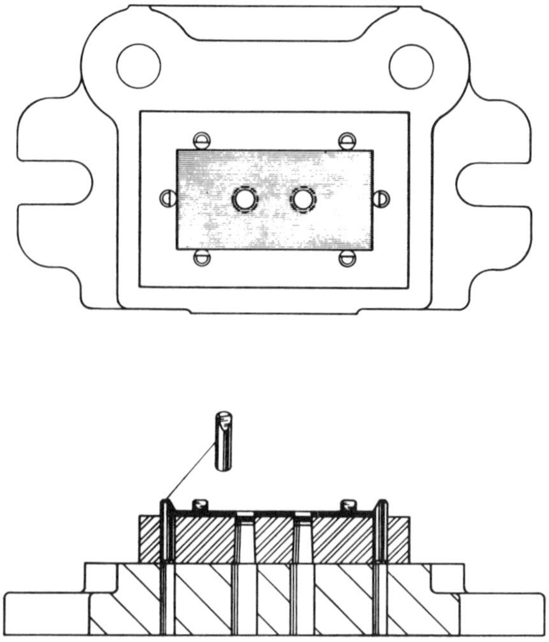

Fig. 12-12. Beveled gage pins facilitate quick positioning for higher production requirements.

12-13. TURNED BEVELS

Perhaps a better method of applying a bevel to gage pins is to taper turn the ends of the pins as shown. Thus, even if one pin should loosen and turn, blank positioning would not be affected.

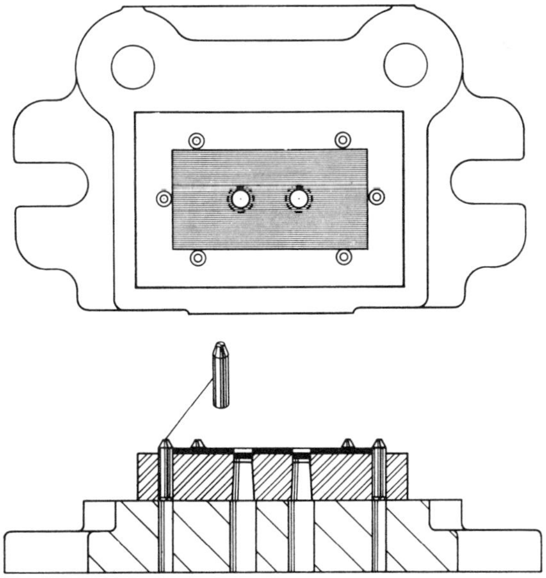

Fig. 12-13. Alternate method of applying bevel to pins.

12-14. DISAPPEARING PINS

If the nature of the operation would cause the punch to strike the locating pins, they are made of the disappearing type. Springs, backed up by socket set screws, act against shoulders machined in the locating pins.

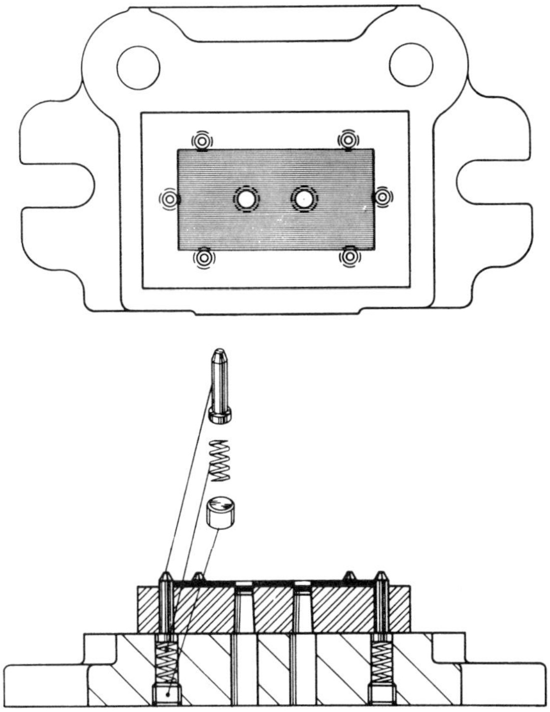

Fig. 12-14. Locating pins may be spring-backed if interference is expected.

12-15. SPRING PUSHERS

When dimensions **A** and **B** of the part must be held very accurately, three spring pushers **C**, confined in spring housings **D**, locate the part against gages **E**.

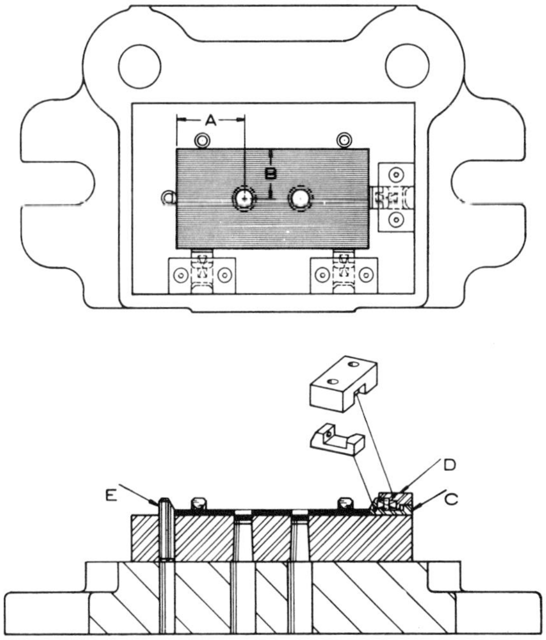

Fig. 12-15. Spring pushers (**C**) provide accurate positioning.

12-16. LOCATING PADS

For high production and long life, the part would be located against locating pads **A**, held in housings **B** instead of against pins as in previous examples. These pads are hardened and ground and they are retained by socket button-head screws.

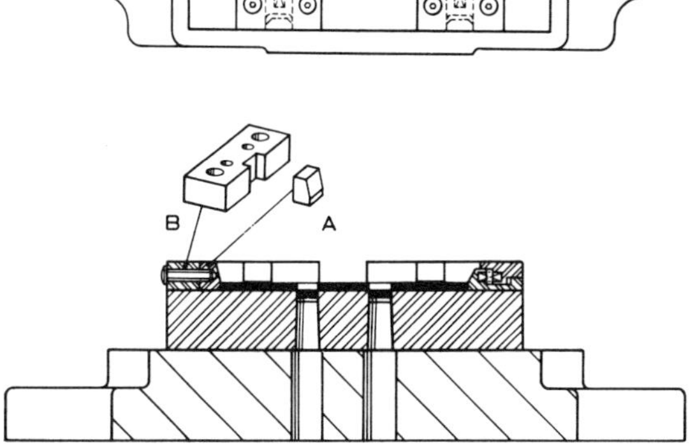

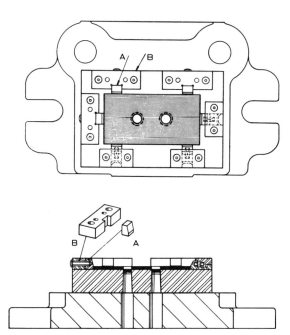

Fig. 12-16. Locating pads (**A**) may be used in lieu of pins for high production and long life.

12-17. PILOT GAGING

Use pilots for location when the part contains holes. Pilots provide quick part positioning and are inexpensive. Frequently used sizes are tabulated in Fig. 11-11 of the previous section of the book.

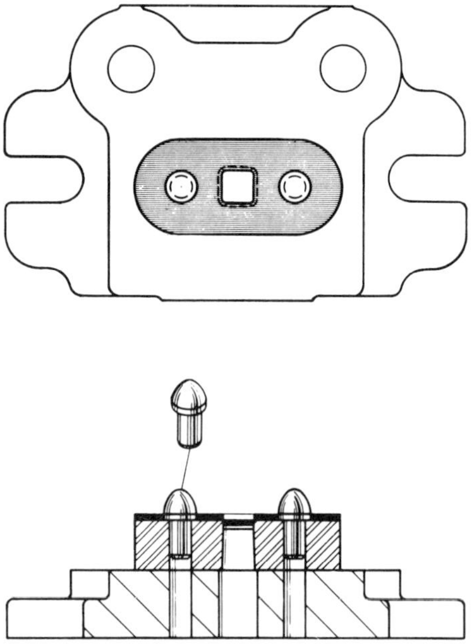

Fig. 12-17. Pilots provide quick part positioning.

12-18. RADIUS GAGING

Many parts contain internal radii somewhere around their peripheries. Pilots, engaging in these radii, effectively locate the blanks for subsequent operations.

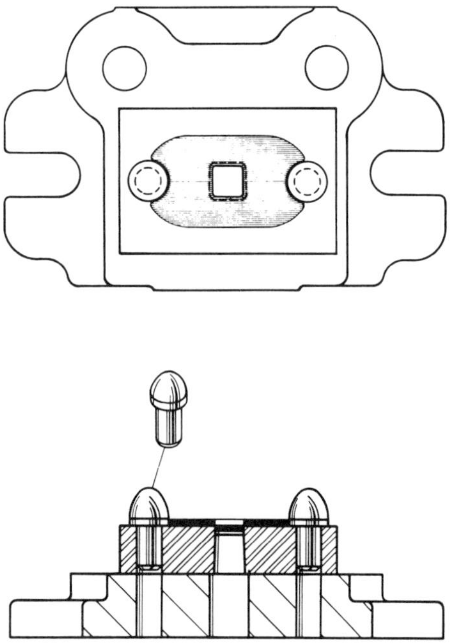

Fig. 12-18. Pilots used on outside periphery for positioning part.

12-19. V GAGING

Parts with opposed outside radii are located in V gages as shown. Engaging faces of each V are tapered for quick part insertion. A straight land, equal in length to the blank thickness, is left for proper positioning of the part.

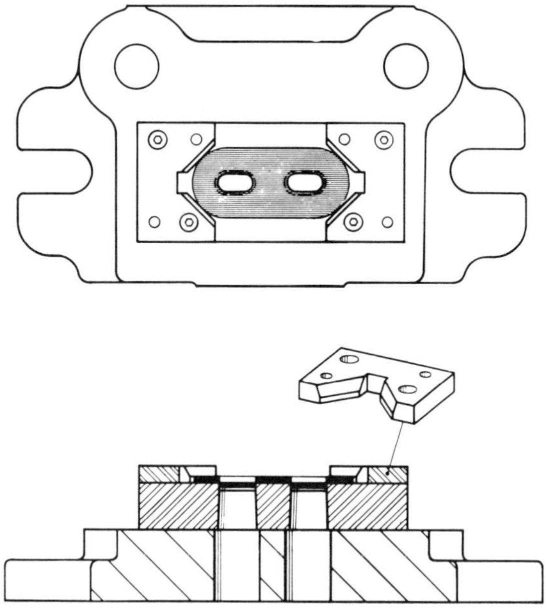

Fig. 12-19. Positioning part with V gages.

12-20. RELIEVED GAGES

Parts with irregular outside contours are located in gages machined to fit the contour, but relieved so that they bear only at important points.

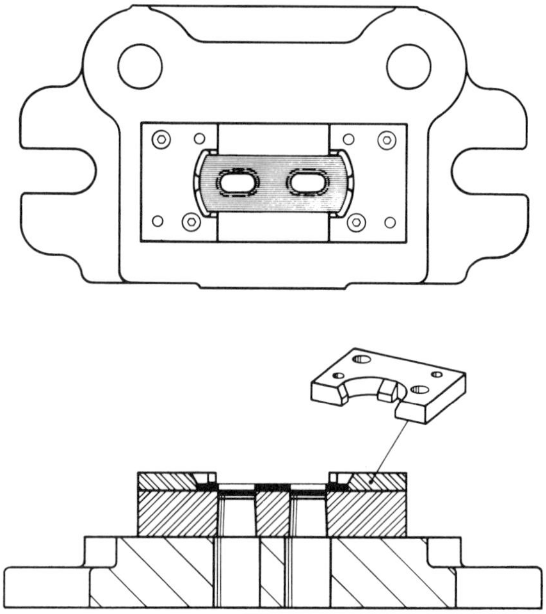

Fig. 12-20. Gages machined to the outside contour of the part are used for positioning irregularly shaped pieces.

12-21. INTERNAL GAGES

Formed or drawn parts are located for further processing by gages machined to fit the inside contours, but relieved so as to bear only at critical points. This die trims the flange of a previously drawn shell.

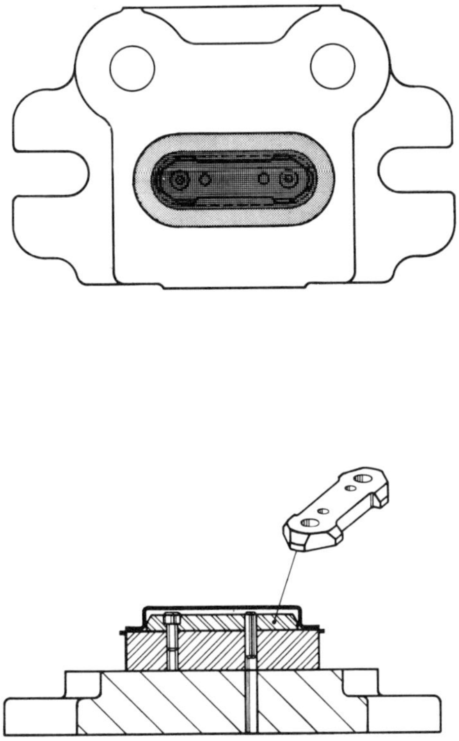

Fig. 12-21. Gage machined to fit the inside coutour of formed or drawn parts.

12-22. GAGES FOR SHAVING DIES

Gages for shaving dies are made to fit the outside contours of the blank, but relieved so they bear only at required points. Bearing areas are beveled to provide room for the curled chip produced by shaving action. Depth of this relief should be two-thirds of the part thickness. For shaving, die sets with floating adapters should be used, as shown.

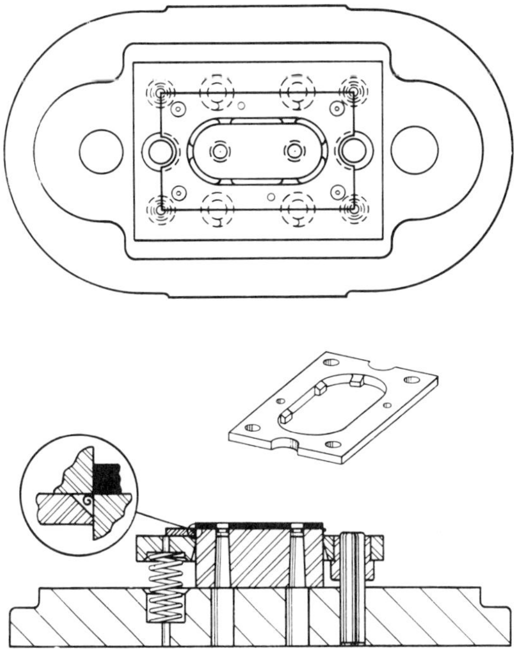

Fig. 12-22. Typical gage for shaving die.

Section 13

HOW TO DESIGN FINGER STOPS

Finger stops, or primary stops as they are sometimes called, are used in dies with two or more stations. They register the strip for performing operations prior to strip engagement by the automatic stop or roll feed. The number of finger stops used depends upon the number of stations in the die. For hand feeding it is always one less than the total number of stations. For automatic feeding only one finger stop is required. Finger stops are made of cold-rolled steel, cyanide hardened.

In the early days of press work, numerous vertically-acting primary stops were used. The hazard of placing fingers between upper and lower die members has caused them to fall into disrepute. Presently, almost the only finger stops used in modern plants are the horizontal types to be described.

Illustrated are fifteen standardized finger stops fully tabulated to aid the designer in selecting the right one for the conditions encountered. Machining data are given for accompanying front spacers. In addition general rules are outlined to help in the correct selection and application of these die components. This further explains Step 8 in Section 5, "Fourteen Steps to Design a Die."

13-1. OPERATION

Taken together, this illustration and Fig. 13-2 explain the operation of a typical finger stop. As shown in this plan view of a two-station die, two holes are pierced at the first station, and the blank is removed from the strip at the second station. Finger stop **A** has been advanced to operating position; the strip is pushed against its toe by the operator, and the press is tripped, piercing the two holes. The toe of automatic stop **B** has been pulled to the right by the automatic stop spring.

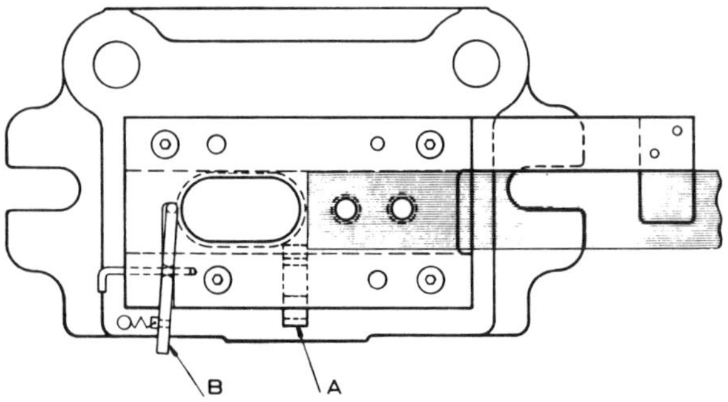

Fig. 13-1. Finger stop (A) is in position to stop the strip for the piercing operation.

13-2. WITHDRAWING THE STOP

The finger stop has now been pulled back by the operator, allowing the strip to be moved toward the left until it contacts the toe of the automatic stop, "setting" it. Tripping the press produces a full blank and two pierced holes. Subsequently, the operator simply keeps the strip firmly against the automatic stop until all blanks have been removed. Usually, conventional front and side section views of the die are used to show the form of blanking and piercing punches. So, on the die drawing the side view of the finger stop is projected to the right as a partial section view, **A**.

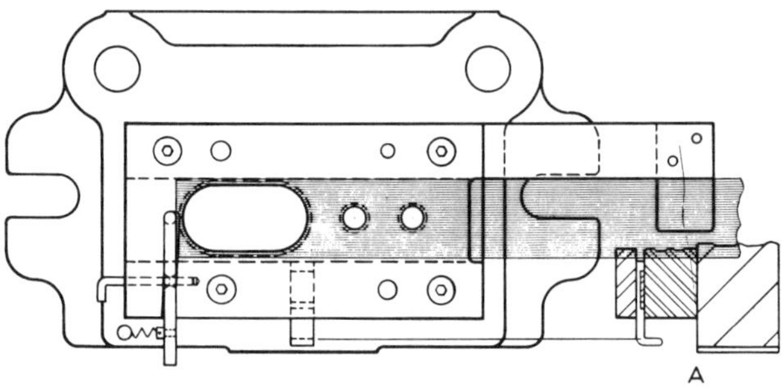

Fig. 13-2. Finger stop in pulled back position allows strip to be moved to the automatic stop.

13-3. CONSTRUCTION

Three common methods of making finger stops are illustrated. At **A** the bottom of the stop is milled to provide a slot for limiting stop travel, and to retain the stop in the front spacer. The stop at **B** has an end-milled slot machined along its center. A dowel engages this slot to limit stop travel. Similarly, the stop at **C** has a partial slot cut along its edge to limit travel. Because it does not require a dowel, the stop at **A** is preferred.

The designer should always be on the lookout for ways to eliminate unnecessary parts. Also, end-milling of long, narrow slots is slow and therefore expensive.

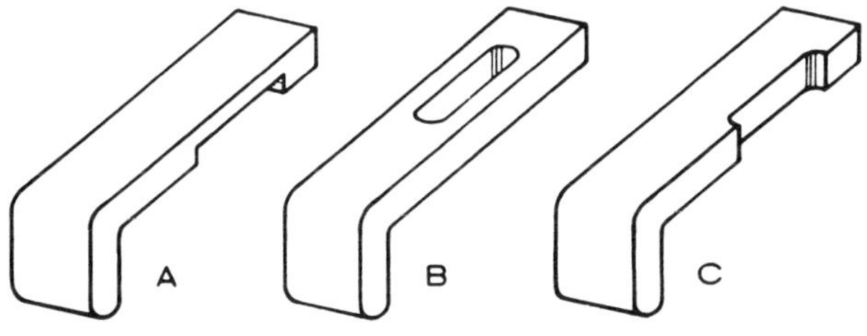

Fig. 13-3. Three common methods of making finger stops.

13-4. MULTIPLE STOPS

In multiple station dies designed for hand feeding, finger stops locate the end of the strip for each station except the final automatic stop station. In this die two extruded bosses are applied to the strip at the first station, stop **A** positioning the strip. Two holes are pierced at the second station, Stop **B** engaging the end of the strip for locating them. At station 3 the part is blanked, automatic stop **C** locating the strip end.

When a roll feed is used, only one finger stop is required, applied at the first station. The roll feed advances and positions the strip for all subsequent stations. Pilots perform the final accurate positioning.

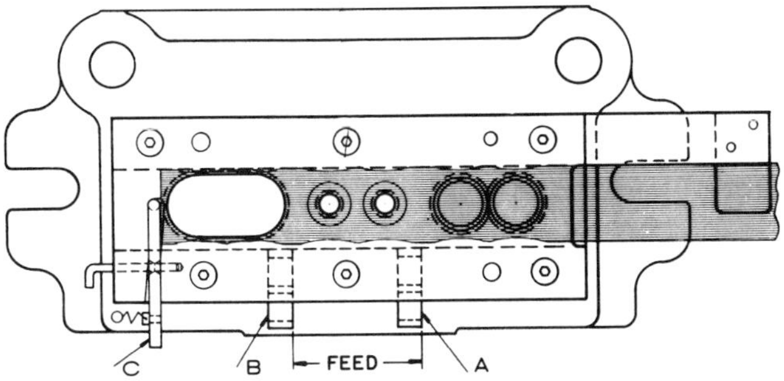

Fig. 13-4. Multiple station die employing two finger stops.

13-5. BEVELING THE STOP

For some part contours it is necessary to shear the end of the strip at an angle for starting it through the die. In such applications the end of the finger stop is beveled to the angle applied to the strip end.

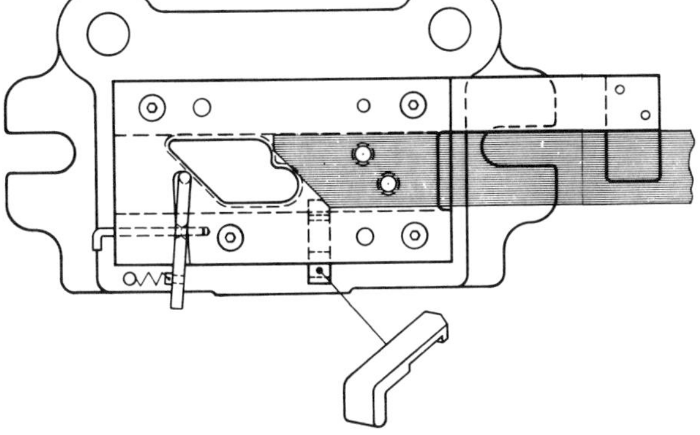

Fig. 13-5. Finger stop with bevel to conform to pre-sheared strip.

13-6. INTERFERENCES

Always check carefully to make sure that the corner of the finger stop will not be sheared off by the blanking punch in its downward travel. Where interference occurs, bevel the end of the finger stop.

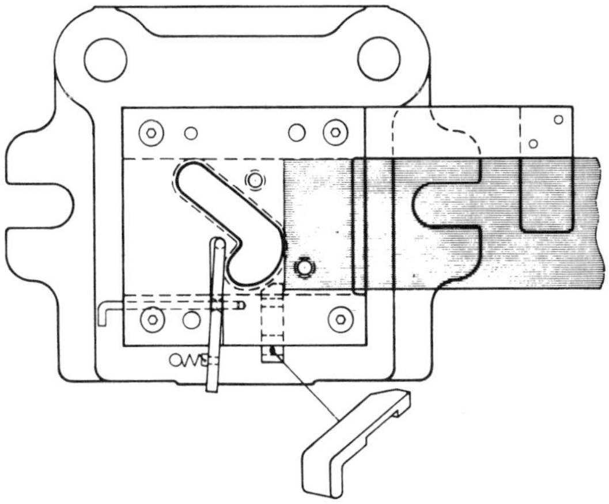

Fig. 13-6. End of finger stop is beveled to avoid interference with punch.

13-7. RETURN SPRING

A return spring is not ordinarily required on finger stops. However, when the front edge of the material is notched, and a possibility exists that the stop might work inward under vibration and engage the notch to cause a misfeed, a return spring would be used. A small guide pin, riveted to the finger stop, holds and guides the spring.

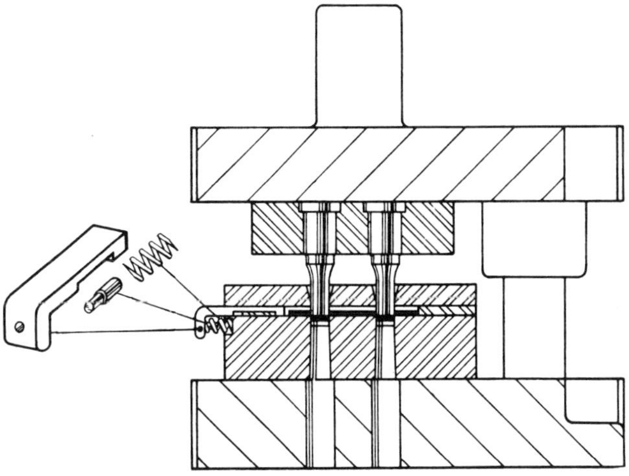

Fig. 13-7. Finger stop with return spring for avoiding misfeeds on notched strips.

13-8. SPRING STRIPPER

When a spring stripper is used, the slot in the finger stop is inverted. This provides a convenient means of retaining the stop in the front stock guide.

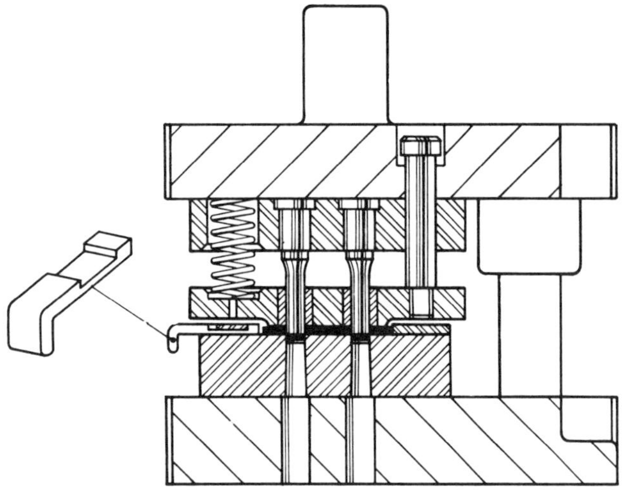

Fig. 13-8. Slot in finger stop is inverted when spring stripper is used.

13-9. PROPORTIONS OF DIE BLOCKS

Finger stop proportions can only be determined after the width of the front spacer has been established. Front spacer width, in turn, is governed by the minimum distance **C**, of the die block, which can be used for the particular job. Minimum distance **C** of the die block depends almost entirely on the contour of the die hole. Secondary considerations are:

1. Extent of straight lands. Where these are long the die block is subjected to considerable side pressure during the cutting process. It is often advisable to use a minimum distance **C** in the thicker ranges regardless of die-hole contour

2. Size of the die hole opening. When openings are large and material strip is thick, it is wise to go to the thicker **C** ranges regardless of die hole contour.

For die holes with smooth, or rounded contours, view 1, minimum distance **C** is generally 1-1/8 times the thickness **B** of the die block. When the die hole contains inside corners, view 2, minimum distance **C** is generally 1½ times die block thickness **B**. View 3 shows severe inside corners in the die hole contour. Minimum distance **C** is then made twice the thickness of the die block. These minimum distances are tabulated for recommended die block heights, which in turn are governed by strip thickness **A**.

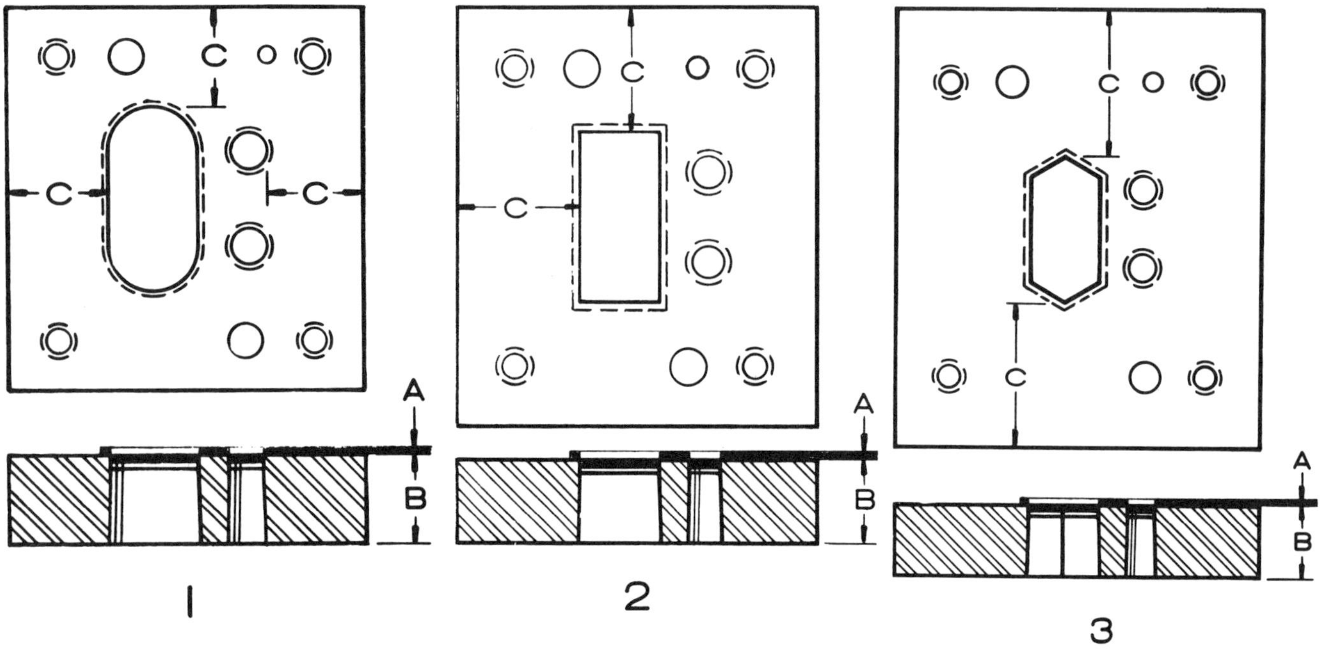

A	B	C		
		MINIMUM DISTANCE - DIE HOLE TO OUTSIDE EDGE		
		1	2	3
STRIP THICKNESS	DIE BLOCK HEIGHT	SMOOTH DIE HOLE CONTOUR (1 1/8 B)	INSIDE CORNERS (1 1/2 B)	SHARP INSIDE CORNERS (2 B)
0 to 1/16	15/16	1.0547	1.4062	1.875
1/16 to 1/8	1 1/8	1.2656	1.6875	2.250
1/8 to 3/16	1 3/8	1.5469	2.0625	2.750
3/16 to 1/4	1 5/8	1.8281	2.4375	3.250
over 1/4	1 7/8	2.1094	2.8125	3.750

Fig. 13-9. Recommended minimum **C** distances for various die hole contours and die block heights (**B**).

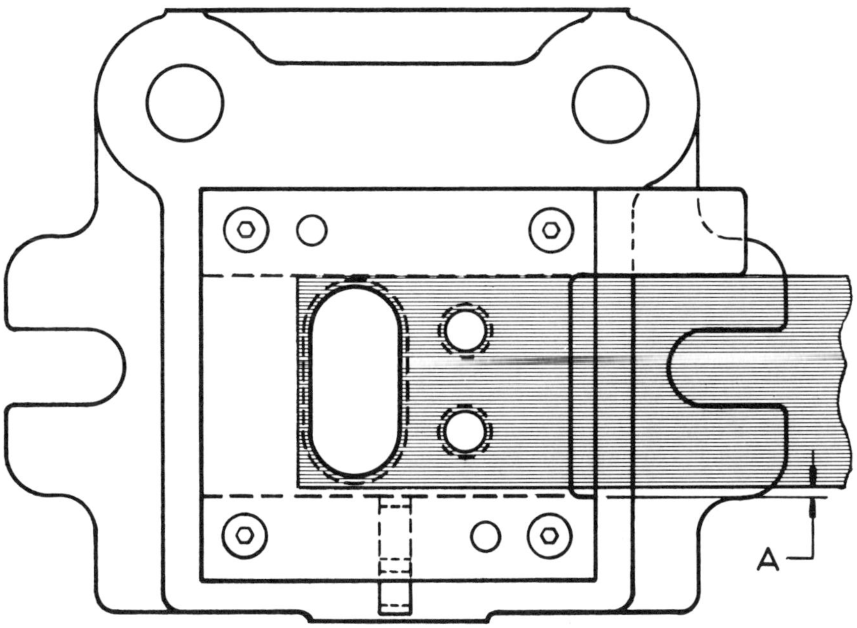

STRIP THICKNESS	A HAND FEED	A POWER FEED
0 to 1/16	1/16	1/32
1/16 to 1/8	3/32	1/32
1/8 to 3/16	1/8	1/32
3/16 to 1/4	5/32	1/32
over 1/4	3/16	1/32

Fig. 13-10. Table of recommended **A** distances for both hand and power feeds.

A STRIP THICKNESS	B FRONT SPACER THICKNESS
0 to 1/16	1/8
1/16 to 1/8	3/16
1/8 to 3/16	1/4
3/16 to 1/4	5/16
1/4 to 5/16	3/8

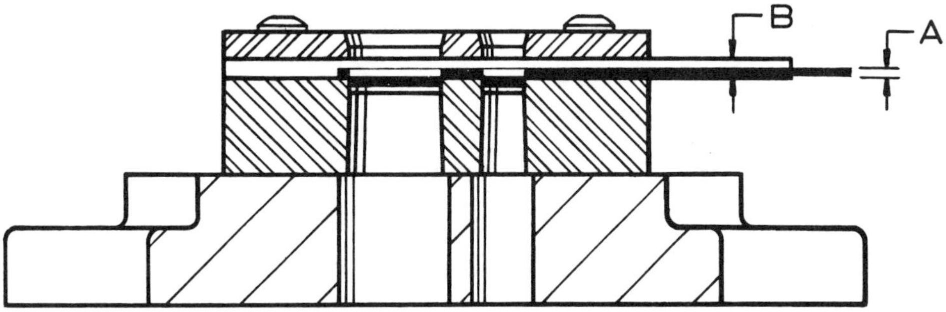

Fig. 13-11. Table of recommended front spacer thicknesses.

13-10. STRIP CLEARANCE

Another factor must be known before finger stop proportions can be determined. Distance **A** between the strip edge and the front spacer must be established because this determines the amount of finger stop travel required to stop the strip in a positive manner. Tabulated are recommended distances **A** for hand feeding using an automatic stop, and power feeding using a roll feed or hitch feed. Distances **A** are given for various strip thicknesses.

13-11. FRONT SPACER THICKNESS

Recommended front spacer thicknesses are tabulated. These allow a minimum of 1/16 inch clearance between the top of the strip and the underside of the stripper plate to provide for possible curvature in the strip.

13-12. PROPORTIONS OF FINGER STOPS

Proportions of these fifteen finger stops enable ready selection for almost any die design and they assure positive stopping of the strip. In both the forward and return positions the maximum thicknesses of the stops remain confined in the front spacer for strength.

This table corresponds, for practical purposes, to the one in Fig. 13-9, and from it the designer can choose the most suitable finger stop for the conditions confronting him. For example, if 3/32 inch thick strip is to be run, and the die hole contour is smooth and curved, it would fall in the second line: Strip Thickness **A** – 1/16 to 1/8. Recommended front spacer width for this condition is 1¼ inches, and finger stop No. 2 should be used. The 1¼ inch dimension corresponds roughly to line 2 of table 13-9 for smooth die hole contour with a dimension of 1.2656 inches. For 1/32 inch thick strip, with sharp inside corners in the die hole, front spacer width, line 1, would be 2 inches and finger stop No. 11 should be used. Of course, slight modifications may be necessary for some dies. When in doubt as to correct classification of the die hole contour, use the next greater minimum distance. Only the front spacer width and thickness have been mentioned, but it is understood that the back gage is made the same width and thickness.

13-13. DIMENSIONS

All dimensions necessary are given for making finger stops ranging from No. 1 to 15. From this table the designer can apply dimensions quickly, or the finger stop can be specified by number when finger stops have been standardized. Note that:

1. Stops 1 to 5 are used when smooth contours are present in the die hole
2. Stops 6 to 10 are used when the die hole contains inside corners
3. Stops 11 to 15 are used when the die hole contains sharp inside corners.

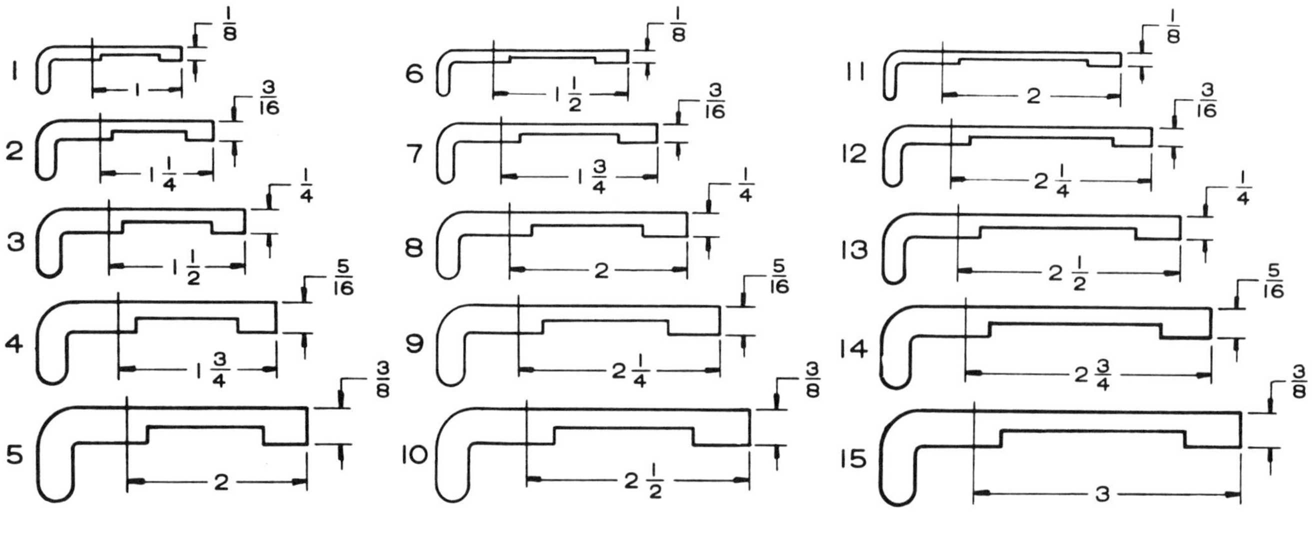

A	1 SMOOTH DIE HOLE CONTOUR		2 INSIDE CORNERS		3 SHARP INSIDE CORNERS	
STRIP THICKNESS	Front Spacer Width	Finger Stop No.	Front Spacer Width	Finger Stop No.	Front Spacer Width	Finger Stop No.
0 to 1/16	1	1	1 1/2	6	2	11
1/16 to 1/8	1 1/4	2	1 3/4	7	2 1/4	12
1/8 to 3/16	1 1/2	3	2	8	2 1/2	13
3/16 to 1/4	1 3/4	4	2 1/4	9	2 3/4	14
over 1/4	2	5	2 1/2	10	3	15

Fig. 13-12. Proportions of fifteen finger stops that assure positive stopping of the strip in almost any die design.

NO.	A	B	C	D	E	F
1	.125	1/4	21/32	1 15/32	.062	1.820
2	.187	5/16	13/16	1 3/4	.093	2.259
3	.250	3/8	31/32	2 1/32	.125	2.635
4	.312	7/16	1 1/8	2 5/16	.156	3.012
5	.375	1/2	1 9/32	2 19/32	.187	3.388

NO.	A	B	C	D	E	F
11	.125	3/8	1 7/16	2 1/2	.062	2.914
12	.187	7/16	1 19/32	2 25/32	.093	3.290
13	.250	1/2	1 3/4	3 1/16	.125	3.666
14	.312	9/16	1 29/32	3 11/32	.156	4.043
15	.375	5/8	2 1/16	3 5/8	.187	4.420

NO.	A	B	C	D	E	F
6	.125	3/8	15/16	2	.062	2.414
7	.187	7/16	1 3/32	2 9/32	.093	2.790
8	.250	1/2	1 1/4	2 9/16	.125	3.166
9	.312	9/16	1 13/32	2 27/32	.156	3.543
10	.375	5/8	1 9/16	3 1/8	.187	3.920

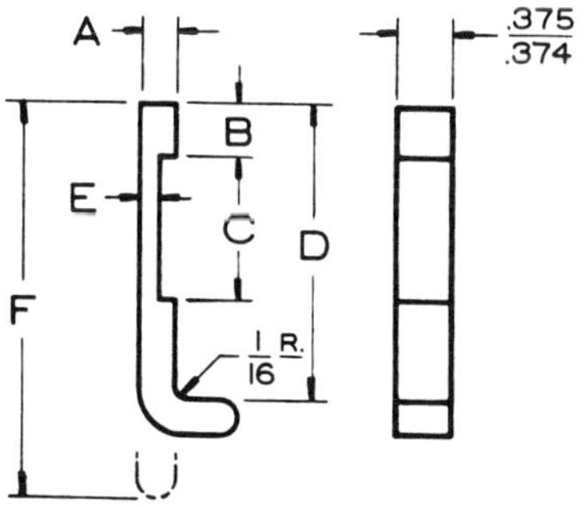

Fig. 13-13. Tables of all necessary dimensions for making finger stops.

13-14. SLOT MACHINING DIMENSIONS

Slot machining dimensions are tabulated to correspond with the finger stops in Fig. 13-13. Machining the front spacer in this way does not affect its function because it is simply a spacer between the die block and stripper plate.

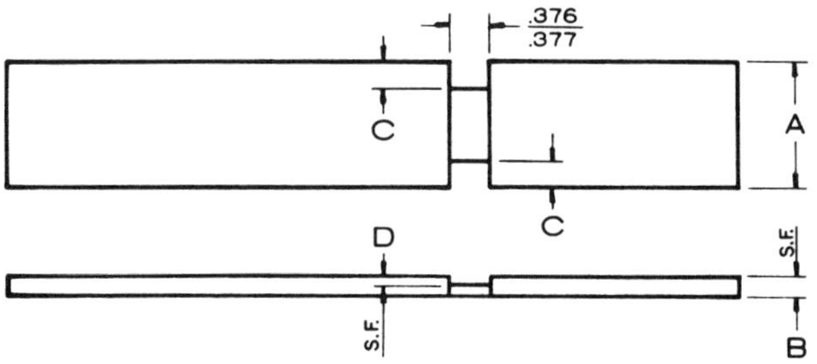

NO.	A	B	C	D
1	1	1/8	1/4	.064
2	1 1/4	3/16	5/16	.095
3	1 1/2	1/4	3/8	.127
4	1 3/4	5/16	7/16	.158
5	2	3/8	1/2	.189

NO.	A	B	C	D
6	1 1/2	1/8	3/8	1/16
7	1 3/4	3/16	7/16	3/32
8	2	1/4	1/2	1/8
9	2 1/4	5/16	9/16	5/32
10	2 1/2	3/8	5/8	3/16

NO.	A	B	C	D
11	2	1/8	3/8	1/16
12	2 1/4	3/16	7/16	3/32
13	2 1/2	1/4	1/2	1/8
14	2 3/4	5/16	9/16	5/32
15	3	3/8	5/8	3/16

Fig. 13-14. Tables of dimensions for machining slots in front spacer to accommodate the standard finger stops given in Fig. 13-13.

SPRING FINGER STOPS

Finger stops occupy a good position to act as stock pushers for keeping the strip firmly against the back gage in its travel through the die. Stock pushers are not ordinarily required for hand feeding because the operator can position the strip against the back gage while advancing it. However, their use eliminates the necessity for side pressure and more uniform strip runs are assured.

Stock pushers are indispensible when the strip is to be fed automatically with a roll or hitch feed. Their use makes possible some reduction in scrap bridge allowance with a saving in material cost. For cut-off dies, in which the edges of the strip become edges of the finished blanks, the use of stock pushers results in more accurate parts.

In the following illustrations is shown the method of modifying standard finger stops and of making actuating springs. Applied one way, the spring makes the stop a combination finger stop and stock pusher. Applied another way, the stop becomes a spring-actuated finger stop.

13-15. MACHINING SPRING FINGER STOPS

Conventional finger stop **A** has a slot milled in its underside to retain it in the front spacer and to limit stop travel. Shown at **B**, the stop is modified by end-milling, or spot-facing, radial pockets in both the heel and the toe of the stop to the same depth as the previously machined slot. Dimensions **C** of both stops remain the same.

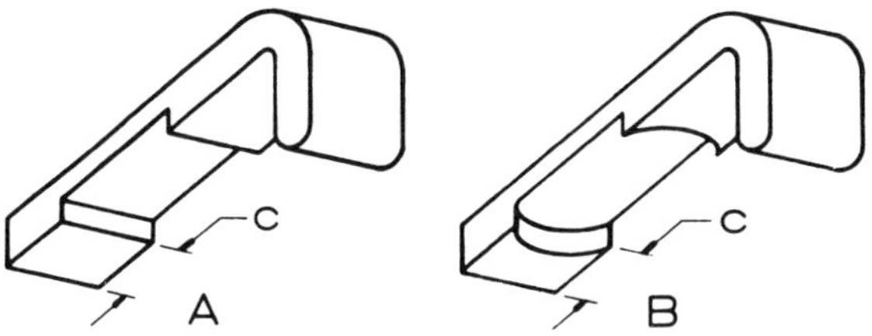

Fig. 13-15. Conventional (**A**) and modified (**B**) finger stops.

13-16. CONICAL SPRINGS

A conical spring, such as the one shown at **A**, can be compressed until it is completely closed, the coils slipping one into the other. A common application of this principle is the flashlight spring. A small conical spring like the one at **A** is used for the heavy finger stops with toe dimensions of 3/8 by 3/8 inch. Shown at **B** is a flattened conical spring, used for the thinner finger stop ranges.

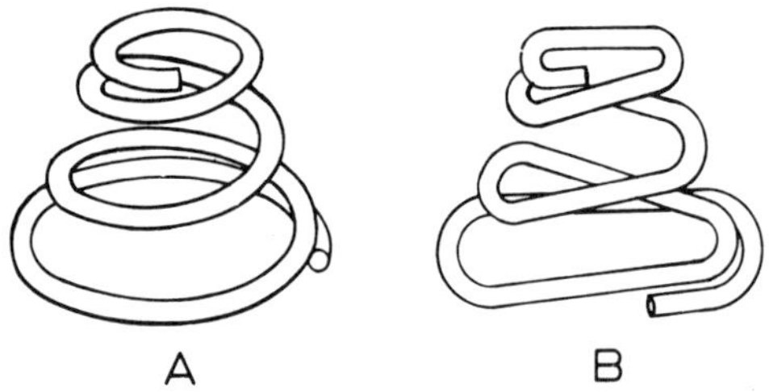

Fig. 13-16. Conical (**A**) and flattened conical (**B**) springs for use with spring finger stops.

13-17. SPRING APPLICATION

This illustrates the application of a conical spring to a finger stop to convert it into a combination finger stop and stock pusher. Spring **A**, acting against the face of the radial pocket in the toe of stop **B**, keeps it in a normally advanced position toward the back gage. Both stop and spring are retained in front spacer **C**. The strip has been brought against the toe of the stop for piercing holes at the first station. The enlarged view shows the stop, spring, and front spacer with the stripper plate removed.

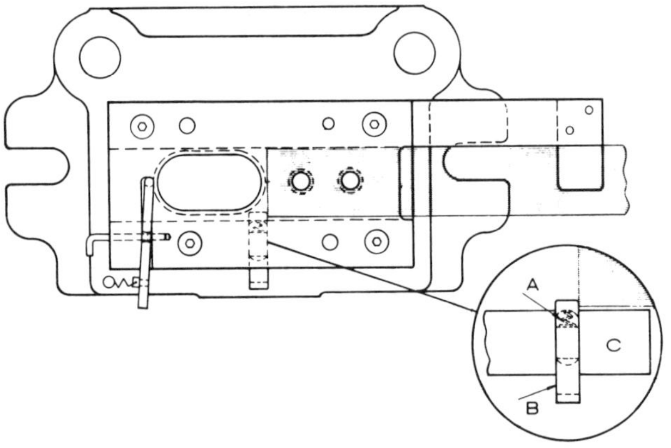

Fig. 13-17. Method of application of a conical spring to a finger stop making it a combination finger stop and stock pusher.

13-18. STOCK PUSHER OPERATION

The stop has now been retracted by the operator, compressing the spring to allow the strip to advance against the automatic stop. Releasing the stop causes the spring to push the strip firmly against the back gage. It now acts as a stock pusher until all blanks have been removed from the strip. When a new strip is started it is used as a finger stop again.

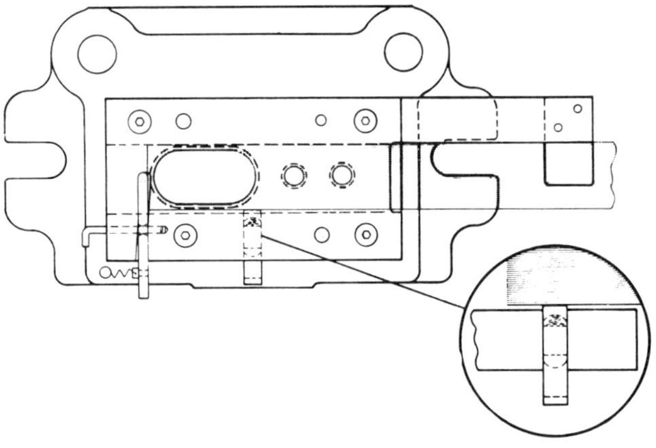

Fig. 13-18. Finger stop in use as a stock pusher.

13-19. SPRING FINGER STOP

When the same spring is assembled in the back radial pocket of the stop, spring pressure acts to keep the stop away from the strip, as shown. In this view the strip is running through the die with only the automatic stop modifying and limiting its travel.

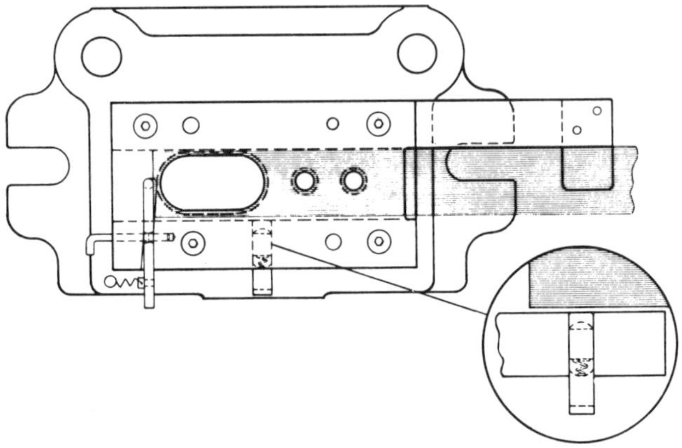

Fig. 13-19. Conical spring in back radial pocket keeps stop away from strip.

13-20. SPRING FINGER STOP OPERATION

To stop the strip for piercing two holes at the first station the stop is pushed in by the operator, compressing the spring. Upon release it moves back automatically to allow feeding of the strip.

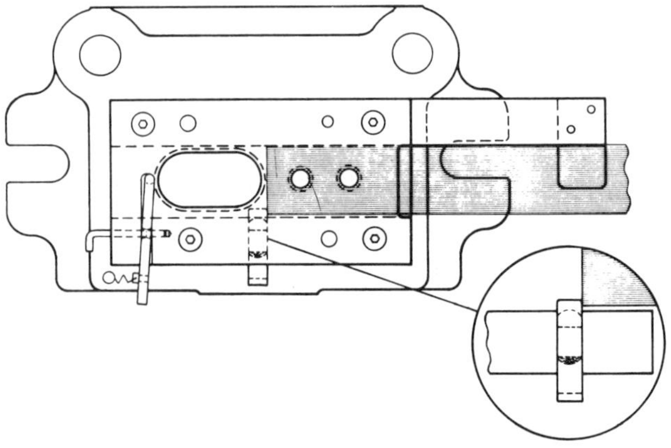

Fig. 13-20. Spring finger stop is pushed in by operator to stop strip for first piercing operation.

13-21. DIMENSIONS OF RADIAL SLOTS

Tabulated are machining dimensions for applying radial pockets to the line of finger stops described in Fig. 13-13. These can be end-milled, or spotfaced using a simple drill jig with guide bushings.

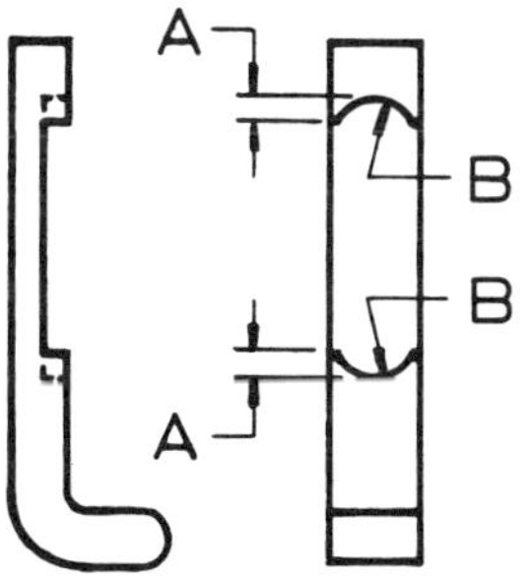

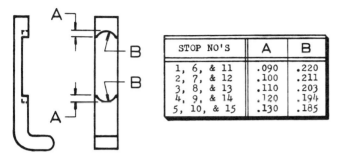

STOP NO'S	A	B
1, 6, & 11	.090	.220
2, 7, & 12	.100	.211
3, 8, & 13	.110	.203
4, 9, & 14	.120	.194
5, 10, & 15	.130	.185

Fig. 13-21. Table of machining dimensions for applying radial pockets in finger stops of Fig. 13-13.

13-22. MULTIPLE STOPS AND STOCK PUSHERS

This practical application is a four-station progressive die for producing pierced and stamped links. The two outside finger stops have been assembled to act as stock pushers as well. The center stop was assembled as a spring finger stop to reduce excessive drag on the strip. When a number of finger stops are used, only the end ones need be usually assembled as stock pushers. Thus, the strip is located against the back gage as early as possible in its travel through the die.

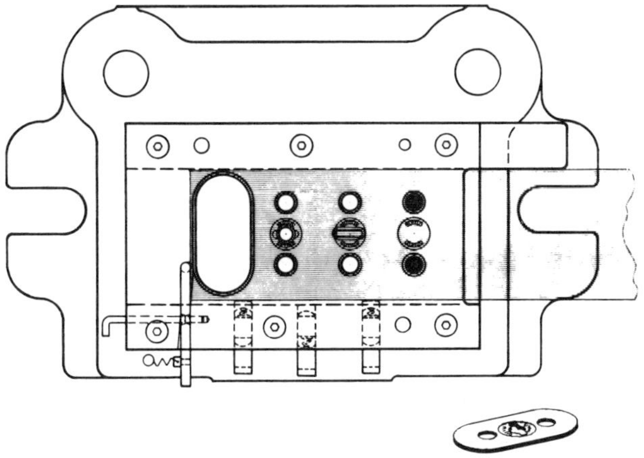

Fig. 13-22. A four-station progressive die utilizing two stock pushers and a spring finger stop.

13-23. CUT-OFF DIES

When are finger stops not needed in a die? For most cut-off dies, finger stops are not required. Illustrated is a simple cut-off die for producing rectangular blanks. In operation the end of the strip is advanced until it projects slightly past the cutting edge. Tripping the press trims the end of the strip square. The strip is then advanced against stop **A**, which also backs up the cut-off punch to prevent deflection while cutting. No finger stop is needed because trimming the end of the strip prepares it for register against stop **A**.

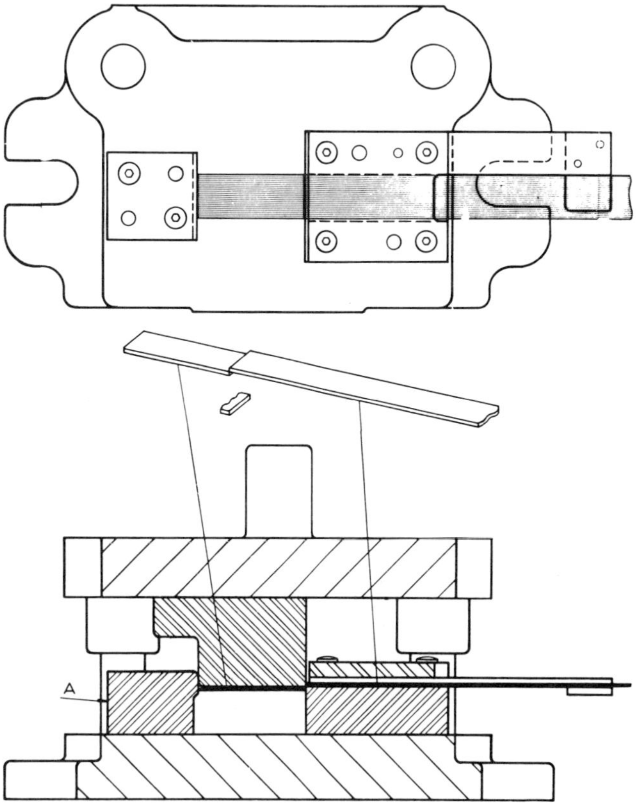

Fig. 13-23. Cut-off die in which finger stops are not required

Section 14

HOW TO DESIGN AUTOMATIC STOPS

Automatic stops, or trigger stops as they are sometimes called, register the strip at the final die station. They differ from finger stops in that they stop the strip automatically, the operator simply keeping the strip pushed against the stop in its travel through the die. For this reason they are always used when an operator is to feed the strip by hand. Automatic stops can be made of cold-rolled steel or machine steel, cyanide hardened, but when long runs are anticipated they should be made of tool steel, hardened after machining. Design considerations include:

1. Fast, positive action under high-speed, high-shock conditions.
2. Minimum machining of the stripper plate for strength.
3. Sturdy, "gadget-free" design. Automatic stops perform grueling service in operation, and weak design can be a source of trouble.

Illustrated are seventeen standardized automatic stops with dimensions tabulated to aid the designer in selecting the right one for the conditions encountered. In addition, general rules are outlined to help in the correct application of these die components. This material further explains Step 9 in Section 5, "Fourteen Steps to Design a Die."

14-1. SIDE-ACTING STOP

Taken together, two plan views **A** and **B**, with a common side section-view **C**, illustrate the operation of a conventional side-acting automatic stop. At **A** the strip has been advanced toward the left. Previously blanked strip edge **D** contacts the toe of the automatic stop, moving it to its extreme left position as shown, "setting" the stop. Descent of the press ram causes the square-head set screw **5** to raise the stop toe to the position shown in section view **C**. Now, the tension spring **3**, acting at an upward angle, turns the stop to the position shown in view **B**. When the press ram goes up the toe of the stop falls on top of the scrap bridge, allowing the strip to slide under it. After the scrap bridge has passed completely under it, the toe drops to the top surface of the die block, acted upon by spring **3**. Now the stop is ready to be reset upon contact of the next blanked strip edge.

These motions occur at extremely high speeds. On fast runs the motions cannot be followed by the eye. Six parts make up the stop assembly. They are:

1. Automatic stop
2. Fulcrum pin
3. Tension spring
4. Spring post
5. Square-head set screw, usually ¼ in. diameter
6. Jam nut.

As shown in the inset of the pictorial view, the hole for the fulcrum pin is taper-reamed from both sides to allow rocking. The slot in the stripper plate is machined angularly to allow stop movement. It is not machined entirely through the stripper plate except at the toe and opposite the fulcrum-hole portion for strength.

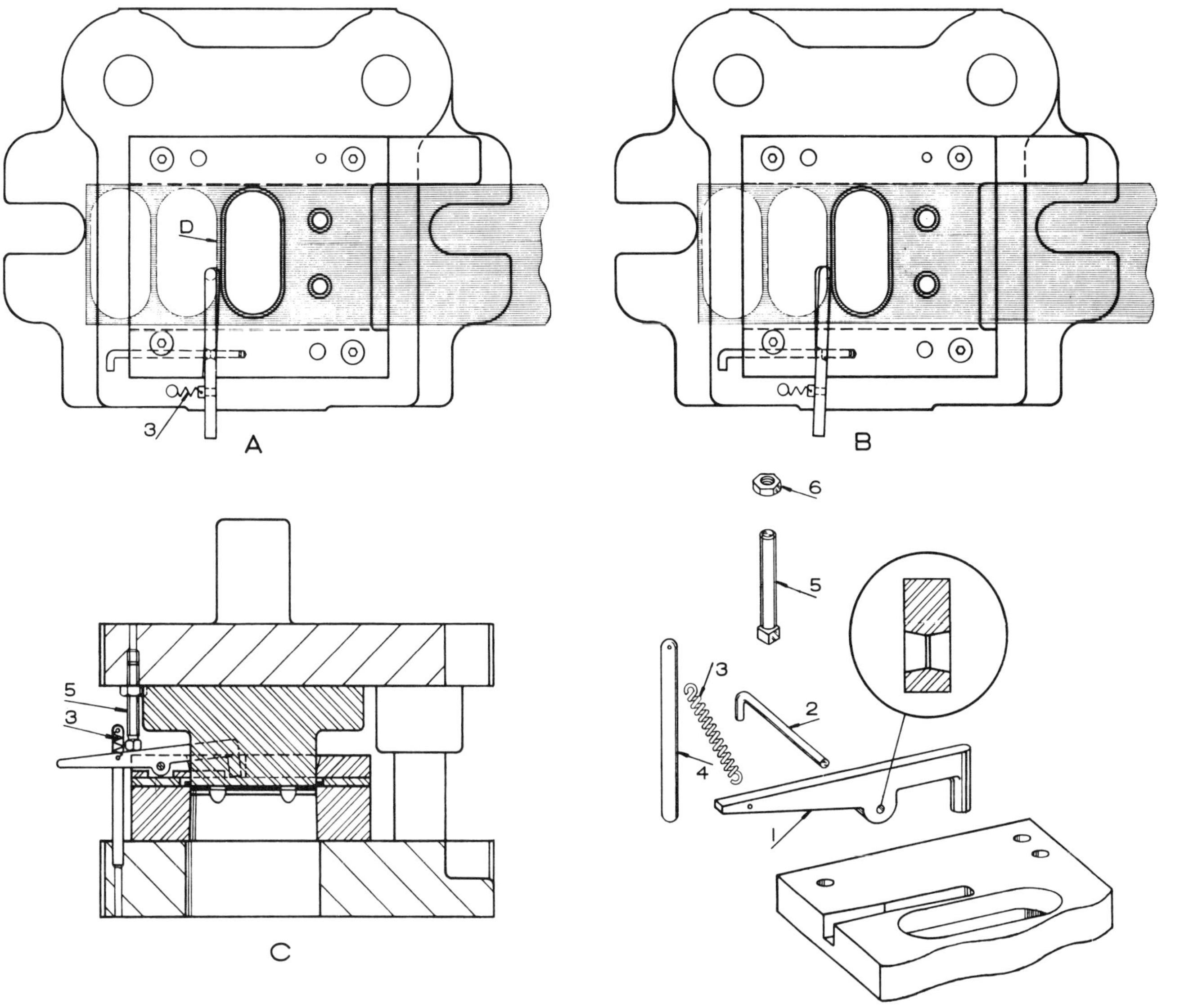

Fig. 14-1. Typical side-acting automatic stop.

14-2. STOP HOLDER

Another method of applying a side-acting automatic stop is to confine the stop in a holder. Here are the features of this construction:

1. The holder can be easily hardened to provide long life
2. Very little machining of the stripper plate is required
3. The stop is a self-contained unit, and it can be quickly removed and used in several dies
4. There is no post and exposed spring. Instead, the stop has husky parts and simple, clean lines.

View **A** shows the automatic stop "set" and ready for blanking of the hole. At view **B** the press has descended, releasing the stop and causing it to swing above the scrap bridge. The pictorial view shows stop construction. Stop **1** fits in a tapered slot in holder **2**, held by fulcrum pin **3**. Compression spring **4** provides the required movement. As in Fig. 14-1 a square-head set screw **5**, locked by jam nut **6**, is applied to the punch holder for operating the stop. In this case the fulcrum-pin hole is taper reamed from one side only to allow the spring to provide side thrust, as well as up and down movement.

14-3. END-ACTING STOP

The same type of stop can be designed as an end-acting automatic stop. End-acting automatic stops are easier to standardize because they don't have the great range of lengths required in side-acting stops. The primary modification is an end-milled slot instead of a tapered hole to engage the fulcrum pin. Views **A** and **B** show the stop "set," the strip having pushed it back to its maximum left position. Descent of the press ram causes the square-head set screw to turn the stop to the position shown at view **C**. The spring has now pushed the stop toward the right, the end-milled slot allowing movement. It is obvious from this view that when the upper die goes up the toe of the stop will drop on top of the scrap bridge, allowing movement of the strip toward left until the toe is again engaged by the strip. View **A** is a plan view of the die, while

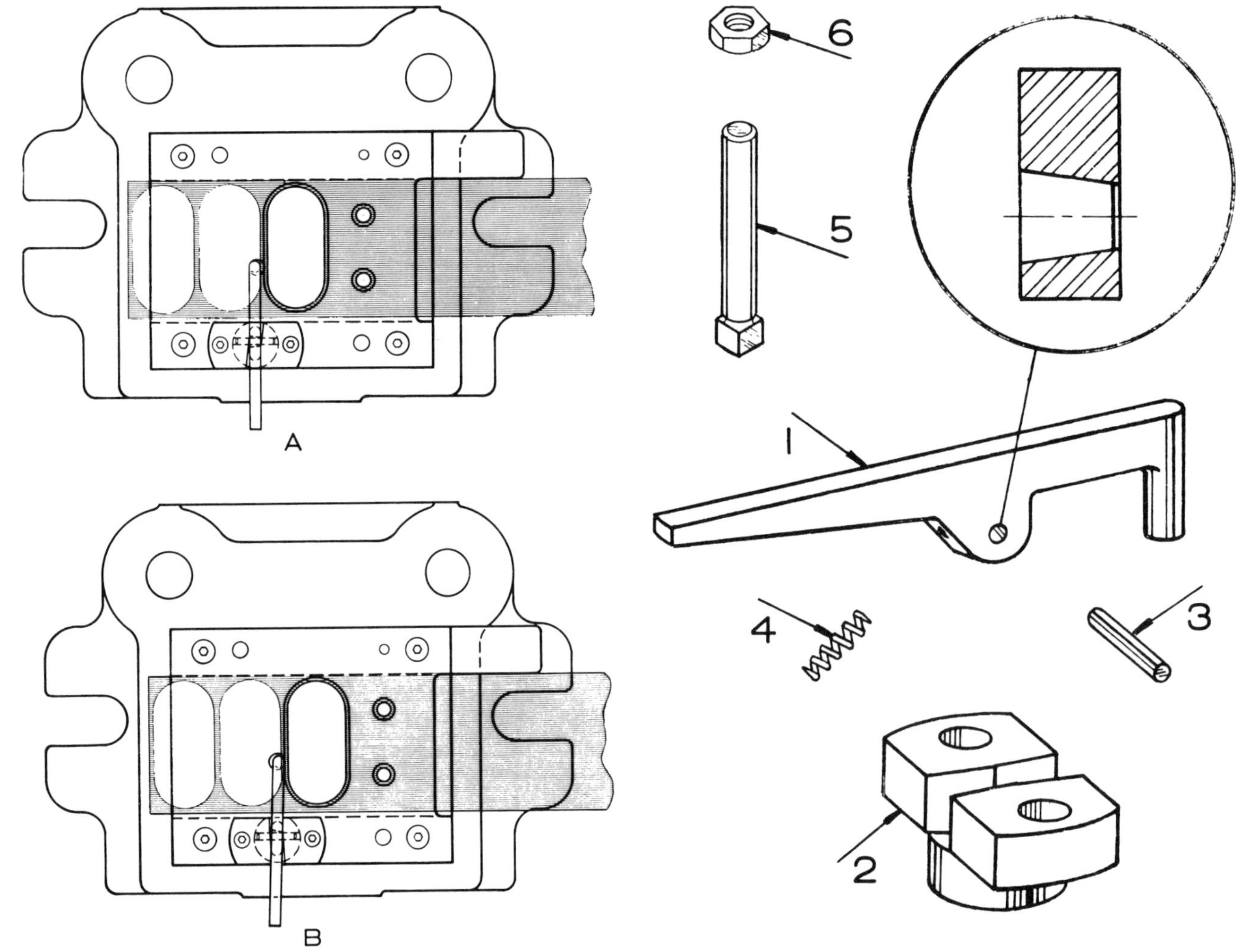

Fig. 14-2. Side-acting automatic stop that is incorporated into a holder.

views **B** and **C** are section views showing operation of the stop.

Dimension **D** is the sum of the following:

½ Feed
1 Scrap Bridge Allowance
0.010 inch

The allowance causes the strip to be stopped 0.010 inch past its required position. Pilots, engaging in previously pierced holes, bring the strip back this amount for final accurate location before blanking occurs.

14-4. SPRING PLUNGER

Using a square-head set screw for actuating automatic stops is a time-honored practice that usually works well. One disadvantage is that the set screw must be backed up practically every time the die is sharpened by the amount removed from punch and die members. Many automatic stops have been smashed by the set screw through failure to retract it sufficiently after die sharpening. View **A** shows a Vlier spring plunger, applied as stop actuator. These are available from Vlier Engineering Co. The spring plunger has been backed up by a socket lock screw, although a jam nut would be equally effective. The spring-loaded toe of the Vlier plunger actuates the automatic stop. The heavy series of these standard components should be used to assure positive action. The view at **B** shows the same die in closed position after repeated sharpening. The spring plunger has not been reset in any way. After actuating the stop, the spring loaded end retracts harmlessly as shown.

14-5. STRIPPER PLATE THICKNESS

Automatic stop proportions can only be determined after we know what stripper plate thickness will be used. The correct value is found by the formula:

$$A = \frac{W}{30} + 2T$$

In which: A = Thickness of stripper plate
W = Width of strip
T = Strip thickness

Shown in Table 1 are stripper plate thicknesses **A** for representative strip sizes. Table 2 gives recommended commercially available plate thicknesses and it corresponds, for practical purposes, with Table 1.

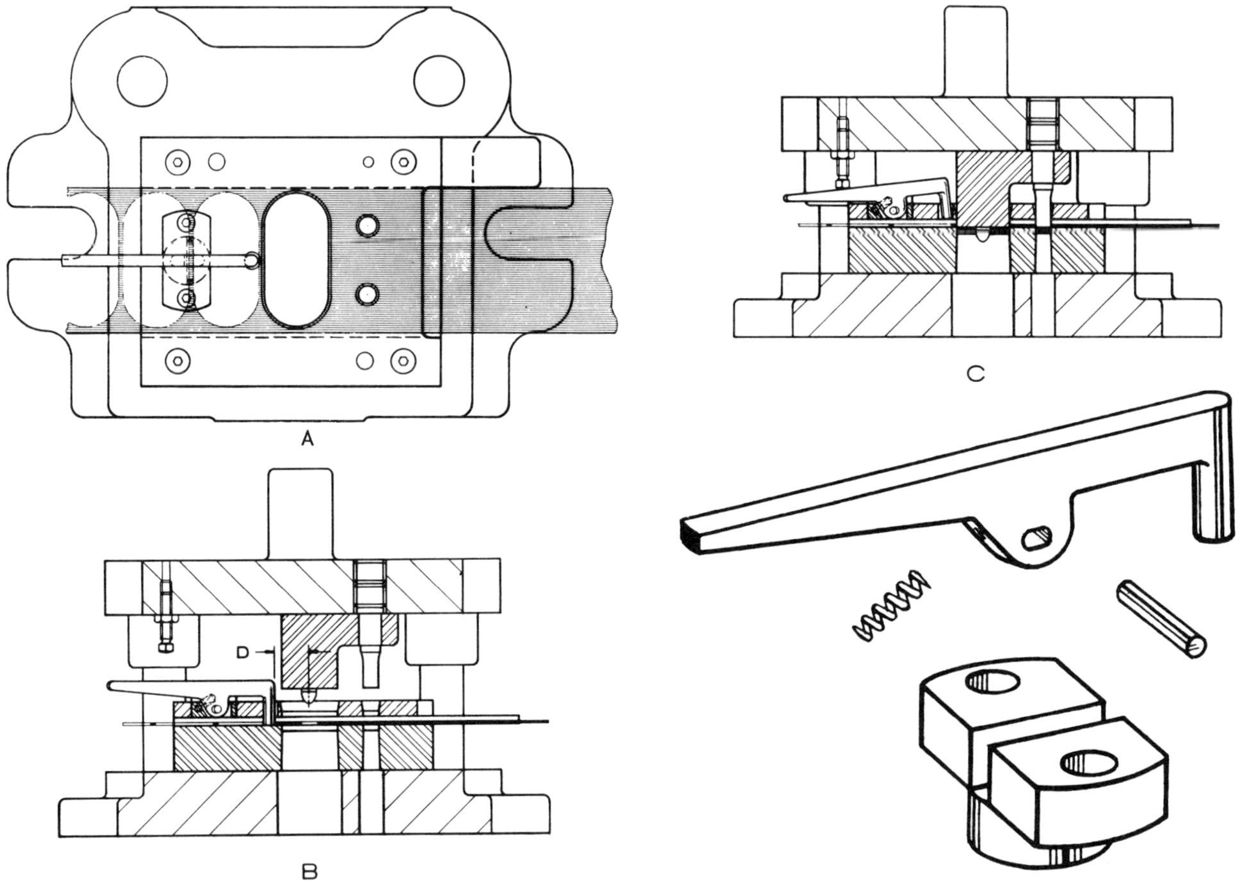

Fig. 14-3. Typical end-acting automatic stop.

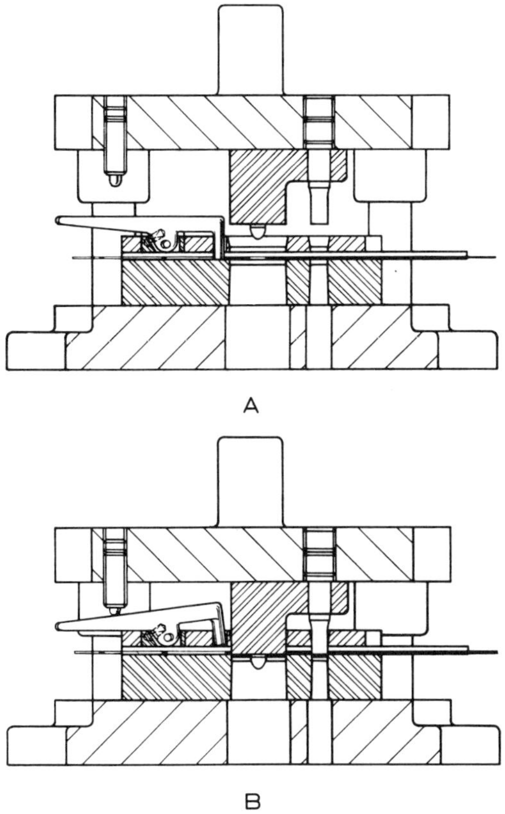

Fig. 14-4. Actuating an automatic stop with a spring plunger.

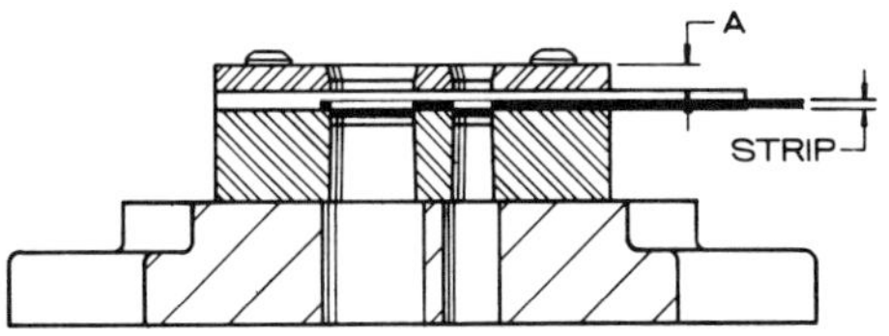

1

STRIP	A
1/16 x 3	.225
1/16 x 6	.325
1/16 x 9	.425
1/16 x 12	.525
1/8 x 3	.350
1/8 x 6	.450
1/8 x 9	.550
1/8 x 12	.650
3/16 x 3	.475
3/16 x 6	.575
3/16 x 9	.675
3/16 x 12	.775
1/4 x 3	.600
1/4 x 6	.700
1/4 x 9	.800
1/4 x 12	.900
5/16 x 3	.725
5/16 x 6	.825
5/16 x 9	.925
5/16 x 12	1.025

2

STRIP	A
1/16 x 3	1/4
1/16 x 6	3/8
1/16 x 9	1/2
1/16 x 12	5/8
1/8 x 3	3/8
1/8 x 6	1/2
1/8 x 9	5/8
1/8 x 12	3/4
3/16 x 3	1/2
3/16 x 6	5/8
3/16 x 9	3/4
3/16 x 12	7/8
1/4 x 3	5/8
1/4 x 6	3/4
1/4 x 9	7/8
1/4 x 12	1
5/16 x 3	3/4
5/16 x 6	7/8
5/16 x 9	1
5/16 x 12	1 1/8

Fig. 14-5. Tables of stripper plate thicknesses for representative strip sizes (1) and corresponding commercially available plate thicknesses (2).

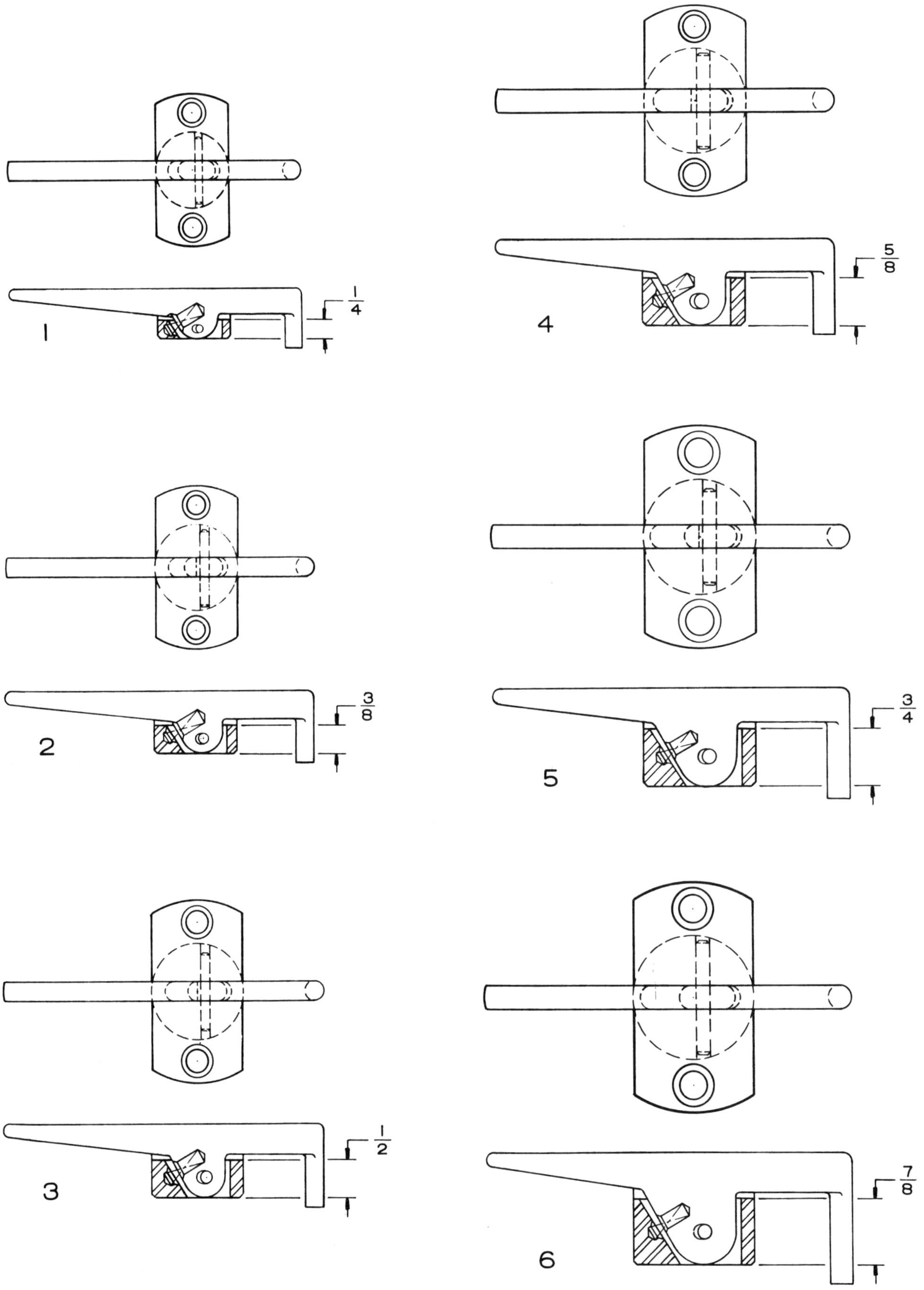

Fig. 14-6. Proportions for six standard automatic stops.

From this table the designer can quickly select correct stripper plate thickness for the conditions facing him. For example, if strip 1/8 inch by 5 inches is to be run, select the 1/8 by 6 size listed in the table and use a 1/2 inch stripper plate thickness. For 3/32 by 4 inch strip, use the value given for 1/8 by 3 inch strip given in the table, and a 3/8 inch stripper plate thickness can be used safely. When in doubt as to correct corresponding size, use the next thicker plate. Of course, these are minimum thicknesses for adequate strength. Other factors may cause the designer to choose thicker plate. For example, if the fulcrum pin of the automatic stop is to be retained in the stripper plate, the 1/4 inch thick plate may be considered thin and a 3/8 plate used instead.

14-6. STANDARDIZED STOPS AND HOLDERS

Proportions of these six standardized automatic stops enable ready selection for almost any die design as they can be used in stripper plates varying in thickness from 1/4 to 7/8 inch, in increments of 1/8 inch. Note that first, the correct stripper plate thickness is selected from Table 2 of Fig. 14-5. Then, from this table, select the corresponding stop to use.

14-7. DIMENSIONS OF STOPS

All necessary dimensions are given for making automatic stops ranging from Nos. 1 to 6. From this table the designer can apply dimensions, or the automatic stop can be specified by number. If a side-acting stop like the one shown in Fig. 14-1 is to be designed, it can be given the same general proportions.

14-8. DIMENSIONS OF HOLDERS

All necessary dimensions are supplied for holders to be used with stops Nos. 1 to 6. These holders would be made of machine steel unless unusually severe duty is anticipated, in which case they would be made of tool steel and heat treated.

14-9. HOLES IN STRIPPER PLATES

This table gives dimensions for machining the holes in the stripper plate to receive the automatic stop assembly. This type of automatic stop is a self-contained unit and it can be removed quickly from the die by simply removing two screws.

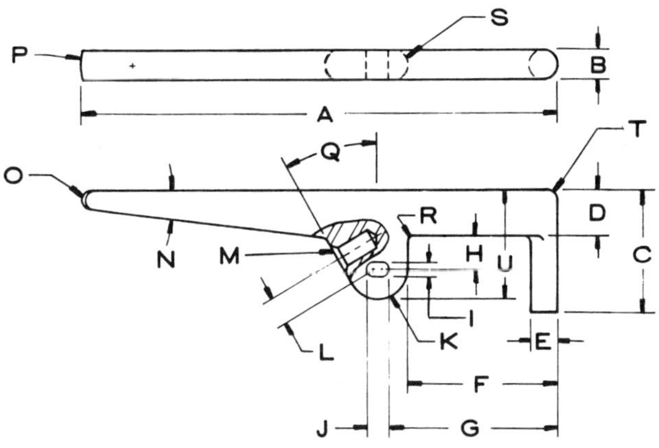

NO.	A	B	C	D	E	F	G	H	I	J	K	L
1	4	1/4	25/32	11/32	1/4	1 3/16	1 3/8	3/16	3/32	1/8	9/32 R.	3/16
2	4 3/16	1/4	15/16	3/8	1/4	1 1/4	1 7/16	1/4	1/8	5/32	9/32 R.	1/4
3	4 3/8	1/4	1 3/32	13/32	1/4	1 3/8	1 9/16	5/16	1/8	5/32	9/32 R.	1/4
4	4 9/16	5/16	1 1/4	7/16	5/16	1 15/32	1 11/16	3/8	3/16	7/32	11/32 R.	9/32
5	4 13/16	5/16	1 15/32	15/32	5/16	1 17/32	1 13/16	7/16	3/16	7/32	13/32 R.	5/16
6	5	5/16	1 11/16	1/2	5/16	1 5/8	1 15/16	1/2	3/16	7/32	7/16 R.	3/8

NO.	M	N	O	P	Q	R	S	T	U
1	3/16 Dr. 3/8 Dp. 45 C/sink 1/16 Dp.	6°	1/16 R.	1/2 R.	30°	3/64 R.	1/8 R.	1/16 R.	21/32
2	3/16 Dr. 3/8 Dp. 45 C/sink 1/16 Dp.	6°	5/64 R.	1/2 R.	30°	3/64 R.	1/8 R.	5/64 R.	13/16
3	3/16 Dr. 3/8 Dp. 45 C/sink 1/16 Dp.	6 1/2°	5/64 R.	1/2 R.	30°	3/64 R.	1/8 R.	3/32 R.	31/32
4	3/16 Dr. 3/8 Dp. 45 C/sink 1/16 Dp.	6 1/2°	3/32 R.	1/2 R.	30°	3/64 R.	5/32 R.	7/64 R.	1 1/8
5	3/16 Dr. 3/8 Dp. 45 C/sink 1/16 Dp.	7°	3/32 R.	1/2 R.	30°	3/64 R.	5/32 R.	1/8 R.	1 9/32
6	3/16 Dr. 3/8 Dp.	7 1/2°	3/32 R.	1/2 R.	30°	3/64 R.	5/32 R.	5/32 R.	1 7/16

Fig. 14-7. Tables of dimensions for making the six standard automatic stops given in Fig. 14-6.

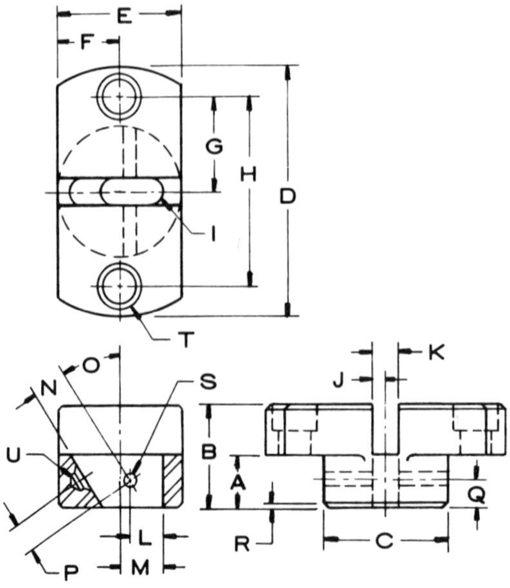

NO.	A	B	C	D	E	F	G	H	I	J	K	L	M	N
1	1/4	21/32	1	2	1	1/2	3/4	1 1/2	1/8	1/8	1/4	5/16	23/64	5/16
2	3/8	13/16	1 1/8	2 1/8	1 1/8	9/16	13/16	1 5/8	1/8	1/8	1/4	11/32	13/32	11/32
3	1/2	31/32	1 1/4	2 3/8	1 1/4	5/8	29/32	1 13/16	1/8	1/8	1/4	11/32	7/16	3/8
4	5/8	1 1/8	1 3/8	2 1/2	1 3/8	11/16	31/32	1 15/16	5/32	5/32	5/16	13/32	1/2	7/16
5	3/4	1 9/32	1 1/2	2 7/8	1 1/2	3/4	1 3/32	2 3/16	5/32	5/32	5/16	15/32	9/16	15/32
6	7/8	1 7/16	1 5/8	3	1 5/8	13/16	1 5/32	2 5/16	5/32	5/32	5/16	1/2	5/8	17/32

NO.	O	P	Q	R	S	T	U
1	33°	7/32	1/8	1/32 x 45°	3/32	17/64 Dr.-13/32 C'bore 1/4 Dp.	3/16 Dr. 3/32 Dp. 45° C'sink 3/64 Dp.
2	33°	17/64	3/16	1/32 x 45°	1/8	17/64 Dr.-13/32 C'bore 1/4 Dp.	3/16 Dr. 3/32 Dp. 45° C'sink 3/64 Dp.
3	33°	17/64	1/4	1/32 x 45°	1/8	21/64 Dr.-15/32 C'bore 5/16 Dp.	3/16 Dr. 3/32 Dp. 45° C'sink 3/64 Dp.
4	33°	5/16	5/16	1/32 x 45°	3/16	21/64 Dr.-15/32 C'bore 5/16 Dp.	3/16 Dr. 3/32 Dp. 45° C'sink 3/64 Dp.
5	33°	11/32	3/8	1/32 x 45°	3/16	25/64 Dr.-19/32 C'bore 9/16 Dp.	3/16 Dr. 3/32 Dp. 45° C'sink 3/64 Dp.
6	33°	3/8	7/16	1/32 x 45°	3/16	25/64 Dr.-19/32 C'bore 9/16 Dp.	3/16 Dr. 3/32 Dp. 45° C'sink 3/64 Dp.

Fig. 14-8. Tables of dimensions for holders to be used with the six standard automatic stops.

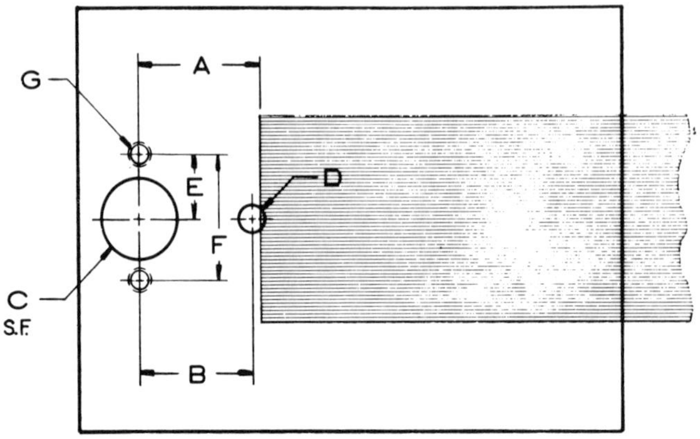

NO.	A	B	C	D	E	F	G
1	1.4687	1.3750	1	5/16	3/4	1 1/2	1/4-20 Tap
2	1.5625	1.4687	1 1/8	5/16	13/16	1 5/8	1/4-20 Tap
3	1.7187	1.6406	1 1/4	11/32	29/32	1 13/16	5/16-18 Tap
4	1.8750	1.7656	1 3/8	13/32	31/32	1 15/16	5/16-18 Tap
5	2.0000	1.8906	1 1/2	13/32	1 3/32	2 3/16	3/8-16 Tap
6	2.1562	2.0625	1 5/8	7/16	1 5/32	2 5/16	3/8-16 Tap

Fig. 14-9. Table of dimensions for machining automatic stop assembly holes in the stripper plate.

14-10. SET SCREW LOCATION

Tabulated are dimensions **A** between automatic stop and actuating square-head set screw. By standardizing the position of the actuating screw, more uniform results are assured.

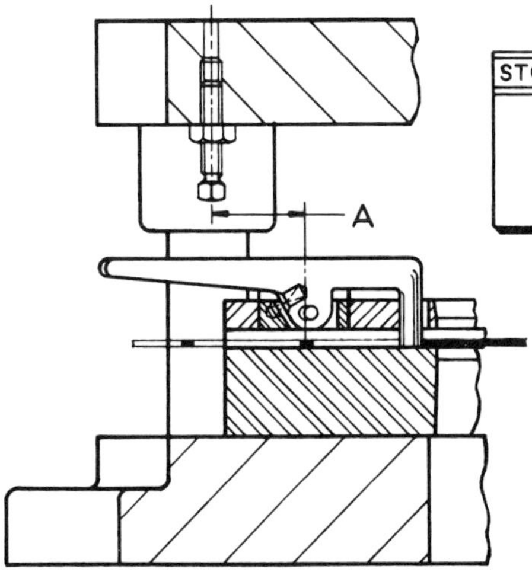

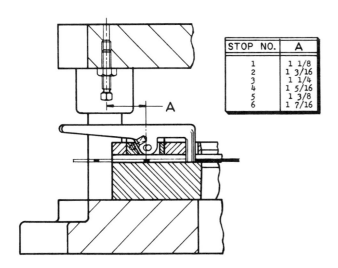

STOP NO.	A
1	1 1/8
2	1 3/16
3	1 1/4
4	1 5/16
5	1 3/8
6	1 7/16

Fig. 14-10. Tabulated dimensions (**A**) of distance between automatic stop and square-head set screw for the six standard automatic stops.

14-11. TOE LENGTHS

Toe lengths **A** are given for all stops incorporating the variations described in Fig. 14-12. We now have 17 standardized automatic stops, many of which vary only in respect to dimension **A**.

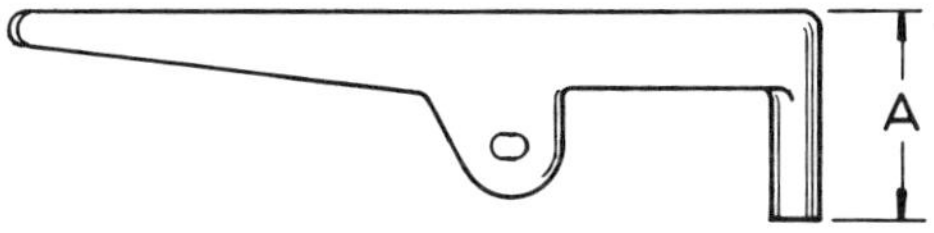

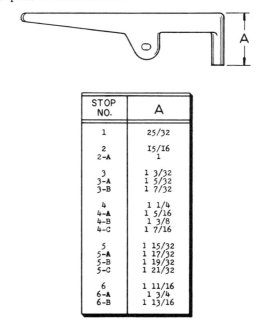

STOP NO.	A
1	25/32
2	15/16
2-A	1
3	1 3/32
3-A	1 5/32
3-B	1 7/32
4	1 1/4
4-A	1 5/16
4-B	1 3/8
4-C	1 7/16
5	1 15/32
5-A	1 17/32
5-B	1 19/32
5-C	1 21/32
6	1 11/16
6-A	1 3/4
6-B	1 13/16

Fig. 14-11. Tabulation of toe length (**A**) dimensions.

14-12. BACK GAGE THICKNESS

Still another factor must be taken into consideration when specifying toe length **C** of Fig. 14-7 and **A** of Fig. 14-11. This is the thickness **B** of the back gage and front spacer, because in Table 2 of Fig. 14-5, the same stripper plate thickness can be used for more than one strip thickness. For example, a stripper plate 3/8 inch thick is used for 1/16 by 6 inch strip. But it is also used for 1/8 by 3 inch strip which would require a thicker back gage and front spacer, raising the stop.

In this table further automatic stop numbers are applied to allow for these variations. For example, stripper plate thickness 1/2 inch can have a spacer thickness **B** of 1/8 inch which calls for stop No. 3. It may also have a spacer thickness of 3/16 inch in which case stop No. 3-A would be used. Still another spacer thickness is 1/4 inch, with which stop No. 3-B would be used.

STRIPPER PLATE THICKNESS A											
1/4		3/8		1/2		5/8		3/4		7/8	
B	NO.	B	NO.	B	NO.	B	NO.	B	NO.	B	NO.
1/8	1	1/8	2	1/8	3	1/8	4	3/16	5	1/4	6
		3/16	2-A	3/16	3-A	3/16	4-A	1/4	5-A	5/16	6-A
				1/4	3-B	1/4	4-B	5/16	5-B	3/8	6-B
						5/16	4-C	3/8	5-C		

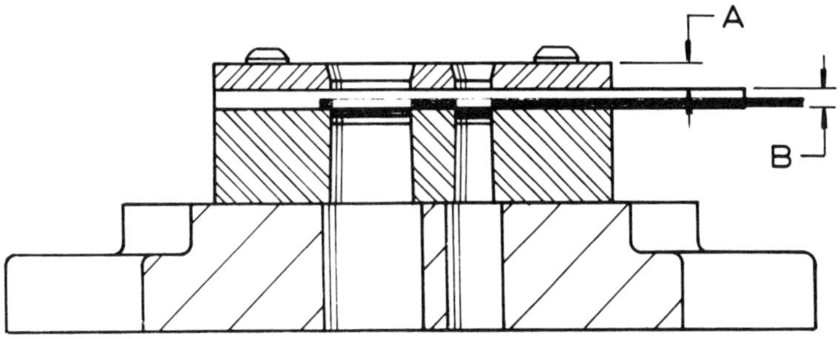

Fig. 14-12. Modifications of six standard automatic stop numbers to allow for varying thicknesses of back gage and front spacer.

14-13. FULCRUM PIN

Dimensions are given for fulcrum pins for all stops. Fulcrum pins are ordinarily made of cold rolled steel, but they would be made of drill rod for long runs.

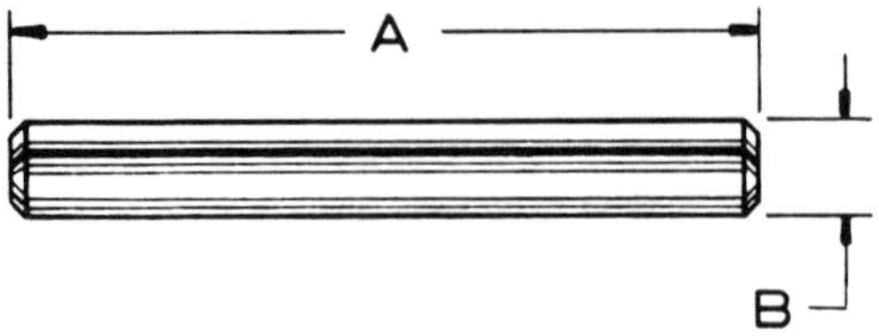

STOP NO.	A	B
1	7/8	3/32
2	1	1/8
3	1 1/8	1/8
4	1 1/4	3/16
5	1 3/8	3/16
6	1 1/2	3/16

Fig. 14-13. Table of fulcrum pin dimensions.

14-14. SPRING DIMENSIONS

Outside dimensions of springs used in these automatic stops are now given. All stops use the same size spring, but pressure can be varied by using different wire diameters.

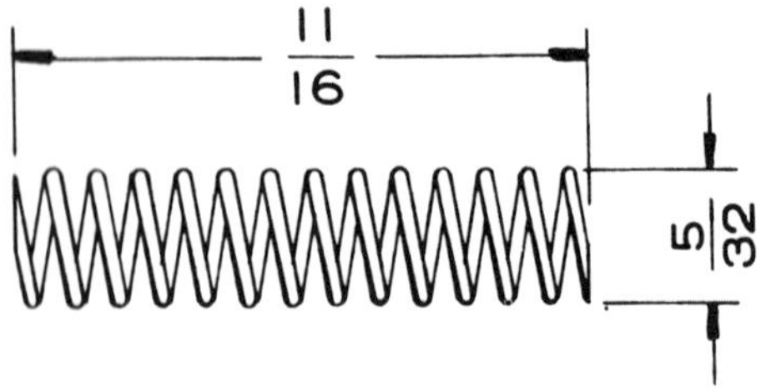

Fig. 14-14. Spring dimensions for use in standard automatic stops.

14-15. PIN STOP

Trigger type automatic stops previously described are used for all but very wide blanks. Wide blanks, run in slow presses, can be located by a simple pin stop pressed into the die block. In operation the strip clings around the blanking punch and is removed from it upon contact with the underside of the stripper plate. The operator applies pressure against the strip tending to move it toward the left so that, as it is released, it falls with the scrap bridge on top of the pin stop to allow feeding. A sight hole should always be applied to the stripper plate so that the operator can see stop action.

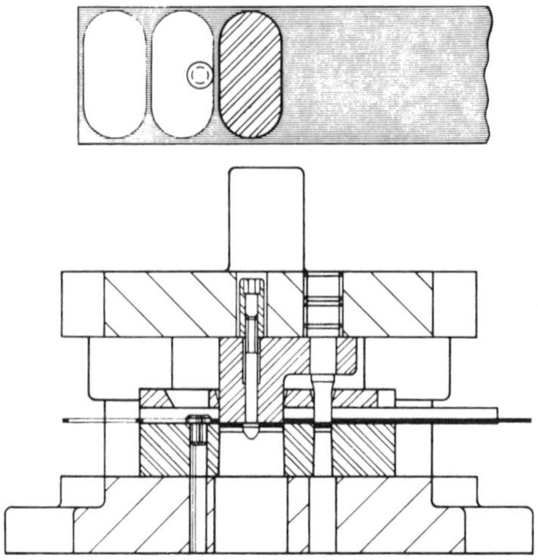

Fig. 14-15. Simple pin stop for wide blanks run in slow presses.

Section 15

HOW TO DESIGN STRIPPERS

Stripper plates remove the material strip from around blanking and piercing punches. Severe adhesion of strip to punches is characteristic of the die cutting process. Because of their low cost, solid strippers are the most frequently used type, particularly when running strip stock. Spring strippers, though more complex, should be used when the following conditions are present:

1. When perfectly flat, accurate blanks are required, because spring strippers flatten the sheet before cutting begins.
2. When blanking or piercing very thin material, to prevent uneven fracture and rounded blank edges.
3. When parts are to be pressed from waste strip left over from other operations, spring strippers provide good visibility to the operator for gaging purposes.
4. Because stripping occurs immediately, small punches are not as subject to breakage.
5. In secondary operations, such as in piercing dies, increased visibility provided by spring strippers allows faster loading of work and increased production.

Stripper plates may be made of cold-rolled steel if they are not to be machined except for holes. When machining must be applied to clear gages, the plates should be made of machine steel, which is not as subject to distortion. Illustrated and described in this section are eighteen methods of applying stripper plates and their components. These methods further explain Step 10 in Section 5, "14 Steps to Design a Die."

15-1. SOLID STRIPPERS

Here is the most common method of applying a solid stripper. Plate **A**, machined to receive blanking and piercing punches, is fastened in position on top of the back gage and front spacer with four button head socket screws. Two dowels accurately locate the stripper plate in relation to the die block and back gage. A small, short dowel locates the other end of the back gage to the stripper plate. Notch **B** is machined in the stripper edge to provide a shelf for starting new strips through the die.

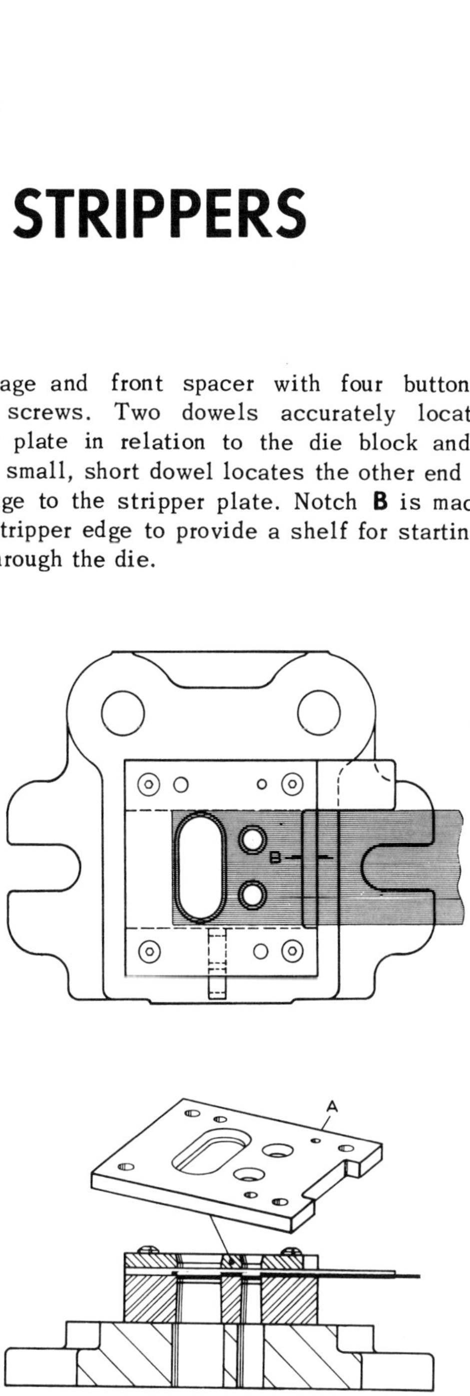

Fig. 15-1. Common method of applying a solid stripper.

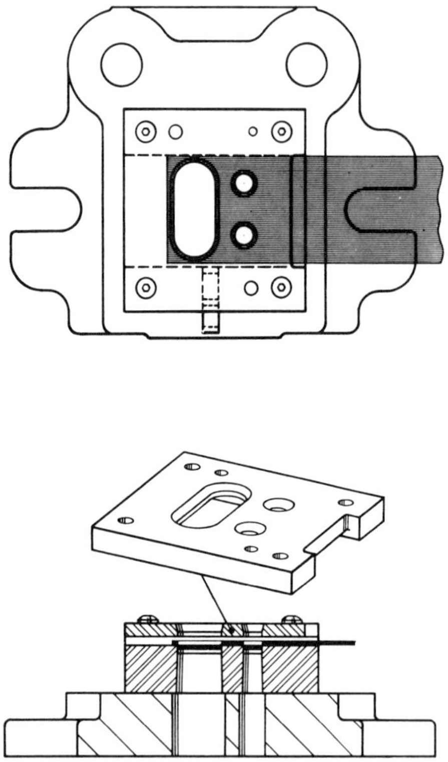

Fig. 15-2. Alternate design of solid stripper used now only for very small dies.

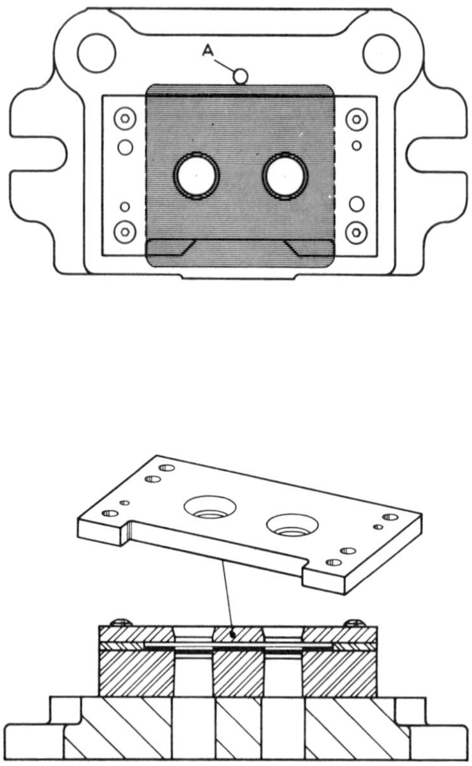

Fig. 15-3. Stripper plate for secondary operations.

15-2. ALTERNATE METHOD

An alternate method of designing a solid stripper is to make it thicker and machine a slot in its underside slightly larger than strip width. In its travel through the die, the strip is located against the back edge of the slot. Once widely used, this method has now become obsolete except for very small dies.

15-3. SECONDARY OPERATIONS

For secondary-operation work, stripper plates are fastened on top of two guide rails set at either side. This die pierces two holes in a rectangular blank. Gage pin **A** locates the blank endwise, while it is confined sidewise between the guide rails. The stripper plate is relieved at the front to provide a shelf for easy insertion of the blank. The die block is relieved at the front to provide finger room.

15-4. MACHINING PUNCH OPENINGS

Three methods are used for machining punch openings in the stripper plate. At **A**, a 1/8 inch straight land is applied from the bottom of the plate. Above the land, angular relief is provided to clear the punch radius when the punch is lowered in die sharpening. At **B** the cutting diameter of the small punch is kept short for rigidity. The stripper plate is counterdrilled for clearance. At **C** small punches may be guided in hardened bushings pressed into holes machined in the stripper.

15-5. SPRING STRIPPERS

Views **A**, **B**, and **C** illustrate the operation of a spring stripper plate. Springs, arranged around the blanking punch, provide stripping pressure. Four stripper bolts, located at the corners, limit stripper travel. View **B** shows the die in open position, while view **C** shows the die as it would appear at the bottom of the press stroke. Springs have been compressed ready to strip the material from around the punch upon movement of the punches. View **A** shows the punch holder, blanking punch, and punch plate inverted as they would appear in the upper right hand view of the die drawing.

For large dies, cost of the die set becomes important. So the stripper plate corners are beveled to clear die posts and guide bushings, thereby allowing use of a smaller die set. Springs are retained in pockets counterbored in the punch holder and in the stripper plate. The holes are countersunk 1/8 inch by 45 degrees in the punch holder and 1/16 inch by 45 degrees in the stripper to guide the spring coils. A small hole is drilled completely through the punch holder and stripper plate while the two are clamped together. This hole provides for engagement of the counterbore pilot.

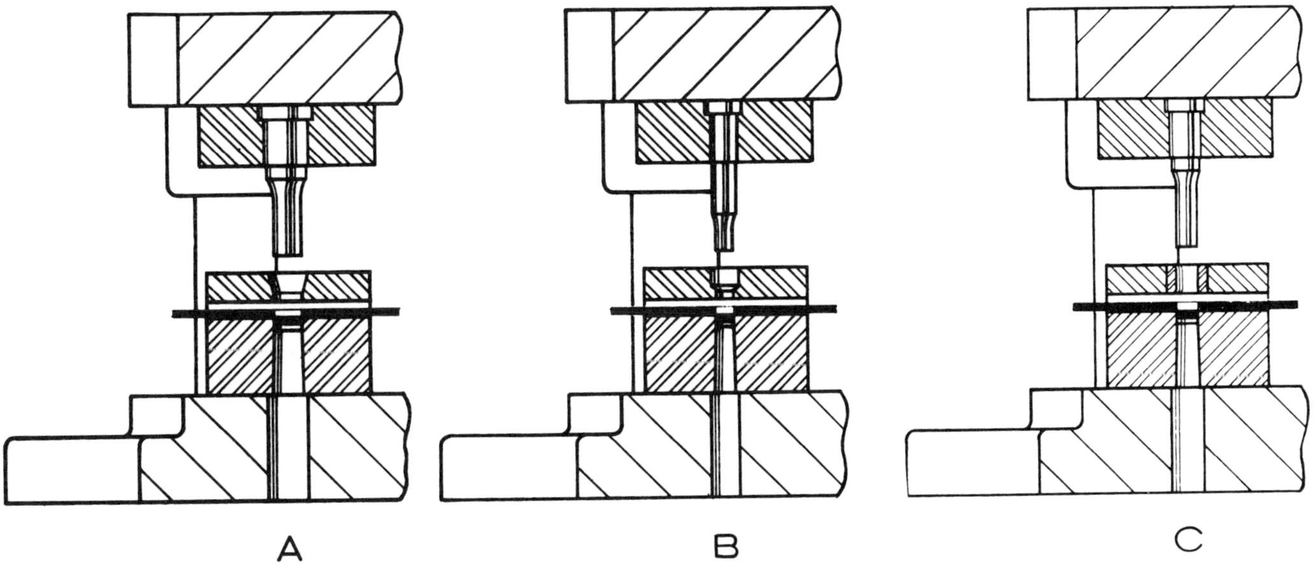

Fig. 15-4. Three types of punch openings for strippers.

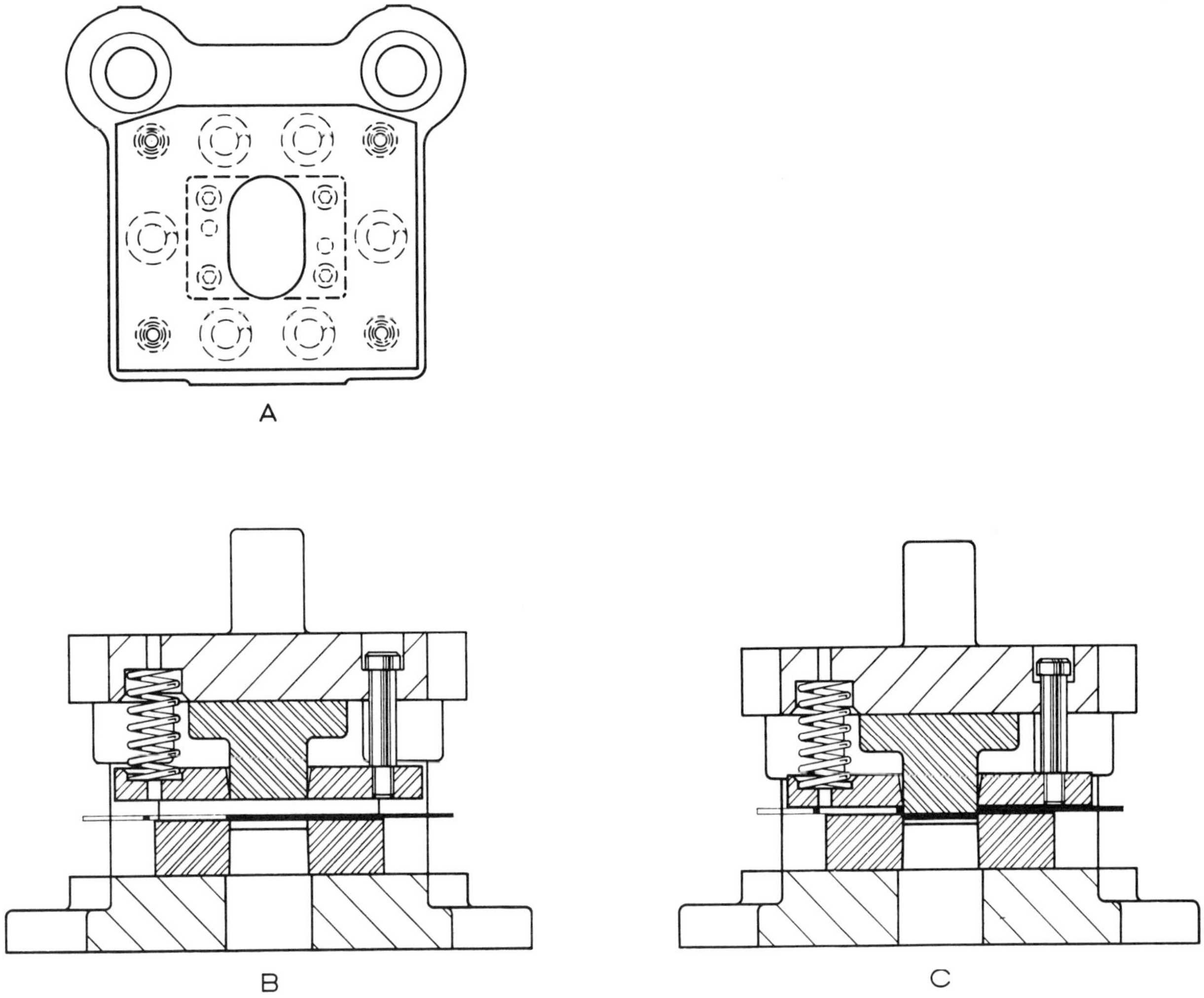

Fig. 15-5. Typical spring stripper.

15-6. SPRING PILOTS

You can avoid counterboring the stripper plate to retain springs by the use of spring pilots. These can be made to suit conditions, or they can be purchased from commercial sources that offer a standardized line of these components.

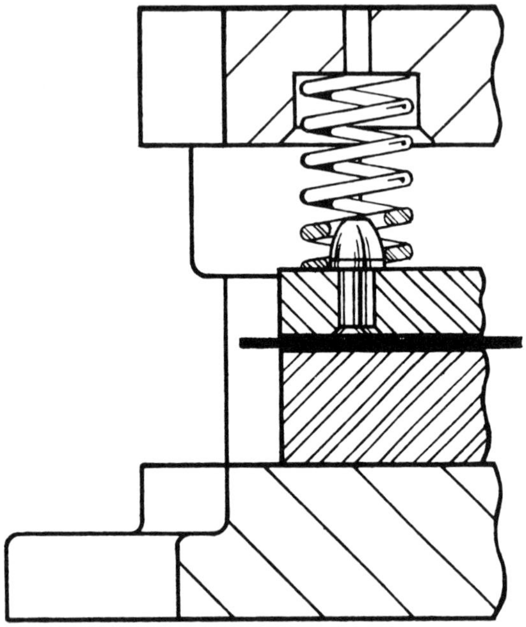

Fig. 15-6. Spring pilot retains stripper plate spring.

15-7. MACHINING THE PUNCH PLATE

When a punch plate is used to retain piercing punches, holes are bored through the punch plate to hold stripper springs. This construction avoids counterboring the punch holder of the die set.

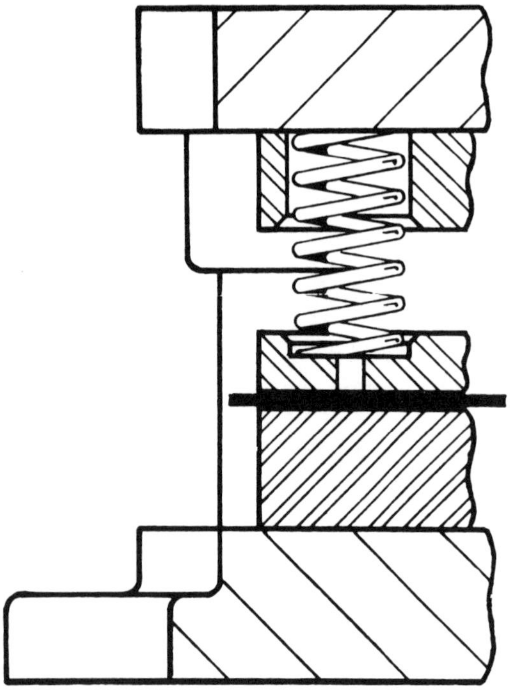

Fig. 15-7. Hole bored in punch plate retains stripper spring.

15-8. SHORT STRIPPER SPRINGS

When stripper springs are short, it is not necessary to counterbore the stripper plate. The springs are retained, either by holes in the punch plate or in counterbored holes in the punch holder.

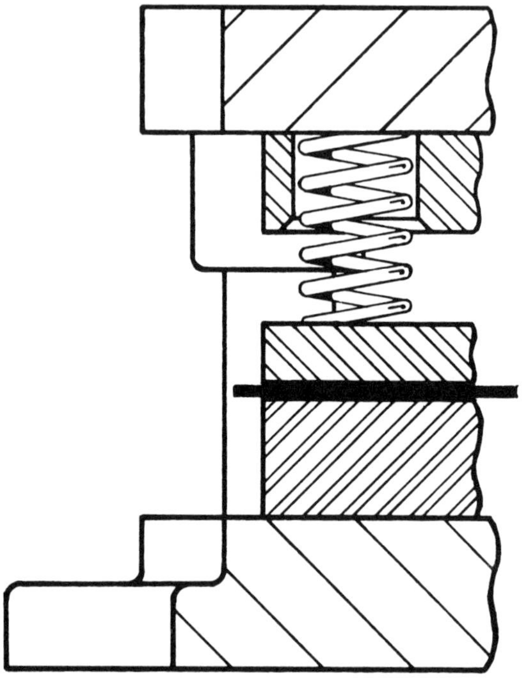

Fig. 15-8. Short stripper spring does not require hole in stripper for maintaining position.

15-9. SPRINGS RETAINED BY STRIPPER BOLTS

For medium-production dies, springs can be applied around stripper bolts as shown. This method is not recommended for long runs because of increased wear on the stripper bolts, and because of the need to remove the bolts in the event of broken springs.

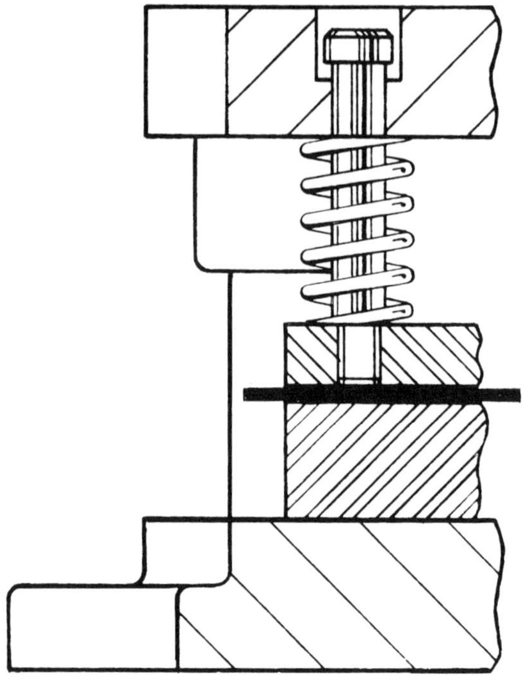

Fig. 15-9. Spring retained by stripper bolt is used in medium-production die.

15-10. APPLYING STRIPPER BOLTS

For severe applications stripper bolts are better applied with their bearing shoulders confined in short counterbored holes in the stripper plate for strength. The counterbore is usually made 1/8 inch deep and a press fit is specified for the diameter of the hole.

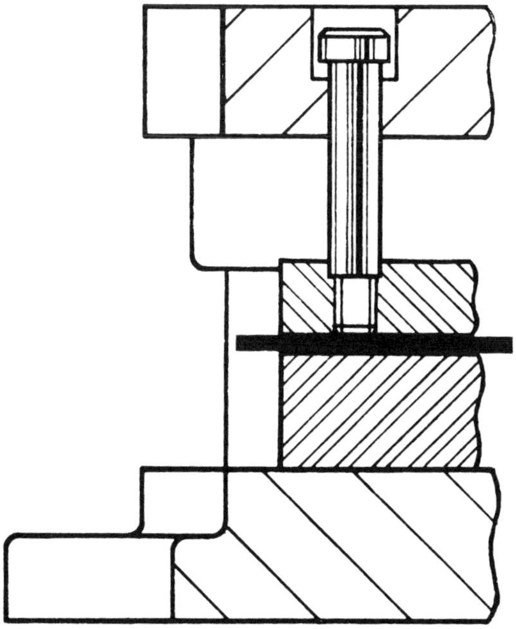

Fig. 15-10. Method of applying stripper bolt for severe applications.

15-11. SPACER WASHERS

When punches are sharpened, spacer washers are applied under stripper bolt heads to maintain correct relationship between the underside of the stripper plate and the faces of blanking and piercing punches. The stripper usually extends 1/32 inch past the faces of cutting punches to flatten the strip properly before cutting occurs.

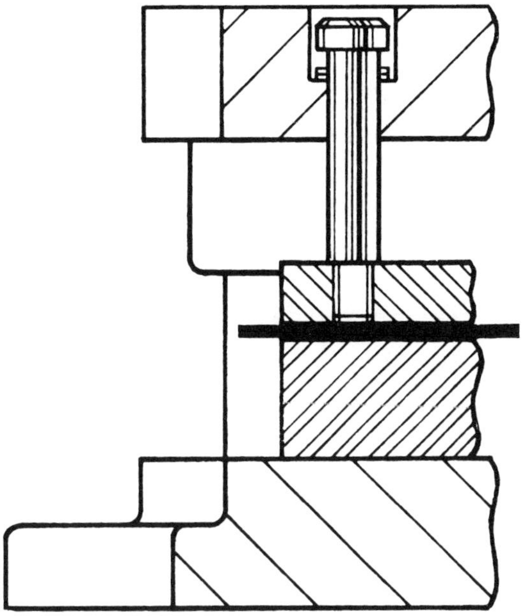

Fig. 15-11. Washers are applied under stripper bolt head when punches are sharpened.

15-12. "STRIPPIT" SPRING UNITS

"Strippit" spring units are self-contained, commercially available assemblies that allow removal of the stripper plate without dismantling springs. Socket cap screws, or socket flat head screws for thin plates, retain the stripper plate to the "Strippit" units. Because pressures are self-contained, thinner stripper plates can be used and stripper bolts are not required.

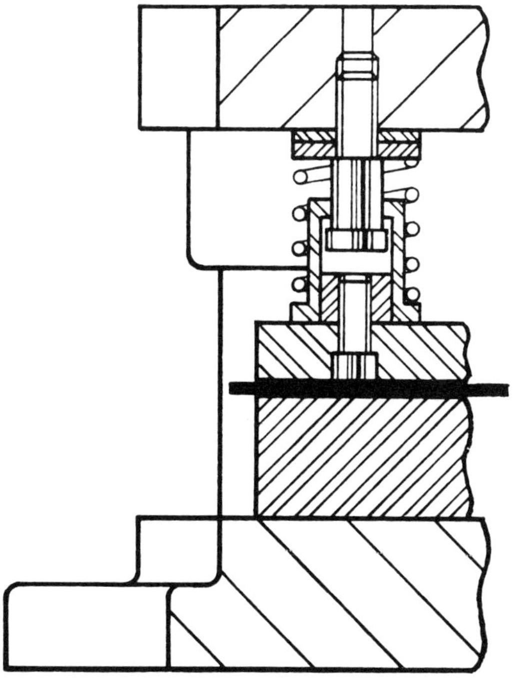

Fig. 15-12. "Strippit" spring unit allows removal of stripper without dismantling springs.

15-13. ALTERNATE METHOD

Another method of applying stripper plates to "Strippits" is to insert short socket cap screws in the units. The cap screw heads engage holes in the stripper plate to prevent lateral movement. Stripper bolts limit travel.

15-14. RUBBER SPRINGS

For medium and low production dies, rubber springs may be used. These rubber components are available from commercial sources. Dowel pins, pressed into the stripper, retain the rubber springs in position.

15-15. FLUID SPRINGS

Where extremely high stripping pressures are required, fluid springs reduce the number of spring units required in the die, an important factor where space

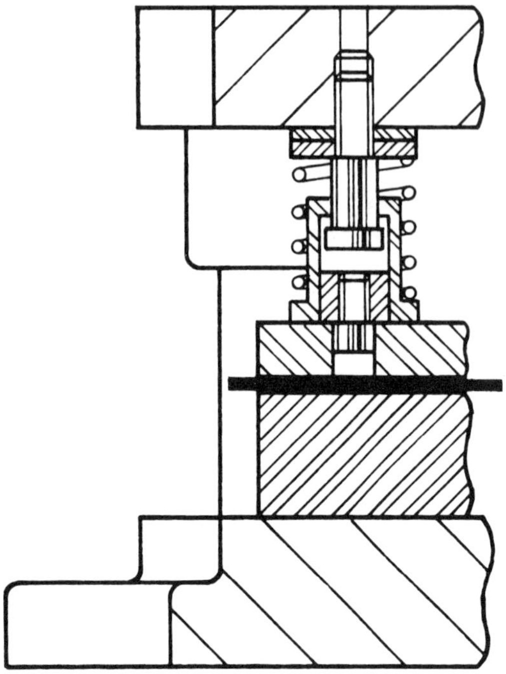

Fig. 15-13. Alternate method of applying "Strippit" spring unit to stripper.

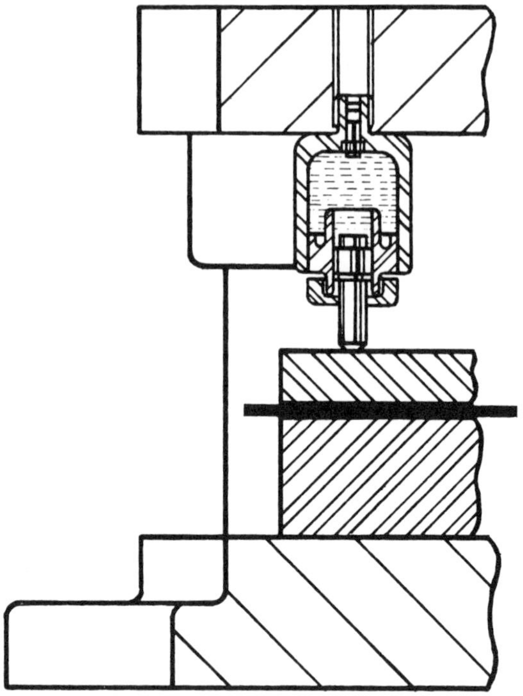

Fig. 15-15. Fluid springs are used where extremely high stripping presures are required.

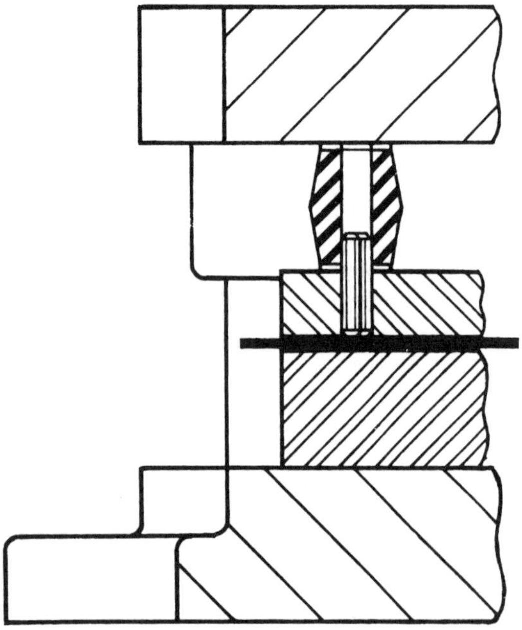

Fig. 15-14. Rubber spring for medium and low production dies.

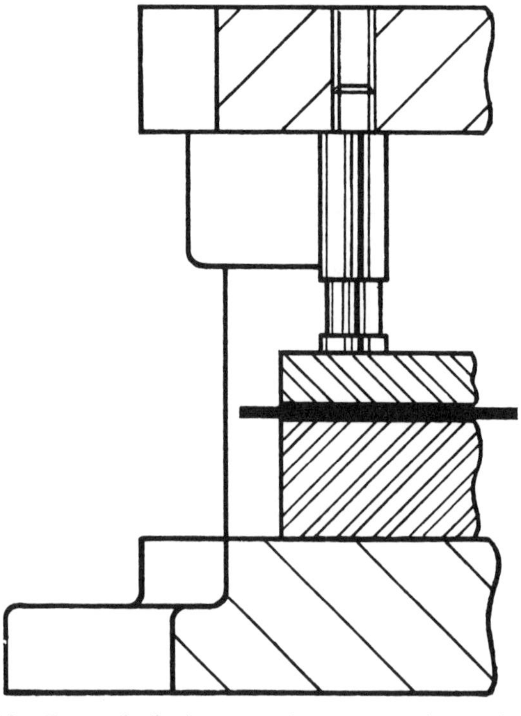

Fig. 15-16. Type of fluid spring that is interchangeable with standard springs.

is limited. Fluid springs are filled with an emulsion of silicones in oil. The one illustrated is available from commercial sources.

15-16. ANOTHER FLUID SPRING

Another type of fluid spring is made interchangeable with some sizes of standard springs. These are also available commercially. Both fluid springs, Figs. 15-15 and 15-16, are fastened to the die by threading their shanks into holes tapped in the die set.

15-17. INVERTED DIES

In inverted dies the blanking punch is fastened to the lower die holder of the die set, instead of to the punch holder as in conventional dies. In such applications the spring stripper is reversed. Reversing the stripper plate does not alter application of the components previously described except that they are inverted also.

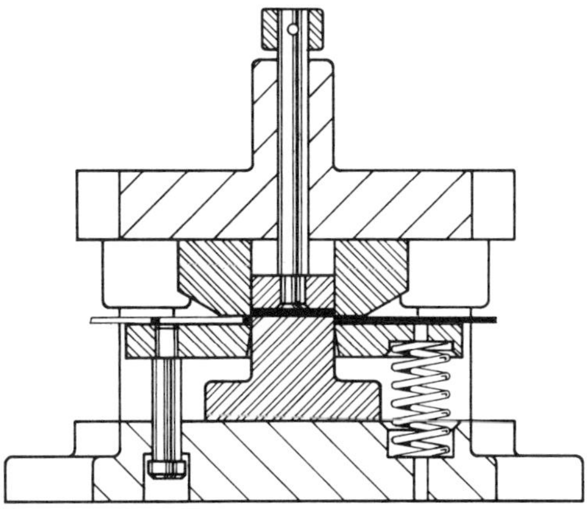

Fig. 15-17. Typical inverted die.

15-18. STRIPPING FORCE

When spring strippers are used it is necessary to calculate the amount of force required to effect stripping. Stripping force is found by the formula:

$$\mathbf{P} = \mathbf{L} \times \mathbf{T} \times 855$$

Where:

L = Length of cut. In piercing operations this is the the sum of the perimeters of all perforator faces.

T = Thickness of stock

P = Force, in pounds, to effect stripping.

The constant 855 was derived from an empirical formula: $\mathbf{P} = \dfrac{\mathbf{L} \times \mathbf{T}}{0.00117}$

This formula has been in use for many years in a number of plants and it has been found to be satisfactory for most work. The constant 855 (the reciprocal of 0.00117) simplifies calculations.

These formulas are for "full stripping". In blanking dies and progressive dies in which only strips are to be run and thin, weak scrap bridges are present in the scrap strip, the calculated figure may be reduced somewhat, depending upon the number and extent of the weak areas. But the value of **P** should never be reduced in applications where there is any possibility of scrap pieces from other operations being stamped in the die.

After the total stripping force has been determined, the stripping force per spring must be found in order to establish the number and sizes of springs required. Force per spring is listed in manufacturers' catalogs in terms of pounds per 1/8 inch deflection. In some catalogs it is given in pounds per 1/10 inch deflection, and must be converted to pounds per 1/8 inch deflection by simple proportion.

Three types of spring deflection must be taken into consideration. Illustrated at **A** is initial compression, usually 1/4 inch, which compresses the springs to apply a preload. At **B** is shown working compression, which is further deflection of the springs while work is performed. At **C** is illustrated grinding compression, usually 1/4 inch, which is the amount allowed for sharpening punches during the life of the die.

If a spring 1 1/2 inches in diameter by 6 inches long is tentatively selected, and initial compression is 1/4 inch, the force for this deflection will be twice the listed amount (as the listed amount is for 1/8 inch deflection for that size of spring). To this is added the force for the first 1/8 inch of working compression;

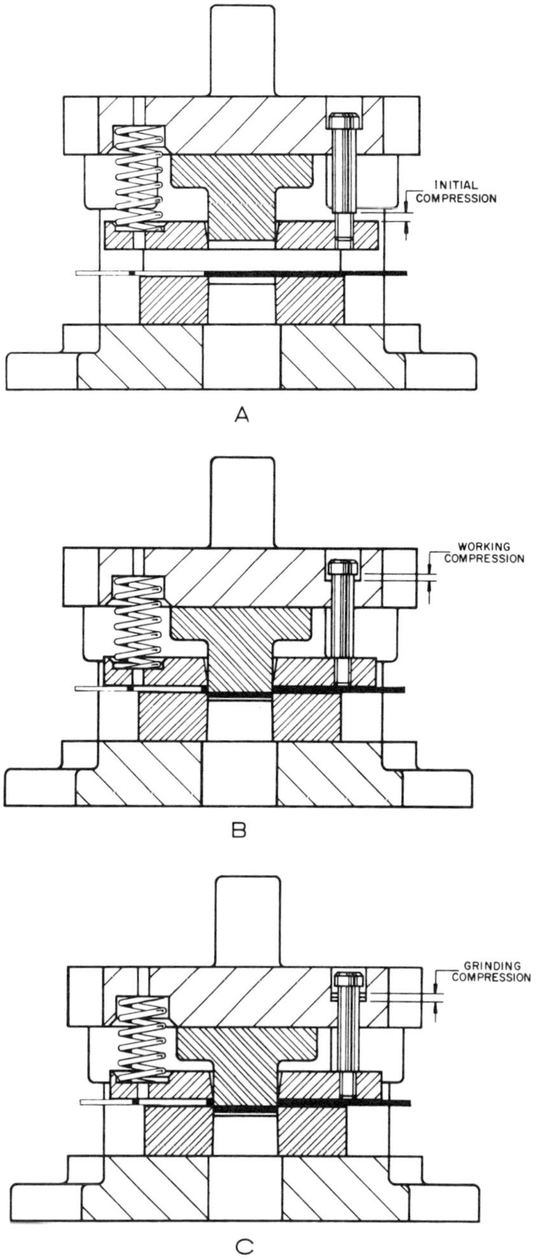

Fig. 15-18. Three types of spring deflection which must be considered when determining stripping force.

no more force is added because too high a value would result, and the force would fade away near maximum travel. Should the working compression be less than 1/8 inch, say 1/16 inch, only one-half of the listed force would be used in the calculation. For example:

Listed force per 1/8 inch compression:	20 pounds
1/4 inch initial compression: (2 × 20)	40 pounds
1/16 inch working compression: (1/2 × 20)	10 pounds
1/4 inch grinding compression: (2 × 20)	40 pounds
Total force per spring:	90 pounds

This value represents the total amount of force exerted by the compressed spring after 1/4 inch has been removed in sharpening. It is the maximum force and the value should be used in any calculation of strength of members.

To determine the number of springs required to effect stripping, we must know the force exerted by each spring *before* sharpening. Therefore, referring to the example:

Listed force per 1/8 inch compression:	20 pounds
1/4 inch initial compression: (2 × 20)	40 pounds
1/16 inch working compression: (1/2 × 20)	10 pounds
Force per spring:	50 pounds

The number of springs required is found by dividing the total stripping force by the force per spring. If the number arrived at is out of proportion to the die, use fewer and larger springs, or perhaps more springs of smaller size. Or pressure may be increased by applying more initial compression. Manufacturers' catalogs list the maximum amount of compression to apply, and their recommendations should be followed. In general they suggest:

1. For high-speed work both "medium pressure" and "high pressure" springs should not be deflected more than 1/4 of their free lengths

2. For heavy, slow-moving presses use "medium pressure" springs with a total deflection not to exceed 3/8 of their free lengths.

KNOCKOUTS

Knockouts remove, or strip completed blanks from within die members. They differ from stripper plates in that stripper plates remove the material strip from around punches. There are three types of knockouts:

1. Positive knockouts. These eject the blank upon contact of the knockout rod with the knockout bar of the press.

2. Pneumatic knockouts. These are actuated by an air cushion applied under the bolster plate of the press.

3. Spring knockouts. These employ heavy springs as the thrust source.

The knockout plate or block in contact with the part is usually made of machine steel, but would be made of heat-treated tool steel when it also performs a forming operation.

Knockouts can be applied in two ways. In the first, Direct knockouts, the force is applied directly from source. In the second, Indirect knockouts, the force is applied through pins arranged to clear other die components, such as piercing punches.

Illustrated are 21 methods of applying knockouts to dies, as well as details of their construction, and methods of finding the center of stripping force for correct design.

15-19. OPERATION OF A KNOCKOUT

Taken together, Figs. 15-19 and 15-20 illustrate the operation of a positive knockout. This is an inverted blanking die, with the blanking punch fastened to the lower die holder of the die set, and the die block fastened to the upper punch holder. The knockout assembly consists of knockout plate, **A** knockout rod **B**, and stop collar **C**. At the bottom of the press stroke, the blanking punch has removed the blank from the strip and inserted it into the die block, raising the knockout assembly.

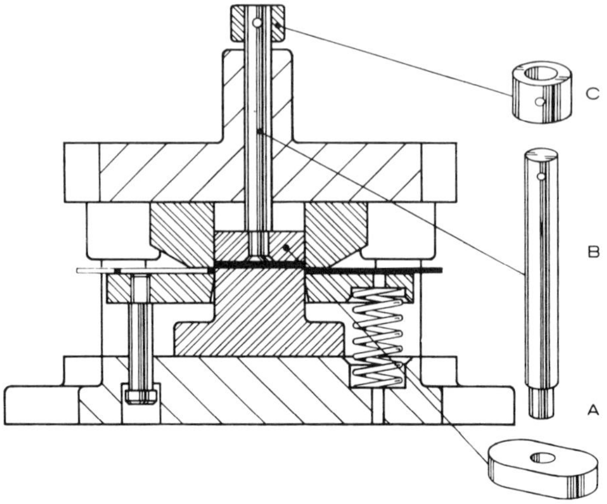

Fig. 15-19. Inverted blanking die with positive knockout.

15-20. STRIPPING THE BLANKS

Near the top of the press stroke the knockout rod contacts the stationary knockout bar of the press. Continued ascent of the upper die causes the knockout to remove the blank from within the die cavity. If the job is run in an inclined press, the blank falls to the rear of the press by gravity. Thin blanks may be blown to the rear of the press by air. Blanks produced from oiled stock tend to cling to the face of the knockout. When this condition is present, a shedder pin applied to one side of the knockout plate will break the adhesion and free the blank. Three types of shedder pins were illustrated in Fig. 8-15 in the section on Blanking Punches.

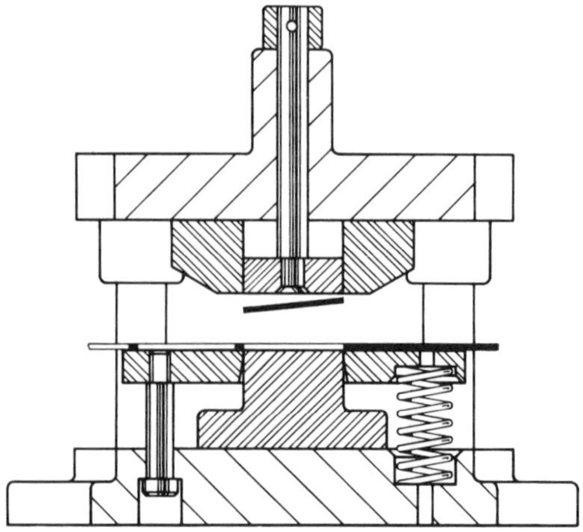

Fig. 15-20. Knockout removes blank near top of press stroke.

15-21. CENTER OF STRIPPING FORCE

Before designing the knockout, the center of stripping force must be found. If the knockout rod is not applied at the exact center of stripping force, the rod will be stressed and possibly bent in operation.

Symmetrical blanks present no difficulty, but when the blank outlines are irregular here is the method to use:

Place a sheet of cardboard (board for show cards is best) under the part drawing. Insert carbon paper between the drawing and cardboard and trace the part outline, as well as all holes and openings. With scissors cut out a cardboard blank as shown in the plan view. All holes and openings may be cut out of the blank as shown at **A**. The blank is then balanced over a point, (a pencil will do). The center of balance is the center of stripping force.

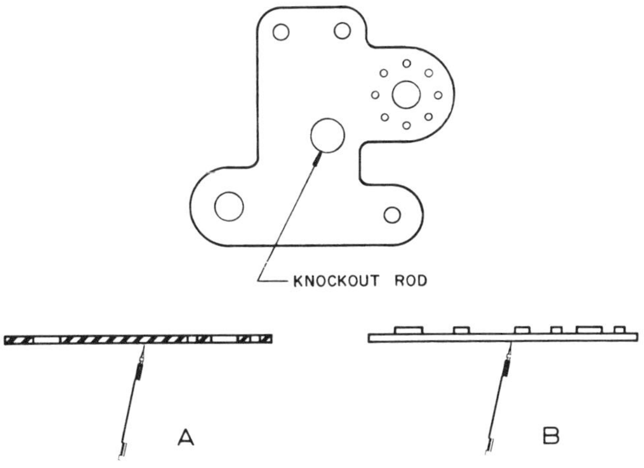

Fig. 15-21. Ways of determining center of stripping force.

Cutting out small holes is difficult, so here is an alternate method: From the same weight cardboard cut slugs the shape and size of all holes and openings. Paste these in position on top of the blank as shown at **B**. Balancing the blank as before will establish the center of stripping force.

15-22. ALTERNATE METHOD

For very large blanks, which would be difficult to balance, pierce three small holes, **A**, close to the edge of the blank. Suspend the blank from a vertical surface, using a pin or thumbtack. With a triangle. draw a vertical line directly under the hole from which the blank is suspended. Turn the blank around and, suspending it from one of the other holes, draw another vertical line crossing the suspension hole. The intersection of the two lines is the center of stripping force. Suspend the blank from the third hole to provide a check for accuracy.

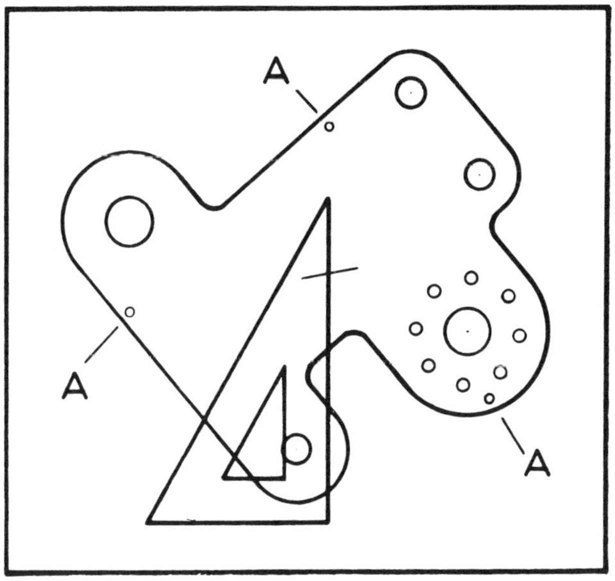

Fig. 15-22. Alternate method of determining center of stripping force.

15-23. SPRING DAMPER

In applying a positive knockout, many designers prefer to provide a relatively weak spring around the knockout rod. This spring is not strong enough to strip the part. Its function is to prevent unnecessary travel and bounce of the knockout to reduce wear.

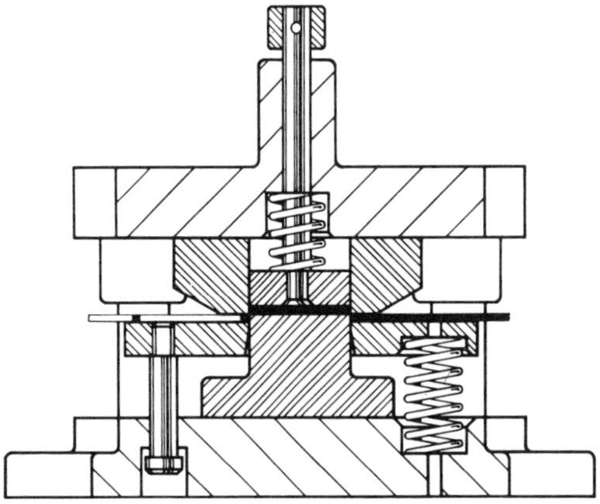

Fig. 15-23. Spring around the knockout rod is too weak to strip but prevents needless travel and bounce.

15-24. GUIDING IN THE KNOCKOUT

Slender piercing punches may be guided in the knockout by providing hardened bushings pressed into the knockout plate. Close fits between the knockout and other die components must be maintained.

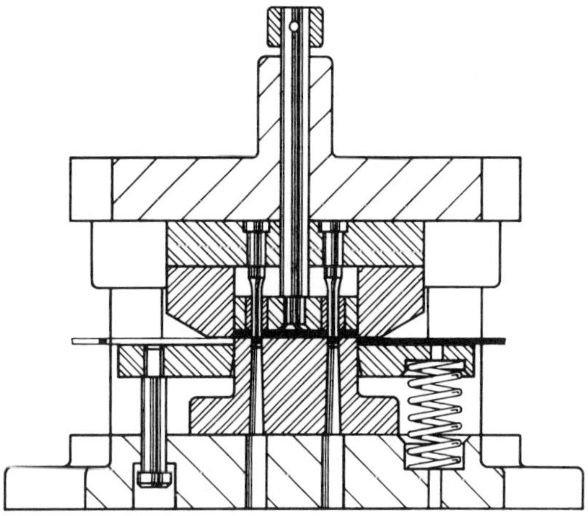

Fig. 15-24. Slender piercing punches are guided by hardened bushings in the knockout plate.

15-25. EJECTING CUPS AND SHELLS

Positive knockouts may be used to eject drawn shells. In this combination die the upper punch blanks a disk from the strip, and in further descent draws it into a flanged shell. Lower knockout **A** is raised by pins actuated by the air cushion of the press, and it strips the shell from around draw punch **B**. Positive knockout **C**, actuated near the top of the stroke, removes the shell from within the die and it falls to the rear of the press.

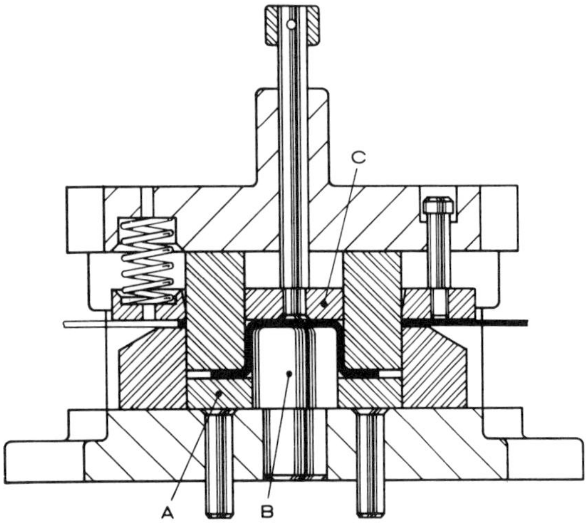

Fig. 15-25. Positive knockouts are used to eject drawn shells.

15-26. TRIMMING OPERATIONS

In this trimming die for a previously drawn flanged cup, a positive knockout, relieved to clear the shell body, removes the shell from within the die hole. Whenever a knockout is used to remove formed or drawn stampings, it should be relieved so that stripping force is applied only near cutting edges to prevent distortion of the parts.

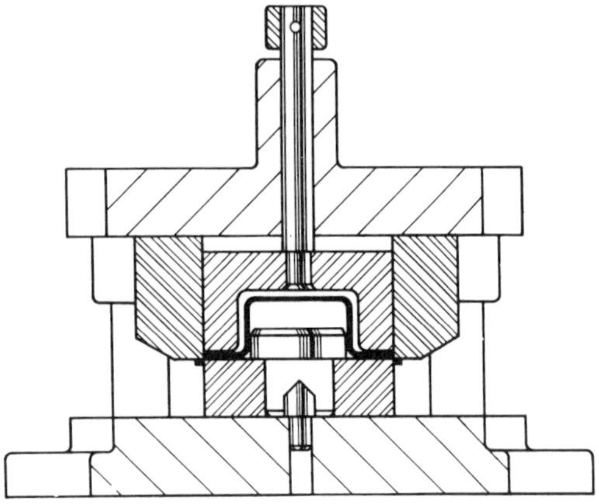

Fig. 15-26. Positive knockout is relieved so as to apply stripping force near trimmed edge.

15-27. FORMING IN THE KNOCKOUT

For some types of work the knockout provides the final forming operation. This combination die produces a flanged cover by blanking a disk and drawing a shallow flanged shell. At the bottom of the stroke the knockout, in conjunction with the lower embossing punch **A**, embosses a shallow recess in the part. When knockout plates do forming they are made of hardened tool steel and are backed up by a plate to "spank," or set the form. A shedder pin, backed up by a spring and socket lock screw, prevents adhesion of the part to the knockout face.

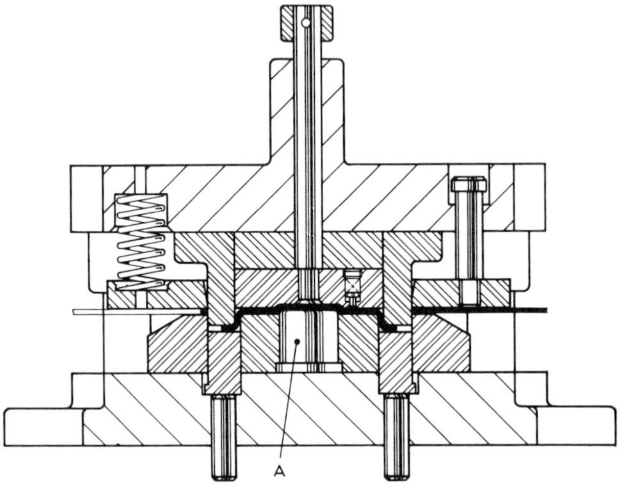

Fig. 15-27. Die in which knockout is used for forming or embossing.

15-28. BOTTOM KNOCKOUTS

Bottom knockouts, operated by the press air cushion as in Figs. 15-25 and 15-27, have their pins applied in seven ways. At **A**, pins transmit force from the face of the air cushion to the underside of the knockout ring. This method proves suitable for very long press runs. The pins are loose and may become lost if the die is removed often. At **B**, the pins are peened, then machined to form beveled heads to prevent dropping out when the die is removed from the press. At **C**,

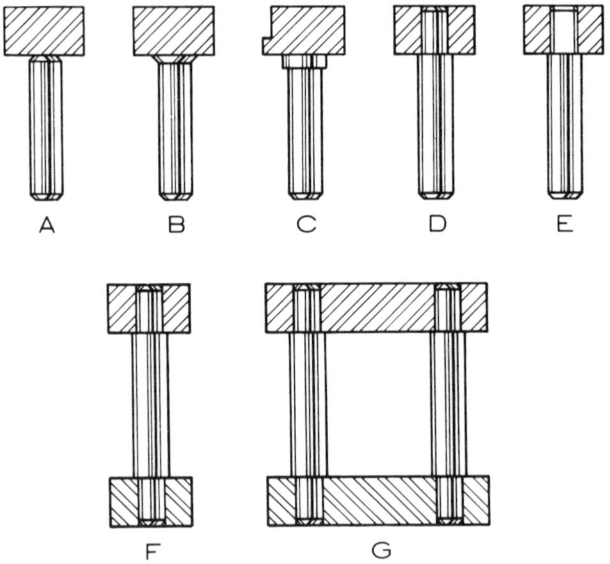

Fig. 15-28. Several methods of pinning bottom knockouts.

turned heads retain the pins in the die set. The knockout ring has a flange to retain it in the die. At **D** the ends of the pins are turned down and pressed into the knockout ring, while at **E** the pins are turned down and threaded into the knockout ring. At **F** the tops of the pins are turned down and are pressed into the knockout ring. The pins are also turned down at their lower ends and pressed into collars. In the up position the collar seats against the bottom of the die set to limit travel. It also retains pins and knockout ring to prevent loss. At **G**, long, rectangular knockout plates used in bending and forming dies are retained in the die set by two or more pins with turned down ends pressed into the knockout bar at the top, and also into the bottom retaining bar.

15-29. SPRING KNOCKOUTS

Spring knockouts are used in dies too large for the positive types. Stripper bolts limit travel. One disadvantage is that the blank is returned into the strip and it must be removed subsequently. In some progressive dies the blanking station is provided with a spring knockout to return the blank into the strip for further operations.

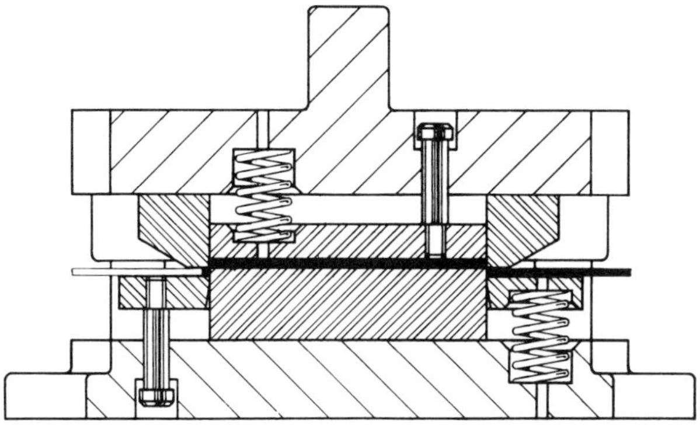

Fig. 15-29. Typical spring knockout used in large dies.

15-30. INDIRECT KNOCKOUTS

The knockouts described so far have all been the direct-acting types. Indirect knockouts are used when piercing or other types of punches are in line with the knockout rod. This illustration shows an indirect

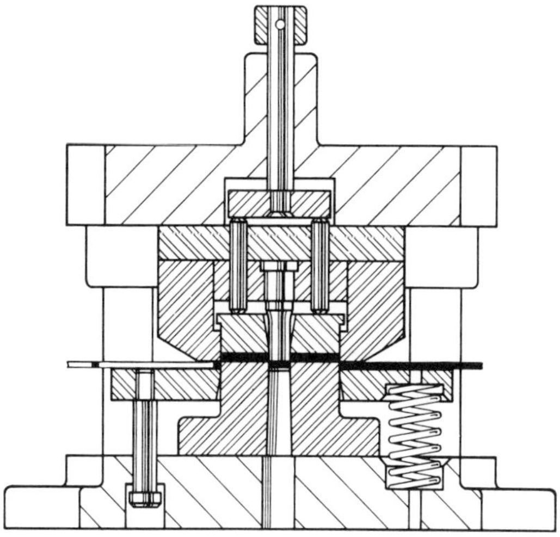

Fig. 15-30. Typical indirect knockout.

knockout with force transmitted through pins to clear a central piercing punch. The knockout plate moves in a recess milled in the upper punch holder of the die set. Through the pins, it actuates the knockout block to push the blanks out of the die hole.

15-31. PRESSURE PINS AND STOP COLLARS

The number of pressure pins used and their arrangement depends upon part contour and size. At **A**, knockouts for round blanks have three actuating pins. At **B**, blanks with a roughly triangular shape are also provided with three actuating pins. As shown at **C**, blanks which are roughly rectangular, or square, require the use of four pins.

There are three ways of applying a stop collar to the knockout rod. At **A**, a collar is pressed over the end of the knockout rod and retained by a dowel pressed through both. At **B**, the knockout rod is machined to form a solid shoulder. At **C** a dowel is pressed through the knockout rod. Although often used, this method is not recommended because, should the press not be set up properly, the dowel could be sheared with consequent damage to die components.

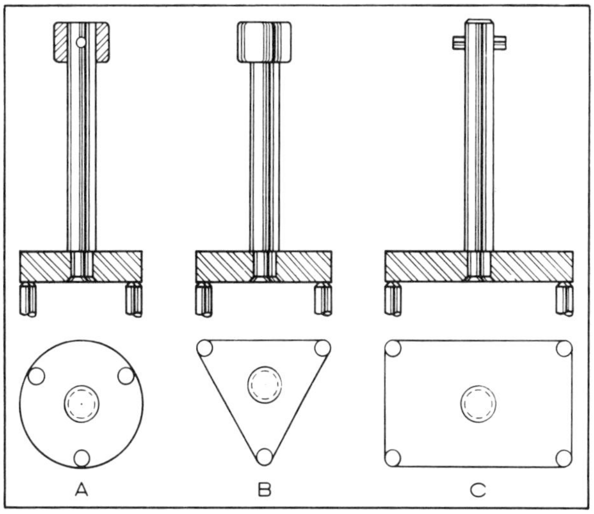

Fig. 15-31. Arrangement of pressure pins and stop collars for indirect knockouts.

15-32. GUIDE PINS

Slender piercing punches may be guided in the knockout block of indirect knockouts. Guide pins **A**, pressed into the knockout block, transmit stripping force and also guide the block. They are fitted in hardened bushings **B**. The knockout plate travels in a recess machined in the punch holder of the die set.

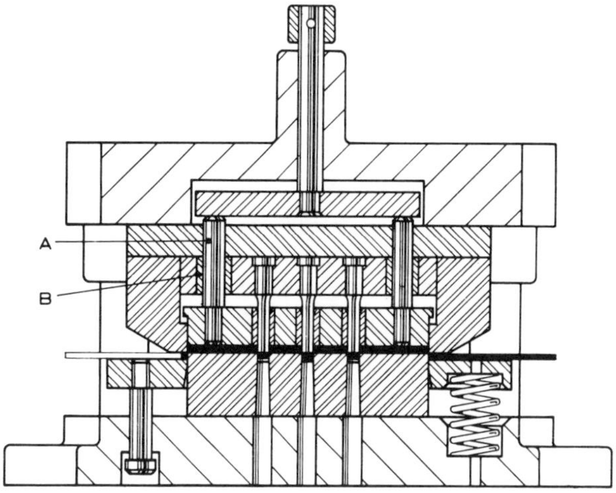

Fig. 15-32. Pins (A) guide and transmit force to the knockout block.

15-33. AUXILIARY PUNCH SHANK

When the press has sufficient opening, an auxiliary punch shank may be fastened to the punch holder of the die set. The knock plate travels in a recess machined in the bottom of this auxilliary shank.

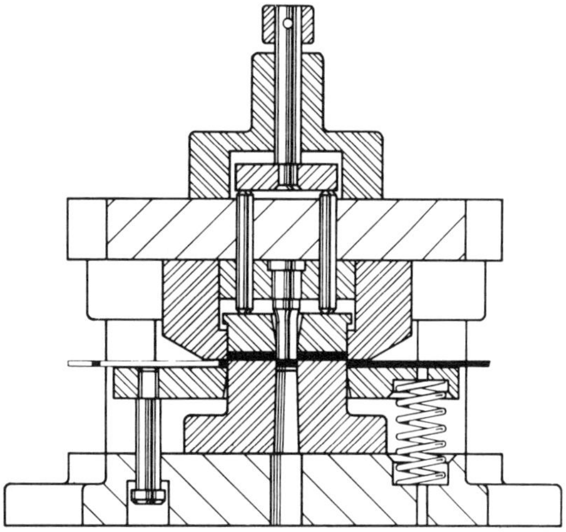

Fig. 15-33. Die in which auxiliary punch shank is fastened to the punch holder of the die set.

15-34. BACKING BLOCKS

In another method, the soft steel backing block **A** can be machined to accommodate the knockout plate. This die produces ring shaped parts.

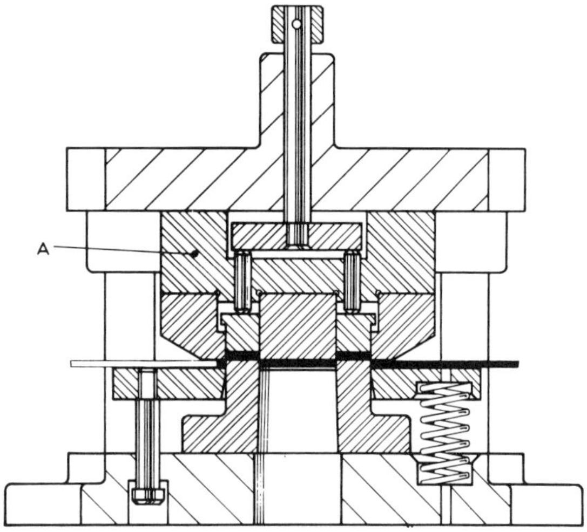

Fig. 15-34. Soft steel backing plate (A) machined to accommodate the knockout plate.

15-35. SPIDER KNOCKOUTS

When holes are to be pierced in ring-shaped parts, the knockout plate has a spider shape and the punches are retained between the arms of the spider. On the drawing one arm of the spider is drawn at one side, and a piercing punch at the other.

15-36. SPIDER KNOCKOUT PLATES

The number of arms contained in knockout spiders such as the one used for the die Fig. 15-35 depends on the number of piercing punches required. When three punches are applied, the spider has three arms to clear the punches. This type is shown at **A**. For four punches a four-armed spider, at **B**, would be used. Piercing punches, applied at other than radial locations are cleared by holes in knockout frames such as the one shown at **C**. The shape of the knockout frame would depend upon the number and arrangement of the punches.

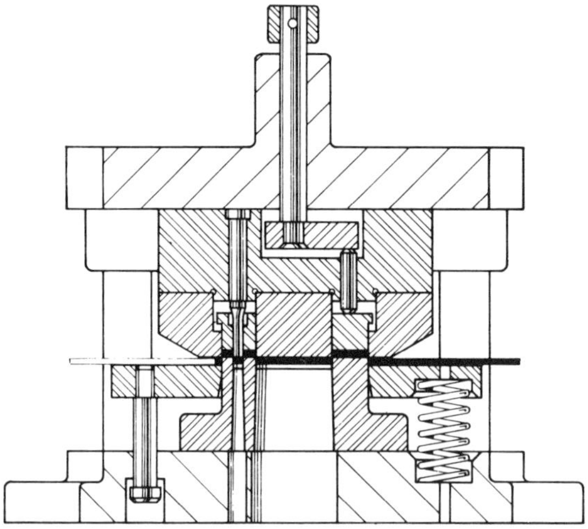

Fig. 15-35. Knockout plate is of spider shape to facilitate piercing ring-shaped parts.

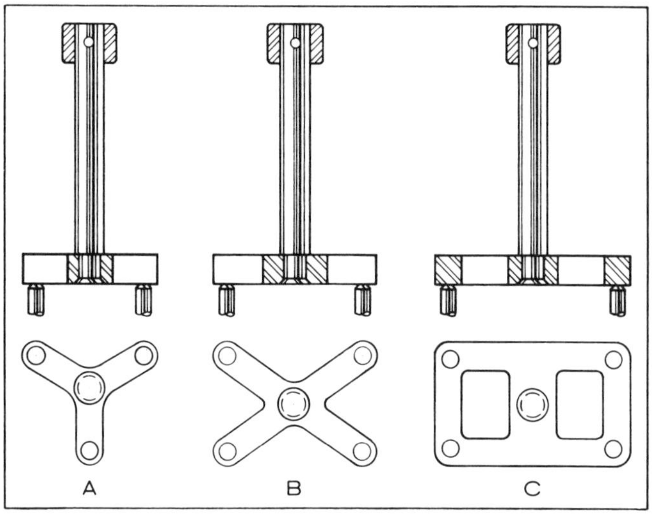

Fig. 15-36. Various shapes of spider knockout plates.

15-37. FLAME-CUTTING KNOCKOUTS

One method frequently used to save material is to flame cut the spider knockout entirely through the backing plate. The spider is removed from the plate and then machined thinner to allow up-and-down movement. Since the knockout pocket is cut completely through the plate, the pins must be securely fastened to the spider arms, in this case by pressing and riveting their ends.

Still another method of applying large spider knockouts is to flame cut the spider through the punch holder of the die set. A steel die set must be specified, and the flame cutting must be done by the die set manufacturer before stress relieving and final accurate machining.

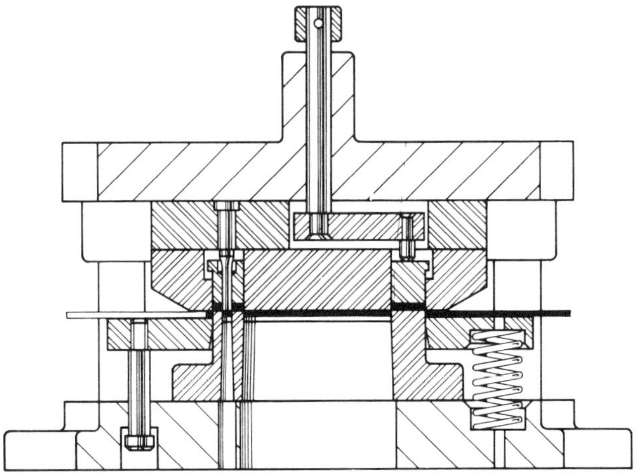

Fig. 15-37. Spider knockout plate in this die has been flame cut.

15-38. KNOCKOUT RODS

These are the three commonly used methods of securing the knockout rod to the knockout plate. At **A** the rod end is turned down, pressed into the plate, and riveted over. When heavy knockout pressures exist, the knockout rod is provided with a shoulder to prevent it from sinking into the knockout plate as shown at **B**. In this method also the end is turned, pressed in, and peened over as in the previous example. At **C** is shown still another method of fastening heavy knockout rods. The end is provided with a shoulder, threaded into the knockout plate, and prevented from loosening by a dowel pressed through the flange and into the knockout plate. The dowel hole is carried through the plate, but with a smaller diameter to prevent the dowel from working out in operation.

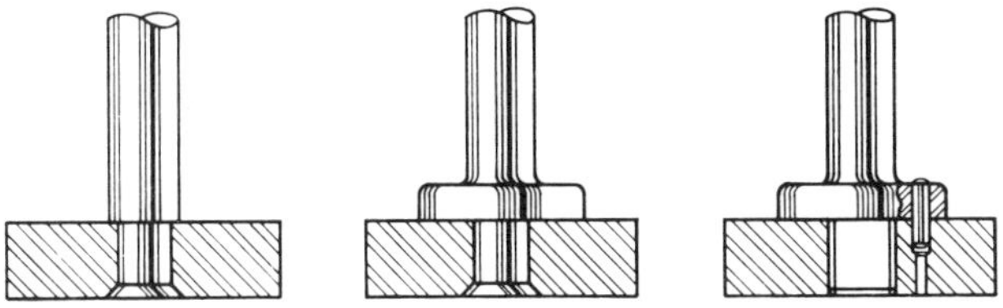

Fig. 15-38. Three methods of securing the knockout rod to the knockout plate.

15-39. KNOCKOUT PLUNGERS

Indirect knockouts for small dies may be operated by a knockout plunger **A**, applied within the punch shank. Cap **B**, fastened to the punch shank with socket cap screws, provides an outboard bearing for the knockout plunger and also keeps it confined within the die.

15-40. SPRING KNOCKOUTS

Small knockouts may be of the spring-operated variety. One disadvantage is that the part is returned into the strip and it must be removed as an extra operation. However, the blanking station of some progressive dies is purposely made in the above manner; the part is returned to the strip for other operations, and removed from the strip at the last station.

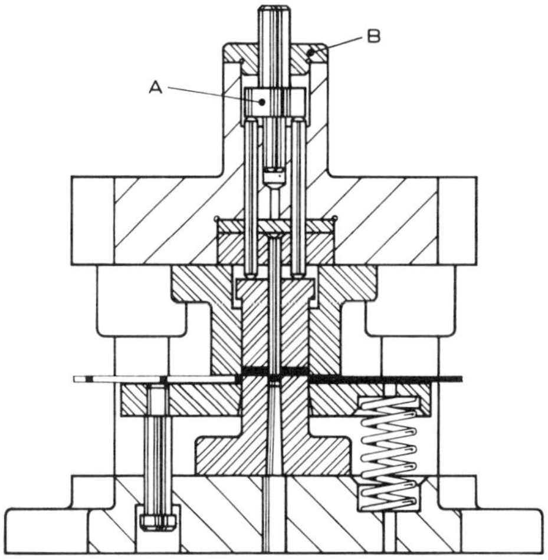

Fig. 15-39. Knockout plunger (**A**) contained within punch shank operates indirect knockout.

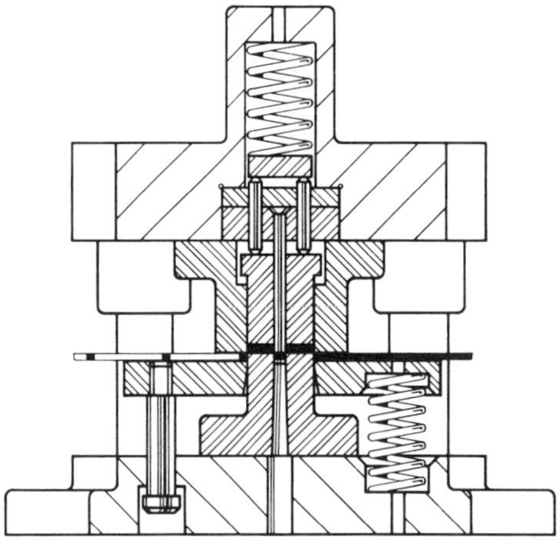

Fig. 15-40. Typical small knockout of the spring-operated variety.

15-41. SPRING-ACTUATED KNOCKOUTS

Spring actuated knockouts may be applied to the lower die in a variety of ways. These are used in progressive dies at bending, forming, and embossing stations. At **A** the knockout is operated by a spring applied in a counterbored hole in the die holder of the die set. Shown at **B** the hole is carried through the die set and the spring is backed by a plate fastened in the die holder. This provides greater travel. At **C** knockout blocks of irregular shape may be held by one or more stripper bolts, and pressure is applied by a spring retained in a counterbored hole in the die holder. **D** shows one method of applying the spring within a spring housing fastened under the die set. This construction is used when considerable travel is required. At **E**, the spring is held under the die set by a stripper bolt, and pressure is transmitted to the knockout through pins. This design facilitates the use of a very heavy spring when high pressure is required and when the press is not equipped with an air cushion.

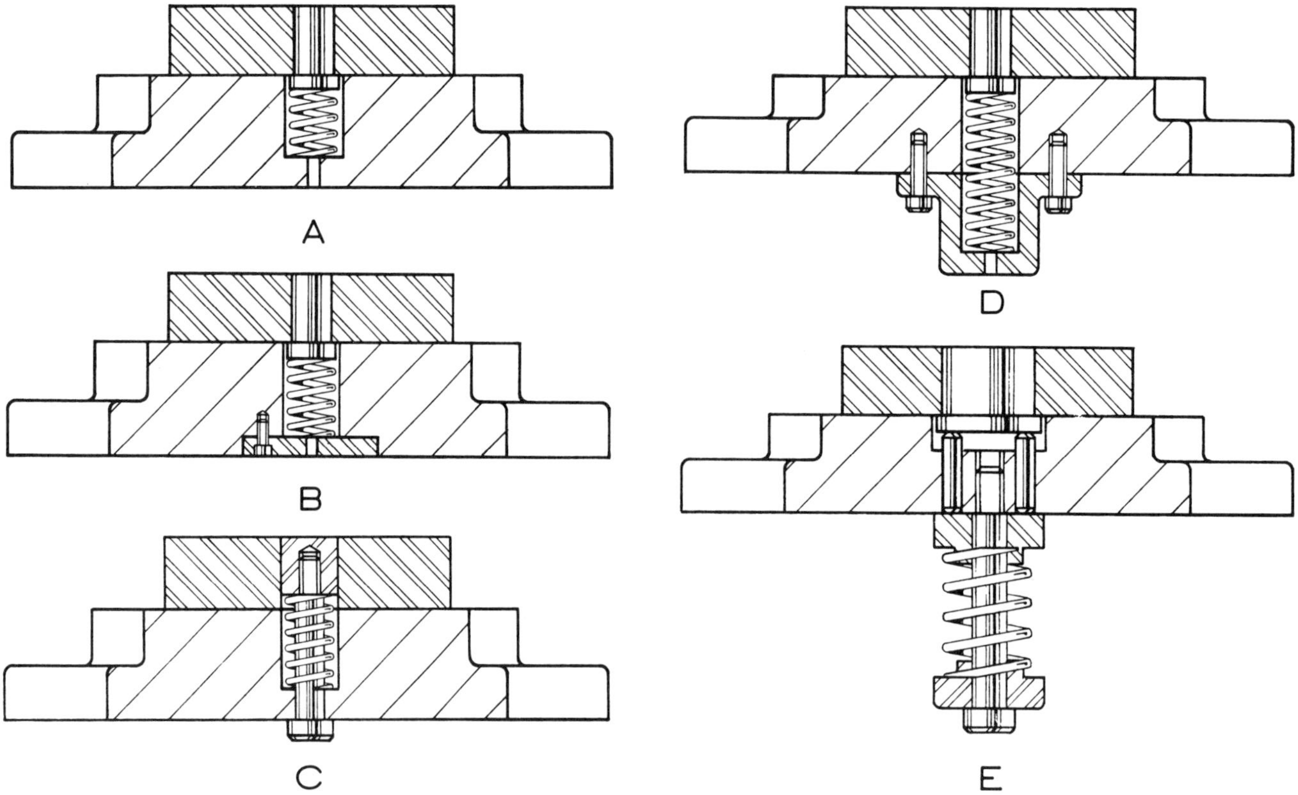

Fig. 15-41. Various ways of applying spring-actuated knockouts to the lower die.

Section 16

HOW TO APPLY FASTENERS

The subject of fasteners is an important one because these components are applied so frequently and employed in such large quantities. Although small, they perform important functions. In the design of tools and dies, fasteners are often the "weakest link" in the tool and, if they are not selected and applied correctly, they can become the cause of failure of the entire tool or die.

In applying fasteners, an experienced designer seemingly follows no rules for size, location, or number. But if two designers were to select and apply fasteners for the same job, their choices would be almost identical. In turn, the checker would approve their selections.

Obviously, these men have developed a sense of *proportion*. When a designer looks over a layout and he decides that screws are too small, too close together, or too close to edges, he is subconsciously being guided by observations of tool components that failed and had the same proportions.

Fortunately, definite rules for application of fasteners can be used by the inexperienced designer or student to avoid many pitfalls. These pitfalls include hardening cracks and breaks, stripped threads, distortion by release of internal stresses, and mis-alignment of holes. By the use of these rules, the less experienced man can avoid trouble and quickly develop a correct sense of proportion.

16-1. DIE FASTENERS

In this exploded view of a typical die for producing blanks from metal strip, all fasteners have been shown removed from the components which they locate and hold. From this drawing, it is apparent that fasteners, although small individually, form a substantial portion of the entire tool when taken together.

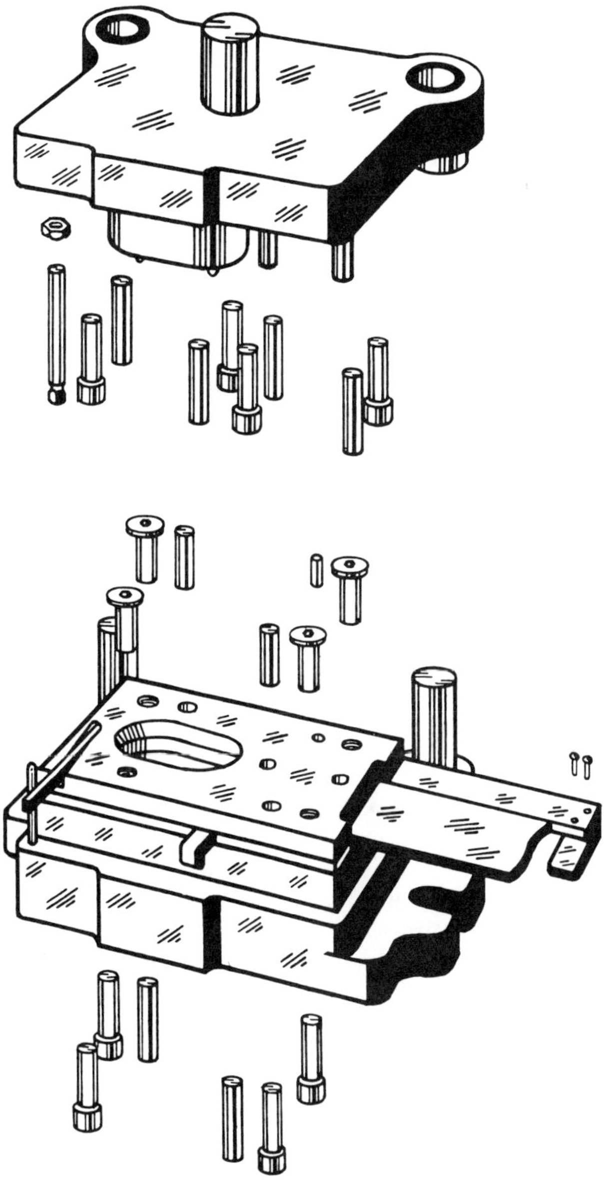

Fig. 16-1. Exploded view of die showing number of fasteners used.

16-2. TYPES OF FASTENERS

Illustrated here are the types of fasteners most commonly used in die construction. They are:

1. Socket cap screws
2. Dowels
3. Socket button-head screws
4. Socket flat-head screws
5. Stripper bolts
6. Socket set-screws
7. Allenuts.

Less frequently employed types include the following: hexagon nuts, washers, studs, rivets, and wood-screws.

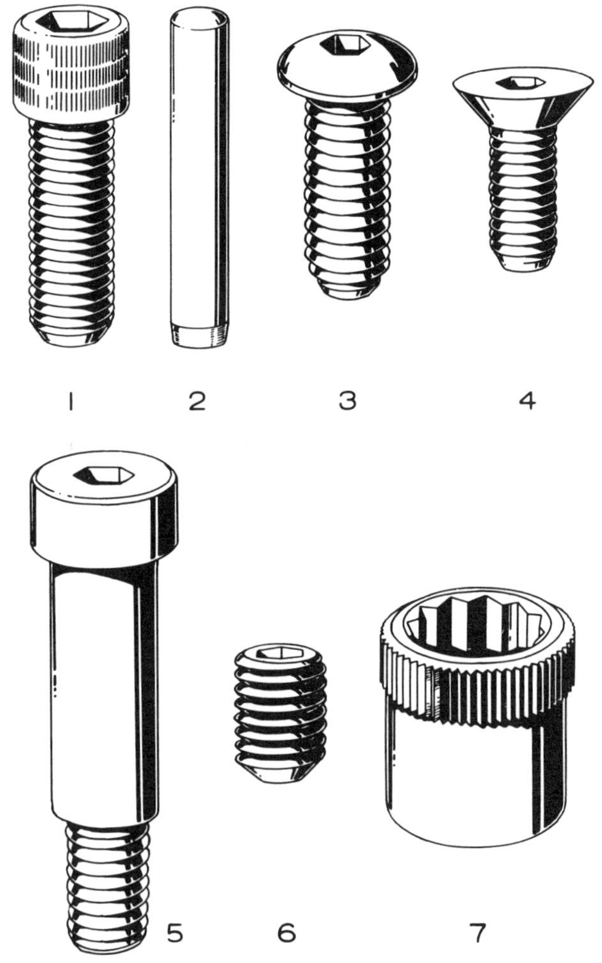

Fig. 16-2. Types of fasteners used in die construction.

16-3. THREADED FASTENERS

When components of any mechanical device must be assembled securely, and must be dismantled occasionally for repair, adjustment, or replacement, threaded fasteners are the most effective. Socket cap screws are most often used in tool work, followed by dowels.

Fundamental rules govern application of screws and dowels. Screws are used to hold components together. They are not intended to locate components sideways relative to each other. Study of the illustration will show why this is so. Two blocks are fastened together with two screws and two dowels. Clearance holes for screws are drilled 1/64 inch larger in diameter than body diameter of the screws, and counterbored holes for the screw heads are 1/32 inch larger in diameter than the heads. This clearance has been shown slightly exaggerated at the left in the section view. Obviously, these clearances will allow side shift if the screws are loosened. This is exactly what can happen when a tool is taken apart for sharpening or repair. A small amount of side movement of this nature may be permissible in many mechanical assemblies, but in precision jigs, fixtures, and dies, it could cause serious damage. For this reason, closely fitted pins called dowels are applied to effect accurate relative positioning. Dowels permit no movement between parts. They can be pressed out for repair, then replaced to restore relative positioning to original accuracy.

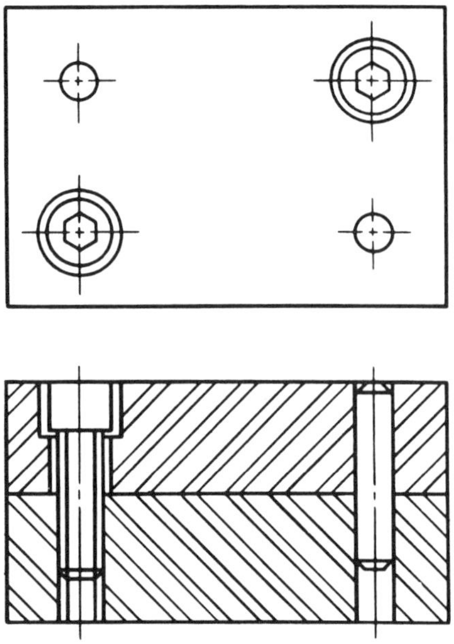

Fig. 16-3. Socket cap screws and dowels are used in holding these two blocks together.

16-4. TO APPLY FASTENERS

The first method considered is shown at **A**. Screws are applied at two diagonal corners and dowels at the other two corners. This method is employed for small and medium-size blocks and plates designed to withstand only small and medium forces. For larger blocks and where larger forces are encountered, the method shown at **B** should be selected. Screws are applied at all four corners and dowels are offset. When still larger forces are present, a fifth screw is applied to the center of the block, as shown at **C**.

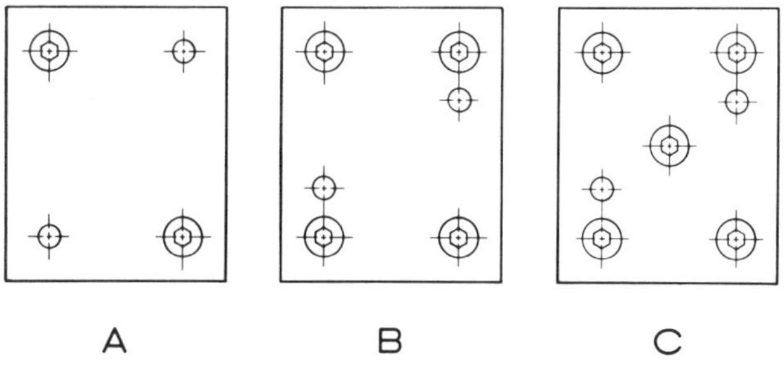

Fig. 16-4. The number of fasteners depends on the magnitude of the the anticipated force.

16-5. FLANGED PUNCHES

When parts have a projection along the center as in flanged forming punches, two screws and two dowels are applied at opposite corners when punches are short, as at **A**. For longer punches, four screws are applied at the corners, and dowels are offset, as shown at **B**. Long punches may be fastened with six screws, **C**, applied three to each side. Dowels facilitate lateral location and are applied in the same manner as for the punch at **B**.

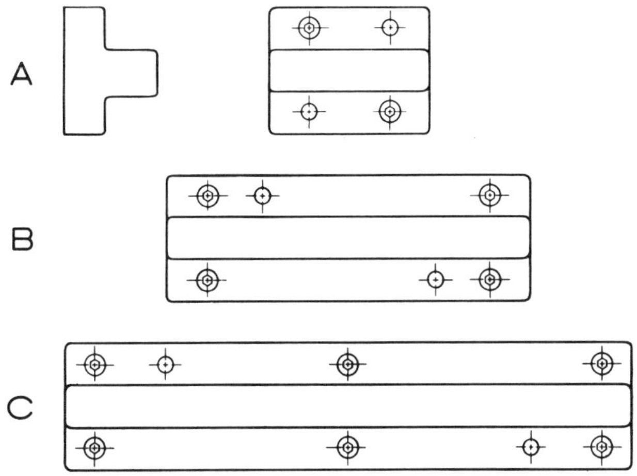

Fig. 16-5. Method of fastening flanged punches.

16-6. SPACING OF FASTENERS

Proper spacing between holes and between holes and edges of parts is particularly important for tool steel parts to be hardened. If too little space is allowed, there is a strong possibility of the block cracking in the hardening process. But on the other hand, it is often desirable to have screw holes as close to edges as possible, to keep dowels far enough apart for accurate positioning.

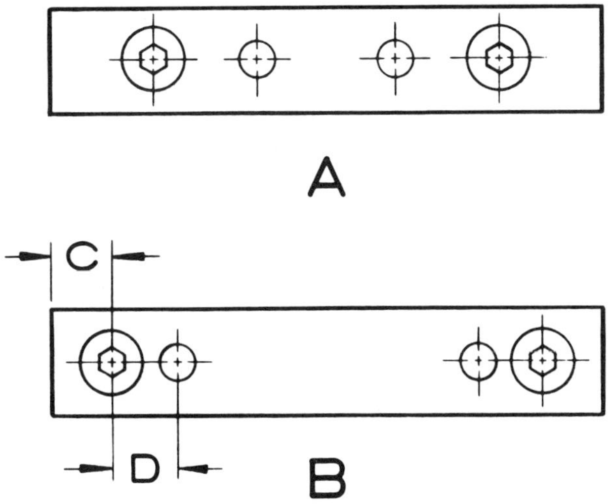

Fig. 16-6. Ineffective (A) and effective (B) spacing of fasteners.

At **A**, screws have considerable space between them and outside edges. Also, dowels have adequate space between them and their nearest screw holes. Unfortunately, the dowels are too close together for effective positioning of the component. Block **B** shows screws and dowels positioned properly. Space between dowels has increased considerably. We need to know the safe minimum distances **C** and **D**.

16-7. SPACING GUIDE

This is an illustrated guide which gives correct *minimum* proportions for applying holes in machine steel and tool steel parts. You will find it invaluable for checking to determine if correct spacing has been applied in your designs, and in time you will come to recognize good proportions instantly. At **A** is specified correct minimum spacing of holes applied at corners. Note that holes may be positioned closer to edges of machine steel parts than for parts to be made of tool steel. The extra material applied for tool steel components assures that corners will not crack in the hardening process, if it is properly done.

When a hole in tool steel or machine steel is located a greater distance from one edge than in the previous example, it may be positioned closer to the adjacent edge, as shown at **B**. This condition occurs frequently in the application of screw holes in die blocks and in other tool steel parts.

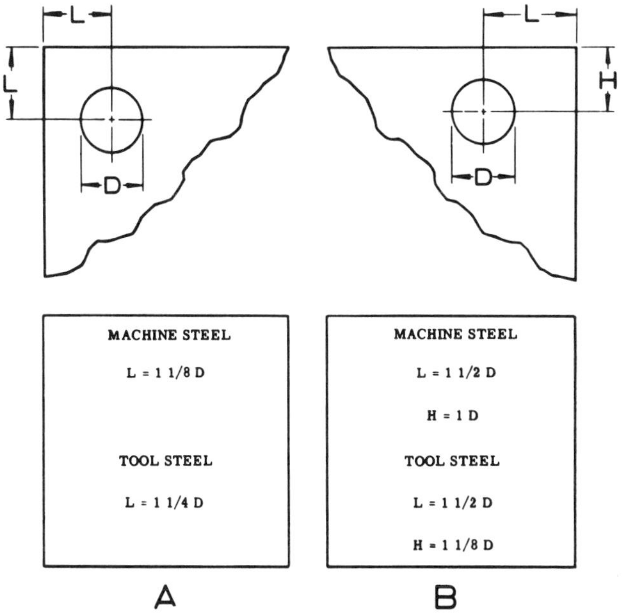

Fig. 16-7. Guide which gives *minimum* proportions for the spacing of holes from corners in machine and tool steel parts.

16-8. DISTANCE BETWEEN HOLES

Minimum proportions for positioning adjacent holes having the same size are given at **A**. Note that diameter **D** on view **B** applies to the small hole, and that distance **L** is taken from the center of the small hole to the edge of the large hole. This is the common application of drawing holes for a socket cap screw and its adjacent dowel. Under normal conditions, measure distance **L** from the center of the dowel to the edge of the cap screw head. For crowded conditions, measure to the edge of the clearance hole for the screw body.

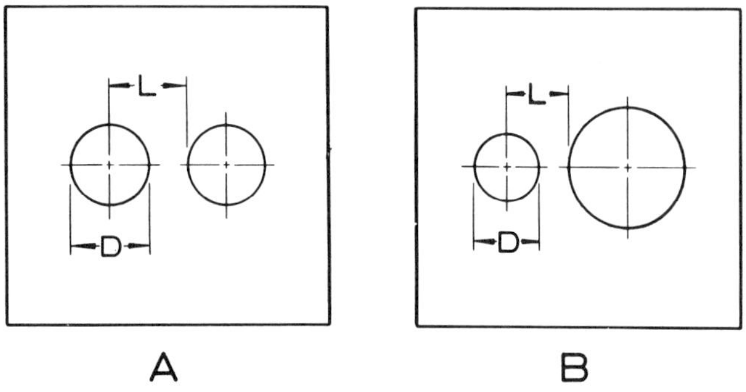

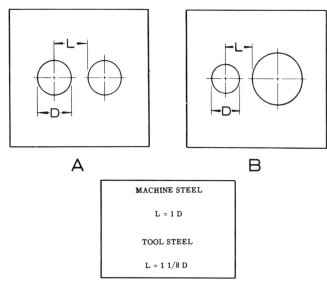

MACHINE STEEL

L = 1 D

TOOL STEEL

L = 1 1/8 D

Fig. 16-8. Minimum proportions for positioning adjacent holes in machine and tool steel parts.

16-9. LONG, NARROW PARTS

Screws and dowels are applied to long, narrow parts in several ways, At **A** is shown the most frequently used application. Distances **E**, **F**. and **G** are given in Figs. 16-7, and 16-8. Components to be taken apart for repairs are foolproofed by offsetting one of the dowels as at **B**.

When greater strength is required, a third screw is applied in the center, as at **C**. However, this addition does not affect positions of dowels. Short, narrow plates may be fastened with a single screw applied at the center. Dowels at each side provide accurate lateral location. This application is shown at **D**.

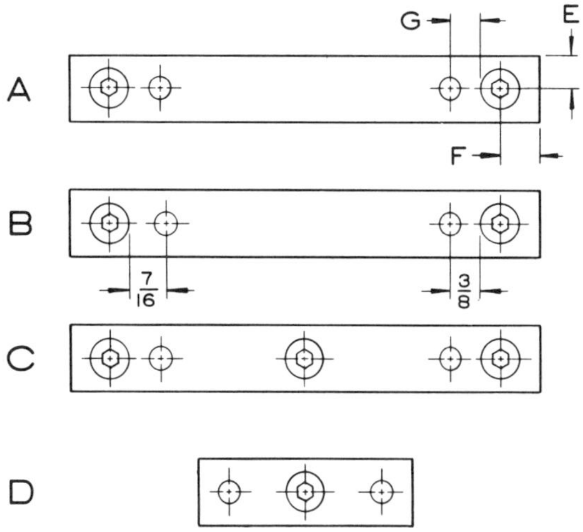

Fig. 16-9. Ways of applying screws and dowels in long narrow parts.

16-10. PROPORTIONS

In applying a row of holes in a bar, employ the following procedure:

1. Measure length **A**
2. Decide upon the number of holes required
3. Divide length **A** by the number of holes
4. The answer is the distance between holes

One-half of the amount found in 4 is the distance between end holes and part edges. Thus, hole locations are properly proportioned. For example:

1. Five holes are required
2. Length **A** is twenty inches
3. Twenty divided by 5 is 4. Distance between holes is therefore 4 inches. One-half of four is two. Distance between end holes and part edges is therefore 2 inches.

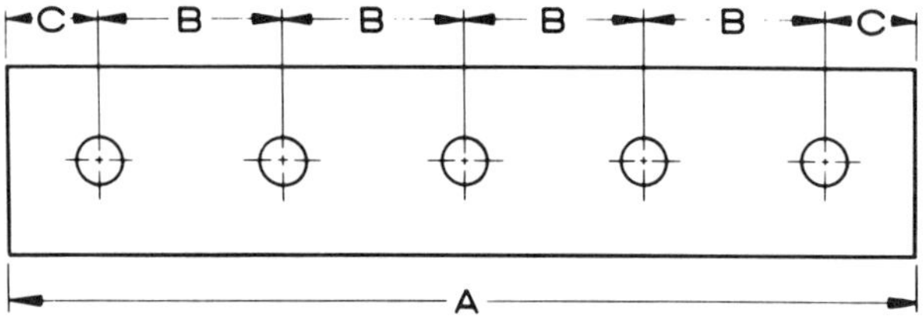

Fig. 16-10. Applying a row of holes in a bar.

16-11. FORCE ON SCREWS

In deciding upon the number of screws required, consider the size of the details in addition to any forces which will act upon the screws. The component being fastened must be pulled down evenly and squarely. Observe these rules:

1. Keep dowels as far apart as possible
2. Make sure that the screws hold down the part securely flat.

In this segment of a sectional die, the construction at **A** is incorrect because screws should act somewhere along line **C-C** for stability. Shown at **B** is the correct application, even though dowels are somewhat closer together.

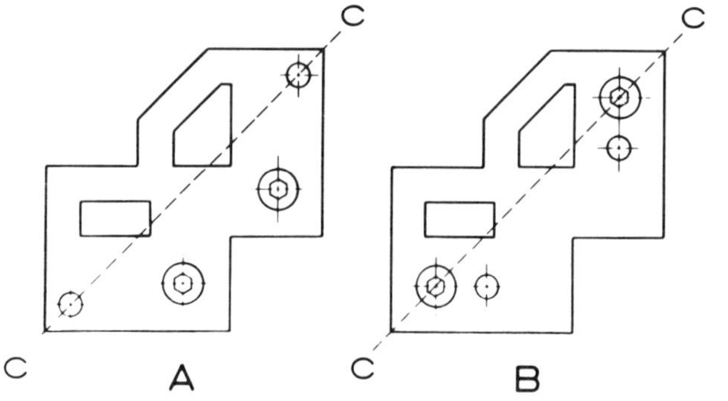

Fig. 16-11. Incorrect (A) and correct (B) method of applying fasteners in a die segment.

16-12. FOOLPROOFING

A simple way to foolproof parts which might be reassembled incorrectly in die repair is to reverse the relative positions of dowels. This method is applied to gages **A** in this piercing die. Obviously, gage positions cannot be reversed accidentally, nor could the gages be assembled upside-down because of the holes counterbored for the heads of the screws.

16-13. SCREWS ON DRAWINGS

This is the way screws appear in the plan and front section views of the representative die. Observe that in the flange of the punch a dowel is drawn at one side and a socket cap screw at the other. The die block is fastened to the die set with long socket cap screws applied from the bottom. The stripper plate, back gage, and front spacer are fastened to the die block with socket button-head screws applied from the top. Double dowels illustrated at the other side of the view provide accurate lateral positioning of components.

Observe that stripping load against the screws which hold the stripper to the die block is equal to stripping load against screws which hold the blanking punch. When only two screws and two dowels are employed to hold and locate the blanking punch, make the screws larger in diameter than those in the die block where a minimum of four screws are always employed. Compare holding strengths as given in a manufacturer's catalog. In general, screws one size larger, will have to be employed to realize approximately equal holding strength.

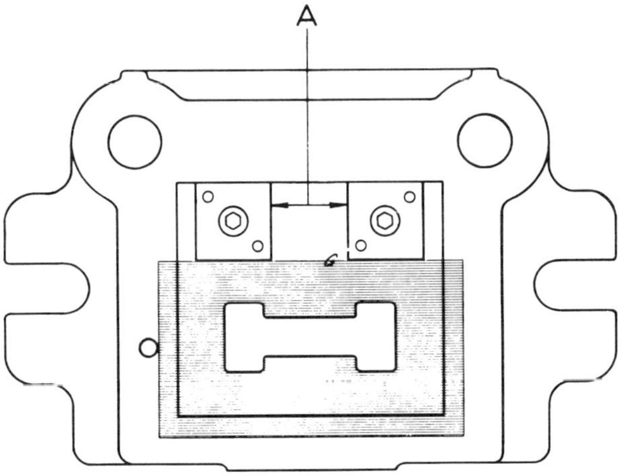

Fig. 16-12. Simple method of foolproofing back gages (A) to assure correct positioning upon reassembly.

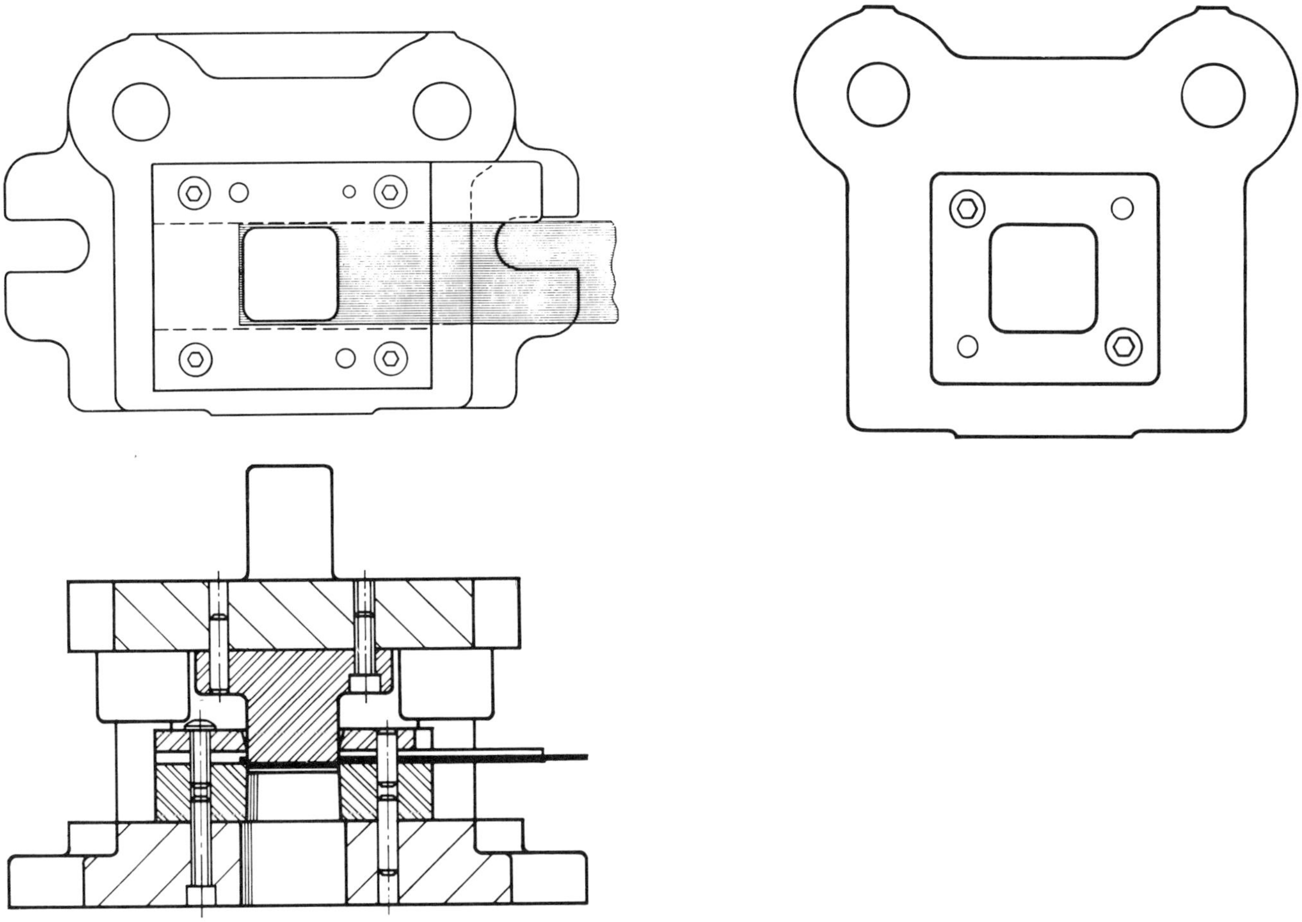

Fig. 16-13. Method of application of and appearance of fasteners in a typical die drawing.

16-14. HOLES FOR SCREWS

In specifying holes for socket screws, observe the following rules:

1. Holes **A** which engage the screw bodies are specified 1/64 inch larger than body diameter
2. Counterbored holes **B** are specified 1/32 inch larger than the diameter of the screw head
3. Counterbore depth **C** is the same as the height of the head of the screw
4. Countersink diameter **D** is made the same as the head diameter of the flat-head screw.

In the illustration, view 1 shows the section through a hole for a socket cap screw; view 2 shows the hole for a socket button head screw, and view 3 the hole for a socket flat head screw.

SOCKET CAP SCREWS

Socket cap screws are the most frequently used fasteners for tools and dies and they should be specified whenever it is possible to employ them. A socket cap screw is provided with a head within which has been broached a hexagonal socket for driving. Threads of all socket screws in the size range normally used are held to a Class 3 fit, a very accurate fit having precise tolerances. After machining they are heat-treated; a hardening and tempering process is applied to produce a correct combination of toughness without brittleness. The final stage in their manufacture consists of careful inspection for uniformity and accuracy.

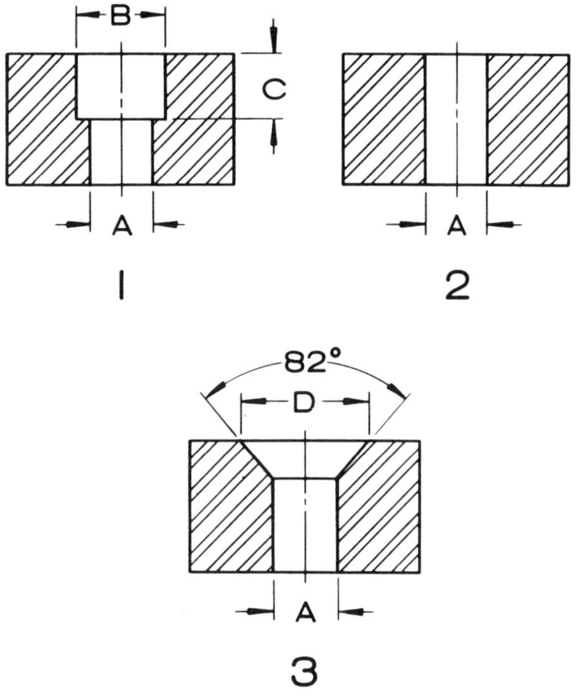

Fig. 16-14. Sectional views of holes for various socket screws.

Some differences may be noted in socket cap screws obtained from different manufacturers. Some have plain heads; others are knurled for ease in starting screws by hand; some stamp the size on the head; others are provided with two sizes of heads, conventional, and oversize for severe applications. Socket screws are also available in stainless steel for use under corrosive conditions.

Nylock screws are socket provided screws with a projecting nylon pellet inserted permanently in the body. When the threads are engaged, the nylon is compressed and displaced providing a locking thrust to prevent loosening under vibration.

THREAD ENGAGEMENT

It is important that thread engagement for socket screws be applied correctly. If too little is specified, it is possible to strip the threads in the tapped hole. On the other hand, excessive thread engagement should be avoided because no greater strength is provided and it is difficult to tap deep holes. Also, the deeper a hole is tapped, the greater the possibility of tap breakage.

16-15. MINIMUM THREAD ENGAGEMENT

This table specifies the minimum amount of thread engagement which should be applied for various materials. The values recommended for steel and cast iron should be memorized because they are employed so frequently.

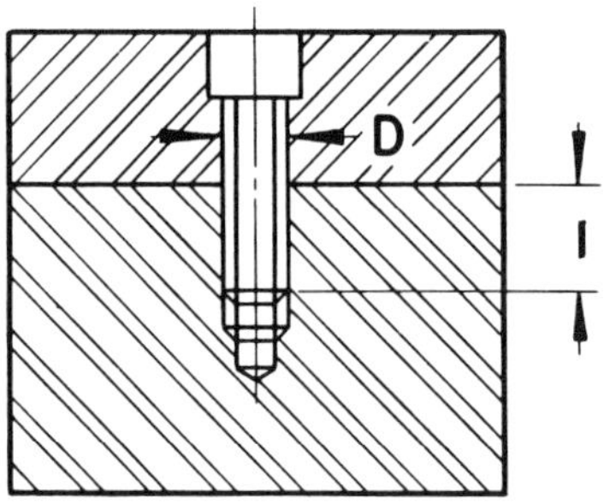

Steel	I = 1 1/2 D
Cast Iron	I = 2 D
Magnesium	I = 2 1/4 D
Aluminum	I = 2 1/2 D
Fiber & Plastics	I = 3 D & UP

Fig. 16-15. Table for determining minimum thread engagement for various materials.

FORMULAS FOR THREAD LENGTH

Simple formulas establish thread lengths. Let **L** equal screw length, **I** equal thread length, **D** equal screw diameter. For Coarse-Thread Series (UNC) threads; **I** equals either **2D** plus ½ inch or ½ **L** whichever is greater. For Fine-Thread Series (UNF) threads **I** equals either 1½ **D** plus ½ inch or 3/8 **L** whichever is greater.

16-16. PROPORTIONS OF SOCKET CAP SCREWS

Socket cap screws are drawn to the following proportions: **A** = length of the screw; **B** = thread length; **C** = head height, **D** = the body diameter; (Note also that that **C** = **D**); **E** = root diameter of the thread; **F** = thread chamfer, drawn 1/32 to 3/32 inch wide, depending on screw size; **G** = angle of chamfer, 45 degrees.

When the block to be fastened is made of hardened tool steel, distance **H** should never be less than 1½ **D**. For machine steel, it need only be thick enough for adequate strength. Length of thread engagement **I** is 1½ **D** for steel, with a minimum of 1 **D** under certain conditions, and 2 **D** for cast iron and some non-ferrous metals.

Depth of the tapped hole **J** is applied in increments of 1/16 inch at least, never in increments of 1/32 or 1/64 inch. Distance **K** between the end of the screw and the bottom of the thread, and between the bottom of the thread and the bottom of the tap drill hole, is normally made 1/8 inch. Bottoming taps have from 1 to 1½ imperfect threads, and this fact must be taken into consideration when drawing blind holes. The thread must extend at least 1½ times the pitch of the thread

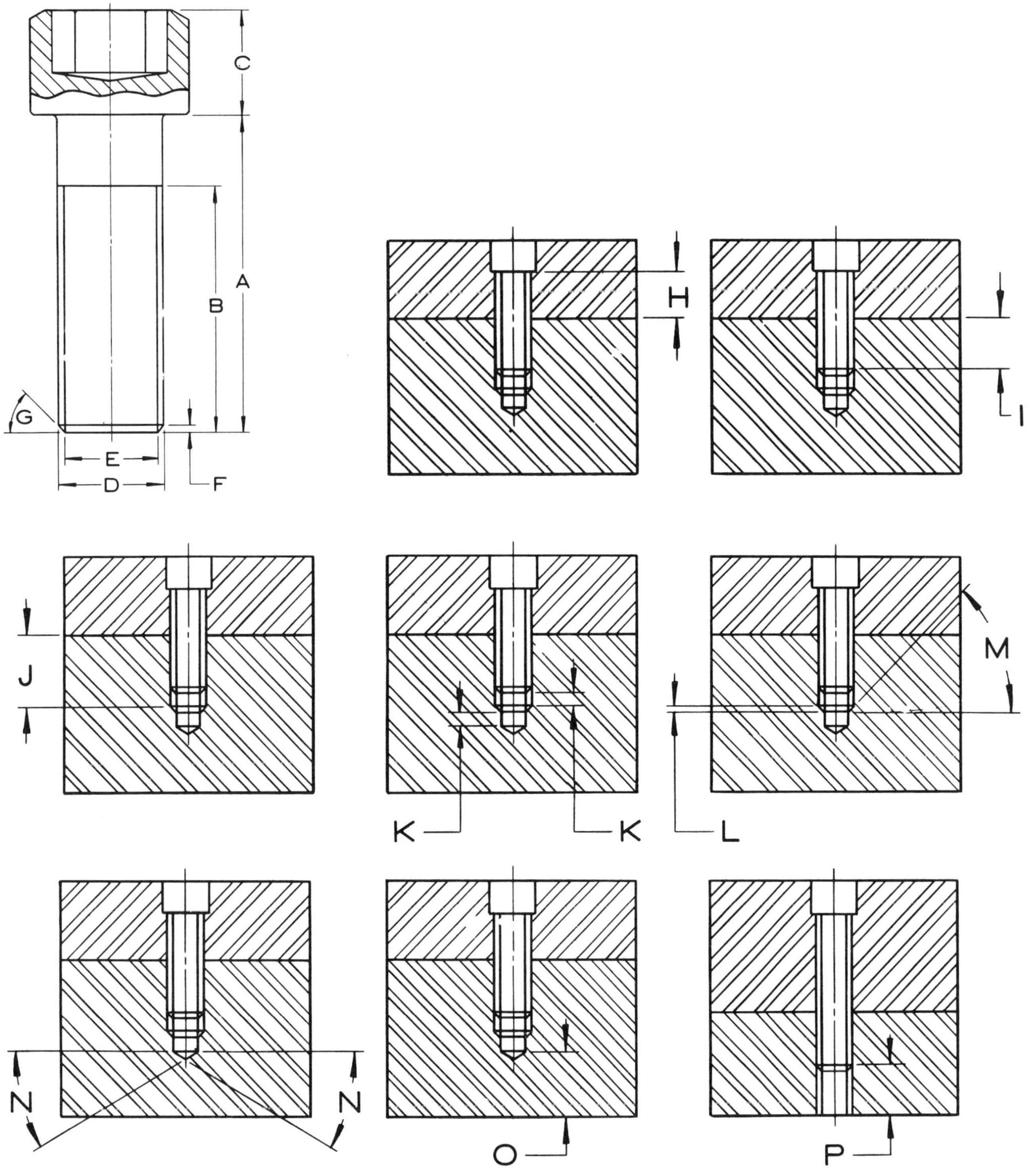

Fig. 16-16. Proportions of socket cap screws.

past the end of the screw. Length **L** of the thread chamfer is made 1/16 inch. Chamfer **M** is 45 degrees. At the bottom of the tap drill hole are drawn two lines at angles of 30 degrees, dimension **N**. They represent the conical depression produced by the end of the tap drill.

For hardened tool steel parts, distance **O** between the end of the tap drill hole and the lower surface of the block must be greater than 1 **D** (one diameter of the screw body). When this distance is less than 1 **D**, show the tap drill running completely through the part. If this is not done, it is possible for the thin, circular section of steel to crack in hardening and fall out as a rough-edged disk.

The hole which a screw engages is tapped all the way through when distance **P** from the end of the screw to the lower surface of the block is 1 **D** (one diameter of the screw), or less.

16-17. APPLICATION OF SCREWS

There are three methods of applying socket cap screws:

1. The most commonly used method is to counterbore the hole for the screw as at **A**. The screw head engages this counterbored hole and its top comes flush with the surface after assembly.

2. In a variation of the foregoing, the hole is not counterbored to full depth, and the head protrudes a certain amount as at **B**. This is employed for fastening thinner plates.

3. In the third method, the hole is simply drilled and the screw head is left to protrude, as at **C**. This would be used for thin parts and in covered places.

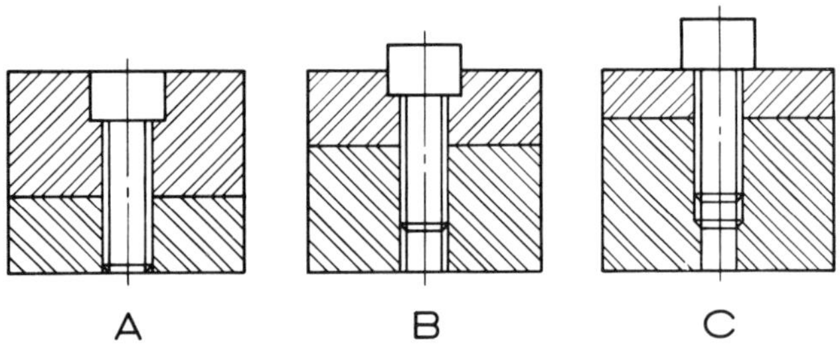

Fig. 16-17. Three methods of applying socket cap screws.

16-18. FASTENING PLATES

When components such as plates are fastened to both sides of a block, tap the block all the way through. Screws engage the block from both sides to hold the plates, as shown at **A**. When the center block is not too thick, it is permissible to hold three parts by threading one and fastening the three with relatively long screws, as at **B**. Sometimes it is desirable to fasten two details together through a third component. The screw head is reached for fastening through a hole which clears it, as at **C**.

OTHER FASTENERS

Other types of fasteners commonly used in the design of tools and dies would include the following:

Socket flat head screws
Socket button head screws
Socket set screws
Socket lock screws
Socket shoulder screws
Dowels
Rivets.

Although these types of fasteners are not employed so frequently, the designer should understand the specialized conditions which require their use. Dowels are also treated in detail in the remainder of this section, as well as rivets as they apply to tools and dies.

16-19. SOCKET FLAT HEAD SCREWS

Heads of these screws are machined to an 82 degree included angle, dimension **A**. They are employed for fastening thin plates which must present a flat, unbroken surface. Avoid their use when possible, because they cannot be tightened as securely as cap screws. Employ them only for flush applications when plates to be fastened are too thin for counterboring. For tool work, *socket* flat head screws are always specified in preference to the slotted type.

To draw the side view, first look up the head diameter in a handbook or manufacturer's catalog, and

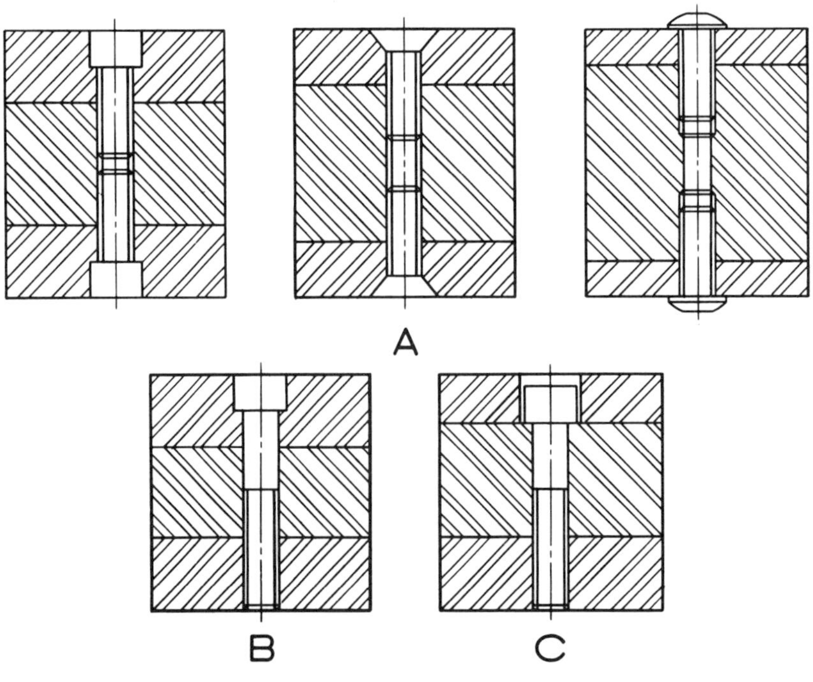

Fig. 16-18. Different methods of fastening plates.

mark ends of head diameter to the specified dimension. Then the tapered lines of the head are drawn with the protractor set to an angle of 41 degrees from the screw axis, dimension **B**.

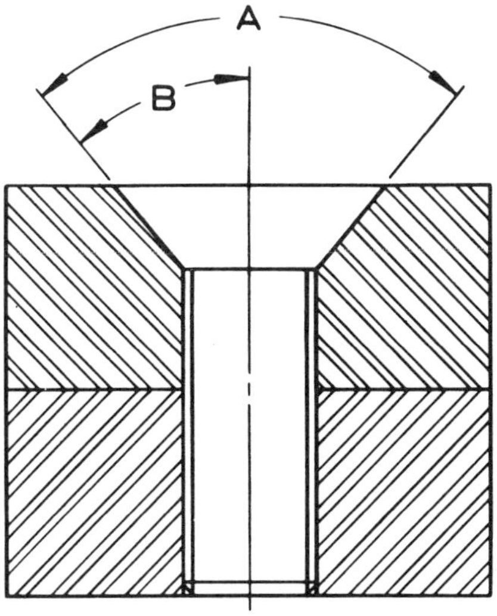

Fig. 16-19. Application of a socket flat head screw.

16-20. SOCKET BUTTON HEAD SCREWS

These screws are employed for fastening plates in applications where a raised head is not objectionable. They should be used when plates are too thin for counterboring for cap screws, and surfaces need not be flush, or flat. In the design of small and medium size dies, they fasten the stripper plate, back gage, and front spacer to the die block. Button head screws project only slightly above the surface. Their rounded contours prevent injuries to operators' hands.

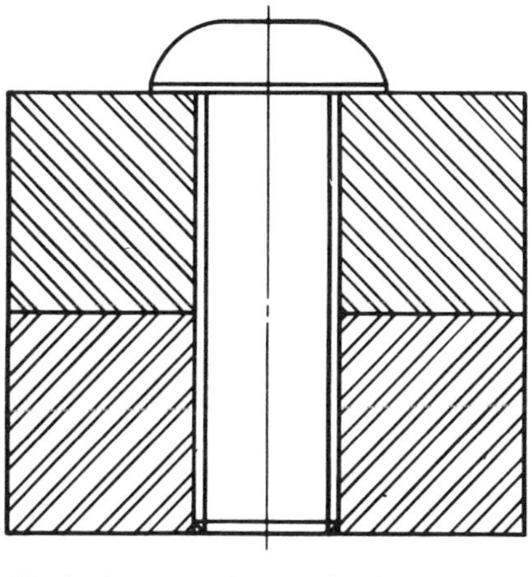

Fig. 16-20. Application of a socket button head screw.

16-21. SOCKET SET SCREWS

When first developed, socket set screws were called "safety" screws. They were employed to lock rotating machine parts to their shafts. They replaced screws with protruding heads which were dangerous because clothing could become caught by the whirling projection. A socket set screw is threaded its entire length, and it is provided with an internal driving socket at one end.

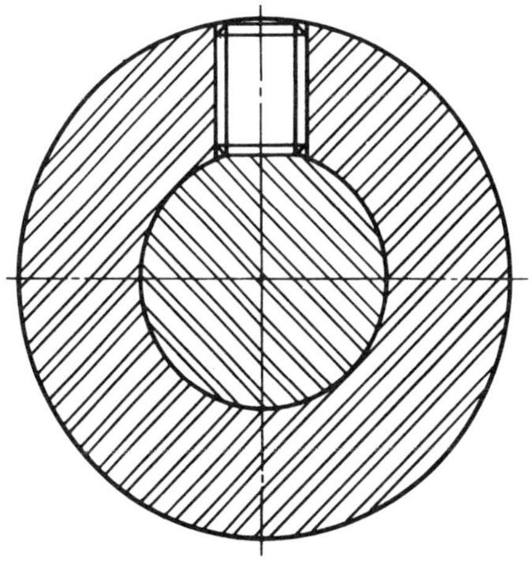

Fig. 16-21. Application of a socket set screw.

16-22. POINT STYLES FOR SET SCREWS

There are six styles of set screw points. The designer must be able to specify the correct style of point for the specific application.

1. The flat point is the most commonly used type for jigs, fixtures, and dies. Flat-point set screws are employed as adjustable stops, clamp screws, and to lock hardened shafts.

2. Cup-point set screws are used to lock pulleys, collars, gears, and other parts on soft shafts. The sharp edges cut into the metal of the shaft to effect more or less permanent positioning.

3. Cone-point set screws may be employed for the same applications as cup-point screws. However, a much more positive lock is effected because the shaft is first spotted or drilled to engage the conical point of the screw.

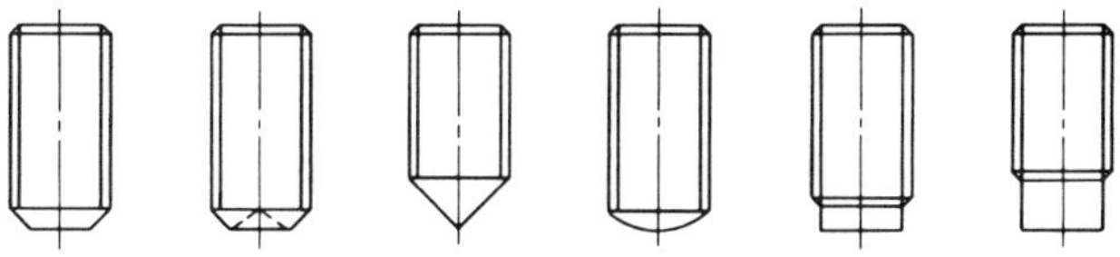

Fig. 16-22. Six point styles for set screws.

4. Oval-point set screws are employed to lock parts which are to be adjusted frequently relative to each other. A groove is ordinarily provided of the same general contour as the set screw point which bears against it. This groove may be machined lengthwise, angularly, or in any other direction to the shaft axis.

5. Half dog-point set screws are frequently employed to engage slots milled longitudinally in shafts. They allow lengthwise movement, but prevent rotation. The point also acts as a stop to limit travel.

6. Full dog-point set screws are employed for exactly the same purposes as half dog-point set screws. They are not appreciably more efficient and therefore are now seldom used, and they must be specially ordered.

16-23. PUNCH-RETAINING SET SCREWS

This table facilitates selection of the correct set screw size after punch head diameter **A** has been established. It will help to eliminate errors because, in every instance, tap drill size **B** is larger than head diameter **A** of the punch. This method provides quick removal and replacement of nicked or broken punches.

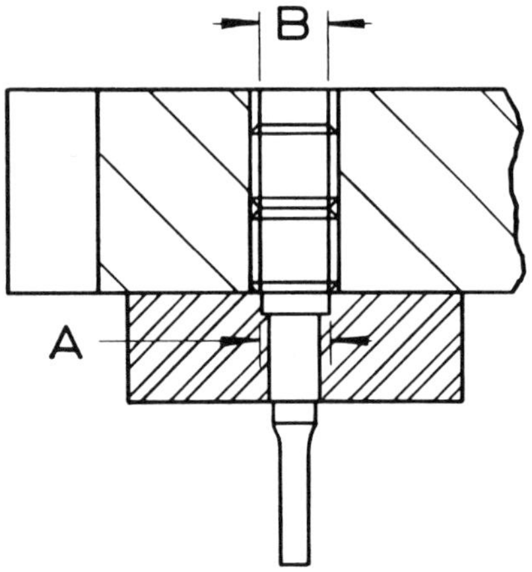

PUNCH HEAD DIA. A	TAP DRILL DIA. B	TAP
3/16	#7 (.201)	1/4 - 20
1/4	#F (.257)	5/16 - 18
5/16	5/16	3/8 - 16
3/8	27/64	1/2 - 13
1/2	17/32	5/8 - 11
5/8	21/32	3/4 - 10
3/4	49/64	7/8 - 9
7/8	7/8	1 - 8

Fig. 16-23. Table for selecting tap drill diameter and set screw thread size when punch head diameter is known.

16-24. SOCKET LOCK SCREWS

Lock screws have the same dimensions as socket set screws, except that they are much shorter, and the hexagonal driving socket is broached clear through the screw. The length is one-half the diameter for most sizes. They are employed to lock set screws to prevent their loosening.

A big advantage for some applications is that the lock screw need not be completely removed for re-setting the set screw. It is simply backed up a turn or so and the set screw socket is reached through the lock screw hole for re-setting to a new position.

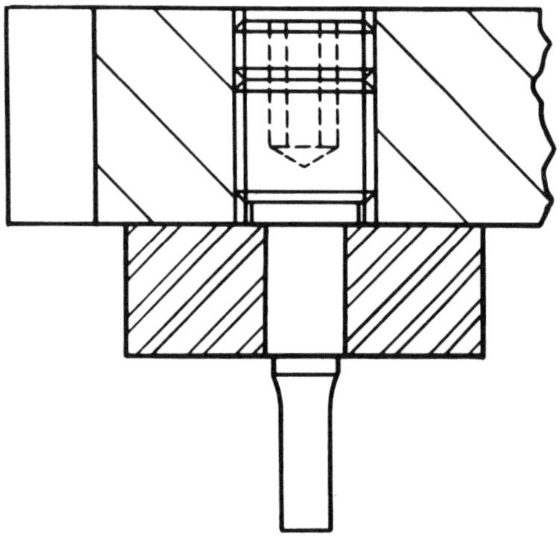

Fig. 16-24. Application of a socket lock screw.

In the design of dies, lock screws are employed to lock punch-retaining set screws under crowded conditions.

16-25. SQUARE-HEAD SET SCREWS

In die design, only one application remains for such screws. This is as actuator for the automatic stop. This right section view of a representative die

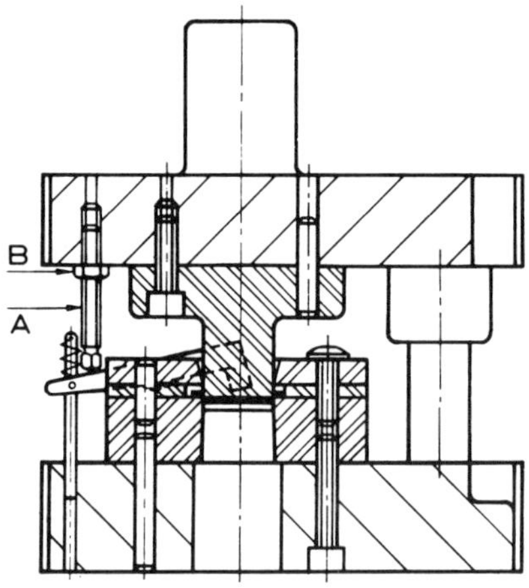

Fig. 16-25. Application of a square head set screw (A) for actuating the automatic stop.

illustrates the manner in which a square head set screw, **A**, is applied to operate an automatic stop. A jam nut, **B**, locks the screw against rotation. Note that the hole for the set screw is tapped ¼ inch deeper than necessary. This permits re-setting the screw back as punches are shortened in sharpening.

A square head set screw is measured from under the head to the end and this is the specification listed in the bill of material.

16-26. SHOULDER SCREWS

Shoulder screws are used to provide pivots for rocking members of jigs and fixtures and to limit travel of components. A shoulder screw is provided with

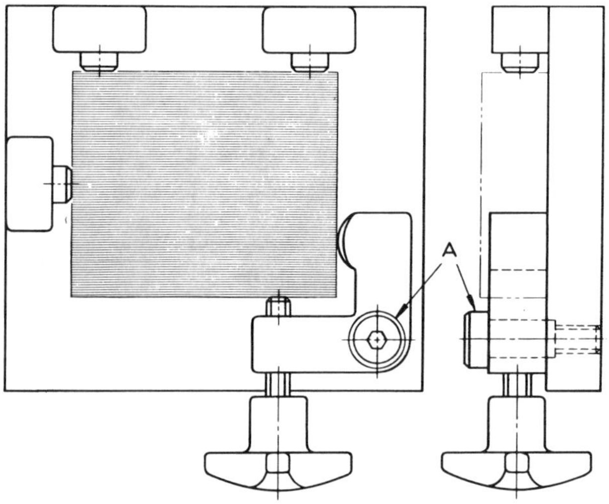

Fig. 16-26. Application of a socket shoulder screw.

a body ground to accurate size, a head with an internal driving socket, and, at the other end, a smaller threaded portion.

The illustration shows a corner clamp employed to clamp square and rectangular workpieces against locating buttons for accurate positioning. The corner clamp pivots about a shoulder screw, **A**, which is threaded into the base.

16-27. STRIPPER BOLTS

When shoulder screws are employed in dies, they are called stripper bolts, because they find their most common application in limiting travel of spring strippers.

This front section view of a blanking die shows an application of stripper bolts **A**, employed to retain a spring stripper and to limit its travel. Four or more stripper bolts are used, but it is common practice to draw only one at one side in order to show one of the springs at the other side of the view.

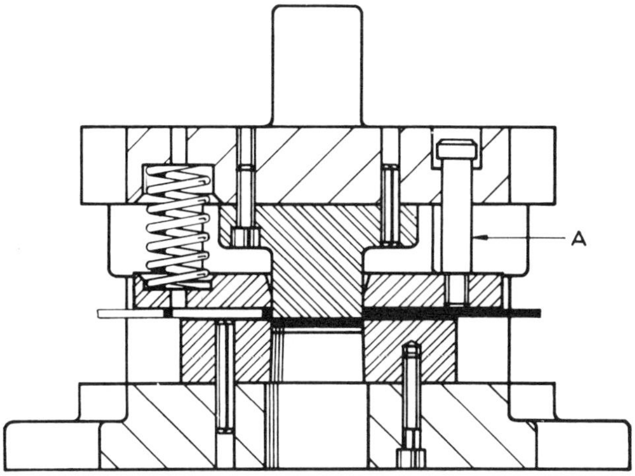

Fig. 16-27. Application of a stripper bolt (A) to limit travel of a spring stripper.

16-28. TELESCOPING SLEEVE

When stripper plates or pressure pads require long travel, but stripper bolts cannot extend below the die set because the bolster plate of the press is not provided with a clearance hole, a telescoping sleeve may be employed to increase the amount of travel. At **A**, the pressure pad is illustrated in raised position. At **B**, it is shown at the bottom of the press stroke with the sleeve telescoped over the stripper bolt.

16-29. HOLES FOR STRIPPER BOLTS

When specifying holes for stripper bolts, observe these rules:

1. Holes **A** which engage stripper bolt bodies are specified a slip fit, or sliding fit, by giving nominal diameter followed by the abbreviation S.F. Example: ½ DR. & RM. THRU – S.F.

2. Counterbore diameter **B** is specified 1/32 inch larger than the diameter of the head of the screw.

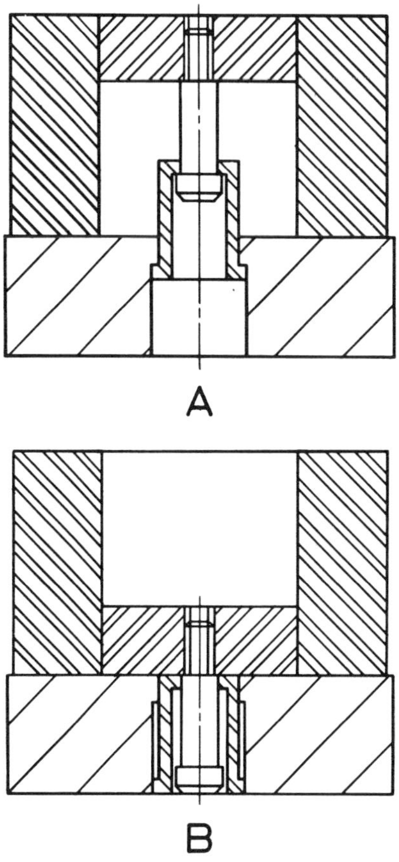

Fig. 16-28. Application of a telescoping sleeve provides long travel of a stripper bolt.

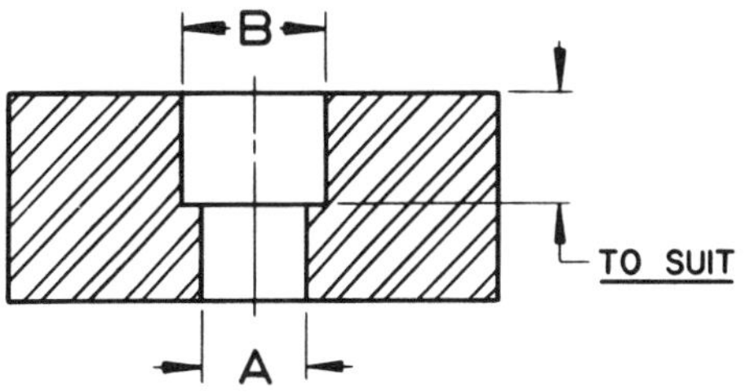

Fig. 16-29. Hole for a stripper bolt.

16-30. SAFE STRENGTH OF SCREWS

As a general rule, the strength of a socket screw is comparable to the strength of an ordinary screw of the next larger standard diameter. For example, a 5/16-18 socket cap screw is about as strong as a 3/8-16 hexagon head cap screw.

Many factors enter into the determination of strength of screws. In designing, we are not concerned about the strength of a screw in its free state. Instead, we must know the amount of strength *remaining* in it after it has been tightened. A considerable proportion of the strength of a screw is expended in tightening. What is left is the effective load-carrying capacity. This table lists load ratings for socket cap screws, socket flat-head screws, and socket button-head screws.

The table is based on a breaking strength of 180,000 pounds per square inch to which most socket screws are manufactured. Read the values directly in selecting die fasteners intended to resist specific loads. These values will be found of particular importance in determining the sizes and number of screws required for fastening punches and stripper plates.

SCREW SIZE	SOCKET CAP SCREWS		SOCKET FLAT HEAD SCREWS		SOCKET BUTTON HEAD SCREWS		AFTER TIGHTENING: EFFECTIVE STRENGTH, IN POUNDS, TO RESIST LOAD.
	N.C.	N.F.	N.C.	N.F.	N.C.	N.F.	
# 4	540	585	465	....	....	....	
6	810	910	700	....	....	....	
8	1,250	1,315	1,080	....	1,010	1,060	
10	1,565	1,790	1,350	1,545	1,260	1,445	
1/4	2,850	3,260	2,460	2,805	2,300	2,625	
5/16	4,620	5,200	4,045	4,480	3,785	4,190	
3/8	6,950	7,900	5,595	6,790	5,595	6,300	
7/16	9,250	10,400	8,215	9,185	....	....	
1/2	12,400	14,000	10,975	12,375	10,250	....	
9/16	15,500	17,200	....	....	....	....	
5/8	19,150	21,700	17,485	19,800	16,350	....	
3/4	27,500	30,750	25,880	28,860	....	....	
7/8	38,500	41,900	....	....	....	....	
1	48,500	54,500	....	....	....	....	

Fig. 16-30. Table of effective strengths of socket cap screws, socket flat head screws and socket button head screws.

After the stripping force has been calculated, turn to the table and read values directly. When selecting stripper bolts, choose values given for socket cap screws of the same diameter and threads per inch as the threaded portion of the stripper bolt.

16-31. DOWELS

Dowels hold parts in perfect related alignment by absorbing side pressures and lateral thrusts. Also, they facilitate quick disassembly of components and reassembly in their exact former relationship.

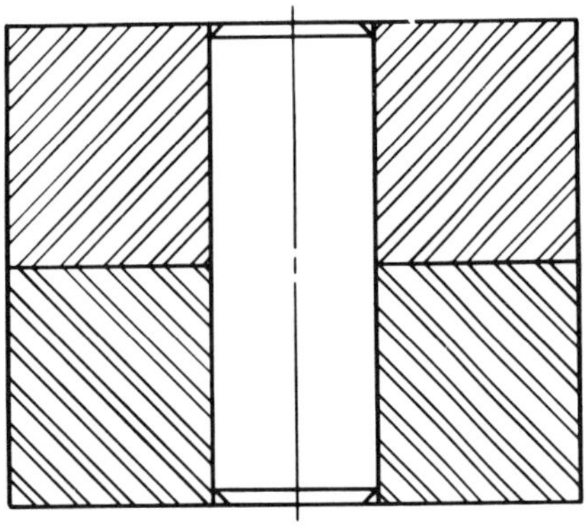

Fig. 16-31. Typical application of a dowel.

Present day dowels are precise tool components, carefully designed and engineered. They are produced with exacting accuracy, both dimensionally and in their physical characteristics. Dowels are made of alloy steel, heat treated to produce an extremely hard exterior surface with a somewhat softer, but tough core to resist shear and spread, or mushrooming, when they are driven into tight holes. Surface hardness is Rockwell C 60 to 64; core hardness C 50 to 54. Depth of the hard exterior case extends from 10 to 20 thousandths of an inch depending on size, smaller sizes having a thinner case. Dowels are available in a range of sizes from 1/8 inch diameter by 3/8 inch long, to 1 inch diameter by 6 inches in length.

STRENGTH

Single shear strength ranges from 150,000 to 210,000 pounds per square inch. To find the shear strength of a dowel, multiply the dowel area by the above values.

OVERSIZES

Dowels are manufactured in two amounts of oversize:

1. Regular dowels, employed for all new jigs, fixtures, and dies are made 0.0002 inch oversize to provide a secure press fit.

2. Oversize dowels are made 0.001 inch oversize. They are used for repair work when dowel holes have been enlarged through repeated pressing of dowels in and out, and when holes have been accidentally machined oversize.

SURFACE FINISH

Manufacturers precision grind dowel surfaces to a diameter tolerance of plus and minus 0.0001 inch. Surface roughness is held to a finish of 4 to 6 microinches average, maximum. This extremely smooth finish reduces the possibility of galling or seizing when dowels are driven in or out of their holes. A rust preventative coating is then applied.

16-32. DOWEL SHAPE

Standard dowels are given a 5 degree taper at one end for easy starting when they are pressed in, as shown at **A**. A small radius is applied to the other corner. However, to save time, they are drawn conventionally by showing a chamfer at each end, as shown at **B**.

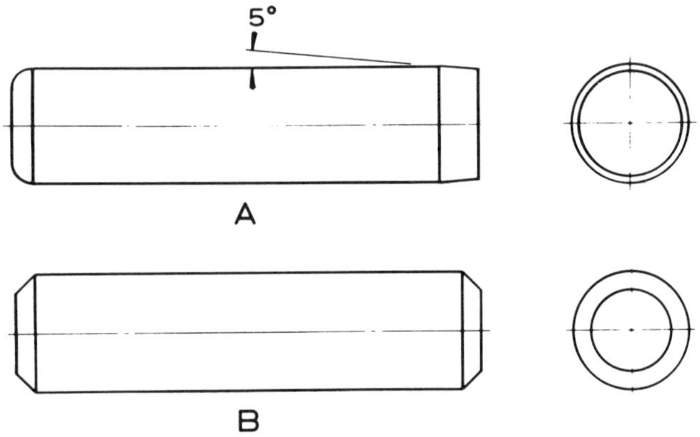

Fig. 16-32. Dowel shape in actuality (A) and as shown on a drawing (B).

16-33. SHEAR STRENGTH OF DOWELS

The safe load that dowels can resist in shear is determined by dividing the ultimate strength by the area of the dowel. This table lists safe shear strengths

DOWEL DIA.	SAFE LOAD IN POUNDS
1/8	164
3/16	368
1/4	655
5/16	1,022
3/8	1,473
7/16	2,004
1/2	2,618
5/8	4,090
3/4	5,890
7/8	8,017
1	10,472

Fig. 16-33. Table of safe loads for alloy steel dowels in single shear.

of dowels from 1/8 to 1 inch in diameter. Ultimate shear strength is taken at 190,000 PSI, and a safety factor of 12 has been applied. Therefore, these are safe loads for dowels in single shear under shock conditions as encountered in the design of dies. For double shear applications, values should be doubled. The table lists strengths of alloy dowels, and not of the less expensive cold-drawn steel dowels. Alloy dowels should always be used for dies because they are considerably stronger.

16-34. REAMING DOWEL HOLES

When a hole is to be reamed for press fitting a dowel, it is first drilled with a reamer drill, then reamed. Reamer drills have the same nominal size as the corresponding reamers, but their diameters are actually smaller. For instance, a 5/16 inch reamer drill has a diameter of 0.307 inch and actual reamer size is 0.3125 inch, leaving 0.0055 inch of metal for the reamer to remove. The table lists sizes of commonly used reamer drills and their corresponding reamers.

REAMER DRILL DIAMETER		REAMER DIAMETER	
NOMINAL SIZE	DECIMAL SIZE	NOMINAL SIZE	DECIMAL SIZE
5/16	.307	5/16	.3125
3/8	.366	3/8	.375
7/16	.427	7/16	.4375
1/2	.489	1/2	.500
5/8	.616	5/8	.625
3/4	.734	3/4	.750

Fig. 16-34. Table of commonly used reamer drills and corresponding reamers.

16-35. PROPORTIONS OF DOWELS

Conditions under which dowels are employed determine the type of application chosen. These are four:

1. *Through dowels.* In this application the hole is reamed all the way through the components, and dowels can be pressed out from either side. Dimension **A** is two inches or less. Dowel engagement **B** is between 1½ and 2 times diameter **D**

2. *Semi-blind dowels.* In this application the dowel hole is drilled and reamed from one side at least 1/8 inch deeper than dowel length. A smaller hole is drilled through the block and the dowel can be pressed out from one side only. Dimension **C** of the knockout hole is made 1/2 **D** plus 1/64 inch, or one-half dowel diameter with clearance for a standard diameter hand punch for pressing out

3. *Blind dowels.* This dowel is applied in a blind hole, one not drilled and reamed completely through. The application should be avoided whenever possible. Blind dowels are more difficult to fit because of trapped air, and removal can be troublesome. Diameter **E** is made a press fit. Diameter **F** at the blind side should be a slip fit

4. *Relieved dowels.* When doweling blocks over two inches thick (dimension **G**), standard length dowels are employed and the hole **H** is specified 1/32 inch larger than the diameter of the dowel for relief. This relief is applied to that portion of the hole not in actual contact with the dowel surface. Engagement length *L* is 1½ to 2 **D**.

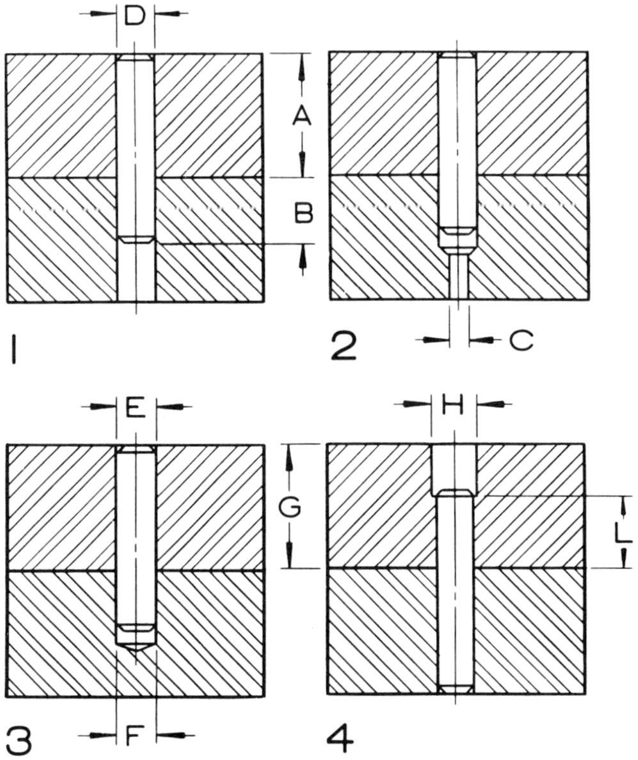

Fig. 16-35. Four ways of applying dowels: through dowel (1); semi-blind dowel (2), blind dowel (3), relieved dowel (4).

Normally, dowels are press fitted into both members. Holes are drilled and reamed after the jig, fixture, or die has been completely assembled, and often even after it has been tried out. However, when parts are subject to frequent disassembly, as for instance for sharpening, dowels are press fitted in one component and made a sliding fit in the other for ease of disassembly.

16-36. DOWELS FOR MULTIPLE PARTS

In precision tool design where clearances are held to extreme accuracy, good doweling methods must be employed. When more than two parts are to be doweled, the method shown at **A** may be used when plates are relatively thin. Dowel length is the same as the thick-

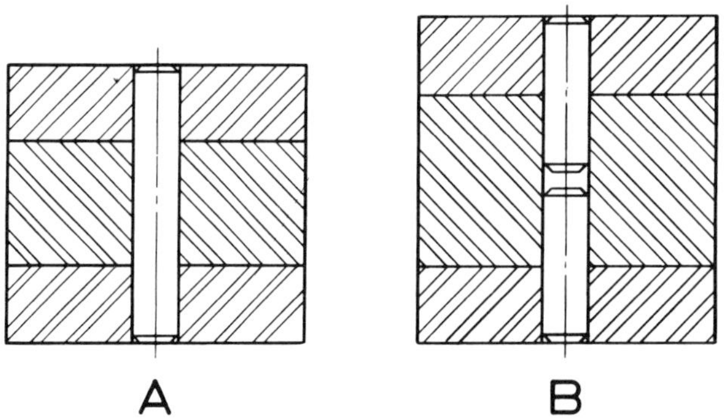

Fig. 16-36. Application of dowels for multiple parts.

ness of the combined plates. For thicker plates and blocks, the method illustrated at **B** is preferred. Two dowels engage each dowel hole. The outer plates are thus doweled to the center block.

It is common practice to make the length of a dowel four times its diameter, when possible. For example, a 3/8 inch diameter dowel would be 1½ inches long.

16-37. DOWELING HARDENED PARTS

There are three methods of doweling hardened tool-steel blocks. In the first, shown at **A**, holes are drilled and reamed before hardening. After hardening, they are either jig-ground or lapped for accurate engagement of dowels. In a second method **B**, soft plugs of machine steel are pressed into oversize holes in the hardened blocks. Holes for dowels are drilled and reamed through the soft plugs in a conventional manner.

When doweling a machine steel block to a hardened tool steel block **C**, the hardened block only may be provided with a soft plug pressed into a large hole. Dowel location is transferred from the machine steel plate to the soft plug for accurate location and fit of dowels.

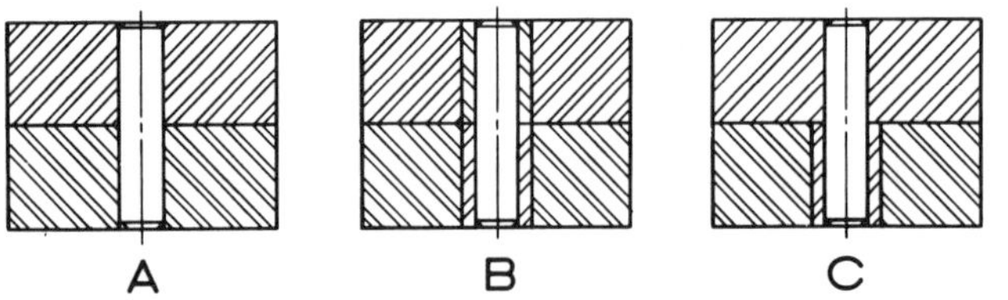

Fig. 16-37. Methods of doweling hardened tool-steel blocks.

16-38. DOWEL DIAMETER

For jigs, fixtures, and gages, always make dowel diameters one size smaller than corresponding screw diameters. For dies, dowels are made the same diameter as the screws because of the high speed and shock conditions present in operation. This table lists correct dowel sizes for screws ranging from number 8 to ¾ inch in diameter.

SCREW DIAMETER	DOWEL DIAMETER	
	TOOLS	DIES
# 8	1/8	1/8
# 10	1/8	3/16
1/4	3/16	1/4
5/16	1/4	5/16
3/8	5/16	3/8
7/16	3/8	7/16
1/2	7/16	1/2
5/8	1/2	5/8
3/4	5/8	3/4

Fig. 16-38. Screw diameters and corresponding dowel diameters as applied to tools and dies.

16-39. REMOVABLE DOWELS

One type of removable dowel is illustrated at **A**. These dowels are used in blind applications where the dowel holes cannot be drilled entirely through the component. A threaded hole is provided in one end as shown. To remove the dowel, a length of pipe or tubing (**B**) is placed over it, then rotation of the capscrew acting against a washer (**C**) removes it. Longer lengths of pipe can be used to increase travel.

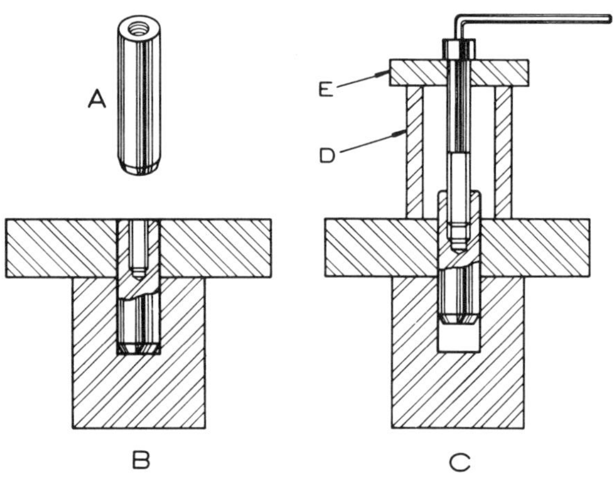

Fig. 16-39. One type of removable dowel for use in blind hole applications.

16-40. ANOTHER REMOVABLE DOWEL

A different type of commercially available removable dowel is illustrated here. This dowel **A** is provided with an axial hole tapped the entire length of the dowel. Threaded into the hole is a long socket set screw **B**. In section view **C**, the dowel is shown pressed into a blind hole. For removal, the set screw is turned as shown in view **D** and this jacks the dowel upward out of the hole.

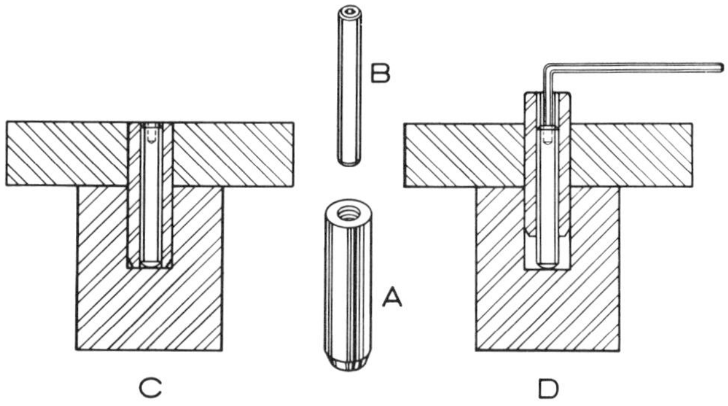

Fig. 16-40. Another type of removable dowel for use in blind hole applications.

16-41. RIVETS

Rivets are fasteners which derive their holding power from deformation or upsetting of a portion of their structure. Numerous types have been developed because they provide a fastening method well adapted for joining parts produced in quantities. In the design of tools and dies, however, only two types of rivets are commonly employed. They are the button-head rivet shown at **A**, and the countersunk rivet shown at **B**. They are employed for fastening thin plates which are not likely to require dismantling for repair. When inserted and firmly seated, the rivet end projects. This projection is then deformed by pressure or peening, as shown at **C**.

16-42. RIVET APPLICATIONS

Riveting is not often employed for fastening die parts. There are two exceptions:

1. The knockout rod is usually turned down at its end, pressed into the knockout plate, and the end is then peened or riveted over, as shown at **A**

2. In another application, the strip support is often riveted to the back gage, as shown at **B.**

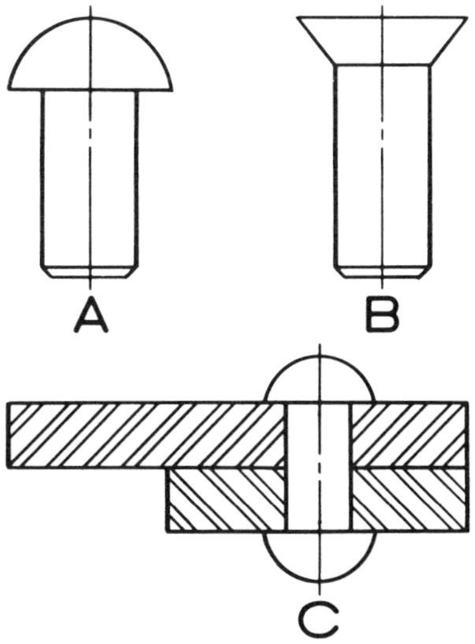

Fig. 16-41. Two types of rivets commonly used in tools and dies.

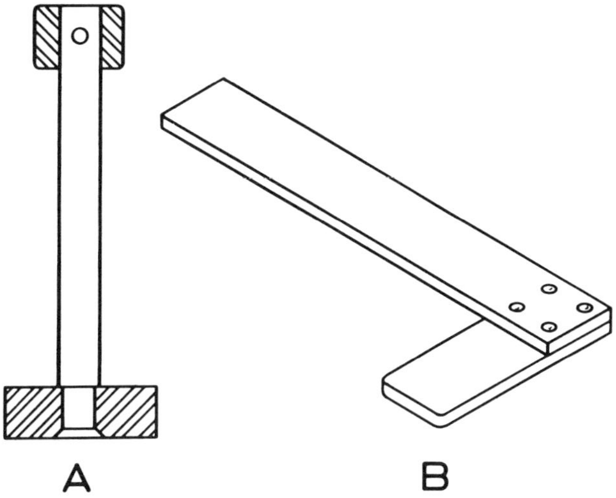

Fig. 16-42. Two instances where riveting is used to fasten die parts.

16-43. RIVET PROJECTION

In applications which require riveting, an important consideration is the amount that the rivet end must project for upsetting or riveting. If this amount is insufficient, the riveted joint will be weak. If too long, excessive pressure or peening will be required and an unsightly joint will be formed. These tables list correct lengths of projections for rivets from 1/8 to 3/4 inch in diameter. Note that when a tool component is turned down for riveting, as for instance a knockout rod, the same amount of projection would be applied, determined by its diameter.

Riveting of die components is done with a hand rivet set and sledge. The work is performed by a skilled diemaker, so more material can be allowed than for machine riveting. Flat-head riveting is done by peening with the round end of a ballpeen hammer. After riveting, any excess metal is removed by machining to provide a flat surface.

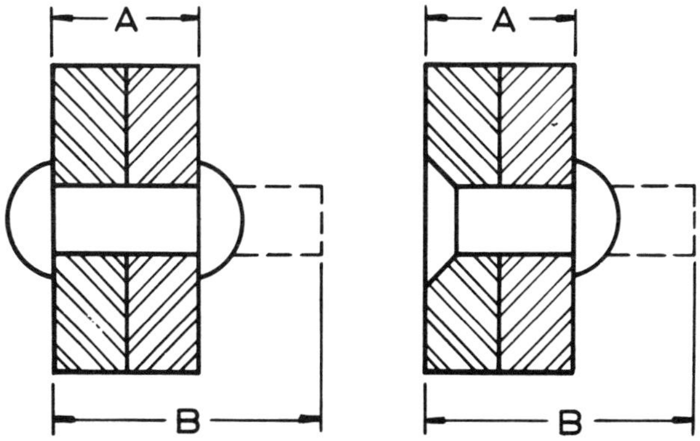

GRIP A	RIVET DIAMETERS							LENGTH B
	1/8	3/16	1/4	3/8	1/2	5/8	3/4	
1/4	5/8	3/4	7/8	1	1 3/16	1 3/8	1 1/2	
3/8	3/4	7/8	1	1 1/8	1 5/16	1 1/2	1 5/8	
1/2	7/8	1	1 1/8	1 1/4	1 7/16	1 5/8	1 3/4	
5/8	1	1 1/8	1 1/4	1 3/8	1 9/16	1 3/4	1 7/8	
3/4	1 1/8	1 1/4	1 3/8	1 1/2	1 11/16	1 7/8	2 1/16	
7/8	1 1/4	1 3/8	1 1/2	1 5/8	1 13/16	2	2 3/16	
1	1 3/8	1 1/2	1 5/8	1 3/4	1 15/16	2 1/8	2 3/8	
1 1/8	1 1/2	1 5/8	1 3/4	1 7/8	2 1/16	2 1/4	2 1/2	
1 1/4	1 5/8	1 3/4	1 7/8	2	2 3/16	2 3/8	2 5/8	
1 3/8	1 3/4	1 7/8	2	2 1/8	2 3/8	2 1/2	2 3/4	
1 1/2	1 7/8	2	2 1/8	2 1/4	2 1/2	2 11/16	2 15/16	
1 5/8	2	2 1/8	2 1/4	2 3/8	2 5/8	2 13/16	3 1/16	
1 3/4	2 1/8	2 1/4	2 3/8	2 1/2	2 3/4	3	3 1/4	
1 7/8	2 1/4	2 3/8	2 1/2	2 5/8	2 7/8	3 1/8	3 3/8	
2	2 3/8	2 1/2	2 5/8	2 3/4	3 1/16	3 1/4	3 1/2	

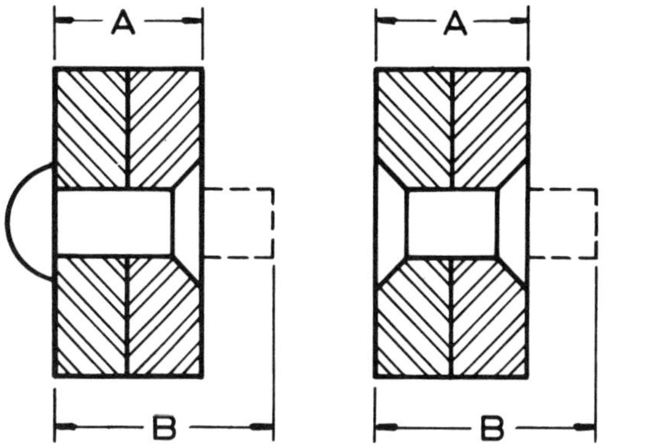

GRIP A	RIVET DIAMETERS							LENGTH B
	1/8	3/16	1/4	3/8	1/2	5/8	3/4	
1/4	3/8	1/2	5/8	3/4	13/16	7/8	7/8	
3/8	1/2	5/8	3/4	7/8	15/16	1	1	
1/2	5/8	3/4	7/8	1	1 1/16	1 1/8	1 1/8	
5/8	3/4	7/8	1	1 1/8	1 3/16	1 1/4	1 1/4	
3/4	7/8	1	1 1/8	1 1/4	1 5/16	1 3/8	1 3/8	
7/8	1	1 1/8	1 1/4	1 3/8	1 7/16	1 1/2	1 9/16	
1	1 1/8	1 1/4	1 3/8	1 1/2	1 9/16	1 5/8	1 3/4	
1 1/8	1 1/4	1 3/8	1 1/2	1 5/8	1 11/16	1 3/4	1 7/8	
1 1/4	1 3/8	1 1/2	1 5/8	1 3/4	1 13/16	1 7/8	2	
1 3/8	1 1/2	1 5/8	1 3/4	1 7/8	1 15/16	2	2 1/8	
1 1/2	1 5/8	1 3/4	1 7/8	2	2 1/8	2 3/16	2 5/16	
1 5/8	1 3/4	1 7/8	2	2 1/8	2 1/4	2 5/16	2 7/16	
1 3/4	1 7/8	2	2 1/8	2 1/4	2 3/8	2 1/2	2 5/8	
1 7/8	2	2 1/8	2 1/4	2 3/8	2 1/2	2 5/8	2 3/4	
2	2 1/8	2 1/4	2 3/8	2 1/2	2 11/16	2 3/4	2 7/8	

Fig. 16-43. Tables of lengths of projections necessary for good round head and flat head riveting.

Section 17

HOW TO SELECT A DIE SET

After all die details have been designed, a die set of the proper size and style is selected from a manufacturer's catalog and drawn in position. Between five and ten per cent of total design time is spent in selecting and drawing the views of the die set. This allowance may be increased considerably if the designer does not thoroughly understand the principles underlying die set selection and representation.

Die sets are manufactured in a bewildering variety of sizes and shapes and it is the purpose of this section to acquaint you with the various styles as well as to indicate proper methods of selection and placement.

Advantages realized when die components are retained in a properly selected die set are:

1. Members are kept in proper alignment during the cutting process, even though some looseness may exist in the press ram. Thus, uniform clearances are maintained around cutting edges for producing blanks free of burrs
2. Die life is increased
3. Dies can be installed in the press in a minimum amount of time because they are self-contained units
4. Storage is facilitated. There is no possibilitv of loss of loose parts
5. Properly designed dies can be sharpened without removal of cutting members.

Standard die sets range from 3 by 3 inches to 45 by 60 inches. Die holder and punch holder thicknesses range from 1 to 3½ inches, by quarter inches.

ACCURACY

Die sets are manufactured to two standards of accuracy: *precision* and *commercial*. Punch-holder and die-holder tolerances are the same for both. The difference between them occurs in the closeness of fit between bushings and guide posts. For precision sets, tolerances between bushings and guide posts are maintained from 0.0002 to a maximum of 0.0004 inch. This tolerance assures extremely accurate alignment between punches and corresponding holes in die blocks. For this reason, precision die sets should be specified for all dies which perform cutting operations.

Commercial die sets are given more liberal clearances between bushings and guide posts. These range from 0.0004 to 0.0009 inch. Commercial die sets should be specified only for dies which perform bending, forming, or other non-cutting operations.

MATERIALS

Selection of the material from which the die set is to be made will depend upon strength requirements. There are three choices:

1. Semi-steel
2. All steel
3. Combination – in which the punch holder is semi-steel and the die holder is all steel.

SEMI-STEEL

In manufacturers' catalogs the material of the die set is listed as either semi-steel or steel. Semi-steel contains only about 7 per cent of steel in its composition and is considered to be cast iron. Semi-steel die sets are cast to shape and then machined. Some manufacturers may cast punch holders and die holders of Meehanite which may be considered a high-grade cast iron.

STEEL DIE SETS

When a large hole is to be machined through the die set for blank removal, it is considered good practice to specify a steel die holder. This prevents fracture of the die holder if placed over a large hole in the bolster plate, which is done occasionally even in the best press shops. It happens too frequently that a cast-iron die holder is actually broken in two because of the weakening effect of a large hole in conjunction with insufficient support under pressure.

Steel die sets are thoroughly stress-relieved by manufacturers before final machining or grinding. Stress relieving removes any stresses introduced in the material in rolling at the mill and other stresses added during rough machining. If such residual stresses are not removed, they are gradually released with consequent distortion and dimensional change, which can ruin a precision die.

Obviously, it behooves the designer not to incorporate anything in the design which can introduce stresses in the die set while the die is being built. Welding anything to a die set must be avoided. Rough machining of deep pockets should be done by the die set manufacturer before the stress relieving operation, and a print showing necessary machining operations should accompany the purchase order. To illustrate the importance of stress relieving in the manufacture of die sets with deep milled pockets and through holes, here is a representative order of operations actually employed for a larger die holder

1. Flame-cut holes
2. Stress relieve
3. Surface grind
4. Rough machine pockets
5. Stress relieve
6. Surface grind
7. Finish-machine.

SELECTING THE DIE SET

Ten elements of die-set information must be decided before a die set can be ordered:

1. Make or manufacturer
2. Type
3. Size
4. Material
5. Thickness of die holder
6. Thickness of punch holder
7. Type and lengths of bushings
8. Lengths of guide posts
9. Shank diameter
10. Grade of precision.

In selecting a die set from a catalog, first consider the dimensions from front to posts and from side to side. This is the die-set area or usable space, to which die details can be fastened. Next in importance is the thickness of the die holder and of the punch holder.

17-1. DIE SET COMPONENTS

These are:

A. Punch holder
B. Guide bushings
C. Guide posts
D. Die holder.

When the die set is assembled, the lower ends of the guide posts are pressed securely into the die holder and the turned down portions of the guide bushings are pressed into the punch holder. The bushings engage the guide posts with a close sliding fit to provide accurate alignment.

The illustration typifies small and medium-size die sets made of both cast iron and steel, although different manufacturers may incorporate slight variations.

17-2. PUNCH HOLDERS

The upper working member of the die set is called the punch holder. The name is easy to remember because of its relationship with the punches, which are normally applied above the strip and fastened to the underside of the punch holder. Surfaces **A** are finished. They are employed by the die maker for squaring and locating punch components of the die. Surfaces **B** are also finished surfaces. The upper one bears against the underside of the press ram. Punch components are fastened to the lower finished surface.

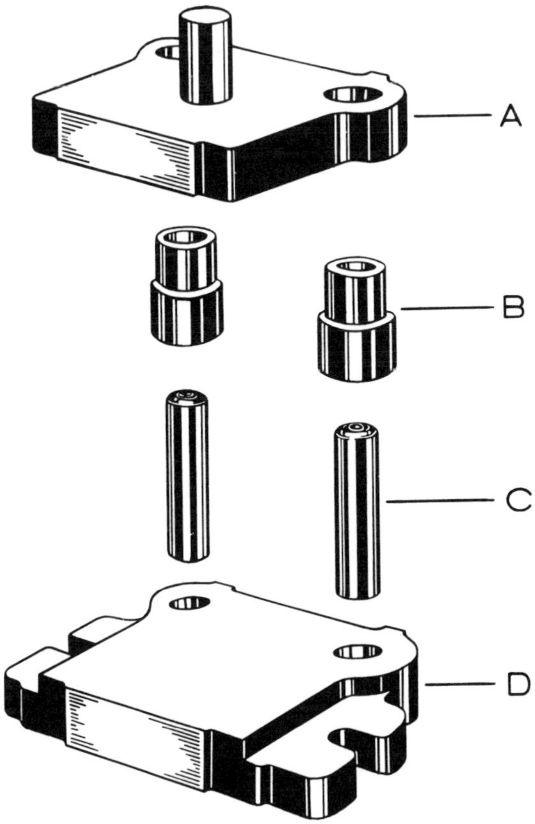

Fig. 17-1. Components that make up a die set.

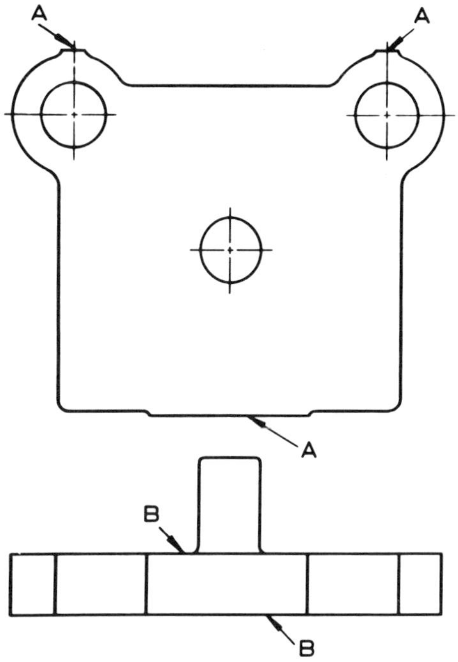

Fig. 17-2. A typical punch holder.

17-3. INVERTING THE PUNCH HOLDER

On a die drawing the punch holder is shown inverted or turned over. At the upper portion of the illustration the die holder is shown at the left and the punch holder at the right, exactly as they appear on the drawing. At the bottom is shown how the punch holder is removed from the guide posts and inverted to an upside down position for drawing.

At the upper right view the punch shank is represented by a dotted circle and the bushings by concentric solid circles. The punch holder is drawn inverted in this manner because this is the position in which it is placed on the die maker's bench for assembly of punches. Also, punches can be drawn with solid object lines, which makes the drawing easier to draw and read.

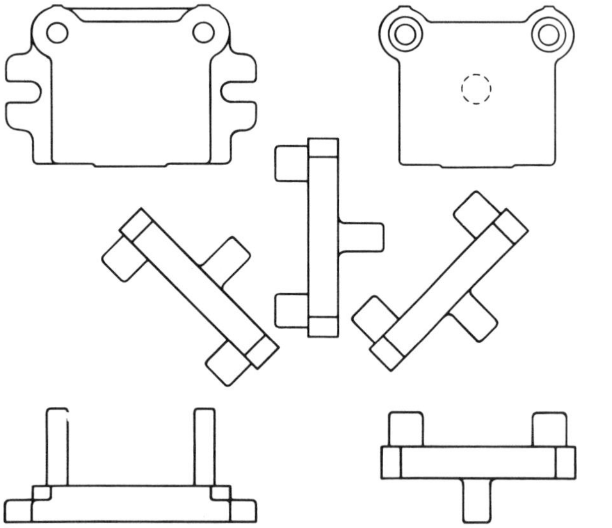

Fig. 17-3. How a punch holder is inverted and shown on a drawing.

17-4. PUNCH SHANK

The punch shank projects above the punch holder and it aligns the center of the die with certerline of the press. In operation, the shank is clamped securely in the press ram and it drives the punch portion of the die, raising and lowering it for performing cutting and other operations.

For semi-steel die sets, the punch shank is cast integrally with the body of the punch holder and it is then machined. For steel die sets, it is electrically welded to the punch holder and then machined.

Punch shanks may also be ordered separately. These are turned down at one end and threaded for engagement in a large tapped hole in the punch holder. Punch-shank diameter depends upon the press selected. It is usually determined from a company standards book and it should be checked carefully for accuracy. After the diameter is known, the length can be found listed in a die-set catalog. The round **A** at the top of the punch shank and the fillet **B** at the bottom where it joins the punch holder are given a 1/8 inch radius on the drawing.

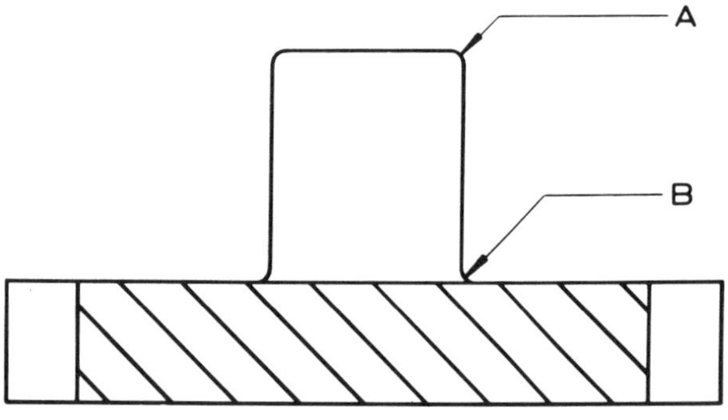

Fig. 17-4. Punch shank projecting above punch holder is given a 1/8 inch radius at (A) and (B).

Larger die sets are not ordinarily provided with a punch shank, or the shank is employed only for centering the die and not for driving. Instead, such die sets are clamped or bolted to the underside of the ram because of the considerable weight of large punch holders and punch members. The relatively small punch shank would not be a safe method of driving.

To supplement the holding power of the shank, socket cap screws are often inserted upward through the punch holder to engage holes tapped in the press ram. Where this practice is followed, the designer specifies and dimensions the mounting holes to match the hole pattern in the ram, and he must make certain that they clear punch components. Dimensions for mounting holes are ordinarily taken from a company standards book.

17-5. DIE HOLDERS

The die holder is the lower working member of the die set. Its shape corresponds with that of the punch holder except that it is provided with clamping flanges **A** having slots for bolting the die holder to the bolster plate of the press.

Machined surfaces **B** are employed for squaring and locating die components. Surfaces **C** are also finished. The lower one rests on the bolster plate, and the die block and other components are fastened on the upper surface.

Usually, the die holder is made thicker than the punch holder to compensate for the weakening effect of slug and blank holes which must be machined through it. Common proportions for small and medium-size dies are:

Punch holder thickness – 1¼ inches
Die holder thickness – 1½ inches.

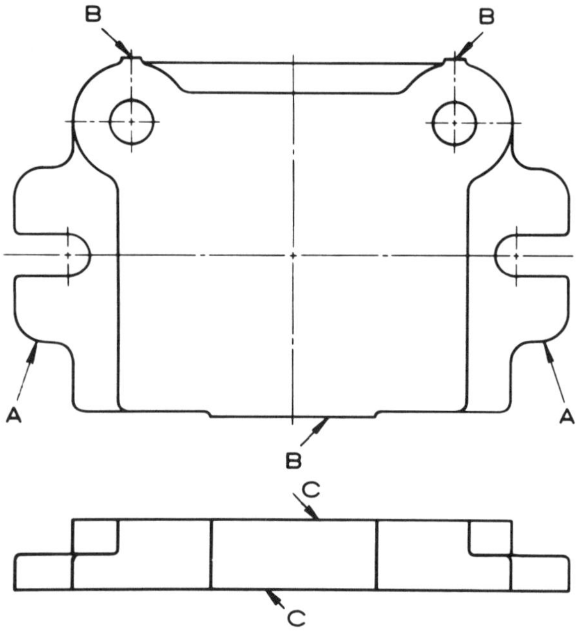

Fig. 17-5. Typical die holder with clamping flanges (A) and machined surfaces (B) and (C).

17-6. GUIDE POSTS

Guide posts are precision-ground pins which are press-fitted into accurately bored holes in the die holder. They engage guide bushings to align punch and die components with a high degree of closeness and accuracy. Illustrated are six types.

1. Small guide posts are usually hardened and centerless ground, particularly for the commercial die-set grades
2. Larger diameter posts are ground between centers after hardening
3. Posts may be relieved at what will be the die set surface. This relief is usually applied to precision posts
4. A non-sticking post end may be incorporated. This provides for quick and easy assembly and disassembly
5. Shoulder guide posts are employed in conjunction with shoulder guide-post bushings. The large shoulder is the same diameter as the press-fit portion of the guide bushings. In the manufacture of special die sets, the punch holder and die holder are clamped together and holes are bored through both for engagement of bushings and guide posts
6. Removable guide posts can be easily removed from the die for sharpening. They are employed for large dies and for dies having more than two posts.

Guide posts for precision die sets are hard-chromium plated to provide a high degree of resistance to wear. Also, the addition of a chromium surface reduces friction by more than fifty per-cent.

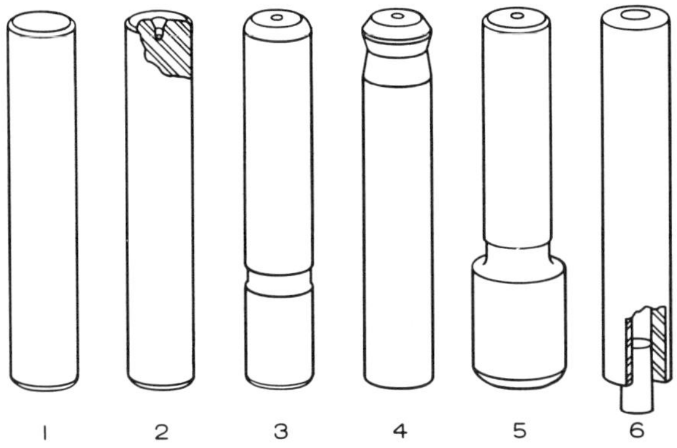

Fig. 17-6. Six types of guide posts.

For secondary-operation dies, guide posts should have sufficient length so that they never leave their bushings in operation. This is a safety feature to prevent possible crushing of fingers accidentally introduced between posts and bushings as the die is operated.

Guide posts are specified at least ¼ inch shorter than the shut height of the die as listed on the drawing, (the shut height being the distance from the bottom surface of the die holder to the top surface of the punch holder, excluding the shank, and measured when the punch holder is in the lowest working position). This provides a grinding allowance to assure that the top of the posts will not strike the underside of the press ram when the upper die is lowered as punches are sharpened.

17-7. REMOVABLE GUIDE POSTS

Often guide posts must be removed for die sharpening, especially in large dies and in dies having more than two posts of the back-post style. We will look at three types:

1. The first kinds of removable guideposts have an axial hole machined through them and are tapered at one end to engage a taper pin **A**. The post end is slotted. By driving the taper pin, the post is expanded against the walls of the hole in the die holder. To remove the post, a long rod called a drift is inserted from the top and the taper pin is pressed out.

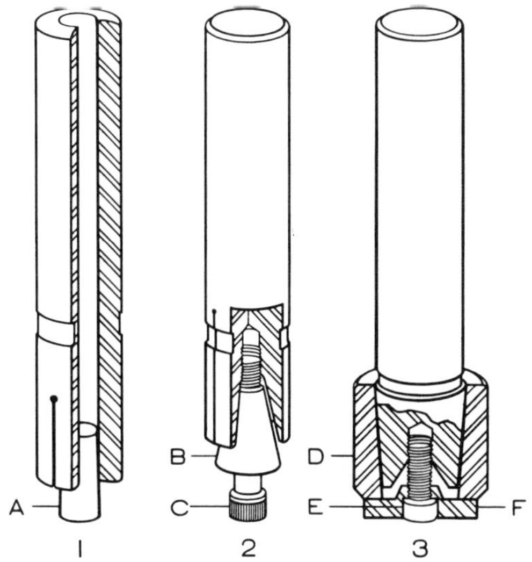

Fig. 17-7. Three types of removable guide posts.

2. In the second type of removable guide posts, the taper pin **B** is advanced for locking the post by means of a socket cap screw **C**.
3. The third removable post has a taper at the lower end to engage a sleeve for bushing **D**, which is pressed into the die holder. A socket cap screw **E** engages a retaining cap **F** to clamp the post to the bushing. Removal of the socket cap screw allows the post to be lifted up and removed.

17-8. NON-STICKING GUIDE POSTS

Sticking or jamming in initial stages of engagement of punch holder and die holder has long been a problem because of the close fits maintained. Sticking occurs until the bushings have engaged the posts sufficiently for complete alignment. Dies must be assembled and disassembled a great number of times in their manufacture, tryout, and in sharpening.

Illustrated at 1 is a popular, as well as a commercially available, post that features the following characteristics:

A. A ground taper guides the bushing over the post.

B. A narrow land of the same diameter as the post centers the bushing. The land is narrow enough to allow rocking of the bushing over it.

C. This clearance area represents the sticking range. Because metal has been removed, sticking cannot occur.

D. This is a ground lead which guides the bushing to engagement with the full diameter of the post.

Shown at 2 is a post that features a radius at the leading edge to align the bushing.

Fig. 17-8. Two types of commercially-available guide posts developed to overcome sticking or jamming in initial stages of engagement of punch and die holders.

17-9. OFFSET POST ENDS

In another method of assembly employed by a commercial supplier, one of the guide posts is made longer than the other. The punch holder engages the long post first and it is thus aligned before engagement of the other post occurs. Dimension **A** is usually made ½ inch.

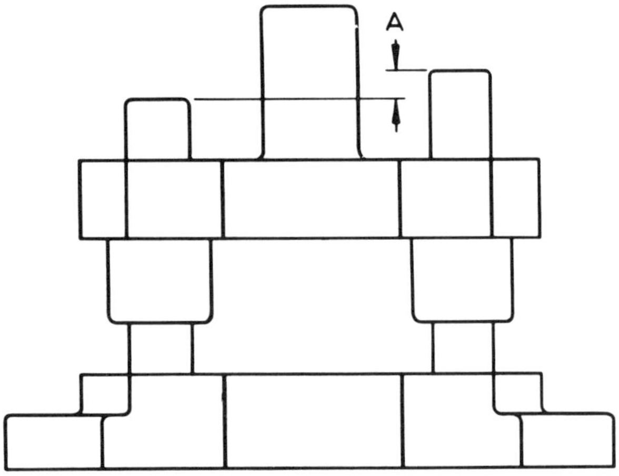

Fig. 17-9. Use of guide posts of different lengths facilitates engagement of punch and die holders.

17-10. GUIDE BUSHINGS

Accurately ground sleeves, or guide bushings, engage guide posts for aligning the punch holder with the die holder. Most bushings are made of tool steel although they are also available in bronze. There are two types:

1. Plain bushings are simple sleeves pressed into the punch holder
2. Shoulder bushings are turned down at one end and they are pressed into the punch holder against the shoulder thus formed. They are recommended for all dies which perform cutting operations.

Lengths of guide bushings vary, depending upon the manufacturer. In general, we may recognize two different lengths for plain bushings – regular and long. Shoulder bushings are furnished in three lengths – regular, long, and extra long. The length selected will depend upon the accuracy requirements of the die. The longer the bushing, the more accurate will be the alignment of punch and die members. This is particularly important in cutting operations, especially for thin stock when clearances between cutting edges are small.

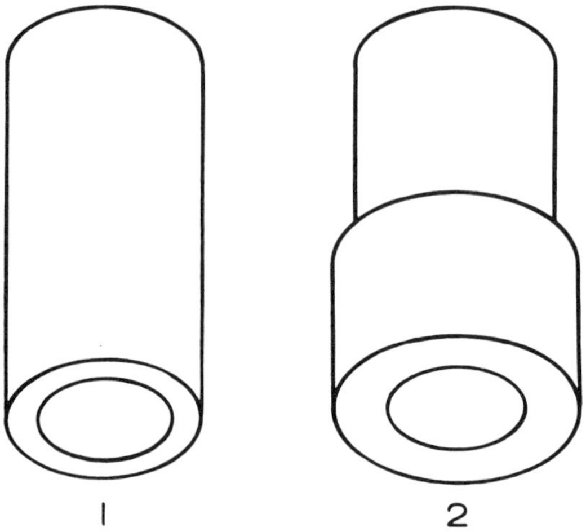

Fig. 17-10. Two common types of guide bushings.

Posts and bushings are assembled by shrink fitting into holes bored in the punch holder and die holder. The posts and bushings are subjected to deep freezing, thereby reducing their diameters. They are then inserted in the punch holder and die holder and upon warming to room temperature, they expand to provide a tight fit between componets.

Each guide bushing is provided with a fitting for lubrication. Helical grooves are machined in inside surfaces for retention and distribution of the lubricant.

17-11. SELF OILING GUIDE BUSHINGS

Shown is a guide bushing made of porous powdered alloy steel. Internal pockets are cored in the walls, and these are filled with oil at manufacture. In use, the oil meters through the porous walls by capillary action. Stored lubrication is sufficient for the life of the bushing.

17-12. DEMOUNTABLE GUIDE BUSHINGS

These are shoulder bushings provided with clamps that engage an annular groove machined in the bushing wall or shoulder. Socket cap screws are threaded into the punch holder to effect clamping. The turned-down portion of the bushing is not a press fit into the punch holder. Instead, it is ground to an accurate sliding fit for ease in disassembly.

These bushings are available in both steel or bronze, and they are provided with either two clamps **A** or three Clamps **B**, depending on size. Demountable guide bushings are specified for long runs, when it is anticipated that bushings and posts will require replacement.

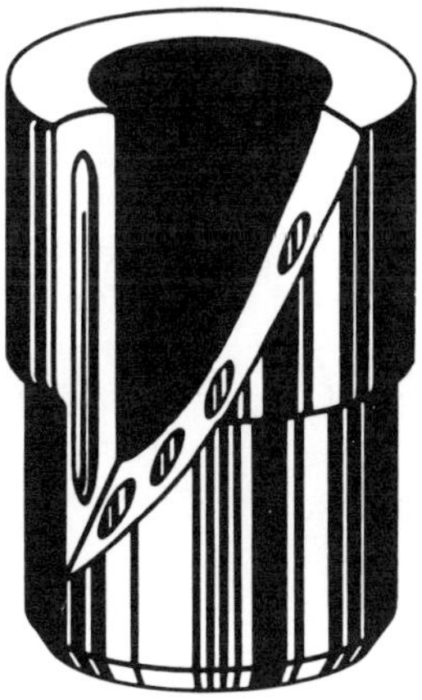

Fig. 17-11. A commercially-available self oiling guide bushing made of porous powdered alloy steel.

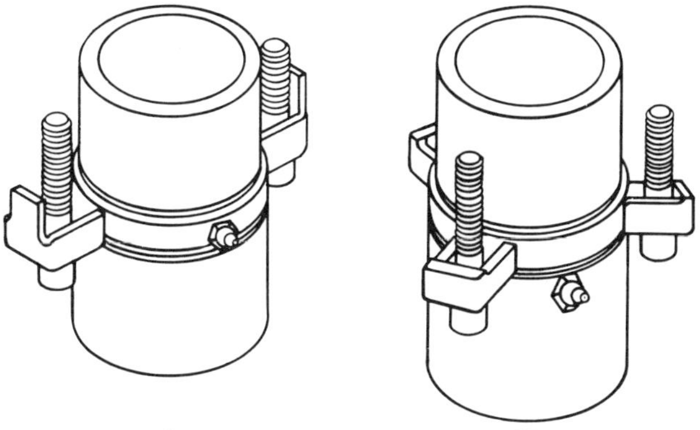

Fig. 17-12. Demountable guide bushings are used for long runs.

17-13. BOSS BUSHINGS

Demountable bosses may be employed as guide bushings in large die sets. They are used for heavy-duty work when long runs are expected. The bosses

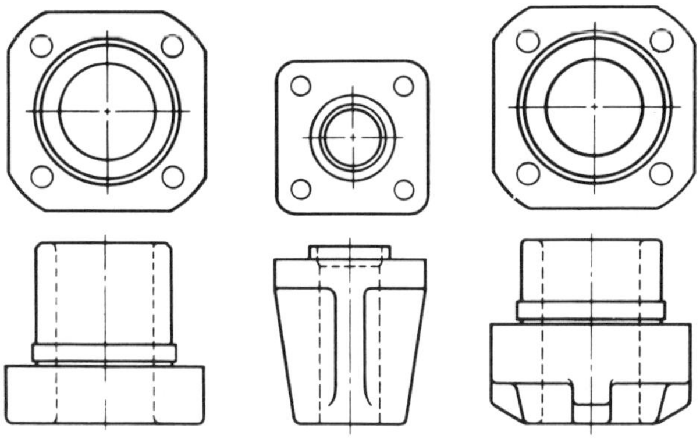

Fig. 17-13. Three types of demountable boss bushings for heavy-duty work in long runs.

are turned down for location in holes in the die set and they are fastened with socket cap screws for easy replacement. There are three types of boss bushings:

1. Flange mounted – the greater portion of the bearing surface is within the die set
2. Demountable – employed as bearings and also as guide-post supports
3. Long bearing – these have a bearing surface extending below the mounting flange and supported by ribs.

17-14. BALL-BEARING DIE SETS

Some die sets are provided with ball bearings instead of guide bushings. Guide posts are pressed into the punch holder and they engage linear ball bearings **A**, which in turn are guided in hardened sleeves **B** pressed into the die holder. The bearings are preloaded to remove looseness or side play. Lubrication is by cup grease applied at set up and this is usually sufficient for the entire run. Ball bearings take up more room than conventional guiding methods and they reduce die space a small extent.

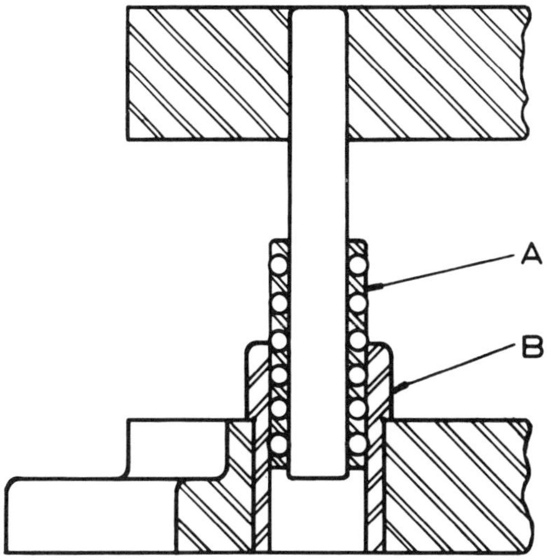

Fig. 17-14. Set up in which ball bearings are used instead of a guide bushing.

17-15. DIRECTION OF FEED

Direction of feed of the strip will influence selection of the die set. Strip may be fed through a press in any of three directions:

1. Front to back. This method may be employed for long runs when strip is fed automatically

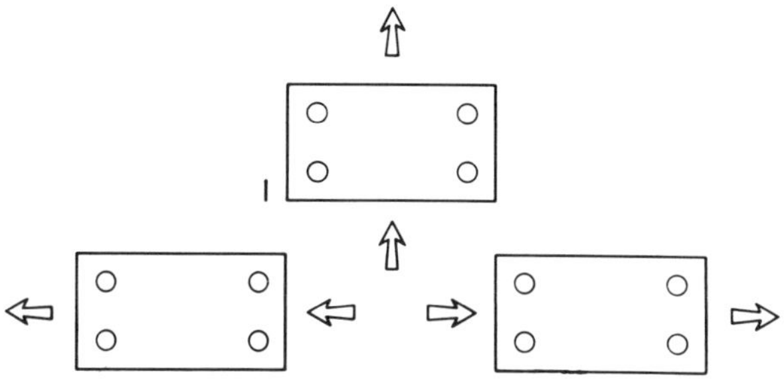

Fig. 17-15. Three directions in which the strip may be fed through the press.

2. Right to left. This is the most commonly used feeding direction. It is always employed when the strip is advanced by hand

3. Left to right. This direction is occasionally used when the strip is fed automatically.

Feed direction must always be ascertained before design of a die is started because it will affect the sequence of operations and location of stops.

17-16. POST ARRANGEMENT

Guide posts may be positioned in any one of six ways:

A. Two posts are applied at the back of the die set. This is the most commonly used two-post arrangement.

B. Posts are applied at the sides for feeding strip from front to back.

C. The posts are positioned diagonally, and at **D** four posts are used. The foregoing are standard post arrangements as listed in die-set catalogs.

When rectangular steel die sets are ordered, any post arrangement may be supplied by the die set manufacturer. For feeding strips sideways in long runs, some designers prefer posts applied at the front and at the back as shown at **E**. Others specify three posts for stability as shown at **F**.

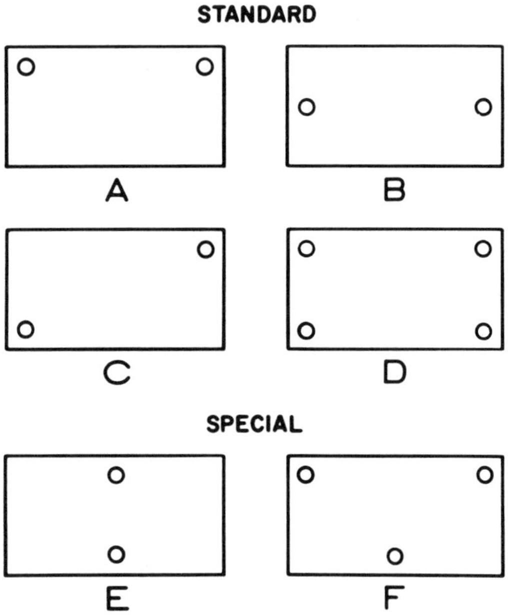

Fig. 17-16. Six ways of arranging guide posts in a die set.

17-17. PRESS DATA

After a die has been tentatively designed or roughed out, the next step is to consider the specifications of the press in which it is to operate. This should be done before the die set is selected because the available space may influence die-set size and type. It is very important that a die fit the press for which it was designed, and it is the designer's responsibility to ascertain that there will be no interferences. The three most important considerations in determining the dimensions of a die set are:

1. Punch shank diameter. Check the press data sheet carefully to make sure that the recess in the press ram will accommodate the punch shank selected.

2. Shut height of die. Make certain that the shut height dimension is well within the available die space without the ram adjustment being taken up to its limit. In this connection, make certain that grinding clearance has been taken into consideration.

3. Distance from the center of the shank to the back of the die. Make certain that this dimension is at least ¼ inch less than the distance from the center of the ram to the frame of the press. The make and model number of the press are marked on the route sheet, and specifications can be found in the manufacturer's catalog or in the company standards book.

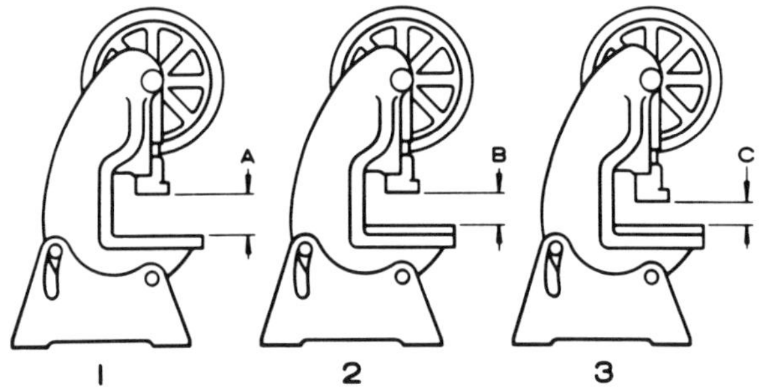

Fig. 17-17. Terms applied to presses: die space, (**A**); shut height, (**B**); and height of shortest die (C) that press will accommodate.

Look first for the "Die Space." This is usually specified as the distance from the bed of the press to the underside of the ram with the stroke down and the adjustment up, dimension **A.**

Next look for the thickness of the bolster plate. This must be subtracted from the die space to give the shut height from the top of the bolster plate, dimension **B.** This is the height of the *tallest* die which will fit into the press. However, some manufacturers give the die space directly as the distance from the top of the bolster plate to the underside of the press ram, and caution should be exercised.

Next, it will be necessary to determine the *shortest* die which the press will accommodate. Look up the dimension for "Adjustment of Slide," The ram of a press is usually provided with an adjustment to accommodate a range of die heights. Subtract the dimension given for adjustment of slide from the shut height. This will be the height of the shortest die which the press will accommodate, **C.** However, a die shut height ¼ inch higher must be used to allow for lowering the upper die as punches are sharpened from time to time.

17-18. SPECIFICATIONS

So that your understanding will be complete in every respect, I have included a representative specifications page from a press catalog. Study those specifications which apply in the selection of a die set and actually look up the dimensions as you proceed to review the example to follow.

Assume that a die is to be designed for use in a Federal press No. 4. The manufacturer's catalog lists the "Die Space" **C** as 9¼ inches, and "Bolster Plate Thickness" **B** as 1¾ inches. Subtracting 1¾ from 9¼ gives the maximum shut height – 7½ inches. The "Adjustment of Slide" is listed as 2½ inches. Sub-

SPECIFICATIONS

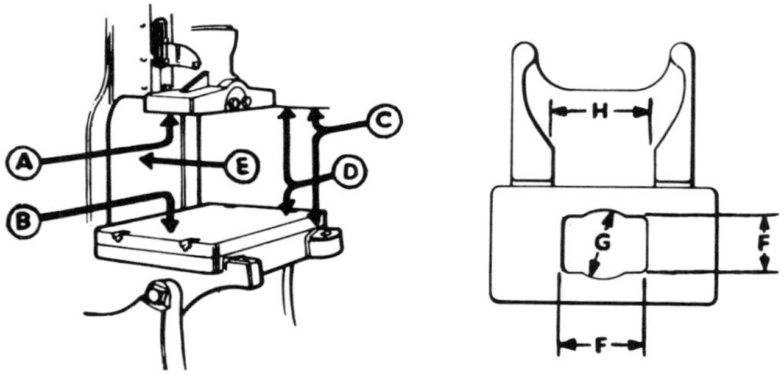

	Federal OBI Press No.	0	1	2	3	33	3½	4	44	5	55	6
	Tonnage, capacity near bottom of stroke	7	15	20	27	27	35	43	43	56	56	60
	SLIDE, standard stroke	1¼	1½	2	2½	2½	3	3	6	4	4	4
	maximum stroke	3	4	5	6	6	8	8	10	8	12	6
	adjustment of slide	1½	1½	1½	2	2	2½	2½	2½	2½	2½	2½
	round punch shank hole (sq. hole optional)	1	1 9/16	1 9/16	1 9/16	1 9/16	1 9/16	1 9/16	2½	2½	2½	2½
A	face area F. to B., R. to L. (flanges available)	3⅞ x 3⅝	5 x 4⅝	5½ x 5	7¼ x 5⅞	7⅝ x 18	8¾ x 7½	8¾ x 7½	8½ x 24	10 x 8¾	11⅛ x 24	11⅝ x 12
B	BOLSTER PLATE area F. to B., R. to L.	6 x 9¾	8 x 15	10 x 17½	12¾ x 21½	16 x 32	14¾ x 27	14¾ x 27	21 x 33	18½ x 29½	28 x 36	25½ x 33
	thickness	1	1¼	1¼	1¾	1¾	1¾	1¾	2	2¼	2¾	2¾
C	DIE SPACE, bed to slide, stroke down adj. up	5¾	7½	7¾	8¾	9½	9¼	9¼	10	10¼	15	13
D	bolster plate to slide, stroke down adj. up	4¾	6¼	6½	7	7¾	7½	7½	8	8	12¼	10¼
	additional shut height w bed extension	1 to 4	1 to 5	1 to 10	1 to 12	1 to 6	1 to 6	1 to 6	1 to 10	1 to 6	1 to 21	1 to 6
E	BED depth of throat, ram center to frame	3½	4½	5½	7¼	8¾	8	8	11½	10	15 or 17	13½
F	Std. opening in bed F. to B., R. to L.	3 x 5	4 x 6	5 x 7	5 x 11	7 x 21	7 x 12	7 x 12	7 x 21	8 x 14½	10 x 22	14 x 18
G	Std. round opening	....	5	7	8	....	10	10	....	11¾	....	16
H	Std. opening through back	5¼	7½	8½	10¾	20½	12½	12½	21	13½	22 or 26	16
	distance bed to gibs	7	9	10¼	11½	14	12¾	12¾	17½	15¼	21½	18½
	reclines from upright	40°	40°	40°	40°	40°	40°	40°	30°	30°	36°	36°
	CRANKSHAFT, dia. at main bearings	1⅜	2 1/16	2 5/16	2¾	2¾	3¼	3½	3½	4	4	4 5/16
	diameter at crank bearing	2¾	2 5/16	2 9/16	3	3	3¾	3¾	3¾	4⅜	4⅜	4⅞
	FLOOR SPACE overall F. to B., R. to L.	24 x 23	28 x 26	34 x 30	42 x 35	45 x 35	45 x 41	45 x 41	57 x 46	50 x 48	59 x 49	60 x 58
	legs only, F. to B., R. to L.	24 x 23	27 x 21	32 x 21	38 x 29	40 x 39	40 x 34	40 x 34	48 x 41	48 x 36	57 x 48	57 x 40
	height from floor to bed	36	31	32	33	32	32	32	32	32	34	33
	height from floor to shaft center	54	54	59	63	62	67	67	73	72	81	81
	height from floor to top of wheel	62	64	70	76	77	83	83	91	92	98	102
	FLYWHEEL TYPE PRESS											
	Weight, approximate	580	1300	1750	2800	3300	4300	4500	7400	6700	10500	11000
	Shipping weight, approximate	655	1400	1850	2900	3450	4450	4650	7650	6950	10900	11400
	Flywheel—weight	75	180	225	450	450	700	720	820	1000	1000	1150
	speed (strokes per min.)	175	150	150	125	125	120	120	90	90	90	75
	diameter x width	16 x 2½	20⅛ x 3¼	22⅛ x 3½	27½ x 4	27½ x 4	32 x 5	32 x 5	36 x 5¼	36¼ x 6	36¼ x 6	42½ x 6
	MOTOR H.P. and speed	½-1200	1-1200	1½-1200	2-1200	2-1200	3-1200	3-1200	5-900	5-900	5-900	5-900

Federal Press Co.

Fig. 17-18. Representative specifications page from a press catalog.

tracting 2½ from 7½ gives a minimum shut height of 5 inches. Therefore, this press will accommodate dies ranging from 5 inches to 7½ inches high. However, a die with a 5 inch shut height, the minimum dimension, would not operate very long. After sharpening, the members would not come together because the press adjustment would be all taken up. Any die designed for this press should have a shut height of at least 5¼ inches, thus allowing ¼ inch of material for sharpening.

In effect then, the shut height of the die to be designed should be between 5¼ and 7½ inches.

Next, it will be necessary to look up dimensions for the recess in the slide for the punch shank. For a No. 4 Federal press, this is listed as 1 9/16 inch diameter. Punch shank diameter must be 1 9/16 also.

Still another dimension to be taken into consideration is the stroke of the press. This is particularly important for bending, forming, and drawing dies. Should the stroke be too short, it might be impossible to place the part into the die or to remove the stampings from it. The stroke for a No. 4 press is listed as 3 inches, and it is called "Slide, standard stroke,"

One entry in the press catalog may be puzzling. This is "Maximum stroke of ram," or "Slide, maximum stroke," and the dimension is always greater than the dimension for "Standard stroke of ram." For a No. 4 Federal press, it is given as 8 inches. This entire entry can be disregarded. It lists the maximum stroke for which the press can be built and the press can be modified to exert any stroke within this range. However, if a press is built with a stroke other than standard, it will have a special number.

Another dimension to be considered is the "Depth of Throat," **E**. This is the distance from the center of the press back to the frame. Since the punch shank is located at the center of the press, the distance from its center to the back of a die set must be less than the listed dimension. For the press under consideration, depth of throat is given as 8 inches. The corresponding dimension for the die set should be at least ¼ inch shorter.

17-19. ESTABLISHING THE DIE-SET CENTER

Ten design steps are necessary in selecting and applying the views of a die set for a specific die design. Consider the following sequence carefully, because it provides a proper working method:

1. Determine the diameter of the punch shank. Punch shank data is usually found in a company standards book or manufacturer's catalog, although occasionally it may be necessary to get it directly from the press room. On an appropriate sheet of paper, draw a circle of the required punch-shank diameter
2. On the upper left plan view of the die, draw vertical and horizontal centerlines. Their intersection represents the ideal center of the die; the one we should prefer to use if possible. For most dies, the ideal center would be the center of the die block, measured from side to side and from front to back.
3. Transferring measurements, draw corresponding centerlines on the upper-right inverted view of the punches
4. Slip the sheet on which the punch-shank circle

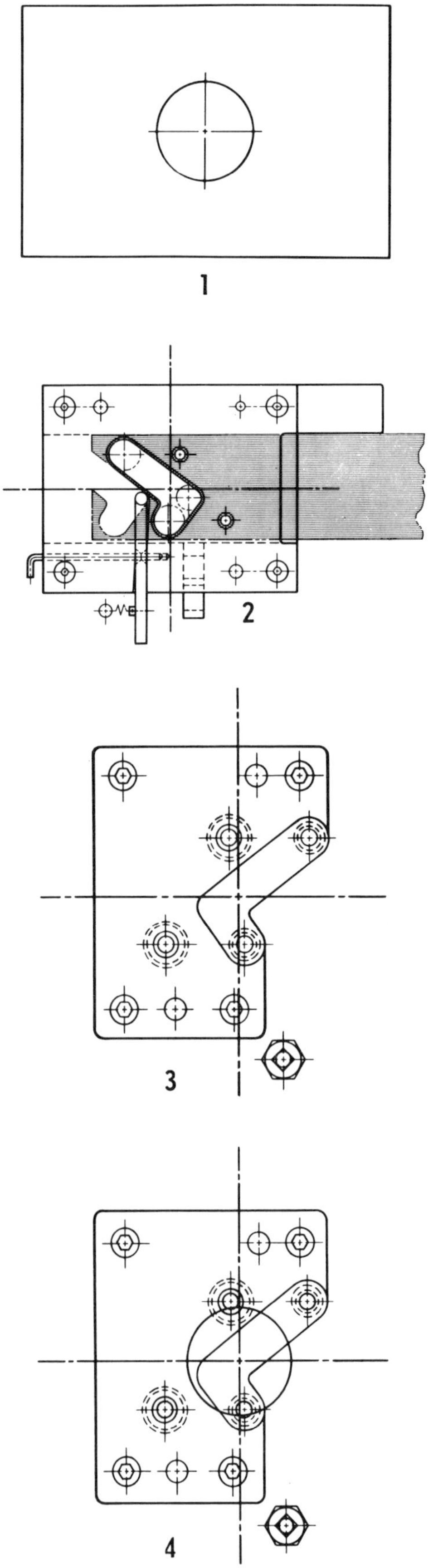

Fig. 17-19. Steps necessary in selecting a suitable die set for a specific die design: determine punch shank diameter, (1); draw centerlines, (2); transfer centerlines to punch holder view, (3); and superimpose punch shank circle drawing on punch holder view, (4).

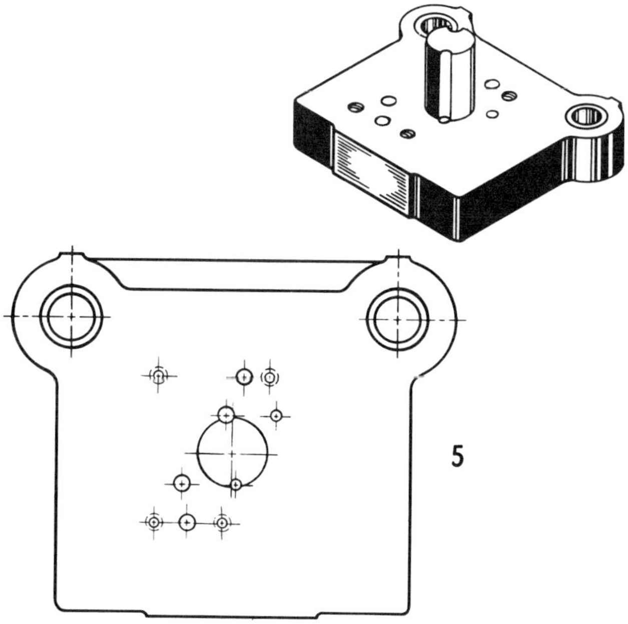

5

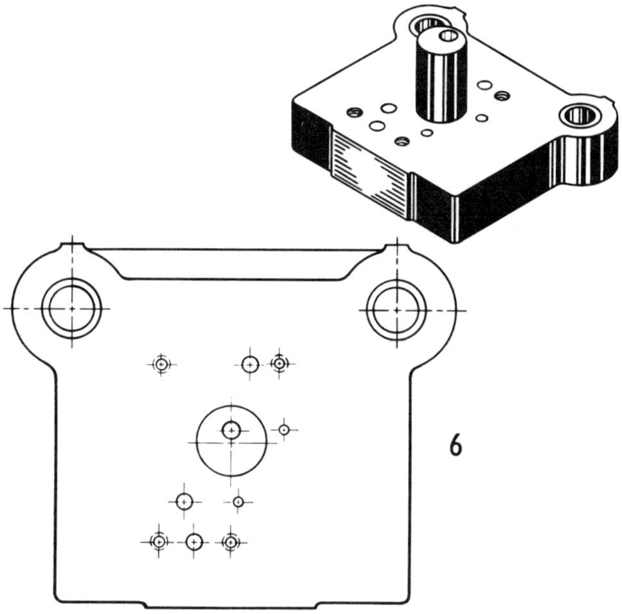

6

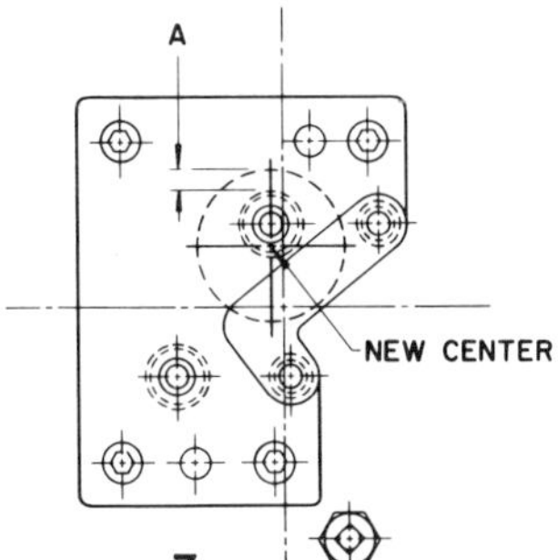

7

Fig. 17-19. (cont.). Steps necessary in selecting a suitable die set for a specific die design: inspect superimposed drawings, (5); change position of superimposed drawings, (6); place new center position on punch holder view, (7); and place new center position on die drawing, (8).

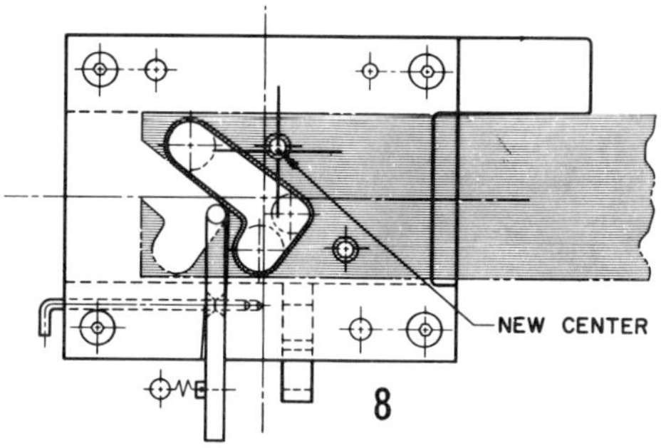

8

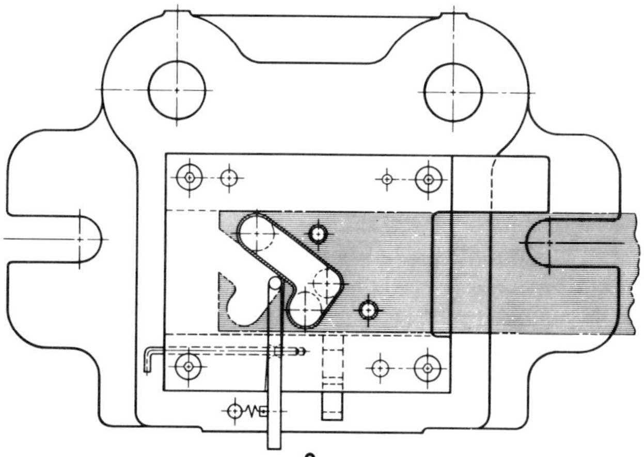

9

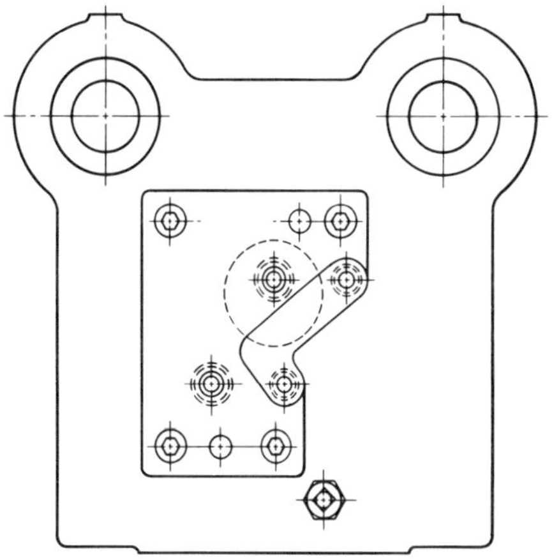

10

Fig. 17-19. (cont.). Steps necessary in selecting a suitable die set for a specific die design: select suitable die set and draw its views, (9) and complete view of punch holder, (10).

was drawn under the die drawing and move it to the upper-right plan view representing the inverted punches. Apply the center of the circle directly under the intersecting lines representing the ideal center

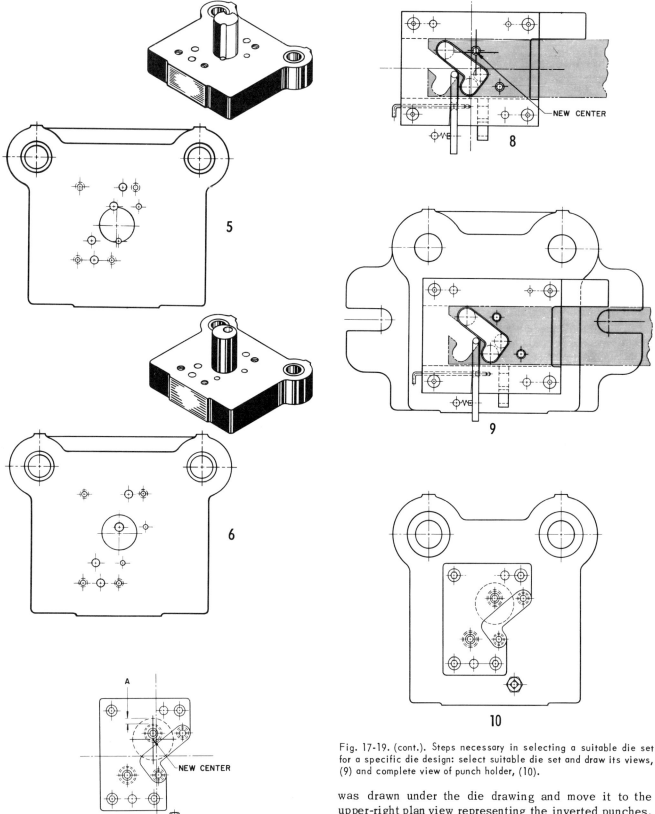

5. Inspect to establish whether or not all holes to be machined through the punch holder will pass outside of the punch shank or inside of it. In the illustration, the punch holder has been turned upside down for viewing the punch shank from the top. Observe that two

holes are machined partly in the edge of the punch shank. Machining away portions of the punch edge in this manner is considered poor practice

6. In this illustration, relative positions of holes and punch holder have been altered so that one of the holes passes entirely within the shank and the other entirely outside of it

7. Referring back to the drawing, slide the sheet on which the punch-shank circle was drawn until it clears holes so that they pass entirely outside or entirely inside of it. The best position found, closest to the ideal center, is shown. Dimension **A**, the wall thickness between the holes and the outside surface, is made 1/8 inch minimum

8. Transfer the new center to the left plan view of the die by measurement. Always remember that because the punch is inverted, horizontal dimensions are reversed

9. Select a suitable die set and draw its views. Observe that the die block is slightly off center, but that it is positioned as close to the ideal center as possible

10. Complete the view of the punch holder. Front and side section views are then drawn by projection.

In actual practice, the foregoing steps can be performed quickly. They provide the logical method of selecting a suitable die set for a specific die design.

17-20. CENTER OF CUTTING LOAD

When blanks are large, the cutting loads may be great and unbalanced. The center of cutting load must be determined before selecting the die set. This then represents the ideal center, the one we would use if no punch-shank interference existed. To determine the center of cutting load:

Step 1. Draw the scrap strip for a die in which cutting loads are unbalanced

Step 2. From heavy cardboard, cut blanks and slugs the sizes and shapes of all cut-out portions. Leave thin webs between blanks to maintain relative positions or paste thin strips across them

Step 3. Place a square or rectangle of cardboard over a pivot and move it until it is in balance

Step 4. Position the cut blanks on the cardboard and slide them until they balance. The point of balance will be the center of cutting load or close enough to it for practical purposes.

17-21. MISSING DIMENSIONS

Study of any die-set catalog will reveal that a number of dimensions are not given. There are three ways of establishing dimensions which are not listed in a catalog:

1. Dimensions may be estimated. Those dimensions which are not listed are not critical and may be approximated to proportions printed in the catalog

2. Dimensions may be established with proportional dividers. The point relationship of the divider arms may be set to one of the given dimensions. Points are transferred from the catalog views to the views of the drawing

3. When a component must be drawn at frequent intervals, missing dimensions may be measured and recorded in a standards book for future use.

In this illustration are given all dimensions which are not ordinarily listed in die-set catalogs. These dimensions may be used directly when applying the views of the die set to your drawings.

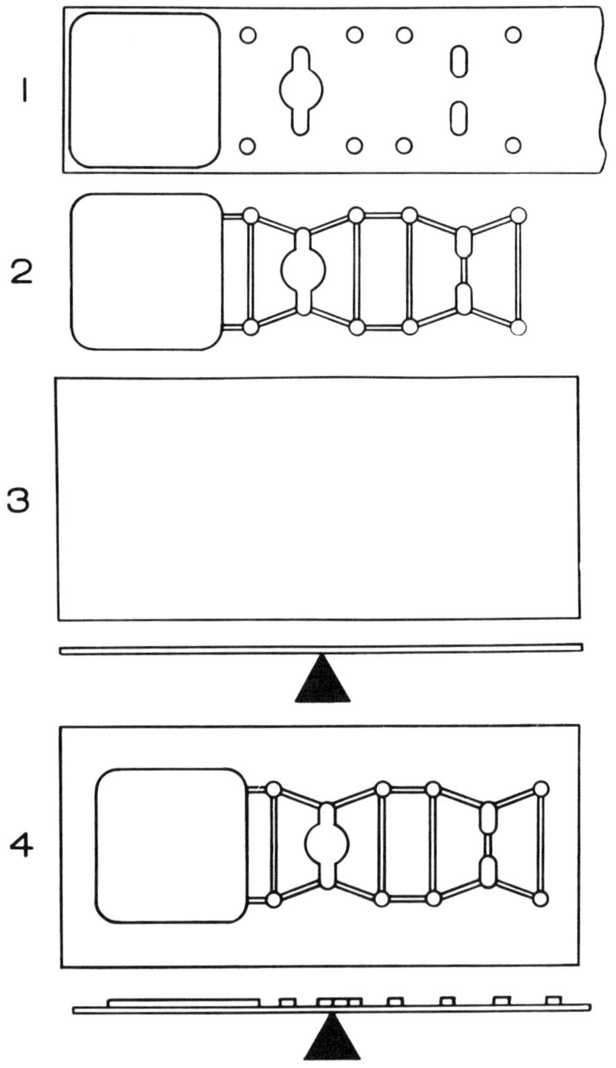

Fig. 17-20. Method of determining center of cutting load.

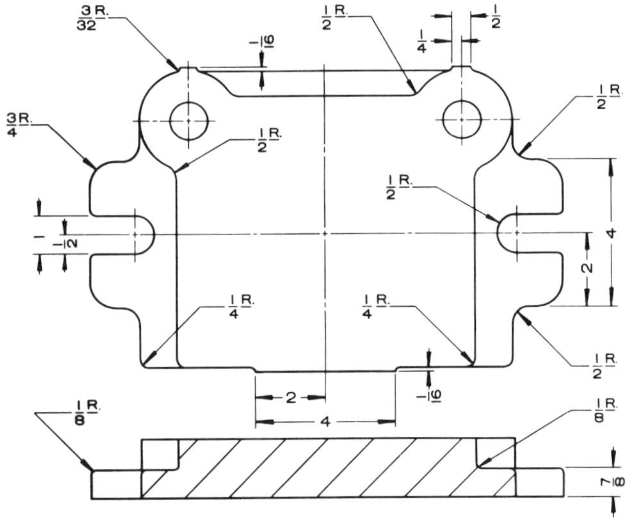

Fig. 17-21. Dimensions not ordinarily listed in die-set catalogs.

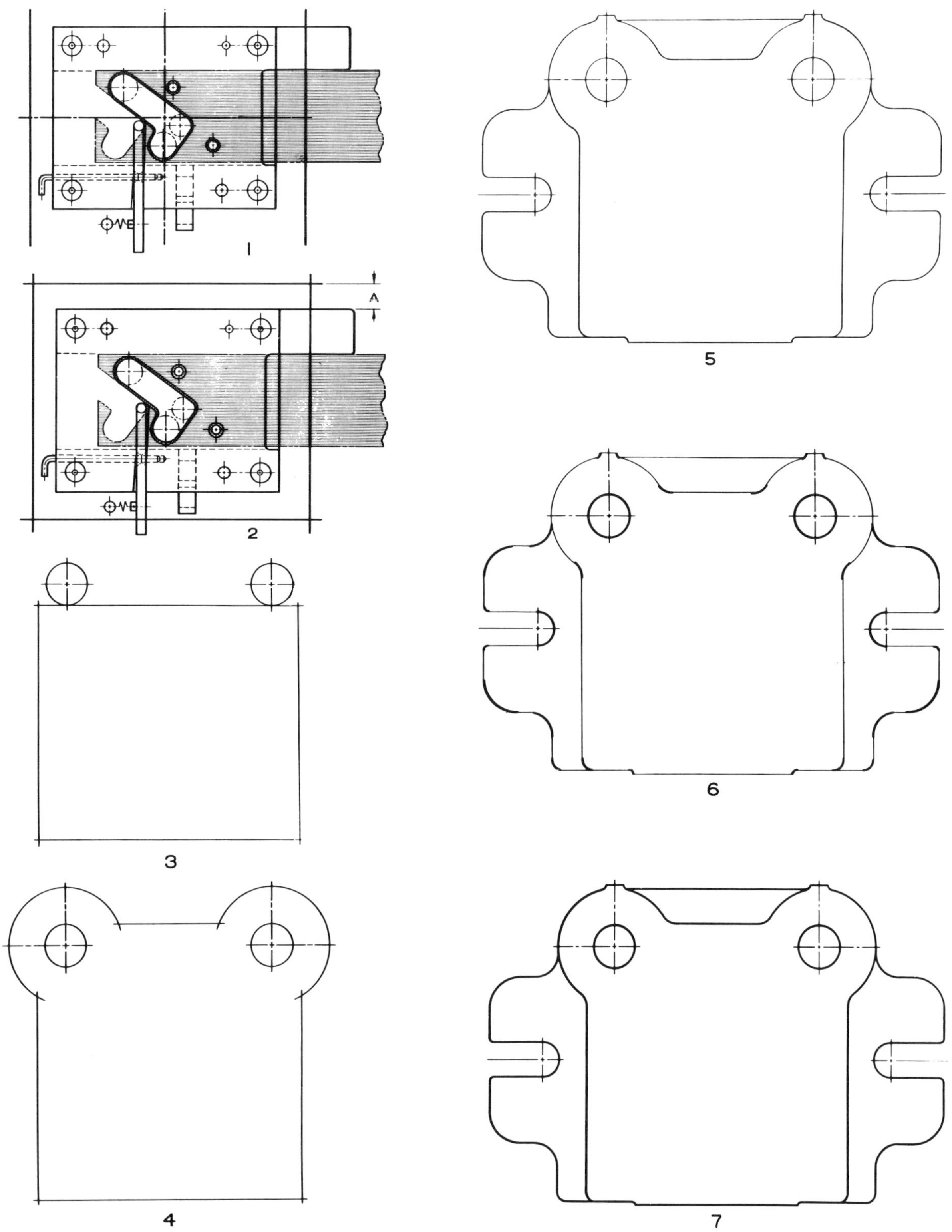

Fig. 17-22. Steps taken in laying out a die set: represent left and right sides of die set with vertical lines, (1); represent front of posts and front of die set with horizontal lines, (2); draw circles to represent post posts, (3) and draw circles to represent post bosses, (4). Steps taken in laying out a die set: block out remainder of die set with light lines, (5); draw small arcs with heavy lines, (6); and darken all remaining lines, (7).

17-22. DRAWING THE DIE SET

A proper working procedure reduces loss of time in laying out die sets. Seven steps are required:

1. As we have developed the layout in Fig. 17-19 so far, the left and right sides of the die set have been represented by vertical lines, as shown in the illustration

2. In addition, the vertical center of the die set has been established. Note that preferably the die would be centered between the posts and the front of

the die set. Look up this dimension in the catalog and draw horizontal lines to represent the front of the die set. Dimension **A** between posts and die block should be 5/8 inch minimum, to allow clearance for the grinding wheel nut when the die block is sharpened.

3. Look up the distance between centers of posts and their diameters and draw circles to represent them

4. Look up the radii of post bosses and draw them with light lines

5. Block out the rest of the die set with light lines

6. Draw all small arcs with heavy lines using a radius template

7. Darken all remaining lines to final object line width.

The punch holder is drawn in the same manner. Less time will be required because it does not have clamping flanges.

17-23. VIEWS FOR CAST DIE SETS

Four views are drawn of a back-post die set made of semi-steel or cast iron. These are the views ordimarily shown on a die drawing. Observe that the punch holder and die holder are castings and therefore radii are applied to all corners where the adjacent surface has not been machined. Corners of guide post bosses and of the flange are given large blending radii, a characteristic of this type of die set. The punch holder at the upper right has been inverted and therefore the punch shank appears as a dotted circle. Because bushings are viewed directly, they are represented by two solid circles.

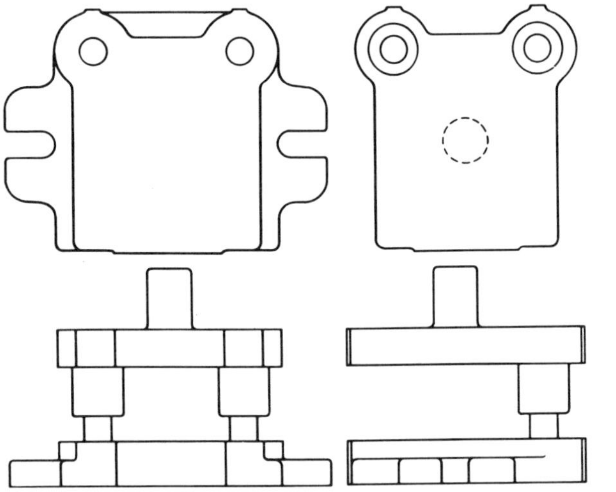

Fig. 17-23. How four views of a cast back-post die set are shown on a drawing.

17-24. STEEL DIE SETS

Steel die sets are drawn somewhat differently and it is necessary to understand the method of manufacture to draw them properly. The first step in producing a steel die holder is to flame-cut the shape from plate as at **A**. Note that edges have straight sides all around, and that the plate from which it is cut is the die-holder thickness with allowance for machining. In actual practice, a number of blanks would be cut simultaneously in an automatic flame cutting machine, with the cutting heads guided by a template.

In the next operation the bolting flanges are milled as at **B**. A five inch diameter cutter is employed, and therefore a 2½ inch radius is left at the end of the cut. Corners of the cutter are ground to a 1/8 inch by 45 degree chamfer, and a corresponding angle would be left in the corners of the die holder.

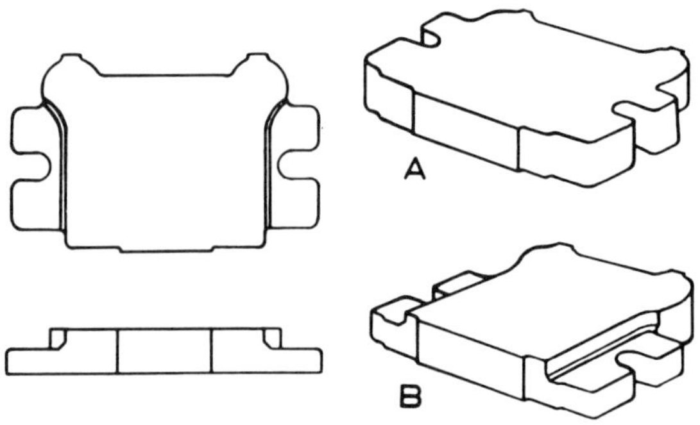

Fig. 17-24. Steel die sets are first flame cut to shape (A); then bolting flanges are milled, (B).

17-25. VIEWS FOR STEEL DIE SETS

Here are the four views of a steel die set. Comparison with the views of a semi-steel die set will reveal three significant differences. The first is the large radius **A**, and it is 2½ inches. Another is the absence of a flange at the back of the die holder **B**, and a third is the small angle **C**, applied in the corner of the milled cut. It is drawn 1/8 by 45 degrees. Whenever a steel die set is selected, the views should be drawn in this style and to proportions given. In addition, sectioning for steel would be applied.

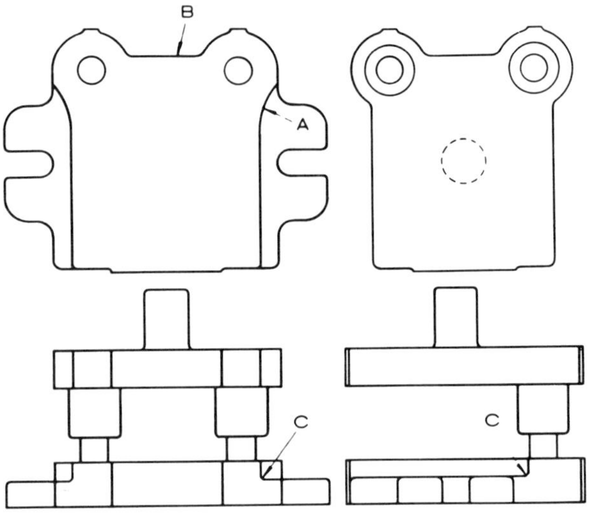

Fig. 17-25. How four views of steel back-post die set are shown on a drawing.

17-26. SECTIONING

The front view and also usually the side view of die drawings are sectioned to reveal internal construction. The first step in sectioning is to draw lines at 45 degrees across die set surfaces in contact with the cutting plane to indicate that they have been cut. Inclination of section lines for the punch holder and die holder should be opposite, as shown at **A**. This is important for balance. If section lines for both are inclined in the same direction, an optical illusion is introduced and the view will appear to lean.

Section lines for other details are then drawn, alternating their directions from top and bottom *toward the strip,* as at **B**.

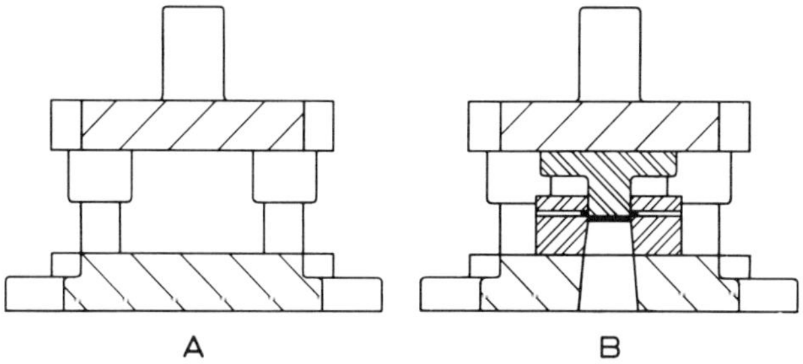

Fig. 17-26. How section lines are drawn in a die drawing.

17-27. SPACING OF SECTION LINES

Draw section lines for die sets to the following proportions: For semi-steel die sets, position them approximately 5/8 inch apart, as shown at **A**. For steel die sets, draw section lines in sets, 3/16 inch apart. The sets are positioned with about 5/8 inch between them, as at **B**.

When sectioning combination die sets, those with a semi-steel punch holder and a steel die holder, apply appropriate section lines to indicate material.

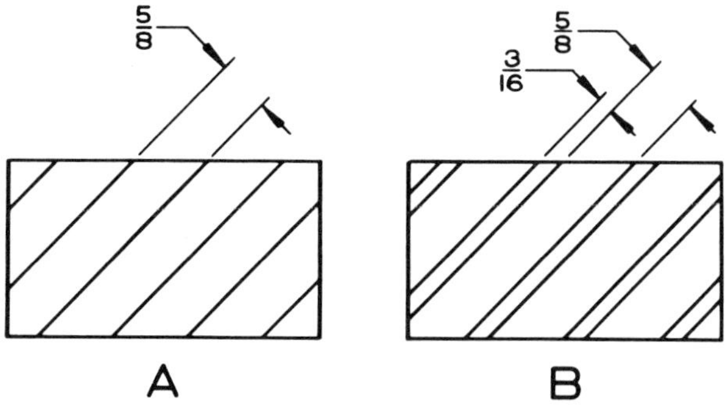

Fig. 17-27. Proper spacing of section lines.

17-28. LISTING THE DIE SET

In the bill of material, the die set is always given detail number 1. The information to be specified is too lengthy for the space available in the bill of material, and is therefore given in the form of a note on the drawing itself, as at **A**. The box in the bill of material is filled in as shown at **B**, and the reader of the drawing is thus referred to the note.

(1) DANLY DIE SET
CAT. NO. 0603 -A1
STEEL SHL'D. BUSH.
1" DIA. x 5 1/4 GUIDE POSTS

A

DET.	REQ'D	PART NAME	MAT.	SPECIFICATIONS
1	1	DIE SET	PUR.	SEE NOTE

B

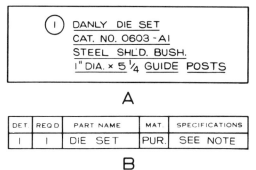

Fig. 17-28. Die set on a drawing is described in a note, (A) and listed as detail 1 in bill of material, (B).

The die set note should contain the following information:

1. The detail number, applied within a detail circle 7/16 inch in diameter
2. Manufacturer's name followed by the words "die set"
3. The catalog number
4. The type of bushings
5. Diameter and length of guide posts.

The die set note is applied in a clear space near the center of the die drawing.

17-29. DIE SET STAMP

In another method of specifying die set information, a box is printed on the drawing sheet with a rubber stamp and information is lettered in the spaces provided. Stamps are available from die set manufacturers and they vary somewhat in detail. You will notice from the example that some dimensions are not absolutely necessary for standard die sets. However, applying extra dimensions such as those for die space tends to reduce errors because a mistake in specifying the catalog number would be discovered.

DIE SET DATA

CAT. NO. OR SERIES, PRECISION ....0808 -A1.... COMMERCIAL ....

DIE SPACE -- A ....8 1/2.... (LEFT TO RIGHT) B ....8.... (FRONT TO BACK)

THICKNESS -- J ....1 1/2.... (DIE HOLDER) K ....1 1/4.... (PUNCH HOLDER)

GUIDE POSTS -- L ....8 3/4.... (OVERALL LENGTH)

BUSHINGS -- TYPE ....STEEL SHOULDER....

SHANK -- DIA. ....1 9/16.... LENGTH ....2 1/8....

IF NONE IS REQUIRED STATE NONE

ORDER FROM

DANLY MACHINE SPECIALTIES, INC.

2100 So. LARAMIE AVE., CHICAGO 50, ILLINOIS

(Or Nearest Branch Office)

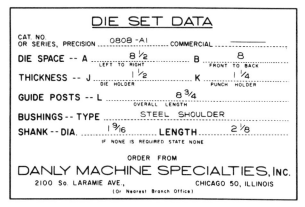

Fig. 17-29. Filled in rubber stamp print may be used to specify die set data on drawing.

17-30. MACHINING THE DIE SET

There are two methods of applying holes in the die holder for passage of slugs. At **A**, slug relief holes are machined with straight walls. Dimension **C** is 1/16 inch for blanks up to No. 16 gage (0.0625 inch), and proportionately more for thicker blanks.

The method shown at **B** is preferred for blanking and piercing soft materials, which have a tendency to stick together and form thick slugs which could jam. The holes in the die set are die filed to the same angle applied to the die block for relief.

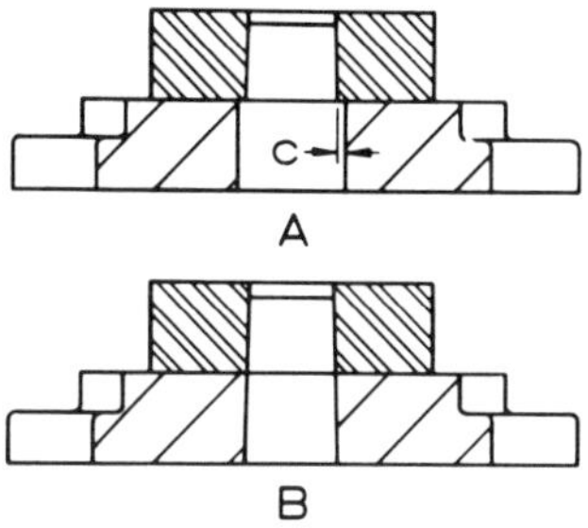

Fig. 17-30. Two methods of applying holes for the passage of slugs.

17-31. STRIPPER BOLT HOLES

Counterbored holes for stripper bolts should be proportioned carefully because considerable pounding occurs against the bottoms of the counterbores in operation of the die. Also, a spring stripper may occasionally stick or become jammed. When this happens, a pry bar is used to free it and the stripper then slams up with all the stored energy in the springs. Apply the following *minimum* proportions:

Dimension **A** = Strip thickness + Grinding allowance

Dimension **B** = $\frac{\textbf{D} \text{ for a semi-steel die set}}{\frac{3}{4}\,\textbf{D} \text{ for a steel die set}}$

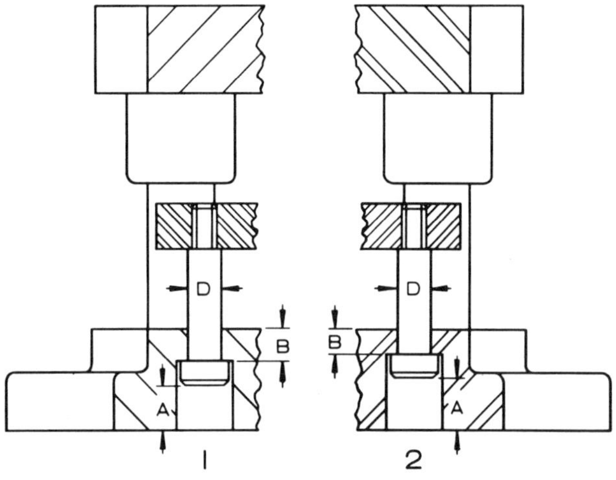

Fig. 17-31. Proportions of counterbored stripper bolt holes.

17-32. PROJECTIONS

All projections in a die block must be supported by corresponding projections applied to the die holder. In this illustration, the dotted lines represent the hole machined in the die holder for blank removal. Observe that the die block projections are well supported to prevent overhang and possible breakage under pressure.

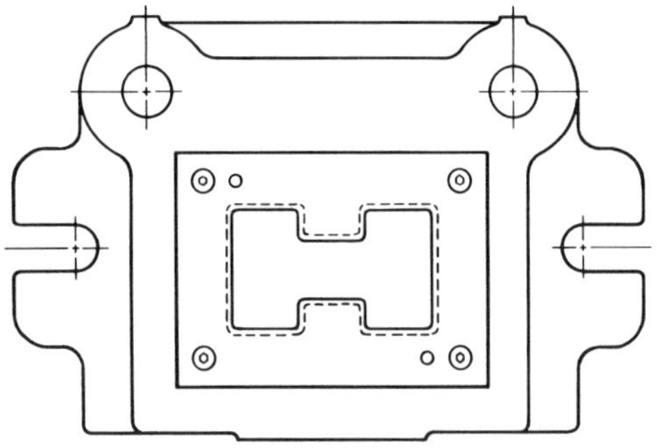

Fig. 17-32. All projections of this die block are supported by similar projections in the die holder.

17-33. SLUG SLOTS

When the hole in the bolster plate is smaller than the blank, a slot may be machined in the under side of the die holder. At the rear of the die set, it is made slightly wider than blank size. At the front, it need be only wide enough to accommodate a thin bar for pushing blanks to the rear of the press.

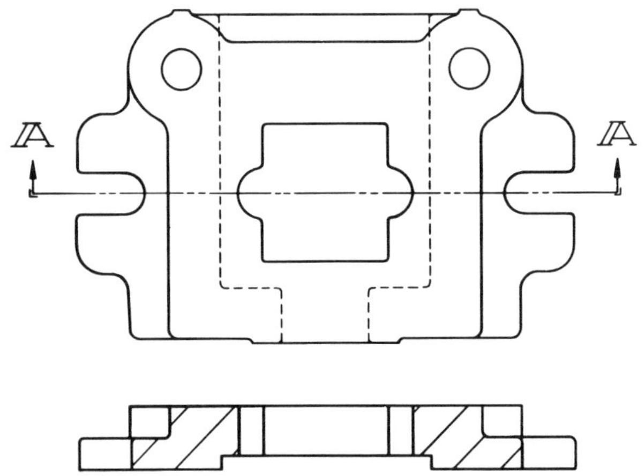

Fig. 17-33. Slot machined in the underside of the die holder facilitates removal of blanks when hole in bolster plate is too small.

17-34. KNOCKOUTS

When a large spider knockout is incorporated in the design of the die, it can be flame-cut directly through the punch holder of the die set. A steel die set must be specified, and the flame-cutting is done by the die-set manufacturer before stress relieving and accurate machining. After the spider has been cut from the punch holder, it is machined thinner to allow travel and then it is re-inserted in the punch holder. The knockout pins are retained to the spider and knockout plate by socket cap screws.

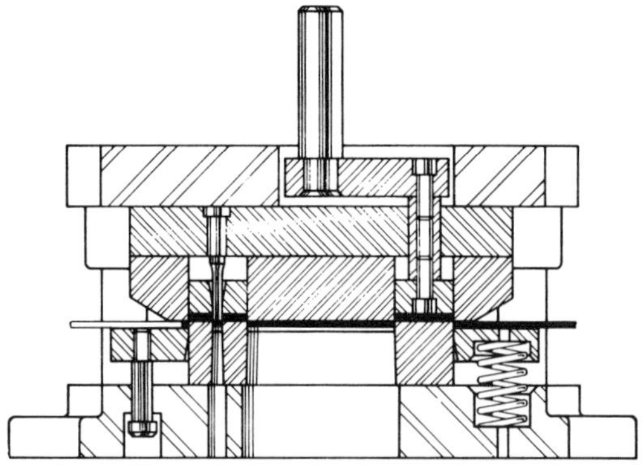

Fig. 17-34. Large spider knockout of this steel die set has been flame-cut from the punch holder of the die set.

17-35. TWO POST DIE SETS

Most dies designed for hand feeding of strip are provided with two guide posts applied at the back of the die set because this type gives maximum visibility and accessibility since it is open on three sides. A back-post die set is also used when scrap stock is to be employed for producing small blanks. Scrap material is usually very irregular in shape and other guide post arrangements would interfere with positioning.

There are three distinct types of back-post die sets:

1. Regular. This is employed for dies with average proportions
2. Long, This type is used for dies which are long and narrow
3. Reverse. This type is used for dies which are relatively longer in measurement from front to back than their measurement from side to side.

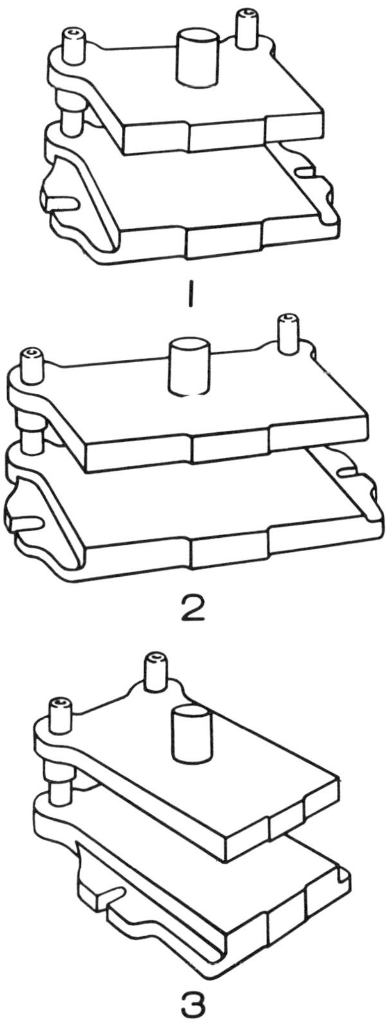

Fig. 17-35. Three types of back-post die sets: regular, (1); long, (2); and reverse, (3).

17-36. STYLES

Back-post die sets are made in five different styles or shapes:

1. This style is the most common. It is used for small medium-size die sets ranging from 3 by 3 inches to about 16 by 18 inches in both semi-steel and steel

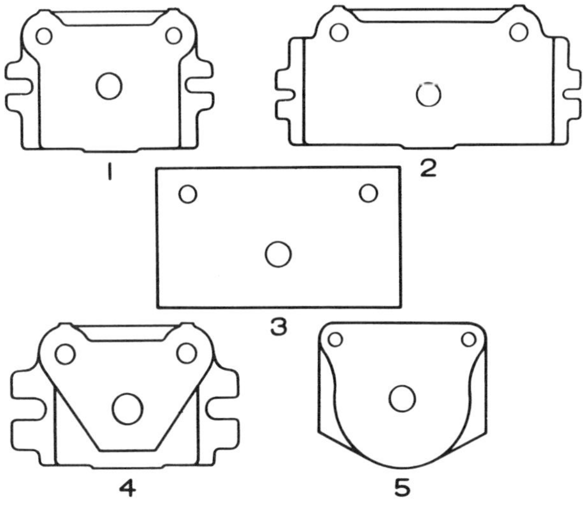

Fig. 17-36. Five styles of back-post die sets.

2. Large, semi-steel die sets ranging from 22½ by 6 to 25 by 14 inches have sides wider than the distance over the posts, as shown.

3. The larger ranges of steel die sets are made square or rectangular in shape

4. Many dies have relatively small punch members which occupy little punch holder room. For such dies, die sets with V-shaped punch holders provide a better proportioned design as well as greater visibility for loading and unloading work

5. For round punch members a round die set may be used.

17-37. THREE-POST DIE SETS

The addition of a front post to a back-post die set provides increased stability for unbalanced cuts and when greater precision is required. These are incorporated only in square or rectangular steel sets. For hand feeding, the extra post is applied at the front, left corner as at **A**. When the feed is automatic, it is centered as at **B**.

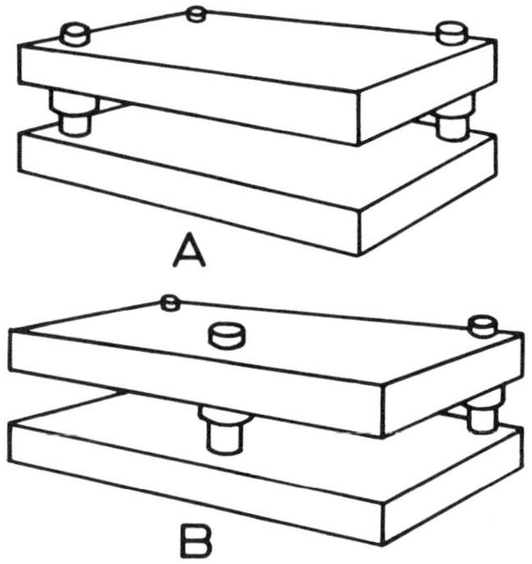

Fig. 17-37. Three-post die sets for hand, (A) and automatic, (B) feeding provide more stability.

17-38. FOUR-POST DIE SETS

Large die sets are ordinarily provided with four posts. There are two styles: At **A** is illustrated the con-

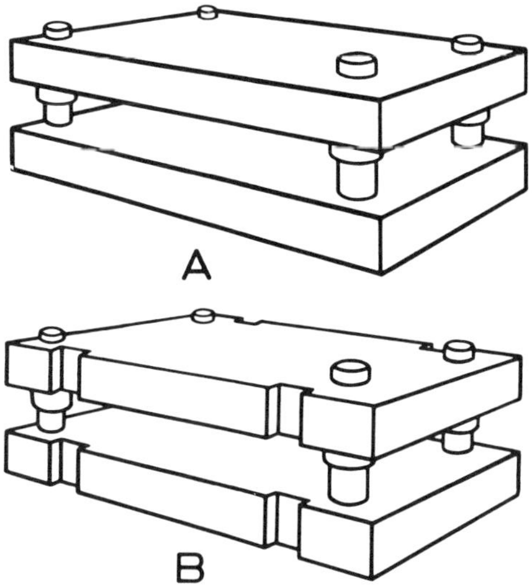

Fig. 17-38. Large die sets have four guide posts, some having slots at side, (B) to prevent slippage as the die is lifted.

ventional type with unbroken edges, employed for small and medium-size four-post sets. At **B** is shown the safety type provided with chain slots milled into the sides to facilitate lifting the die with a chain fall. The slots prevent possible slippage as the die is lifted.

For foolproofing, one post may be offset 1/8 inch towards the edge of the die set, or one post may be made over-size. This prevents accidental reversal in assembly.

Four-post sets are not suitable for hand feeding. They should always be used in conjunction with an automatic feed. They are now widely employed for progressive dies and carbide dies because they provide rigidity.

17-39. LONG, NARROW DIE SETS

This type of die set is used to retain dies for cutting, bending, and forming of long, narrow parts. They are back-post sets, and they are available with either two or three guide posts. Two posts are specified for sets ranging from 12 to 72 inches in length, and three posts for sets ranging from 84 to 240 inches in length.

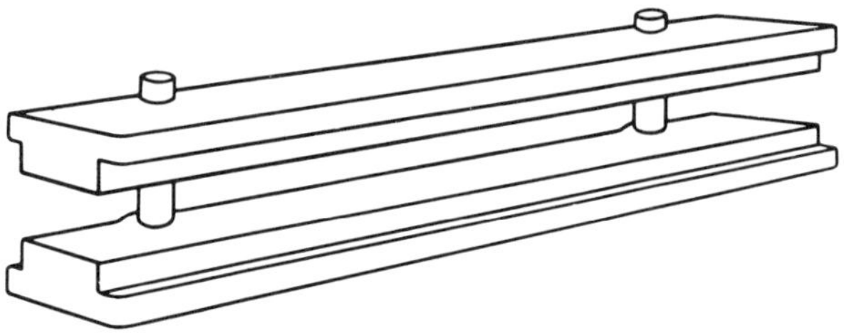

Fig. 17-39. Die set for cutting, bending and forming of long, narrow parts.

17-40. ROUND DIE SETS

These die sets are selected for retaining round dies such as drawing dies, trimming dies, and the like. There are two styles: Back-post style as shown at **A** and center post style as shown at **B** are available in diameters ranging from 4 to 48 inches.

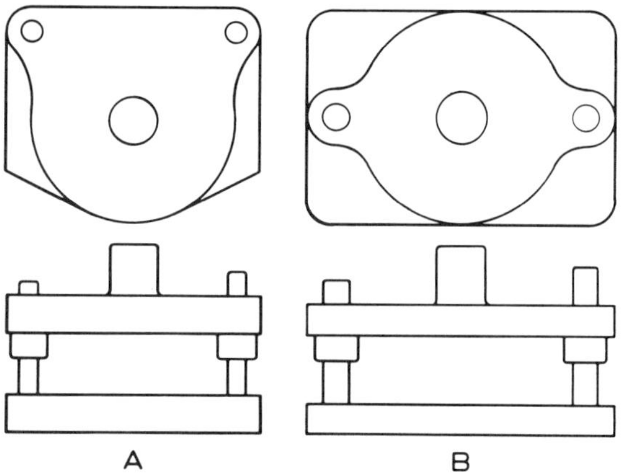

Fig. 17-40. Die sets for drawing and trimming round parts.

17-41. CENTER-POST DIE SETS

These die sets are ordinarily employed for secondary-operation work such as piercing, coining, and the like. Parts are loaded from the front. The die sets are available in semi-steel in the style illustrated at **A**, and in steel in the style shown at **B**. Components may be supplied in combination, with a steel die holder used in conjunction with a semi-steel punch holder as at **C**.

Another important application for center-post die sets is the performing of secondary operations on workpieces having a right hand and a left hand. Parts of one hand may be conveniently loaded from one side. When the other hand is to be run, the die set is turned around 180 degrees in the press for ease in loading.

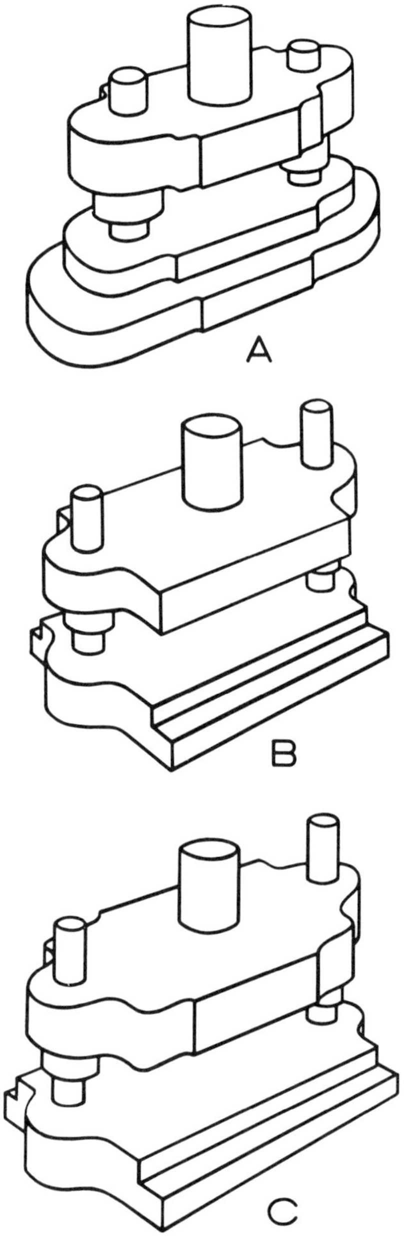

Fig. 17-41. Die used for secondary operation work such as piercing and coining.

17-42. FOOLPROOFING

Center-post and diagonal-post die sets are provided with different-diameter posts, dimensions **A** and **B**. Thus, the punch holder cannot be reversed on the die holder. This is an important precaution for symmetrical dies.

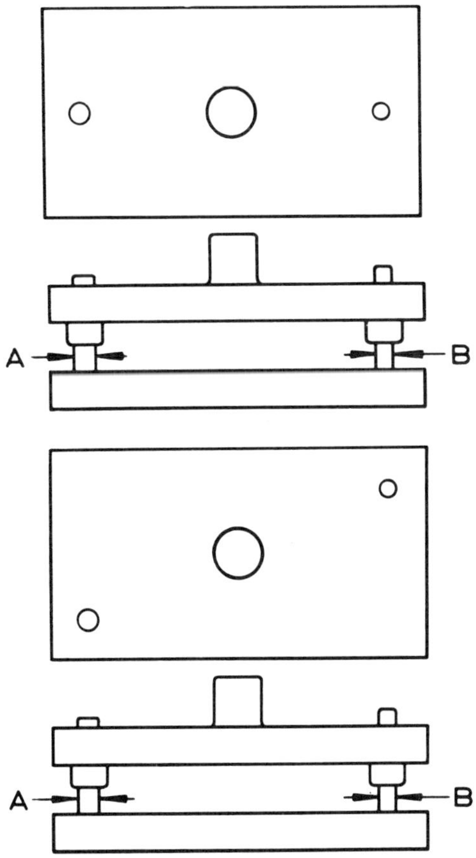

Fig. 17-42. Die sets are foolproofed by using different-diameter guide posts.

17-43. FLOATING-ADAPTER DIE SETS

In blanking and piercing thin stock and for shaving and broaching operations, very little clearance can be allowed between punch and die members. The slightest lateral movement would cause nicked or dulled cutting edges. The floating-adapter shank **A** is clamped in the ram of the press in the regular way. However, by using this adapter the ram can only impart an up and down motion to the punch holder. Any inaccuracy or wear in the slide of the press will not be transmitted as stresses on the die set guide bushings and guide posts. The punch holder, therefore, is actuated independently of the press slide. Long shoulder bushings should be used with these die sets because, in operation, the guide posts must always be guided within them.

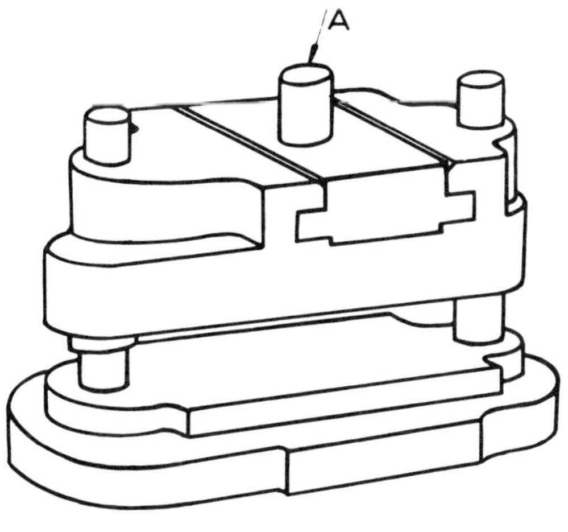

Fig. 17-43. Die set with floating adapter shank, (**A**), prevents lateral movement of punch holder normally the result of inaccuracies in the press slide.

17-44. LARGE DIE SETS – SEMI-STEEL

Large semi-steel die sets are available in the back post **A**, center post **B**, diagonal post **C**, or four post **D** styles. All are provided with clamping flanges for mounting in the press. They are assembled with steel shoulder bushings unless otherwise specified.

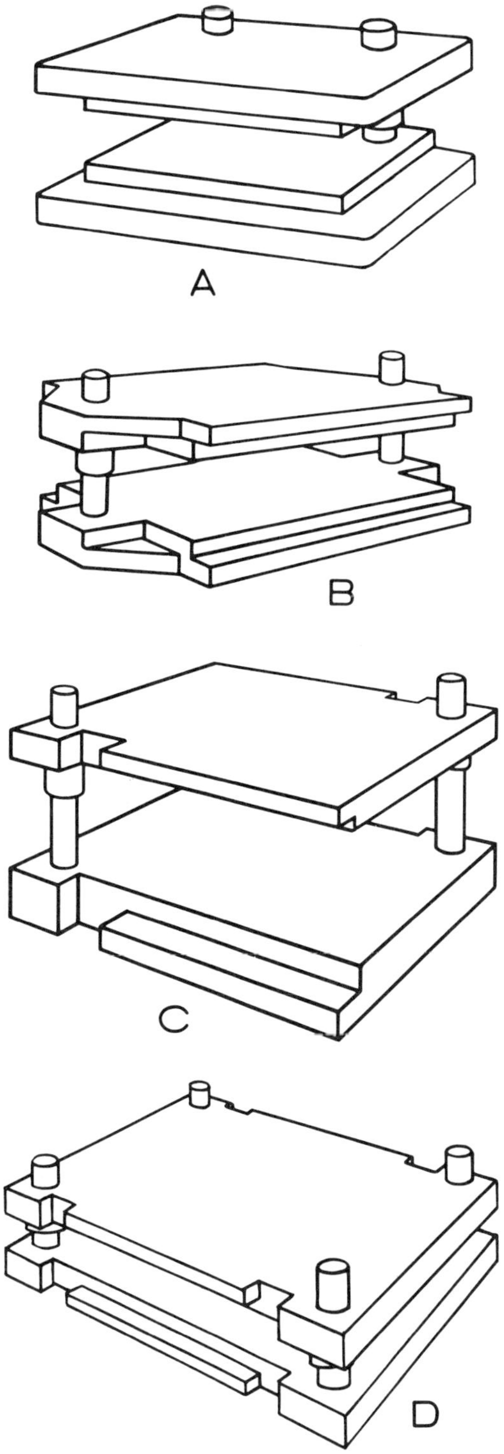

Fig. 17-44. Four styles of large semi-steel die sets.

17-45. LARGE DIE SETS – STEEL

Large steel die sets are made of plate. They have ground surfaces and they are square or rectangular in shape. Two-post sets are given one of three post arrangements. At **A** is shown the back post, at **B** the center post, and at **C** the diagonal post styles. Sizes are not limited. That is, they may be specified to any length, width, and thickness of punch holder and die holder.

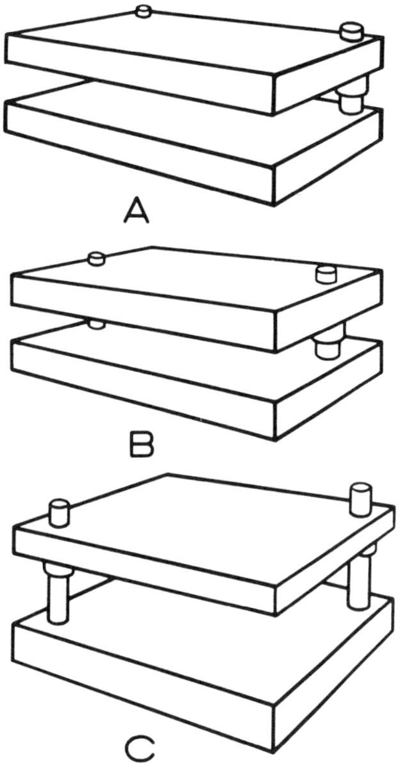

Fig. 17-45. The three post arrangements of large two-post steel die sets.

17-46. RECOMMENDED THICKNESSES

The die holder and punch holder of a large die set must be given sufficient thickness. Die set catalogs recommend specific thicknesses in relation to side-to-side and front-to-back dimensions and these recommendations should be followed. When plates are too thin in relation to their width and length, they will warp causing misalignment of punch and die members and binding of guide posts in guide bushings. Conversely, when plates are too thick the overall die cost increases.

This table provides a useful guide to the specification of punch holder and die holder thicknesses. Observe that there are two considerations, the die-space dimensions **A** and **B**, and the force in tons required to perform the work that is to be done by the die. Select the values for **C** and **D** opposite whichever is greater.

Example: If the die set area for a particular die measures 30 by 20 inches and the force in tons is less than 30, the values of 1¾ inches for **C** and 2 inches for **D** would be selected. However, if the force in tons were 60, we would use the values opposite pressure in tons of 50 to 70, and the value for **C** would be 2½ inches and for **D** 3 inches.

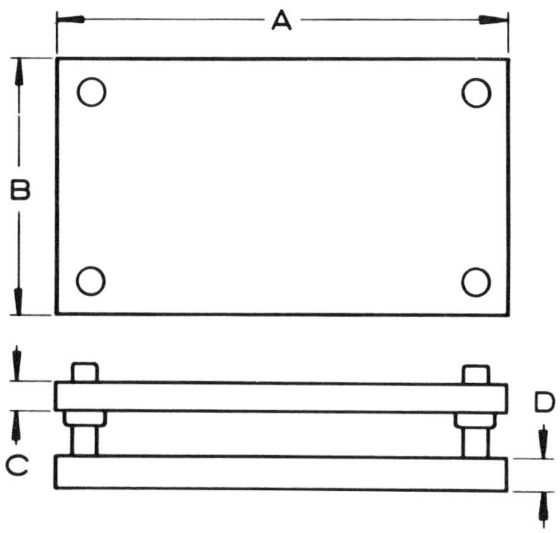

DIE SPACE		PUNCH HOLDER THICKNESS	DIE HOLDER THICKNESS	FORCE IN TONS	
A	B	C	D		
15	10	1 1/4	1 1/2	0	10
30	20	1 3/4	2	10	30
45	30	2	2 1/4	30	50
60	40	2 1/2	3	50	70
75	50	3	3 1/2	70	90
90	60	3 1/2	4	90	110
105	70	4	4 1/2	110	130
120	80	4 1/2	5	130	150
135	90	5	5 1/2	150	200
150	100	5 1/2	6	200	over

Fig. 17-46. Table for determining punch and die holder thickness.

17-47. HEAVY-DUTY DIE SETS

This type of die set features an exceptionally large and thick die holder, which in effect becomes the bolster plate of the press. Heavy-duty die sets are particularly useful for long production runs. They are assembled with removable boss bushings to provide adequate alignment between punch holder and die holder.

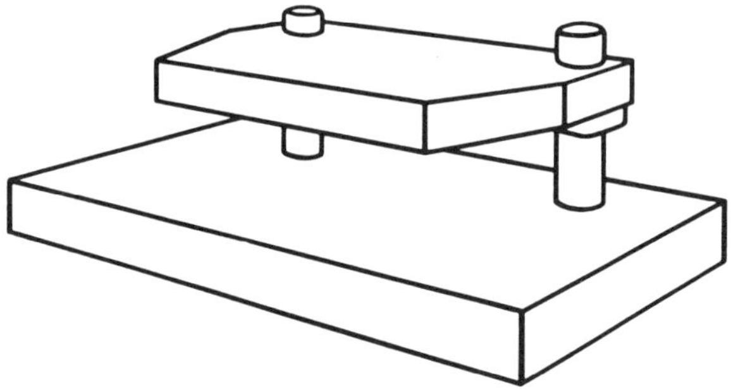

Fig. 17-47. Typical heavy-duty die set.

SPECIAL DIE SETS

Despite the large number of styles and sizes of standard die sets available, it is occasionally necessary to design a special die set for a specific job. This occurs particularly for parts which are exceptionally large or which contain severe offsets. Provide adequate strength by applying ribs or gussets at highly stressed sections. Specific rules cannot be given because of the variety of conditions encountered.

Special die sets are designed by the die designer. and a print is sent to a die set manufacturer where the die set is actually built.

Section 18

DIMENSIONS AND NOTES

After the layout of a die has been drawn, dimensions and notes must be applied to complete the information that the diemaker will require in order to build the die exactly as the designer planned it. Some dimensions are simple; others must be calculated from considerable background information and experience.

There are two methods of detailing a die. In assembly detailing, all dimensions and notes are given on the assembly drawing. The dimensions can be of two kinds. The first includes dimensions that establish relationships between the various components, as needed for assembly of the die. Additional dimensions are applied for critical operations performed after assembly to maintain accuracy. Assembly detailing should be used only on designs suited to that method because of the difficulties encountered in building the die if dimensions are vague.

The second method of detailing is to draw and dimension each component individually. Separate detailing is used for more complex dies, and it is the best method in most cases because the diemaker can be furnished with more complete information. Dimensions should not have to be calculated in the toolroom, because while the diemaker is working on dimensional problems his expensive equipment is standing idle.

The shut height of the die, the distance from the top of the punch holder to the bottom of the die holder, should always be given on the drawing. It is noted with a fractional dimension followed by the abbreviation S.H. for shut height.

Fractional dimensions on the part print are converted to decimal dimensions on the jig borer layout. This ensures that the die will produce parts well within the required limits. Decimal dimensions are given to three places ordinarily. Often, the ten thousandths in the fourth place are left out if they are less than five. When they are five or more, the digit in the third place is increased by one.

TRIGONOMETRY

For applying dimensions to die drawings, it is frequently necessary to compute problems involving trigonometry. This is the determination of unknown sides or angles of triangles. Our approach to the study of trigonometry will be a practical one. We will employ it as a tool for solving specific problems, and charts will be provided for simplifying the subject and to avoid the requirement for memorizing functions or formulas.

18-1. RIGHT TRIANGLES

Most problems encountered in die design involve the solution of right triangles. A right triangle has a 90-degree corner as shown at **A**. The inclined line is the longest of the three and it is called the hypotenuse. The side directly across from any given angle is called the side opposite, while the side nearest to a given angle is called the side adjacent, as shown at **B** and **C**.

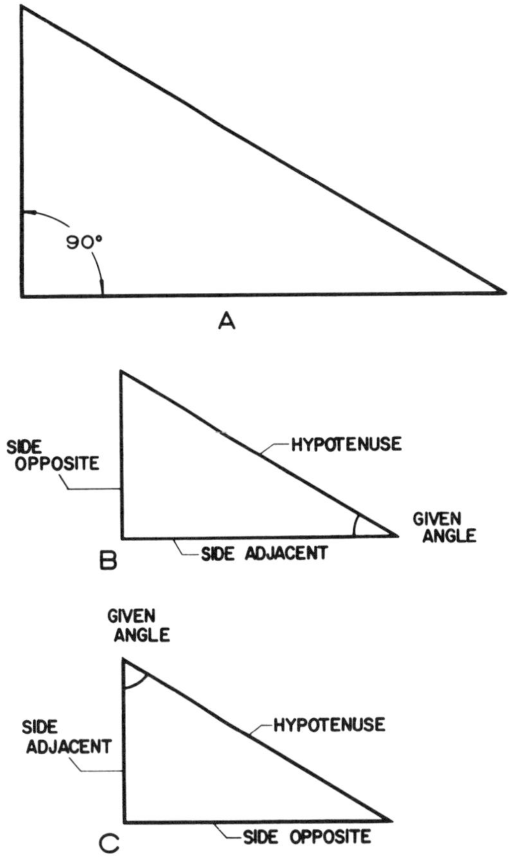

Fig. 18-1. Terms relating to right triangles.

18-2. GRAPHIC REPRESENTATION

In this illustration, those functions of angles that we will use are represented graphically. A circle is drawn with its center at the large apex of a triangle. A vertical line is extended downward from the intersection of the hypotenuse and the circle, line length **A**, and another vertical line from the outside of the circle, line **C**. The following, then are the functions of the angle (designated with the circular arc) of the right triangle whose hypotenuse is the radius of the circle with a value of 1:

A – sine
B – cosine
C – tangent
D – cotangent.

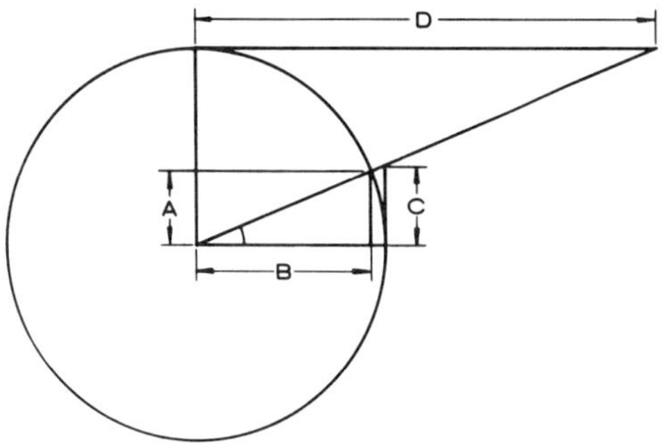

Fig. 18-2. Graphic representation of the functions of an angle of a right triangle.

18-3. MATHEMATICAL RELATIONSHIPS

The functions of right triangles may be calculated by the following formulas:

1. The sine of an angle is equal to the side opposite divided by the hypotenuse.

$$\text{sine } A = \frac{a}{c} \qquad \text{sine } B = \frac{b}{c}$$

2. The cosine of an angle is equal to the side adjacent divided by the hypotenuse.

$$\text{cosine } A = \frac{b}{c} \qquad \text{cosine } B = \frac{a}{c}$$

3. The tangent of an angle is equal to the side opposite divided by the side adjacent.

$$\text{tangent } A = \frac{a}{b} \qquad \text{tangent } B = \frac{b}{a}$$

4. The cotangent of an angle is equal to the side adjacent divided by the side opposite.

$$\text{cotangent } A = \frac{b}{a} \qquad \text{cotangent } B = \frac{a}{b}$$

In actual practice, functions of triangles are seldom calculated. Instead they are taken directly from a table of trigonometric functions in a handbook such as MACHINERY'S HANDBOOK. Make sure that you use the table entitled 'Natural Trigonometric Functions' and not the one entitled 'Logarithms of Trigonometric Functions'. For angles from 0 to 45 degrees, the table is read downward. At the top of the page the number of degrees is given in bold type, as for instance, 20°. The left column, marked M, lists minutes from 0 to 60. At the top of the page, above the columns of numerals are marked Sine, Cosine, Tangent, Cotangent, and other less frequently used functions. For a whole number of degrees, that is, one without minutes or seconds, read the function directly on the top line as for instance, 20° – 0 minutes. When the number of degrees is followed by some minutes, turn to the appropriate page and read down the **M** column to the given number of minutes. Functions are then read on that line. For instance, the tangent of 20°32' would be 0.37455. Angles from 45° to 90° are listed at the *bottoms* of the pages and minutes are read upward in the column at the extreme right. Names of functions are located at the bottoms of the columns and you must trace upward to the line for the appropriate number of minutes for reading values.

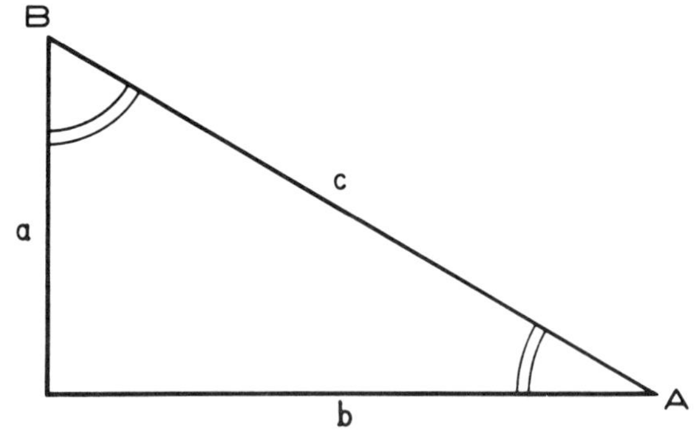

Fig. 18-3. Letter designations for use in calculating functions of a right triangle.

18-4. IDENTIFYING KNOWN AND UNKNOWN SIDES AND ANGLES

It will be necessary to learn the method of identifying the various sides and angles. In the illustration, observe that capital letters denote angles and lower case letters denote sides as follows:

A – acute angle
B – acute angle
a – side
b – base
c – hypotenuse.

In our method of identification, a heavy black line denotes the side or angle to be calculated and double lines indicate other unknown sides and angles. In the example, the side **a** would be the one requiring solution. Side **b** would be unknown. We would therefore know the values for angle **A**, angle **B**, and hypotenuse **c**, and it would be a simple matter to solve for the value of side **a** as will be shown.

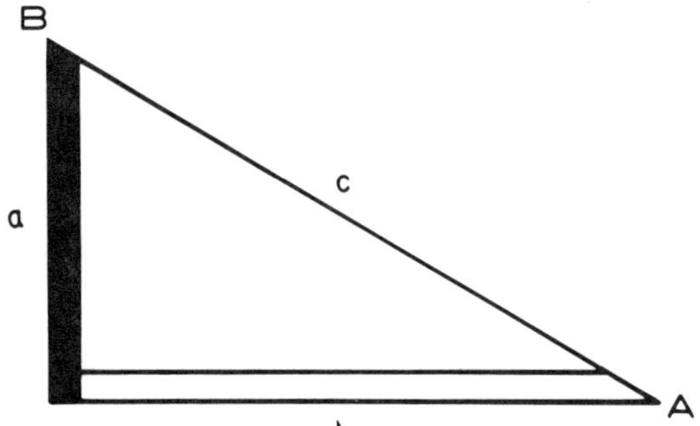

Fig. 18-4. Solid black side a of right triangle is the side to be calculated. Double lines indicate side b is unknown. Hypotenuse c and angles A and B are known.

TRIGONOMETRIC EQUATIONS

HEAVY LINES REPRESENT SIDES AND ANGLES TO BE CALCULATED
DOUBLE LINES REPRESENT OTHER UNKNOWN SIDES AND ANGLES

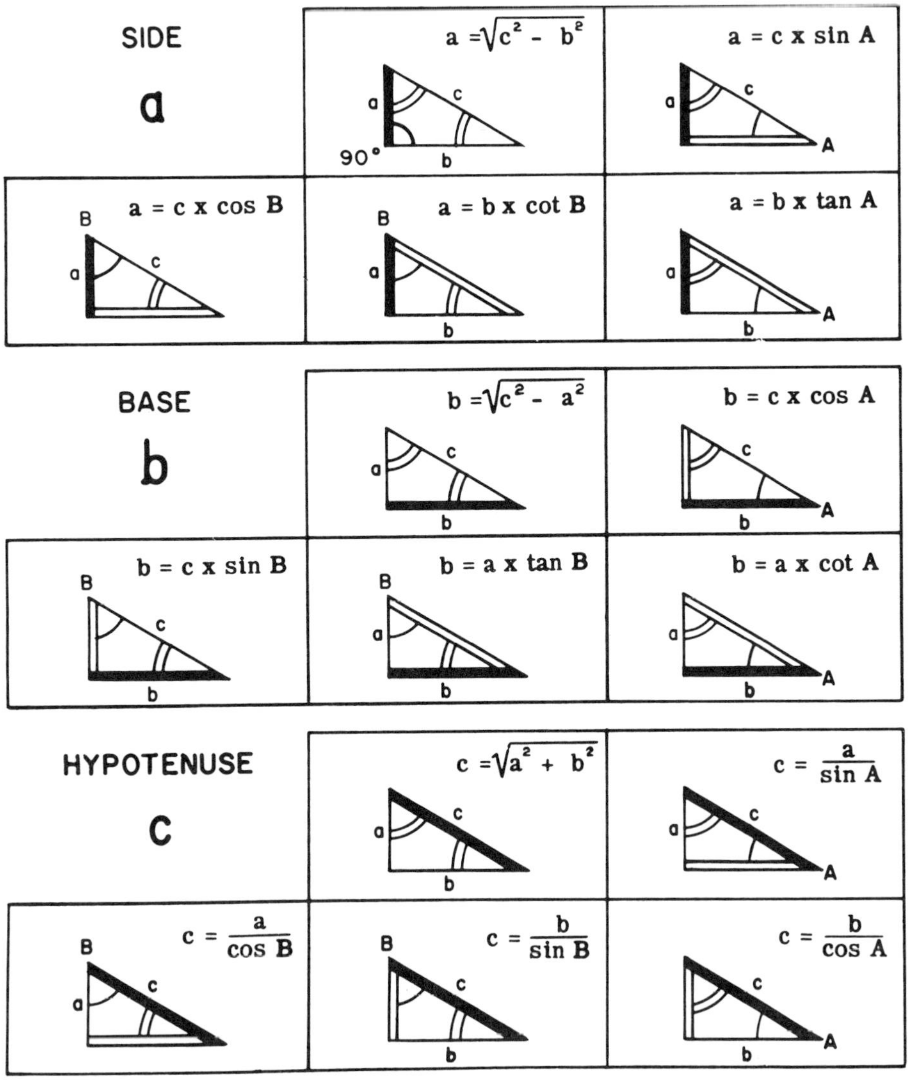

Fig. 18-5. Trigonometric equations used in computing sides and angles of triangles.

First however, we must know exactly what information will be required before any triangle can be solved. To compute the length of one side of a triangle, the length of the other two sides must be known or the length of one side and one acute angle must be known. Given this information, we can determine the values of the other sides and angles.

18-5. TRIGONOMETRIC EQUATIONS

This chart has been prepared to provide a simple method of selecting equations in the solution of trigonometry problems. Let us enter into a careful analysis of its features because this will enhance its value to you in the development of orderly methods. Note the five rectangles labeled "side **a**" at the top of Fig. 18-5. Within each rectangle is a triangle and an equation. In every one of these five triangles, side **a** is the unknown side, the one requiring solution. In the first triangle, sides **b** and **c** are known. Angles other than the 90° angle are unknown and they are identified as such by double lines. The formula to employ in solving for **a** when only the base **b** and hypotenuse **c** are known

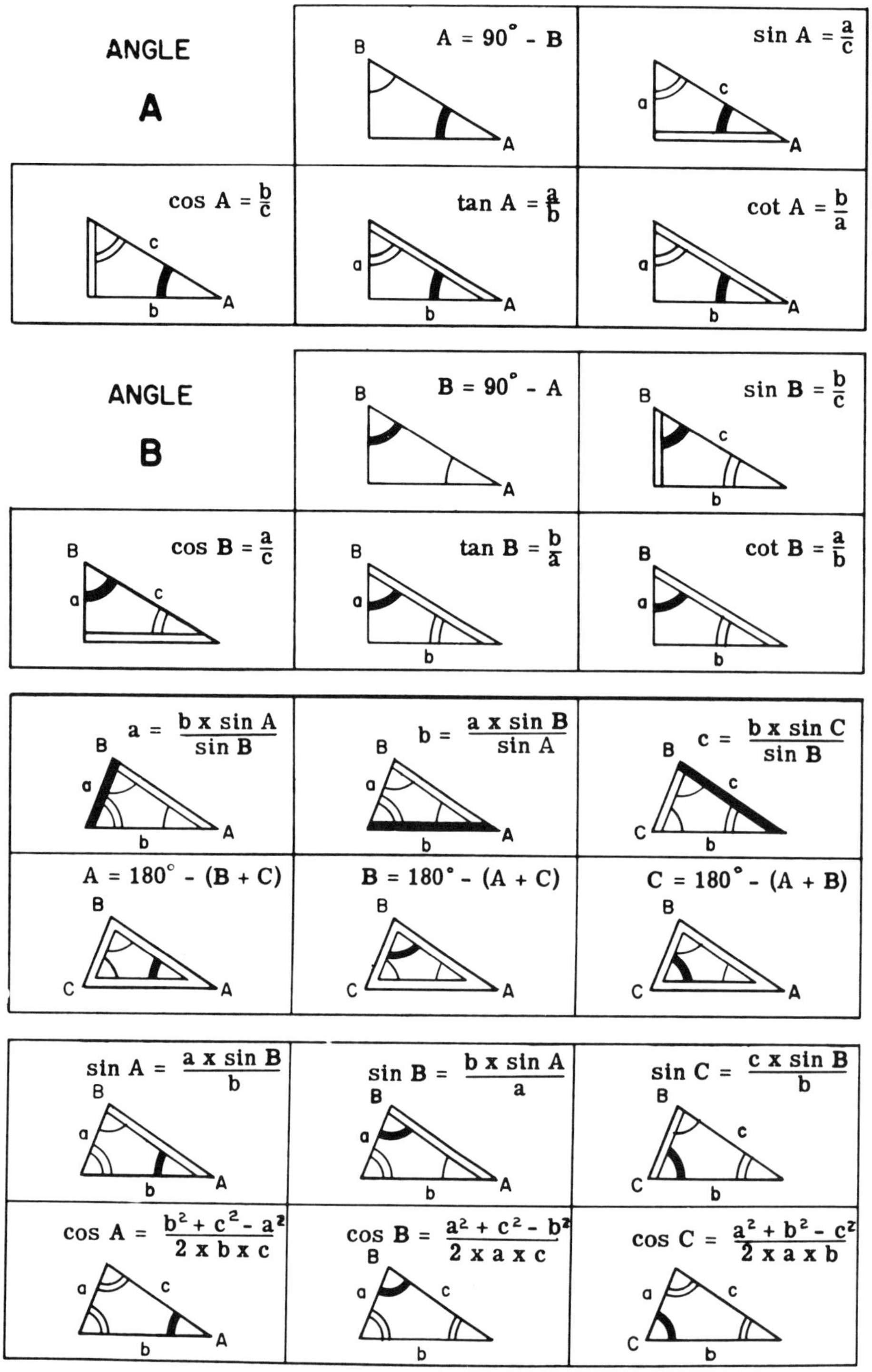

Fig. 18-5. (cont.) Trigonometric equations used in computing sides and angles of triangles.

is given above.

In the second triangle, only angle **A** and hypotenuse **c** are known and the formula is given when this condition is present. The same method is followed for the succeeding triangles, and formulas are given for the various combinations of known and unknown sides and angles.

In the next block of triangles, formulas are given for solving for the unknown base **b**, and in the third block for the hypotenuse **c**.

At the top of the next group of triangles formulas are given for solving for angles **A** and **B**. Underneath this, formulas are given for solving for other than right-angle triangles. Observe that in every instance the angle known, the one used in the formula, is identified on the triangle by a single thin arc.

DIE TRIGONOMETRY

The solution of problems in trigonometry is a simple procedure when formulas given in Fig. 18-5 are understood and employed. It is not always so simple to set up or identify the triangles that will require solution for applying dimensions to drawings of dies. This is because most blanks have to be nested or inclined to conserve material. Establishing the triangles that will require solution can be difficult unless you acquire a clear understanding of the entire process of triangulation. The following outline or guide will increase your knowledge of this important subject.

18-6. PART DIMENSIONS

On part drawings for sheet metal workpieces, dimensions are normally applied horizontally and vertically as shown at **A** for a simple representative part. Note that a triangle is formed as illustrated at **B**. The unknown dimensions of this triangle can be easily calculated by trigonometry because its base and side have been given.

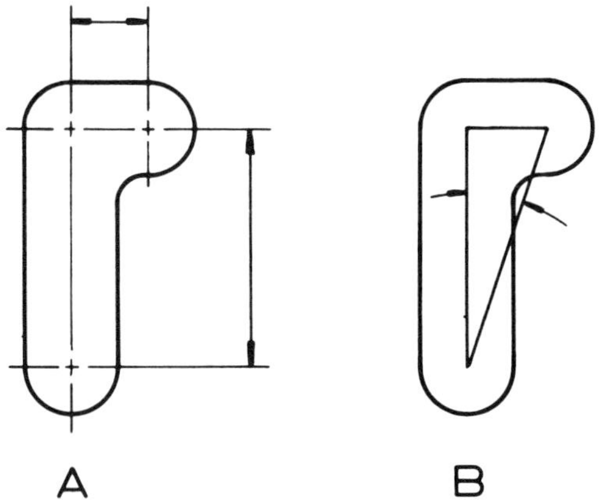

Fig. 18-6. Applying trigonometry to part drawing to solve for unknown dimensions.

18-7. SCRAP STRIP

This is a good scrap strip design for the part illustrated in Fig. 18-6. The blank is drawn in an inclined position to conserve material. Angular positioning of workpieces is required for most parts except simple round, square, or rectangular blanks, which may be run side by side, positioned either vertically or horizontally.

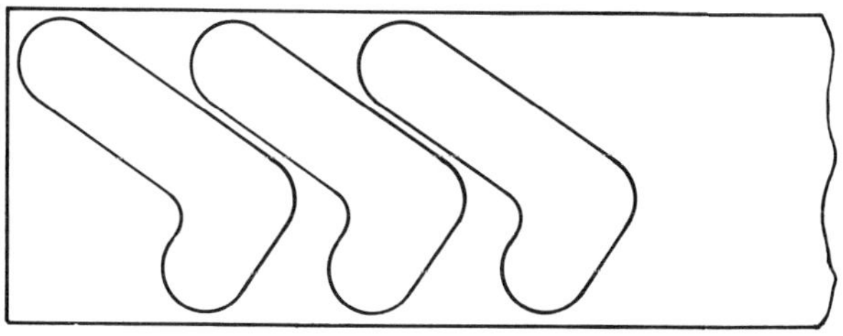

Fig. 18-7. Scrap strip design for part shown in Fig. 18-6.

18-8. JIG BORER LAYOUT

Holes in die blocks are dimensioned for jig borer layouts. In this type of dimensioning, all horizontal dimensions are given from the line representing the left surface and all vertical dimensions are given from the line representing the upper surface. Grind marks are applied to extension lines to indicate surfaces from which accurate measurements can be taken. In a variation of the method, the first hole is located with fractional dimensions, both horizontally and vertically, Other holes are then located from it with decimal dimensions in the same manner as shown here.

All internal radii in the die-hole contour are completed as full circles with phantom lines. Notes with leaders are employed to indicate that holes are to be jig bored at those locations. Observe that horizontal dimensions **A** and **B**, and vertical dimensions **C** and **D** cannot be applied directly from dimensions given on the part drawing because of the inclined position of the blank. Their lengths must be calculated.

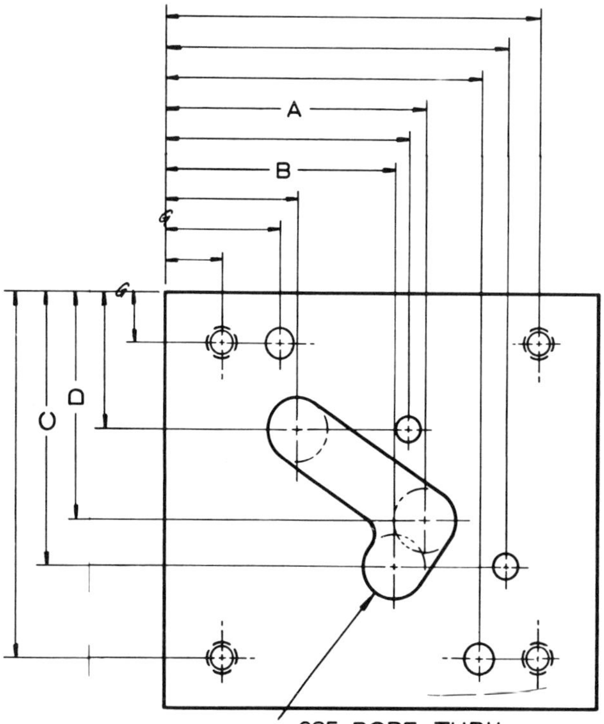

Fig. 18-8. Typical dimensioning of die block for jig boring operation.

18-9. DIE BLOCK

At **A** is shown the plan view of a die block after holes have been jig bored. Note that the large holes will form part of the actual die-hole contour or outline. Jig boring holes to produce internal radii provides a very accurate beginning or basis for laying out and machining irregular die holes. Precise lines are scribed tangent to the jig bored holes. The center is sawed out in a metal-cutting band saw, and the sides are then accurately dic filed to "split the line", thus completing the opening as shown at **B**.

18-10. TRIANGLES IN DIE DIMENSIONING

When a part is tilted for best nesting in the scrap strip, Fig. 18-7, many dimensioning problems can occur when preparing the jig borer layout. Note that when the inscribed triangle is tilted, and horizontal and vertical lines are drawn from the vertices of the acute angles of the inscribed right triangle a second and adjacent triangle is produced. Tilting the part shown in Fig. 18-6, with its triangle established by the vertical and horizontal dimensions produces this effect. Observe carefully the arrangement and direction of adjacent right triangles formed. Their positions will depend upon the direction and inclination of the part in the scrap strip.

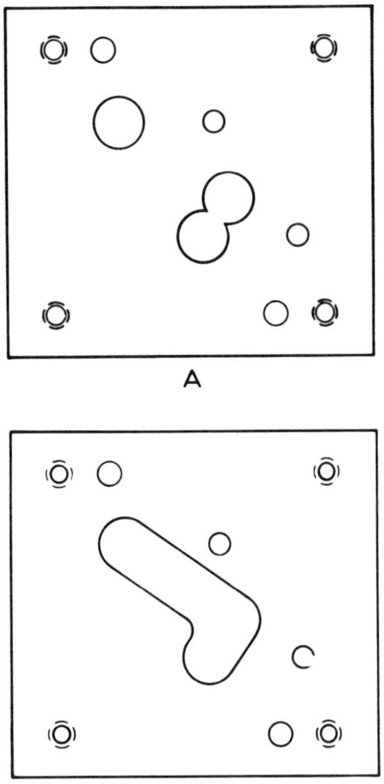

Fig. 18-9. Plan view of die block after jig boring, (**A**) and after bandsawing and die filing, (**B**).

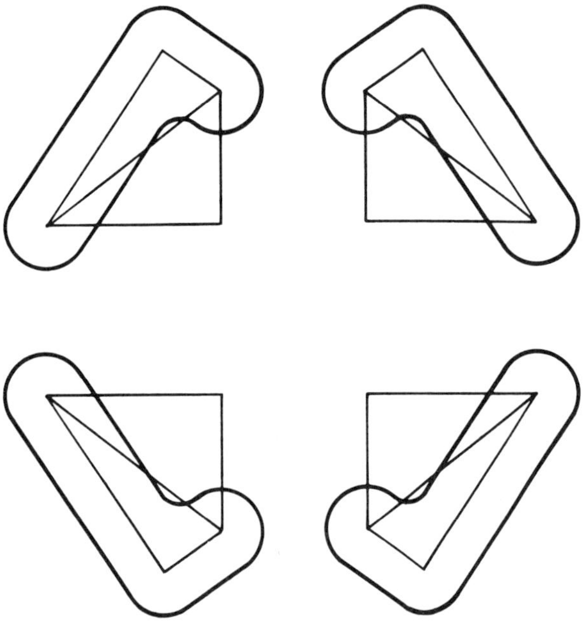

Fig. 18-10. A second adjacent triangle is constructed by drawing horizontal and vertical lines from the vertices of the acute angles of the inscribed right triangle which will facilitate dimensioning of jig borer layout.

18-11. SOLVING ADJACENT TRIANGLES

You will find this chart invaluable in the solutions of adjacent triangles. Formulas are given for solving all the sides and also for determining the large angle **X** when sides are known. It is often difficult to establish triangles on drawings because of the confusion of lines

FORMULAS FOR ADJACENT TRIANGLES

TRIGONOMETRIC FIGURE IS SHOWN IN EIGHT POSITIONS TO AID IN VISUALIZING APPLICATION.

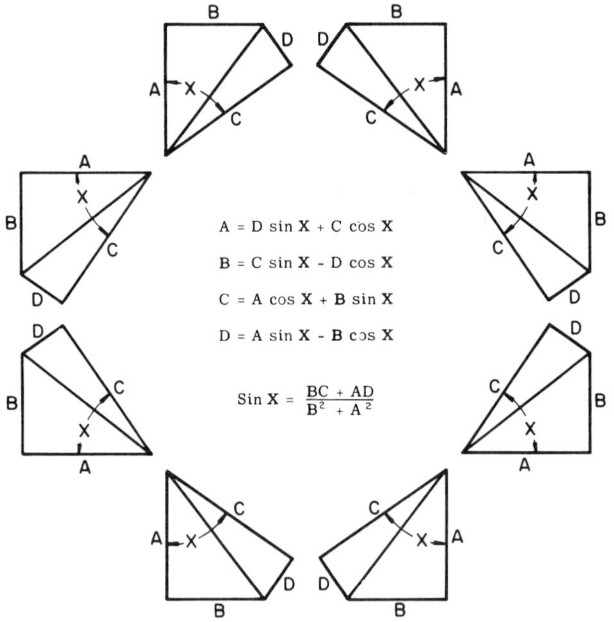

Fig. 18-11. Chart which gives formulas for solving adjacent triangles.

and the numerous positions which triangles may assume. Therefore the trigonometric figure is shown in eight positions to aid in visualizing application.

18-12. ENLARGED LAYOUT

To establish triangles, draw as large a layout of the part as possible to be certain that small triangles will not be overlooked. The sides of some of these triangles may be only a few thousands of an inch long and would not be detected on an actual-size drawing. If they are ignored, final dimensions on the jig borer layout will be incorrect. For most small

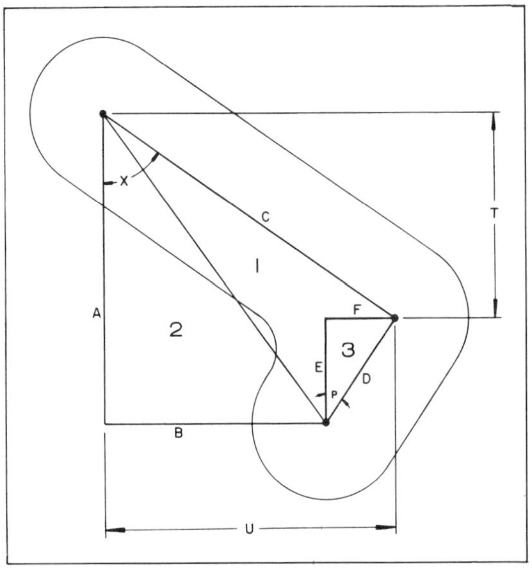

Fig. 18-12. Enlarged part layout for determining dimensions for jig borer layout.

blanks a ten-to-one layout will be satisfactory. It is a convenient scale because dimensions for the large layout are established by simply moving the decimal point one numeral. For example, an actual dimension of 0.093 would become 0.930 on the ten-to-one layout.

Another reason for making a large layout is that it provides a check for accuracy of calculated dimensions. Scaling the layout will often reveal mistakes which might otherwise remain undetected.

After the layout has been drawn, fasten a sheet of thin tracing paper over it with drafting tape. Triangles are established on this outer tracing paper. Often the paper will become covered with numerous lines before it is discovered that a wrong start was made. When this happens the tracing paper can be removed and a new one substituted. The layout itself will not be marked and it need not be redrawn. Draw the first triangle and identifying letters and dimensions with black lead. Succeeding triangles may be drawn in different colors to help in identification. The practice in most tool design offices is to establish all triangles which will require solution, set up formulas for the entire job, and then "run them off" on a calculator or computer.

In establishing triangles on the tracing paper or tissue, observe the following general rules:

1. Connect centers of circles with light lines
2. From centers draw horizontal and vertical extension lines. These may complete required right triangles
3. Extend oblique lines until they intersect horizontal and vertical lines to define triangles
4. Add vertical and horizontal dimensions to establish lengths of longer lines which may become sides of larger triangles
5. When two triangles have a common side or angle, solution of one triangle may form the basis for solving the other
6. When two circles are tangent to each other, the distance between centers is the sum of the radii
7. When solving for centers of arcs, it may be helpful to draw the full circles
8. When a line is tangent to a circle, draw the following two lines in attempting a solution:
   a. The radius to the tangent point
   b. A line parallel to the line of tangency and through the center. This line usually will be helpful when the angle made by the tangent line is known
9. When making a ten-to-one layout, first draw the part in the position in which it is dimensioned on the part print. Draw circles to represent all holes and draw all portions of circles that form a portion of the part outline or are contained wholly within the part outline. Through the centers of these circles or portions of circles, draw long vertical and horizontal lines
10. Unfasten the sheet and rotate it to the selected angle of tilt. Next, draw horizontal and vertical lines through centers to establish triangles for solution. At the same time, draw strip edges to establish final strip width.

In Fig. 18-12 you will note that angle **X** is equal to the angle of tilt, and that angle **P** is its complement. Solutions for values **A** and **B** of adjacent triangles **1** and **2** are determined by formulas given in Fig. 18-11. In all, three separate triangles are formed, numbered **1**, **2**, and **3**. Following is the procedure for solution:

Given **D** and **P**: Solve for **E** and **F**

Final dimensions are determined as follows:

A is read directly
B is read directly
T equals **A** - **E**
U equals **B** + **F**.

18-13. MULTIPLE TRIANGLES

When the corner radius of a part similar to the one shown in Fig. 18-12 is small, other triangles must be solved before jig borer dimensions can be determined. Taken together, views **A** and **B** illustrate perfectly the number and often difficult arrangement of triangles which require solution for even relatively simple workpieces. It should emphasize the need for a large layout and systematic methods of operation. View **B** is an enlarged portion of view **A** to reveal small triangles more clearly. Observe that six separate triangles are established. Angle **X** is the angle of tilt. Angle **P** is

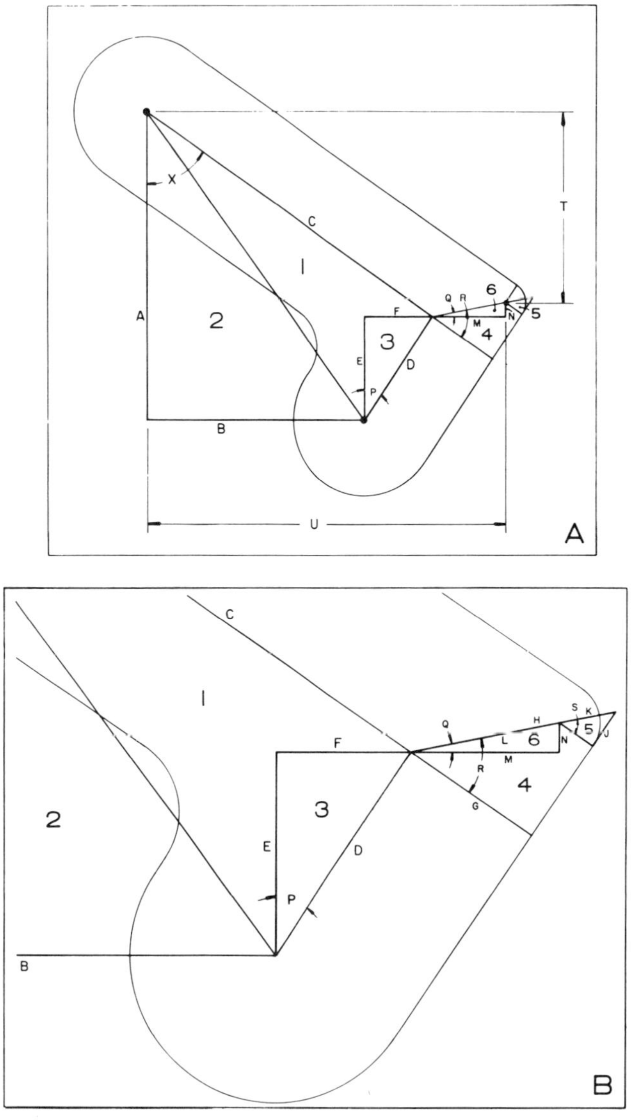

Fig. 18-13. Enlarged part layout in which multiple triangles are used for determining dimensions for jig borer input.

its complement and angle **R** is a 45-degree angle. Angle **Q** may be found by subtracting **P** from **R**. Following is the procedure for solution:

Given **C**, **D**, and **X**:	Solve for **A** and **B**
Given **D** and **P**:	Solve for **E** and **F**
In enlarged view **B**:	
Given **G** and **R** in triangle 4:	Solve for **H**
Given **J** and **S** in triangle 5:	Solve for **K**
Subtract **K** from **H** to	Solve for **L**
Given **L** and **Q** in triangle 6:	Solve for **M** and **N**

Final dimensions are determined as follows:

A is read directly
B is read directly
T equals **A** – (**E** + **N**)
U equals **B** + **F** + **M**

18-14. DIE CLEARANCES

Another factor must be considered in applying die dimensions. This is the amount of clearance between punch and die members. For a blank to part cleanly from the material strip, there must be exactly the correct space between the edge of the punch and the cutting edge of the die. If too little clearance exists, power consumption to operate the press will be excessive. Also, when the punch enters the material strip, the fractures which originate from both sides of the stock – punch side and die side – will not meet, and a ragged edge will be formed on the blank, or on the inside edge of the hole being pierced.

Excessive clearance will dish the blank and produce long, stringy burrs all around the edge. Application of correct clearances will result in a blank free of burrs, and with the burnished portion of its edge extending to the greatest possible depth. This burnished part of the edge should be approximately one-third of the blank thickness.

The proper clearance to apply depends upon the material, its degree of hardness, and its thickness. The accompanying table gives the formula and table of constants by which clearances may be calculated. The formula says that the clearance is equal to the stock thickness (in inches) divided by the constant. The values arrived at by the use of this table and formula apply to overall clearances or diameters. When clearance "on a side" is desired, as when laying out dies having an irregular contour or for cutting out only portions of a blank, divide the answer by two. For example, if 16-gage (0.0625 inch) hard steel is to be punched in the die, look under *Hard Steel* in the table, and the constant 14 is given. Divide 0.0625 by 14, and the answer 0.0045 inch is applied either to the punch or to the die hole.

Below the table of constants of Fig. 18-14 is given the punch or die allowance to compensate for part size change. The use of this information is discussed further along under "Secondary Allowances."

Constants for Various Materials

Formula: $\frac{\text{Thickness of Stock}}{\text{Given Constant}}$

MATERIAL	CONSTANT
Copper	21
Brass	20
Soft Steel	17
Medium Steel	16
Phosphor Bronze	16
Hard Steel	14
Boiler Plate (over ¼ in. thick)	10
Soft and Medium Steel (over ¼ in. thick)	10
Aluminum (to ⅛ in. thick)	10
Aluminum (over ⅛ in. thick)	8

PUNCH OR DIE ALLOWANCE TO COMPENSATE FOR PART SIZE CHANGE

STOCK, THICKNESS, GAGE	ALLOWANCE IN.
50 to 22	0.001
22 to 16	0.0015
16 to 10	0.002

Fig. 18-14. Table of constants for computing clearances and table of allowances to compensate for part size change.

18-15. TABLE OF DIE CLEARANCES

This table lists clearances directly. The values apply to overall clearances or diameters. Stock thicknesses employed by industry are in terms of gages or decimal thicknesses. In either case, the clearance can be interpolated by reference to values given. For clearance "per side", divide the given amounts by two.

18-16. APPLYING CLEARANCES

For dies of irregular shape the clearance must be *added* to the required dimension under certain conditions, while at other times it must be *subtracted* from it. This illustration shows how to apply clearances.

Clearance is applied to either the punch or the die; never to both. Here is the rule to follow: When a slug is produced to be thrown away as scrap, the punch must be to size and clearance is applied to the die. When a blank is produced, which will be kept, and the strip from which it is removed will be thrown away as scrap, the die opening is made to size, and the clearance is applied to the punch. At **A** is shown a punch and die hole to which clearances are to be applied. Observe these rules:

1. *When clearance is applied to the punch:* Subtract clearance from all radii with centers inside the punch. Add clearance to all radii with centers outside. Subtract from all dimensions between parallel lines. Angles and dimensions between centers remain constant.

2. *When clearance is applied to the die:* Add clearance to all radii with centers inside die. Subtract clearance from all radii with centers outside. Add to

STANDARD PUNCH AND DIE CLEARANCES

STOCK THICKNESS	SOFT STEEL	MEDIUM STEEL	HARD STEEL	STAINLESS STEEL	PHOSPHOR BRONZE	BRASS	COPPER	ALUMINUM
0.010	0.0006	0.0006	0.0007	0.0008	0.0006	0.0005	0.0005	0.001
0.020	0.0011	0.0012	0.0014	0.0016	0.0012	0.001	0.0009	0.002
0.030	0.0017	0.0018	0.0021	0.0024	0.0018	0.0015	0.0014	0.003
0.040	0.0023	0.0025	0.0028	0.0032	0.0025	0.002	0.0019	0.004
0.050	0.0029	0.0031	0.0035	0.004	0.0031	0.0025	0.0023	0.005
0.060	0.0035	0.0037	0.0043	0.0048	0.0037	0.003	0.0028	0.006
0.070	0.0041	0.0043	0.005	0.0056	0.0043	0.0035	0.0033	0.007
0.080	0.0047	0.005	0.0057	0.0064	0.005	0.004	0.0038	0.008
0.090	0.0052	0.0056	0.0064	0.0072	0.0056	0.0045	0.0042	0.009
0.100	0.0058	0.0062	0.0071	0.008	0.0062	0.005	0.0047	0.010
0.110	0.006	0.0069	0.0078	0.0088	0.0069	0.0055	0.0052	0.011
0.120	0.007	0.0075	0.0085	0.0096	0.0075	0.006	0.0057	0.012
0.130	0.0076	0.0081	0.0093	0.0104	0.0081	0.0065	0.0062	0.0162
0.140	0.0082	0.0087	0.010	0.0112	0.0087	0.007	0.0066	0.0175
0.150	0.0088	0.0093	0.0107	0.012	0.0093	0.0075	0.0071	0.0187
0.160	0.0094	0.010	0.0114	0.0128	0.010	0.008	0.0076	0.020
0.170	0.010	0.0106	0.0121	0.0136	0.0106	0.0085	0.008	0.0212
0.180	0.0105	0.0112	0.0128	0.0144	0.0112	0.009	0.0085	0.0225
0.190	0.0111	0.0118	0.0135	0.0152	0.0118	0.0095	0.009	0.0237
0.200	0.0117	0.0125	0.0142	0.016	0.0125	0.010	0.0095	0.025
0.210	0.0123	0.0131	0.015	0.0168	0.0131	0.0105	0.010	0.0262
0.220	0.0129	0.0137	0.0157	0.0176	0.0137	0.011	0.0104	0.0275
0.230	0.0135	0.0143	0.0164	0.0184	0.0143	0.0115	0.0109	0.0287
0.240	0.0141	0.015	0.0171	0.0192	0.015	0.012	0.0114	0.030
0.250	0.0147	0.0156	0.0178	0.020	0.0156	0.0125	0.0119	0.0312

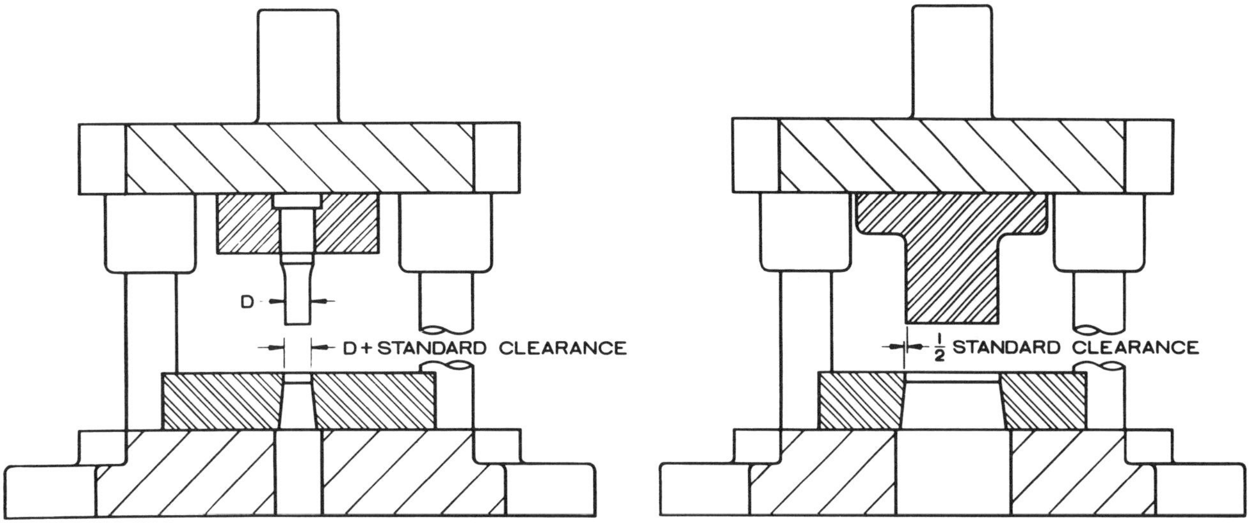

Fig. 18-15. Table of standard punch and die clearances and drawings showing how clearances are applied.

all dimensions between parallel lines. Angles and dimensions between centers remain constant.

Let us consider the actual application of clearances to a die drawing.

At **B** and **C** are shown a blanking punch within a die hole with clearance greatly exaggerated. The layout at **B** is a blanking station. Therefore, the die hole must be made to sizes given on the part print and clearances are applied to the punch and it will be smaller by the amount of clearance. In applying dimensions observe that:

1. The amount of clearance is subtracted from each of the radii **A**

2. The amount of clearance is added to each of the radii **B**

3. Distances between centers remain the same for both the punch member and die hole.

The layout at **C** is a piercing station. Therefore, the punch must be made to sizes given on the part print. Clearances are applied to the die hole and it will be larger by the amount of the clearance. Observe that the order is reversed. For radii at **A**, the amount of clearance is added to the radius. For radii at **B**, the amount of clearance is subtracted from the given radius. Distances **C** remain constant.

Until facility in applying clearances is acquired, it is advisable to make a similar layout, allowing about 1/8 inch clearance between lines representing the punch and die members. Dimensioning directly on this layout will reduce the possibility of error because

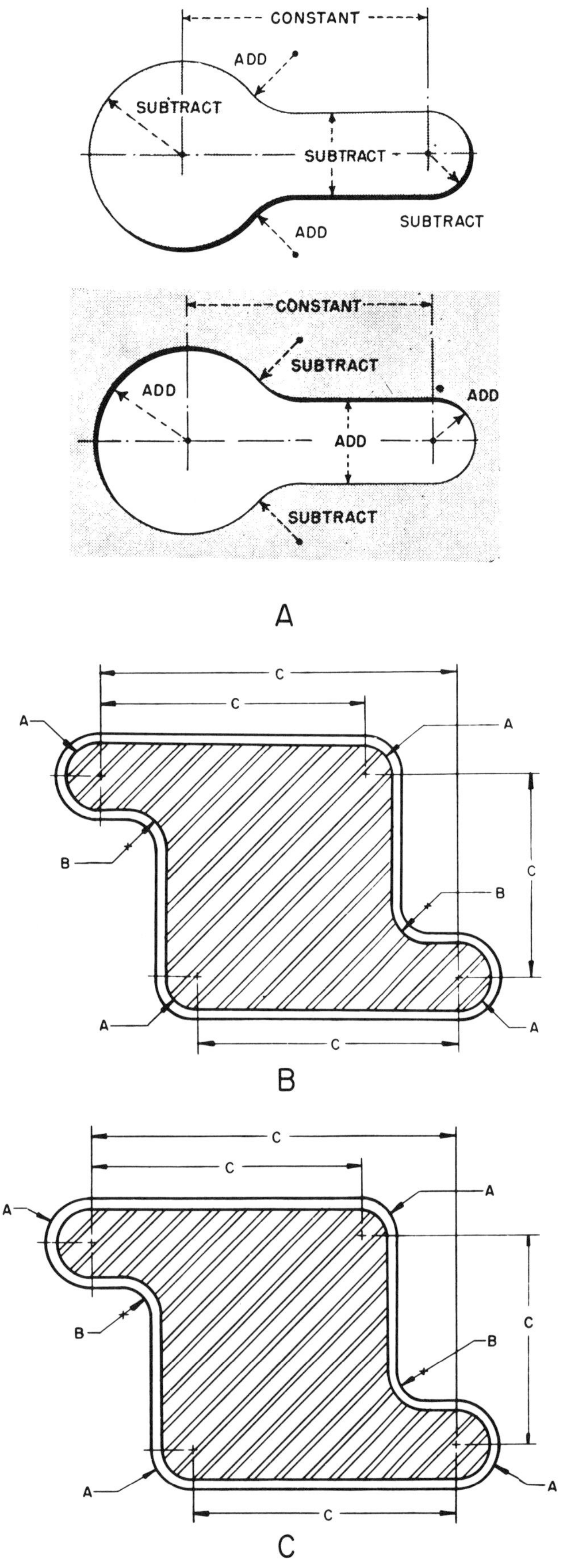

Fig. 18-16 Method of applying clearances to punch and die hole of a die.

it will be readily apparent whether the amount of clearance should be added or subtracted from any given dimension.

Cutting faces of blanking punches are fitted to the die and therefore they do not ordinarily require dimensioning. Also, in the plan view of the punches, do not give locating dimensions. The die maker will know that all punches must fit in their corresponding die openings and he will locate them accordingly.

SECONDARY ALLOWANCES

After they have been punched out, holes close in a small amount if they are under 1 inch in diameter. Blanks under 1 inch in diameter have the reverse characteristic and become larger. A second table in the lower portion of the illustration Fig. 18-14 lists the amount to either add to the punch or subtract from the die in order to produce an accurate blank.

When the blank is required, the allowance is subtracted from the diameter of the die hole. When accurate piercing is required, the allowances must be added to the punch diameter. For punches and dies of irregular shape, one-half the given value is either added or subtracted all around. Apply the allowance, then add or subtract the clearance. For example:

In piercing a 0.500-inch diameter hole in 16-gage (0.0625) steel, the allowance (0.002) is added to the punch and it is made 0.502 inch in diameter. The clearance (0.004) is added to this dimension and the hole in the die block is made 0.506 inch in diameter.

For a 0.500-inch diameter blank, the allowance (0.002) is subtracted from 0.500 and the die hole is made 0.498 inch in diameter. The clearance (0.004) is subtracted from this dimension and the punch is make 0.494 inch in diameter.

Holes or blanks larger than one inch diameter will not enlarge or shrink appreciably and no allowance need be applied.

When tolerances are liberal, as when hole dimensions are given fractionally, make piercing punch diameters 0.005 inch larger than nominal size. This allowance takes care of closing in of holes after piercing and of punch wear. When dimensions are held more accurately, specify punch diameters to the high side of the tolerance.

18-17. JIG BORER LAYOUT

A jig borer layout guides the jig borer operator in machining holes in die blocks and corresponding holes for punches. In this representative layout, note the arrangement of dimensions, all of which are given decimally. All internal radii, those with their centers within the large die hole, are completed as full circles with phantom lines and they are specified as jig bored holes. These accurately positioned holes provide a basis for laying out and machining the irregular die opening. Center to center dimensions which would be identical for the punch view and for the die view need not be repeated. On the punch view are given only sizes of holes to retain piercing punches and actual punch dimensions and radii not duplicated on the die view.

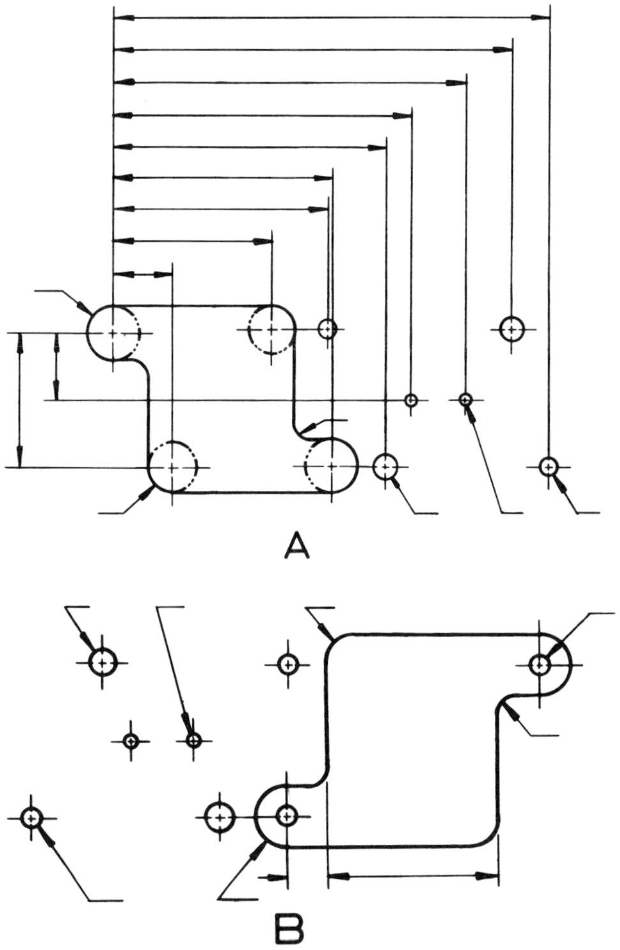

Fig. 18-17. Die view (A) and punch view (B) of a typical jig borer layout.

18-18. BLANK DEVELOPMENT

Blank development entails the designing of the flat blanks from which bent, formed, and drawn workpieces are made. The technique used is to analyze the finished workpiece and in a series of steps transform it into the flat blank from which it was stamped. The technique is called blank development. The designing of developed blanks is necessary in order for dimensions to be properly calculated and so cut-off, blanking, bending or forming dies can be designed for them. To acquire a thorough understanding of the process of blank development, it will be necessary to learn exactly what occurs when metal is bent. Fig. 18-18 illustrates the action. Note the following details:

1. That portion of the metal on the side of arc **A** has been *stretched*

2. That portion of the metal defined by arc **a** and shown solid black has been *compressed*

3. Bending may be considered to occur along the inside line **B**. This is the neutral line or axis along which neither stretching nor compression would take place.

To determine the length of material in the bent arc, it is necessary to compute the length of arc along the neutral line. For calculation purposes, the distance **B** will be considered as either 1/4, 1/3 or 1/2 of thickness **T**, depending on the size of radius **R**. Note that adding **A** (measured along the neutral axis), **C**, and **D** gives the length of the blank.

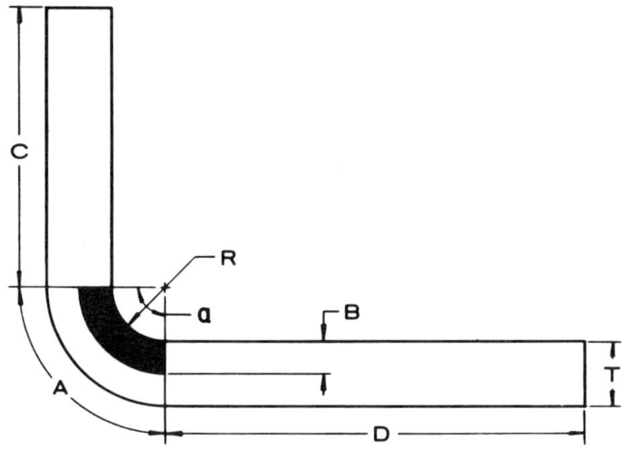

Fig. 18-18. Length of blanks is C plus D plus bend A measured along neutral axis.

18-19. BEND DEVELOPMENT

To develop a bent or formed blank **A** in an orderly way, proceed as follows:

1. Sketch a side view or section of the part, to enlarged scale if necessary, and apply dimension lines as shown

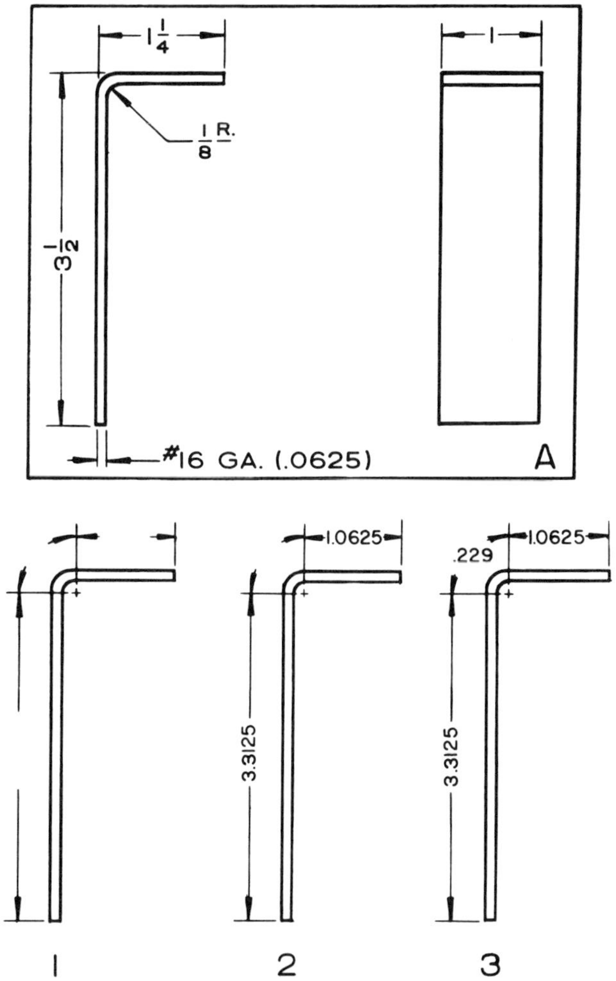

Fig. 18-19. Method of determining blank length.

2. From dimensions given on the part drawing, add the thickness of the stock to the given radius and subtract this from outside dimensions. Fill these in decimally on the sketch

3. Compute the length of arc and write it in the proper position. Note that adding all dimensions gives the over-all length of the part. (See chart in Fig. 18-21.)

(For the part under consideration the formula: $A = \left(\frac{T}{3} + R\right) \times 1.5708$ is used, as the radius is 2 times the stock thickness.)

18-20. HOLE DIMENSIONS

To establish the developed distance to a hole when it is dimensioned from the surface of the bent edge, subtract the sum of the part thickness and the inside radius from the given dimension 2, in this case. To this value, add the developed radius, taken from the sketch, and the length of the straight arm.

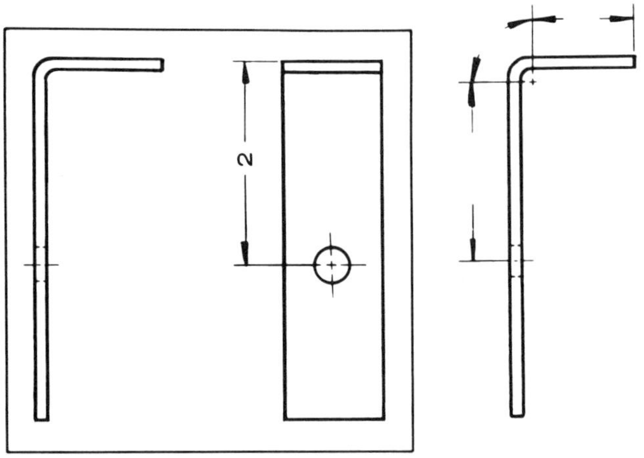

Fig. 18-20. Method of determining hole dimension for developed blank.

18-21. FORMULAS FOR BENDS

This chart provides all the formulas that you will require for developing corners of bent and formed workpieces. Observe that there are three possible conditions and that each requires the use of a different formula. In the first, the arc has a radius *smaller* than the stock thickness and appropriate formulas are given below the illustration. In the second, the arc is between one thickness and two thicknesses of stock, and in the third the arc radius is greater than twice the stock thickness. The upper formulas apply for 90-degree bends, which are the most common. The lower formulas apply for bends of one degree and they are used for computing the lengths of bends at angles other than 90 degrees. Multiply the value computed by the actual number of degrees through which the arm of the part is bent.

18-22. TYPICAL EXAMPLE OF BLANK DEVELOPMENT

At the upper portion of the illustration is shown a drawing of a part containing a number of bends. Two sections, a horizontal one marked **A – A** and a vertical one marked **B – B** are taken through the part and drawn below it. Dimensions are applied directly to the sections. Horizontal and vertical dimensions are found by addition and subtraction of part drawing dimensions. Dimensions of arcs are found by calculation, using the formulas given. After all dimensions have been applied, the developed flat blank can be easily drawn, as illustrated below the sections. Note that adding all dimensions for both sections gives the length and width of the blank, and a rectangle can be drawn which will be the length and width of the finished blank. The drawing is then completed by taking dimensions directly from the sections and the part drawing.

18-23. FORMED PART DEVELOPMENT

Although no more difficult, the development of a formed part requires more steps than one which is simply bent. The difference between bending and forming basically occurs in the straightness or curvature of the bend line. In bending, portions of the blank are raised to some angular position and the line of bend is straight. A forming operation is similar except that the line is curved instead of straight.

A formed workpiece is developed by dividing it into sections and finding the length of each section

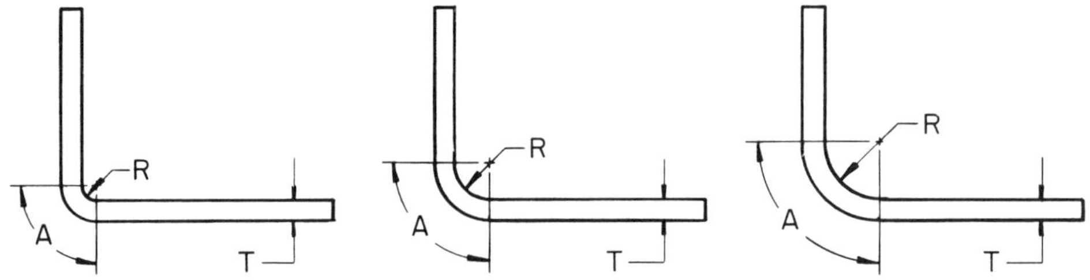

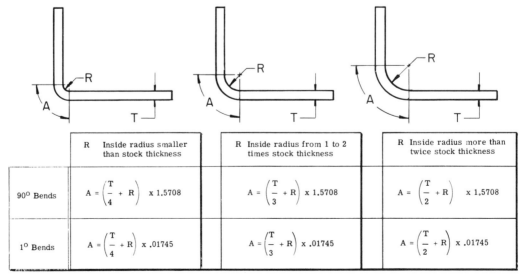

	R Inside radius smaller than stock thickness	R Inside radius from 1 to 2 times stock thickness	R Inside radius more than twice stock thickness
90° Bends	$A = \left(\frac{T}{4} + R\right)$ x 1.5708	$A = \left(\frac{T}{3} + R\right)$ x 1.5708	$A = \left(\frac{T}{2} + R\right)$ x 1.5708
1° Bends	$A = \left(\frac{T}{4} + R\right)$ x .01745	$A = \left(\frac{T}{3} + R\right)$ x .01745	$A = \left(\frac{T}{2} + R\right)$ x .01745

Fig. 18-21. Formulas for computing developed lengths of bends.

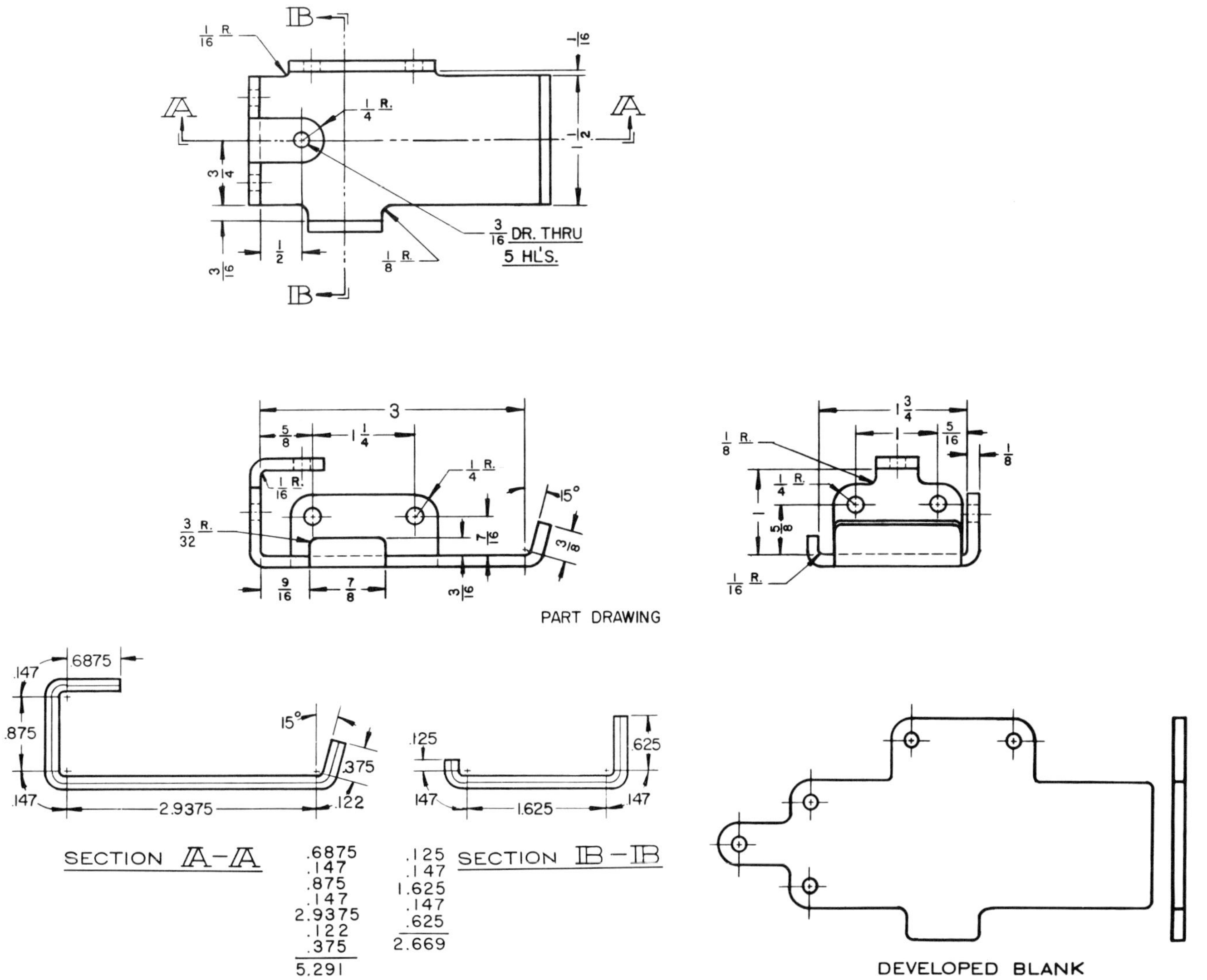

Fig. 18-22. Typical example of blank development for bent part.

by the methods employed for developing a blank for a bent part. Lengths of arcs are determined by employing the formulas given in Fig. 18-21.

At **A** is shown a drawing of a formed workpiece. Wherever the bend occurs in a straight line, it is considered as being bent and wherever the line of bend is curved, it is considered as being formed. Note, however, that any part which contains a form is called a formed part regardless of whether or not it also contains bends.

The first step in developing the flat blank is to draw an accurate layout of the top view and front view as shown at **B**. For small parts, this layout is made to an enlarged scale for increased accuracy. Next, draw evenly spaced lines to divide the formed portions of the part into a convenient number of divisions. Extend the lines so they cross both views. These are actually cutting-plane lines. Sections are to be taken through each.

Obviously, the more sections taken the more accurate will be the development. However, this should not be carried to extremes. Large workpieces may require more divisions, while small parts may need fewer divisions to achieve equal accuracy in the development.

On the front view of the layout, draw a line lengthwise to divide the bottom of the part in two. This is shown as line **X** in the illustration.

Now draw the various sections. Observe that the bottoms of the sections are revolved, that is, they are shown as the actual thickness of the part instead of being thicker as cutting-plane lines in the front and top views would appear to indicate.

Dimensions are applied directly to the sections in the same way as for ordinary bends. First apply dimensions that can be taken from the part drawing. Then scale the layout for other dimensions. Measure carefully along each cutting-plane line, taking a reading from the top of the part to the bottom where it intersects center line **X**. In the section views, this is the distance from the top of the section to the center of the horizontal bottom portion. Lengths of arcs are calculated in the same manner as for regular bends. Under each section, enter the various lengths and add them together. These will be developed lengths across the workpiece as measured along each cutting plane line.

Now determine linear or length dimensions. The length of line **X** must be measured because it is the

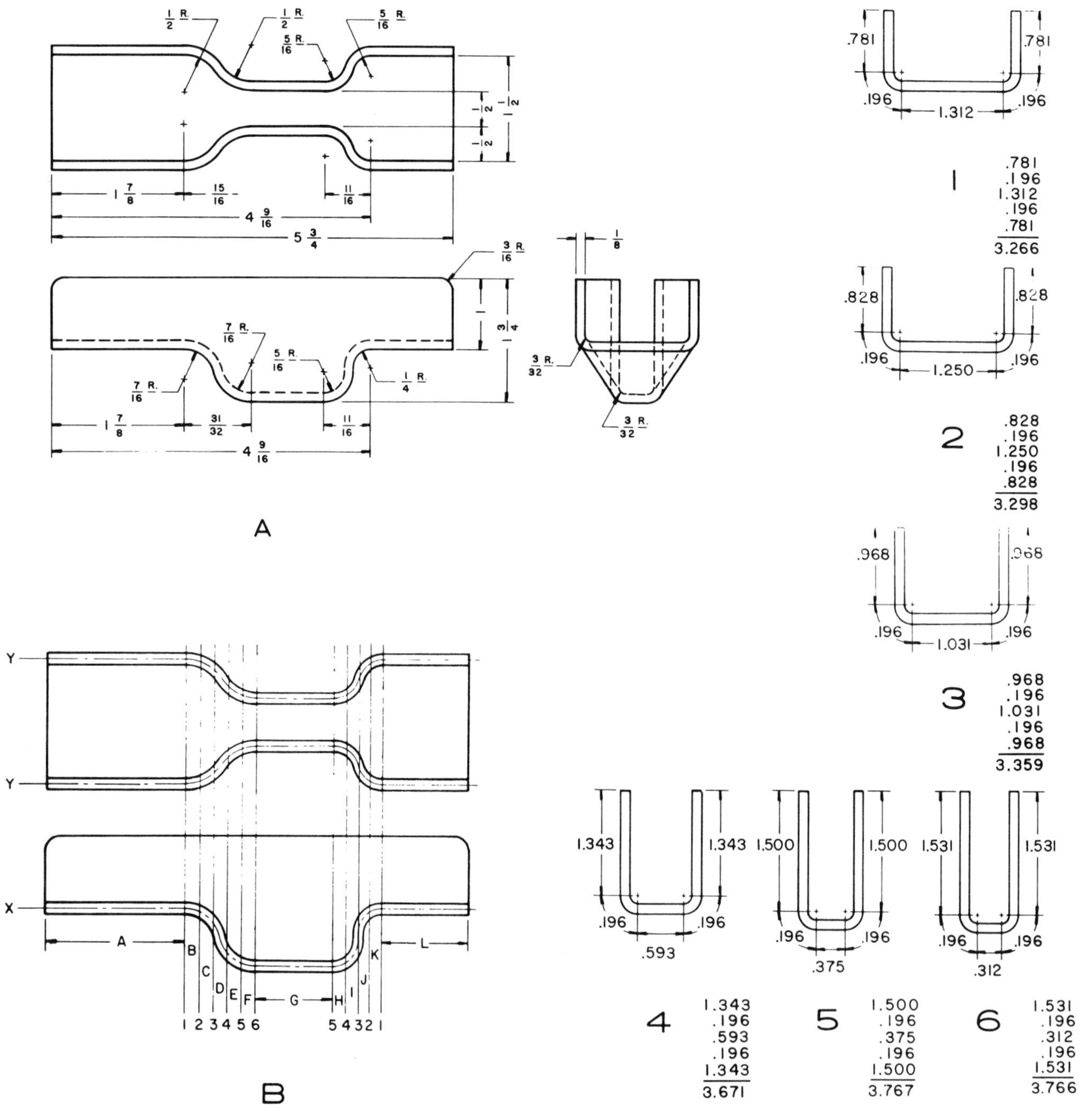

Fig. 18-23. Typical example of blank development for formed part.

same as that of the developed blank as measured along its center line.

The next step is to draw the blank layout **C**, proceeding as follows: Refer to the developed lengths of the sections and select the *longest* dimension. On a sheet, draw a center line and two light horizontal lines the same distance apart. This will be the maximum width of the developed blank. On the layout **B**, measure distance A and on the blank drawing **C**, apply two vertical lines the same distance apart. Next, measure distances B, C, D, etc., and draw vertical lines the same distances apart on the blank drawing. Observe that these distances are measured along the curve of the part and on line X, view **B**. In blank layout **C** they represent distances along the center line. Provide yourself with a diemaker's flexible steel scale. Carefully bend the scale to the contour of the line before taking a reading. Values for arcs may be calculated instead.

When you have finished laying out vertical grid lines, mark points on the vertical lines to the respective dimensions of the sections. Dimensions are marked an equal distance from the center line because the blank is symmetrical.

Several things must be done before an accurate blank layout can be produced. On another sheet, measure the formed portions of the workpiece along line Y and draw the divisions as shown on the layout

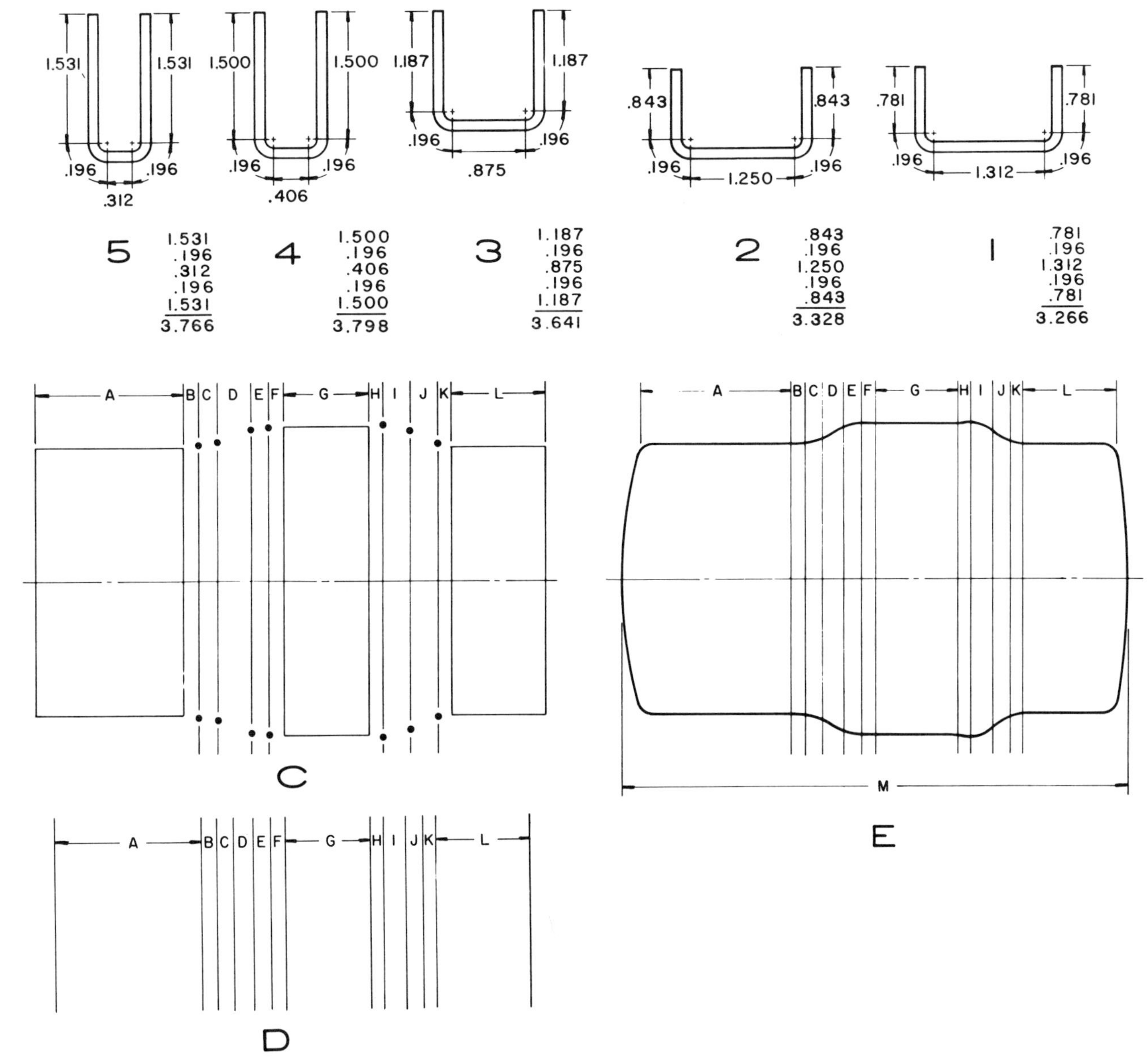

Fig. 18-23 (cont.) Typical example of blank development for formed part.

at **D**. The developed layout is then constructed as in **E**, with the edge distances A,B,C, etc. taken from layout **D**, the length of the centerline from **C**, and respective vertical widths from layout **C**.

This is necessary because the distances A, B, C, etc. along lines Y, which were originally the edges of the blank are not necessarily the same, (in some blanks they may be the same) as A, B, C, etc., measured along line X which is also the center line of the developed blank. Points are connected with a French curve.

Observe that the left and right sides are arcs with large radii instead of straight lines because of the difference in length of the center line as compared with lengths of the upper and lower edges. The small arcs at the corners are 3/16 inch, as taken from the part drawing.

Next, the drawing of the developed blank would be fully dimensioned. This drawing is used for tracing or laying out the opening in the blanking die. However, the die opening is not dimensioned on the die drawing. Instead, a print of the blank development is sent to the shop along with the die print. The diemaker will lay out and cut two trial blanks to dimensions given. These will be of the same material and gage thickness as the part drawing specifies for finished workpieces.

The forming die is always completed before the blanking die is made and one of the trial blanks would be actually formed in it. Should the formed part be accurate and within the limits established by the part drawing, the diemaker then uses the other trial blank as a template for machining the die hole. More frequently, some modification is necessary because of the way in which the metal flows in forming. The diemaker would then make two more trial blanks, adding or removing stock in an attempt to correct any irregularity. One of these would be formed and checked for accuracy. This process is continued until an accurate blank is produced.

18-24. DEVELOPING DRAWN PARTS

Before a die for producing a drawn cup or shell can be dimensioned, it is necessary to develop the form, that is, to determine the diameter of the flat blank from which the shell is to be drawn. This dimension must be calculated before the design is begun because the diameter to which the first cup can be drawn has a direct relationship with the diameter of the flat blank. Also, the blank diameter must be known before the blanking die can be laid out.

First, you must realize that blanks for drawn parts cannot be developed in the same manner as blanks for bent or formed work. In drawing, metal is gathered or moved from all sides simultaneously and the developed length will be shorter than for corresponding bent or formed workpieces. In the illustration, observe that the developed length of the bent part is 10 inches, but that the diameter of a drawn shell having the same proportions is considerably less. Therefore, for drawn shells, simply adding lengths of portions of sections will not provide an accurate dimension for the flat blank. Instead, we must determine the *areas* of various sections of the shell and compare their sum with the area of the flat blank. The two must be equal.

There are two methods of determining diameters of flat blanks for drawn shells:

1. They may be calculated mathematically. First the drawn workpiece is separated into its component rings and disks and the area of each is determined by appropriate formulas

2. Some forms are better developed by a graphical layout. This method is accurate and relatively fast when it is properly understood. We will now undertake the study of both methods.

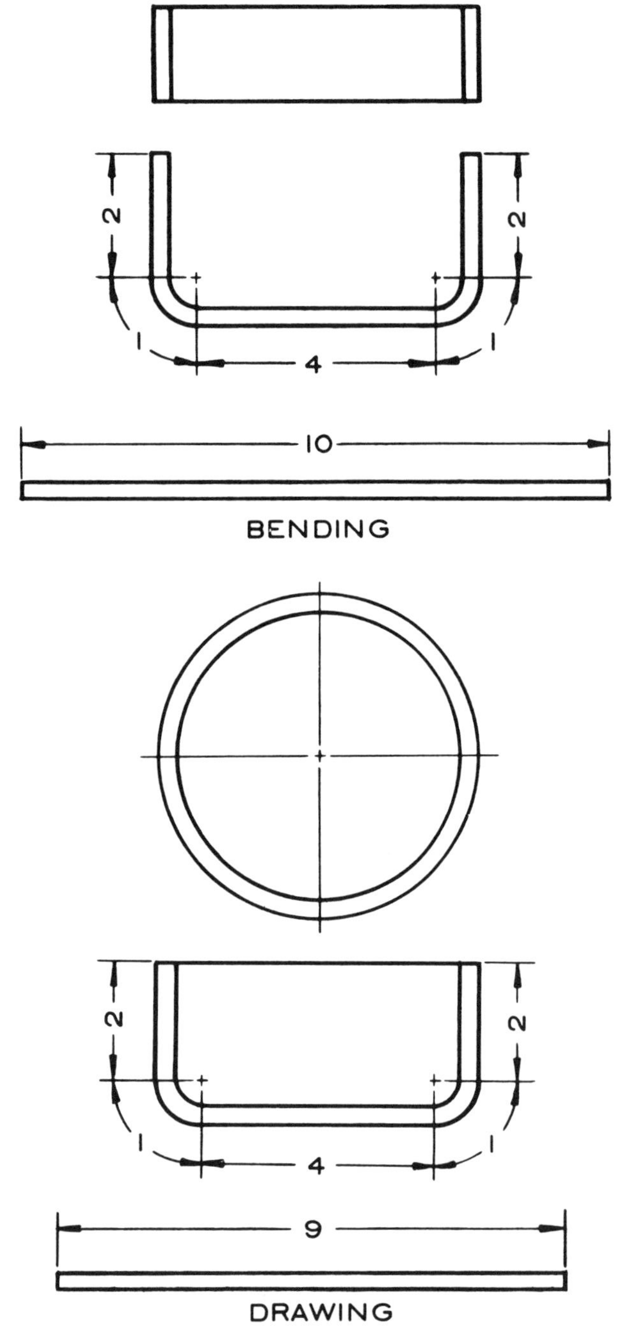

Fig. 18-24. Different amounts of material are needed for bending as compared to drawing.

18-25. MATHEMATICAL METHOD

The flanged shell at **A** is to be drawn to several diameters. Divide the shell into flat disks and ring-shaped sections. The area of each of these sections must be calculated. Their sum equals the area of the developed blank. The diameter of the blank is then found in a table of diameters, circumferences, and areas of circles in a handbook such as MACHINERY'S HANDBOOK, or it may be calculated. (The blank diameter equals the square root of the area multiplied by 1.128.)

Formulas are given for solving for the areas of each of the nine representative sections. These formulas determine the area of the neutral surface represented by a line in the center of each section and drawn along its length.

When you are confronted with the problem of developing the flat blank for a round shell, first divide it into elementary forms as shown. Then it is a simple matter to calculate the areas of each. Their sum will represent the area of the entire shell at the line drawn along the center of its thickness. The sum will also represent the area of the flat blank if no stretching occurs. The corresponding diameter is given on the drawing of the blanking die followed by the work TRY. The die maker will make a blank by hand and actually try it in the drawing die before beginning to build the blanking die.

18-26. BOTTOMS OF SHELLS

When a shell has a flat bottom, its division into component parts is a round, flat disk and the formula for calculating its area was given in the previous illustration. When the bottom is spherical in shape, different formulas must be employed, depending upon the extent of the spherical surface. This illustration lists appropriate formulas for use.

18-27. GRAPHICAL METHOD

Shells may be developed graphically, that is, by plotting the diameter of the flat blank with lines instead of computing areas mathematically. The method is an

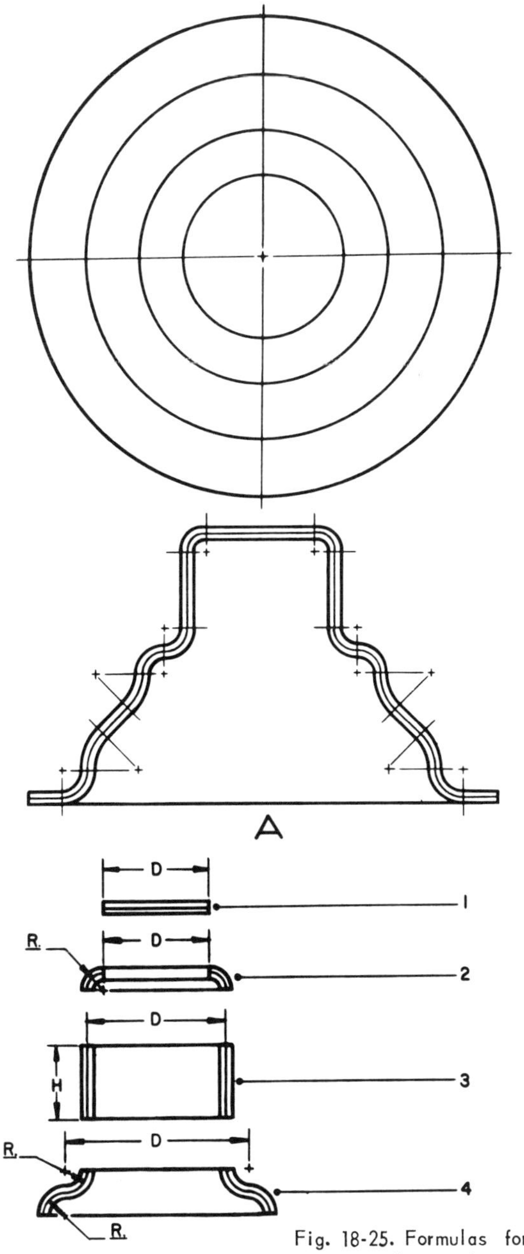

Area =

1. $\dfrac{\pi D^2}{4}$

2. $\dfrac{\pi^2 D R}{2} + 2 \pi R^2$

3. $\pi D H$

4. $\pi^2 D R$

5. $\pi (DL - 2RH)$

6. $\pi L \left(\dfrac{D + E}{2}\right)$

7. $\pi (DL - 2RH)$

8. $\dfrac{\pi^2 D R}{2} - 2 \pi R^2$

9. $\dfrac{\pi (D^2 - E^2)}{4}$

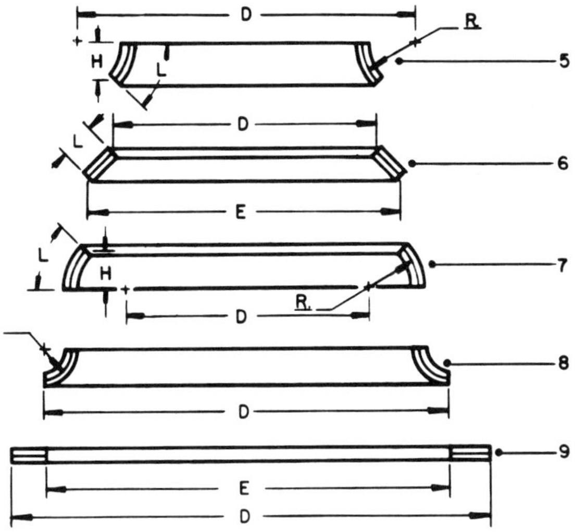

Fig. 18-25. Formulas for solving for non-stretched areas of nine representative sections of a drawn shell.

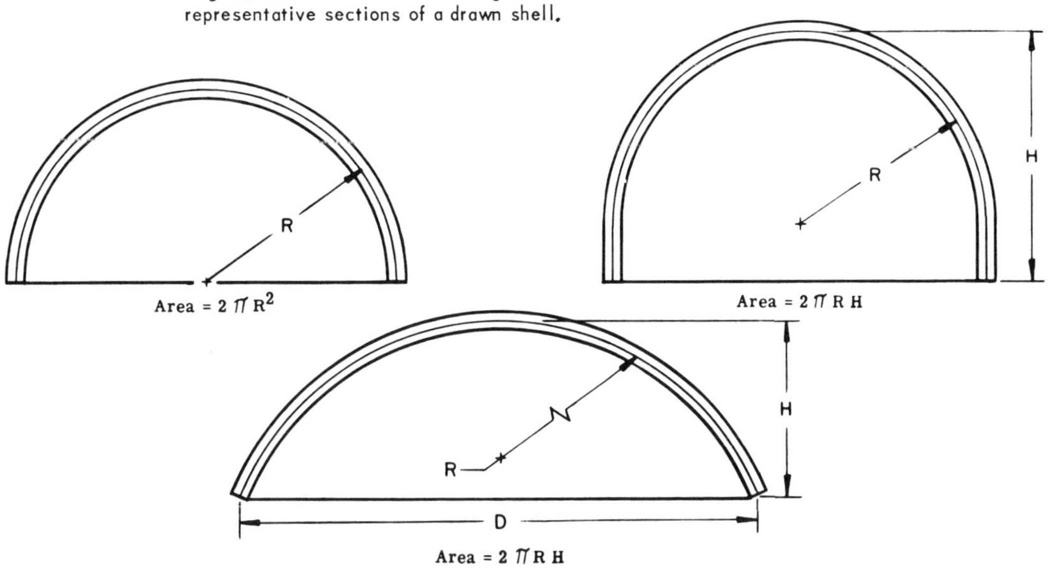

Fig. 18-26. Formulas for solving for areas of spherical shape.

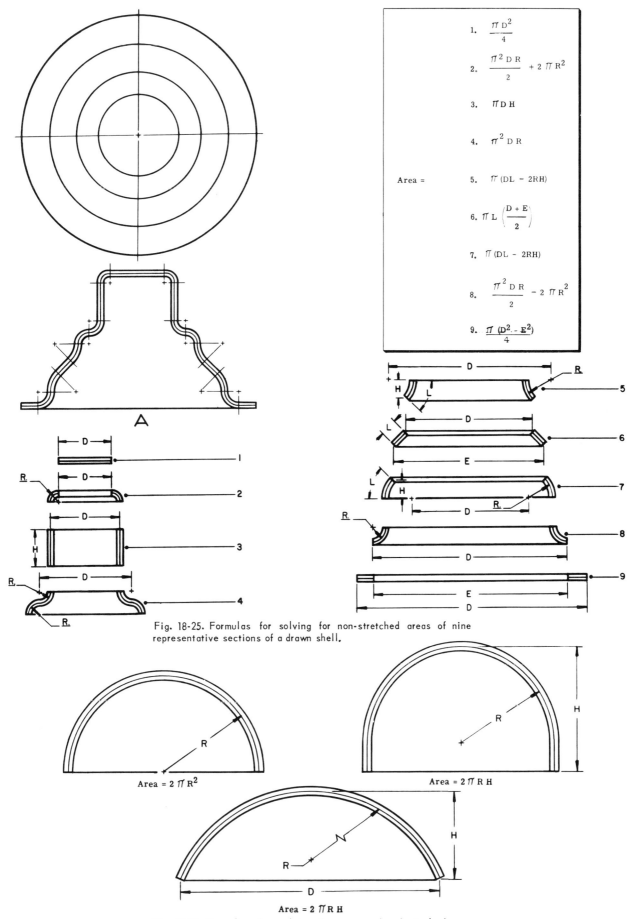

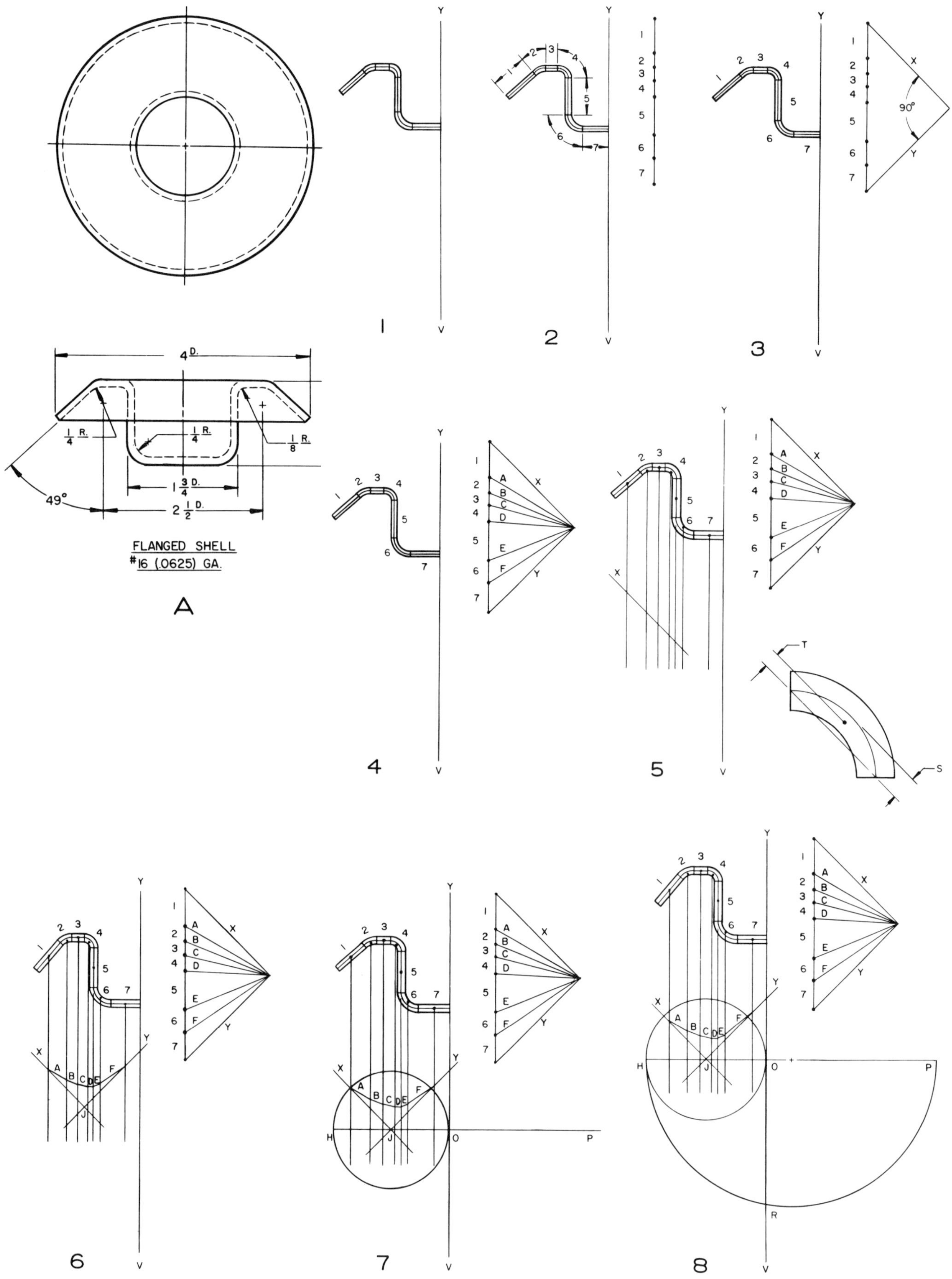

Fig. 18-27. Graphical method for obtaining radius of developed blank for a shell.

application of the theorem of Pappas and Guldinus, which states that the volume of a body generated by revolving a plane section about an axis in the same plane of the section may be found by the formula:

$V = 2\pi \times D \times A$

where: V = Volume of shell
D = Distance of the center of gravity of the section from the axis of rotation
A = Area of section.

The method is relatively simple. Let us apply it to a flanged shell **A.** Eight steps are taken in developing the blank size, as follows:

1. Draw a section through the left half of the shell and divide it into its component arcs and straight sections as shown. Also draw a longitudinal line along the center of the thickness. Next apply a centerline **Y – V** at the center of the shell. If the shell is small, draw the section to enlarged scale

2. Number each section. At the right of the view, draw a vertical line and divide it into lengths to correspond with the lengths of the shell sections 1 to 7, measured along the center of the thickness. Solve for lengths of arcs using formulas given in Fig. 18-21, or measure them along the center using a flexible diemaker's scale

3. Draw lines **X** and **Y**, each at an angle of 45 degrees

4. Extend lines from division points on the vertical line to meet the intersections of lines **X** and **Y** as shown, and label them **A, B, C,** etc.

5. Mark the center of gravity of each section of the shell as shown by heavy dots. Note that the center of gravity of rectangular sections is at the center of each section. The center of gravity of a circular arc is 1/3 of arc thickness **S,** measured from the chord. This is shown as distance **T** in the inset. Extend vertical lines downward from the center of gravity of each section. Below the section view, draw a line **X** at the same angle as line **X** in the diagram at the right

6. Set the protractor to the angle of line **A** in the diagram. With this setting, draw a line **A** below the section view. Locate it from the intersection of line **X** and the vertical line from section 1, and extend it until it intersects the vertical line from section 2. Next, set the protractor to the angle of line **B** in the diagram, and on the section view draw line **B** from the intersection of line **A** and section 2 to where it intersects the vertical line from section 3. Continue in this manner until all lines in the diagram have been transferred to below the section view and drawn to the same angular positions. Next draw line **Y** and continue it until it intersects line **X** at **J**

7. With **J** as center and with **J-O** as radius, draw a circle **O-H**. Then draw a long, horizontal centerline to cross point **J**

8. Make line **O-P** the same length as the vertical line 1 to 7 in the diagram. With the compass point on line **H-P**, and with the compass set to one-half its length, draw an arc with the left end tangent to circle **H-O.** The length of the vertical line **O-R** is one-half the diameter of the flat blank required for the shell if the section view was drawn actual size.

18-28. SQUARE AND RECTANGULAR SHELLS

Square and rectangular shells are developed by a combination of the methods described for developing blanks for formed workpieces and for round drawn shells. At the top of the illustration is shown a part drawing for a rectangular drawn shell to be developed to a flat blank. Three steps are required:

1. Sections **A – A** and **B – B** are taken through the long and short sides of the shell and dimensioned from dimensions given in the part drawing and by employing the formulas given previously

2. Section **C – C,** taken through the corner of the shell to the center of the radius, is drawn and developed by the graphical method. Radius **O-R** is called the blank radius

3. As shown at **A,** a rectangle is drawn to represent the length and width of the flat blank. Its length equals the sum of all dimensions of the sections **A – A,** and its width equals the sum of all sections at **B – B.** Centered within the rectangle is drawn an inverted top view of the finished shell. As shown at **B,** 45° lines are drawn at the corners to show the corner metal removed. Dimension **D** is made 0.9375 times the blank radius and it is measured from the center of the corner radius of the finished shell. In other words, multiply length **O-R** at Section **C – C** by 0.9375 and this figure will be dimension **D.** As shown at **C,** radii are drawn at all corners of the flat blank. Radius **E** of the blank is made the same as distance **D.**

NOTES

Notes are employed to supplement information given by views and dimensions. Individual companies may have one or more special notes that would apply particularly to the products they manufacture. In your first day in any job, you should be very observant to determine what special methods are followed. In a large plant you will be supplied with a standards book. Study this carefully for special ways of preparing drawings. In smaller plants you would do well to study a few of their drawings or blueprints.

In addition to conventional notes which apply for tool drawings, die drawings usually have one or more special notes that apply for dies only.

IDENTIFYING CALCULATED DIMENSIONS

There are three ways of identifying calculated dimensions on drawings. Above the dimension line, and immediately following the dimension, may be lettered one of the following:

1. TRY
2. DEV. (Develop)
3. APPROX. (Approximate)

Select the one in use in the plant for which the die is being designed. Where there is no particular preference, I always use 'TRY' because it describes better what is actually to be accomplished. Any of the foregoing indicates to the die maker that he is to make a sample blank and actually bend, form, or draw the metal to make sure that dimensions of the formed part are within limits established by the part drawing.

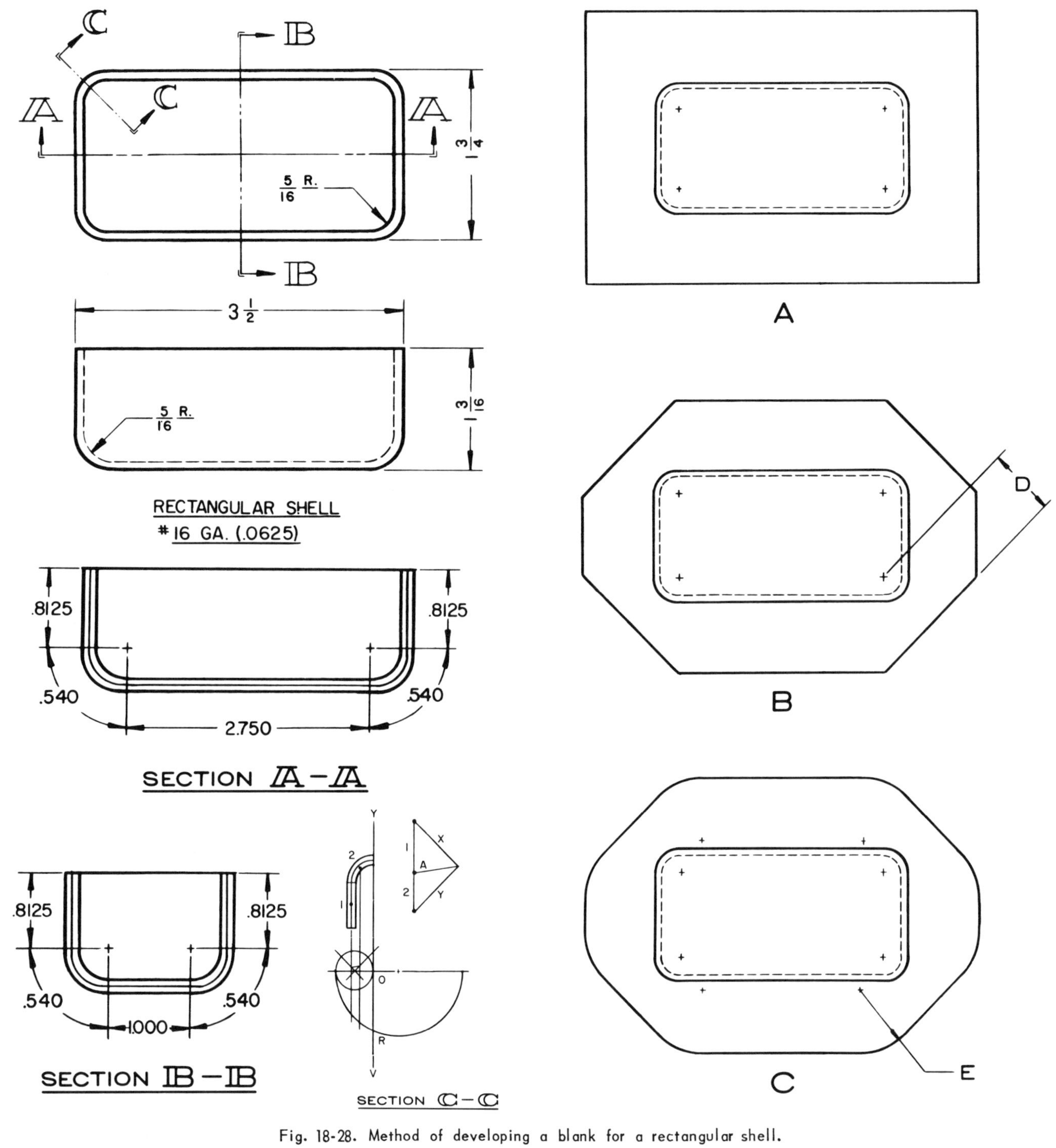

Fig. 18-28. Method of developing a blank for a rectangular shell.

18-29. TOOL IDENTIFICATION NOTE

This note gives the tool number and it directs that it is to be stamped or marked on the die. In addition, it shows the approximate location in which it is to be placed. The note is written by lettering the word, 'STAMP' or 'MARK', and applying the tool number directly underneath. A leader points to the finished pad on the die set where the note is to be applied.

18-30. HARDEN AND GRIND NOTE

On assembly drawings, the fact that a component is to be hardened and ground is indicated by applying the abbreviation H. & G. above the leader of the detail number as at **A**. When a part is detailed individually, the abbreviation H. & G. is lettered immediately follow- the part and material. It is applied under the views of the detail drawing, as shown at **B**.

WORK TO PART PRINT

This note is applied to drawings which do not contain dimensions for those portions of the punches and die blocks which pertain to the blank or workpiece. The note informs the die maker that he is to obtain all such dimensions directly from the part print.

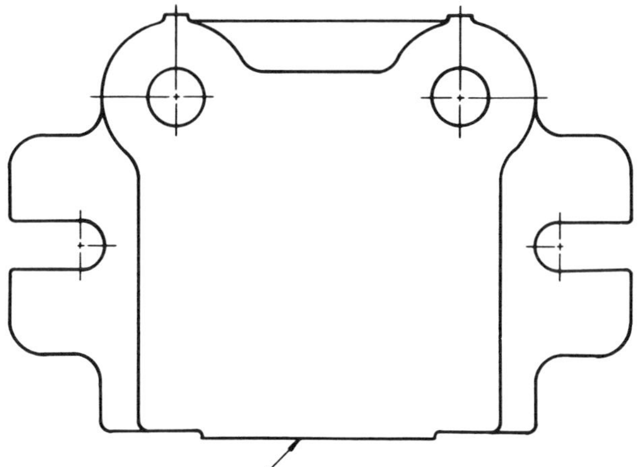

Fig. 18-29. Manner in which a tool number note is placed on a drawing.

NO ALLOWANCE HAS BEEN MADE FOR SPRING-BACK

This note is lettered on most bending and forming dies and it informs the die maker that spring-back cannot be tolerated in the workpiece. After the die has been built, he is to try it out and make appropriate corrections. Spring-back varies between 1/4 degree and 2 degrees and it is the amount that a bent or formed portion of a workpiece deflects backward after bending or forming. For some parts, spring-back may not be objectionable and the note is then omitted.

DIE MUST PRODUCE PART TO PRINT

This note is applied to drawings of dies which are to form a complete part. It is a clear indication to the die maker that he is to try out the die after it has been built and apply all necessary adjustments so that workpieces will meet tolerances indicated on the part print.

WORK TO TEMPLATE

When contours of a part are very irregular, this note may be applied on the drawing and a leader is added to indicate the contour against which a template is to be used for checking. Dimensions for making the template are ordinarily taken directly from the part drawing. A template is made from sheet steel. Lines are scribed accurately to given dimensions and unwanted portions are then cut away. As work progresses, components are checked against the template until contours match perfectly.

DEVELOP BLANK

This note may be applied on layouts of bending, forming, or drawing dies, or a calculated dimension

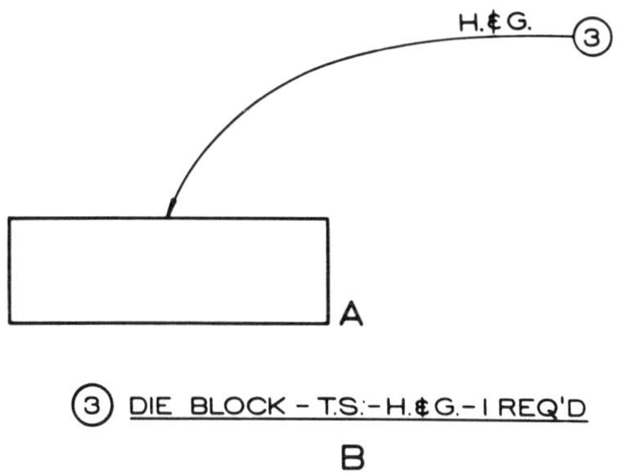

Fig. 18-30. Manner in which a harden and grind note is placed on an assembly drawing (A) and below the views of a detail drawing (B).

may be given followed by the work 'TRY' as previously explained. Both have the same meaning. The bending, forming, or drawing die is to be made first before the blanking die is built. Sample blanks are to be cut by hand and formed to establish final dimensions of the blanking die opening.

ALLOW FOR TRIMMING OPERATION

This note is applied on layouts of drawing dies and it means that sufficient material is to be provided for a trimming operation to follow the drawing or forming operation. After blank development, this allowance is added for determining final dimensions of the blanking die opening.

SHAVE ENTIRE CONTOUR

This note specifies that a shaving die is to be designed in addition to a blanking die and that suitable extra material must be allowed for the shaving operation.

READING A PART DRAWING

From the foregoing it should be apparent that in reading a part drawing the die designer must pay particular attention to notes because many of them, even short ones, are important far in excess of the amount of space they occupy. For instance, the note MUST BE FLAT on a drawing often means that a compound die must be designed instead of a progressive die which might be decided upon if the note were absent. The note MUST BE SQUARE applied to the edge of a drawn or formed workpiece means that the edge must be trimmed in a trimming die or by some other means and that material must be provided for this operation. Therefore, all notes should be considered analytically before a design decision is made.

Section 19

THE BILL OF MATERIAL

Considerable knowledge, and/or experience, is necessary for completing the bill of material. The bill of material, or BOM, determines the materials from which the various die members are to be constructed. These decisions can influence success or failure of the completed die in operation. In addition, the designer must know the names of the various components that make up the die and he must know which materials have proved successful for similar members in previous work. Also, he must be familiar with standard and purchased components, the sizes in which they are available, and the conventional methods of listing them. Filling in the bill of material column, therefore, is an important element in the preparation of a die drawing and a die designer must become proficient at it.

CONTENTS

The bill of material is a list of the following:

1. Rough sizes of blocks of steel or other materials that will be required for making special components of the die
2. Standard parts which are to be taken from stock
3. Parts to be purchased specifically for the job. These are standard components that are not ordinarily carried in stock.

The bill of material, then, is a complete list of every component in the tool or die.

19-1. DIE DRAWING

The final step in preparing a die drawing is to fill in the bill of material column. On drawings for many die shops, the bill of material is placed at the upper right corner and it is read downward as shown. For others, it is located at the lower right corner and it is read upward.

The bill of material is divided into five columns, usually. When extending the printed lines to complete columns, draw them exactly the same width. If the sheet has one or two horizontal lines printed for the first details, make all succeeding boxes the same height. When the sheet does not have starting lines, space horizontal lines 5/16 inch apart. First extend the left vertical line and mark 5/16 inch spaces along its length with small dividers. Then draw horizontal lines, and complete the columns by extending vertical lines. Draw as many horizontal lines as there are detail numbers in the assembly, and no more.

In the first column marked DET., the abbreviation for detail, write detail numbers, beginning with number one and continuing for the total number of details in the assembly. The second column is marked REQ'D, the abbreviation for required. This lists the number of parts needed for each detail number. Fill in these amounts very carefully because it is easy to miss parts that do not show in every view. The third column marked PART NAME lists the name of each component. Learning names of parts is just as important as learning to draw them. They form an important portion of the language of the die designer which you are now learning to understand. In the fourth column, MAT., are listed the materials from which the parts are to be made. For parts available commercially, this space indicates whether they are to be purchased or are available from stock. In the final column. SPECIFICATIONS, stock sizes are listed, as well as catalog numbers of purchased items.

There are two methods of specifying stock for special parts:

1. An allowance is applied for machining wherever it is required
2. All parts are listed exact size, and the stock cutter applies extra stock where it is required for machining.

About three-quarters of all plants use the first method, and the remaining quarter use the second method. Note, however, that when exact sizes are given, (method number 2), a note is usually printed to that effect near the bill of material column.

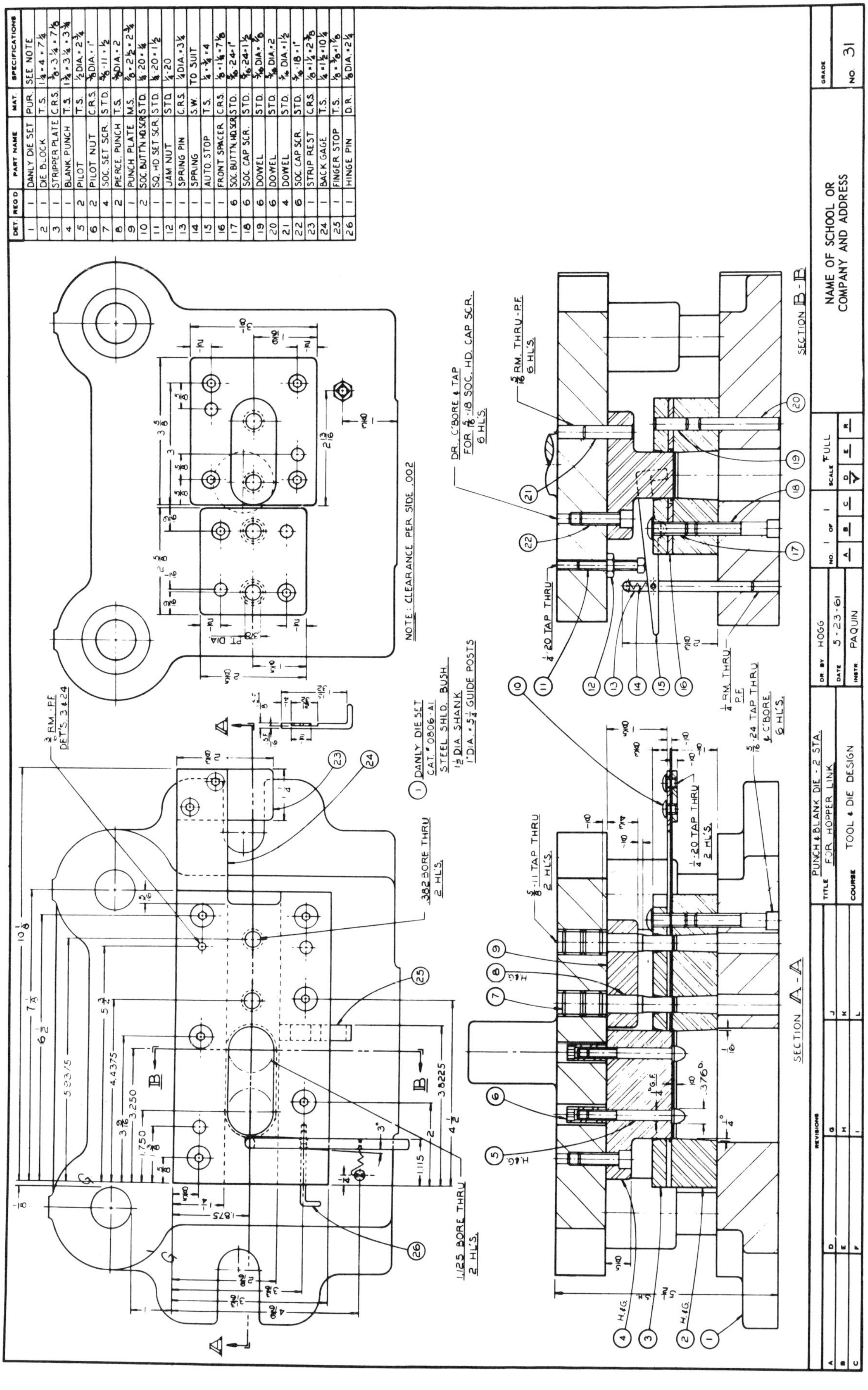

DET.	REQ'D	PART NAME	MAT.	SPECIFICATIONS
1	1	DANLY DIE SET	PUR.	SEE NOTE
2	1	DIE BLOCK	T.S.	1¼ × 4 × 7¼
3	1	STRIPPER PLATE	C.R.S.	3/8 × 3¼ × 7⅛
4	1	BLANK. PUNCH	T.S.	1¾ × 3¼ × 3¾
5	2	PILOT	T.S.	½ DIA. × 2¾
6	2	PILOT NUT	C.R.S.	3/8 DIA. × 1"
7	4	SOC. SET SCR.	STD.	5/8-11 × ½
8	2	PIERCE. PUNCH	T.S.	3/8 DIA. × 2
9	1	PUNCH PLATE	M.S.	7/8 × 2½ × 2¾
10	2	SOC. BUTT'N HD. SCR.	STD.	¼-20 × ¼
11	1	SQ. HD. SET SCR.	STD.	¼-20 × 1½
12	1	JAM NUT	STD.	¼-20
13	1	SPRING PIN	C.R.S.	¼ DIA. × 3¼
14	1	SPRING	S.W.	TO SUIT
15	1	AUTO. STOP	T.S.	¼ × ¾ × 4
16	1	FRONT SPACER	C.R.S.	⅛ × 1¼ × 7⅛
17	6	SOC. BUTT'N HD. SCR.	STD.	5/16-24 × 1"
18	6	SOC. CAP SCR.	STD.	5/16-24 × 1½
19	6	DOWEL	STD.	5/16 DIA. × ½
20	6	DOWEL	STD.	5/16 DIA. × 2
21	4	DOWEL	STD.	5/16 DIA. × 1½
22	6	SOC. CAP SCR.	STD.	5/16-18 × 1"
23	1	STRIP REST	C.R.S.	⅛ × 1¼ × 2⅜
24	1	BACK GAGE	T.S.	¼ × 1½ × 10¼
25	1	FINGER STOP	T.S.	⅛ × 3/8 × 1⅛
26	1	HINGE PIN	D.R.	⅛ DIA. × 2¼

Fig. 19-1. Bill of material is shown in upper right hand corner of this die drawing.

19-2. TYPES OF COMPONENTS

Referring once again to the representative die which has formed the basis for these studies, we find that eleven types of components are to be listed in the bill of material, as follows:

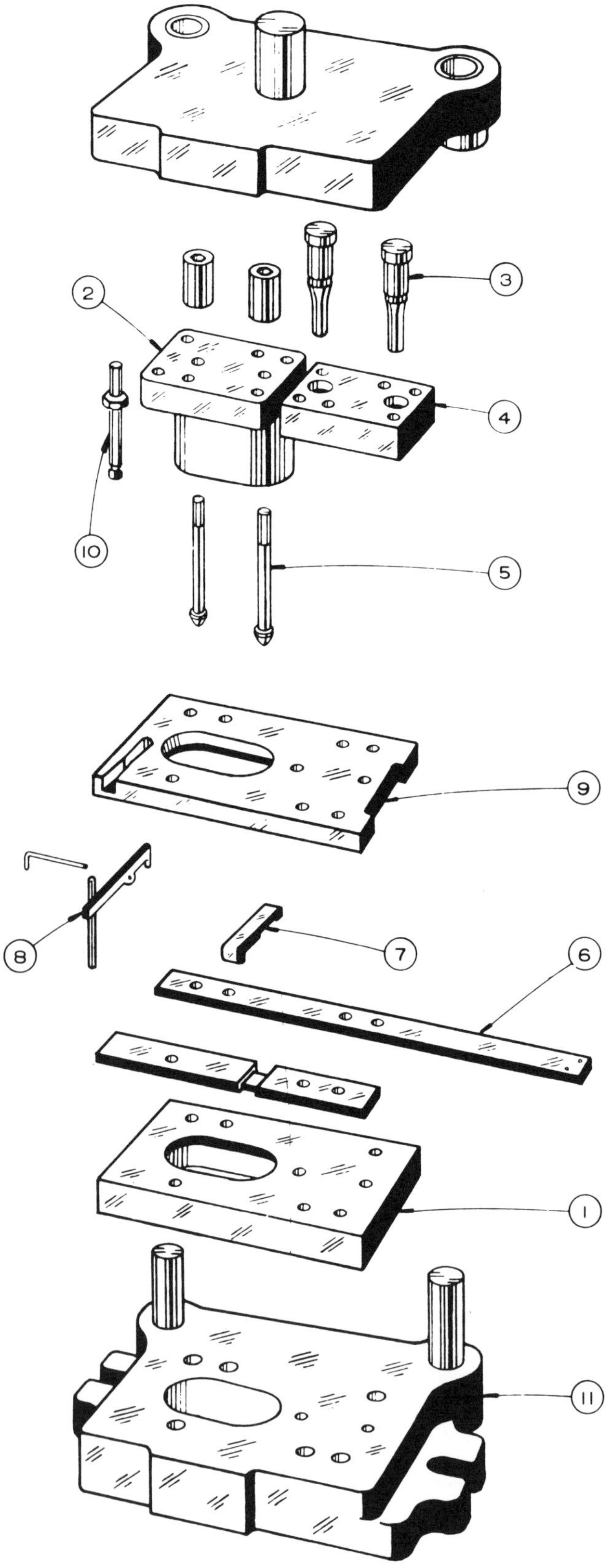

Fig. 19-2. Types of components that are listed in the bill of material.

1. Die Block
2. Blanking Punch
3. Piercing Punch
4. Punch Plate
5. Pilot
6. Back Gage
7. Finger stop
8. Automatic Stop
9. Stripper
10. Fasteners
11. Die Set.

Each of these classifications would have other die components associated with it by function. Illustrations to follow will show exactly how each of the eleven basic components should be listed. In addition, listings for related die parts are included so your understanding will be complete.

19-3. DIE BLOCK

This shows how the first component, the die block, is listed in the bill of material. In addition the representative bill of material lists those members which could properly be associated or identified with the die block. Observe that many words are abbreviated and compare the abbreviations with the following list which corresponds to the illustrated list:

1. DIE BLOCK
2. DIE SECTION
3. INSERT
4. COMPOSITE SECTION
5. DIE BUTTON
6. FORMING BLOCK
7. DRAWING RING
8. HORN
9. SPACER.

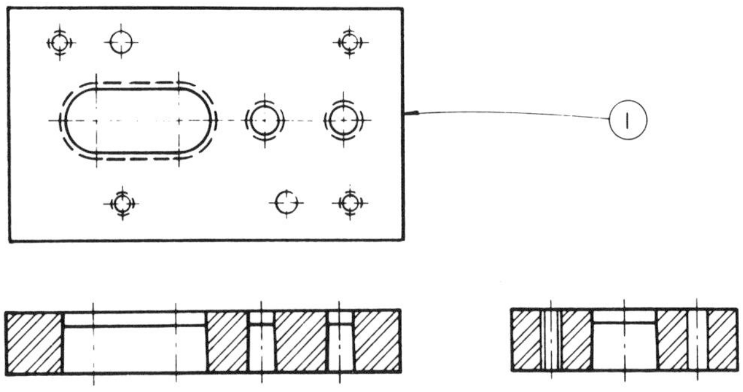

DET.	REQ'D	PART NAME	MAT.	SPECIFICATIONS
1	1	DIE BLOCK	OH.T.S.	1 1/4 X 4 X 4 5/8
2	4	DIE SECTION	T.S.	1 1/4 X 3 X 5
3	2	INSERT	H.C.H.C.	1/2 X 1 X 1 1/4
4	6	COMP. SECT.	PUR.	SEE NOTE
5	4	DIE BUTT'N	T.S.	1 1/4 DIA. X 1 1/2
6	1	FORM. BLOCK	T.S.	1 1/2 X 3 X 5 1/4
7	1	DRAW. RING	T.S.	8 DIA. X 2 1/2
8	1	HORN	T.S.	3 DIA. X 6 1/4
9	2	SPACER	M.S.	3/4 X 4 X 7

Fig. 19-3. How die block members are listed in the bill of material.

19-4. BLANKING PUNCH

The punch produces a blank, or portion of a blank, and it is the male member or component of any die. The punch is positioned above the die block in all but a few types of inverted dies. It derives its name from the type of die in which it is applied. The punch of a blanking die is called a blanking punch. The punch of a trimming die is called a trimming punch, etc. Following are listed seventeen types of punches to correspond with seventeen types of dies. In the illustration, note carefully how the names of punches are abbreviated in the bill of material column.

1. BLANKING PUNCH
2. CUT OFF PUNCH
3. TRIMMING PUNCH
4. SHAVING PUNCH
5. BROACHING PUNCH
6. BENDING PUNCH
7. FORMING PUNCH
8. DRAWING PUNCH
9. CURLING PUNCH
10. EXTRUDING PUNCH
11. SWAGING PUNCH
12. PARTING PUNCH
13. NOTCHING PUNCH
14. LANCING PUNCH
15. STAKING PUNCH
16. COINING PUNCH
17. BURNISHING PUNCH.

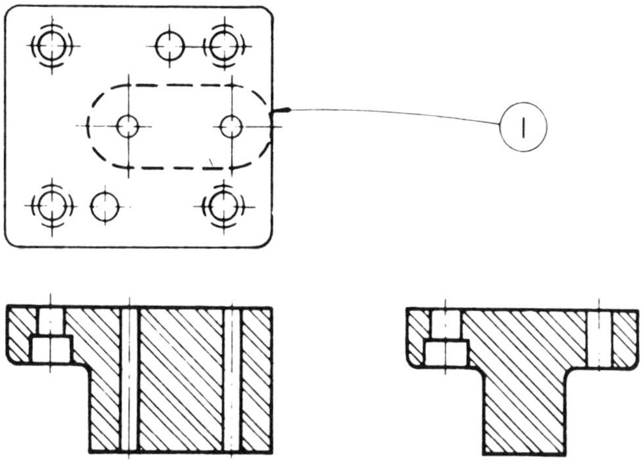

DET.	REQ'D	PART NAME	MAT.	SPECIFICATIONS
1	1	BLANK. PUNCH	O.H.T.S.	1 3/4 x 3 x 4 1/2
2	1	C'OFF PUNCH	T.S.	1 3/4 x 4 x 6
3	1	TRIM. PUNCH	T.S.	8 1/2 DIA. x 2
4	1	SHAVE. PUNCH	T.S.	6 DIA. x 1 3/4
5	1	BROACH.PUNCH	T.S.	1 3/4 x 2 x 3
6	1	BEND. PUNCH	T.S.	3 x 4 1/2 x 5
7	1	FORM. PUNCH	T.S.	2 x 4 x 6 3/4
8	1	DRAW. PUNCH	T.S.	9 DIA. x 3
9	1	CURL. PUNCH	T.S.	10 DIA. x 4 1/4
10	1	EXTR. PUNCH	T.S.	1 1/2 DIA. x 2
11	1	SWAGE. PUNCH	T.S.	1 DIA. x 2 1/8
12	1	PART. PUNCH	T.S.	1 1/2 x 3 x 7
13	1	NOTCH. PUNCH	T.S.	1 3/4 x 2 x 3
14	1	LANCE. PUNCH	T.S.	1 DIA. x 3
15	2	STAKE. PUNCH	T.S.	3/4 x 1 x 1 3/4
16	1	COIN. PUNCH	H.S.S.	1 1/2 DIA. x 2
17	1	BURN. PUNCH	T.S.	3 DIA. x 3 3/8

Fig. 19-4. Seventeen types of punches and how each would be listed on a bill of material.

19-5. PIERCING PUNCH

A piercing punch pierces holes in blanks or strips. Such holes are ordinarily round, but they may have any contour. This illustration shows how a piercing punch is listed in the bill of material. In addition, five components that may be associated with the piercing punch are also listed:

1. PIERCING PUNCH
2. PERFORATING PUNCH
3. HOLECUTTING PUNCH
4. COUNTERSINK PUNCH
5. QUILL
6. KEY.

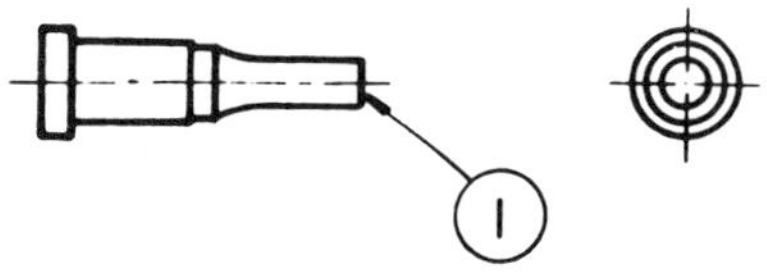

DET.	REQ'D	PART NAME	MAT.	SPECIFICATIONS
1	2	PIERCE. PUNCH	T.S.	3/4 DIA. x 1 3/4
2	4	PERF. PUNCH	D.R.	3/32 DIA. x 1 5/8
3	1	H'L'CUT PUNCH	T.S.	3 1/4 DIA. x 1 3/4
4	1	C'SINK PUNCH	T.S.	1/2 DIA. x 1 3/4
5	2	QUILL	T.S.	3/4 DIA. x 1 3/4
6	1	KEY	M.S.	1/4 x 1/2 x 1

Fig. 19-5. How piercing punches and their associated components are listed in a bill of material.

19-6. PUNCH PLATE

A punch plate is a plate or block used to retain piercing punches. A simple square plate may retain a

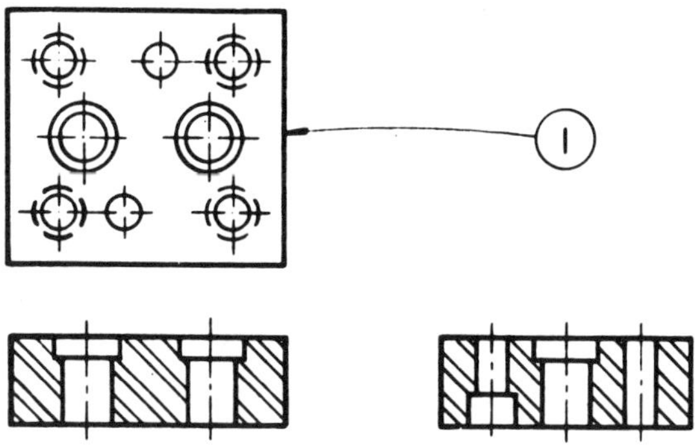

DET.	REQ'D	PART NAME	MAT.	SPECIFICATIONS
1	1	PUNCH PLATE	M.S.	3/4 x 8 x 10
2	1	BACK. PLATE	T.S.	1/4 x 3 x 4 1/4
3	1	SPACER	C.R.S.	1 x 4 x 6 1/2

Fig. 19-6. How a punch plate, backing plate and spacer are listed in a bill of material.

single punch, while a large punch plate may contain hundreds of precision-bored holes for retaining a corresponding number of piercing punches. As the following list indicates, backing plates and spacers are closely associated with punch plates.

1. PUNCH PLATE
2. BACKING PLATE
3. SPACER.

19-7. PILOTS

Pilots provide a method of accurate location of the strip. Associated with a pilot would be its pilot nut and in one type of spring-backed pilot, one or more detents. A locating plug, or locating pin and diamond pin, would perform the same function of precision location for some types of secondary-operation dies. Following is a list of details related to the pilot:

1. PILOT
2. PILOT NUT
3. DETENT
4. LOCATING PLUG
5. LOCATING PIN
6. DIAMOND PIN.

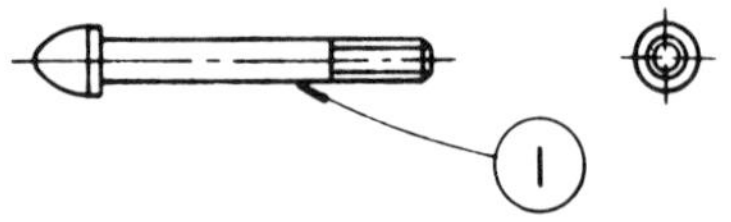

DET.	REQ'D	PART NAME	MAT.	SPECIFICATIONS
1	2	PILOT	T.S.	3/8 DIA. X 1 3/4
2	2	PILOT NUT	C.R.S.	1/2 DIA. X 1
3	1	DETENT	D.R.	3/16 DIA. X 3/8
4	1	LOC. PLUG	T.S.	1 1/2 DIA. X 4 1/8
5	1	LOC. PIN	T.S.	5/8 DIA. X 1 5/8
6	1	DIAMOND PIN	T.S.	5/8 DIA. X 1 5/8

Fig. 19-7. How pilot details are listed in a bill of material.

19-8. BACK GAGE

In its travel through the die, the strip is positioned against the back gage. Associated with the back gage is the front spacer and strip support. When the strip must be centered, an equalizing device is designed for positioning it exactly over the center of the die hole. For secondary operations, gages or nests are employed for locating the workpieces. Here is a list of details related to the back gage:

1. BACK GAGE
2. FRONT SPACER
3. STRIP SUPPORT
4. EQUALIZING BAR
5. GAGE
6. NEST.

19-9. FINGER STOP

The finger stop positions the strip for the first stroke or operation. Related to it would be the stock pusher which keeps the strip registered against the back gage. Some finger stops serve the dual purposes of stop and stock pusher. A stop block is used in cut off dies.

1. FINGER STOP
2. STOCK PUSHER
3. STOP BLOCK

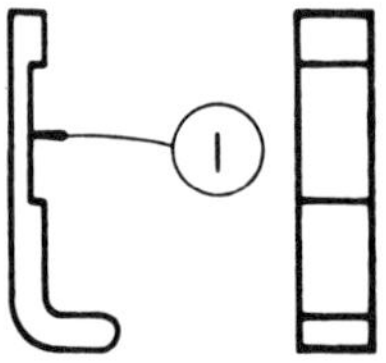

DET.	REQ'D	PART NAME	MAT.	SPECIFICATIONS
1	1	FINGER STOP	C.R.S.	1/8 X 3/8 X 1 7/8
2	1	STOCK PUSH.	T.S.	1/8 X 5/8 X 2
3	1	STOP BLOCK	T.S.	1 1/2 X 2 X 2 1/8

Fig. 19-9. How a finger stop, stock pusher and stop block are listed in a bill of material.

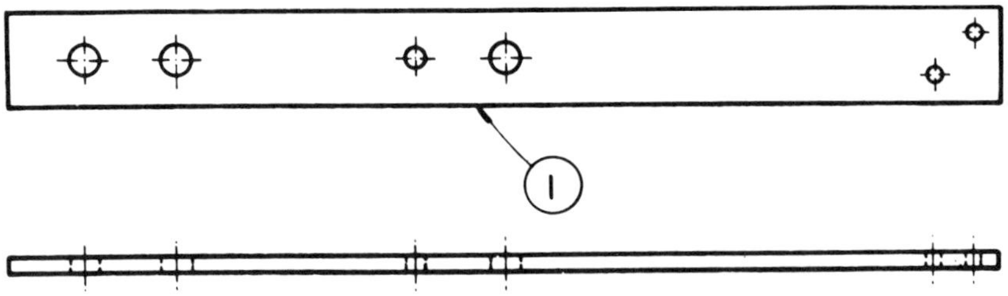

DET.	REQ'D	PART NAME	MAT.	SPECIFICATIONS
1	1	BACK GAGE	T.S.	1/8 X 1 X 8
2	1	FRONT SPACER	C.R.S.	1/8 X 1 X 5 1/4
3	1	STRIP SUPPORT	C.R.S.	1/8 X 1 1/4 X 3
4	1	EQUAL. BAR	C.R.S.	1/4 X 1 X 5
5	2	GAGE	T.S.	1/4 X 1 3/4 X 3
6	1	NEST	T.S.	1/4 X 4 X 6 1/2

Fig. 19-8. How details related to the back gage are listed in the bill of material.

19-10. AUTOMATIC STOP

Dies designed for hand feeding of strip are provided with an automatic stop. Large blanking dies, run in slow moving presses, are provided with a stop pin instead. Six parts are included in the conventional automatic stop assembly:

1. AUTOMATIC STOP
2. FULCRUM PIN
3. SPRING PIN
4. SPRING
5. SQUARE-HEAD SET SCREW
6. JAM NUT
7. STOP PIN.

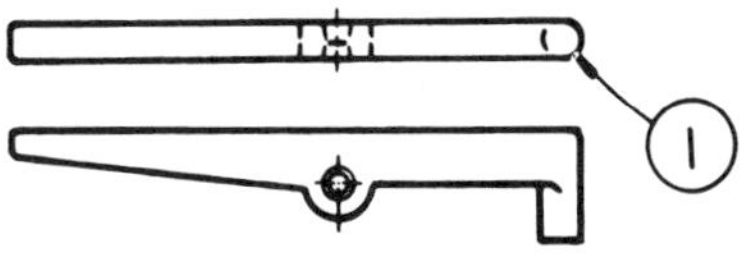

DET.	REQ'D	PART NAME	MAT.	SPECIFICATIONS
1	1	AUTO. STOP	T.S.	1/4 x 7/8 x 4
2	1	FULCRUM PIN	D.R.	1/8 DIA. x 3
3	1	SPRING PIN	C.R.S	1/4 DIA. x 3 1/4
4	1	SPRING	S.W.	TO SUIT
5	1	SQ.HD.SET SCR.	STD.	1/4-20 x 2 1/4
6	1	JAM NUT	STD.	1/4-20
7	1	STOP PIN	D.R.	1/4 DIA. x 2

Fig. 19-10. How parts of an automatic stop assembly and a stop pin are listed in a bill of material.

19-11. STRIPPER PLATE

A stripper, whether of the solid type or the spring-operated variety, is the die member that strips or removes the material from around punches. Associated in function with it are ejectors, knockouts, and their accessories, as shown by the following list:

1. STRIPPER PLATE
2. BLANK HOLDER
3. PRESSURE PAD
4. EJECTOR
5. KNOCKOUT PLATE
6. KNOCKOUT BLOCK
7. KNOCKOUT COLLAR
8. KNOCKOUT ROD
9. PRESSURE PIN
10. GUIDE PIN
11. GUIDE BUSHING
12. DIE SPRING.

19-12. FASTENERS

This shows the method of listing the most frequently used types of fasteners. Observe that fasteners are marked STD., or Standard, in the Material column. This means that they are carried in stock. In the Specifications column, screw sizes are noted by giving the diameter, followed by the number of threads per inch, and the length. Stripper bolt sizes are noted by giving the body diameter, followed by the length from under the head to the shoulder. Dowels are listed by giving the diameter followed by length. Sizes of nuts are given by listing the diameter of the engaging bolt and the number of threads per inch. Sizes of washers are given by listing the diameter of the engaging bolt. Sizes of rivets are given by listing the diameter followed by length. Compare the following list with the abbreviations in the illustration:

1. SOCKET CAP SCREW
2. SOCKET SET SCREW
3. SOCKET LOCK SCREW
4. SOCKET BUTTON HEAD SCREW
5. SOCKET FLAT HEAD SCREW
6. STRIPPER BOLT
7. DOWEL
8. HEXAGON NUT
9. JAM NUT
10. WASHER
11. RIVET – FLAT HEAD.

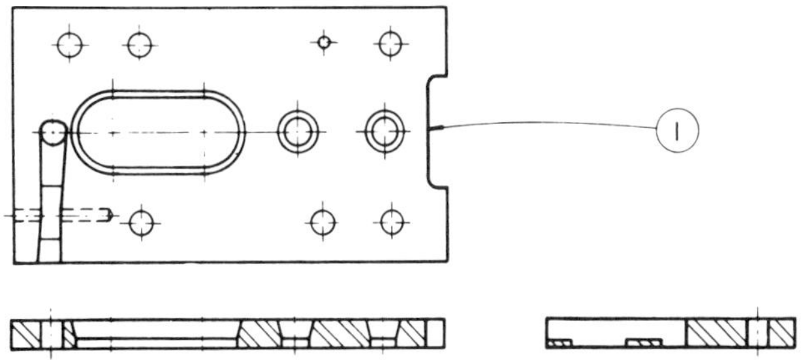

DET.	REQ'D	PART NAME	MAT.	SPECIFICATIONS
1	1	STRIP. PLATE	M.S.	1/2 x 6 x 8
2	1	BLANK HOLD.	T.S.	3/4 x 8 1/2 x 10
3	1	PRESS. PAD	T.S.	1 x 2 1/2 x 4
4	1	EJECTOR	T.S.	3/4 x 1 3/4 x 3
5	1	KN'OUT PLATE	M.S.	3 1/2 DIA. x 5/8
6	1	KN'OUT BLOCK	M.S.	4 DIA. x 3 1/8
7	1	KN'OUT COLLAR	C.R.S	1" DIA. x 3/4
8	1	KN'OUT ROD	C.R.S	1/2 DIA. x 7 3/16
9	2	PRESS. PIN	C.R.S.	1/4 DIA. x 2 1/8
10	2	GUIDE PIN	D.R.	1/2 DIA. x 4 1/4
11	2	GUIDE BUSH.	T.S.	1" DIA. x 7/8
12	4	"STD" SPRING	PUR.	#05-YH-10

Fig. 19-11. How the stripper and details associated with it are shown in a bill of material.

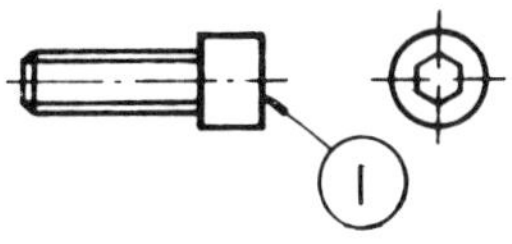

DET.	REQ'D	PART NAME	MAT.	SPECIFICATIONS
1	4	SOC.CAP SCR.	STD.	3/8-16 x 2 1/4
2	2	SOC.SET SCR.	STD.	1/2-13 x 3/4
3	2	SOC.LOCK SCR.	STD.	1/2-13 x 1/4
4	4	SOC. BTT'N. HD.	STD.	5/16-18 x 1 1/2
5	2	SOC.FL.HD.SCR.	STD.	3/8-16 x 2
6	4	STRIPPER BOLT	STD.	1/2 DIA. x 2 1/2
7	2	DOWEL	STD.	3/8 DIA. x 1 1/2
8	4	HEX. NUT	STD.	1/2-13
9	4	JAM NUT	STD.	3/8-16
10	2	WASHER	STD.	1/2 DIA.
11	4	RIVET- FL. HD.	STD.	1/4 DIA. x 1/2

Fig. 19-12. Listing fasteners in a bill of material.

19-13. DIE SET

There is usually not enough room to list all the die set information required. The reader of the drawing is therefore directed to a note on the drawing itself in which specifications of the die set and its component parts are given. In some types of dies, a side cam or scrap cutter may be fastened to the die set and these are listed here. Both are usually made of water-hardening tool steel, given simply as the abbreviation, T.S.

1. DIE SET
2. SIDE CAM
3. SCRAP CUTTER.

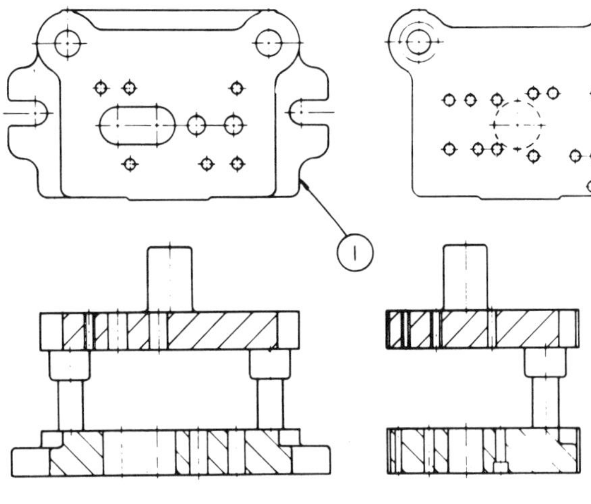

DET.	REQ'D	PART NAME	MAT.	SPECIFICATIONS
1	1	DIE SET	PUR.	SEE NOTE
2	2	SIDE CAM	T.S.	2 × 3 1/2 × 7
3	1	SCRAP CUT.	T.S.	1 3/4 × 2 1/2 × 3

Fig. 19-13. How the die set, side cam and scrap cutter are listed in a bill of material.

COLUMNS

Let us now consider the main divisions of information contained in the bill of material. As shown in previous illustrations, the bill of material is divided into five columns:

1. DET. (Detail)
2. REQ'D (Required)
3. PART NAME
4. MAT. (Material)
5. SPECIFICATIONS.

DETAIL NUMBER (Column 1)

The first column, DET., lists numbers that have been assigned to the components of the die. Observe these rules:

1. One number identifies all identical parts. For example, all 5/16 dia. by 1¼ inch long dowels would have the same number. It is lettered only once on the drawing, enclosed within a detail circle with a leader pointing to one of the components.

2. All parts that are different, however slightly, are given individual numbers. For example, a ¼ dia. by 1 inch long dowel would have one number, while a ¼ dia. by 1¼ inch long dowel would be given a different number.

3. Purchased assemblies, although composed of several parts, are given a single detail number.

4. Weldments are given a single detail number.

NUMBER REQUIRED (Column 2)

Before specifying the number required, study all the views to determine exactly how many of the particular component are required. In many cases a single view will not show the total number and other views must be considered as well.

PART NAME (Column 3)

In listing the name of a part, give the general name first, followed by any word or abbreviation qualifying it. For example, a right-hand V block would be listed as V BLOCK – R.H. Note that the name, V Block, is listed first, followed by the abbreviation for Right-Hand because the 'hand' qualifies or limits the type of V Block that is specified.

It is frequently necessary to shorten the part name because of the limited space available. For instance, when specifying a key, we may turn to the Lodding catalog and find a suitable one listed as Plain Fixture Key. In addition to this rather long name, we must add the word Lodding, which makes the part name entirely too long for the space provided. The name is better shortened to LODDING KEY. This is sufficient identification when given in conjunction with the catalog number listed in the SPECIFICATIONS column.

19-14. MATERIAL (Column 4)

In the material column is listed the material from which the component is to be made. The name of the material is usually abbreviated because of limited space. For dies, the most commonly employed materials are tool steel and machine steel.

Blanks for making cutting members of dies are sawed from bars of tool steel. At least 1/8 inch of material should be allowed per side for machining. This is measured from the outside of the bar to final size. Shading in the illustration shows the depth of this layer of decarburized steel and iron oxide, or scale. If not removed previously, the hardening operation would leave soft spots and produce surface cracks.

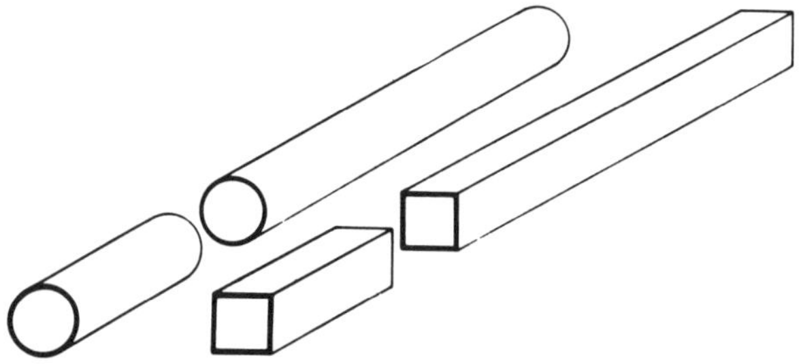

Fig. 19-14. Shaded areas of these tool steel bars denote outside layer of decarburized steel, iron oxide, or scale and are removed by machining in making cutting members of dies.

19-15. DIRECTION OF GRAIN

Blanks for making punches and small die blocks are preferably cut with the grain of steel at right angles to cutting faces to reduce hardening distortion. In the illustration, the grain runs in the direction of the parallel lines, always along the length of steel bars. Cutting faces **A** will be at right angles to the grain in finished punches. Of course, positioning cutting faces across the grain is possible only for small components within commercial tool steel sizes.

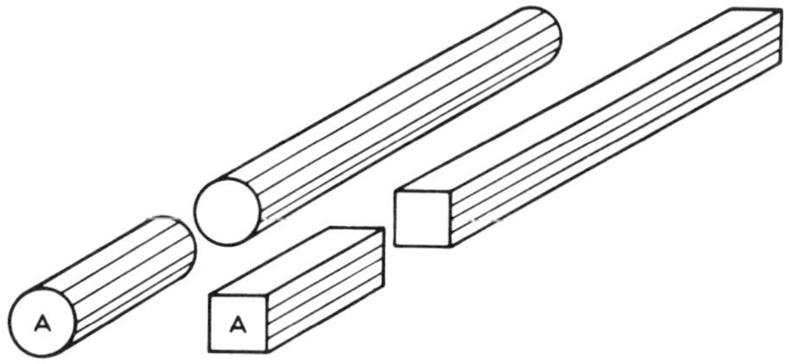

Fig. 19-15. Direction of grain is parallel to the axes of these steel bars and is at right angles to the cutting faces of punches made therefrom.

19-16. LARGE CUTTING MEMBERS

When ordering tool steel for large die blocks, consider that distortion is greatest lengthwise with grain direction and stock should be ordered so distortion will be kept to a minimum. Die hole contour will govern the decision. The rule is: Place the longest dimension of a narrow die hole opening across the grain. Distortion in the slot at **A** will be more extensive than if it is located across the grain as at **B**. This means that swelling or shrinking distortion will shorten or lengthen the slot at **A** more than it would be affected if positioned across the grain as at **B**.

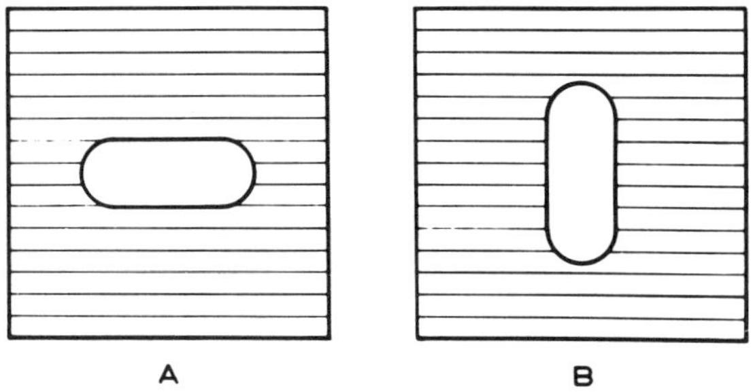

Fig. 19-16. Less distortion will be experienced if longest dimension of die hole is positioned across the grain as at (B).

19-17. AVOIDING CRACKS IN HARDENING

Cracks tend to occur *along* the grain of the material. When sharp corners are present in the die hole, order the stock so the grain will be *across* the corners as at **A**, and not in line with them as at **B**. Sharp corners provide a focal point for fractures and correct application of grain direction will help to eliminate this source of trouble.

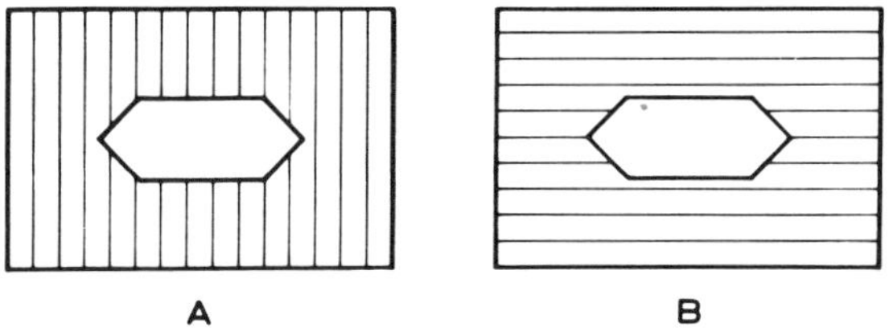

Fig. 19-17. Since cracks tend to occur along the grain of the material, best position of die hole with sharp corners is shown at (A).

TOOL STEELS

Tool steel is specified for numerous die components and it may be well to discuss briefly the most commonly used types. They are:

1. Water Hardening Tool Steel
2. Oil Hardening Tool Steel
3. Air Hardening Tool Steel
4. High Carbon-High Chromium Tool Steel
5. High Speed Steel
6. Shock Resisting Tool Steel
7. Hot Work Die Steel.

1. Water Hardening Tool Steel

As its name indicates, water hardening tool steel is hardened by quenching it in water after it has first been heated to proper hardening temperature. It is employed for parts which can be ground after hardening. Water hardening tool steel is subject to distortion in the hardening process and it should not be specified for parts with internal contours that must remain accurate and which cannot be ground after hardening.

2. Oil Hardening Tool Steel

Oil hardening tool steel contains chromium and it is quenched in oil in the hardening process. Warpage or distortion is much less than for corresponding grades of water hardening steels. When accurate surfaces cannot be ground after hardening, and anticipated production rates are average, oil hardening tool steel should be specified. The abbreviation is O.H.T.S.

3. *Air Hardening* Tool Steel

Air hardening tool steel need not be quenched in either oil or water for hardening to occur. After heating beyond the critical range, it is simply exposed in air until cool. Air hardening tool steels have minimum warpage and this is combined with greater toughness and wear resistance than corresponding grades of oil or water hardening steels.

4. High Carbon, High Chromium Tool Steel

High carbon, high chromium steels have about the same properties as air hardening steels except that they posses a greater degree of resistance to wear. High carbon-high chromium steels should be specified for die parts when long production runs are anticipated.

5. High Speed Steel

The outstanding quality of high speed steel is its toughness, combined with a high degree of wear resistance. It should be specified for weak die parts such as frail inserts, small diameter punches, and the like. Another excellent application is in dies for cold working, coining and upsetting of metal.

6. Shock Resisting Tool Steel

Stock resisting tool steel contains a smaller amount of carbon and therefore it is tougher than other types. It is employed for heavy cutting and forming operations where steels with a higher carbon content would be subject to breakage.

7. Hot Work Die Steel

These steels are employed in dies designed for forming hot materials because they possess high resistance to softening under heat.

TYPE OF STEEL	Non Deforming Properties	Safety in Hardening	Toughness	Wear Resistance	Machineability	Resistance to Softening Under Heat
WATER HARDENING TOOL STEEL	POOR	FAIR	GOOD	FAIR	BEST	POOR
OIL HARDENING TOOL STEEL	GOOD	GOOD	FAIR	FAIR	GOOD	POOR
AIR HARDENING TOOL STEEL	BEST	BEST	FAIR	GOOD	FAIR	FAIR
HIGH CARBON - HIGH CHROME	BEST	BEST	POOR	BEST	POOR	FAIR
HIGH-SPEED STEEL	GOOD	BEST	BEST	GOOD	FAIR	GOOD
SHOCK RESISTING TOOL STEEL	FAIR	GOOD	BEST	FAIR	FAIR	FAIR
HOT WORK DIE STEEL	BEST	BEST	BEST	FAIR	FAIR	GOOD

Fig. 19-18. Guide for the proper selection of tool steel.

19-18. PROPERTIES OF TOOL STEELS

This chart provides a guide for the selection of the proper tool steel for any given application. Observe that seven types are listed in the first column. In the second column is given the non-deforming property for each type. This is an important factor for many die blocks and punches. Other important properties are given in succeeding columns to aid in selecting the type of tool steel having exactly the properties desired.

S.A.E. NUMBERING SYSTEM

The S.A.E. system of numbering steel was originated by the Society of Automotive Engineers and it is widely used. You should be familiar with the system because the material of many stampings, as given on part drawings, is often specified by S.A.E. number. Following is a brief summary:

LOW CARBON STEELS, S.A.E. 1006 to 1015

This group of steels weld readily, but they do not machine freely, especially when smooth surfaces are required.

LOW CARBON STEELS, S.A.E. 1016 to 1030

This group of low carbon steels generally go under the general name of machine steel. They can be readily welded, easily machined, and have sufficient strength for most tooling applications. When hard surfaces are required, they may be case-hardened, either by carburizing or by cyaniding.

MEDIUM CARBON STEELS, S.A.E. 1033 to 1052

These are sometimes called low carbon tool steels. They can be hardened a certain amount by heating and quenching in oil. For example, S.A.E. 1040 will harden to about Rockwell C-45. They machine readily and they can be welded if allowed to cool slowly to avoid cracking.

HIGH CARBON STEELS, S.A.E. 1055 to 1095

High carbon steels go under the general name tool steel and they are specified when good wear characteristics are required. When purchased, tool steels are in the soft state and they machine fairly well. Hardening is accomplished by heating and quenching. After hardening, any further machining must be accomplished by grinding. Tool steel should not be welded.

SPECIFICATIONS (Column 5)

The final step in filling in the bill of material is to give the specifications of the various components. For square and rectangular bars, this consists of giving the thickness, width, and length. For round bars, the diameter is given, followed by the length. Standard parts such as fasteners are listed by giving the diameter, followed by the number of threads per inch and the length. For purchased components, the catalog number is given. For small springs, the note TO SUIT is applied. When there is not enough space to list the specifications, the words SEE NOTE are lettered in the box in the bill of material and specifications are given in a note on the drawing.

Section 20

TYPES OF DIES

In previous sections of this book, you have learned the elements that go into building a complete die. In addition, you have learned how to design a die, that is, how to arrange those elements – the die block, punches, stops, gages, die set, and all the others into a functioning die. Also, the preparation of a die drawing was explained in detail so your comprehension would be a thorough one.

The next step is to learn about the types of dies, their function, and how they operate. There are twenty types of dies and each is distinct and different from all the other types. However, as you study the descriptions to follow, observe how the elements that you learned previously are applied and reapplied with suitable modifications to adapt them for each particular job to be performed.

20-1. BLANKING DIES

A blanking die produces a blank by cutting the entire periphery in one simultaneous operation. Three advantages are realized when a part is blanked:

1. Accuracy. The edges of blanked parts are accurate in relation to each other
2. Appearance. The burnished edge of each blank extends around its entire periphery on the same side.
3. Flatness. Blanked parts are flat because of the even compression of material between punch and die cutting edges.

The inset at **A** shows a material strip ready to be run through a blanking die. At **B** is shown the top view of the die with punches removed. The section view at **C** shows the die in open position with the upper punch raised to allow advance of the strip against the automatic stop. At **D** the die is shown closed with a blank pushed out of the strip.

Blanking dies may produce plain blanks as shown in inset **E**, but more frequently holes are pierced at one station and the part is then blanked out at the second station. Such dies are called "pierce and blank" dies and they have been described fully in preceding sections of the book.

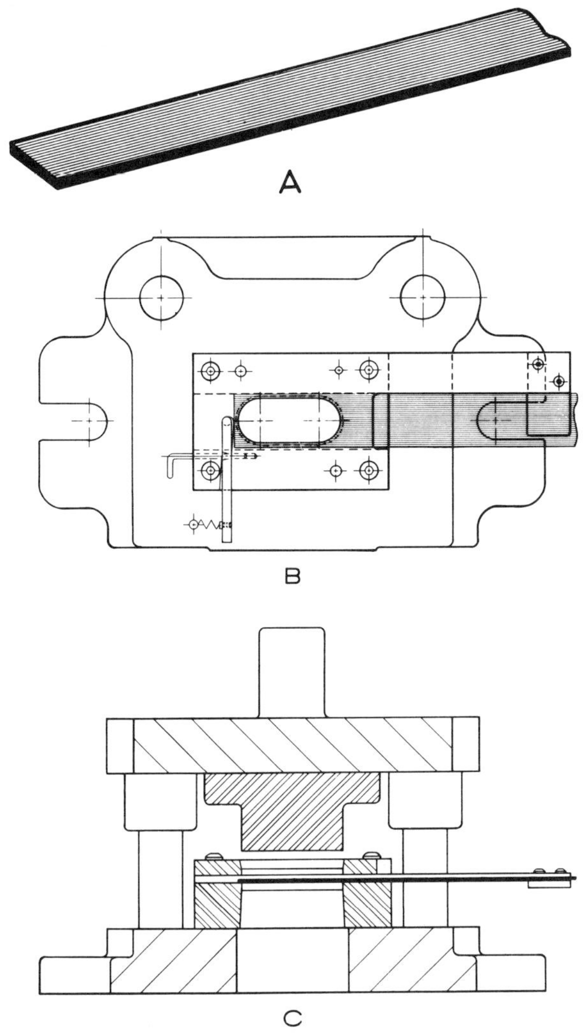

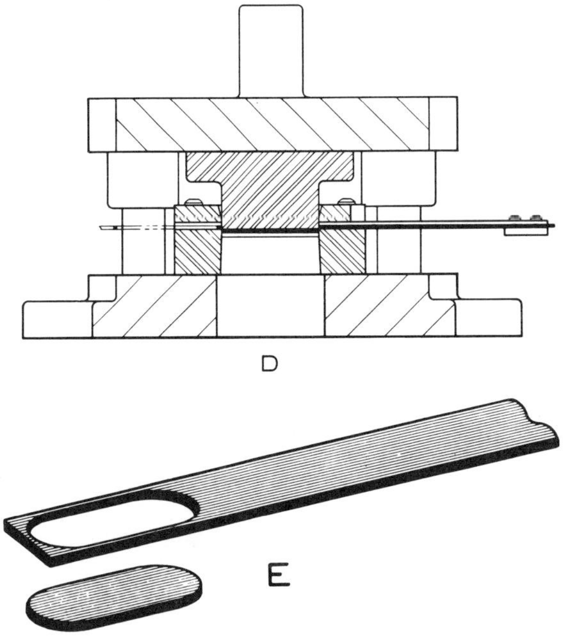

Fig. 20-1. Blanking die.

20-2. CUT OFF DIES

The basic operation of a cut off die consists in severing strips into short lengths to produce blanks. The line of cut may be straight or curved, and holes or notches or both may be applied in previous operations. Cut off dies are used for producing blanks having straight, parallel sides because they are less expensive to build than blanking dies. In operation, the material strip **A** is registered against stop block **B**. Descent of the upper die causes the cut off punch **C** to separate the blank from the strip. Stop block **B** also guides the punch while cutting occurs to prevent deflection and excessive wear on guide posts and bushings. A conventional solid stripper is employed.

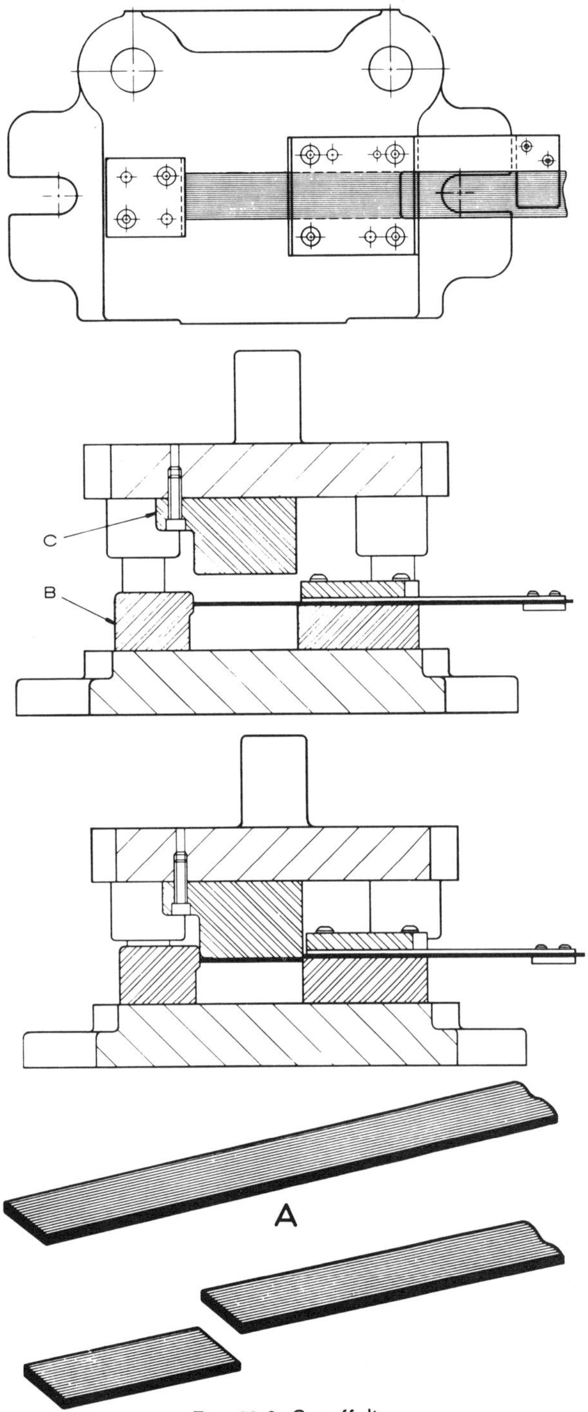

Fig. 20-2. Cut off die.

20-3. COMPOUND DIES

In a compound die, holes are pierced at the same station as the part is blanked, instead of at a previous station as is done in a pierce and blank die. The result is greater accuracy in the blank. Whatever accuracy is "built in" the die will be duplicated in every blank produced by it.

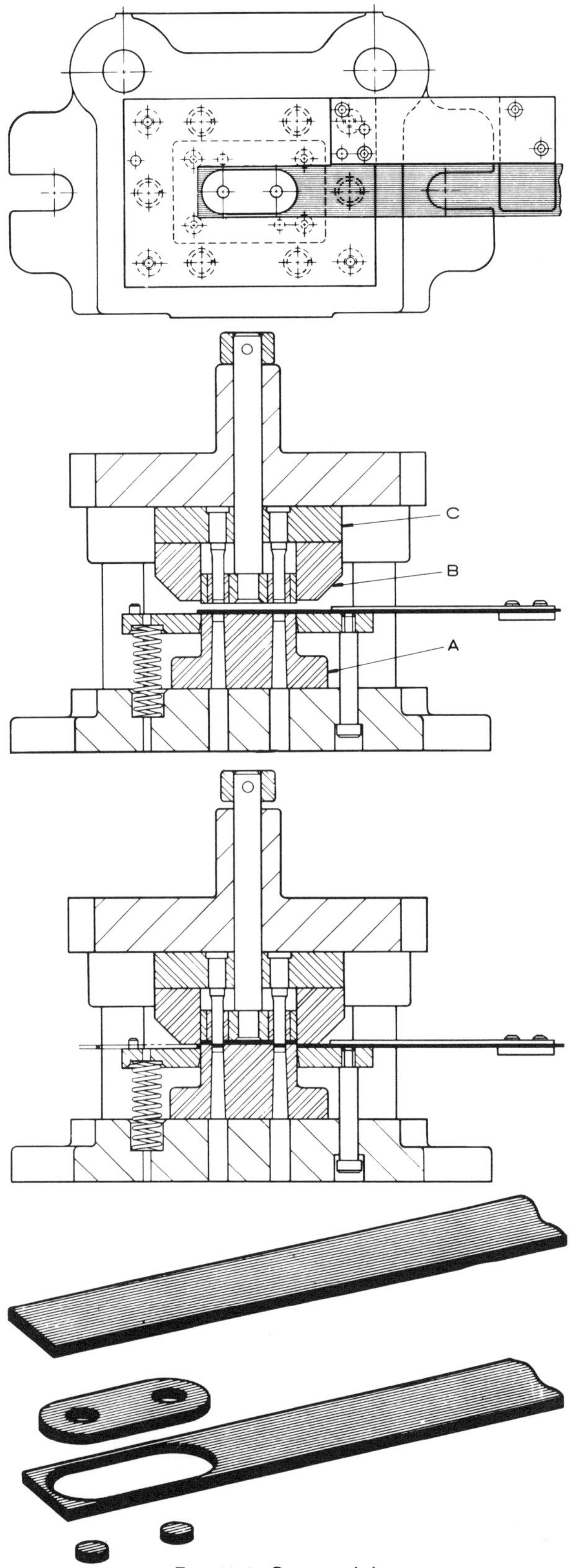

Fig. 20-3. Compound die.

Compound dies are inverted dies. The blanking punch **A** is located on the die holder of the die set instead of being fastened to the punch holder as in conventional dies, and it is provided with tapered holes for disposal of slugs.

The die block **B** is fastened to the punch holder and it is backed up by a spacer **C** which retains piercing punches. A positive knockout removes the blank from within the die cavity near the top of the press stroke. A spring stripper removes the material strip from around the blanking punch.

Although most compound dies are designed for producing accurate, flat blanks, they are occasionally used for producing blanks that are too large for production in more than one station. Since all operations are performed at the same station, compound dies are very compact and a smaller die set can be applied.

20-4. TRIMMING DIES

Trimming dies cut away portions of formed or drawn workpieces that have become wavy and irregular. This condition occurs because of uneven flow of metal during forming operations. Trimming removes this unwanted portion to produce square edges and accurate contours.

The illustration at **A** shows a flanged shell after the drawing operation. A trimming die is required to trim the irregular edge of the flange. The shell is placed over a locating plug **B** and descent of the upper die causes the scrap ring to be cut from around the flange. After trimming, the shell is carried up in the upper die and a positive knockout ejects it near the top of the stroke. The scrap rings are forced down around the lower trimming punch until they are split in two by scrap cutters **C** applied at the front and back of the die. The scrap pieces fall to the sides, away from the operation of the press.

20-5. PIERCING DIES

Piercing dies pierce holes in stampings. There are two principal reasons for piercing holes in a separate operation instead of combining piercing with other operations:

1. When a subsequent bending, forming, or drawing operation would distort the previously pierced hole or holes

2. When the edge of the pierced hole is too close to the edge of the blank for adequate strength in the die section. This occurs in compound and combination dies in which piercing and blanking are done simultaneously.

In the inset at A is shown a flanged shell requiring four holes to be pierced in the flange. If the holes were pierced before the drawing operation they would become distorted because of the blankholder pressure applied to the flange in the drawing process.

The shell is located in an accurately ground hole in the die block. Piercing punches are retained in a punch plate fastened to the punch holder, and a knockout effects stripping after the holes have been pierced.

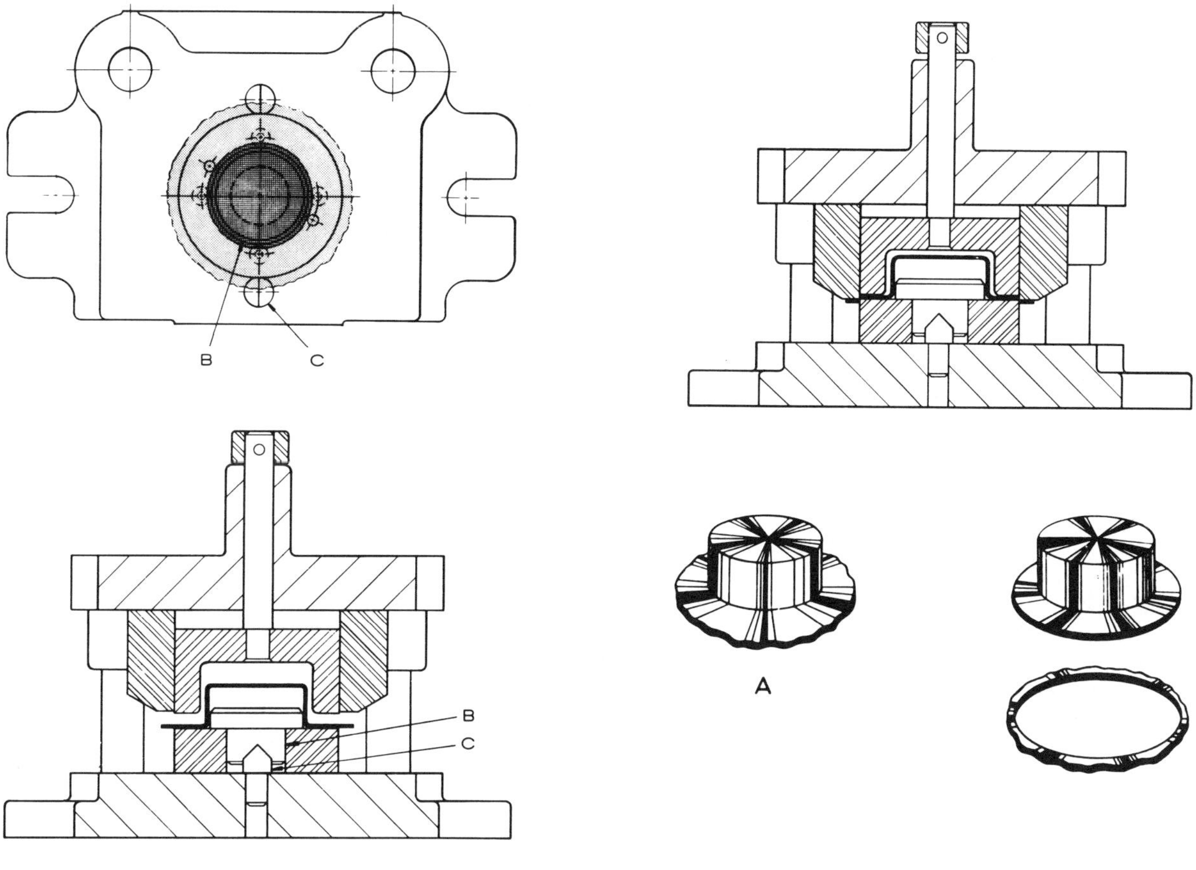

Fig. 20-4. Trimming die.

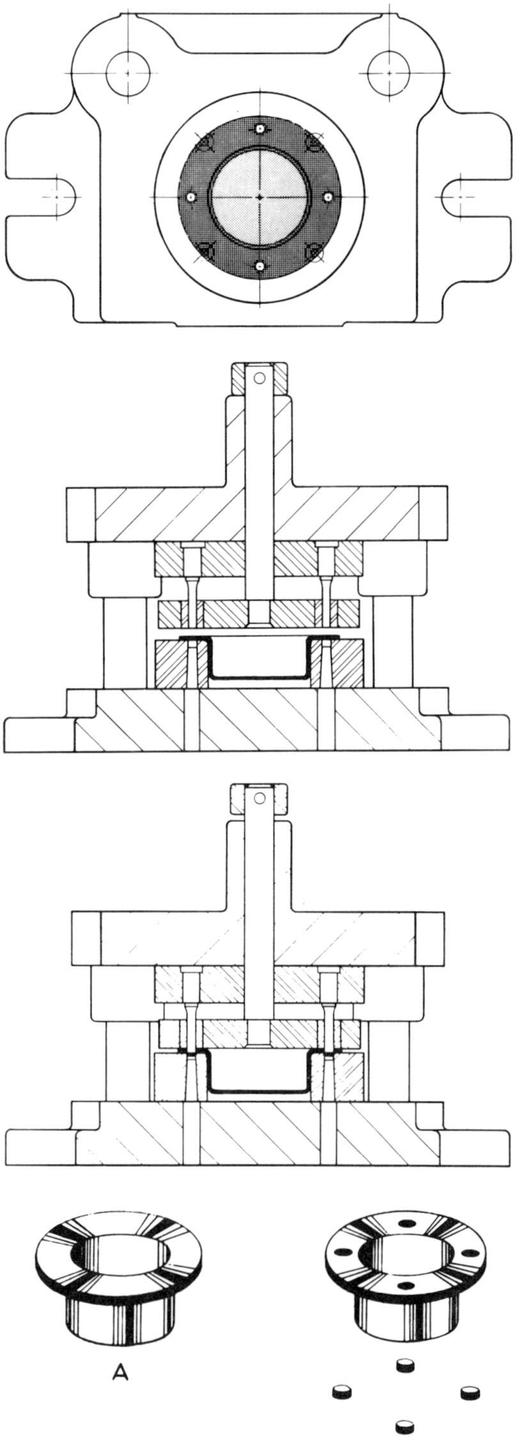

Fig. 20-5. Piercing die.

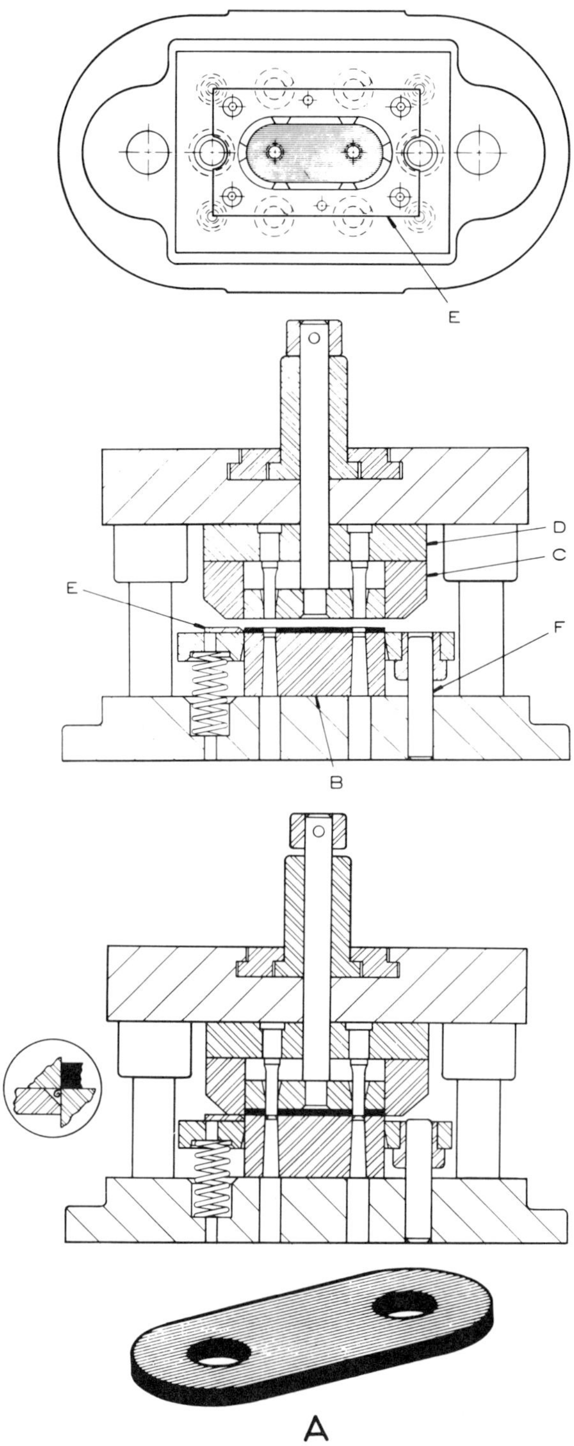

Fig. 20-6. Shaving die.

20-6. SHAVING DIES

Shaving is the operation of removing a small amount of metal from around the edges of a blank or hole in order to improve the surface. A properly shaved blank has a straight, smooth edge and it is held to a very accurate size. Many instrument, business machine, and other parts are shaved to provide better functioning and longer wear.

In the illustration, a blank **A** is to be shaved, both along outside edges and in the walls of the two holes. The shaving die for this workpiece consists of an inverted shaving punch **B** fastened to the die holder, and a shaving die block **C** fastened to the punch holder. A spacer **D** backs up the die block and it retains the shaving punches for the holes. The blank is located in a nest **E** beveled to provide clearance for the curled chip. The nest is mounted on a spring stripper plate guided on two guide pins **F**. The shaved blank is carried up, held in the die block with considerable pressure, and it is ejected near the top of the stroke by a positive knockout. Shaving dies are ordinarily held in floating adapter die sets for better alignment. This is necessary because no clearance is applied between punches and die block.

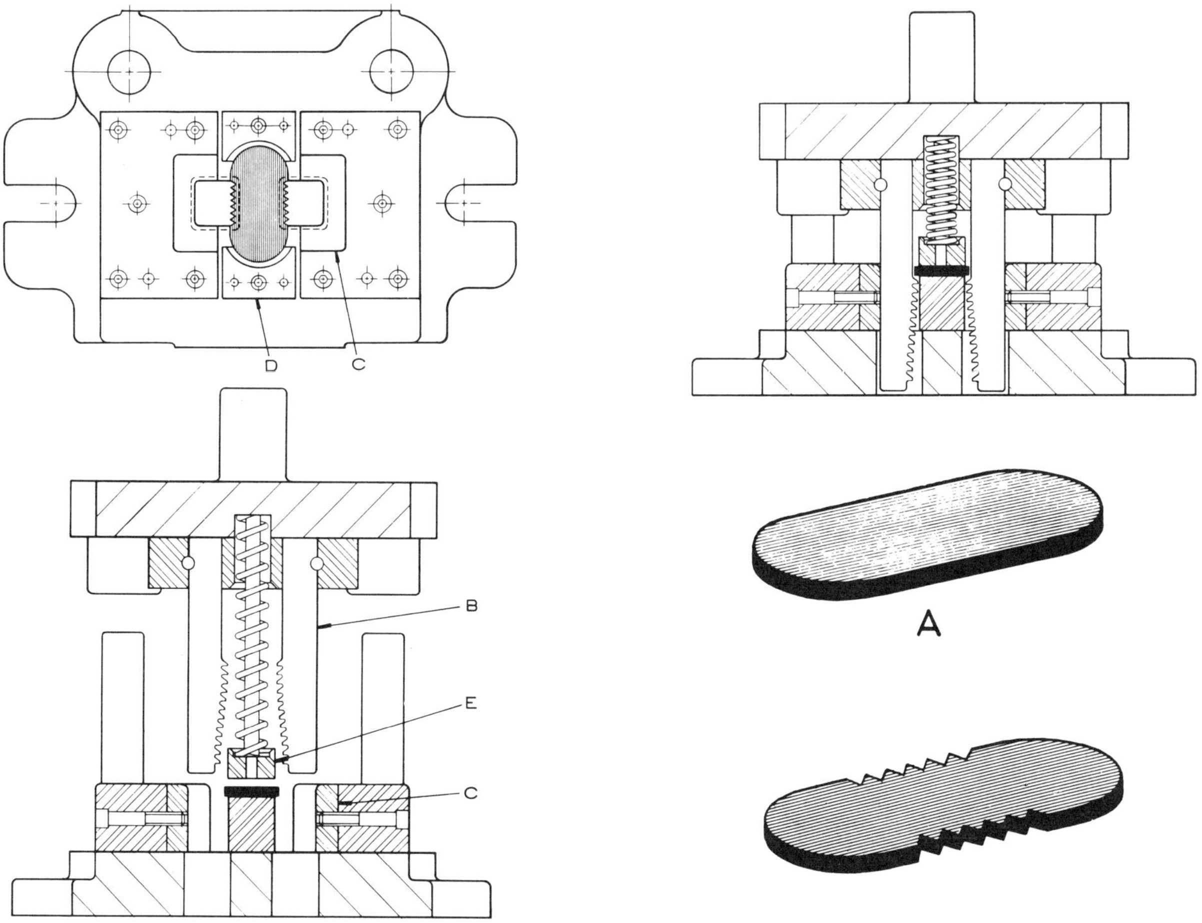

Fig. 20-7. Broaching die.

20-7. BROACHING DIES

Broaching may be considered to be a series of shaving operations performed one after the other by the same tool. A broach is provided with a number of teeth, each of which cuts a chip as the broach traverses the surface to be finished. Internal broaches finish holes; surface or slab broaches finish outside surfaces. Two conditions make broaching necessary:

1. Blanks are too thick for shaving. If considerable metal must be removed from the edges of thick blanks, a series of shaving dies would be required to produce a smooth finish. It would then be more economical to use a broaching die.

2. When considerable metal must be removed. This occurs when ridges or other shapes are required in the edges of the blank. It is often impractical to blank such shapes directly because the cutting edges would be weak and subject to breakage.

In the illustration, a blank at **A** must have small pointed serrations machined in the sides. The die is provided with two broaches **B** supported during the cutting process by hardened backing blocks **C**. The blank is located in a nest **D** composed of two opposed plates machined to fit the contour. Pressure pad **E**, backed up by heavy springs, clamps the blank securely before cutting begins. The first three or four teeth of the broach are made undersize and they ordinarily do no cutting except if an oversize blank is introduced into the die. The last three or four teeth are sizing teeth. Intermediate teeth are called working teeth and they take the successive chips to machine the serrations.

20-8. HORN DIES

A horn die is provided with a projecting post called a horn. Bent, formed, or drawn workpieces are applied over the horn for performing secondary operations.

In the illustration at **A**, a blank has been reverse-bent in a previous operation and the ends are to be hooked together and seamed in a horn die. The horn **B** is retained in a holder **C** fastened to the die holder. When the ram descends, seaming punch **D** strikes the workpiece to form the seam.

Many other operations such as piercing, staking, and the like are also performed in horn dies.

20-9. SIDE CAM DIES

Side cams transform vertical motion from the press ram into horizontal or angular motion and they make possible many ingenious operations. In the illustration at **A**, a flanged shell requires two holes pierced in its side. The shell is placed over die block **B** of the die. Descent of the upper die causes pressure pad **C** to seat the shell firmly over the block. Further descent causes side cams **D** to move the punch-carrying slides **E** for piercing the holes. Spring strippers **F** strip the shell from around the piercing punches as they are withdrawn.

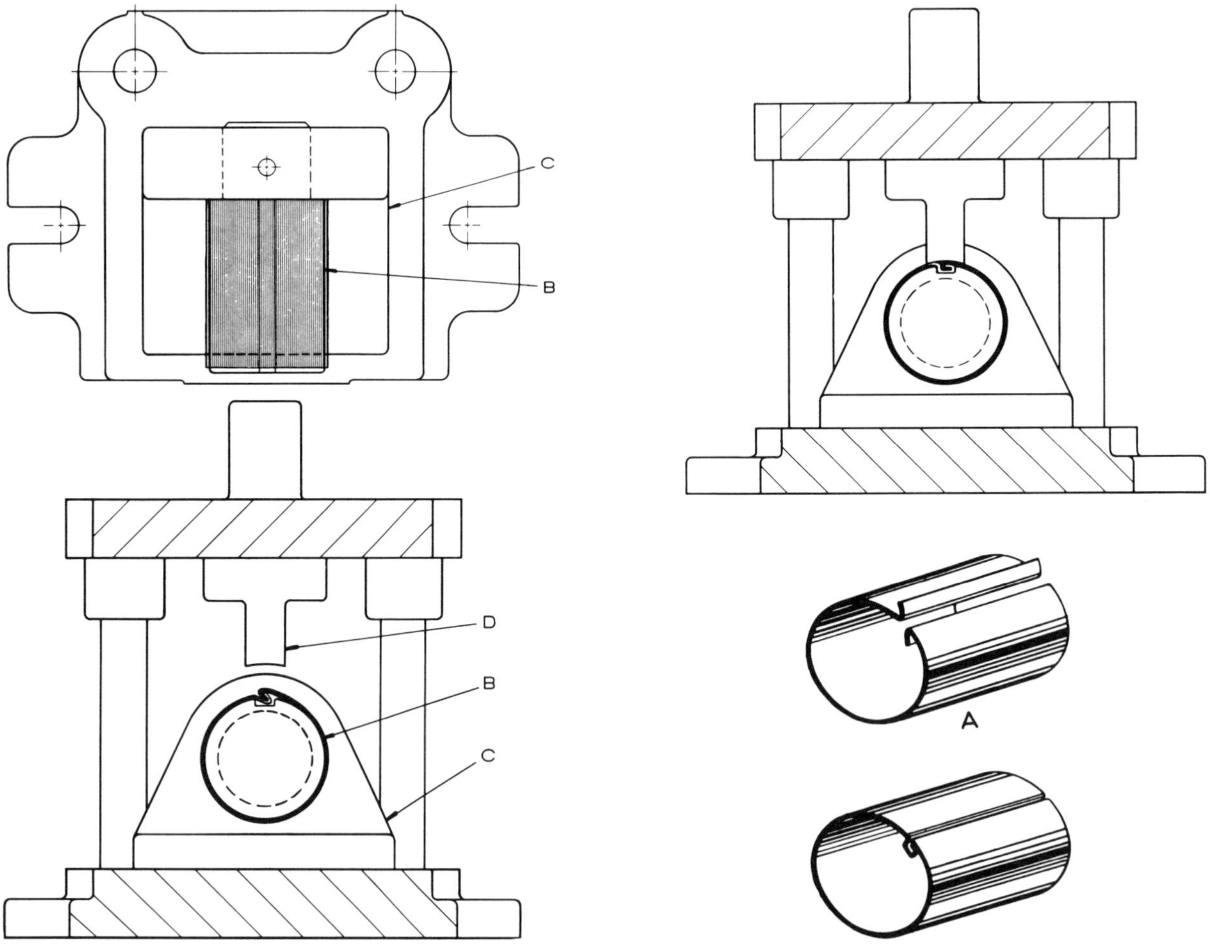

Fig. 20-8. Horn die.

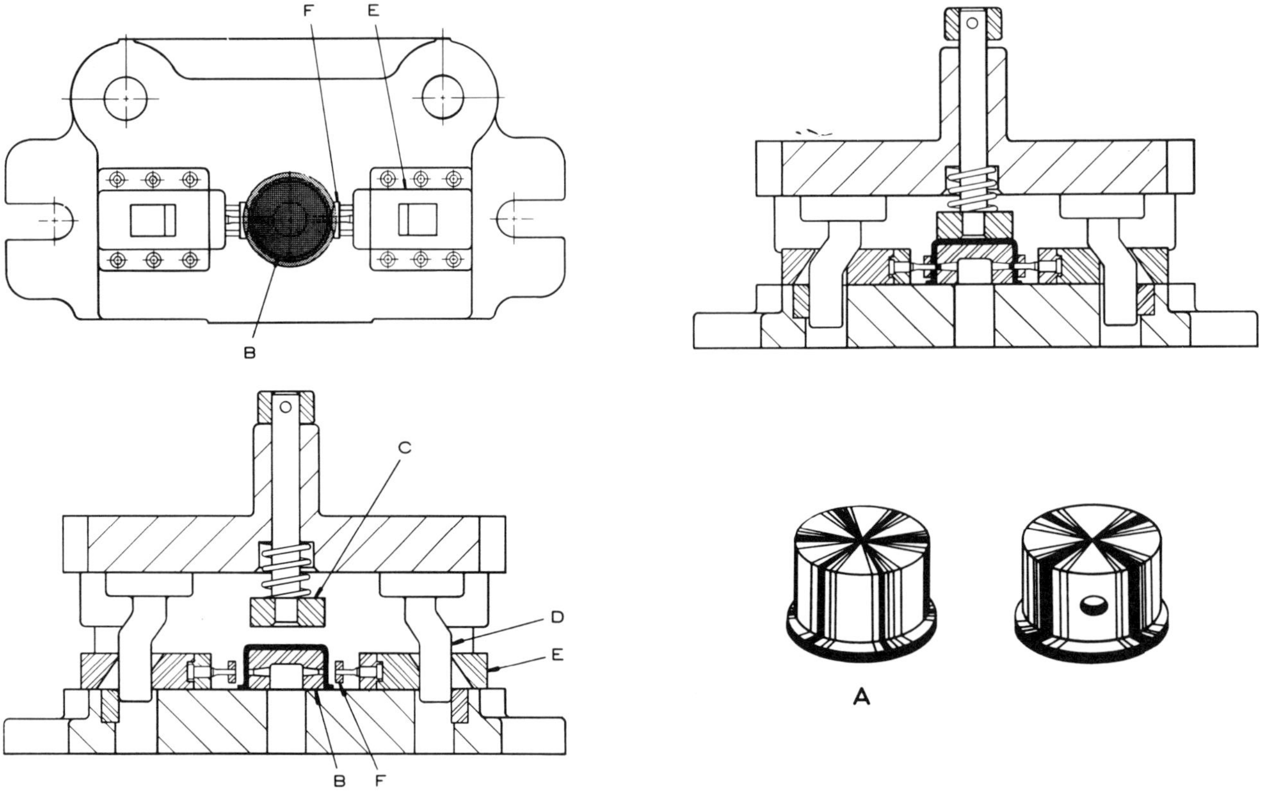

Fig. 20-9. Side cam die.

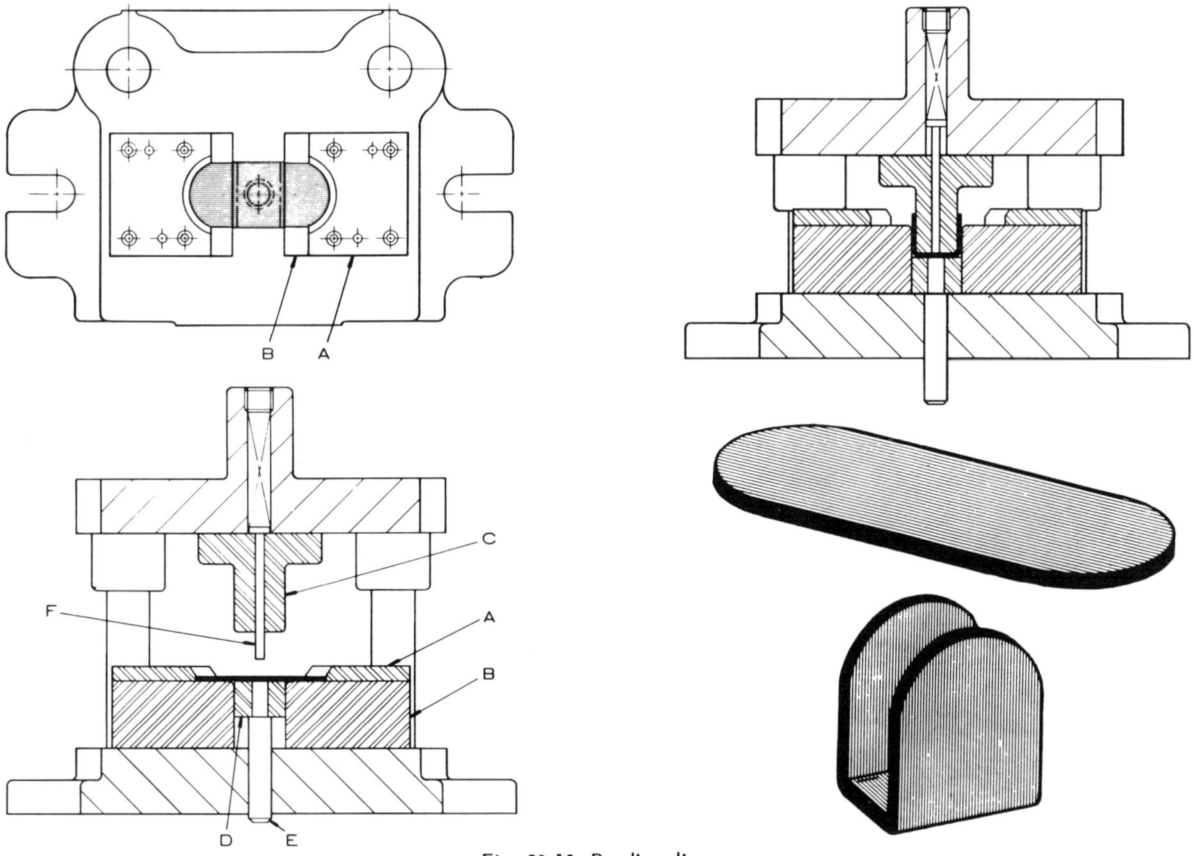

Fig. 20-10. Bending die.

20-10. BENDING DIES

A bending die deforms portions of flat blanks to some angular position. The line of bend is straight along its entire length, as differentiated from a forming die which produces workpieces having a curved line of bend. In the illustration, a flat blank is to be given a double bend to form a U shape. The blank is inserted in gages **A** fastened on bending blocks **B**. The bending blocks, in turn, are fastened to the die holder. Upon descent of the upper die, the bending punch **C** grips the blank between its lower face and pressure pad **D**. Pins **E** extend to the pressure attachment of the press. Shedder **F** strips the workpiece from the punch.

20-11. FORMING DIES

The operation of forming is similar to bending except that the line of bend is curved instead of straight and plastic deformation in the material is more severe. In the illustration the flat blank at **A** is to be formed into a part having a curved contour. The blank is positioned in nest **B** composed of two plates mounted on pressure pad **C**. When the ram descends, the blank is gripped between the bottoms of forming blocks **D** and the surface of pressure pad **C**. Further descent causes the sides of the blank to be formed to the curved shape of forming blocks **D** and forming punch **E**. At the bottom of the stroke, knockout block **F** applies the final form. It bottoms against a hardened spacer fastened to the punch holder thus "setting" the form. When the die ascends, the part is carried up within form blocks **D**. Near the top of the stroke it is ejected by knockout **F**.

20-12. DRAWING DIES

The operation of drawing is similar to forming, although usually there is more severe plastic deformation in the material. The difference between the two occurs in the extent of closure in the form. Consider a drawn cup such as a metal drinking cup. The material extends all around the sides and therefore the part is said to have been drawn. In a formed part the material does not extend completely around to surround a space, even though the formed contour may be quite intricate.

In the illustration at **A**, a flat disk is to be drawn into a cup. The blank is placed on pressure pad **B** of the drawing die and it is located by four spring-loaded pins **C**. Descent of the upper die causes the blank to be gripped securely between the surface of pressure pad **B** and the lower surface of draw ring **D**. Further descent of the ram causes the blank to be drawn over punch **E** until it has assumed the cup shape shown in the closed view at the right. Pressure pins **F** extend to the pressure attachment of the press.

The amount of pressure must be adjusted carefully. Excessive pressure would cause the bottom of the cup to be punched out. Insufficient pressure would allow wrinkles to form. With the proper amount of pressure, a smooth, wrinkle-free cup is produced. Drawing is extensively used for producing stampings ranging from tiny cups and ferrules to large shells for pressure vessels, ships, aircraft, and missiles.

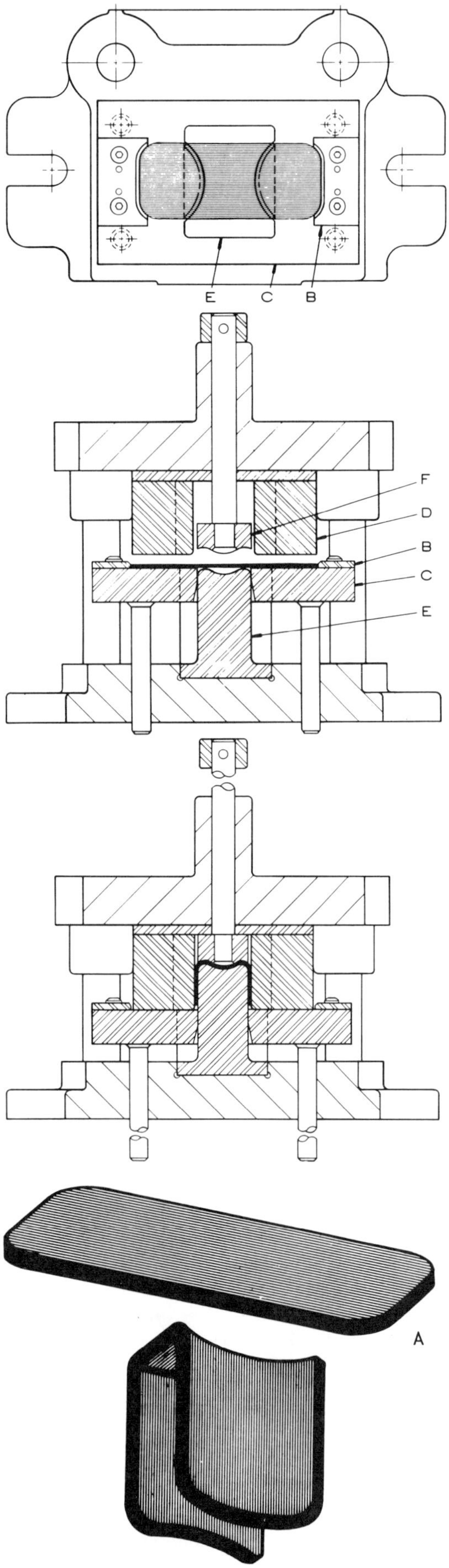

Fig. 20-11. Forming die.

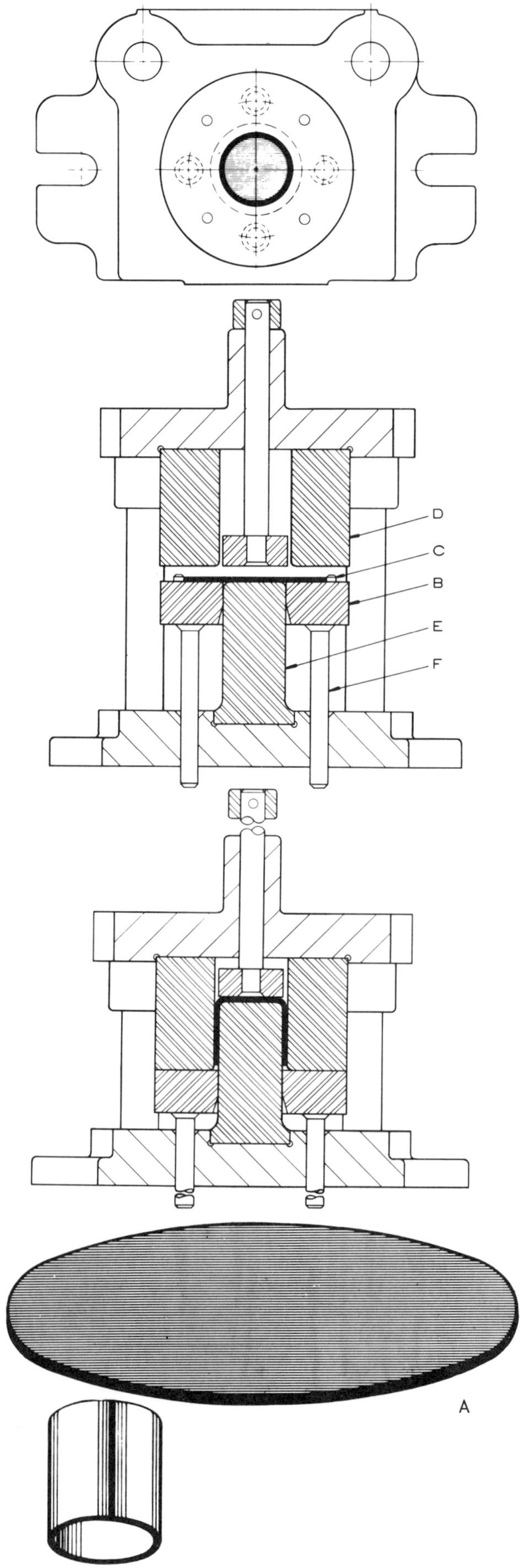

Fig. 20-12. Drawing die.

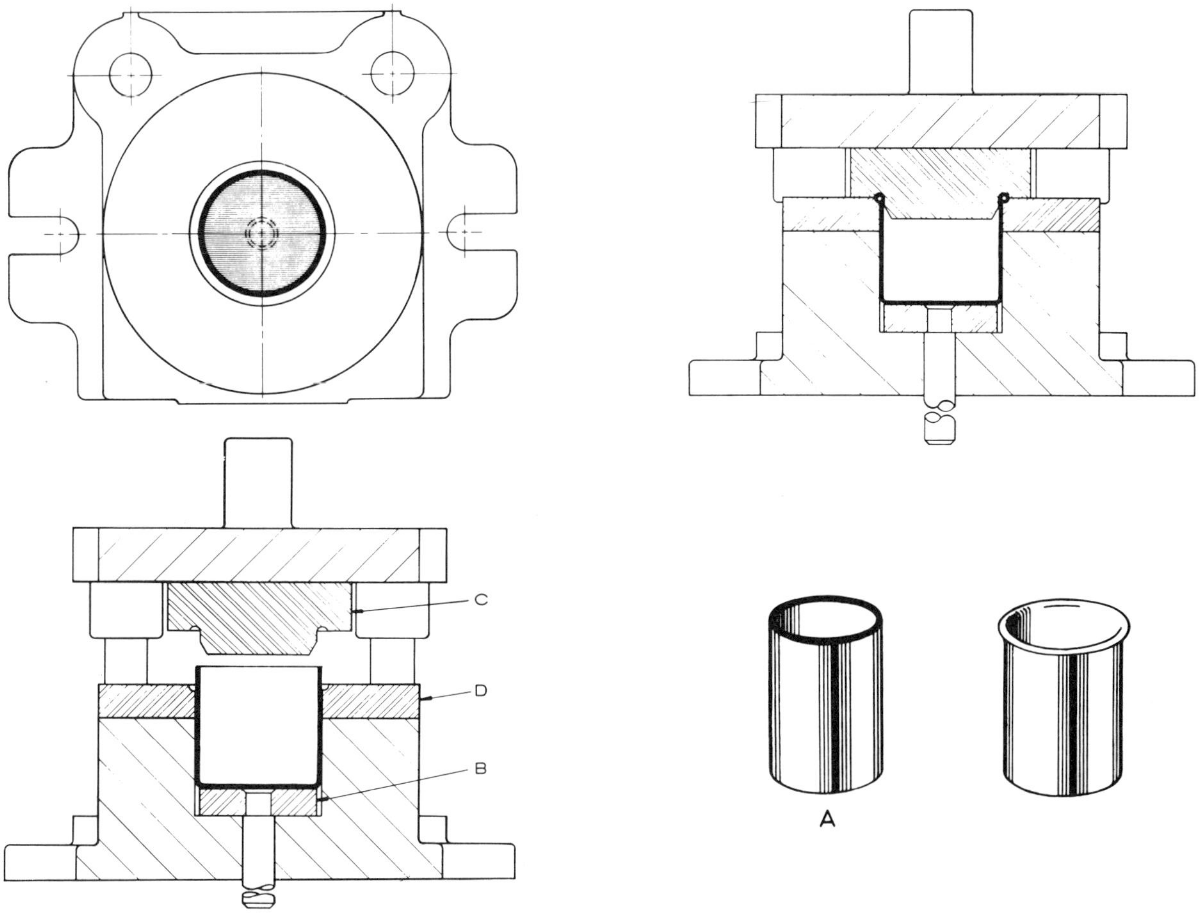

Fig. 20-13. Curling die.

20-13. CURLING DIES

A curling die forms the material at the edge of a workpiece into a circular shape or hollow ring. Flat blanks may be curled; a common application is a hinge formed of two plates each of which is curled at one side for engagement of the hinge pin. More often, curling is applied to edges of the open ends of cups and shells to provide stiffness and smooth, rounded edges. Most pans used for cooking and baking foods are curled.

In the illustration, a drawn shell shown at **A** is to be curled. The shell is placed in the curling die where it rests on knockout pad **B**. Descent of the upper die causes the knockout pad to be pushed down until it bottoms on the die holder. Further descent causes curling punch **C** to curl the edge of the shell. Near the bottom of the stroke, the lip of the material contacts an angular surface machined in curling ring **D** to complete the curl. When the punch goes up, the knockout raises the shell for easy removal.

20-14. BULGING DIES

A bulging die expands a portion of a drawn shell causing it to bulge. There are two types: fluid dies and rubber dies. Fluid dies employ water or oil as the expanding medium and a ram applies pressure to the fluid. In rubber dies, a pad or block or rubber under pressure moves the walls of the workpiece to the desired position. This is possible because rubber is virtually incompressible. Although it can be made to change its shape, the volume remains the same.

In the illustration at **A**, a drawn shell is to be bulged at its closed end. The shell is placed over punch **B** of the bulging die and its lower end is confined in lower die **C**. The upper end of punch **B** is a rubber ring within which is applied a spreader rod **D**. This rod is conical at its upper end and it helps the rubber to flow outward to the desired shape. When the press ram descends, the upper die applies a force to the shell bottom and since the rubber cannot compress, it is forced outward bulging the walls of the shell. When the ram goes up, the rubber returns to its original shape and the bulged shell can be removed from the die. After bulging, a shell is shorter than it was previously.

20-15. SWAGING DIES

The operation of swaging, sometimes called necking, is exactly the opposite of bulging. When a workpiece is swaged a portion is reduced in size and this causes the part to become longer than it was before swaging. In the illustration at **A**, a shell is to be swaged at its open end. It is inserted in the swaging die where it rests on knockout pad **B** and its lower end is surrounded by the walls of block **C**. When the ram descends, swaging die **D** reduces a portion of the diameter of the shell and this becomes longer.

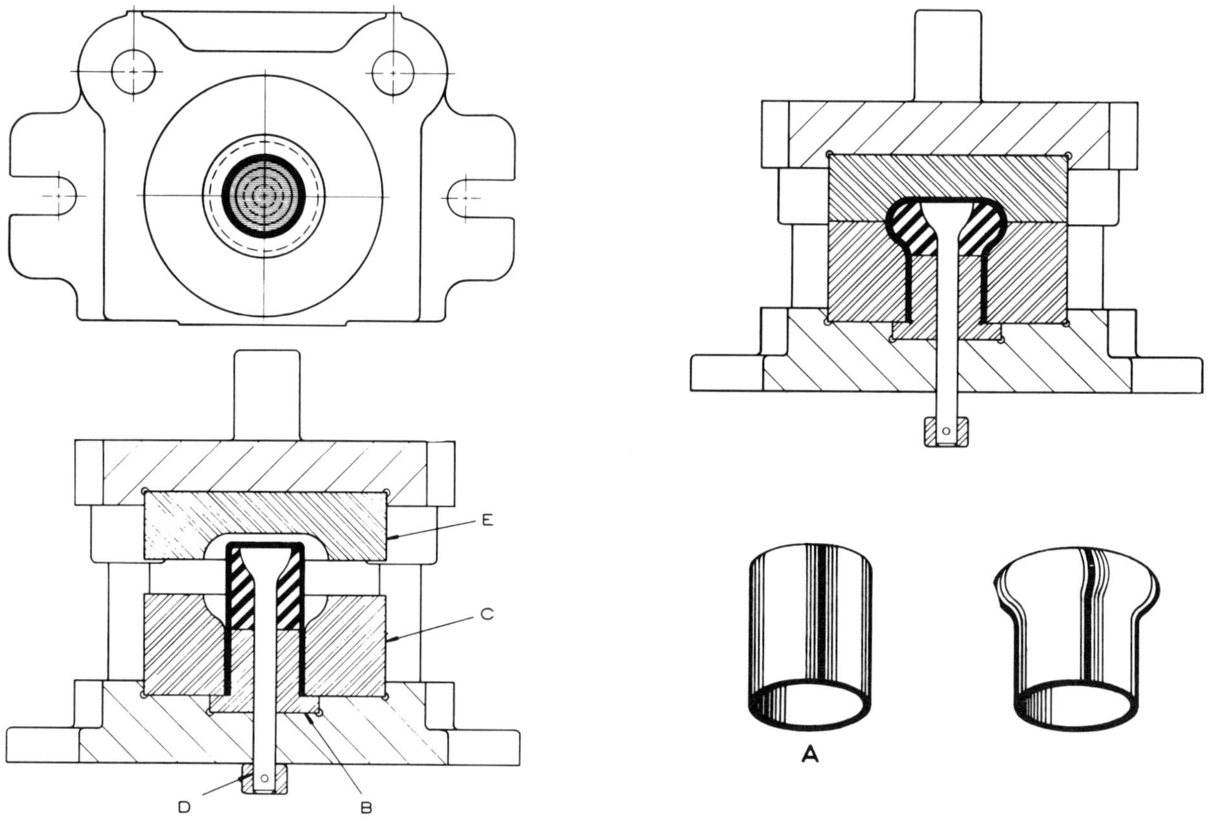

Fig. 20-14. Bulging die that employs rubber as the bulging medium.

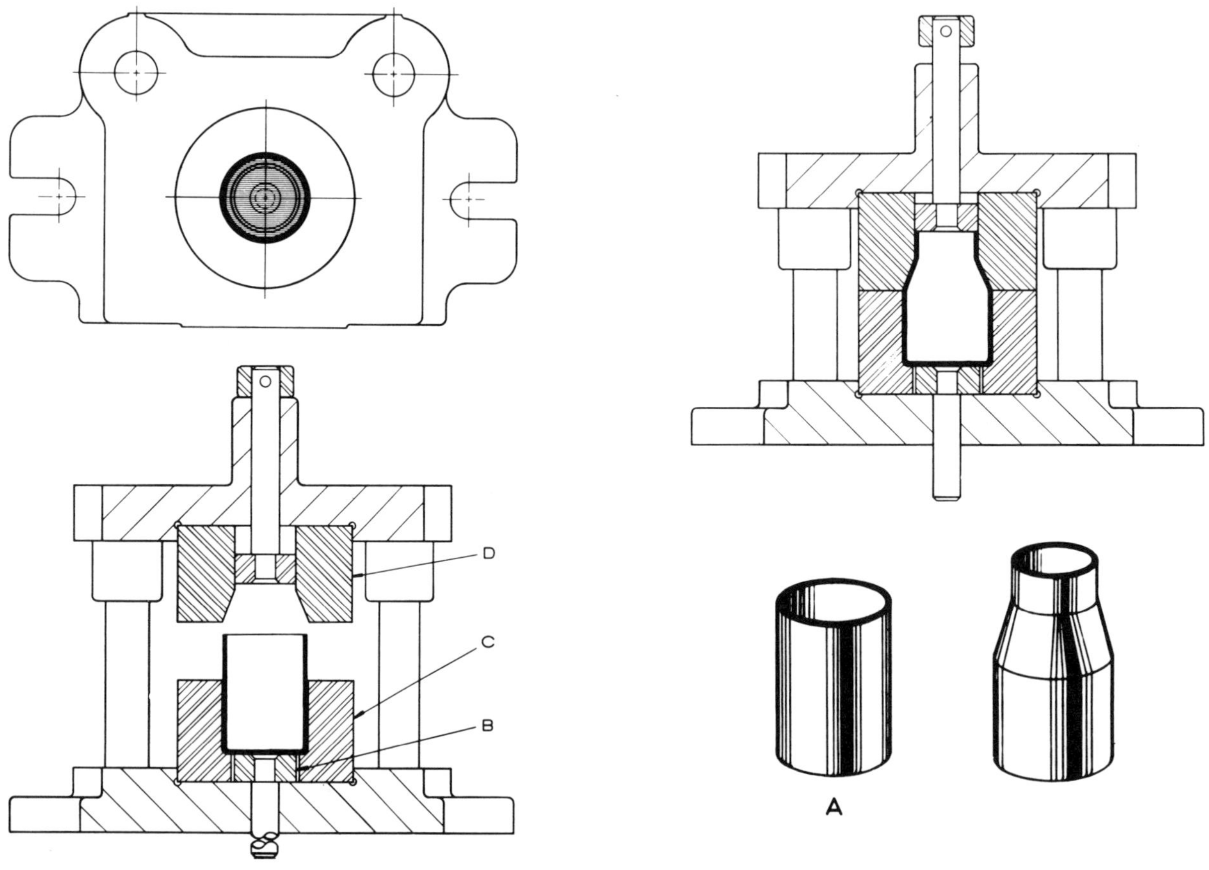

Fig. 20-15. Swaging die.

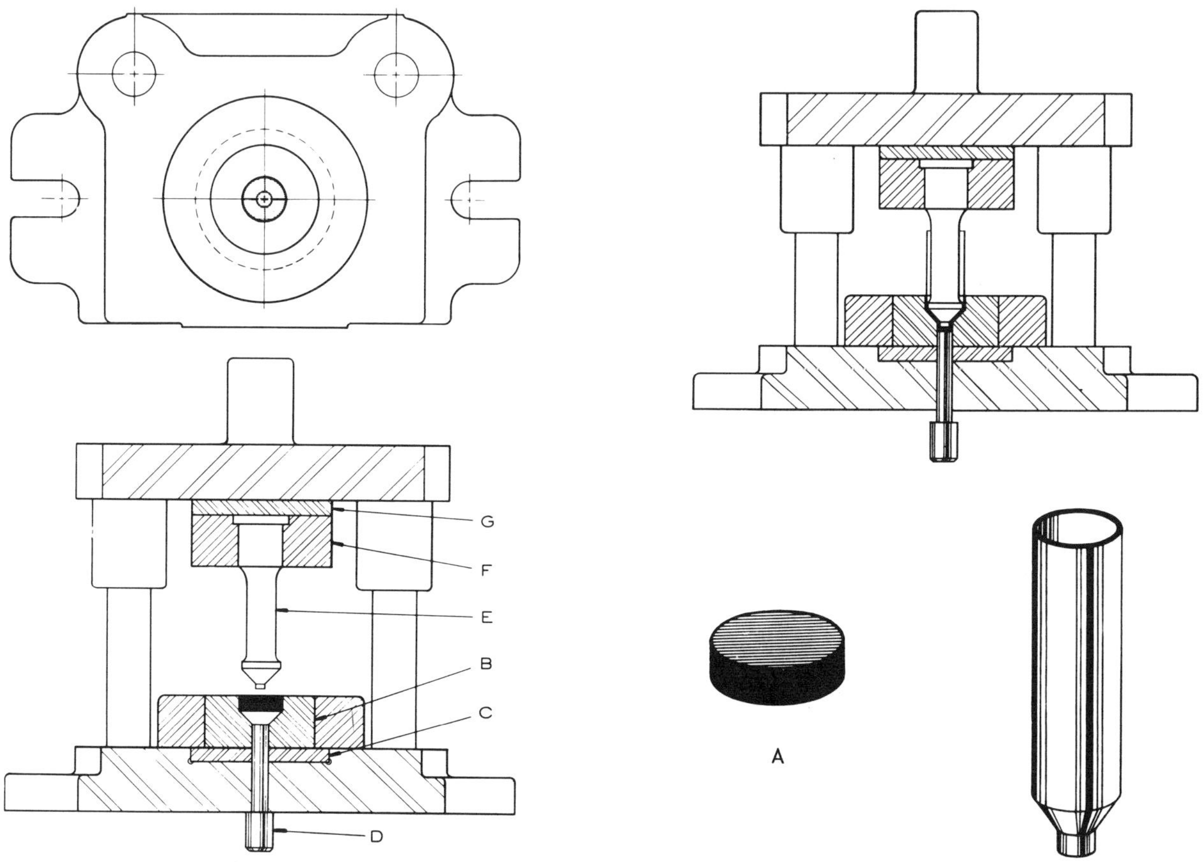

Fig. 20-16. Extruding die.

20-16. EXTRUDING DIES

The function of all the dies discussed so far is to perform work on sheet material – to cut sheet material into blanks, to perform further operations upon the blanks, or to perform operations on workpieces bent, formed, or drawn from the blanks. We come now to interesting classes of dies that perform secondary operations on small thick blanks called slugs. In these dies the slugs are severely deformed to make parts having no resemblance to the slugs from which they were made. The first class is called extruding dies. In this type of die each slug is partly confined in a cavity and extremely high pressure is applied by a punch to cause the material in the slug to extrude or squirt out, much like toothpaste is extruded when the tube is squeezed. In the illustration the slug **A** is to be extruded into a thin-walled shell having a conical closed end. The slug is placed in die block **B**, backed up by a hardened plate **C**. The bottom of the cavity in the die block is formed by the end of knockout rod **D**. When the press ram descends extruding punch **E** first squeezes the material in the slug until it assumes the shape of the die cavity and of the working end of the extruding punch. Continued descent causes the material to extrude upward between the wall of the punch and the wall of the die cavity. The amount of clearance between the two determines the thickness of the wall of the extruded shell. The extruding punch is retained in punch plate **F** and because of the high pressure involved, it is backed up by backing plate **G**.

20-17. COLD FORMING DIES

Cold forming dies produce workpieces by applying pressure to blanks, squeezing and displacing the material until it assumes the shape of the punch and die. In the illustration at **A**, a slug is to be formed into a flanged part in a cold forming die. It is placed on punch **B** located within spring-loaded V gages **C**. Descent of the upper die causes the material under the upper die block to be displaced outward to form the flange. As the flange increases in diameter, the gages are pushed back as shown. When the die goes up, the part is carried upward within it and it is ejected near the top of the stroke by knockout plunger **D** actuated by knockout rod **E**.

20-18. PROGRESSIVE DIES

In a progressive die the strip is moved in stages from station to station. Different operations are performed on it at each station except at idle ones applied to provide room for components. A complete workpiece is removed from the strip at the final station. All of the operations described previously may be performed in progressive dies. For example, a single die of this type may do piercing at the first station, trimming at the second station, bending at the third, forming at the fourth etc. A progressive die may thus be considered as a series of different dies placed side by side with the strip passing through each successively. This analogy has some merit although it does not give a true picture of the extremely close

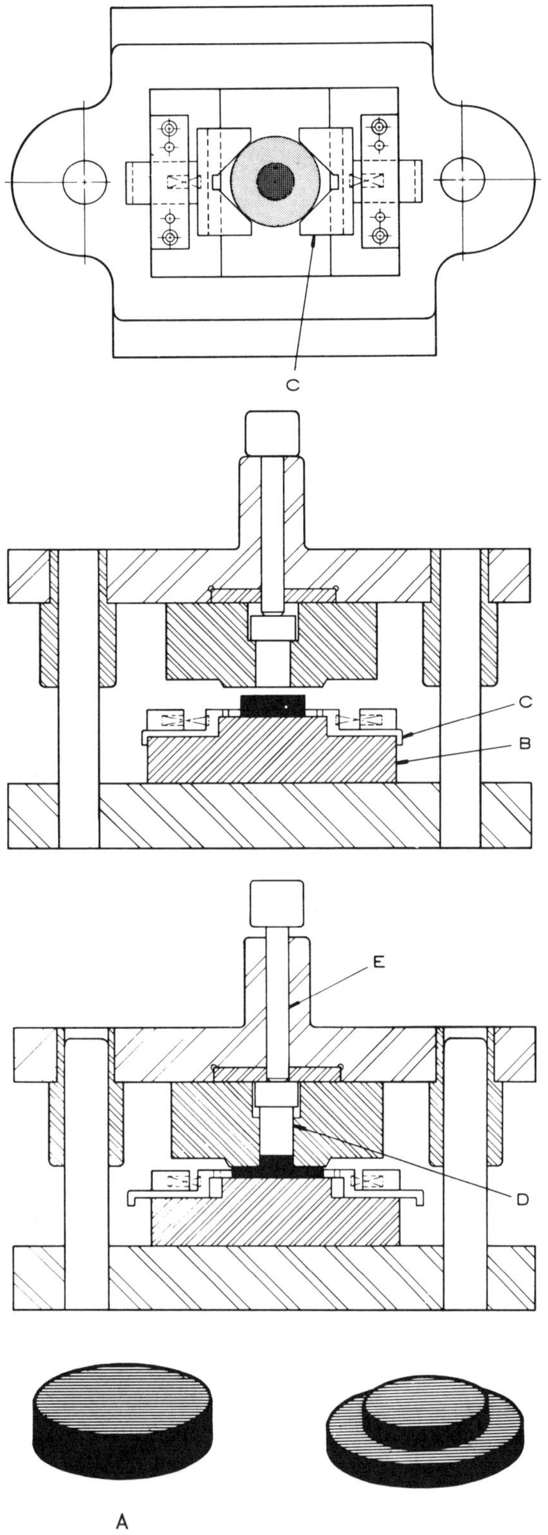

Fig. 20-17. Cold forming die.

interrelationship between the various stations.

In the illustration at **A**, a pierced, trimmed and bent part is to be produced complete in a simple progressive die. At the first station the strip is notched and pierced and at the second station the blank is cut off and bent. You should easily recognize all of the elements in this die – the die block, piercing punch, trimming punch, knockout, stop block, and all the others.

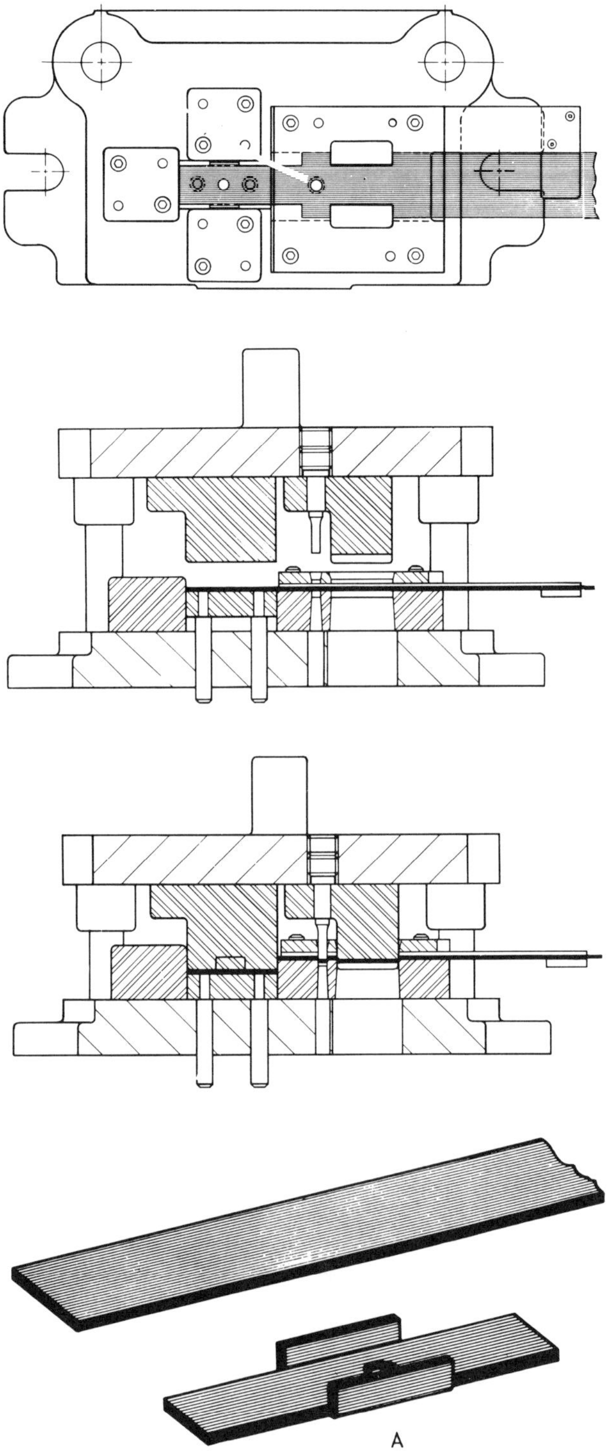

Fig. 20-18. Progressive die.

20-19. SUB-PRESS DIES

Sub-press dies blank and form very small watch, clock, and instrument parts. An example would be the small instrument cam shown at **A**. The die components are retained in a subpress which is, as its name implies, actually a small press operated in a larger one. The sub-press is composed of base **C**, barrel **B**, and plunger **D**. A long, tapered babbit bearing **E** provided with longitudinal key slots guides the plunger and prevents rotation. Tightening spanner nut **F** against

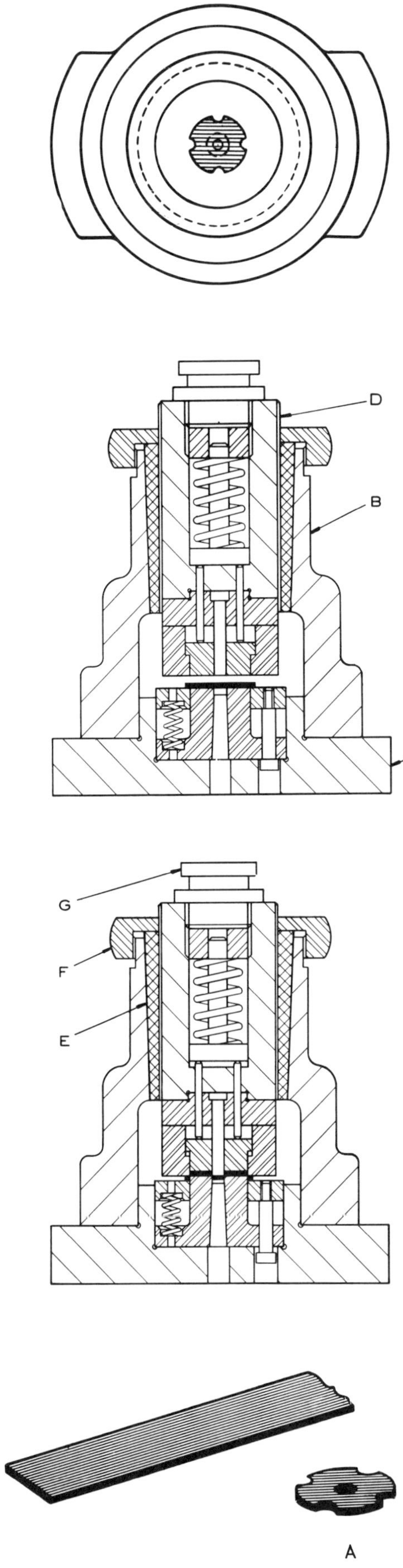

Fig. 20-19. Sub-press die.

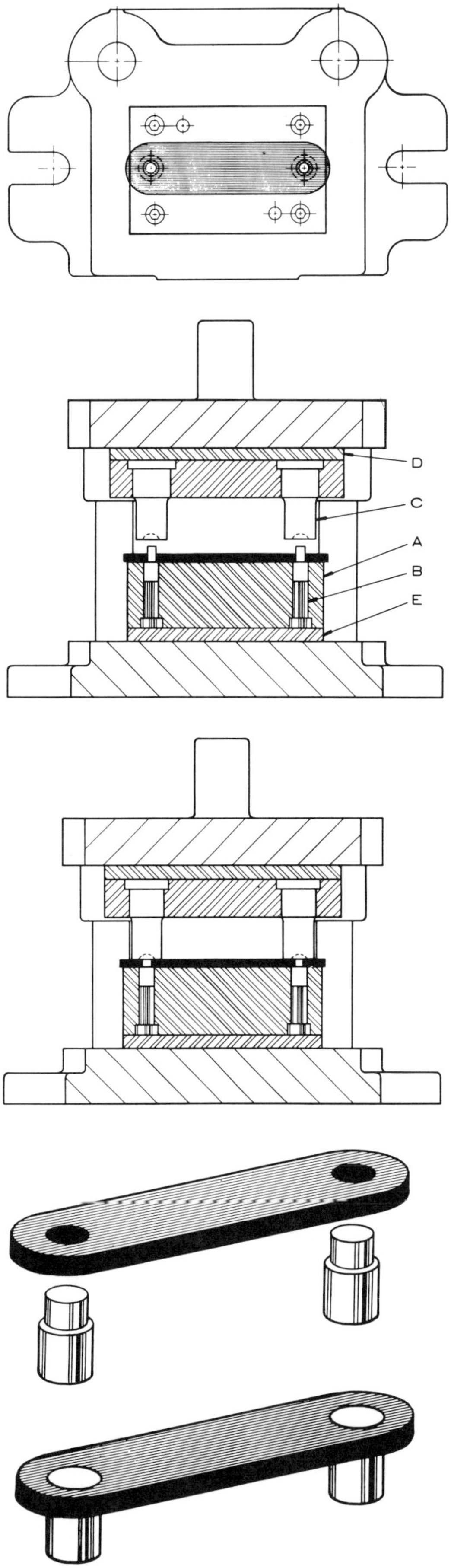

Fig. 20-20. Assembly die.

bearing **E** causes it to close around plunger **D** to remove all looseness. The top portion of plunger **D** is engaged by actuator **G** threaded into a central tapped hole. The slot of the actuator is engaged loosely by a yoke fastened to the press ram. Thus the press ram does not guide the sub-press in any way. It simply applies the up and down motion. Sub-press dies are usually of the compound type because of the considerable accuracy obtained.

20-20. ASSEMBLY DIES

Assembly dies assemble two or more parts together by press-fitting, riveting, staking, or other means. Components are assembled very quickly and relationships between parts can be maintained closely. In the left inset are shown a link and two studs that are to be riveted together in an assembly die. The studs are positioned in die block **A** and they seat on plungers **B**. The link is then positioned over the studs, the turned-down ends of the studs engaging in holes in the link. Descent of the press ram causes riveting punches **C** to deform the ends of the studs into the shape of rivet heads. A hardened plate **D** backs up the punches to prevent the heads from sinking into the relatively soft material of the die set. Another hardened plate **E** backs up the plungers.

Index

T